Fighting Words

THE ENTIRE POPULATION IN THE STREETS.

THE UNION FOREVER! "Nobody Hurt" on Our Side.

struggling for existence and liberty.

THE ENEMY IN FULL FLIGHT AND CLOSELY PURSUED! War is upon us.

INDEPENDENCE, NOW and FOREVER!

A reckless and unprincipled tyrant Mothers of my much loved native South.

A CARNIVAL OF FIRE AND BLOOD REBELS COMPLETLY ROUTED.

WHAT ARMING NEGROES HAS DONE. depravity which finds no parallel

Virginians! the invaders are upon you.

We turn to you in mute agony! The Enemy's Loss Terrific

"Could'nt Stand Abe."

bloody standard of tyranny Shocking Barbarities Perpetrated by the Rebels.

MORE TROOPS WANTED!!

Rebels Defeated at all Points.

REIGN OF THE RABBLE.

Fighting Words

An Illustrated History of Newspaper Accounts of the Civil War

Andrew S. Coopersmith

THE NEW PRESS
NEW YORK
LONDON

Requests for permission to reproduce selections from this book should be mailed to: Permissions Department, The New Press, 38 Greene Street, New York, NY 10013

Published in the United States by The New Press, New York, 2004
Distributed by W. W. Norton & Company, Inc., New York

LIBRARY OF CONGRESS CATALOGING-IN-PUBLICATION DATA
Coopersmith, Andrew.
Fighting Words: an illustrated history of newspaper accounts of the Civil War / Andrew Coppersmith.
p. cm.
Includes bibliographical references (p.) and index.
ISBN 1-56584-796-2 (hc.)
1. United States—History—Civil War, 1861–1865—Press coverage. 2. United States—History—Civil War, 1861–1865—Journalists. 3. Press and politics—United States—History—19th century. 4. Journalism—United States—History—19th century. 5. American newspapers—History—19th century. 6. United States—History—Civil War, 1861–1865—Pictorial works. I. Title
E609.C66 2004
070.4'499737—dc22
2004049945

The New Press was established in 1990 as a not-for-profit alternative to the large, commercial publishing houses currently dominating the book publishing industry. The New Press operates in the public interest rather than for private gain, and is committed to publishing, in innovative ways, works of educational, cultural, and community value that are often deemed insufficiently profitable.

www.thenewpress.com

Book design by Lovedog Studio

Printed in Canada

2 4 6 8 10 9 7 5 3 1

for my mother and father

Contents

List of Newspapers Cited

Alabama
(Mobile) *Army Argus & Crisis*
Montgomery Advertiser [daily and weekly editions]
Montgomery Mail
Selma Morning Reporter
South-Western Baptist

Georgia
Augusta Chronicle & Sentinel
Augusta Constitutionalist
Christian Index
Columbus Sun
Countryman
Macon Telegraph [also appears as *Macon Telegraph & Confederate*]
Rome Weekly Courier
Savannah Republican
Southern Christian Advocate
(Atlanta) *Southern Confederacy*
(Milledgeville) *Southern Federal Union* [also appears as *Confederate Union*]

Illinois
Chicago Tribune

Kentucky
Louisville Courier
Louisville Journal

Louisiana
(New Orleans) *Black Republican*
New Orleans Bee
New Orleans Crescent
(New Orleans) *Delta*
Shreveport Weekly News

Massachusetts
Barre Gazette
Boston Evening Transcript
Hampshire Gazette & Northampton Courier
Liberator
Pittsfield Sun
Springfield Republican

Michigan
Detroit Free Press

Mississippi
(Jackson) *Daily Southern Crisis*

(Paulding) *Eastern Clarion*
Mississippian [daily and weekly editions]
Natchez Courier [daily and weekly editions]
Vicksburg Evening Citizen
Vicksburg Whig

North Carolina
Church Intelligencer
Greensborough Patriot
Hillsborough Recorder
Milton Chronicle
North Carolina Standard [daily, semi-weekly, and weekly editions]
Raleigh Confederate
Wilmington Journal

New York
Albany Atlas & Argus
Albany Evening Journal
Anglo-African
Evangelist
Frank Leslie's Illustrated Newspaper
Harper's Weekly
Independent
National Principia
New York Evening Day-Book
New York Evening Post
New York Herald
New York News
New York Times
New York Tribune
New York World
Troy Times
Weekly Caucasian

Ohio
Cincinnati Enquirer
Cincinnati Gazette
Cleveland Plain Dealer
(Columbus) *Crisis*

Pennsylvania
Harrisburg Patriot & Union
Harrisburg Telegraph
Philadelphia Inquirer
Philadelphia North American & United States Gazette

Rhode Island
Providence Post

South Carolina
(Spartanburg) *Carolina Spartan*
Charleston Courier
Charleston Mercury
(Columbia) *South Carolinian*

Tennessee
Memphis Appeal
Memphis Avalanche
Nashville Union & American

Texas
Galveston Tri-Weekly News
Houston Telegraph [weekly and tri-weekly editions]
(Marshall) *Texas Republican*

Vermont
Rutland Herald

Virginia
Religious Herald
Richmond Dispatch
Richmond Enquirer
Richmond Examiner
Richmond Whig
Southern Illustrated News
Wellsburg Herald
Wheeling Intelligencer

Acknowledgments

I have racked up many debts in completing this project. John Dower has been an inspiration to me intellectually, and his unfailing encouragement and good cheer made both my graduate school days and my time writing this book far richer and more enjoyable than they would have been otherwise. My work also bears the indelible imprint of the late William Gienapp. His nineteenth-century history courses at Harvard University sparked my own interest in the Civil War period, and it was he who first pushed me to pay serious attention to the newspapers of the time. Apart from shaping me as a scholar, Bill was responsible for singlehandedly creating an extraordinary microfilm collection of Civil War newspapers at Harvard, which was a veritable gold mine of source material. The staff at Harvard's Government Documents & Microform Division, which until recently managed the university's newspaper holdings, offered assistance to me every step of the way. Most of my research, however, was conducted at the University of Pennsylvania's Van Pelt Library. Lee Pugh, who heads the interlibrary loan office there, was my saving grace. She readily fielded all of my research needs and succeeded in procuring even some of the more obscure titles I requested. Without her efforts, my job would have been infinitely more difficult. Kimberly Scheckner, Eva Sheppard-Wolf, Michelle Shienbaum, Silvana Siddali, Michele Taillon Taylor, and Susan Wyly have been both cherished friends and insightful critics. They read (and reread) drafts of the manuscript and challenged me to refine my thinking, and the book is the better for it. Lisa Cardyn, Lisa Lauterbach Laskin, and Chandra Manning lent their expertise to helping me contextualize some of the trickier documents. At The New Press, Marc Favreau and Maury Botton dutifully kept me on track and shepherded the manuscript to completion. My greatest debts, however, are to my family. The entire Coopersmith clan has brought tremendous joy to my life, but my parents, Norman and Roslyn Coopersmith, deserve special mention. In so many ways, too many to count, they have made this book possible, and it is lovingly dedicated to them.

Introduction

This Is a War of Opinion

Springtime in 1861 started off dismally for the American Union. Far from being a season of hope and renewal, it seemed to promise nothing more than a continuation of tensions and troubles from the previous winter. Between December and February, after decades of discord between the North and South over slavery, the seven states of the Deep South had thrown off their allegiance to the United States and embarked on a mission to create their own independent nation. Despite the revolutionary nature of these acts, they had all proceeded peaceably, without any attempt by the federal government to put a stop to them. But now, as April began, all attention was focused on Charleston, where military forces for the newly established Confederate States of America were engaged in a decisive showdown with United States troops defending Fort Sumter, a small stronghold in Charleston Harbor that remained one of the few bastions of federal authority still standing in the region. At stake was more than just control over the fort; the larger issue was whether the North and South would finally throw down the proverbial gauntlet and go against each other in an all-out war.

With so much hanging in the balance, everyone was eager for reports from Charleston. While people there were able to monitor the situation with their very own eyes and ears, others in the North and South had to keep their fingers on the pulse of events in the only way they could—by reading the daily newspapers. The prominent New York attorney George Templeton Strong, who kept a diary throughout the conflict, wrote continually of the information he was gleaning from the city papers, and when word of the Confederate attack on Fort Sumter and the outbreak of war reached him, it was the *New York Herald* that served as the messenger. "*War* has begun, unless my extra *Herald* lies," Strong wrote wryly in his journal at the end of the day on April 12, 1861. Although he was well aware of how critical the situation at Fort Sumter was, the commencement of actual hostilities seemed to take him by surprise. Indeed, as Strong recounted, the evening had begun innocuously enough—dinner with his wife at a friend's home, followed by a committee meeting at church—but as he walked uptown afterward, the feeling in the air had changed dramatically. "The streets were vocal with newsboys," he recalled, blaring their shouts of "Extry—a *Herald*! Got the bombardment of *Fort Sumter*!!!" Strong initially suspected that it was just an overblown rumor and tried to resist the impulse to buy a copy, but after walking a few blocks amid the commotion, he "could not stand it longer" and "sacrificed sixpence" to check out the story for himself. Over the next several days, he would spend much time scouring the newspapers—not just the *Herald*, but also the *Evening Post*, the *Tribune*, and the *Times*, among others, to keep up with what was happening. "So Civil War is inaugurated at last," Strong told his diary, in a tone of calm that belied the true severity of the conflict now under way.[1]

Although Strong was in many ways an exceptional individual—distinguished, well connected, socially and economically privileged—his unremitting desire for the latest war news made him no different from the other millions of Americans living in the Northern and Southern states. As the Confederate battery in Charleston mounted its assault on Fort Sumter, newspaper offices in cities all across the country were themselves "besieged" by throngs of anxious patrons. The news carried an urgency that was irresistible. "We shall never forget the scene presented yesterday, when the fact became known . . . that the bombardment of Fort Sumter had actually commenced," the *Montgomery Daily Advertiser* proclaimed. "The people seemed wild with excitement, and congregated around the telegraph office in vast numbers for the purpose of ascertaining the news." In New Orleans, the Confederacy's largest city, the papers tried to satisfy the public's demand for information by posting brief notices on their bulletin boards, but that only seemed to stir up their excitement for fuller reports. As the editor of the *New Orleans Picayune* described, "at about the usual hour of the publication of the afternoon edition," the office "was literally besieged"—so much so that even after patrons had purchased their papers, they had difficulty squeezing their way back toward the doors to make their exit. It was the same story in the North. On the Monday after the fighting began, "crowds began to assemble on street corners to discuss the prospects of the country, and to besiege the newspaper establishments," the *Cincinnati Gazette* reported. "We can speak for the Gazette office, and say, that a more anxious congregation has never passed into our counting room in demand for the latest news." It was practically impossible to print enough papers to keep pace with consumer demand. An observer in central Massachusetts noted that within the first week of the conflict, circulation of the major New York dailies in the area had doubled, and even though local papers were cranking out their own extra editions, those were snatched up "almost instantly" as people clamored "to get the news at the earliest moment" possible. "War, war, is the all-absorbing topic of thought and conversation."[2]

Public interest in war news would not always be so intense. After large-scale battles or pivotal political events, sales would spike and then settle. Regardless of these fluctuations, though, newspapers were a constant part of life during the war. Although millions of men participated personally in the fighting, and countless numbers of civilians—particularly in the South—endured its hardships directly, most Americans experienced the Civil War on a daily basis not through combat but by reading about it in the papers. As they were living in an era prior the advent of electronic media, newspapers often were the only way in which Northerners and Southerners could stay abreast of what was happening in the war. This was particularly true in rural areas, where families were isolated even from the channels of gossip that might otherwise carry war-related information their way. Civilians were therefore voracious readers of the dailies and weeklies, sometimes scouring several different papers in order to understand developments as thoroughly and accurately as possible.

In a letter to the editor of the *Augusta Chronicle & Sentinel*, one female reader in 1862 described just how important newspapers were to her efforts to remain connected to the war. As she explained, "I live in the country, far removed from the excitement and the bias of city life. I hear nothing of what is going on, and my knowledge of passing events is derived entirely from the daily papers; my judgment upon them made up from a comparison of the facts, therein set forth." The press was her lifeline to the outside world; "I watch for the papers eagerly," she declared. "I read them with avidity."[3] She certainly was not the only one who depended on the press in this way. Over 3,700 newspapers were in publication in the Northern and Southern states on the eve of the Civil War. The dailies alone, which constituted only around 10 percent of all the papers, had a combined circulation of 1.4 million issues each day.[4] If we want to understand what the Civil War meant to the men and women who lived through it—if we want to see events as they themselves grasped them—we too have to read what they were reading, and learn about the war as they were learning about it. We have to look at the newspapers.

Just to glance at a Civil War paper is to be transported to a different era from the one in which we live today. Accustomed as we are to newspapers that are thick with articles and embellished with high-quality professional photographs, Civil War papers appear almost primitive by comparison. The typical daily newspaper consisted of just a single sheet, which was hand-fed though a steam-powered press and then folded to create a four-page edition. Only the major dailies such as the *New York Times* were longer in length, generally eight pages per issue. Although scanty by modern standards, at the time this was ample. The United States in 1860 was not yet a major world power, so with the exception of important events in Canada, England, France, and Latin America, there was little interest in international news. And as national intelligence was limited to what could be reported in short telegraph dispatches, papers rarely needed more space. In addition to being smaller in scope, Civil War newspapers were visually monotonous. Since the technology for transforming photographs into printable images did not exist, every page was virtually an unbroken sea of typeset words. It was rare for one of the dailies to publish a map, a woodcut, a cartoon, or any other type of graphic image. Just a handful of weekly papers—notably *Harper's Weekly* and *Frank Leslie's Illustrated Newspaper*—had the artistic staff, as well as the longer production schedule, to offer readers visual depictions of wartime events.

Newspapers also functioned differently. Unlike today, nineteenth-century papers did not even aspire to offer objective, balanced reporting. Rather than attempting to conceal their personal points of view, editors expressed them openly, with an eye toward actively shaping popular opinion. Some editors used their papers to focus public attention on certain social problems, as William Lloyd Garrison did with the *Liberator*, his famous antislavery sheet. Others targeted specific racial or ethnic audiences, such as the *Anglo-African*, the preeminent black newspaper of the Civil War period. Still others worked to advance the views of particular religious denominations, churning out titles like the *Christian Observer*, the *Christian Advocate*, and the *Christian Index*, which offered readers not only biblical instruction but spiritual counsel, along with secular news. Several of these religious papers sold upward of fifteen thousand copies each week, and constituted for some families their main source of reading material.[5]

More than anything else, though, newspapers were devoted to the expression of political opinion. Like practically all other men of voting age, the editors of the mainstream dailies and weeklies identified strongly with one of the major political parties of the day. Henry Jarvis Raymond, for instance, who helped launch the *New York Times* in 1851 and went on to edit it throughout the Civil War, also was a founding member of the Republican party in New York and was a delegate to the Republican National Convention in 1860 that nominated Abraham Lincoln for the presidency.

Similarly, one of the *Times*' main competitors, the *New York News*, was headed by Benjamin Wood, a prominent Democrat who served two terms in the U.S. House of Representatives during the Civil War. Not just in New York but throughout the country, newspaper editors were immersed in politics, and in running their presses, they made no effort to hide their partisan loyalties and agendas. Rather, they consciously used their papers to serve important political ends—to rally voters at election time, debate matters of public policy, and agitate for legislative change.

Among the various types of papers from which to choose, Americans were never at a loss for news during the Civil War. But the perspectives the newspapers offered were not uniform. Each had its own distinctive personality that reflected the social attitudes, political biases, and personal ambitions of the men who ran it. At the same time, the papers also mirrored the temperament of those who read them. Editors worked not just for themselves, but for profit, and expected to find their main commercial audience among like-minded readers. Republican papers were geared toward Republicans, and Democratic papers toward Democrats. Abolitionist papers circulated primarily in circles that supported abolition, just as black newspapers catered to Northern free blacks. Consequently, newspapers give us a window—a proxy—for pondering how people from different segments of society looked at the sectional crisis between the North and South, a crisis that developed into the most devastating and divisive war in our country's experience.[6]

The war itself was many years in the making—the culmination of a fateful political struggle that came to focus on a single issue: slavery. Because this political drama is so fundamental to the chapters that follow, it is important to clarify the different actors involved, including the role that newspaper editors played in it.

In the years leading up to the Civil War, two parties dominated American politics: the Democrats and the Whigs. Both parties were national in scope, with solid bases of support in all sections of the country, but their platforms and values differed vastly. Although each of them drew voters from every economic class, the Whigs appealed particularly to more prosperous, business oriented Americans, including many large slaveholders in the South. The Whig party aspired to see the United States become a more modernized society; to that end, it supported the use of federal funds for building roads, canals, and other improvements, and desired a strong national banking system to foster economic development. Whigs also tended to endorse social reform. They worked to improve education, outlaw alcohol, and at least in the North, voiced concerns about slavery. Democrats, by contrast, were less enamored with industrialization and urban growth. They disputed the use of federal finances for making internal improvements and were suspicious of "moneyed interests" such as banks. Therefore, the Democratic creed appealed especially to small farmers, although the party attracted support from immigrant Irish and German workers as well, who were at odds with the Whigs' teetotalism and aggressive reform efforts. Compared to their Whig rivals, the Democrats also supported the South's interest in slavery more completely and consistently. The sizeable differences between the two parties made for a dynamic political culture, and both developed national networks of partisan newspapers to discuss current issues and woo voters.

For decades, this national two-party system helped link Northerners and Southerners together. However, in the 1850s, bitter and bloody disputes over the westward spread of slavery—particularly in the territory of Kansas—upended it. As the crisis unfolded, slavery went from being just one of many political questions up for debate to being the primary issue. The Democrats, who had always been more supportive of slavery, navigated the crisis with relative success. The Whig party, however, collapsed, as many Southern members became increasingly strident in defending slavery and went over to the Democratic side. In its place, the

Republican party emerged in 1854. It was an exclusively Northern and antislavery party dedicated to blocking the expansion of slavery into any new lands in the American West.

By 1860, the Republicans had become the prevailing party in the North, while Democrats predominated in much of the South. These sectional majorities dictated the course of events that eventually led to the creation of the Confederacy. When the seven states of the Deep South—the stretch extending from South Carolina to Texas—withdrew from the Union in the winter of 1860–61, it was Southern Democrats who led the way. Their decision to secede was a direct reaction to the victory of Abraham Lincoln, the Republican candidate, in the 1860 presidential election. Determined to never live under the authority of an antislavery Republican president, Democratic leaders in the Deep South quickly ushered their states out of the Union before Lincoln even had the chance to take office. As these states made their exit, Democratic newspapers in the region issued impassioned editorials defending secession, lambasting Lincoln as a threat to slavery, and calling upon the common people of the South to lend their full support to making the Confederacy a glorious slaveholding empire.

Despite the boldness with which these states seceded, the entire South was not a solid unit. The states of the Upper South—Virginia, North Carolina, Tennessee, and Arkansas—still retained strong contingents of men who identified with the former Whig party, even though the party itself was defunct. Some of these Southerners were die-hard Unionists, and through newspapers run by Unionist editors, they proclaimed their loyalty to the federal government and blasted secession as treason. This brand of unconditional Unionism, however, prevailed among only a minority in the Upper South. Most people in the region believed that secession was legal in theory; nevertheless, they still wanted to give Lincoln the opportunity to prove that he could be a friend to the South before they considered withdrawing from the Union. Therefore, while their sister states in the Deep South seceded, the Upper South states stayed put, and among the local papers, most editors encouraged their readers to hope that Lincoln could find some way to de-escalate the crisis peacefully.[7]

Northerners were equally divided over secession. Republicans naturally resented the attempt by the Deep South states to evade Lincoln's constitutional authority, which he had earned through a legal and fair election. As the Republican press at the time made clear, they insisted upon preserving the integrity of the Union and wanted to punish the renegade politicians in the South who had engineered secession. But Northern Democrats, whose cooperation would be necessary to force the seceded states back into the Union, saw the situation differently. In keeping with their tolerance for slavery, they remained sensitive to the concerns of their Democratic brethren in the South. They understood why Southern secessionists saw Lincoln as a menace to their interests and believed their fear of Republican rule was justified. Democratic newspapers in the North therefore let Lincoln know that they would not support a military effort to impose his antislavery administration on any Southern states that refused to accept it willingly.[8]

All told, as the North and South drifted toward a showdown in April 1861, they did so as divided societies. The outbreak of armed hostilities at Fort Sumter, however, radically altered the situation on both sides. Once the Confederate battery in Charleston opened fire on the fort, almost everyone in the North, Republicans and Democrats alike, seemed to explode with anger and appeared wild for war. The men who ran the Northern newspapers were as riled up as their readers and took it upon themselves to ensure that the martial zeal of the moment lasted. Most Republican and Democratic editors put their political differences aside and embarked on a bipartisan crusade to support Abraham Lincoln in crushing the rebellion. Indeed, the papers were blunt in asserting that their greatest duty now was to cooperate in maintaining the public's enthusiasm for the coming fight and encouraging every citizen to do his part in it. As the Democratic *New York World* emphasized in the opening days of the conflict, "It is for the press to fire, assimilate, and give expression to—as nothing else can—that national spirit without which no land was ever saved when danger threatened." By summoning the unity and patriotism of the North, the loyal press was to be "the most effective auxiliary of the government" in Washington.[9]

A similar transformation occurred in the South. As Abraham Lincoln took steps to mobilize Northern men and resources for war, the pro-Union sentiment that previously had prevailed in the Upper South states gave way. Disgusted by Lincoln's attempt to restore the Union by force, they quickly seceded and joined the Confederacy. The entire region from Virginia to Texas now appeared determined to defend Southern independence, come what may. Southern editors, while joining in the frenzied chorus of approval for war, also took responsibility for sustaining it. With words that echoed the sentiments of his Northern counterparts, one Alabama editor candidly acknowledged, "This is a war of opinion as well as of arms." While the Confederate military was busy "deal[ing] in bayonets, bombshells, blood and sinews" and managing the nation's physical resources, the press would take charge of the psychological aspects of war-making, as its work "marshals the spirit of the revolution" and "inspires the courage" of the people to fight for victory.[10] In the North and South alike, editors aspired to be what we today would call war propagandists. Consensus was their goal, and in the moral calculus of most of them, saying or doing anything that would divide public sentiment or reduce popular support for the war was treasonous.

The Civil War was indeed a "war of opinion." As the newspapermen of the time clearly understood, victory was not simply a matter of military might. It depended on the will of the people doing the fighting. When the war began, every aspect of it was voluntary. The conversion of industries from peacetime to wartime production, the collection of food and other needed supplies, and the raising of money to finance war operations all depended on the patriotism of individual citizens. Even military service was not compulsory. Therefore, to get the war going and to keep it going, both the Union and Confederate governments would need to have public opinion on their side. They would need a level of popular support that was as steady and united as it was generous.

In their role as opinion leaders, Northern and Southern editors took up the task of soliciting this cooperation by defining, in idealistic terms, what the war was about—what their side was fighting for. It was a job that entailed invoking commonly held values and sentiments that could cut across political, religious, gender, and class lines. In the North, this meant that talk of slavery and abolition was virtually tabooed; these topics were just too controversial. Instead, newspapers focused attention on principles and goals that all Northerners could share: defending the national government, vindicating the Constitution, protecting their country from upheaval, and punishing Southern traitors. Likewise, in the South, the press portrayed the war in terms that formed a universal language for all Southerners—as a struggle not just for the maintenance of slavery, but for other goals as well: defending state sovereignty, vindicating the right of self-determination, protecting themselves from invasion, and punishing Yankee aggressors.

While appealing to these shared ideals and objectives, editors on both sides also aspired to draw their countrymen together by intensifying their fear and hatred of the enemy. Even before any large-scale military confrontations had occurred, Southern papers issued dire reports to their readers, warning them that the Union's plan for subduing the rebellion was vicious beyond comprehension. As they described it, Southern homes were to be raided and their female inhabitants raped. Civilian property was to be confiscated and given over to Yankee owners. The slaves were to be armed and incited to kill their masters. For Union soldiers, the war would be an orgy of bloodletting and crime; they would not rest until the Southern people were ruined. As the Union armies actually started advancing into the Confederacy, the press only became more strident in using these conjoined themes—Yankee barbarity on the one hand, Southern dishonor and humiliation on the other—to enlist and sustain public support for the war. The Northern press, meanwhile, indulged in its own war hates. After the Battle of Manassas in the summer of 1861—the first major contest of the war and an important victory for the Confederacy—Northern papers began circulating stories of battlefield atrocities by Confederate soldiers. Although these allegations were almost certainly false, they nevertheless became enduring symbols of Southern depravity. In the minds of many Northerners, they justified the Union's effort to prosecute the war until the rebels were fully prostrated and punished.

In whipping up popular enthusiasm for the fight, these Northern and Southern editors saw themselves as waging a "war of opinion"—a struggle to keep their readers unified and focused on victory. However, it was a struggle they could not sustain. Despite all efforts to the contrary, the Civil War became a war of opinion of a totally different sort, as angry and sometimes violent dissent flourished on both sides and found expression in the press.

Within the Union, slavery became the breaking point. The war that Northerners went to fight in 1861 was purely for the preservation of the Union. The coalition that existed between Republicans and Democrats rested on the notion that in disarming and subduing the rebels, the Union had no intention of undermining slavery or promoting its abolition. Abraham Lincoln, in keeping with public opinion on the matter, agreed that when the rebels were brought back into the Union, their slavery rights would be intact.

Such assurances notwithstanding, divisions within the Union appeared immediately. Despite the danger of being branded as disloyal, the most conservative and proslavery wing of the Democratic party refused to give themselves over to the war fever that had overtaken the vast majority of Democrats in 1861. Convinced that the federal government had no legal right to coerce the sovereign states of the South to remain within the Union, and fearful that Lincoln and his fellow Republicans—whom they saw as a "negro worshipping party"—would eventually use the war as a pretext for destroying slavery, these Peace Democrats (dubbed "Copperheads" by their opponents for the poisonous influence they theoretically exerted) believed they had their own patriotic mission to fulfill. Through press organs like the *New York News*, the *Louisville Courier*, and the *Crisis* in Columbus, Ohio, they aspired to "arouse the people, demand peace, and save our endangered country" from abolition and fratricidal self-destruction.[11] It was a position from which they never strayed, and throughout the entirety of the conflict, the Copperheads agitated against the war as a vicious, dishonorable, evil, and regrettable act of aggression.

Disagreements also emerged on the other end of the political spectrum. Whereas the Copperheads protested that the Union war effort was cruel and aggressive, free blacks and their white abolitionist allies in the North felt that it was not nearly forceful enough. They certainly supported Lincoln and applauded his determination to suppress the rebellion, but they believed his goals were too limited. Fighting just for the preservation of the Union was shortsighted, they argued. To fully disarm the rebels, the government had to destroy the one thing that had started them on the road to secession in the first place: slavery. Through the *Anglo-African*, the *Liberator*, and other abolitionist papers, they rightly insisted that to restore harmony between the North and South, Lincoln needed to finally settle their differences over slavery by demolishing the institution altogether.

Initially, these voices of dissent did not trouble the Union much. Copperheads and abolitionists, while shrill and unyielding in their beliefs, did not constitute large segments of the Northern population. For almost eighteen months the Union prosecuted the war with the widespread support of its people, and with the near-universal approval of the Northern press. However, this wave of good feeling completely collapsed in September 1862 when Lincoln shocked the country by announcing his Preliminary Emancipation Proclamation, promising freedom to all the slaves residing in rebel territory. As the president had come to recognize, what the abolitionists had asserted at the start of the war was true. It was impossible to destroy the rebellion without obliterating slavery too. Once the president endorsed emancipation, the abolitionists went from being marginalized dissenters to adoring fans of the Lincoln administration. Practically the entire Republican camp, in fact, rallied behind his new policy, and party papers hailed it as the rebellion's death knell.

This groundswell of support, however, was almost outweighed by the firestorm of opposition the Emancipation Proclamation provoked not just from Copperheads but from virtually all Democrats, who came to detest Lincoln for it. Whereas most Democratic editors had joined hands with Republicans in 1861 to back the president and unite Northerners behind him, they now broke from the ranks and began vilifying Lincoln. They had signed on to fight a war for the Union, not a war for emancipation, and felt betrayed by the president. Without necessarily turning against the war itself, many leading voices within the Democratic party branded Lincoln as a dangerous tyrant who had single-handedly transformed a glorious national struggle into a disgusting racial revolution. Some went even further and joined the Copperheads in calling for an immediate end to the fighting, before the Emancipation Proclamation could go into effect. The Democrats' outrage over emancipation was explosive. It carried a spillover effect and poisoned the way they viewed practically every other step Lincoln took in his quest to defeat the rebels. By 1864, when Lincoln was up for reelection, the Democratic press was organized solidly against him and urged Northern voters to unseat him from power. Republican papers fired back with invective of their own, denouncing Democratic criticisms as treasonous, distracting, and hostile to the Union's success. But they never did manage to staunch the angry flood of opposition. As united as Northerners seemed when the war started, they actually spent much of it arguing and fighting fiercely among themselves.

The Confederacy was no more successful in holding itself together. Although most Southerners entered the conflict determined to defend themselves and their new nation from invasion, the harsh realities of wartime eventually shattered their spirit of unity. The Union military campaigns through Southern territory were, in and of themselves, destructive, fearsome, and destabilizing. But the Confederacy also experienced devastating economic problems that pitted Southerners against each other. Shortages of food, clothing, and other basic necessities, combined with galloping wartime inflation, ruined the livelihoods of many ordinary Southerners and left them mired in poverty. Instead of charitably coming to their aid, wealthy merchants and planters generally ignored their plight, fueling their feelings of bitterness and frustration. By 1863, the widespread privation led to the outbreak of violent bread riots by women in several Southern cities and fed a desire for peace that was particularly powerful in North Carolina, northern Alabama, eastern Tennessee, western Virginia, and northern Georgia. The discontent of Southerners on the home front, which they then conveyed in letters to men on the battle fronts, also contributed to an alarming desertion rate among soldiers who felt duty-bound to return home and help their now destitute and desperate families.

Members of the Southern press fought against these forces of disintegration with all their might and tried to keep the Confederacy unified. Heedless of the true suffering that many civilians endured, editors were horrified by the upsurge in dissension and peace feeling, and repeatedly upbraided Southerners for "croaking" against the war. To revive the popular will to fight, newspapers sought to remind their readers of all that was at stake for them. As they had at the start of the conflict, they bombarded Southerners with stories detailing the dreadful consequences of defeat. In frenzied tones, the papers constantly reiterated that if the Yankees succeeded, they would seek to humiliate, brutalize, and perhaps even exterminate the Southern people. These were messages meant to frighten Southerners into ceasing their sniveling and rededicating themselves to the Confederate cause. However, in repeatedly scolding Southerners for their war weariness, editors actually helped give voice to the despondency and misery people were experiencing. Indeed, one can only wonder if the press, in harping on the atrociousness of the Yankee enemy, only added to the sense of despair that crept through the Confederacy. As the papers themselves conceded, they never did succeed in squelching it. While most editors became increasingly shrill in supporting the war effort, expressions of public discontent and disillusionment remained unabated. The picture of the Confederacy that thus emerges from the newspapers is one of a society pushed to extremes. While the war brought some Southerners to soaring heights of militant zeal, it plunged others into irrepressible frustration, hopelessness, and anger.

Looking at the Civil War through the newspapers, it becomes evident that the struggle was more than one of North versus South. The lines of opposition were not so neatly drawn. In actuality, the war was the seedbed for a multiplicity of conflicts. Certainly the sectional crisis between the North and South was the main event. But within this larger contest, other equally bitter struggles raged along political, social, and racial lines, pitting Republicans against Democrats, whites against blacks, rich against poor, women against men, and soldiers against civilians. The newspapers, in exposing these various points of friction, enable us to see the war as the complex and divisive affair it was.

In addition to chronicling the rifts that tore through the Union and Confederacy, the newspapers also reveal timeless challenges that the United States has faced again and again in going to war. In its divisiveness and contentiousness, the Civil War was hardly unique. Its history fits a pattern that other American wars share. The initial burst of martial enthusiasm, with its idealistic appeals and crusading spirit; the persistent attempt to enforce patriotism; the branding of all freely spoken opposition as traitorous and wicked; followed, ultimately, by the emergence of critical, dissenting views that defy all efforts to stifle or silence them—all of these things are characteristic of America in wartime. This crumbling of internal unity appeared most stunningly, perhaps, a full century after the Civil War, during the conflict in Vietnam. But it has been part of the American way of war since Revolutionary times. There is an inherent tension between the nature of American democracy, which respects pluralism, independent thought, and individual freedom, and the demands of war mobilization, which put a premium on conformity, unity, and self-sacrifice. Even during the Civil War—arguably the greatest crisis the United States has ever faced—it proved impossible for Americans on either side to maintain the level of unanimity with which they entered the fight. Their failure to do so, however, says as much about the controversial nature of the war as it does about the nature of American civilization itself.

The chapters that follow are based on a reading of around a thousand editorials and articles from over eighty Civil War newspapers. These, of course, represent only a fraction of the papers that circulated across the Northern and Southern states. Several criteria helped determine which ones to include here. For the sake of narrative consistency, I focused my attention on newspapers that remained in publication throughout the duration of the war. In covering the Confederacy, this was not always easy, for as the Union armies penetrated more extensively throughout the Southern states, newspapers often were driven out of circulation or were indefinitely suspended until Unionist editors could be found to run them. Even those newspapers that were relatively untroubled by the fighting still had to deal with wartime shortages of paper and ink, which eventually forced many out of business. Nevertheless, most of the newspapers used in this book survived at least until 1864. At the same time, I strived to canvass the Union and the Confederacy geographically—to give views from both the eastern and western theaters of the war and from smaller communities as well as the major cities. In the attempt to survey newspaper opinion as broadly as possible, I came up against certain limitations. While most of the documents in the book highlight the different political views and racial attitudes of the times, some attention is also given to religion. However, it simply is not feasible to account for all of the religious denominations that existed—that alone could fill an entire book. My efforts therefore concentrate on some of the more prevalent ones: Presbyterians and Congregationalists in the North, Baptists and Episcopalians in the South. Moreover, since black newspapers were few in number and inadequately preserved for posterity, black voices are less well represented here than white voices are. Finally, choices also had to be made concerning which topics to explore. The newspapers reported on practically every event of the war; no book could possibly discuss them all. My goal here is to cover the war chronologically while tapping into important episodes in its military, social, ideological, and political history. Much like the newspapers themselves, this book is a product of editorial selection and design, and in and of itself can tell only some of the stories that together constitute our country's Civil War experience.

Fighting Words

THE NEW YORK DAILY NEWS.

VOL. VI......NO. 306 | NEW YORK, SATURDAY, APRIL 13, 1861. | PRICE TWO CENTS

WAR! WAR!

COMMENCEMENT OF HOSTILITIES

BOMBARDMENT OF SUMTER.

ANDERSON REPLIES.

BRISK CANNONADING ALL DAY.

Reported Breach in the Walls of Fort Sumter.

GALLANT CONDUCT OF ANDERSON

Bravery of the Confederate States Troops.

TWO OF SUMTER'S GUNS SILENCED.

Heavy Fire From the Various Batteries.

THREE WAR VESSELS OUTSIDE.

Correspondence Between Beauregard and his Government.

KENTUCKY VOLUNTEERS CALLED ON.

Pennsylvania Army Bill Signed.

HOW THE NEWS IS RECEIVED

IMPORTANT FROM WASHINGTON.

The Confederate States Congress.

EXTRA SESSION CALLED.

Great Excitement All Over the Country.

FIRST DISPATCH.

CHARLESTON, April 11, 1861.

Intercepted dispatches disclose the fact that Mr. Fox, who had been allowed to visit Major Anderson on the pledge that his purpose was pacific, employed his opportunity to devise a plan for supplying the fort by force, and that this plan had been adopted by the Washington Government and was in progress of execution.

SECOND DISPATCH.

CHARLESTON, April 12, 1861.

The ball has opened. War is inaugurated.

The batteries of Sullivan's Island, Morris Island and other points were opened on Fort Sumter at 4 o'clock this morning. Fort Sumter has returned the fire, and a brisk cannonading has been kept up. No information has been received from the seaboard yet.

The military are under arms, and the whole of our population are on the streets. Every available space facing the harbor is filled with anxious spectators.

THIRD DISPATCH.

CHARLESTON, April 12, 1861.

Civil war has at last begun. A terrible fight is this moment going on between Fort Sumter and the fortifications by which it is surrounded.

In my last dispatch I stated that negotiations had been reopened between Gen. Beauregard and Major Anderson. This was done with a view to prevent an unnecessary effusion of blood.

The issue was submitted to Major Anderson of surrendering as soon as his supplies were exhausted, or of having a fire opened on him within a certain time.

This he refused to do, and accordingly at 4.27 this morning Fort Moultrie began the bombardment by firing two guns. To these Major Anderson replied with three of his barbette [guns, firing] against him. The remainder of the batteries are held in reserve.

Some fifteen or sixteen shots have struck the Floating Battery, but made not the slightest impression upon their iron-cased sides. The Stevens Battery is also eminently successful, and does terrible execution on Fort Sumter.

Breaches, to all appearance, are being made in the several sides exposed to fire. Portions of the parapet have been destroyed, and several of the guns there mounted have been shot away.

Major Anderson is at present using his lower tier of casemate ordnance.

The fight is going on with intense earnestness, and will continue all night.

It is not improbable that the fort will be carried by storm.

The soldiers are perfectly reckless of their lives, and at every shot jump upon the ramparts and then jump down cheering.

A party on the Stevens battery are said to have played a game of the hottest fire.

The excitement in the community is indescribable. With the very first boom of the gun thousands rushed from their beds to the harbor front, and all day every available place has been thronged by ladies and gentlemen, viewing the solemn spectacle through their glasses. Most of these have relatives in the several fortifications, and many a tearful eye attested the anxious affection of the mother, wife and sister, but not a murmur came from a single individual.

The spirit of patriotism is as sincere as it is universal. Five thousand ladies stand ready to-day to respond to any sacrifice that may be required of them.

The brilliant and patriotic conduct of Major Anderson speaks for itself, and silences the attacks lately made at the North upon his character and patriotism.

Business is entirely suspended. Only those stores open necessary to supply articles required by the army.

Governor Pickens has all day been in the residence of a gentleman which commands a view of the whole scene. General Beauregard commands in person the entire operations, and thus far they have moved with the utmost system and success.

It is reported that the Harriet Lane has received a shot through her wheelhouse. She is in the offing. No other Government ships in sight up to the present moment, but should they appear, the entire range of batteries will open upon them.

Troops are pouring into the town by hundreds, but are held in reserve for the present, the force already on the island being ample. People are also arriving every moment on horseback and by every other conveyance. Within an area of fifty miles, where the thunder of the artillery can be heard, the scene is magnificently terrible.

FOURTH DISPATCH.

The firing has continued all day without intermission.

Two of Fort Sumter's guns have been silenced, and it is reported that a breach has been made in the southeast wall.

The answer to Gen. Beauregard's demand by Major Anderson was that he would surrender when his supplies were exhausted—that is, if he was not re-enforced.

Not a casualty has yet happened to any of the forces.

Of the nineteen batteries in position, only seven have opened fire on Fort Sumter, the remainder are held in reserve for the expected fleet.

Two thousand men reached this city this morning, and embarked for Morris Island and the neighborhood.

FIFTH DISPATCH.

The bombardment of Fort Sumter continues.

The floating battery and Stephens battery are operating freely, and Fort Sumter is returning the fire.

It is reported that three war vessels are outside the bar.

SIXTH DISPATCH.

The firing has ceased for the night but will be renewed at daylight in the morning, unless an attempt is made to re-enforce, which ample arrangements have been made to repel.

The Pawnee, Harriet Lane and a third steamer are reported off the bar.

Troops are arriving by every train.

SEVENTH DISPATCH.

The bombardment is still going on every [illegible]

HIGHLY IMPORTANT CORRESPONDENCE

CHARLESTON, April 12, 1861.

The following is the telegraphic correspondence between the War Department at Montgomery and Gen. Beauregard immediately preceding the hostilities. The correspondence grew out of the formal notification by the Washington Government, which is disclosed in Gen. Beauregard's first dispatches:

[No. 1.]

CHARLESTON, April 8, 1861.

L. P. Walker, Secretary of War:

An authorized messenger from President Lincoln just informed Gov. Pickens and myself that provisions will be sent to Fort Sumter peaceably or otherwise by force.

(Signed) G. T. BEAUREGARD.

[No. 2.]

MONTGOMERY, April 10, 1861.

Gen. G. T. Beauregard, Charleston:

If you have no doubt of the authorized character of the agent who communicated to you the intention of the Washington Government to supply Fort Sumter by force, you will at once demand its evacuation; and if this is refused, proceed in such manner as you may determine to reduce it. Answer.

(Signed) L. P. WALKER, Secretary of War.

[No. 3.]

CHARLESTON, April 10, 1861.

L. P. Walker, Secretary of War:

The demand will be made to-morrow at 12 o'clock.

(Signed) G. T. BEAUREGARD.

[No. 4.]

MONTGOMERY, April 10, 1861.

Gen. Beauregard, Charleston:

Unless there are especial reasons connected with your own condition, it is considered proper that you should make the demand at an early hour.

(Signed,) L. P. WALKER, Secretary of War

[No. 5.]

CHARLESTON, April 10, 1861.

L. P. Walker, Secretary of War, Montgomery

The reasons are special for 12 o'clock.

(Signed,) G. T. BEAUREGARD.

[No. 6.]

CHARLESTON, April 11, 1861.

L. P. Walker, Secretary of War:

Demand sent at 2 o'clock—allowed till 6 o'clock answer.

(Signed.) G. T. BEAUREGARD,

[No. 7.]

MONTGOMERY, April 11, 1861.

Gen. Beauregard, Charleston:

Telegraph the reply of Major Anderson.

(Signed) L. P. WALKER, Sec'y of War.

[No. 8.]

CHARLESTON, April 11, 1861.

L. P. Walker, Secretary of War:

Major Anderson replies: "I have the honor to acknowledge the receipt of your communication demanding the evacuation of this fort, and to say in reply thereto, that it is a demand with which I regret that my sense of honor and my obligations to my Government prevent my compliance." He adds: "probably I will await the first shot, and if you do not batter us to pieces we will be starved out in a few days." Answer. G. T. BEAUREGARD.

[No. 9.]

MONTGOMERY, April 11, 1861.

General Beauregard, Charleston:

We do not desire needlessly to bombard Fort Sumter if Major Anderson will state the time at which, as indicated by him, he will evacuate, and agree that, in the meantime, he will not use his guns against us, unless ours should be employed against Fort Sumter. You are thus to avoid the effusion of blood. If this, or its equivalent, be refused, reduce the fort as your judgment decides to be the most practicable. (Signed) L. P. WALKER, Secretary of War.

[No. 10.]

CHARLESTON, April 12, 1861.

L. P. Walker, Secretary of War:

He would not consent. I write to-day.

G. T. BEAUREGARD.

The Confederate States Congress.

MONTGOMERY, April 12, 1861.

An extra session of the Confederate States Congress has been called for April 29.

Pennsylvania Legislature.

HARRISBURG, April 12, 1861.

The War bill passed both Houses to-night without amendment. Governor Curtin waited at the Executive Office to sign it. It is signed.

The Charleston dispatches about hostilities were announced in both Houses, and produced profound sensation.

Mr. Smith, a Democratic member of the House, after the Charleston dispatches were received, changed his vote to aye on the War bill. All the Democrats of both Houses voted against it.

The bill appropriates $500,000 for the purpose of arming and equipping the military, authorizes a temporary loan, provides for the appointment of an Adjutant General, Commissary General, and Quartermaster General, who, with the Governor, are to have power to carry the act into effect.

Excitement in Mobile.

MOBILE, April 12, 1861.

There is an intense excitement and rejoicing here. Fifteen guns have been fired in honor of the attack on Fort Sumter.

The Kentucky Volunteer Regiment [illegible]

From Washington.

WASHINGTON, April 12, 1861.

It is denied that any portion of the Confederate States loan has been offered in New York. More than the entire amount has been arranged at par within the limits of the Confederacy.

The expedition for the relief of Fort Sumter, it is said, has been undertaken against the advice of Lieut. Gen. Scott. He has urged the evacuation of both Forts Sumter and Pickens.

Senator Sumner called on Mr. Seward to-day with James Redpath, the agent of the Government of Hayti, and made known the passage of the resolution by the Legislature of Massachusetts, instructing its Senators and Representatives to use their influence to obtain the recognition of the Haytien independence.

Mr. Sumner stated that this resolution was adopted on the petition of all the merchants of Boston having trade with Hayti, and added his own personal desires to those thus expressed by the Legislature. He also said that Governor Andrew warmly approved of this policy. It was also suggested that such a recognition was calculated to have a good effect in counteracting the reported Spanish movement against Dominica.

The Virginia Commissioners arrived in this city this morning, and during the afternoon they visited the President, but not in their official capacity, and were received by him directly after the Cabinet meeting adjourned.

The President has made the following Massachusetts appointments:

Charles A. Phelps, Surveyor of the Port of Boston, in place of Fletcher Webster, who was removed at the earnest request of the Massachusetts Congressional delegation.

Eugene L. Norton, Navy Agent at Boston; Richard H. Dana, District Attorney, John S. Keys, Marshal; John A. Goodwin, Postmaster at Lowell.

O. C. P. Baldwin, Marshal, and Geo. Howe, Attorney for Vermont.

Jas. C. Aiken, Marshal; and Ed. G. Bradford, Attorney for Delaware.

Lansing G. Vance, Postmaster at Norristown, Penn.

Harmon Bennett, Postmaster at Norwich, N. Y.

From Vera Cruz.

NEW ORLEANS, April 12, 1861.

The steamship Tennessee, from Vera Cruz, with dates to the 9th, has arrived here, bringing $170,000 in specie.

A conducta of $3,000,000 arrived at Vera Cruz on the 13th, and $2,500,000 was taken by British packets.

Lacrdo de Lajada is dead.

The roads to the Capital were newly patrolled.

Juarez has certainly been elected President.

It is reported that Mr. Weller, United States Minister, had tendered his resignation.

Virginia Convention.

RICHMOND, April 12, 1861.

The fourteenth resolution was adopted with Mr. Scott's amendments.

This being the last resolution, the committee took up the proposed amendments to the Constitution.

The Wise substitute was rejected. Adjourned.

The Hon. John Tyler received this afternoon from Montgomery copies of official dispatches between Gen. Beauregard, Maj. Anderson and Secretary of War Walker. These were printed and circulated in the Convention. Considerable sensation was caused, but there was no indication that the Union men will consent to secede without the co-operation of the Border States. The public mind is greatly excited.

The State Canals.

SYRACUSE, April 12, 1861.

At a meeting of the Board of Canal Commissioners, held in this city to-day, the following resolution was adopted:

Resolved, That the Canals of this State shall be opened and ready for navigation on the 1st of May next.

The Vagrancy Bill.

ALBANY, April 12, 1861.

The bill relating to cases of vagrancy in the Police Courts of New York and continuing the Police Justices, originates with the Commissioners of Charities and Correction, suggested by their experience of the good management of the present Police Justices over vagrancy cases.

The new system of special sessions is working well, and the Police Justices being all experienced, it is thought by the Commissioners that public interests will be better secured by continuing the present Justices until the change by appointment under the new Constitution is made. If this conservative principle is adopted, they say this important branch of the administration will not be surrendered to ward politicians without regard to competency.

Failures and Suspensions.

BOSTON, April 12, 1861.

The Boston Commercial's list of the business changes in the United States for the last week gives 11 failures and suspensions in New York, 7 in Boston, 5 in Springfield, 2 in Baltimore, 2 in Detroit, and 19 in other places, being a total of 46.

The Brig War Eagle.

PHILADELPHIA, April 12, 1861.

The steamer Keystone State, from Charleston, has arrived here with the captain and crew of the brig War Eagle. The War Eagle was bound from Port-au-Prince for Philadelphia, and was wrecked on Cape Hatteras shoals on Monday night. George Brown, seaman, of Boston was drowned.

Philadelphia Stock Board.

PHILADELPHIA, April 12, 1861.

Stocks inactive. Pennsylvania State 5s, 87; Reading Railroad, 19; Morris Canal, 50; Long Island Railroad, 10; Pennsylvania Railroad, 31½. Sight Exchange on New York at par @1-10 ¼ cent. discount.

Markets.

PHILADELPHIA, April 12, 1861.

Flour firm. Wheat dull; sales 9,000 bushels at $1 32@$1 34. Corn firm; sales 8,000 bushels at 66@68c. Mess Pork $17 50. Lard advancing; 10¾c. refused. Whisky steady at 17½@18c.

BALTIMORE, April 12, 1861.

Flour steady; Howard street and Ohio $5 37½; City Mills held at the same rate. Wheat firm; red $1 30@$1 36; white $1 40@$1 70. Corn firm; mixed at 66@68c.; yellow 19@60c.; white 61@63c. Provisions firm and rates unchanged. Coffee firm; Rio 12½@13½c. Whisky 17¼@17½c.

NEW ORLEANS, April 12, 1861.

Cotton—Sales to-day 1,800 bales at 12@12½c. for middling; sales of the week, 11,250 bales; receipts do., 14,800 bales. Decrease of receipts, 322,800 bales; and at all Southern ports, 775,800 bales. Exports, 37,000 bales; total exports of the season, 1,113,100 bales. Stock in port, 119,400 bales. Coffee—Sales of the week, 7,410 bags at 10½@13½c. Stock in port, 10,100 bags, against 20,000 bags the same time last year.

[illegible] 1861. The year 1861 will [illegible]

THE WAR CLOUD.

SHIPS AND TROOPS STILL MOVING.

THE TEXAN SOLDIERS GONE.

CHIEF ENGINEER KING DETACHED.

LOCAL MILITARY AND NAVY NEWS.

THE COATZACOALCAS TROOPS.

At seven o'clock yesterday morning, the steamer Coatzacoalcas hauled alongside the wharf at the foot of Warren street, and the troops on board commenced to disembark. The luggage was first removed and put on board the towboats B. L. Mabey and Pope Catlin. By noon all the men had left the Coatzacoalcas, the Washington detachments being the last to leave. Annexed is a tabular distinction of the companies as they departed:

FOR WASHINGTON.

	Men.
Company D, Second Cavalry	59
Company H, Second Cavalry	41
Total	100

FOR CARLISLE.

Company B, Second Cavalry	64
Company J, Second Cavalry	50
Company G, Second Cavalry	64
Company E, Second Cavalry	48
Total	232

FOR FORT HAMILTON.

Company I, First Infantry	83
Grand total	417

The arrival of the infantry at Fort Hamilton was the signal for a repetition of the bustle and excitement occasioned by the garrisoning of that fortress some time since. The rooms occupied by the Artillery Companies from Texas were prepared by the Sergeant in charge for these new residents, who are now comfortably located in them. A guard was mounted in the afternoon, and sentinels told off for their duty as though the poor fellows had just returned from furlough, instead of harrassing service. The $50,000 appropriated by the Government for the extension of the Fort Hamilton batteries are beginning to be used, in the employment of workmen, etc.

GOVERNOR'S ISLAND.

The increasing preparations which have been making on the Island for some days to receive troops, were not made for nothing, as we anticipated. No sooner had the arrival of the Coatzacoalcos been announced on Thursday than Fort Columbus was in a ferment. Off-duty men rushed to the beach to cheer their returned comrades, police parties threw by their work and followed suit, even the day's guard forgot the dignified disregard of events going on off their post—which sentinels generally observe—and went as far from the guard room as they dared. The band, having been tired playing the Girl I Left Behind Me for departing troops, were glad to have a chance of altering it to a less melancholy strain. (See the Conquering Hero Comes is the time usually played on the occasion of re-enforcements, but it did'nt exactly suit the case.) Paddy Carey was performed with spirit. The barracks, mess rooms and baggage rooms received a hasty brush up, and missing belt pegs and musket racks were supplied. Yesterday morning the continual arrival and departure of officers and messengers from the city betokened active movements, the nature of which Providence and Gen. Scott only know.

THE NAVY YARD.

The business at the Navy Yard continues with unabated vigor. In all the departments bustle and activity are visible. The machine shops have the engines and machinery of the Wabash and Roanoke in hands. The former is approaching completion rapidly, and will probably be finished on Tuesday; the latter is not being hurried. The Marine barracks still have about 86 troops, none having been detached for some time. They are drilled every day, sometimes along with the guard of the receiving ship. Instead of one commanding officer, one executive captain and three lieutenants, the commissioned officers of the post consist of Capt. Brevoort and Major Doughty. Sergeant McDonald has been acting officer of the day in his turn for weeks, but the honor is all trouble and no profit. In the Paymaster's Department, Mr. Belknap, the new incumbent, has just "got the hang of things," Mr. Nixon keeping him posted during his initiation term.

The late Acting Clerk in the Purser's office, Mr. Murray, who has gone to Mare Island with his father, is replaced by Mr. Belknap's son, an intelligent, gentlemanly fellow. The visitors who daily throng the premises minutely examine all the attractions of the yard, from that "old curiosity shop," the Lyceum, to the magnificent launching ways, which have been bridged over and completed. The new gun ground, which will be one of the finest "ornamental squares" at the station, when completed, is quite ready for the cannon, but they have not yet been brought down. The skids are all laid.

THE ARMORY.

Tightly bound, and hid from the gaze of outsiders, is the Armory. Since the memorable night on which the capture of the Navy Yard was decided upon by some desperadoes, whom the Commandant is reported to have seen in a dream, the doors of this building have been shut up, and no one but the "Keeper of the Keys" can tell how the arms look now. The muskets, cutlasses, carbines, pistols, boarding pikes, and the rails filled with cartouche boxes are [illegible]

pound heavy howitzers (for the launches), 2 twelve pound light howitzers (for the [illegible]). This battery will, of itself, weigh over [illegible] and will have attached to it little less than [illegible] rounds of shot, shell, &c. It will soon be [ready] for work. The Wabash is to get her [illegible] to-day or Monday, and will have steam up [this] afternoon.

THE SAVANNAH.—The armament of the Savannah recently consisted of quite a large [illegible] of comparatively light guns. It will be changed. The impression seems to be now that she [will] have 22 nine inch guns, which will make [her] battery nearly equal in power, as regards weight of metal, to the spar deck of the Wabash, excepting pivots. The authorities [seem] to think, like Napoleon, that Providence [and] victory are on the side of the big artillery. Hence the Savannah's improved arma[ment]. She is progressing fast, and will be re[ported] ready about the 15th of May—not before.

THE PERRY.—The Perry will have six [thirty-]two pounders, weighing 27 cwt. each, and [a] light twelve pound howitzer; quite a formidable armament for a little brig. Her shot rails, perhaps, contain some 2,890 shot, shell[s]. The rigging of this vessel is almost up, [and she] can be ready for sea in a few days.

THE RECRUITING OFFICES.

The business at the recruiting offices [since our] notice on Wednesday, has not mate[rially] changed. Cedar and Chatham streets are each about thirty men per week, who are [sent] over to Fort Columbus, when sworn in [and] "refreshed." The cavalry rendezvous in [Hudson] street is not doing much. When a dozen recruits are obtained at the [depot], they are dispatched to the "horse soldiers' depot," Carlisle, Penn., where riding masters [and] green steeds await them. After going th[rough] the initiatory service of a mounted tro[oper], they are then drafted for California, O[regon] and other distant regions, where the in[fantry] needs assistance. There are generally [150] to 200 men at Carlisle, and a large [stable] filled with horses, many of which, notorio[us for] their wickedness, are kept permanently [to in]ure the new military man into the difficult[ies] of his profession.

BOSTON, MASS.—Six men were sent to the [Naval Renderzvous?] cal depot, Governor's Island, on Monday, [and] six on Wednesday. The rendezvous w[as al]most besieged by aspirants for military [service]. Any number of men could be enlisted, bu[t the] same rule obtains there as in this city, a[nd] first class men are rejected. We unders[tand] that the naval recruiting rendezvous in Bo[ston] and Charlestown are in full operation.

THE STEAMERS SUPPOSED TO BE CHARTERED [BY] GOVERNMENT.

Whatever supposition might have be[en en]tertained regarding the Vanderbilt, [Ocean] Queen, or Daniel Webster, the present [condi]tion of those steamships effectually sets a[side] the idea of their being put to any imme[diate] use. The Vanderbilt has been sent ro[und to] the East River to have new condensers p[ut in], the Daniel Webster is regularly up for the [next] trip to New Orleans, and the Ocean Quee[n was] yesterday occupied by one watchman only, [the] workmen being taken off her, and s[he is] shored up for a lengthened berth at the [wharf] side. What started the rumor that those [ves]sels were engaged by Government, or [that] soldiers could have been found near New [York] to send out in them, it would be impossib[le to] say.

THE ARMSTRONG COURT MARTIAL.

Commodore Breese, the Commandant o[f the] Brooklyn Navy Yard, who has been to W[ash]ington on the Armstrong Court Martial, [re]turned to town on Thursday, and assumed [com]mand of the yard. The trial has concluded, [and] the sentence of the Court been submitted [for] the approval of the President. In the abs[ence] of any authoritative statement of its result [we] may say that there is little likelihood of the [Com]modore being cashiered. Assisted by his c[oun]sel, Mr. Phillipps, he got up a very able defe[nce] which is reported to have had great effect on [the] Court.

The launches, which were brought down f[rom] the Navy Yard to go in the Baltic and Illi[nois], and two-third cutters were yesterday retu[rned] and hauled up on the wharf.

SHUCKED HIMSELF.—A correspondent o[f a] Nashville paper tells a story, which may be [pos]sibly untrue, about a person who was goin[g to] Chattanooga on the railroad. When the [train] entered the tunnel and total darkness, said [per]son asked a stranger how long it would be g[oing] through. Stranger was a bit of a wag, and [re]plied, "two hours." Person thought he w[ould] avail himself of the opportunity to don a c[lean] shirt, and about the time he had "shucked [him]self" the train dashed out into daylight, ex[pos]ing his person to the astounded gaze of s[ome] hundred pair of male and female eyes belong[ing] to passengers. He had on no linen, and ab[out] as much other clothes as the Apollo Belvid[ere] —and no chance to run.

—Why is it impossible for men born b[lind] to be carpenters? They never saw.

—The accounts of the peach and fruit c[rop] generally in the State of Virginia are, so [far] favorable.

—All the State Conventions of the South[ern] Confederacy, except Florida, have now rat[ified] the new Constitution.

—According to the reports in Turin, the c[ost] of the bombardment of Gaeta to Sardinia a[lone] amounts to £1,000,000 sterling.

—"Mountain Maid," a racing mare, [well] known to horse fanciers and sporting men, [died] at Lancaster, Pa., last week.

—The Hon. A. H. Boteler of Va. announ[ces] himself an independent Union candidate for election to Congress.

—Dr. Holmes tells of "Men so utterly mo[an]"[illegible]

Part One Why They Fought

Chapter 1

First Shots

After thirty years of bitter debate over the future of slavery in America, the North and South finally came to blows in 1861 over a very different question of property—the right to possess Fort Sumter, a military outpost perched off the coast of Charleston. The outbreak of civil war could not have occurred at a more fitting venue. South Carolina had been the birthplace of the movement for Southern independence—or, as Northerners would come to see it, the seedbed of treason and rebellion. On December 20, 1860, a state convention had unanimously dissolved South Carolina's ties to the rest of the Union and repealed its 1788 ratification of the Constitution, touching off a final crisis between the North and South that culminated at Fort Sumter and brought them, at long last, to war.

Political leaders in the South had been debating the possibility of secession throughout the 1850s, and South Carolinians had been flirting with it for even longer. The issue for most Southerners was not *whether* they had the right to withdraw from the Union. They agreed that the individual states were sovereign and could, at will, dissolve their relationship to the federal government. Rather, it was a question of when, and under what circumstances, the Southern states could justify striking out on their own. For South Carolina, the decision to secede came as a direct reaction to the 1860 presidential election, which had placed Abraham Lincoln, the Republican candidate, in the White House. The Republican party was still new at that time; it had come together only a few years previously, in 1854, as an explicitly antislavery party. Republicans had always been clear, however, that while they regarded slavery as an evil thing, they were not abolitionists—they did not advocate its complete eradication from American soil. They conceded that the Constitution protected slavery in the Southern states where it currently existed, but they were determined to prevent it from spreading into any new territories in the American West. Still, in the eyes of the South, the Republican party's hatred of slavery posed a potentially lethal threat to the region's economic prosperity, social stability, and strict racial order.

The prevailing view in South Carolina was that the election of an antislavery president was reason enough to put the wheels of secession into motion. Lincoln's electoral victory in 1860—which he achieved without carrying a single Southern state—betokened the political disfranchisement of the South. With the North clearly holding the reins of political power now, it seemed only a matter of time before the federal government started creating laws to restrict slavery's westward expansion, perhaps as a precursor to assailing it everywhere, even in the Southern states. As South Carolina's secession convention declared, the nonslaveholding states of the North, in voting the Republican party into power, "have assumed the right of deciding upon the propriety of our domestic institutions" and "have denounced as sinful the institution of Slavery." Since the 1830s, when abolition societies first appeared in the North, "this agitation" against slavery "has been steadily increasing," and with Lincoln's triumph, "it has now secured to its aid the power of the common Government." The secessionists in South Carolina envisioned that with the inauguration of Lincoln's presidency, "the equal rights of the States" to regulate slavery would be lost. "The Slaveholding States will no longer have the power of self-government, or self-protection, and the Federal Government will have become their enemy."[1] Rather than face such a dire future, the state made a preemptive strike to secede.

With South Carolina's withdrawal from the Union in 1860, the secession movement rapidly gained momentum, as the other six states of the Deep South—Georgia, Florida, Alabama, Mississippi, Louisiana, and Texas—followed in tow. Together, they drafted a new national constitution, and on February 7, 1861, they officially conjoined their fates as the Confederate States of America, selecting Jefferson Davis of Mississippi as their provisional president. Even before they established the Confederacy, the Southern states, in their determination to throw off all signs of federal authority, had started seizing federal properties located within their boundaries: the national mint in New Orleans, as well as the military forts, naval yards, treasury offices, and customs houses that had once linked the South to the rest of the United States. By February, only four military forts in the South remained under Union control, including Fort Sumter. The commander there, Major Robert Anderson, was a devoted Unionist from Kentucky and would not surrender his garrison willingly.

The situation at Sumter quickly slid into a stalemate. The Confederacy, reluctant to provoke a war that it was unprepared to wage, did not try to militarily force Anderson to abandon the fort. At the same time, the lame-duck president, James Buchanan, whose term in office would not end until March, refused to order Anderson to surrender it. In hopes of temporarily mollifying the South, though, he did agree not to resupply the fort with provisions unless Anderson explicitly requested it. It was a tenuous and obviously imperfect truce.

Lincoln inherited this standoff when he assumed the presidential seat on March 4, 1861. In the months between his electoral victory and his accession to office, Lincoln had been silent on what he intended to do about the sectional crisis. His inauguration gave him an opportunity to finally take a public stand, and the address he delivered that day was firm: he would not yield Sumter to the Confederacy. Rather, he vowed "to hold, occupy, and possess the property and places belonging to the government" and to ensure that all federal laws were enforced in the Southern states.[2] It remained an open question, however, whether he would have the popular support he needed to actually accomplish these objectives.

Lincoln's words, which conveyed a clear determination to vindicate the rights and honor of the federal government, stood in stark contrast to the state of public opinion in the North. Throughout the winter of

1860–61, Northerners had been angrily divided on how to respond to the secession crisis. Lincoln's fellow Republicans agreed that secession was illegal—that the Southern states had no right to unilaterally withdraw from the Union and that the government could not allow them to flout its authority. Many Democrats saw the situation differently. Believing that the Union was indeed a voluntary compact and that the Lincoln administration posed a credible threat to the interests of the South and the survival of its slave-based civilization, they seemed willing to let the seceded states go. The commercial interests of the Northern states gave pause too. Northern merchants who controlled the trade in Southern cotton, and the textile manufacturers who depended on it for their businesses, wanted to preserve amicable relations with the South at all costs. With the stalemate over Sumter looming, the North was nowhere close to a consensus on what to do.

Neither was the South sure of how to proceed, for that matter. At this point, the Confederacy consisted of only the seven states of the Deep South. The other eight slave states still remained within the Union, and even within the Deep South, many questioned the wisdom of starting a war, given the decisive advantages of the Union in terms of manpower and material resources. The stressfulness of the situation was enormous, for so much was at stake, but neither side was willing to back down or move forward decisively.

Although the North and South were not ready to take action, events at Fort Sumter quickly went beyond their control. The day after Lincoln gave his inaugural speech, he received alarming news from Anderson: the garrison's supplies of food were nearly exhausted, and unless the government sent provisions, he would be forced to capitulate. Anxious to find some way of maintaining control over Sumter, Lincoln took the suggestion offered to him by Captain Augustus V. Fox of the U.S. Navy, to send a relief effort of food, but not military supplies, to Anderson and his troops. For Lincoln, the move was a calculated risk. Perhaps the Confederates would let Fox's fleet resupply Sumter. But if they did not—if they chose to counter with a military strike and initiate a war—they would do so on ships serving a humanitarian mission.

Jefferson Davis chose war. Knowing that the expedition was on its way, he ordered General P. G. T. Beauregard, the commander of the shore batteries at Charleston, to demand Anderson's surrender. On April 12, after Anderson refused, and before the Union fleet reached Charleston Harbor, Beauregard's forces, with the president's approval, fired the first shot at Fort Sumter. Davis reasoned it was better to initiate hostilities and potentially rally Southerners to the drums of war than to ignominiously allow Lincoln's relief expedition to succeed. Thirty-three hours later, with the fort now in flames from the Southern cannonade, Anderson finally was left with no option but to acquiesce. Despite the length of the engagement, not a single life was lost on either side during the fighting—testimony to both the inaccuracy of the artillery pieces and the inexperience of the soldiers in using them. It was a bloodless beginning to what would become, in terms of American lives, the bloodiest war in the nation's history.[3]

The Northern response to the outbreak of hostilities was nothing short of spectacular. After months of waiting and waffling over what to do, the public seemed to explode with pent-up emotions. Now that the Confederacy had disgraced the national flag and aggressively taken control of Sumter, Northerners were suddenly hot for a fight. Many Democrats, who before had wanted the federal government to negotiate with the rebels and find a peaceful way to resolve the crisis, clasped hands with Republicans in clamoring for war. "The telegrams announcing the bombardment of Fort Sumter created a feeling in this city of the most intense character," a reporter in Philadelphia noted. "With the first fire that was opened on Major Anderson, all desire for conciliating the South seemed to have passed from the masses.—Men who were ardent for compromise a few days previous" had become "most belligerent" now. It was the same story

THE SIEGE OF SUMTER.

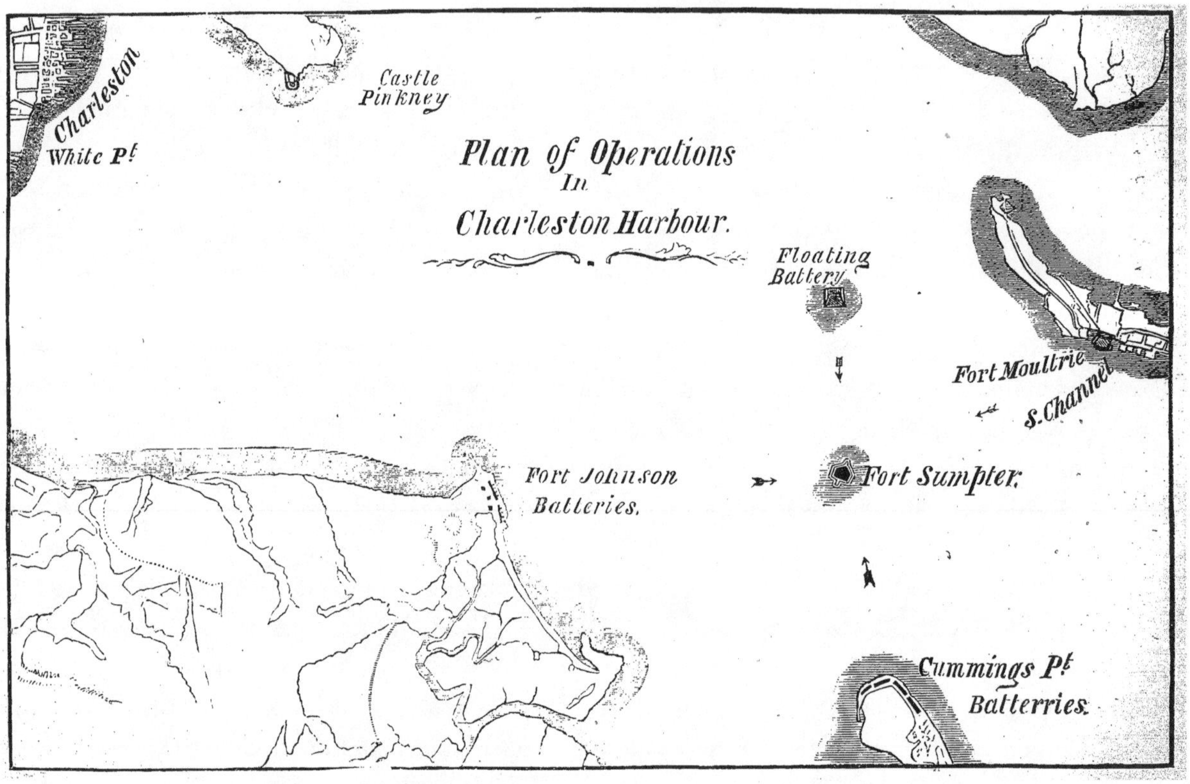

TOP *Cleveland Plain Dealer*, April 15, 1861.
In 1861, the technology for taking photographs of battle scenes and reproducing them on newsprint did not exist. Newspapers that wanted to give readers a visual image of the bombardment of Fort Sumter therefore had to rely on woodcuts or drawings.

BOTTOM *Frank Leslie's Illustrated Newspaper*, April 27, 1861.
Map of the theater of operations around Fort Sumter.

in practically every Northern community. The people were almost joyful, and definitely relieved, that the standoff had finally ended. On April 15, when the president called for 75,000 volunteers to help put down the rebellion, Northerners enlisted in droves, enthusiastic for the chance of making Southerners pay for their audacity.

Patriotic displays appeared everywhere. As one newspaper described, the entire North seemed to be convulsed with "a severe attack of the Star-Spangled Banner on the brain." At public demonstrations in towns and cities across the North, bands pounded out the American anthem, while people draped the national colors from their windows, doors, and rooftops, even decorating their horses and carriages with them. "Men walk the streets with badges of red, white, and blue on their breasts. Flags float from every public edifice, from every newspaper office, from every hotel, from every church spire, from almost every store, and from thousands of private dwellings," an observer wrote of the scene in New York City. "Fifth avenue has decorated her brown-stone fronts with star-spangled banners as gaily as she decorates her fashionable daughters for an evening party." The feeling was electric. "Patriotic devotion is the one dominating feeling everywhere," exulted the *New York World*. "We have, at last, thank God—and most reverently do we say it—we have, at last, a united North."[4]

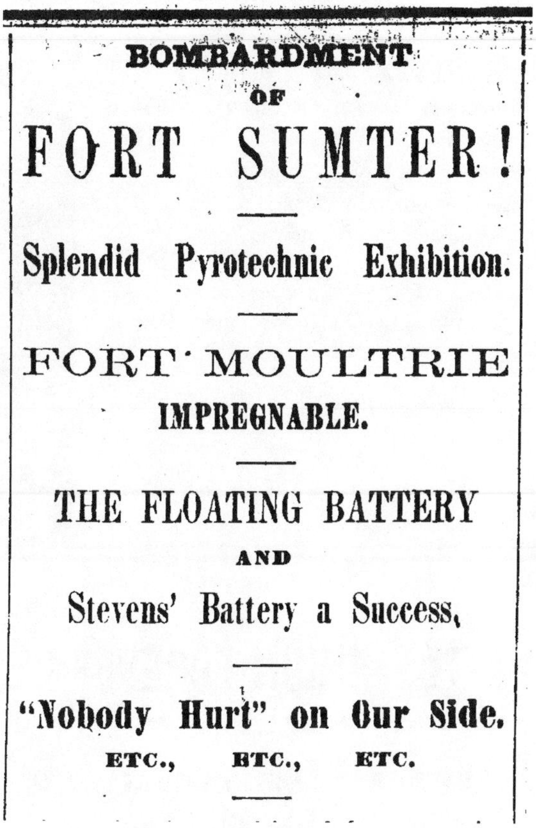

BOMBARDMENT

OF

FORT SUMTER!

Splendid Pyrotechnic Exhibition.

FORT MOULTRIE

IMPREGNABLE.

THE FLOATING BATTERY

AND

Stevens' Battery a Success,

"Nobody Hurt" on Our Side.

ETC., ETC., ETC.

Charleston Mercury, April 13, 1861.
Instead of using bold headlines that spread across the entire width of the front page, newspapers used a "pyramid" style of headlining that ran lengthwise down one column. Even this pivotal announcement, marking the start of the Civil War, did not warrant anything grander or more dramatic.

The outpouring of patriotism was so intense and so universal that practically every newspaper felt compelled to comment on it. Given the aimless way in which the Union had been drifting, as if too timid or too distracted to defend itself against secession, the sudden displays of national pride and martial zeal were like a revelation. Some people had been starting to wonder if, after enjoying many decades of economic growth and material prosperity, Northerners had become so self-absorbed as to stop caring about the fate of their country. The truth, as the *Harrisburg Patriot & Union* reported, was far different:

> Persons who have been accustomed to indulge in doleful lamentations at the supposed dearth of patriotism in this country . . . have lived long enough to have their painful apprehensions dissipated. The events of the past ten days demonstrate beyond question the intense love of country, which, in peaceful times, appears latent in the breast of American freemen; but when the cause of country calls [them] to arms is ardent and irrepressible. Where on the face of the earth can another nation be found to present the same spectacle as the American people at this

RIGHT *Harper's Weekly,* May 4, 1861. New Yorkers congregated in Union Square on April 20, 1861, for a patriotic rally that brought together all citizens—men and women, Republicans and Democrats—in support of the Union.
(© Applewood Books, Inc. Reproduced by permission of Applewood Books and harpersweekly.com)

BELOW *New York Times,* April 21, 1861.

THE UNION FOREVER!

Immense Demonstration in this City.

THE ENTIRE POPULATION IN THE STREETS.

Over One Hundred Thousand People at Union-square.

The Metropolis Streaming with Banners and Streamers.

eventful period of history? . . . Our people appreciate the blessings of Union. They know the immeasurable value of a good Government. They have too long enjoyed the blessings of peace and prosperity to submit to the inauguration of the reign of anarchy without a struggle. . . .

This unanimous uprising of the people of the loyal States did not enter into the calculations of the conspirators now in arms against the Federal Government. They falsely imagined that because a very large element of the Northern people deprecated an appeal to arms, and forbore with unexampled patience to meet force with force, that they might proceed to any extremity against the Government of the Union, without having to confront its vast power. They supposed that we were so absorbed in money-getting that patriotism was extinguished, and the commencement of war upon the Government would rend us into hostile factions. Fatal error! Never did a deluded people commit a more egregious blunder. Reverence for the Union, respect for the laws, detestation of those who would tear the country into fragments, is paramount to every other sentiment in the breasts of the American people. . . . Patriotism is the ruling passion of all true Americans—not money, or party or power. We know this to be true now, and knowing it, we are certain that a Government cannot be overthrown which is founded upon the love of the people.[5]

The zeal for war and the rush to mobilize for it were not confined to the men of the North. Women too were eager not only to show their support for the con-

* Volunteers! Volunteers!! Volunteers!!! *
Young men desirous of rallying round the Standard of the Union, and willing to maintain its time-honored folds unsullied over the ramparts of Fort Sumter, will enroll themselves immediately in the new volunteer Light Artillery Regiment, now rapidly filling up, and ready to march upon the receipt of orders from the Governor. Muster Rolls open every day and evening, at Military Hall, Third street, near Green. By order of Captain J. BRADY, Acting Major.

Philadelphia Inquirer, April 15, 1861.
The United States in 1861 did not have a national draft, so the country had to depend on volunteers to fight its battles. Through advertisements like this, newspapers helped notify citizens where and when to enlist.

flict but to participate actively in it. In keeping with the Victorian notions of the time, though, women's wartime roles were not supposed to extend too far beyond the home. Single women might consider applying for a position in the new corps of army nurses being enlisted by the War Department. More typically, they were encouraged to organize patriotic societies in their hometowns and to raise money and provisions for the soldiers and their families, which were now losing their male breadwinners to the war. Their most essential responsibility, however, was to swallow any feelings of sadness or hesitation and, in a spirit of heroic self-sacrifice, usher the men they loved into the army. By doing their part, women would help empower men to do theirs—a lesson pressed home by newspaper articles such as this one from the *Troy Times*:

> They are mistaken, who think that in the mighty struggle now impending, woman has no share. In this, indeed, as in the other missions of life, her influence is quiet, unobtrusive, but holy and important in the highest degree. War enters the circle of the family. . . . It calls the husband, the brother, the son, from his sphere of activity, to enter new fields, and perform other duties. . . . It calls away the objects upon which affection has been lavished, and devotes them to danger, possibly to death. In such an emergency as this, is it nothing that she who remains behind should willingly, uncomplainingly,—though sorrowfully perhaps,—surrender all she holds most dear at the call of her country? Is it nothing that, with noble resolution, she should bid the husband or the son to go forward and discharge his duty. . . ? A woman's gentle encouragement, and high-souled abnegation of herself, can exercise more influence in determining the conduct of a true man, and making him act in a manner worthy of himself, than any other thing on earth. There is not a soldier [that] will enter the field of battle with firmer step and more invincible will, if the voice of the woman he loves best has cheered him in his departure, and he knows she waits to hear that he has done well his part. . . .
>
> Some work can likewise be found for woman's hand, in this contest. A battle-field always presents its painful features of mangled limbs and bleeding bodies, and these call for attention.—For such purposes, bandages, lint and other things must be provided. These can be made ready by women. . . . So, likewise, extra blankets, felt hats, shirting, rubber capes, and other accessories of comfort in camp life—often very important in the preservation of health—are, we understand, permitted to be carried by each soldier, in addition to the uniform provided by the Government. Some of the men will be unable to procure these for themselves, and what can be more useful than a movement on the part of women to furnish them?. . . Anything that can conduce to the actual value of a soldier on the field, or aid in the preservation of his life, will be of value, and will no doubt be thankfully received. Is there not room enough for women to work? Is there not work sufficient for her to do?[6]

The ebullience with which Northerners greeted the outbreak of war reflected not just the stridency of their patriotism but also a complacent sense of confidence that the Union's ultimate triumph was inevitable. Just in terms of brute resources, the North dwarfed the South in population, food production, and industrial and financial capital. The rebels also appeared weaker in terms of their character and intellect. In Northern eyes, Southern society was composed of wealthy, effete slaveholders and masses of uneducated, poor whites, neither of which were fit for stern military action. All together, then, Northerners believed they had nothing to fear, as this editorial, taken from the *New York World*, suggests:

> First, we have the difference in physical constitution. The people of cold latitudes are naturally more robust, more hardy, possessed of greater physical strength and stamina, than those of warm latitudes; and this, though not so great an advantage as it used to be before the invention of gunpowder, when combats were mainly hand to hand and forced marches were constant, still, so far as it goes, makes positively in favor of the North. . . . Intelligence, too, is an important consideration. The ignorant man always fights with less aptitude and less presence of mind than the man whose mind has had a certain training. Great numbers of the southern rank and file must be taken from the multitudes that are down in . . . the totally illiterate class—that peculiar species of the southern citizen appropriately designated in the southern dialect as "the white trash."
>
> Even more important . . . is the difference superinduced by the fact that the labor of one section is performed by freemen, [and the labor] of the other by slaves. The great majority of the northern volunteer forces will consist of men who at home are engaged in daily manual labor. Their bodies are well developed, well knit, compacted, inured to fatigue; and their minds are trained to the patience and persistence inseparable from habitual labor, and which preeminently fit them for that strict, steady discipline without which an army is little better than a rabble. It is here that volunteers are most apt to fail, but most assuredly the men of the North will be far less exposed to it than the men of the South, few of whom, comparatively, have ever known continuous, systematic labor. The sons of slaveholders, accustomed to a life of ease and to the unrestrained indulgence of their wills, are pretty uncompromising subjects for any kind of subordination; and as for those who have no negroes, they are, in general, without knowledge or enterprise, and quite as impatient of any sort of prolonged effort. It is not possible that a body of volunteer officers and soldiers made of such material should have the efficiency of such men as the North is now marshaling. . . .
>
> There are other points, each of prodigious consequence, in favor of the federal government, which are so obvious that they hardly need an allusion;—the fact that the North, by its great superiority in white population, can furnish at least two, probably three, fighting men for every one of the South—the fact that the federal government, supported by its foreign and domestic credit, . . . has ten times greater resources for the maintenance of its armies—the fact that the federal government has a powerful navy to cooperate in its military operations, while the rebels have none. . . . But better than [all] we have yet mentioned is the fact that the cause in which the North is engaged is a righteous cause. . . . It is the cause of constitutional freedom and social order, and national prosperity, against unhallowed ambition, black conspiracy, wild passion, anarchy and ruin. . . . Were there nothing else in favor of the North than this infinite superiority of the cause for which they are contending, it would be almost a moral impossibility that they should not prevail. But when, superadded to this, are the manifold other advantages we have mentioned, the ultimate result becomes absolutely sure and inevitable. It is not more certain that the earth will revolve than that this government will be maintained.[7]

The North's confidence seemed unbounded. More than just certain of victory, Northern papers assumed that the nation would derive incredible benefits from waging and winning the struggle. By showing their military might and proving their superiority over their Southern brethren, Northerners would emerge from the conflict ennobled and "purified" by the experience. In giving themselves to the national cause, they would learn to think beyond their own narrow, selfish needs and appreciate their higher responsibilities as citizens:

> War is an expensive luxury. However humanely and discreetly waged, it is a serious drain upon the life of a nation. We shall come out of the present struggle impoverished in many ways. With the best of success, we shall expend hundreds of millions of treasure and sacrifice thousands of lives. We shall feel the bruises of the conflict for years after the rebellion has been crushed and peace has been restored. Thousands of fortunes will be wrecked—thousands of homes made desolate—thousands of bright careers will be arrested. The mourners will go about the streets. There will be sorrow and anguish. . . .
>
> Will it pay the cost? Yes—a hundred—a thousand fold—if we come out of the struggle conquerors! If we succeed in crushing out this miserable rebellion—if we exterminate the fatal heresy of secession—if we . . . succeed in convincing the world that we have a government strong enough, vigorous enough, determined enough, to overcome all combinations and attacks, . . . the war, no matter how long or how desperately waged, will be the cheapest enterprise upon which the nation ever embarked. Every drop of blood. . . . will fructify into future blessings. We shall emerge from the conflict stronger in all that goes to make up the life of a great people. We shall resume the calm pursuits of peace, chastened by the trial through which we have passed—purified by the affliction with which we have been visited. We shall find ourselves elevated to a higher moral plane, and quickened by nobler impulses to the performance of nobler deeds. We shall find ourselves purer, more self-reliant, more self-poised, more able to grapple with future issues, and avoid future dangers. We shall find ourselves less bound up in selfishness, less the slaves of toil and business, less grovelling in our tastes, less earthly in our aspirations.[8]

As the newspapers portrayed it, the war was to be welcomed, not regretted—or resisted. Now that the rebels had crossed the proverbial Rubicon in disgracing the federal flag at Fort Sumter, the editors of Northern papers clamored for a swift, unyielding attack on the Confederacy. No "half-way measures" were to be allowed—no offers of conciliation or mercy were to be shown until the rebels agreed to submit unconditionally to the authority of the federal government. "*The South has chosen war, and it must have all the war it wants*," vowed the *New York Times*. An immediate, aggressive invasion was the only way to bring about a speedy reunion between the sections. By hitting the Southern states with overwhelming military force, the Union armies would cow them into submission, dispel their dreams of independence, and restore sectional harmony before the fighting got out of hand. One editor couched it in this way: "The war must be carried on with vigor—with that humane cruelty which restores the blessings of peace by doing the most injury possible in the shortest space of time." In keeping with the angry passions that overtook the North at the time, the Southern people had to be made to feel the harshness of war personally. "We must pierce, fight, and crush the traitors upon their own soil, under the shadow of their own homes—or if need be, amid the glare arising from their blazing domicils," another paper exclaimed.[9] As the *Chicago Tribune* envisioned, in storming the South by land and blockading its ports by sea, there would be no holds barred:

> Let there be no boy's play—no waiting for repentance, for a willing return to patriotism and duty; no

Frank Leslie's Illustrated Newspaper, April 30, 1861. Amid the cheers and salutes of their fellow citizens, the Sixth Regiment of Massachusetts Volunteers prepares to leave Jersey City to help defend Washington. In the early days of the war, the public mood was exuberant and the number of men who wanted to fight for the Union seemed inexhaustible.

sending of sods, no battles with squirt guns and buttered words. The men invoked to sustain the supremacy of the law and to vindicate the majesty of the Republic must be called by the half million in a levy. The credit of our people must be strained to the uttermost to raise the means to equip them. . . . Every port in the South must be blockaded, and wherever by land our army can be driven into the interior, there it should go. The trade of the rebels must be cut off by vigorous and effective means. Their exports must be stopped. "Eat your cotton, d——n you!" is the command that must be addressed to them by every Northern man—a command that every Northern man must be prepared to enforce. . . . With the immense preponderance of wealth, military resources and fighting men enlisted in support of the Government, [we] would close the contest in a short six months. . . . This is a war—not an émeute that a sheriff and a corporal's guard can suppress. . . . All the means legitimate in civilized warfare must be freely employed. If necessary to burn, kill and destroy, let there be no hesitation. Temporizing is out of place, and, in the end, more destructive of life than vigorous and decisive measures. The great object to be attained is a speedy and honorable peace by the restoration of Government authority. If to compass that, Charleston, New Orleans, Mobile or Baltimore must be sacrificed, let the sacrifice be made. If it be necessary to sweep Virginia with the besom of destruction, let no man hold his hand. If Maryland must be obliterated, the command to lay waste should be only a day ahead of its execution.[10]

While the *Tribune* was quick to recommend the sacking of Southern cities as a legitimate form of "civilized warfare," not all Northerners were so sanguine over the prospect of wreaking wholesale destruction. For religious leaders especially, such callous and hate-filled directives smacked of barbarism and suggested that the humane sensibilities of the Northern people were being overwhelmed by the fiery emotions of the moment. Preachers across the Union were resoundingly supportive of the war effort. At the same time, though, they were leery of the passions it aroused and, through both religious and secular newspapers, tried to channel them in a more wholesome and God-fearing direction.

Faithful that the fate of the Union was really in God's hands, they wanted to be sure that the Northern people would prove deserving of His good graces. The following except from a sermon on "the right use of excited feeling," delivered by the Reverend David Pitkin at St. Peter's Church in Albany and published in that city's *Evening Journal*, illustrates the concerns with which some religious men approached the war:

> The subject to which I would direct your attention is THE RIGHT USE OF EXCITED FEELING. It is a subject that is eminently practical and suited to the times. We are passing through a period of intense excitement in which all the deepest feelings of our nature have been stirred. I suppose that nothing like the scenes of the past week have been ever before witnessed in this country. . . . I propose, in the way of Christian counsel, to remind you of the right and proper use of this excited feeling; to show to you what are the channels for its exercise, sanctioned by our holy religion and provided in the Church of our Lord Jesus Christ.
>
> Intense emotion, when it takes possession of great masses of people, is, we may believe, a power that is of God to enable them to do some great thing which is otherwise beyond their reach; but this power when misdirected becomes the occasion of the greatest evils and inflicts innumerable miseries and wrongs. It is never safe to allow mere feeling, when it pervades great masses of people and is concentrated on a single object, to run its course; it soon becomes excessive; soon fanatical; soon ferocious. It must be restrained. It must be directed. . . .
>
> I think that many persons are beginning now to feel that the excitement of our people. . . . is becoming too intense, and is running into violent fanaticism which may soon plunge us into all the brutalities of the lowest and most savage forms of warfare. . . . [We] are in danger, as it seems to me, of inaugurating here, on our own native soil and against our brothers and fellow countrymen, scenes of revolting butchery that will make us blush in after times, and hang our heads in shame as we face our Christian brethren of England and of Europe. . . .
>
> The excitement that sent forth that regiment of soldiers from our city, at so short a notice, was a strong power for good; it was a noble impulse of enthusiasm in the breasts of the brave men, who marched so calmly and steadily through our streets. But that excitement . . . is with them a safe and healthy feeling, working itself off day by day in weary marches, in exposure to the heat and to the rain, in sleeping . . . on bare boards or on the ground; in a constant state of readiness to face the cannon's mouth. Excitement is a very different thing with us, who remain here at our ease and devour with avidity the news, and . . . sit in our comfortable chairs or around our well supplied tables, and talk fiercely and almost savagely about opening batteries at once upon this city or laying immediately that city in ashes.
>
> The sudden demolition of a great city, dearly beloved Christian brethren, is a very fearful thing. It involves the indiscriminate destruction of the innocent and the guilty; of the aged and the helpless; of the sick lying on their beds and the little ones resting in their sweet innocence on their mothers' bosoms. . . . I do not think that we, of this church, are cruel and ferocious and bloodthirsty. We have only been profoundly and intensely moved. We have shared in a general uprising of national feeling which has many of the highest elements of grandeur, but has also many elements of danger to ourselves.
>
> I would, therefore, interpose the caution . . . that fierce expressions of revenge, or of cruel and excessive forms of retaliation towards our fellow-men . . . are not the Christian forms of relieving our surcharged breasts of the intense emotion of indignant patriotism which has animated all alike. . . .
>
> The . . . most natural channel for the outpouring of our feelings, is prayer to God . . . He hears and answers prayer. I believe that the more humbly and

devoutly we pray the less anxious shall we be. . . . Let us call heartily upon God to "stir up His strength and come and help us"—that He will "save and defend our country in this its hour of peril." Be assured, my brethren, there is great power in prayer, when offered in a worthy cause. . . . If . . . we could pray as earnestly as we talk, as we advise, as we direct or as we censure, I believe that God would give us first an answer of peace, allaying our excitement, inspiring trust and confidence, and then would answer our petitions by giving to our rulers wisdom and power to save us.[11]

This did not mean, however, that Northern ministers and pastors were reluctant to strike the South harshly. They simply wanted Northerners to prosecute the war without personal vindictiveness and hatred. Vindictiveness was a sin, but swift punishment for treason was a matter of right and justice. It was a fine line, as these furious words by the Reverend Andrew Leete Stone, who headed the Park Street Church in Boston, make clear:

That which is sometimes called the war spirit, must have no home in our breast. We must watch against its savageness—its hate—its revengefulness—its murderous rancor. When public justice smites with her sword on the neck of crime there is no passion in her stroke—only a stern and awful sorrow. I have read of a minister of the Gospel, who went into battle and dispatched, one after another, a score of unerring bullets; and as each took effect, he apostrophized from afar the victim, "My poor fellow, God have mercy on your soul." That is the spirit in which to fight and in which to wait.

But in this spirit we ought to make the war overwhelming. Not a hundred thousand, but a half a million of men ought to be in motion. We ought to pour our legions forward. It is mercy now to go strong and fight hard. The grapple has come—finish it quick and finish it forever. Let this contest never need to be renewed. Let it be settled from henceforth in this land that a Government has a right to be a Government. Let discontent and treason learn that when they stretch out sacreligious hands to tug at the pillars of the Union, and of all constitutional law, that hand shall be stricken down and forever palsied. Let us meet and settle the issue now, and bury it so deep, in a grave so blood-cemented, that it shall have to the end of time no resurrection. Let us not be so eager for peace as to heal this hurt slightly. Let the laws go with the armies. HANG TRAITORS. Above the terror of sword and bayonet, let there be the terror of the gibbet and the rope. Give not to treason, when it can be helped, the honor of a soldier's death. Widen the streets through riotous cities. Make a broad passage for the country's defenders. Raze the nests of conspirators with ax and fire. This is shortest and surest, time-saving and life-saving. Let the country burn this ulcer out. That is the message today of the law of Love.[12]

Amid the high-pitched emotions of the time, there was little room for expressions of dissent. "The same liberty of speech cannot be tolerated in time of war, as in time of peace," admitted one newspaper bluntly. Patriotism demanded conformity, and those who seemed hostile—or even just lukewarm—toward the Union placed their personal safety at risk. When William Bennett, the editor of the *New York Herald*, a Democratic sheet, refused "to flag out his sentiments" by prominently displaying the Stars and Stripes from his office window, crowds mobbed the building until he relented.[13] Despite such efforts to control public opinion, though, the North was never able to silence all dissent, let alone achieve universal support for the war. Regardless of the evident dangers involved, one small cadre of Democrats—who would eventually come to be known as the Peace Democrats, or "Copperheads"—remained openly critical of any attempt to strong-arm the Southern states back into the Union. While their countrymen welcomed war, the Peace Democrats assented to the right of secession and doubted that any

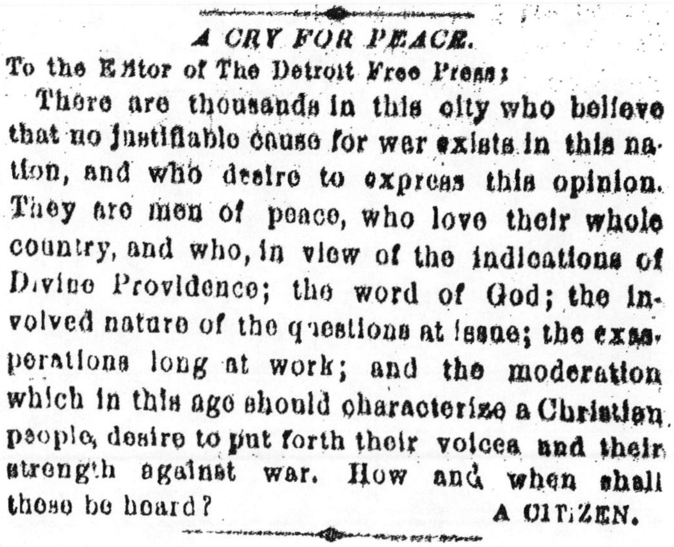

A CRY FOR PEACE.

To the Editor of The Detroit Free Press:

There are thousands in this city who believe that no justifiable cause for war exists in this nation, and who desire to express this opinion. They are men of peace, who love their whole country, and who, in view of the indications of Divine Providence; the word of God; the involved nature of the questions at issue; the exasperations long at work; and the moderation which in this age should characterize a Christian people, desire to put forth their voices and their strength against war. How and when shall those be heard?

A CITIZEN.

Detroit Free Press, April 16, 1861.
Not all Northerners were eager for war. Some, like this resident of Detroit, objected to it on principle and still hoped that a peaceful resolution could be found.

good could ever come from resorting to force. In hopes of encouraging Northerners to pause a moment in their boisterous preparations for war, the *New York News* issued this plea for opening negotiations with the rebels:

> The bristling of bayonets, the heavy tread of artillery, the splendid ostentation of glittering arms and beating drums are witnessed in every city and town of the United States. Wolf-like destruction has not yet begun . . . but the time is approaching when brethren will imbrue their hands in each other's blood. Where is it to end? How far is the "irrepressible conflict" to lead us? The reality of war will prove far different from its magnificent panoply; and the carnage of battle fields, the burning of towns, the shrieks of the widowed and orphaned, the cries of the wounded, [will be] less gratifying than the pomp and magnificence of a dress parade day. And, supposing that the valor of our Northern soldiers should be crowned with victory—that battle after battle should be gained over the armies of Jefferson Davis, what would it all come to? How will the relations of the States to each other be practically bettered, and what positions are conquerors and conquered mutually to assume in the future?
>
> . . . [W]ere all the "places and properties" of the United States once more in the hands of the Government; the troops of the Confederate States disbanded, and a nominal submission everywhere enforced, what then? The States that have withdrawn will be no more than a vast, subjected, unmanageable province, liable to perpetual revolt, and sure to throw off the authority that oppresses them upon the first available occasion. They will contemplate with mournful dismay the havoc and ruin which war has made; every family will yearn to avenge the loss of some missing member . . . and all will bide their time for new outbreaks and military anarchy, rather than [give] tame acquiescence under an abhorred rule.
>
> By peace alone and the utmost measure of concession and conciliation is a solid, reliable reconstruction of the Union, and an obliteration of the memory of past grievances, possible.[14]

While Copperhead papers like the *New York News* still held out a vain hope for a peaceful reconciliation between the sections, others within the Union were wildly in favor of the South's bid for independence. It was a dangerous position to hold, and those who made their Southern sympathies known courted the wrath of their neighbors. According to a report from New Bedford, Massachusetts, for instance, a man flying a rebel flag from his home steadfastly refused his neighbors' demands for its removal, until violence finally forced him into compliance. The standoff ended when the community marched the man out of town, "where a coat of tar and feathers was applied to a part of his person, giving him a handsome set of *tail feathers*." After enduring this humiliation, he then "was compelled to give three cheers for the stars and stripes" and to take a public oath to "never again raise other than the American flag."[15] This volatile mixing of pro-Union and pro-Confederate voices was especially pronounced in the four slave states—Delaware, Maryland, Kentucky, and Missouri—that had resisted secession and remained within the Union. Baltimore, which was evenly divided in its sympathies, was the scene of constant clashes between neighbors of opposite loyalties. Confederate sympathizers there chafed at the Union's authority, especially since the city was occupied by federal soldiers who were helping to defend Washington. One fiercely pro-Confederate woman in Baltimore, in a letter to her friend in Virginia, described the difficulties of coexisting peaceably in such a divided community:

> A huge secession flag floats boldly from my window out on the evening breeze. . . . In gazing on it, I am happy, for it reminds me that hundreds of the best and bravest of Maryland's sons have offered their lives in its defence; and I feel assured that it will be eventually unfurled in triumph over our beloved State. Probably you think it would have been better to have deferred giving this expression to my feelings until that time arrived. Perhaps so; but I was goaded to desperation by the insolent flaunting of dozens of little Union flags in my immediate vicinity; while our own beloved banner was nowhere to be seen; so . . . I purchased a large Confederacy flag, and it has hung at my window for the last three or four days, thereby restoring me to comparative happiness. I do not know how long this luxury may be permitted; for we live in a strong Union neighborhood, and my political enthusiasm has already paid the penalty of two broken panes of glass.
>
> I sincerely wished for you the day I made the purchase. You would have entered fully into the enjoyment of the display I indulged in. Carelessly folded and drooping over the front of my dress in such a way as to admit of no doubt as to its character, I walked up Baltimore street, holding it in my hand.—In the course of my promenade we encountered a squad of Lincoln's beggarly, beastly brutes. . . . I casually raised my hand and accidentally threw the flag across the one nearest me. The party scowled, but were obliged to submit to the indignity of being touched by the rebel banner. It would have done your heart good to see how impotently furious they looked. Why these wretched men should ever make their appearance before a public so utterly hostile to them, I cannot imagine; they subject themselves in so doing to every indignity that can possibly be offered them in a covert way by men, women and children.—The favorite insult on the part of the ladies consists in drawing off to the extreme edge of the pavement, with skirts gathered closely around them to avoid contact. It is done so pointedly that it cannot fail to be observed, and invariably creates a laugh at the expense of the creatures among bystanders, newsboys, etc. To avoid noticing these slights, they have at length adopted the plan of looking neither to the right or left, which makes them look more like escaped convicts than ever.
>
> . . . How I envy the women at the South! It must be an intense comfort to be surrounded by such enthusiastic people, all equally devoted to our glorious cause . . . and inspired with the fullest confidence in its ultimate success. Next door to us there lives an immense family of Unionists, all of whom, not even excepting the baby, possess innumerable Union flags, which they flaunt in our very faces. I really am horror-struck when I think of the emotions those people excite in me sometimes! I am sure it would have given me a sensation of unmixed pleasure to have strangled the young lady (?) of the house, when, a few evenings since, she cheered and kissed her hand to a crowd of Lincoln's rowdy rabble, passing by on their way to Washington. . . . Oh! how I do *hate* the North. I wish I were a volcano or an

earthquake. I would swallow it up so entirely that no one could discover the slightest trace of it.[16]

As this woman acknowledged, the onset of war sparked an outburst of martial enthusiasm in the South that was just as intense and pervasive as the one that had overtaken the North. "It seemed to be regarded a cause of joy rather than sorrow that hostilities had commenced, and almost every countenance was lit up with a smile," wrote the *Montgomery Daily Advertiser* of the public reaction when word first arrived of the assault on Fort Sumter. The delight that Southerners felt in finally taking military action only deepened as news spread of the fort's surrender. "The face of every Southern man was brighter, his step lighter and his bearing prouder, than it had been before," the *Advertiser* noted. In the initial thrill of victory, it was easy to believe that this was just the first of many successes that would eventually force the Lincoln government to recognize the Confederacy's independence. Southern men literally rushed to enlist, eager to get in on the fighting before it was all over.[17]

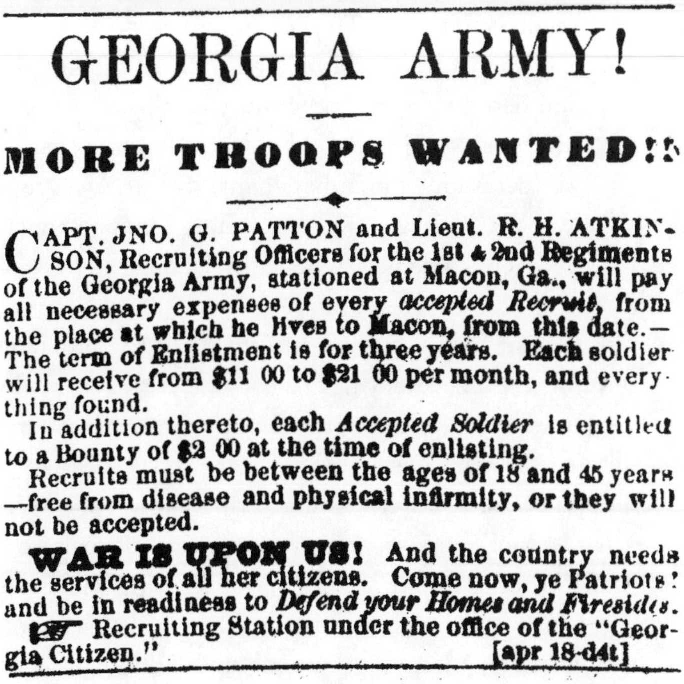

GEORGIA ARMY!

MORE TROOPS WANTED!!

CAPT. JNO. G. PATTON and Lieut. R. H. ATKINSON, Recruiting Officers for the 1st & 2nd Regiments of the Georgia Army, stationed at Macon, Ga., will pay all necessary expenses of every *accepted Recruit*, from the place at which he lives to Macon, from this date.—The term of Enlistment is for three years. Each soldier will receive from $11 00 to $21 00 per month, and everything found.

In addition thereto, each *Accepted Soldier* is entitled to a Bounty of $2 00 at the time of enlisting.

Recruits must be between the ages of 18 and 45 years—free from disease and physical infirmity, or they will not be accepted.

WAR IS UPON US! And the country needs the services of all her citizens. Come now, ye Patriots! and be in readiness to *Defend your Homes and Firesides*.

☞ Recruiting Station under the office of the "Georgia Citizen." [apr 18-d4t]

Macon Telegraph, April 19, 1861.
As with the Union, the Confederacy had to rely on volunteers to fill the ranks of its armies. Soldiers who enlisted were promised a monthly pay of at least $11 and a bounty—essentially a signing bonus—as well as the honor of defending their "homes and firesides" from invasion.

This general feeling of jubilation was matched by total indignation over Lincoln's next moves. His proclamation calling for 75,000 volunteers to put down the rebellion, followed just a few days later by a second declaration establishing a Union blockade of the Confederate coastline, inspired four more slave states—Virginia, Tennessee, North Carolina, and Arkansas—to throw their lot in with the Confederacy. In the months leading up to the showdown at Fort Sumter, these Upper South states had tried to encourage moderation and slow the course toward war. Now newspapers there seethed with hatred against the idea of ever rejoining the Union. With deadly seriousness, the editor of the *Memphis Avalanche* determined that "spies and pimps in our midst" who showed sympathy with the North "should be burnt at the stake" or "nailed to the street doors and public lamp-posts." Those who did not endorse Southern independence were expected to leave for "a more Northern latitude" as soon as possible, or suffer the consequences.[18] These were not empty words, as the reported fate of one Union man—rounded up and lynched by a vigilance committee in Memphis—illustrates:

John Beman is the name of the watchman on the steamer Morrison, who was yesterday hung near Mound City. He was a native of Norway, came to this country in 1811, and lived in Boston, where he has children. He was first examined by a committee, was proven to have said that he hoped Lincoln would come down the river and take everything; that he would die rather than live in the Southern States, and much more of the same sort that it is needless to repeat. The committee proposed to forgive him if he would take an oath to support the Southern States. He indignantly repelled the proposition, and said he would die first. Finding that he was determined and malignant, they threw a rope over the limb of a tree, and strung him up twenty-five feet, where he was hanging last night.[19]

Persistent Unionism was just one of the problems that the Confederacy had to overcome. By practically every standard, the South was comparatively ill-prepared for war. The Northern states boasted a larger population, a vaster manufacturing capacity, a wider network of railroads, and greater reserves of coal, iron, and other essential resources, not to mention a more powerful navy and more replete stockpiles of munitions. Yet, despite their obvious disadvantages, Southerners were perfectly confident that they would triumph eventually. This optimism was not totally unwarranted. The Confederacy did indeed have the benefit of fighting on the defensive. Despite being the weaker party, if the South could just hold out long enough, the Northern people might eventually tire of the war and sue for peace. But for Southerners, hope in victory was not just a matter of strategic advantage; it was a point of faith. In the evangelical perspective that predominated, God was the final arbiter of all things. It was by His will that the Union forces failed to hold Fort Sumter. And just as surely, His power could deliver the South from the evils of invasion and subjugation. "Now, if, as a people, we truly fear the Lord" and "look believingly for His blessing," avowed the *Religious Herald*, "then, when the shock of invasion comes *the Lord will be here* to repel it." The key was twofold, prayer and faith—penitent and devout prayer for God's good graces, and steadfast faith that He would answer by rescuing the South from danger. Southerners imagined themselves to be like David from biblical times, and that just as the young boy felled the Philistine giant Goliath, they too, with God's help, would summon the strength to defeat the North. Speaking before a company of Southern soldiers, one preacher elucidated the encouraging lessons of David's victory in this way:

Goliath was sort of a second Sampson, endowed with almost supernatural physical energy. According to the lowest calculation, his heighth was nine feet nine inches. His coat of mail weighed one hundred and fifty-six pounds four ounces. The head of his spear weighed eighteen pounds twelve ounces; and the staff thereof "was like a weaver's beam.". . . David was a mere stripling, possessing, perhaps, not a tithe of the strength that belonged to his antagonist; and yet Goliath fell prostrate beneath the blow of this stripling. What was the cause of David's victory? We trace it to the spirit that animated his breast, and stirred his soul, and nerved his arm—the spirit of humble boldness, and of unfaltering trust in God. . . . Difficulties and opposition are nothing to a man who has the true spirit in him. . . .

A True Spirit is superior to the greatest Social and Military Prestige of our foes. Goliath had obtained great fame as a warrior. He was renowned not only through Palestine, but likewise throughout all Judea. He was "a man of war from his youth up." The sound of his name, everywhere, would strike terror into the heart of his enemies. . . . But a true spirit will overcome even this. Goliath with all his prestige fell. . . . My Countrymen, those who make war upon us have great social and military prestige. Many of them are brave and chivalrous. It is needless to disguise the fact, that ours is a formidable foe. They have more men than we, more money than we, more provisions than we, more ships than we, more arms and ammunition than we. In these respects they have the advantage. But what of all this! A true spirit, with the blessing of God, can conquer even these odds; yea, and tenfold greater. God helping us, we can drive back the enemy from our native soil, and, if need be, make him "bite the dust.". . .

A True Spirit is Superior to the Completest Accoutrements of our Foes. Goliath was well

C. S. A.

These initials placed after the names of Army officers of the U. S. who have resigned and now belong to the Confederate States Army, are said to signify, "Could'nt Stand Abe."

Southern Federal Union, May 21, 1861.
This notice puts a humorous spin on the conduct of professional military men from the South who, in 1861, resigned their commissions with the United States army and transferred their allegiance to the Confederacy.

armored. . . . His robust frame, with bones like granite and sinews like iron, was thoroughly protected at every point. David had no armor, and no weapon, save only his simple shepherd's sling and fine smooth stones: and yet David was victorious and Goliath was slain. . . . It has been impiously and absurdly claimed, that "Might is Right." No, my friends; reverse the proposition and you will have the truth, Right is Might. A man is never so brave, never so fearless, never so difficult to conquer as when he feels and knows that he is in the right. . . . Our conviction, therefore, of the justness of our cause, must needs strengthen and support us in this dreadful conflict. We know the South has been wronged. We demand only our rights; we simply ask to be let alone. We appeal to the "Judge of all the earth.". . . This spirit, I verily believe, is more than equal to all the implements and munitions of war that can be brought against us. Hence I confidently expect this struggle to issue in the acknowledgment of the independence of the Southern Confederacy.[20]

Southerners entered the war hopeful of victory and eager for the fight. Like their Northern brethren, they saw war as an ennobling experience, one that would rouse them "from lethargy and selfishness" and raise them "to sentiments of honor, patriotism and glory." Personal greed would give way to feelings of national duty. The war would bring the Southern people together and nourish the land with a spirit of self-sacrifice that would more than counterbalance the physical cost of it. As the *Rome Weekly Courier* counseled:

> For the consolation of a certain class of timid and *old fogies*, now growing smaller in number, we submit a few observations to show that there is a bright side to the present gloomy aspect of affairs. There are times and circumstances in the development and history of all nations when wars are beneficial, if not absolutely necessary. This may appear strange and paradoxical to many, yet war has had its advocates in all ages of the world.
>
> So far as the South is concerned, there is reason to believe that the present war will be especially useful. Not alone because of the great object sought to be attained—the security of our national independence, but on account of the salutary influence of the war upon the popular mind in all the civil, moral, and social relations of life.
>
> In times of peace, money making . . . becomes the ruling passion of the people. In the competition of trade and the rivalry of conflicting interests, men grow selfish and overbearing toward their fellow men. On the contrary, in time of war men of all classes are drawn toward each other, loseing their selfishness in their efforts for mutual defence and safety. There is more social feeling, more equality among the classes, less regard for the restraints of

fashion, and a far greater exercise of charity, and other christian graces. There may be more deaths, more bodies lost, as the result of physical conflict; but there are not so many souls ground down by the canker worm of avarice. Widows and orphans may become more numerous, yet fewer of them are ground down and made wretched by the sordid, miserly conduct of men of small souls. . . .

Again, when war exists there is less extravagance, less of the enervating influences of luxury and dissipation; the youth of the land grow ardent, robust and active, and a generation is raised up, which makes its impress upon the habits and spirit of the masses for long years to come.[21]

The fight for independence was to be truly enriching—psychologically, for certain, but economically too. For years, Southern politicians had complained that the North's greatness was built on the South's hard labors. Northern merchants had grown fat on the sales of *their* crops; Northern textile mills had flourished by producing goods made of *their* cotton; revenue earned from the export of *their* agricultural staples helped finance the roads, rail lines, and other structural improvements that spurred the growth of Northern cities. As the *Richmond Enquirer* now boasted, independence would allow the Southern states to finally reap these benefits for themselves:

> There is scarcely an interest or element in Southern society, which will not derive advantage from the established independence of the Confederate States. At the lowest calculation, the South has furnished two-thirds of the revenue of the Federal Government, while scarcely one-third of that revenue has been expended in the Southern States. It was said, some months ago in Richmond, . . . that in round numbers, the exports of the United States, for 1859, amounted in value to $316,000,000, of which $216,000,000 were of Southern products, chiefly . . . cotton, rice, sugar and tobacco; that the duties on the importations of foreign goods bought with these exports, amounted to $70,000,000; and that of this sum, $50,000,000 were distributed in expenditures through the Northern States, and only $20,000,000 in the Southern. . . . With this immense golden current of wealth and power flowing into the North, it is not surprising that large and splendid cities have there sprung up. . . ; that magnificent manufactories, in every branch of mechanic art, have risen even to the successful rivalry of the long established institutions of the old world; that schools and colleges and valuable libraries every where greet the eye; that a vast reading public has been created; that extensive publishing houses and newspaper establishments have flourished as never before in human history; that [savants] in every department of science, and authors in every walk of literature, have won wealth and fame, . . . and that thus, . . . there should have grown that affluence and splendor . . . which have marked the progress of Northern development. . . . Now, all this is in great part to be changed, and, so far as the South is concerned, changed to its infinite advantage. That fecund tide of overflowing wealth which rolled Northward, must and will henceforth fertilize the fair fields and bright savannahs of its origins. We may expect to have our own commerce and our own manufactures. . . . What we make will be our own, and be accumulated or expended in our own midst. Great cities will rise upon solid foundations. Institutions of learning, of the arts and sciences, will flourish and multiply. All the elements and appliances of intellectual development and the elevation and diffusion of knowledge and literature will be enlarged and improved a thousand fold. What . . . our agriculturalists and planters have done for feeding and clothing the *world* and the gratification of its tastes, . . . our merchants and manufacturers, and miners, our men of science and literature and art, will now achieve . . . in the light of the noble dawn of Southern Independence.[22]

While holding out dreams of future riches, Southern newspapers were also quick to point out that for the time being, the Confederacy was still in a very vulnerable economic position. The South's economy centered on staple crops; most manufactured goods had always been imported from the Northern states or from abroad. Now that the sections were at war and Southern seaports were to be blockaded by the Union navy, Southerners suddenly had to depend on themselves for all of these products. This opened up new avenues for female labor. While men had to be ready to enroll in the army and do the actual fighting, the Southern press emphasized that women had to be prepared to support them in every way possible—by giving them words of encouragement, surely, but also by supplying and sustaining them with the material goods they needed:

> It is all well to present flags to our brave soldiery, . . . but men cannot fight unless *fed* and *clothed*. How is this to be done? Where shall they get shirts, socks, pants, havelocks, &c.? The answer we have in part in the willing hands of Southern women. . . . We must clothe *ourselves* and well as the *soldiers* with home-made goods. The spinning wheel and the hand loom must be hauled out from their dusty retreats, and the low hum that was a familiar sound in the houses of our grandmothers, must be heard in ours. Let us look this matter squarely in the face and meet it at once. *Socks* must be knit, and the busy needle and ball of cotton yarn be daily companions in the quiet home, the social circle, and the larger gathering. The time may come when, like our ancestors in the days of '76, we shall sit in the sanctuary and listen to the words of life from the preacher while busy fingers ply the knitting needle.
>
> *Comforters* must be made ready for winter, so that, if needful, we can give our blankets to our troops in the field. The money that has been paid for bonnet ribbons and gentlemen's fancy cravats, would go far to provide for the little items that are indispensable to a soldier—a few cents' worth of scraps can, by our skill, supply the lack of expensive neckcloths. Shoes for ourselves and children *must be had; where shall we get them?* . . . Cloth scraps are all that we need; and there are several ladies in and about Columbus, who have made their own shoes and slippers for a long time past, and they will freely teach others how to do the same. For thirty or forty cents, they can make a pair of slippers equal in appearance and durability to those costing $1.25. If a like economy can be put in practice in other ways, who can estimate the benefit?
>
> I call upon you, *young women of the South*, to come up to this work! This is no time for idle leisure, or profitless occupation: your duties at home are in their place as important as those of your brothers in the field; and your action or inaction may work for weal or woe to them. If you do not [do] all that you can at home—if you live in listlessness and indolence, it is so much towards wasting the effective strength of our armies, and paralyzing the efforts of our government in the mighty struggle before us.[23]

At least in the early days of the conflict, before the coming devastation left so many Southern families utterly destitute, women eagerly seized the opportunity to contribute to the war effort. As this public letter by a Georgia woman to her Southern sisters conveys, the outbreak of war afforded them a sense of usefulness—of independence—that they had never before enjoyed:

> We have outwardly assumed the garb of independence, and now let us walk in the path our State has chosen. And shall man tread it alone? Shall he go forth to his daily toil and labor until his strength is almost spent, and on his return find perhaps his three blooming daughters in the very excess of idleness—one lounging on a sofa, with a novel in her hand, and one thumping on her piano, and the other nursing her favorite lap dog? . . . No, no, no, a thousand times no. Sisters of the South, let us hurl the

INDEPENDENCE, NOW and FOREVER!

Nashville Union & American, June 5, 1861. As the state of Tennessee prepared to vote on secession, pro-Southern images and slogans helped rally public support for joining the Confederacy.

destructive novel in the fire, and turn our poodles out of doors, and . . . convert our pianos into spinning wheels, or, which is more proper, have a wheel for a substitute, whose music is rendered almost as beautiful by its copious produce. . . . It holds good, the old saying, that "what is made is that much saved." Now I, for one, intend to lead a more useful life; if I can't make money by my work, I can save what little I have. I am pretty well acquainted with the implements of home industry, and I expect to cultivate a better acquaintance. Let us centre our thoughts and desires within the circle of home and its employments, and we will be a more contented and happy and useful people. Let us manufacture as much as possible our own goods, and we will soon be worthy of the independence we have assumed. Will none of my Southern friends join me in my work of reformation? . . . I feel a new life within me, and my ambition aims at nothing higher than to become an ingenious, economical, industrious housekeeper, and an independent Southern woman.[24]

Independence was the word of the day. It was the mark of a true Southern woman, the war cry of men who enlisted in the army, and the resplendent end goal for the Confederate nation. Yet there was also a lingering fear among many of the leading voices in the Confederacy, including those who ran the newspapers, that too many Southerners retained some feelings of attachment to the old Union. They hoped the war would cure this problem. Perhaps in that way a long, bitter war was exactly what the Confederacy needed, to help its people more fully appreciate the blessings of independence:

> A three-years war would be better for the South than that immediate peace which [would] restore friendly relations and renew trade and intercourse with the North. We have been so long dependent on New England in almost every department of business, and the affairs of our citizens are so mixed up and inter-ramified with theirs, that an early peace . . . would be sure to restore, in a great measure, our former dependence. Again we should be flooded with Yankee goods, Yankee manufactures, Yankee teachers, preachers, pedlers and drummers. . . . Again would our merchants flock to their cities, our youth to their schools, colleges and universities, and our rich and fashionable men and women to their watering places. A peace attended with these consequences, or even a part of them, would be worse than a three-years war; for such a peace would rob the South of its money and its mind, destroy its nascent manufactures and prevent the growth of its foreign commerce. Such a peace would impoverish the South and restore the wealth of the North. In all but name, we should again become their slaves and tributaries. . . . Whilst a

speedy peace is almost sure to make us again the tributaries of Northern trade and Northern centralization, a three-years war would be certain to make us sufficiently independent of all nations, by teaching us to live within ourselves, to do our own handiwork and our own head-work, to write our own books and make our own shoes, to manufacture our own doctors, professors and pill-venders, to build our own houses and make our own clothes. In effecting all this, we should necessarily establish centres of trade, of manufactures, of education, of thought and of fashion. . . .

We desire peace as much as most men, and would not have the war continue one moment after its legitimate purposes have been attained. But this is a war of independence—we are independent whilst it lasts; and if peace is to restore dependence, we say, then, better fight on—fight forever![25]

Certainly it would be inaccurate to say that both the North and the South were *completely* united in 1861 as they prepared to go to war. The dissent that existed, however, paled in comparison to the overwhelming and heady consensus that the war was necessary, unavoidable—and good. With few exceptions, both sides rushed headlong into it with the greatest of expectations and the conviction that in taking up arms, they were paving a path toward power and glory. Looking forward, all they could see were the shining possibilities.

UNION AND AMERICAN---Extra.

To the People of Tennessee.

Your Homes are in Danger! - - - Rouse you to the Great Conflict!!

THE UNDERSIGNED REPRESENTATIVES OF
IE PRESS, secular and religious, at Nashville, aware the great importance of the hour, beg leave to speak to e citizens of Tennessee. Eschewing all names and ar-ments of the past, and uniting our voice in one com-on accent, we desire to utter only such words as shall use the people of Tennessee to realize their danger and e necessity of concurrent, united action. Confident that any of our citizens are not aware of the magnitude of e operations going on at the North to subjugate the uth, duty, patriotism, humanity, and the interest of this mmonwealth, all impel us to speak to you.

FELLOW-COUNTRYMEN! We are in the midst of a great evolution. The election of a sectional administration in ovember last, gave us all cause of apprehension for our stitutions in the South. The country waited with pa-nce for the words of the Chief Magistrate. They came, d to the hopeful promised peace. The country was lled into comparative repose. The people of Tennessee ved the Union, and they were willing to peril life and rtune to preserve its integrity. Four weeks ago all of were looking daily for the evacuation of Sumter. The ws flew on every wire that such was the determination Mr. Lincoln. What was our surprise and the surprise of e whole country to find that so far from a peaceful evac-tion, secret means had been used all along for its rein-cement. At this open perfidy the whole land was ocked. Attention was fixed on Mr. Lincoln from that ur.

Sumter has fallen. What then? The Abolition Ad-nistration at Washington, contrary to the Constitution. d by purely tyrannic power, calls out 75,000 men and 00 of them from our own State, to repossess the Federal operty and put down the rebellion. A new call has en made in the past week of 88,000 men, all of which, with e regular army, constitute a force little short of 180,000 en. These men are mustering and arming to-day. But se are not one-half of those getting ready for this unholy ir on Southern men. The North is at blood-heat from aine to Nebraska. Every city, village, and county is in mps. One continuous roll of drums sweeps the land. They tnumber the South more than two to one. They boast of told millions of wealth, and exhaustless provisions at com-nd. They are armed and equipped; they have monopo-ed always the manufacture of arms on this continent, and, sides this, while they were professing peace two months o to the South, they had an agent in Europe buying 0,000 more arms of the most approved pattern. These h being received by every steamer.

And what is the spirit that moves the vast North? Re-nge and hate stream through every column of their urnals. Conciliation, peace and mercy are banished rds. "War to the knife," "extermination of the reb-," "crush the traitors," are the common forms of their pressions. The South is to be overrun and crushed for-er; her proud spirit broken, her property confiscated, r families scattered and slaughtered, and then to remain rough all time a dependency on the "free and sovereign" orth. Powerful armies of fanatics and plunderers are to quartered in our quiet cities and towns in the South, tating laws to us at the point of the bayonet, and the ves to be turned loose with more than savage atrocity on lpless women and children.

Every friend we had in the North is silenced, the entire ess is against us, and the ministers of religion, without tinction, are praying for the "holy cause"—the utter duction of the rebels. At the bottom of all this lies the sane idea, held by many of the leaders, that it is their ligious duty to exterminate slavery, and make the irrepressible conflict" doctrine universal. The men who ve acted with and for the South—Pierce, Buchanan, lmore, Cass, Everett, and Dickinson—all have bowed fore the torrent of fanaticism—all have left us, and ime their voices in the fearful chorus of Northern indig ation. Aged ministers of the gospel, presidents of Col-ges, and editors of religious newspapers, all without ex-ption, so far as we know, urge on the maddened and oody populace. The vast north staggers under its load wrath, waiting only for orders from the usurper Lin-ln to overwhelm the South with blood and chains.

Countrymen of Tennessee! We say not these sad things excite you. We have no interest in this matter except citizens of a State we love, and now see threatened with e fiercest foes and the most fatal overthrow recorded in story. Baltimore is to submit or be laid in ashes. It is lieved by military men that Virginia is to be attacked

Their Idea of Neutrality.

[From the New-York Evening Post.]

"Men and brethren of the border States! It is no tim now to split words. You must choose between loyalty and treason. You cannot be neutral in a war which is forced upon the Union by that Union's most bitter and determin-ed enemies. If you could maintain your neutrality, no words would express the scorn in which the patriot soldiers of this nation would forever hold you for your cowardice. Neutrals, you would be recreant to every sentiment of honor and patriotism. Neutrals in a war on whose result depends our national existence are simply cowards, to be forever stripped of every honorable privilege of freemen."

The Short Way!

[From the New-York Courier and Enquirer.]

"There are two ways of putting down the present re-bellion and saving the Union. The one is, to call from seventy-five to a hundred thousand troops into the field, and consume two or three years in *scientifically* terminating the war at a fearful loss of life, an enormous cost in money. besides destroying the business of the country pending the war; which, in itself, would amount to untold hundreds of millions of dollars. The other and the wiser, and the cheaper mode is, to call out a quarter of million of volun-teers, and double that number if necessary, and bring the whole matter to a close in a few months. The latter is the cheaper mode; and when accomplished, business would at once resume its natural channels and we should again be a happy, united, and prosperous people—a *Nation* command-ing the respect and admiration of the world. And this latter course, is the one which the people will insist upon. We entreat of the President not to thwart them."

Invade the South!

[From the New York Tribune]

"STRIKE!—We are at war. Let us admit the fact and act accordingly. Let us cease mere fending off, and begin to strike home. Let the war be instantly carried into Africa. Let Washington be defended, but not alone at the Capital. The best spots and the best modes to save Wash-ington are to strike heavy and instantaneous blows at Maryland and Virginia, and thus give the rebels work enough to do at home. Let troops be poured down upon Baltimore, and, if need be, raze it to the ground. Land troops in Southern Virginia immediately, and let them scour Southampton and the adjoining counties with fire and sword. We are at war with these pestilent rebels and traitors. Let us treat them accordingly. Strike home! Let the assassins of Baltimore, and the murderers and thieves of Norfolk and lower Virginia, feel the weight of our blows!

"The people will no longer be content with defending the Federal Capital. By the end of this week patriotism will have planted twenty-five thousand troops in Wash-ington. The stream is only just beginning to pour. By the first of May fifty thousand will be encamped along the Potomac. Will they be satisfied to idle away their time on the northerly bank of that river, waiting for Jeff. Davis to come and attack them? No! They, with the fifty thousand more that will be pressing upon their heels by the last of May, will demand to be led across the river to Richmond! And they will go, and that den of rebels and traitors will be broken up and destroyed. 'On to Richmond!' is the cry"

A Dictator Wanted.

[From the New York Tim .]

The spirit evoked within the last fortnight has no paral-lel since the day of Peter the Hermit. In the last ten days, 100,000 men have sprung to their feet, and, arming and provisioning themselves, are rushing to a contest which can never be quelled till they have triumphed. A holy zeal inspires every loyal heart. To sacrifice comfort, property, and life even, is nothing, because if we fall, we must give up these for our children, for humanity, and for ourselves. Where is the leader of this sublime passion? Can the administration furnish him? We do not question the entire patriotism of every member of it, nor their zeal for the public welfare. The President in the selection of his Cabinet, very properly regarded the long and efficient services of men in the advocacy of the principles that tri-umphed in his election. To him the future was seen in the past. But in the few weeks of his official life all past poli-tical distinctions have been completely effaced. From a dream of profound peace we awake with our enemy at our

No More Parleying.

[From the New-York World.]

We trust our federal authorities will not have another word of negotiation, of any character whatever, with any State or City that is either rebellious or hesitating—nor give ear for one moment to any mediator with his *arrange-ments for sparing* the effusion of blood. The only phrase-ology used by the government should be an unconditional demand; the only phraseology listened to should be that of unconditional submission.

The Kind of Men we have to Fight.

[From the New York Herald]

"We have in the Northern cities at least three hundred thousand of the most reckless, desperate men on the face of the earth. The Goths and Vandals who descended upon Rome and ensanguined the Tiber with patrician blood were angels compared to these fellows, who are known by the generic name of "roughs." Of course they are all in for the war, and the spoils thereof—more particu-larly the spoils. They have no stake in this world, no hope for the future. They will fight like demons for pres-ent enjoyment, and where one is killed twenty more will spring up in his place. It is of such rough material that all invincible troops are made. That we are to have a fight, that Virginia and Maryland will form the battle-ground, and that the Northern roughs will sweep those States with fire and sword, is beyond peradventure. They have already been excited to the boiling point by the rich prospect of plunder held out by some of their leaders, and will not be satisfied unless they have a farm and a nigger each. There is no sort of exaggeration about these state-ments, as the people of the border States will shortly as-certain to their cost. The character of the coming cam-paign will be vindictive, fierce, bloody, and merciless be-yond parallel in ancient or modern history."

No Friends at the North Now.

Mr. Dickinson, of New York, the firm friend of the South heretofore, spoke as follows at the great mass meet-ing the other day in New York city:

"He would have no half-way measures, no compromises. Let us settle this thing speedily and surely. *It may ruin this generation, but we owe it to the next that they should have no such troubles as we have had. He would strike now in our might, and if necessary, wipe the South from the face of the earth.* He knew they would have civil war, and what was far worse, *servile* war, and he would make pro-phecy that by the time this matter was settled the peculiar institution of the South would be swept away. Let us finish things while we are about it, and leave nothing be-hind us."

The South to be Whipped and then Governed.

[From the New York World.]

"But even if the dangers naturally to be apprehended from the passions of four millions of brutal blacks should be escaped (which would be but little short of a miracle,) and the South, after a sharp and exhausting war, should be subdued, as any non slaveholding people might be subdued by superior numbers and resources, a weakened and sul-lenly submissive people, such as they would then be, could certainly be governed by the United States till time should put them in a better humor."

MEN OF TENNESSEE, let us lay aside in this dire hour, the unworthy issues of party; life, home, liberty, and all held dear by man are at stake. The time is short. The blood of the North is up. Friends just from New York say the road thence to Cairo is one vast military camp. Prepa-ration hastens with fatal speed. Threats are made by high abolition journals to set aside Mr. Lincoln as too slow, and set up in his stead a military dictator—some flaming Cali-gula—whose sword shall never drop until sheathed in the last southern rebel's heart. Will men of Tennessee, whose property is in danger, whose helpless families are exposed, and whose right to liberty itself is ignominiously demanded, will you sleep, will you be idle, will you wait till a bloody mob is at your door?

What Can You Do?

1. RAISE PROVISIONS.—We call your earnest attention to the following joint resolution of the Legislature of Ten-nessee, which was adopted a few days ago, and ordered to be transmitted to the Senate:

Resolved by the General Assembly of the State of Tennes-see, That in view of the dearth of the past two years, and the probable extraordinary demand for cereal and forage, to supply the absolute wants of our State and of the entire South, that the agriculturists of the State be, and are hereby requested to devote the breadth of arable land in the State to the culture of grain and grass.

You can put in now large crops of millet, you can put in five, ten or twenty acres of corn each. Cultivate each va-cant square yard—the country will need it—at good prices.

2. Raise companies in every neighborhood—drill every day—hold yourself ready to march when arms are in your hands. The bravest people are not secure unless fully aroused to the actual danger. We, who now address you, ask only to set before you the *actual* state of affairs. We know you will then do your duty. God knows the actual

Chapter 2

Freedoms Worth Fighting For

Every American war, from the Revolution to our twenty-first-century "war on terror," has been waged in the name of liberty. The Civil War was no exception. Everyone involved—whether Northerner or Southerner, Republican or Democrat, white or black—believed that the fate of liberty was tied to the war's outcome. But like any exalted ideal, it did not mean the same thing to all people. Different groups rallied around varied, and often opposing, definitions of the freedoms that were at stake; quite literally, the Civil War became a contest over what liberty meant in America and how best to defend it. Whichever side won the war, in the end, would have the power to decide the answers to those questions.[1]

For the Confederacy, the war was obviously about state sovereignty and national liberation—the right of the Southern states to break away from the Union and establish their own independent government. But this quest was really the culmination of a decades-long struggle over another, more specific freedom: the right to own slaves.[2] Slavery was part of the United States Constitution, alongside all of the fundamental freedoms that Americans enjoyed. That document recognized slavery as a part of American society and established the "three-fifths clause," mandating that each slave would count as three-fifths of a white man in calculating the number of seats delegated to each state in the House of Representatives. Moreover, since the Constitution did not expressly grant the federal government any power to regulate slavery, it implied that slavery was a state institution—only the slave states themselves could pass laws affecting it. Yet, as Southerners saw things in 1861, the North had a galling history of trying to interfere with their slavery rights. First there were the abolitionists, who since the 1830s had been decrying slavery as a sin and agitating for its demise. Then came Northern resistance to the westward expansion of slavery into the territories, culminating in the rise of the Republican party to prominence and power. Although the Republicans swore that they had no interest in ending slavery in the South, in Southern eyes their antislavery beliefs and their opposition to slavery's westward march were dangerous enough. In making their bid for independence, the Southern states asserted that they could no longer tolerate Northerners vilifying, dishonoring, and threatening their "peculiar institution." As one newspaper put it, "We simply desired to be left alone, to conduct our own government free from abolition meddlesomeness."[3] The *Eastern Clarion*, a Mississippi paper, gave a lengthier defense:

> What is now the professed object of those who control the Government of the Union? Is it not the destruction of slavery? Did they not gain possession of the government upon their oft expressed principle of hostility to slavery? That was the very foundation upon which the party which elected Lincoln took form and substance, maintained its existence, and finally usurped the Government.—We contended that under the Constitution of the government, the States were equal, that slaves were property, and that we had a right to expect the fulfillment of the object of all free government, the protection of its Constituents. [The Republicans] said not—that we and our institutions should be placed under the ban of the government. . . .
>
> Finding how radical was the difference between us, and how determined both they and we were not to yield to one-another, we asked and asserted the poor privilege of a peaceful separation—that we might be allowed to set up a government which would be effective for our own protection, adapted to our own wants, and which at the same time would relieve them from the odium which they considered to be resting upon them by reason of their connection with our institutions. Their answer is in effect, "we feel the disgrace of your association, but you are profitable to us—we intend to preserve the connection regardless of your rights and interests—we will send our fleets and armies to keep you in the Union, and subjugate you if necessary."
>
> This is a brief, but we believe, a just statement of the matter. If a war is now forced upon us, all we have to say is let it come. We are clear of the responsibility, and while there is a man in the South who can shoulder a musket or draw a sword, the oppressor and invader may expect resistance. Our people have . . . resolved to endure with composure and fortitude the evils and sufferings the war may entail, in order to vindicate their rights and maintain their honor.[4]

This sense of resignation—that Southerners should just "let the war come"—was pervasive. After thirty years of sectional wrangling over slavery, they were eager to bring the conflict to a head and settle it forever. As this editorial from the *New Orleans Crescent* demonstrates, the Southern states harbored no doubts about their ability to fully free themselves from "abolition domination":

> Abraham Lincoln has formally declared a war of invasion against and upon the Confederate States of the South. . . . For our part, we read the news with unaffected satisfaction. . . . We never could, or will, consent to Abolition domination. Abolition rule destroys the spirit of the Constitution, and seeks to reduce us to the condition of slaves, to be abused and robbed at will. Therefore, we will have none of it; and having set up for ourselves, will vindicate and defend our inalienable rights to the last extremity of human sacrifice.
>
> For exercising these high, holy, and purely constitutional prerogatives of freemen, Abraham Lincoln has declared war upon us, and threatens us with the vengeance of seventy-five thousand soldiers. Well, let him come on. We will welcome him and his myrmidons to the bloodiest banquet the annals of ancient or modern war bear witness to. As "the hart panteth for the water brook," so do the Southern

people, in the full consciousness of right, long to grapple with Lincoln's robber Abolition hordes. Let them come. . . . They will be swept away as chaff is swept before the wind. . . . Lincoln should send along a million of Abolitionists, and even then they would not win the wreath of conquerors—and if they did, it would be over a desert, ruined, devastated, uninhabited. . . . The people of the Confederate States may be destroyed—but they never can be conquered. Never![5]

For the Deep South states, Lincoln's evident determination to conquer the Confederacy came as no surprise; they had seceded from the Union expressly because they did not trust that their rights and interests would be safe under his administration. For those in the Upper South, however, Lincoln's actions following the fall of Fort Sumter were shocking. Throughout the winter of 1860–61, as their sister states of the Deep South seceded, the Upper South had stayed put, hopeful that Lincoln, when he assumed office, would take a conciliatory approach and find a peaceful way of resolving the conflict. Despite their initial decision to remain in the Union, the Upper South states agreed in principle that secession was a legal act—that the individual states were sovereign and that they retained the right to withdraw from the Union. They also agreed that under no circumstances could the federal government coerce a state to remain in the Union; the use of force would be an act of despotism. They simply believed that Lincoln's mere election was not sufficient to justify a move as drastic and revolutionary as secession.

However, with Lincoln now determined to militarily crush the rebellion, Southerners in the Upper South felt that their faith in Lincoln had been betrayed. His actions suggested that he truly was out to create a "Union based upon absolutism," in which the "mammoth centralized Government" he controlled would lord its power over the individual states. Moreover, his policies seemed patently illegal. According to the Constitution, the president did not have the right to requisition troops; only the governors of the various states could call up soldiers, through the state militias, for national service. For Virginia, Tennessee, North Carolina, and Arkansas—the Upper South states that now were beginning to organize for secession—he thus became a blatant usurper of constitutional law. In public appeals such as this one from the *Nashville Union & American*, newspapers denounced Lincoln as a despot and rallied their readers to rise in defiance against him:

The hoary-headed old tyrant whose presence now defiles the honored seat of Washington has usurped powers which the constitution has conferred neither upon the President nor Congress, nor upon both together. He has declared war against the sovereign States of the South, in order to coerce them into subjection. The power is not only not conferred, but was, as every lawyer knows, expressly refused by the framers of the Constitution. . . . And yet Lincoln, lifting himself above Congress, above the law and the Constitution, and in violation of every principle of free Government, has the audacity to call for seventy-five thousand soldiers, for the purpose of subjugating the South, and carrying death and desolation to the family and fireside of all who shall dare resist his will.

We owe no obedience to such a mandate. OURS IS A GOVERNMENT OF THE PEOPLE, AND NOT OF ONE MAN. Not only do we owe no obedience to such a Government, but *we owe it to ourselves, our country and the cause of liberty*, TO RESIST IT BY ALL THE POWER *which God has given us*. "RESISTANCE TO TYRANTS IS OBEDIENCE TO GOD."[6]

Practically every act that Lincoln took to suppress the rebellion confirmed for Southerners that he was a threat to liberty. Between April 15 and July 4, when a special session of Congress was convened by the president to discuss war policy, Lincoln acted completely on his own, under the broad authority granted to him as

Virginians! the invaders are upon you. The bloody standard of tyranny is erected on your soil. They come to butcher and enslave—they come to desolate your homes, to slaughter your children—to pollute your wives and daughters. To arms! let their accursed blood quench the thirst of your fields.

Great God! what rage! what transports of fury should be excited by the mercenary tools of Despots, polluting our sacred soil! Sacred love of country! guide and impel our avenging steel! Liberty! beloved Liberty! rally with thy animating voice Victory to the standard of *thy* defenders!

Down with the tyrants! Let their accursed blood manure our fields!

The telegraph announces that Lincolns' armed mercenaries yesterday morning, invaded the Commonwealth of Virginia and took possession of Alexandria. The fact is enough. If we are worthy of the freedom we have boasted, of the glorious ancestors, who won that freedom for us, we will maintain it or die! TO ARMS!—*Richmond Whig.*

Southern Confederacy, May 29, 1861.
Even before any serious fighting occurred, Southern newspapers constantly warned their readers that the Union would wage a vicious war. As they pictured it, Lincoln's "mercenaries" were on a mission to ruthlessly ravage and annihilate the people of the Confederacy.

the nation's commander in chief. On April 19, he established a blockade of the entire Confederate coastline, with hopes of cutting the South's trading ties with the outside world and economically strangling the rebels into submission. His policies in Maryland—a slave state, but one that never seceded from the Union—were perhaps even more alarming. Maryland was critical to the Union cause, but at the start of the war, its loyalty was tenuous. The southeastern section of the state, where slavery flourished, was filled with Southern sympathizers who hoped to deliver Maryland into the Confederacy. As Virginia had seceded almost immediately after the war began, Lincoln had to keep Maryland in the Union. He could not afford to have the national capital surrounded by enemy territory. Lincoln, exercising powers not granted to him in the Constitution, therefore took it upon himself to impose martial law there. With that, Union soldiers in Maryland shut down pro-Confederate newspapers, jailed and detained Southern sympathizers without due process, and seized their assets. It was a sweeping demonstration of federal force, and in the end, Lincoln achieved his immediate goal of keeping Maryland in the Union. But his willingness to act outside the strict limits of the Constitution, with the evident support of the Northern public, signified to Southern onlookers that liberty and constitutional government were dead in the North.

The Confederacy, by contrast, was to take up the role that the old Union had abandoned, of being a bastion of freedom for all of mankind. A headline from the *Richmond Dispatch*—"Constitutional Liberty Takes Refuge in the South"—summed up their view perfectly. "She comes as a fugitive" from Lincoln's dictatorial rule, the *Dispatch* declared. "It is for her sake that we have come out from the old Union. It is for her sake that we have severed our connection with those who dishonored and repudiated her."[7] In seeking freedom from Northern tyranny, Southerners saw themselves as continuing the battle initiated by their Revolutionary forefathers against monarchical oppression and misrule, as exemplified by this editorial from the *Richmond Whig*:

> Our Revolutionary Sires fought for and secured what they termed "*certain inalienable rights*." These rights they considered worth the most costly sacrifice of blood and treasure. They were—
>
> 1st. Government must *secure* to its subjects *life*, *liberty* and *property*.
>
> 2d. Government must derive its powers from the *consent of the governed*.

3d. Government ceasing to effect these ends may, and *ought to be*, altered or abolished by the people.

The British colonies in America affirmed that King George did not afford them proper protection—that they were not protected in the enjoyment of life, liberty and property—that the government under which they lived derived not its powers from their consent; and hence, they would exercise their inalienable right to establish a government to suit themselves. They desired to part in peace, and only requested that they might be permitted "to choose their own destiny."

King George replied that the Colonies were subjects of the British Government. . . . And if the colonies refused obedience to the laws, they should be treated as rebels, and reduced to submission.

The issues thus made resulted in a long and bloody conflict, which terminated in an acknowledgment of the independence of the American Colonies.

The Colonies, composed of thirteen sovereign and independent States, for mutual protection, organized a GENERAL GOVERNMENT, clothed with certain powers, all of which were derived from the consent of the States. . . . After many years, several of the States from whom the General Government derived its powers in part, declare[d] that *that* Government had ceased, so far as they were concerned, to answer the ends for which they had established it; and that they no longer derived from it protection in "life, liberty, and property;" and that they would withdraw from it. . . .

Did the American colonies . . . affirm "that a *just* government can only derive its powers from the consent of the governed?" The Southern States have affirmed no more. Did the colonies declare "that when Government ceased to afford protection to life, liberty, and property, it is the right of the people to alter or abolish it, and institute a new one . . . to effect their safety and happiness?" The Southern States have declared or asked for nothing more. Did

Liberty—Jefferson—Hamilton.—The first shout of the American freemen is 'liberty!' It is a talismanic word. There are *seven stars* on the blue field of our Confederate flag! Jefferson was the father of democracy, the synonym of of true Republicanism, and the first President of the Confederate States bears, as his given name, that of the great apostle of Liberty and Republicanism. Hamilton was the chief of the old Whig school, Washington's aid in revolutionary struggles, and Washington's friend. Seven stars deck the flag of the Confederate States. *Jefferson* Davis is our President, and *Alexander Hamilton* Stephens is our Vice President. There is a pertinent omen in all this.

Shreveport Weekly News, May 13, 1861. Southerners sometimes went to great lengths to affirm their status as the inheritors and defenders of American liberty. In this odd statement from a Louisiana paper, the seven stars on the Confederate flag signify the seven letters in the word *liberty*, while the names of the Confederate president and vice president–Jefferson Davis and Alexander Hamilton Stevens–evoke the memories of American heroes from Revolutionary times.

the colonies send commissioners and ask most earnestly of the British King, to suffer them to depart in peace, and choose their own destiny? The Southern States have followed in the footsteps of our illustrious Ancestors in all these things. . . . Did King George endeavor to bribe the people into submission, by assuring protection to all who would submit, and by branding all as "Rebels" who would not? So has Lincoln acted towards the South. Did King George attempt to *coerce* the Colonies into submission, by blockading their ports, by invading their borders, by seizing their ships and other property?—So has Lincoln acted toward the South. . . .

Comment on these facts is superfluous. All must see that the battle of American independence must be fought over again. . . . It is a question of *freedom* or *slavery*, of *life* or *death*![8]

In describing the war as a "question of *freedom* or *slavery*," the *Whig*, of course, was considering the fate of white Southerners—whether they would be free to follow their own independent destiny or be driven cruelly back into the Union. But the fact that Lincoln would attempt to impose his rule on the seceded states also signaled that he did not care about any of their rights, including their rights regarding slavery. If Lincoln was willing to strip Southerners of their freedom to choose their own government, why would he hesitate to strip them of their freedom to hold slaves? Therefore, while politicians in Virginia, Tennessee, North Carolina, and Arkansas busily organized secession conventions, newspapers such as the *Memphis Avalanche* conceded that the Deep South had been right all along in suspecting that Lincoln was out to force abolitionist ideas down the unwilling throats of the Southern people:

The country has been startled by the proclamation of Lincoln, declaring his purpose to reduce the Confederate States into subjection by military force, and calling for an army of 75,000 men to carry that purpose into effect. In this extraordinary demonstration against our sister States of the South, Lincoln affects a high and conscientious sense of official duty and a patriotic devotion to the Constitution and the Union and the cause of "popular government," as the motives by which he is actuated. But these flimsy pretexts can deceive none but those who wish to be deceived. . . . The real intentions of the traitorous clique of usurpers at Washington are apparent to all but the wilfully blind.

The immediate purpose of Lincoln is to establish a military despotism over the South—while his ulterior design is to annihilate the institution of slavery, and exterminate, with it, the slaveholders themselves.

Wicked and unscrupulous as are the conspirators at Washington, they are not devoid of sense. . . . They know full well that . . . the Confederate States can only be brought back into their abhorred Union, and held there, as conquered provinces, against their will. And they, also, have reason to anticipate that their dominion can never be secure so long as one patriot heart shall throb in the bosom of a single patriot son of the South; and that the spirit of stern resistance . . . can only be quenched in the blood of the last of her devoted children.

Regarding Lincoln & Co., therefore, . . . we are forced to the conclusion that in adopting the resolution to force the South into submission to their authority, they have also determined to establish over her the despotism of the sword, and to exterminate the last of a heroic race, that will never bow to their sway. The war now proclaimed, is one of subjugation or extermination.

The entire South is the object of this atrocious crusade. . . . The chains now forg[ed] for our Southern brethren will soon clank upon our limbs unless we, the men of the Border slave States, rise as one man, and repel the insolent invader from our shores.

The annihilation of slavery is the ultimate object of this Abolition *raid* upon the South. This, for years, has been the darling scheme of Lincoln and his Black Republican backers. . . . He regards this as the golden opportunity to realize, in practice, the fanatical dream of Abolitionism, and hastens to embrace it. He hopes, by throwing the armies of Abolition incendiaries into the heart of the South, to accomplish at once the establishment of his authority, and the extinction of slavery in the blood of the Southern people.[9]

This visceral image of "the blood of the Southern people" pervaded popular thinking. The viciousness of Lincoln's tyrannical sway—his willingness to literally annihilate the Southern masses for the sake of winning his objectives—was a crucial theme that newspapers drummed into the consciousness of their readers. As the *Memphis Appeal* described vividly, Northerners had determined "that this war shall not close before the last slave is free if the life of the last white man in the South is sacrificed, and the sin of slavery washed out in a baptism of blood." While slaveholders would be made to feel the economic pinch of abolition, the newspapers made it clear that the consequences of war would go well beyond that. The devastation was to be as universal as it was tremendous—wholesale slaughter was imminent. The message was unmistakable: all Southerners had a personal stake in the outcome of the conflict. Their very right to exist was in jeopardy.[10]

There was one phrase, trumpeted repeatedly in the press, that encapsulated all of the horrors that Southerners could expect to face: "beauty and booty"—rape and pillage. Southern homes were to be forcibly invaded and plundered, Southern women were to be terrorized and assaulted, and even the slaves were to be enlisted in this evil work and encouraged to rise in revenge against the men and women who held them in bondage. In issuing their warning cry of "beauty and booty," Southern newspapers reprinted the most vindictive, bloodthirsty statements from the Northern press—particularly from the New York papers, which Southerners continued to scan for war-related news.

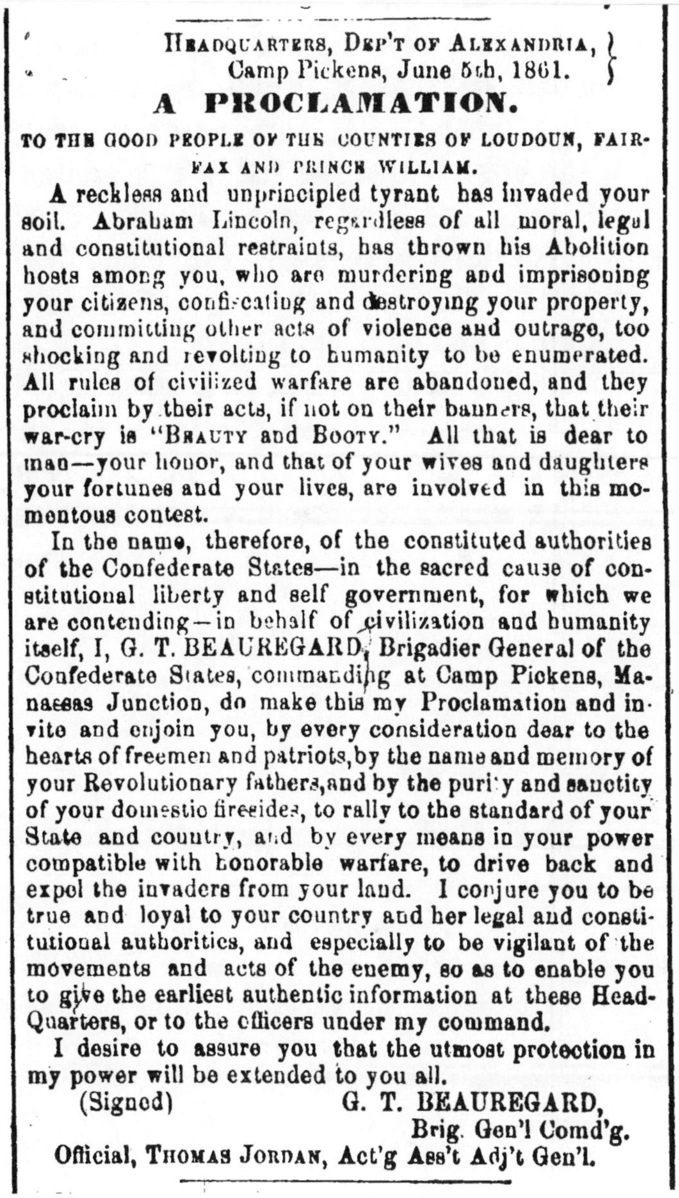

HEADQUARTERS, DEP'T OF ALEXANDRIA,
Camp Pickens, June 5th, 1861.

A PROCLAMATION.

TO THE GOOD PEOPLE OF THE COUNTIES OF LOUDOUN, FAIRFAX AND PRINCE WILLIAM.

A reckless and unprincipled tyrant has invaded your soil. Abraham Lincoln, regardless of all moral, legal and constitutional restraints, has thrown his Abolition hosts among you, who are murdering and imprisoning your citizens, confiscating and destroying your property, and committing other acts of violence and outrage, too shocking and revolting to humanity to be enumerated. All rules of civilized warfare are abandoned, and they proclaim by their acts, if not on their banners, that their war-cry is "BEAUTY and BOOTY." All that is dear to man—your honor, and that of your wives and daughters your fortunes and your lives, are involved in this momentous contest.

In the name, therefore, of the constituted authorities of the Confederate States—in the sacred cause of constitutional liberty and self government, for which we are contending—in behalf of civilization and humanity itself, I, G. T. BEAUREGARD, Brigadier General of the Confederate States, commanding at Camp Pickens, Manassas Junction, do make this my Proclamation and invite and enjoin you, by every consideration dear to the hearts of freemen and patriots, by the name and memory of your Revolutionary fathers, and by the purity and sanctity of your domestic firesides, to rally to the standard of your State and country, and by every means in your power compatible with honorable warfare, to drive back and expel the invaders from your land. I conjure you to be true and loyal to your country and her legal and constitutional authorities, and especially to be vigilant of the movements and acts of the enemy, so as to enable you to give the earliest authentic information at these Head-Quarters, or to the officers under my command.

I desire to assure you that the utmost protection in my power will be extended to you all.

(Signed) G. T. BEAUREGARD,
Brig. Gen'l Comd'g.

Official, THOMAS JORDAN, Act'g Ass't Adj't Gen'l.

Richmond Whig, June 10, 1861.
The famous "beauty and booty" proclamation by General P. G. T. Beauregard, issued after the initial foray of Union troops into Virginia, was carried by newspapers throughout the Southern states to help rouse their men for action.

Organise! Organise!

Eds. Sun: **War is upon us. The ruthless fanatics of the North are calling into the field 75,000 men to subjugate the sons of the South! Shall we bow our necks to the yoke? kiss the rod which smites? cringe in the dust before them? Shall our firesides be invaded and despoiled? Never! To arms, then, ye friends of religious and political liberty! Organise companies with competent officers; fill up the ranks of those partly filled, and form new ones. Get ye all in readiness, for ye know not the day nor the hour when these Northern Huns will be upon you. GEORGIAN.**

Columbus Sun, April 19, 1861.
According to newspapers in the Confederacy, Northerners were fighting a barbaric war of aggression to "subjugate" the Southern people, confiscate their property, and strip them of all their liberties.

Given the angry statements that circulated in the Northern media after the surrender of Fort Sumter, Southern editors had no difficulty finding hate-filled messages to present to their readers. "From all the accounts that reach us," declared the *Richmond Whig*, "the world has never witnessed so fiendish and diabolical a spirit as now animates the Northern people against the South." Determined that Southerners should "appreciate the full extent and character of the danger that menaces them" so that they could "prepare to meet it like men," the *Whig* (among other papers) published the following editorial from the *New York Courier & Enquirer*, threatening not merely mass destruction and privation, but also servile insurrection:

> The game is now fairly opened; and it must be played out with a bold and unflinching hand. And instead of seventy-five thousand volunteers, the government must call forth at least two hundred thousand. With these, occupy such places as are deemed important; and then establish a cordon of posts from Washington to the Mississippi, composed from five to thirty thousand men each, with power to concentrate a large and overwhelming force at any point where circumstances may render it necessary. Let this cordon of posts be along the borders of the secession States; and let no man pass North or South without a military pass. The coast is already blockaded; and that blockade, to be respected by the European Powers, and efficient for the purposes of conquest, must be strictly enforced.
>
> Not a vessel must pass in or out of the ports of the rebel states, and no supplies, of any kind, [can] be permitted to reach them by water. In like manner, not a barrel of flour, a pound of beef, a bushel of grain, or stores, or provisions, or clothing, or munitions of war of any kind or description, must be permitted to reach the rebels from the North by land or water. They must be shut up, penned in and starved into submission to the Government. . . . In the meantime, let the levees on the Mississippi be at once prostrated in a hundred places, while the water is high, and let the Traitors and Rebels living on the lower Mississippi be drowned out, just as we would drown out rats infesting the hull of a ship. Nor is this all. Let the servile population in the Border States understand that all moral obligation on the part of the North to sustain the peculiar institution [of slavery] has ceased; and let the traitors thus be taught at once the price of rebellion and its legitimate fruits.
>
> What we desire to see at once is a call for an additional one hundred and fifty thousand volunteers from the free States, and the establishment of a land blockade of the strictest kind, extending from the Atlantic to the Mississippi—accompanied by the flooding of the country bordering on the lower Mississippi. Do this, and the inevitable consequences . . . will soon bring the rebels to their senses.[11]

As portrayed through the Southern press, not only were the North's objectives brutal, but so too were the military men enlisted to do the dirty work. The word in the South was that the Union's armies were comprised of the "scum" of Northern cities and mercenaries from Europe—men so desperate, poor, or just plain vicious that the thrill of overrunning and plundering the South was all the enticement they needed. Again, Southern papers were quick to borrow words from Northern editors to show that this was not just an extravagant rumor, but a true picture of how horrific the establishment of "Yankee rule" would be. Several Confederate newspapers, for instance, picked up this particular article from the *New York Herald* on "the character of the coming campaign":

> We have in the Northern cities at least three hundred thousand of the most reckless, desperate men on the face of the earth. The Goths and Vandals who descended upon Rome and ensanguined the Tiber with patrician blood were angels compared to these fellows, who are known by the generic term "roughs." Of course they are all in for war, and the spoils thereof—more particularly the spoils. They have no stake in this world, no hope for the future. They will fight like demons for present enjoyment, and where one is killed twenty more will spring up in his place. It is of such rough material that all invincible troops are made. That we are to have a fight, that Virginia and Maryland will form the battleground, and that the Northern roughs will sweep those States with fire and sword, is beyond peradventure. They have already been excited to the boiling point by the rich prospect of plunder held out by some of their leaders, and will not be satisfied until they have a farm and a nigger each. . . . The character of the coming campaign will be vindictive, fierce, bloody, and merciless beyond parallel in ancient or modern history.[12]

It is impossible to overrate the role of the Northern press in helping Southern newspapers elucidate the horrific consequences of invasion and defeat. In using the words of Northerners against them, Southern editors hoped to prove to their readers that each and every one of them had a stake in making the movement for Confederate independence succeed. Victory meant more than simply securing the right to own slaves. Every liberty Southerners cherished was in jeopardy—their right to life, their right to secure homes, their right to happiness. There was no way that Southerners could doubt the extremities that would befall them if they failed to devote themselves completely to the war effort. "The very mildest fate which the leading organs of the fanatical sentiment of the North . . . [assign] to us of the South, is utter and complete subjugation—sacked and burning cities, ruined and deserted villages, and all the indescribable horrors of an unlicensed warfare," one paper warned in summary. "The furious and diabolical spirit which actuates them is abundantly manifested in the tone of their leading newspapers" and could not be mistaken or ignored. Far better, therefore, "that the earth should open and swallow up every white man, woman and child in the Southern States" than ever to yield to the Northern foe.[13]

The freedoms Southerners professed to be protecting were more than just fundamental. They were God-given and holy, and as Southern men left their homes for military camps, Christian ministers sent them off with sermons and prayers exalting the sacredness of their mission, like this one, delivered by the Reverend Benjamin Palmer to soldiers in New Orleans:

> *Gentlemen of the Washington Artillery:*
>
> At the sound of the bugle you are here, within one short hour to bid adieu to cherished homes, and soon to encounter the perils of battle on a distant field. . . . It is fitting that religion herself should with gentle voice whisper her benediction upon your flag and your cause. Soldiers, history reads to us of wars which have been baptized as holy; but she enters upon her records none that is holier than this in which you have embarked. It is a cruel war of

> defense against wicked and cruel aggression—a war of civilization against a ruthless barbarism which would dishonor the dark ages—a war of religion against a blind and bloody fanaticism. It is a war for your homes and firesides—for your wives and children—for the land which the Lord has given us for a heritage. It is a war for the maintenance of the broadest principle for which a free people can contend—the right of self-government. Eighty-five years ago our fathers fought in defense of the chartered rights of Englishmen, that taxation and representation are correlative. We, their sons, contend to-day for the great American principle that all just government derives its powers from the will of the governed. It is the cornerstone of the great temple which, on this continent, has been reared to civil freedom; and its denial leads . . . to despotism, the most absolute and intolerable, a despotism more grinding than that of the Turk or Russian. . . . The alternative before us is, the independence of the South or a despotism which will put its iron heel upon all that the human heart can hold dear. This mighty issue is submitted to the ordeal of battle, with the nations of the earth as spectators, and with the God of Heaven as umpire.[14]

Fired by reports of the devastation that awaited them, the South's newspapermen, like almost everyone else on the home front, were anxious for the Confederacy to take the upper hand. Rather than wait for the Union armies to bring desolation to their doorsteps, the *Augusta Constitutionalist* talked excitedly about turning the tables on their would-be oppressors and making a preemptive, offensive strike for freedom:

> Forced to take up arms as our revolutionary sires were, by the arrogant spirit of would-be tyrants, our policy should be not to wait tamely until the foe invades our soil and comes among us with fire and sword to devastate our homes, to beleaguer us by land and sea, and starve us into submission. We must meet force with force, and give blow for blow. We must strike back with all our strength, and selecting the most vulnerable points of attack, inflict such a deadly evil to every material interest of our enemies which we can reach by our arms, as will make them sick of this contest. We must carry the war into the enemy's country at every point where we can make a lodgement, and by making the evils of war intolerable to him, conquer a peace. . . . We can only thus create a peace party at the North, and give it strength enough to compel Lincoln and his fanatical advisers to call for a truce, and to negotiate a treaty. . . .
>
> We had hoped until the events of the last few days, that the voice of peace, of reason, and of common sense would not be utterly stifled at the North, and that there would be a party there which would sustain our demand for a peaceable settlement of the dispute. We asked simply to be let alone, and to be allowed to inaugurate an independent government under which our people would feel that their interests and their rights would be safe. It was a reasonable request, and it was but reasonable to suppose that the good sense of the North would control its fanatics, and keep even the Abolitionists at the head of the Government in check. Thus far no such result has been accomplished. On the contrary, there is throughout the North one universal howl for blood, for conquest and the utter humiliation of the South. . . . Our armies should not wait until the enemy brings slaughter and devastation into our borders. He should be made to taste the bitterness of war at his own threshold. . . . When the time arrives, Southern armies should cross the line and advance their banners into the heart of the enemy's country. There, they will find ample resources to respond to their expenses. Our Generals can put their cities and towns under contribution, and in default of compliance, lay them in ashes. By keeping open their communications with the South by a line of forts, reinforcements can be sent forward at all seasons, as

long as the war lasts. Foraging on the enemy is a fair game of retaliation for the blockade of our ports. It is a harsh remedy, but it can be vindicated by every principle of justice, and is in strict conformity with the recognized rules of war. . . .

The war inaugurated by the Abolitionists against us is one of extermination. The avowed purpose is to subjugate us—to bring our people into subjection as a conquered race. This is equivalent to a declaration of extermination, for no man living in the South can shut his eyes to the fact that the yoke can never be put on our necks while an arm is left to strike for independence. Our male citizens must first be exterminated! And then, our women will snap up the weapons of their slaughtered husbands, sons, and brothers, and fight for their children's heritage of freedom.[15]

In struggling for independence, the seceded states believed they were indeed fighting for their "heritage of freedom." They were perfecting—not rejecting—the American way of life. Even as the Confederacy prepared for a military showdown with the Union, Southerners in the summer of 1861 planned for a joyous celebration of the Fourth of July, a holiday that they now claimed for themselves as the defenders and inheritors of American liberty:

We note that some discussion prevails as to the propriety of celebrating the 4th [of] July. Why not? That is truly our Independence Day. It is the North which should properly refuse to recognize it. That region has distinctly repudiated all the principles of the 4th July, 1776. We have not. We have steadily adhered to them, and our present war is one undertaken in their defence. What was then our resolve? To be free of a foreign and hostile authority—to govern ourselves—to declare that no government was legitimate which had not the free consent of the governed party—that we would have our rights, and pursue, according to our own notions, the attainment of peace, security, happiness and justice. This is what we aim at now. By our separation from the North, and our defence against its usurpations, we are carrying out all the principles evolved by our ancestors in the Declaration of Independence. We are proving ourselves true to their principles by withdrawing from the [Union], and true to their manhood by meeting our enemies with defiance. The day is properly our own. Let us not surrender it. Let us not give up one tithe of the honorable reputation won by our sires. So far from doing so, let us celebrate it with increased enthusiasm. Let our orators show how truly we assert, and reassert, every principle for which they fought and bled—every truth and principle which they have put on record, as the right reason and governing motive for a free people, in a representative government. This is the true cue for the popular orator. His task is really easy. Look at all the facts in 1776 and 1861, and the analogies are all wonderfully close, even to the brutal war which is now ruthlessly urged against us, with a view to rob us of our liberties.[16]

With equal unanimity and sincerity, Northerners claimed that *they* were the ones waging a holy war for freedom. But for them, fighting for liberty was not about vindicating the rights of states or the rights of individual slaveholders. It meant protecting the integrity of the entire Union. They well understood that the United States—the great palladium of liberty—could not tolerate secession and still survive. As the *Barre Gazette* explained, secession "renders government impossible." If states could withdraw from the Union at their own pleasure, then the country had no cohesive power. It was just a house of cards waiting to fall apart. Unless the North nipped this wave of secession in the bud, "the rebellion of the South will be imitated" by other states in the future, whenever they should become disgruntled with the national government, "and the Union will crumble into atoms."[17]

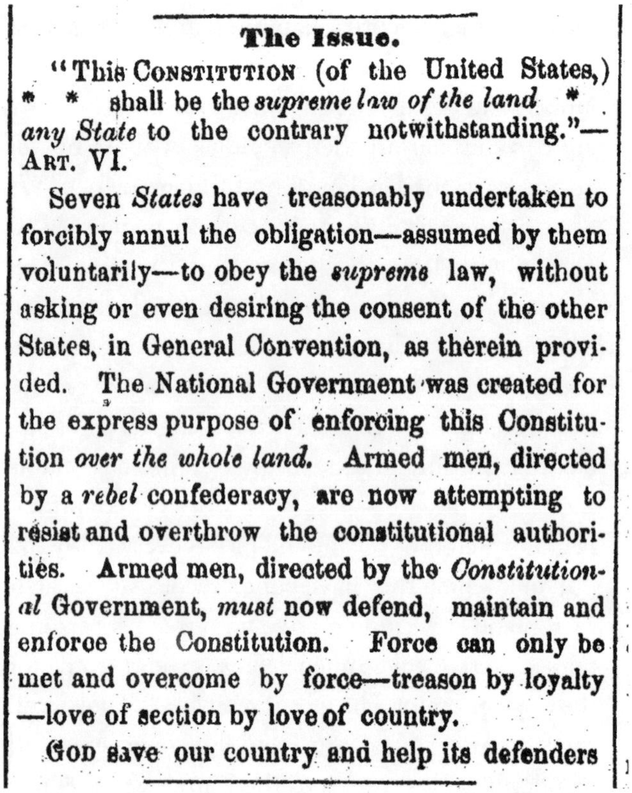

The Issue.

"This Constitution (of the United States,) * * shall be the *supreme law of the land* * any *State* to the contrary notwithstanding."—Art. VI.

Seven *States* have treasonably undertaken to forcibly annul the obligation—assumed by them voluntarily—to obey the *supreme* law, without asking or even desiring the consent of the other States, in General Convention, as therein provided. The National Government was created for the express purpose of enforcing this Constitution *over the whole land.* Armed men, directed by a *rebel* confederacy, are now attempting to resist and overthrow the constitutional authorities. Armed men, directed by the *Constitutional* Government, *must* now defend, maintain and enforce the Constitution. Force can only be met and overcome by force—treason by loyalty—love of section by love of country.

God save our country and help its defenders

Cleveland Plain Dealer, April 19, 1861.
Whereas Southerners defined liberty in terms of states' rights, most Northerners believed that liberty resided in the federal Constitution. Defending Lincoln's lawful authority over the United States—as laid out in the Constitution—was part and parcel of protecting all the rights and principles embodied in that document.

Beyond threatening the survival of the Union, the Southern rebellion also directly challenged the authority of the Constitution, America's charter of freedom. The laws of the Constitution—specifically the voting rights it established—were supposed to make political revolutions unnecessary. Every four years, the people had the opportunity to elect a new head of state; if their chosen candidate failed to win, there was always a next time. In the 1860 election, Abraham Lincoln had come out on top. Although he had won without the support of a single Southern state, his election was honest and lawful. In resisting his authority, Southerners were bucking the legal process and ignoring the will of the people who had voted Lincoln into power. Their rebellion, if successful, therefore would signify that constitutional government did not work. This very thing—the invalidation of constitutional law—was perhaps the most galling, for if constitutional government failed in America, it would be discredited everywhere. Since the inception of the United States, European monarchs had looked at the country as a mere experiment, one that they hoped would fail. Northerners now had to prove that it was viable by keeping all the states within the Union.

For all of these reasons, Northern newspapers made impassioned appeals, like this one by the *Rutland Herald* to the "Green Mountain Boys" of Vermont, rallying the masses to give everything they had to preserve their country and the liberties it enshrined:

> Fellow Citizens:—The time has arrived that is to try men's souls. The epoch in our national history, that is to decide the fate of the noblest Government ever established on earth, has now dawned. . . . It has fallen to our lot to demonstrate to the world the *possibility* or *impossibility* of maintaining a Government, in which the voice of the people shall be the supreme law.
>
> It is our solemn obligation, to vindicate the glorious principles, which the immortal heroes of the Revolution embodied in the Declaration of Independence, and [for] which they poured forth their blood and treasure. It is our sacred duty to maintain the purity, integrity, and honor of this great Republic which our forefathers bequeathed to us, as the richest heritage that the world has ever known, and which is now assailed by the minions of Slavery and despotism, who are infatuated by the wild, chimerical idea that they can subvert this powerful Government, and place the yoke of bondage on this free and enlightened people.
>
> . . . Our national flag, the ensign of liberty, that . . . has carried terror into the hearts of tyrants, and *made the thrones of despots quake beneath them*; this noble

flag beneath whose folds every American citizen has been *proud to live or die*,—this glorious banner beneath which our revolutionary Fathers fought for liberty, . . . is now insultingly torn from Its proud height. . . . *Who is there, that has one spark of patriotism in his breast, and does not burn with indignation at this* sacriligious and dastardly act? *What American citizen, who claims to have one drop of blood*, like that which circulated in the veins of the immortal heroes of '76—is not ready to hasten to the standard of his country, and *die* if need be, to avenge this gross outrage? . . .

Then let every patriot, whose heart throbs for his country, make the solemn vow, to serve her in this hour of peril, and, animated by everything *that he holds sacred*, . . . let him pledge his fealty to a Government which *protects the dearest rights of mankind*, and in whose *success* or *failure*, *[is] involved the destiny of the oppressed throughout the world*.

The eyes of the despots of the Old World have long been turned upon our country, expecting to witness the downfall of our free Government, and if the sun of liberty now sets in darkness, and anarchy shall set upon the ruins of this once mighty and prosperous nation, woe to the oppressed vassals, who so long have been trampled beneath the iron heel of despotism, and in the agony of their thralldom, have looked to this country, as the only asylum, on the face of the earth, where they could be free, and find refuge![18]

This fight for freedom held special meaning for recent immigrants to the Northern states—those "oppressed vassals" who had indeed rankled under "the iron heel of despotism" in Europe. Beginning in the 1830s, a wave of Irish had started making their way to American shores, seeking refuge from widespread famine and British misrule. Thousands of Germans, fearing reprisal for their participation in the failed democratic revolution of 1848 that had erupted in their homeland, took asylum in the United States as well. After braving a difficult transatlantic journey for the sake of enjoying political, religious, and civil liberties, they were ready to fight for the nation's survival, as illustrated in this public letter, written by a German man in Kentucky to his fellow expatriates:

To my German Friends in Kentucky:

You and I are Germans by birth, but we are all American citizens from choice, and as such we are now called upon to aid either in sustaining or overthrowing the Government of our adoption. . . . I warn you, my German brethren and fellow citizens of Kentucky, not to be deceived by those who are trying to overthrow the Government, and reduce you and me to bondage again. We all left our fatherland because we desired to rid our necks of the heel of the tyrant that trampled upon our rights. We have learned to hate tyrants—the proud spirit of our race will never submit to the yoke of bondage which Jeff. Davis and his followers are striving to fasten upon us. My countrymen, beware of all the tricks and treachery of disunionists, for they are traitors to their government. They will approach you pretending to be your best friends, and under the sacred guise of friendship seek to seduce you from your allegiance and your duty. Tell the rebel who may thus approach you that you have left the sacred graves of your ancestors and the homes of your fathers to enjoy the blessings of this free government—that you have crossed the ocean to enjoy its benefits; and tell him also that you have taken a solemn oath to support in good faith its Constitution and laws, and that you intend to make good your obligation and your oath. . . . Having once tasted the sweets of liberty, let us surrender it only with our lives. If this Government is destroyed, liberty will be again banished from the face of the earth. . . .

The plain duty of the United States Government is to protect us, to guard over our rights as its adopted citizens whenever and by whomsoever they may be invaded, and this duty has been performed to the letter. . . . In return for all this, our plain duty is to support the Government that protects us in good faith, to stand by it in this hour of peril, and sustain it, if need be, with [our] fortunes and our lives.[19]

Harper's Weekly, June 8, 1861.
In this cartoon, entitled "Columbia Awake at Last," a wiry Southern aristocrat–sporting pantaloons emblazoned with the words *secession* and *treason*–is throttled by the goddess of liberty while a ghostly George Washington looks on. The Southerner's characteristic straw hat, which is festooned with a Confederate flag and a miniature palmetto (the state symbol of South Carolina), displays his rebel sympathies. Meanwhile, the Southern figure in the background sports a bowie knife and a pirate's flag, drawing attention to the treachery and wickedness of the rebellion.
(© Applewood Books, Inc. Reproduced by permission of Applewood Books and harpersweekly.com)

While almost all Northerners loudly deplored secession as a threat to American liberty, Republican papers were quick to blame the South's behavior on one thing in particular: slavery. The politicians who led the secession movement, they rightly argued, were all slaveholders—haughty men accustomed to lording it over their plantations and oppressing the black men and women they held in bondage. It should have come as no surprise, therefore, that when the Southern states did not get their way in the election of 1860 and failed to prevent Lincoln's accession to the presidency, they would become indignant, unruly, and rebellious. The war thus seemed to embody a clash of cultures and societies, one pitting a liberty-loving North against an arrogant, aristocratic South:

> The *Southern* Republics are not PURE DEMOCRACIES. They contain in their bosom the *feudal* system in its very worst form, embodied in a class of men denominated slaveholders, in number between three and four hundred thousand. . . . Slaveholders . . . possess the ordinary characteristics of a privileged class, such as have been found to exist . . . in every age. Courteous towards equals, generous in their hospitality, sensitive as to their honor, imperious in their bearing, unaccustomed to labor, regarding labor as a badge of servility, having but little sympathy with the doctrine of popular rights, clamorous and very tenacious of their special privileges, and always ready for deeds of chivalry, all aristocratic classes form an order of men by themselves, born to command, but not to obey.
>
> Such, essentially, is the position of the slaveholding order of men at the South, especially the large planters. By education, interest, and habit they are devoted to their peculiar institution. Slavery and

cotton are their two principal ideas. Upon these two connected interests they concentrate their thoughts. They are the men, in the main, who form the South. . . . Though greatly in the minority as to numbers, they are nevertheless the ruling class. They attend to the politics of the South; they manage its government and fill the places of public honor. They have extensive plantations tilled and worked by slaves, among whom they move in the character of feudal lords, acquiring those habits of mind that are peculiar to their position and station. Accustomed to rule over their dependents, they have the instinct of rule everywhere. . . .

This unfortunate legacy of slavery . . . has also its peculiar *governmental* necessities. . . . The slave population must be kept in the state of subjection. They must be taught to submit to the authority of a despotic will. If they have any aspirations towards freedom, these must be promptly suppressed. Law must act upon them with unusual severity. Their movements must be carefully watched. They must have no opportunity for secret combinations or organized action. They must be looked upon, and in many respects treated, as if they were a hostile population. Their mental and moral natures must be thoroughly bent to the yoke. . . . If we are to have an aristocratic and despotic class on the one hand, and an enslaved and degraded class on the other, then the social organism must adjust itself to this state of things. Power must be concentrated in the hands of the former, and taken away from the latter. . . . There must be a broad gulf between the class ruling and the class ruled.

It is hence clear that the Southern Republics with the element of slavery in them, creating a patrician class of slaveholders, . . . are not and cannot be *pure* democracies. The power that governs, is in the hands of a class mainly actuated by one interest; and this constitutes an oligarchy to all intents and purposes. . . .

Look now at the opposite condition as developed in the Free States, where no slavery exists. Here we find a true, practical, thrifty democracy upon the basis of freedom, living, breathing, and moving, under the exclusive inspiration of those great ideas so well stated in the Declaration of Independence. Here there is no governing class, no privileged order, and no institution upon which to build such a class.

Nature of the Contest.—To a person imperfectly acquainted with the real question at issue in this country, the nature of the present contest must be perplexing. Both sides claim to be guided by the purest motives, both to be struggling for existence and liberty. The real position of affairs, however, is simply this, the north are fighting for constitutional liberty, the union and independence, while the south are battling for despotism. A government, founded as is theirs, on negro slavery, cannot be a vehicle of liberty. The elements of despotism are seen from the first inception of the present grand conspiracy. A few men have controlled the whole matter from the first. It did not grow out of the spontaneous action of a down trodden people. It was the careful calculation of a nest of ambitious, unprincipled leaders. Inflated with the desire of forming a grand slave-holding empire, they deliberately forced the people into the rebellion.

Hampshire Gazette & Northampton Courier,
May 21, 1861.
Although the South claimed to be fighting in the name of liberty, the Northern press insisted that the rebellion, initiated as it was by slaveholding elites, really was an aristocratic and despotic movement that did not enjoy the willing support of the Southern masses.

All the people stand upon a common level. The sovereignty is the entire people. The majority rules. Labor is honorable. The masses of the people labor everywhere; and being the sovereign power, they confer dignity upon the idea of labor. In political station and civil rights they are just equal, distinguished from each other only by different grades of talent and industry. . . . This is no fancy-sketch of the Free States. . . . They *are* Free States in fact, as well as by contrast with the Slave States. . . . They constitute the basis and glory of that noble charter of liberty, which our fathers devised for the general government of the whole country. Freedom was their idea, and freedom is the practical idea of the Free States. The Constitution was adopted for the sake of freedom, and not slavery.

What, then, . . . is the real issue pending in this movement of secession? It is the long-standing struggle between different and naturally hostile systems of civilization—the one a system of pure freedom prevailing in the Free States, and the other a system of slavery entering into the structure of society in the Slave States—both existing under one National Government, and . . . now coming into desperate collision with each other. . . . Which of these two spirits shall prevail, freedom and nationality, represented by the Government at Washington; or slavery and rebellion, represented by the usurped Government of Jefferson Davis and his associates? This is the great and immediately urgent question of the hour.[20]

For Southern Unionists, who had never supported secession but who were now citizens of the Confederacy against their will, this struggle against the despotic rule of the slave-owning class was intensely personal. Unionism could be found in every Southern state, but it was especially strong in the western part of Virginia, which in 1861 began taking political action to break away from the Confederacy and rejoin the United States. (The Unionists would eventually accomplish their mission in 1863, with the creation of West Virginia.) The people in western Virginia had been complaining for decades that their state government was too thoroughly under the thumb of slave-owning politicians from the east. The secession ordinance that took Virginia out of the Union in April 1861—an ordinance pushed forward by eastern slaveholders—was for them the final straw. Determined to never again take orders from easterners, western politicians declared their own war of independence, using the newspapers to rally the region against kowtowing slavishly to secession:

Why should the people of North-Western Virginia allow themselves to be dragged into the rebellion inaugurated by ambitious and heartless men, who have banded themselves together to destroy a government formed for you by your patriot fathers, and which has secured to you all the liberties consistent with the nature of man, and has, for near three-fourths of a century, sheltered you in sunshine and storm, made you the admiration of the civilized world, and conferred upon you a title more honored, respected and revered than that of King or Potentate—the title of an American citizen? . . .

If those feelings which actuated our Revolutionary fathers be not all dead in us, we shall exhibit our love for Virginia by repudiating this tyrannical rule which the Richmond Convention has endeavored to impose, and suffer not ourselves to be sold like sheep from the shambles. The people yet hold their destinies in their own hands—it is for them to accept or reject a tyranny worse many times than that from which the war of '76 delivered us. . . . Are we submissionists, craven cowards, who will yield . . . the rich legacy of Freedom which we have inherited from our fathers, or are we men who know our rights, and, knowing, dare maintain them? If we are, we will resist the usurpers and drive from our midst the rebellion sought to be forced upon us. We will, in the strength of our cause, resolutely and determinedly stand by our rights and our liberties, secured to us by the struggles of our Revolutionary fathers and the authors of the Constitution under which we have grown and prospered. . . . We will maintain, protect and defend that Constitution and the Union with all our strength, and with all our powers, ever remembering that "Resistance to tyrants is obedience to God.". . . Let all our ends be directed to the creation of an organized resistance to the despotism of tyrants who have been in session in Richmond, . . . [so] that we may maintain our position in the Union under the flag of our common country, which has for so many years waved gracefully and protectingly over us, and which, when we behold upon its ample folds the stripes and the stars of Freedom, causes our bosoms to glow with patriotic heat, and our hearts to swell with honest love of country. That . . . flag, the symbol of our might, challenges our admiration and justly claims our every effort against those who have dared to desecrate and dishonor it.[21]

The plight of Southern Unionists was well documented in the Northern press; in fact, Northerners were convinced that Unionism was actually the dominant feeling in the South. The rebellion, they believed, was the exclusive handiwork of the slave-owning class and not really representative of the true feelings of most Southerners. Through the Northern press, stories circulated widely of Southern men who were threatened with lynching until they agreed to enlist in the Confederate army, and of Southern women physically assaulted for voicing their love for the Union. The term often used to describe the state of affairs in the Confederacy is one that has become all too familiar to Americans of today: *terrorism.* In the Northern mind, the Southern people were helpless hostages—innocent victims of rebellious slaveholders who had hijacked the Southern states and steered them recklessly out of the Union. Northerners therefore saw themselves as fighting not merely for their own liberties but also for the freedom of their Southern brethren from the tyranny imposed upon them by the rebels:

> This great fact must never for a moment be lost sight of—this truth, that we fight to preserve the whole people against traitors who aim solely to destroy. Our armies are as much the friends of the quiet people of the south as of ourselves. They go to save them from the terrible consequences of the anarchy they have inaugurated. It is to preserve liberty to them, to avert the coming despotism which will soon settle in unrelieved darkness over them, that we take up arms. . . . Let it be understood always, therefore, that we go to liberate the people now resident in the south, not to enslave them. Vast numbers of them detest the rule of the secession traitors not less heartily than we do, yet they are powerless even to protect themselves from enlistment in the war upon us. It is credibly reported that persons refusing to enlist in the confederate army have been killed on the spot. . . . The condition of things in the seceded states is shocking, even horrible, in its despotic and bloody terrorism to those who refuse to join in assailing the Union. We cannot know the real sentiments of men, whatever they may there be driven to do, such is the fierceness of the persecution directed at all who dare to hesitate at embarking in treason. In this most extraordinary case we must strike with all the force we can command at the heads of the rebellion, and prepare to be as tolerant as is possible to the masses there who cannot protect themselves.[22]

The North thus believed it was fighting for the most altruistic of purposes: to save the Southern people from oppression, to preserve democratic government for the entire United States, and to maintain the Union as an asylum of liberty for all the world. As proclaimed by the religious press, these were ends that God Himself would smile upon and bless with success:

Harper's Weekly, April 19, 1862.
This illustration depicts a united North rising out of the fires at Fort Sumter, ready to embark on a struggle in which the fate of liberty and the survival of the Union are equally at stake.
(© Applewood Books, Inc. Reproduced by permission of Applewood Books and harpersweekly.com)

Millions of loyal hearts . . . are swelling with a sentiment which no words can express so fitly as those words of ancient Israel going forth to war for their land and their temple, "In the name of our God we will set up our banners."

Are we right in this feeling? Can we set up our banners and muster our forces in the name of God? Can we, in cheerful and reasonable hope, commend our cause to his protection? Can we, intelligently and with good reason, claim that in the conflict into which we are entering, God is on our side? God is on our side if we are on his side, and not otherwise.

. . . If we were undertaking a war of conquest and subjugation, invading territories not our own for the purpose of extending our empire, we might indeed set up our banners in the name of God, but he would not be with us; for such a war would place us not on the side of justice, which is God's great interest in the world, but on the side of wrong. If we were undertaking a war of passion and hate, in the spirit of mere vengeance, we might indeed inaugurate the war with invocation of the God of battles, but God would not be with us; for . . . he has no fellowship with our malignant passions. . . .

Let it be remembered, first, that our position is on the side of law against violence, and of government against anarchy. . . . Let it be remembered also that our position is on the side not only of an established Government and an existing social order, but of republican self-government against the "architects of ruin." We are called, in the providence of God, to defend the best civil constitution ever given to any people, against disorders which, if allowed, will wreck the cause of freedom throughout the world. . . . Do we not know that in such a conflict God is with us? Are we not on his side? Does he not love and value this balanced and well-ordered liberty which he has given to us in trust for our children and the coming ages? Does he not value . . . the entire inheritance which, under his favor, our fathers won for us, and for which we are ready to lay down not only our treasures but our lives, that it may be the inheritance of others after us? . . . The rebellion against which we stand is indeed a rebellion "to destroy the fairest and the freest Government on earth." Are we not on God's side?[23]

Not all Northerners were so confident in the justness of the Union cause or so complacent about Lincoln's leadership. The fact was that the president's actions—calling up troops to quash the rebellion, establishing the blockade, imposing martial law in Maryland—went beyond the strict limits of his constitutional authority. Most people in the North were willing to overlook this fact. They were ready to support Lincoln in almost any policy that might help the Union win the war. However, papers representing the Peace Democrats, such as the *New York Evening Day-Book*, loudly condemned him as a threat to the survival of America's free government:

The President of the United States derives all his powers from the people; he is the agent of the people, . . . and the Constitution is the law which lays down the rules of his duty. On entering upon his office, he takes a solemn oath to obey and support the Constitution. Does any man pretend that Mr. Lincoln has not violated this oath in usurping the powers which the Constitution gives *to Congress alone*, of calling out and increasing the army and navy of the United States? . . . If the American people tamely submit to the doctrine . . . that the Executive [may] violate the Constitution whenever he thinks it best, then farewell, a long farewell to freedom. We shall lose our liberty—and we deserve to lose it—if we do not resist and condemn every infringement upon the sacred domain of constitutional law. . . . The President of the United States is put in his place, not to make law, but to obey the laws himself, which definitely prescribe and limit his powers. Mr. Lincoln's proclamation blockading the ports, is another and a flagrant violation of the Constitution. . . . If the people fail to rebuke *one* such trespass upon their Constitution, they may soon expect to be called upon to submit to *another*, and to *another*, and *another*, until their liberties have almost imperceptibly slipped away. Down this treacherous and slippery path many Republics have descended to their doom. Great as would be the evil of secession, it [would be] still small compared to the curse of allowing executive usurpation. A thousand times better to lose one-half, or two-thirds, or any number of the States, than to allow the sources of constitutional freedom to be cut off at their fountain head.[24]

Also, as the *New York News* added, the very idea of fighting—in the name of liberty—to *force* the Southern states back into the Union was grossly ironic as well as counterproductive:

All know that war cannot restore fraternal feelings between the States, and that a forced Union is an absurdity. Could the North conquer the South, it would not be a Union, but a *subjugation*. The North would hold the South . . . by the law of *force*, as *subject States*, not as *independent equals*, such as our Government and Constitution made them. Is this what the Administration intends? Are the rights of the States to be invaded, their independence destroyed, and our present form of Government changed to a military despotism, under the assumption of "enforcing the laws" and preserving the Union? . . . Why should not the great and powerful North say to the weaker South, "Put up your sword; let there be no strife between us; we are brethren, and if we cannot live together in peace, let us part in peace?" The cause of justice, humanity, civilization, and free institutions demands this; for when the Union, formed to promote the general welfare, ceases to be a Union of love and concord, but becomes a bond of strife and hate between the States, it no longer subserves the purposes for which it was established. However much we may deplore the unfriendly existing relations of the North and South, all must know that they cannot be changed for the better by war. The forced obedience of States, by the strong arm of military power, was never contemplated by the framers of our Government; and could it now be accomplished, it would change our free republic into an odious military despotism—the stronger States holding the weaker in a degrading bondage—a hated vassalage, to which none but the most tame and ignoble in spirit would be willing to submit.[25]

The Peace Democrats spoke passionately about the horrors of "vassalage" and "bondage," but no group in the North understood these terms more viscerally than the free black community. They knew the meaning of subordination all too well—and knew too that when most of their compatriots spoke majestically of protecting liberty, they actually meant something more specific and exclusive: white liberty. Northerners were rushing to war to defend their Constitution and preserve their beloved Union, not to free slaves or raise the status of blacks in society. Yet, despite this, black Northerners believed that their freedom hung in the balance all the same. Although they were a disdained minority in the North and were not permitted to enlist in the army alongside their white compatriots, free blacks contributed earnestly to the Union cause as laborers, cooks, teamsters, ditch diggers, and nurses. They did so with good reason, for if the proslavery Confederacy defeated the Union, the future for the black race in America would be bleak indeed. The *Anglo-African* explained:

There are men among our people who look upon this as the "white man's war," and such men openly say, let them fight it out among themselves. It is their flag, and their constitution which have been dishonored and set at naught; it is their forts which have been bombarded or stolen; and all they see to is to retake those forts and to restore the Union as it *was!*

This is a huge fallacy. In proof of which, let us ask ourselves some questions. By ourselves, we mean the free blacks of the free States. What rights have we in the free States? We have the "right to life, liberty and the pursuit of happiness." We have the right to labor, and are secured in the fruits of our labor; we have the right to our wives and our little ones; we have to a large extent the right to educate our children—and if in possession of means we can educate them to the fullest extent of their capacities.

Are these rights worth having? If they are then they are worth defending with all our might, and at any cost. It is illogical, unpatriotic, nay mean and unmanly in us to shrink from the defence of these great rights and privileges. To hesitate to defend them, would prove us unworthy to enjoy them.

But some will say that these rights of *ours* are not assailed by the South. Are they not? What in short is the programme or platform on which the South would have consented to remain in the Union? It was to spread slavery over all the States and territories. It was to make slavery co-incident with African descent. It was to make the colored man, wherever found on American soil, a slave. It was to gain for the slave-holder the right to carry his slaves with him securely wherever he wished on American soil.

Against whom did this platform level its guns? We assert that it was against the free blacks of the North, and such freedom as they enjoy. . . . Hence, talk as we may, we *are* concerned in this fight, and our fate hangs upon its issue. The South must be subjugated, or we shall be enslaved. In aiding the Federal government, in whatever way we can, we are aiding to secure our own liberty; for this war can only end in the subjection of the North or of the South. We do not affirm that the North is fighting in behalf of the black man's rights, as such—if this was the single issue, we even doubt whether they would fight at all. But circumstances have been so arranged by the decree of Providence, that in struggling for their own nationality they are forced to defend our rights.[26]

It was true: the Union was not fighting for black men's rights or against slavery. But as the Northern people would discover soon enough, in their efforts to defend liberty they ignored the South's "peculiar institution" at their own risk.

THE LIBERATOR
—IS PUBLISHED—
EVERY FRIDAY MORNING,
—AT—
221 WASHINGTON STREET, ROOM No. 6.

ROBERT F. WALLCUT, GENERAL AGENT.

☞ TERMS—Two dollars and fifty cents per annum, in advance.

☞ Five copies will be sent to one address for TEN DOLLARS, if payment be made in advance.

☞ All remittances are to be made, and all letters relating to the pecuniary concerns of the paper are to be directed (POST PAID) to the General Agent.

☞ Advertisements inserted at the rate of five cents per line.

☞ The Agents of the American, Massachusetts, Pennsylvania, Ohio and Michigan Anti-Slavery Societies are authorised to receive subscriptions for THE LIBERATOR.

☞ The following gentlemen constitute the Financial Committee, but are not responsible for any debts of the paper, viz:—FRANCIS JACKSON, EDMUND QUINCY, EDMUND JACKSON, and WENDELL PHILLIPS.

THE LIBERATOR.

The United States Constitution is "a covenant with death, and an agreement with hell."

☞ "What order of men under the most absolute of monarchies, or the most aristocratic of republics, was ever invested with such an odious and unjust privilege as that of the separate and exclusive representation of less than half a million owners of slaves, in the Hall of this House, in the chair of the Senate, and in the Presidential mansion! This investment of power in the owners of one species of property concentrated in the highest authorities of the nation, and disseminated through thirteen of the twenty-six States of the Union, constitutes a privileged order of men in the community, more adverse to the rights of all, and more pernicious to the interests of the whole, than any order of nobility ever known. To call government thus constituted a Democracy is to insult the understanding of mankind. . . . It is doubly tainted with the infection of riches and of slavery. There is no name in the language of national jurisprudence that can define it—no model in the records of ancient history, or in the political theories of Aristotle, with which it can be likened. It was introduced into the Constitution of the United States by an equivocation—a representation of property under the name of persons. Little did the members of the Convention from the Free States imagine or foresee what a sacrifice to Moloch was hidden under the mask of this concession."—JOHN QUINCY ADAMS.

WM. LLOYD GARRISON, Editor.

Our Country is the World, our Countrymen are all Mankind.

J. B. YERRINTON & SON, Printers.

VOL. XXXI. NO. 17. BOSTON, FRIDAY, APRIL 26, 1861. WHOLE NO. 158[illegible]

Selections.

HENRY WARD BEECHER ON THE WAR.

A SERMON,

Preached at Plymouth Church, Brooklyn, N. Y., Sunday evening, April 14, 1861, and reported for *The Independent* by T. J. ELLINWOOD.

"And the Lord said unto Moses, Wherefore criest thou unto me? speak unto the children of Israel, that they go forward."—EXOD. XIV. 15.

Moses was raised up to be the emancipator of two millions of people. At the age of forty, having through a singular providence, been reared in the midst of luxury, in the proudest, most intelligent, the most civilized court on the globe, with a heart in sympathy with a genuine love of his own race and people, he began to act as their emancipator. He slew one of their oppressors. And, seeing contention among his brethren, he sought to bring them to peace. He was rejected, reproached, and spurned; and finding himself discovered, he fled, and for the sake of liberty, became a witness, a fugitive and a martyr. For forty years, uncomplaining, he dwelt apart with his father-in-law, alone in the wilderness, in the peaceful pursuits of a herdsman. At eighty—the time when most men lay down the burden of life, or have long laid it down—he began his life-work. He was called back by the voice of God; and now, accompanied with companions, he returned, confronted the king, and, inspired by Divine inspiration, demanded, repeatedly, the release of his people. The first demand was answered by a terrific plague; the second by a second terrible judgment; the third by a third frightful devastation; the fourth by a fourth dreadful [illegible]; the fifth by a fifth desolating, sweeping mischief. A sixth, a seventh, an eighth, and a ninth time he demanded their release. And when was there ever, on the face of the earth, a man that, once having power, would let it go till life itself went with it? Pharaoh, who is the grand type of oppressors, held on in spite of the Divine command, and of the Divine punishment. Then God let fly the last terrific judgment, and smote the first-born of Egypt; and there was wailing in every house of the midnight land. And then, in the midst of the first gush of grief and anguish, the tyrant said, "Let them go! let them go!" And he did let them go; [illegible] shoved them out; and they went pell-mell in great confusion on their way, taking up their line of march to escape from Egypt. * * * *

God has raised up many men, at different periods of the world, to bring his cause forth from its various exigencies. Wherever a man is called to defend a truth or a principle, a church or a people, a nation or an age, he may be said to be, like Moses, the leader of God's people or cause. And in every period of the world God has shut up his people, at one time and another, to himself. He has brought their enemies behind them, as he brought the Egyptians behind the children of Israel. He has hedged them in on either hand. He has spread out the unfordable sea before them. He has so beset them with difficulties, when they were attempting to live for right, for duty, and for liberty, that they have been like Israel.

When men stand for the right, their troubles are not a presumption that they are in the wrong. Since the world began, men that have stood for the right have had to stand for it, as Christ stood for the world, suffering for victory.

In the history which belongs peculiarly to us, over and over again the same thing is found. In that grand beginning struggle, in which Luther figured so prominently, he stood in a doubtful conflict. He was in the minority; he was vehemently pressed with enemies on every side; nine times out of ten during his whole life the odds were against him. And yet he died victorious, and we reap the fruit of his victory.

In one of the consequences of that noble struggle—namely, the assertion in Holland and Netherlands of civil liberty and religious toleration—the same thing took place. Almost the entire globe was against that amphibious republic, until England cared for them; and England cared for them but very doubtfully and very imperfectly. All the reigning influences, all the noblest of the commanding men of the Continent, were against them. The conflict was one long and dubious, in which they suffered extremely, and conquered through their suffering.

In the resulting struggle in England, which was borrowed largely from the Continent—the Puritan uprising, the Puritan struggle—the same thing occurred. The Puritans were enveloped in darkness. Their enemies were more than their friends. The issue was exceedingly doubtful. Their very victory began in apparent defeat. For when at last, wearied and discouraged, they could no longer abide the restriction of their liberty in England, they set sail to plant colonies upon these shores. They founded in New England liberal institutions. On the sea did they venture, but the ocean, black and wild, before they left it, was covered with winter.

In every one of these instances, darkness and the flood lay before the champions of truth and rectitude. God in his providence said to them, though they were without apparent instrumentalities, "Go forward! Venture everything! Endure everything! Yield the precious truths never! Live for ever by them! Die with *them* if you die at all."

The whole lesson of the past is that safety and [illegible] very: that the Constitution of the United States, together with the Declaration of Independence, was meant to be as we now hold it, as we now defend it, as we have held it, and as we have been defending it. And at length even this is conceded, as I shall have occasion to say, further on, by the enemies of liberty in this country. The Vice-President of the so-called Southern Confederacy has stated, recently, that there was a blunder made in the construction of our Constitution on this very truth of universal liberty, thus admitting the grand fact that that immortal instrument, as held by the North, embodies the views of those who framed it; and that those views are unmistakably in favor of liberty to all.

2. There can be no disputing the fact that, from the commercial causes, an element of slavery which had a temporary refuge in the beginning in this land, swelled to an unforeseen and unexpected power, and for fifty years has held the administrative power of the country in its hands. No man acquainted with our politics hesitates to say that while the spirit of liberty first suggested our national ideas and fashioned our national institutions, after that work was done, the Government passed into the hands of the Slave Power; and that that power has administered these institutions during the last fifty years for its own purposes, or in a manner that has been antagonistic to the interests of this country.

3. Against this growing usurpation for the last twenty-five years, there has been rising up and organizing a proper, legal, constitutional opposition, wishing not the circumscription or injury of any section in this land, but endeavoring to keep our institutions out of the hands of despotism, and on the side of liberty. For twenty-five years there has been a struggle to see to it that those immortal instruments that were framed for the purposes of liberty should not be wrested from their original intent—that they should be maintained for the objects for which they were created.

4. What is the means that has been employed to maintain our institutions? Free discussion. That simply. We have gone before the people in every proper form. For twenty years of defeat, though of growing influence, we have argued the questions of human rights and human liberty, and the doctrines of the Constitution and of our fathers; and we have maintained that the children should stand where the fathers did. At last the continent has consented. We began as a handful, in the midst of mobs, and derision, and obloquy. We have gone through the experience of Gethsemane and Calvary. The cause of Christ among his poor has suffered as the Master suffered, again, and again, and again; and at last the public sentiment of the North has been revolutionized. What! revolutionized away from the doctrines of the fathers? No; back to the doctrines of the fathers. Revolutionized against our institutions? No; in favor of our institutions. We have taken simply the old American principles. We have merely taken the ground which was taken by our venerated ancestors, and from which, owing to foreign influences, we had lapsed. This is the history very simply stated. The children have gone back to the old landmarks. We stand for the doctrines and instruments that the fathers gave us.

5. The vast majority of this nation are now on the side of our American institutions, according to their original intent. We ask only this: that our Government may be what it was made to be—an instrument of justice and liberty. We ask no advantages; no new prerogatives; no privileges whatsoever. We merely say, "Let there be no intestine revolution in our instruments, and let them stand as they were made, and for the purposes for which they were created." Is there anything unreasonable, anything wrong, in that? Is it wrong to reason? Is it wrong to discuss? Is it wrong to go before a free people with their business, and, in the field, in the caucus, in the assembly, in all deliberative bodies, argue fairly, and express the result by the American means—the omnipotence of the vote? Is that wrong? It is what we have been doing for the last few years. By the prescribed methods of the Constitution, and in the spirit of liberty which it embodied and evoked, we have done our proper work. Before God, we cleanse our hands of all imputation of designing injustice, or of seeking wrong. We have not sought any one's damage. We have aimed at no invidious restrictions for any. We have simply said, "God, through our fathers, committed to us certain institutions, and we will maintain them to the end of our lives, and to the end of time." That is what we have done.

6. Seven States, however, in a manner revolutionary not only of government, but in violation of the rights and customs of their own people, have disowned their country and made war upon it! There has been a spirit of patriotism in the North; but, within my memory, never in the South. I never heard a man from the South speak of himself as an American. Men from the South always speak of themselves as Southerners. When I was abroad, I never spoke of myself as a Northerner, but always as a citizen of the United States. I love our country; and it is a love of the country, and not a love of the North alone, that pervades the people of the North. There has never been witnessed such patience, such self-denial, such magnanimity, such true patriotism, under such circumstances, as that which has been manifested in the North. And in the South the feeling has been sectional, local. The people there have been proud, not that they belong to the nation, but that they were born where the sun burns. They are hot, narrow, and boastful; for, out of China, [illegible]

power of impressing our senses with their mischiefs. I hold that it is ten thousand times better to have war than to have slavery. I hold that to be corrupted silently by giving up manhood, by degenerating, by becoming cravens, by yielding one right after another, is infinitely worse than war. Why, war is resurrection, in comparison with the state to which we should be brought, in such an event. And although war is a terrible evil, there are other evils that are more terrible. In our own peculiar case, though I would say nothing to garnish it, nothing to palliate it, nothing to alleviate it, nothing to make you more willing to have it, nothing to remove the just abhorrence which every man and patriot should have for it, yet I would say that, in the particular condition into which we have been brought, it will not be an unmixed evil. Eighty years of unexampled prosperity have gone far toward making us a people that judge of moral questions by their relation to our convenience and ease. We are in great danger of becoming a people that shall measure by earthly things—by the lowest standard of a commercial expediency. We have never suffered for our principles. And now, if it please God to do that which daily we pray that he may avert—if it please God to wrap this nation in war, one result will follow: we shall be called to suffer for our faith. We shall be called to the heroism of doing, and daring, and bearing, and suffering for the things which we believe to be vital to the salvation of this people.

On what conditions, then, may we retreat from this war, and on what conditions may we have peace?

1. We may do it on condition that two-thirds of this nation shall implicitly yield up to the dictation of one-third. You can have peace on that ground. Italy could have had peace at the hands of Francis II. They had nothing to do but to say to that tyrant, "Here is my neck: put your foot on it," to obtain peace. The people of Hungary may have peace, if they will only say to him of Vienna, "Reign over us as you please: our lives are in your hands." There is never any trouble in having peace, if men will yield themselves to the control of those that have no business to control them. Two-thirds of this nation unquestionably stand on the side of the original articles of our Constitution, and in the service of liberty, and one-third say "No!" Now if the two-thirds will give up to the one-third, we can have peace—a little while.

2. We can have peace, if we can legalize and establish the right of any discontented community to rebel, and set up intestine governments within the Government of the United States. Yield that principle, demoralize government, and you can have peace—for a little while. You cannot yield that principle, and not demoralize government.

If in a family of six children, none of whom are of age, three set up against father and mother and brother and sister, the whole household will be in a constant ferment. Either the children must be subdued, or there is an end of peace in that family. The parents must govern the children, or they will be forever at war.

Now, in our land, it is held that a minority, on becoming discontented with the old Government, have a right to secede and set up a new one. And if this is the right of seven States on the Gulf, it is the right of seven States on the lakes. If it is the right of seven States on the lakes, it is the right of five or three States on the Ohio river. If it is the right of a number of States, it is the right of one State. And if it is the right of any State, there is not a State, a half of a State, a county, or a town, that has not the same right. It is a right that sanctions disintegration. It is a right that aims at the destruction of the attraction of governmental cohesion. It is a right that invalidates all power in government. And if you will grant this right; if you will consent to have this Government broken up; if you are willing that our country should degenerate to the worst form of Jacobinism, you can have peace—for a little while.

3. We can have peace, if we will agree fundamentally to change our Constitution, and, instead of maintaining a charter of universal freedom, write it out as a deliberate charter of oppression.

Mr. Stephens, the Vice-President of the so-called Confederate States, declared, in a formal speech, that our Constitution was framed on a fundamental mistake, inasmuch as it took it for granted that men were born for freedom and equality. And that is the ground taken by those States. It is according to the reading of their new Constitution. They have expunged the doctrine of universal liberty, and put in its place the doctrine of liberty to the strong, and servitude to the weak—for that is just what it comes to. It is said that the African race, by reason of their nationality and savagism, are not fit for liberty, and that the white race, by reason of their nationality and civilization, are fit to govern them. It is merely a plea that weak persons are not fit to take care of themselves, and that strong persons are fit to take care of them; and it is a plea that is just as applicable to any other peoples as to the Anglo-Saxons and the Africans. It is simply a doctrine that might makes right. It may be stated in this form: "You are weak, and I am strong, and I am therefore your lawful master." If it is good with reference to the Africans and the Anglo-Saxons, it is good with reference to all other races. And if it is good in reference to races, it is good in reference to individuals. Therefore, there is not a workman, there is not a poor man, there is not a man that is [illegible]

Milton and Salmasius, and in all the writings of Roman priests that have sought to bolster up sacerdotal rule, these arguments have been put forth far more ably than our unscholarly Southerners have put them forth. But this is the ground which has been taken by the Christian church of the South: that in Christ Jesus all men are not created equal—that white masters are, but that black servants are not!

And that is not all. Not only is this new Government framed on this ground, and not only have all the churches of the South taken this ground, so that it may be said of the Southern Confederacy as it was said of one of the old revolted tribes, "They have a priest to their house"—not only this, but there has just now been raised up in the North a cub of the same kind—a society for the promotion of *national unity*, on the basis of a change of our national instruments of government. This society proposes to restore peace to this country. And how? Exactly as you restore uniformity of color in a room where some things are red, some blue, and some yellow—by blowing the light out so that all things will be of the same color! We are very much divided in this land, one part believing in liberty and the other believing in servitude; and it is proposed to bring these two parts together in unity, by destroying the distinction between them. What is this society's own statement, as contained in the letter which they have put forth with their articles? They make this formal assertion: that that portion of our original Declaration of Independence which makes all men free and equal, has been misinterpreted, or is false. They endeavor to say it soft; but it is a thing that cannot be said soft. To breathe it, to whisper it, makes it louder than thunder.

Indeed, it is true that men are not physiologically equal. No man ever believed that they were. They do not weigh alike. They differ in respect to bone and tissue. They are not the same as regards mental caliber. Their dynamic forces are different. They are not capable of exerting the same amount of political influence. In the nations of Europe it was held that the royal head, *jure Divino*, had privileges which the nobles had not; that there belonged to the nobles prerogatives which did not belong to the commonalty; and that the political rights of the great common people were to be graduated according to their status in society. But our fathers said, "God gives the same political rights to all alike. The people are king, and the people are nobles. They are equal in this: that they all stand before the same law of justice, and that justice is to be the same to one as to another. The richest and the poorest, the wisest and the most ignorant, the highest and the lowest, are on an equality in this regard." And what was meant by the Declaration of Independence was, that every man born into life was born with such dignities, with such a nature, conferred upon him, that, as a child of God, he has a right to confront government, and legislature, and laws, and say, "I demand, in common with every other man, justice, protection, life, liberty, and the pursuit of happiness." And this is what our society in the North for the promotion of national unity undertake, in their first article, to say is a lie!

Now, you can have your American eagle as you want it. If with the South, you will strike out his eyes, then you shall stand with Mr. Davis and Mr. Stephens of the Confederate States; if with the Christians of the South you will pluck off his wings, you shall stand with the Southern churches; and if with the new peace-makers that have risen up in the North, you will pull out his tail-feathers, you shall stand with the society for the promotion of national unity! But when you have stricken out his eyes so that he can no longer see, when you have plucked off his wings so that he can no longer fly, and when you have pulled out his guiding tail-feathers so that he can no longer steer himself, but rolls in the dirt a mere buzzard, then will he be worth preserving? Such an eagle it is that they mean to serve up for the banquet of liberty!

Now if any man is fierce for peace, and is willing to pay the price demanded for it, he can have it. On those conditions you can have peace as long as the Jews did. For three guilty days they were rid of the Savior, and then he rose from the grave, with eternal power on his head, and beyond all touch of weakness or death, and went on high to the source of eternal power, there to live, and to live for ever.

4. We must accordingly, if we go on to purchase peace on these terms, become partners in slavery, and consent, for the sake of peace, to ratify this gigantic evil. We cannot wink at it. We are called to bear overt witness either for or against it. Every State in this Union, according to the new Constitution, must be open to slavery. It is the design of not a few men at the North to make this the issue at the next election: whether we shall not reconstruct this Government according to the Constitution of the Confederate States, one feature of which is that it proposes that slavery shall have liberty to go wherever it pleases—that slavery shall have the right of incursion in any part of this country. If you consent to such a reconstruction as is proposed, you must open every one of your States to the incoming of slavery. Not only that, but every territory on this continent is to be opened to slavery, if a reconstruction like this takes place. We are called to take the executive lancet, and the virus of slavery, and lift up the arm of this virgin continent, and inoculate it with this terrific poison. If you will do these things, you are to be permitted to escape war.

5. Next in order must of course be silence. When [illegible] are instructed in these matters. It is time for every church to make its pews flame and glow with enthusiasm for freedom, and hatred for oppression. While the air of the South is full of pestilent doctrines of slavery, accursed be our communities if we will not be as zealous and enthusiastic for liberty as they are against it! If their air is filled with the storm and madness of oppression, let ours be full of the sweet peace and love of liberty.

2. We must draw the lines. There have been a great many men that have been on both sides. There have been a great many men that have been thrown backward and forward from one side to the other, like a shuttle. But it is time for every man to choose one side or the other. We want no shufflers; we want no craven cowards; we want *men*; we want every man to show his hand, and say, "I am for liberty, and the Constitution, and the country, as our fathers gave them to us," or else, if he does not believe in these, say, "I am against them." It is time that middle men were kicked out! Times are coming in which the lines are being drawn.

Thousands, thank God, of great men have spoken to us; but I think that the voice of Sumter has done more to bring men together, and to produce unity of feeling among them on this subject, than the most eloquent tongued orator that ever was heard in this land.

Thousands, thank God, of great men have spoken to us; but I think that the voice of Sumter has done more to bring men together, and to produce unity of feeling among them on this subject, than the most eloquent tongued orator that ever was heard in this land.

We must say in this matter, my friends, as Christ said, "He that is not for us is against us." I will have no commerce, I will not cross palms, with a man that disowns liberty in such a struggle as is before us! I will not give him shelter or house-room—except as a convicted sinner; then I will take him, as the prodigal was taken, in his rags and nakedness! But so long as he stands up with impudent face against the things that are dearest to God's heart, and dearest to the instincts of this people, I shall treat him as what he is—a *traitor!* There ought to be but one feeling in the North, and that ought to be a feeling for liberty, which should sweep through the land like a mighty wind.

3. We must not stop to measure costs—especially the costs of going forward—on any basis so mean and narrow as that of pecuniary prosperity. We must put our honor and religion into this struggle. God is helping you; for no matter how much you deplore the state of things, you cannot help yourselves. You may talk with your till, and safe, and bank, and you may look at your accounts on both sides, but your talking and looking will make no difference with your affairs. The time is past in which these things could be of any avail. This matter must now be settled. You must have a part in settling it. The question is whether that shall be a manly or an ignoble part.

With the North is the strength, the population, the courage. I stand for this truth: that there is not on this continent that breadth of courage—the courage of a man in distinction from the courage of a brute beast—which there is in the free States of the North.

It was General SCOTT—that noble and heroic patriot, whose life is to be topped off with illustrious and immortal honor, when his days here are ended (and may God long delay the hour of his departure)—it was he that said that the New Englanders were the hardest to get into a fight, and the most terrible to meet in a conflict, of any set of men on the globe.

And we have no braggart courage; we have no courage that rushes into an affray for the love of fighting. We have that courage which comes from calm intelligence. We have that courage which comes from broad moral sentiment. We have no anger, but we have indignation. We have no irritable passion, but we have fixed will. We regard war and contest as the last evils; but when, detesting them as we do, we are roused so as to enter into them, our courage will be of the measure of our detestation. You may be sure that the cause which can stir up the feelings of the North sufficiently to bring them into such a conflict, will develop in them a courage that will be terrific to the men who have to meet it. I could wish no worse punishment to those that decry the courage of the North, than that they shall have to meet her when she is once brought out, and fairly in the field.

4. We must aim at a peace built on foundations so solid, of God's immutable truth, that nothing can reach to unsettle it. Let this matter never come up again. Better have it thoroughly settled, though it take a score of years to settle it, than to have an intermittent fever for the next hundred years, breaking out every five or ten years. It is bad. That has nothing to do with it. Your house is on fire; and the question is, What will you do? You are in the struggle, and the question is, Will you go through it in the spirit of your ancestors, in the spirit of Christians and patriots, in the spirit that belongs to the age of the world in which you live, and settle it so that it shall not be in the power of mischief to unsettle it? Or will you dally? Will you delay? I know which you will do. This question is now going forward to a settlement.

5. Let not our feelings be vengeful nor savage. We can go into this conflict with a spirit just as truly Christian as any that ever inspired us in the performance of a Christian duty. Indignation is needful, that the old spirit would be found y[illegible] church; and that in that patriotism which [illegible] do as well as teach, laymen and officers and [illegible] would be found no whit behind in our day w[illegible] were in the Revolutionary day. At any rat[illegible] God's providence calls so that there can be [illegible] take as to the name that is spelt out, I thi[illegible] is *one* that will be ready to respond!

I do not say these things because I think [illegible] ter is going to such a desperate length, but [illegible] I wish to express the confidence I feel, at a t[illegible] this, in Northern power, Northern zeal, N[illegible] earnestness, and religion therein.

Let me say two things more.

It is trying to be in suspense; to live in [illegible] menting whirl of rumor; now to see the ba[illegible] and now to see it trailing in the dust. Early [illegible] day, things seemed inauspicious. Toward [illegible] all appeared calm and fair. To-day, disastr[illegible] depressing rumors were current. This ev[illegible] came hither sad from the tidings that that str[illegible] which seemed to guard the precious name a[illegible] ing fame of the noble and gallant ANDERS[illegible] been given up; but since I came into this [illegible] have received a dispatch from one of our m[illegible] trious citizens, saying that Sumter is reënfor[illegible] that Moultrie is the fort that has been de[illegible] [Tremendous and prolonged applause, expre[illegible] enthusiastic cheers, clapping of hands, and [illegible] of handkerchiefs.] But what if the rising [illegible] morrow should reverse the message? Wha[illegible] tidings that greet you in the morning should [illegible] the echo of the old tidings of disaster? Y[illegible] in hours in which you are to suffer suspense [illegible] lifted up you will be prematurely cheering, a[illegible] cast down you will be prematurely desp[illegible] Look forward, then, past the individual ste[illegible] the various vicissitudes of experience, to th[illegible] ous end that is coming. Look beyond the [illegible] to that assured victory which awaits us in the [illegible] Let us not be tossed up and down as me[illegible] troubled sea are tossed by chopping waves.

Young men, you will live to see more aus[illegible] days. Later sent, delayed in your voyage ir[illegible] you will see the bright consummation, in [illegible] least, of that victory of this land, by whic[illegible] mortal throe, it shall cast out from itself all [illegible] influences, and cleanse itself from slavery [illegible] you that are in middle life shall see the [illegible] triumph advancing beyond anything that y[illegible] yet known. The sceptre shall not depart [illegible] Government shall not be shaken from its [illegible] tions.

Let us give devout thanks to God, tha[illegible] blindly choosing, we scarcely knew whom, it [illegible] his providence to point out, and lay choi[illegible] not a politician, but a citizen, a true patriot [illegible] man, temperate, forbearing, prudent, but to [illegible] drop of his blood patriotic, who loves his [illegible] more than any party, the Constitution more [illegible] platform, and the original principles of lib[illegible] our articles of confederation more than any [illegible] modern doctrines that have been put forth by [illegible] designing men. Let us thank God for the m[illegible] at last we have at the head of the nation, [illegible] der whose judicious management I doubt no[illegible] will go rightly, successfully, and, in the end, [illegible] riously.

Let no man, then, in this time of peril, [illegible] sociate himself with that cause which is to b[illegible] tirely glorious. Let not your children, as the[illegible] you to your burial, be ashamed to write up[illegible] tombstone the truth of your history. Le[illegible] man that lives and owns himself an America[illegible] the side of true American principles—lib[illegible] one, and liberty for all; liberty now, and libe[illegible] ever; liberty as the foundation of governm[illegible] liberty as the basis of union; liberty against [illegible] lution, liberty against anarchy, and liberty [illegible] slavery; liberty here, and liberty everywhe[illegible] world through!

And now, as the trump of God has sound[illegible] the grand procession is forming; as Italy h[illegible] and is wheeling into the ranks; as Hungary, [illegible] mute, is beginning to beat time and make [illegible] the march; as Poland, having long slept, has [illegible] of liberty again, and is waking; as the [illegible] lion serfs are bearing the roll of the drum, an[illegible] forward into the state of citizenship, let [illegible] your miserable fate, nor mine, to live in [illegible] that shall be reeling, and staggering, and w[illegible] in the orgies of despotism! We, too, have [illegible] to march in this grand procession to libert[illegible] the memory of the fathers; by the suffering [illegible] Puritan ancestry; by every line of the Dec[illegible] of Independence, and every article of our [illegible] tion; by what we are and what our pro[illegible] were, we have a right to walk foremost in [illegible] cession of nations toward the bright and [illegible] millennial future.

Stand, every one of you! Pray much [illegible] while you fight. As the warrior can carry [illegible] elastic plume, that rises at every step with [illegible] beauty, while at the same time he carries a[illegible] on, a battle-axe, or a sword, whose edge s[illegible] cannot turn; so do you, while you have [illegible] courage, and an unwavering purpose, car[illegible] feelings elastic, and move with all the pati[illegible] love and tenderness of a manly nature. A[illegible] ing done all, to stand, and God shall give [illegible] victory.

I am done for to-night. I did not mean to [illegible] much. I could not say less. It has been [illegible]

Chapter 3

Slavery Alone Is the Cause of All the Trouble

Today, the question as to whether the Civil War was about slavery remains a contentious one. Some like to think that that the institution played only a minor role, or perhaps even no role at all, in motivating Southerners to contend for their independence from the Union. As conveyed in the newspapers of the time, though, the centrality of slavery to the Confederacy's sense of national mission and destiny is unmistakable. There was no clearer spokesman on this issue than Alexander Stephens, the vice president of the Confederacy. In the spring of 1861, Stephens visited several cities in his home state of Georgia, delivering to packed houses an oration on the new Confederate Constitution, which contained explicit provisions guaranteeing the security of slave property. His comments on slavery, excerpted here from the *Augusta Constitutionalist*, became the most famous (or infamous) demonstration of the Confederacy's unshakable commitment to black subordination:

> The new Constitution has put at rest, *forever*, all the agitating questions relating to our peculiar institutions—African slavery as it exists among us—the proper *status* of the negro in our form of civilization. This was the immediate cause of the late rupture and present revolution. [Thomas] Jefferson . . . had anticipated this, as the "rock upon which the old Union would split." He was right. What was conjecture for him, is now a realized fact. But whether he fully comprehended the great truth upon which that rock *stood* and *stands*, may be doubted. The prevailing ideas entertained by him and most of the leading statesmen at the time of the formation of the old Constitution were, that the enslavement of the African was in violation of the laws of nature; that it was wrong in *principle*, socially, morally and politically. It was an evil they knew not well how to deal with; but the general opinion of the men of that day

was, that, somehow or other, in the order of Providence, the institution would be evanescent and pass away. . . . Those ideas, however, were fundamentally wrong. They rested upon the assumption of the equality of races. This was an error. . . .

Our new Government is founded upon exactly the opposite idea; its foundations are laid, its corner stone rests, upon the great truth that the negro is not equal to the white man; that slavery—subordination to the superior race—is his natural and normal condition. . . .

This, our new Government, is the first, in the history of the world, based upon this great physical, philosophical, and moral truth.[1]

Negroes for Sale!

I will sell at auction, in the town of Milton, on Saturday the 27th day of April, 1861, a very likely Negro Boy about 17 years old, also a Girl Ten years of age. Terms made known on the day of Sale.

MARTHA R. HAMLETT, Adm'r'x of J. E. Hamlett.

Milton Chronicle, April 12, 1861.
Notices advertising "Negroes for Sale" appeared regularly in Southern newspapers both before and during the Civil War. This one is particularly striking, for in addition to peddling a seventeen-year-old boy, the seller also offered a ten-year-old girl, who evidently was to be sold alone, without parents or other kin.

As Stephens asserted, the prevailing attitude in the South toward slavery had undergone a critical transformation over the course of the nineteenth century. At the time of the American Revolution, it was common for Southerners to regard slavery as a burden, an institution that was not really desirable but which was absolutely necessary for maintaining both the region's plantation economy and a strict separation of the races. By the time the Civil War erupted—in part as a reaction to the persistent criticism from Northern abolitionists—most Southerners had come to embrace and defend slavery as a benevolent institution that brought blessings to blacks and whites alike. The slaves gave their labor for raising the cotton, tobacco, rice, and sugar crops that fueled the South's prosperity; in return, they received what Southerners considered to be generous lifelong care. Northerners, by contrast, remained much more at odds with slavery. Like their Southern compatriots, most believed that blacks were inherently inferior and savage, and recoiled from the idea of allowing them to exist as their equals in American society. But with increasing stridency, the North—particularly with the rise of the Republican party—still maintained that slavery was cruel, wrong, and fundamentally out of touch with America's culture of individual liberty. Free labor, not slave labor, was the ideal building block for a prosperous economy and a happy society.[2]

Looking back on the divergence of opinion that developed between the North and South over the slavery issue, Confederate newspapers in 1861 proclaimed that the two sections were now so different that they could not remain together any longer. "Nature, in all

Hastening to the Wars.

The people of North Carolina, and indeed of all the Southern, States seem to be fully aroused, and on all sides we hear the notes of preparation for the wars. The people of North Carolina are a unit, in their resistance to the tyrant Lincoln; and whatever they may think of the origin of our difficulties, and however they may regret, that civil war is upon us, with all its attendant evils, yet there is a firm determination to make a united effort, and put forth every energy against the abolitionists of the North, who have so long, so wantonly and so wickedly disquieted the country, by trespassing upon the rights of the South.

Greensborough Patriot, May 3, 1861.
Southern papers routinely described the war as a fight against the "tyranny" of Lincoln's rule. However, they also voiced particular disgust for "the abolitionists of the North," revealing their specific concerns about slavery.

Mothers of my much loved native South, will you, by word or deed, keep back your sons from taking part in securing for themselves and their posterity, a country too pure for the impious footprint of Black Republicanism? Oh, deny them not the proud duty of resisting the aggressions of their unnatural enemies—the fanatical abolitionists of the North. Let them not, in future years, when the brave soldier is recounting to his little ones the deeds of daring on the battle-field, be forced in sadness of heart and the reproaches of conscience, to say that in all this they took no part. Force them not, in humiliation to acknowledge that they were unworthy of the liberty and home secured for them by the valor of others. Young men of the South, let patriotism now be above every consideration. Bid adieu for a season to the farm—the office—the store, and the workshops, and rush to rescue your country from the foe now threatening your homes and your firesides. SOUTHERNER.

Augusta Chronicle & Sentinel, May 7, 1861.
Through the newspapers, individual Southerners called upon their countrymen to hurry and join the Confederacy's war of resistance against "the fanatical abolitionists of the North."

her immense laboratory, never produced a conglomerate of more discordant materials than those" that had constituted the former United States, affirmed the *Nashville Union & American*. "Freedom for the negro," as "the chief corner stone of Black Republicanism," had become under Lincoln "the chief corner stone of the Northern Union" too. Accordingly, the Union now stood for "the freedom of the negro, and the equality of the races," whereas the Confederacy was "founded on the reverse theory, that of the superiority of the white race and the subordination of the inferior or black race." Finally freed from their association with the North, Southerners saw themselves as having a rare opportunity to develop a different kind of society—a unique and well-ordered culture that reflected their notions about proper racial hierarchy. Dangerous ideas regarding the evils of slavery and the rights of black men would have no place in the Confederacy. The suitableness of blacks for slavery would never be questioned. "Now, a new civilization, new thought, and a new philosophy will rise among us," the *Richmond Examiner* proudly exclaimed. "Negro slavery will be its foundation."[3]

As the *Examiner* described it, slavery was the only true basis for a good society. Whereas Northern free-market capitalism fostered class rivalry and led to the oppression of workingmen, slavery was based on ties of Christian kindness between generous masters and grateful bondsmen. It was a utopian vision for a harmonious biracial society where justice and goodwill would reign:

> Christian morality is impracticable in free society, and is the natural morality of slave society. Where all men are equals, all must be competitors, rivals, enemies, in the struggle for life, trying each to get the better of the other. The rich cheapen the wages of

the poor; the poor take advantage of the scarcity of labour, and charge exhorbitant prices for their work; or, when labour is abundant, underbid and strangle each other in the effort to gain employment. Were any man engaged in business in free society to act upon the principle of the Golden Rule—doing unto others as he would that they should do unto him—his certain ruin would be the consequence.

"Every man for himself" is the necessary morality of such society, and that is the negation of Christian morality. . . . On the other hand, in slave society, . . . it is, in general, easy and profitable to do unto others as we would that they should do unto us. There is no competition, no clashing of interests within the family circle, composed of parents, master, husband, children and slaves. . . . When the master punishes his child or his slave for misconduct, he obeys the golden rule just as strictly as when he feeds and clothes them. Were the parent to set his children free at fifteen years of age to get their living in the world, he would be guilty of crime; and as negroes never become more provident or intellectual than white children of fifteen, it is equally criminal to emancipate them. We are obeying the golden rule in retaining them in bondage, taking care of them in health and sickness, in old age and infancy, and in compelling them to labour. . . .

'Tis the interest of masters to take good care of their slaves, and not to cheat them out of their wages, as Northern bosses cheat and drive free labourers. Slaves are most profitable when best treated, free labourers most profitable when worst treated and most defrauded. Hence the relation of master and slave is a kindly and Christian one; that of free labourer and employer a selfish and inimical one. It is the interest of the slave to fulfill his duties to his master; for he thereby elicits his attachment, and the better enables him to provide for his (the slave's) wants. Study and analyze as long as [you] please the relations of men . . . in a slave society, and they will be found to be Christian, humane and affectionate, whilst those of free society are anti-Christian, competitive and antagonistic.[4]

Slavery was thus a real matter of pride for Southerners. It distinguished them as a special and morally superior people—a point of faith that the Christian churches in the South fully endorsed. They declared slavery a divine institution, designed by God to bring "barbarous" Africans under the benevolent sway of white masters, who would teach them the benefits of Christian civilization. In defense of their position, Southern ministers turned to the Old and New Testaments, pointing out sections that suggested God's approval.[5] An especially prominent part of this biblical defense of slavery was the "curse of Canaan," found in the ninth chapter of Genesis, within the story of Noah. As the Bible relates, Noah had three sons: Shem, Ham, and Japheth. Canaan, Noah's grandson, was the child of Ham. In rebuilding human society after the flood, the story in Genesis states that Noah "drank of the wine, and became drunk," and fell asleep inside his tent, naked and uncovered. Ham, observing his father's nakedness, did nothing to preserve his modesty, but rather told his two brothers, who then went into the tent and covered Noah, taking care to not look at him directly. When Noah woke up and heard what had transpired, he was mortified and, feeling betrayed by his own son, Ham, issued a curse on Canaan: "Cursed be Canaan; a slave of slaves shall he be to his brothers." Southern defenders of slavery interpreted this passage as both history and prophecy. In their reading of it, Africans were the lineal descendants of Canaan, and as such, they were destined to serve the interests of Japheth, whom they claimed was the father of the Caucasian race. American slavery, in institutionalizing this relationship, brought the "curse of Canaan" to perfect fulfillment, as this editorial from the *South-Western Baptist* proclaimed boldly:

In the providence of God, about four millions of heathen[s] have been thrown upon these Southern

States, in the capacity of slaves, to be trained for usefulness in this world and for the glory of God in the world to come. It is worth observing, too, that these people come from the most degraded race of the earth's population. All travelers concur in saying that the descendants of Ham in the wilds of Africa, are far more degenerated morally, socially and physically, taken as a whole, than any people yet discovered. They seem utterly incapable of working out any form of civilization worth the name.—As the thoughtful traveler stands amongst them, he feels that he is mingling with a race of beings whom he can scarcely recognize as belonging to the *genus homo*. . . . Not the slightest improvement in their manners and customs, their mental, moral, political or religious condition has been achieved by themselves for forty centuries. The same physical inertia, moral degradation, and religious idolatry which enslaved them in the days of Abraham, still maintain their ascendancy over them. . . .

Now place another picture beside this scene of unmingled dreariness. Within the borders of the Southern States of the late Union, there are about four million of the descendants of Canaan exactly fulfilling the condition assigned them by the express decree of the Almighty—servants to the descendants of Japheth. They are happier and better provided for in all respects, than any equal number of laboring classes in any part of the world. In addition to their physical comfort, their moral and religious advantages are ample. The result is, that out of this four million of slaves in these States, not less than five hundred thousand give credible evidence of sincere piety, and are now connected with the several religious denominations of the country. Beside this, the great body of them are brought under the stated ministrations of the Gospel every Lord's day. We suppose that as large a proportion of them are members of our churches as any part of our population. And no man ever preaches the gospel to them without thanking God for that wise providence which brought them within its power. The brightest page which has ever yet been furnished to the history of the world, in regard to the descendants of Ham, is now furnished within these Southern States. . . . Five hundred thousand happy [slave] voices ascend to heaven every Sabbath, thanking God that He brought them out from the most degraded form of heathenism that now curses the world, into a land of Bibles and sanctuary privileges, where they are taught to worship him without let or hindrance. Is it at all marvelous that Christians of the South are so perfectly united in a movement, which will relieve the country of [the abolitionists'] perpetual agita-

Again : To the South has been committed the responsible task of working out a civilization compatible alike with the ordinations of heaven and the interest and happiness of our two races. There is no truth more patent in the Word of God than that which has doomed the race of Ham to a condition of servitude. Nor is there any truth more susceptible of proof than that which from moral, mental and physical constitution, assigns to this race the divinely prescribed condition. In this condition, they are healthy, long lived, useful and happy—out of it they are squalid, short-lived, imbecile and miserable.—It is time that an institution that is working out the civilization and Christianization of the most degraded race of this earth's population should be vindicated before the world.

South-Western Baptist, November 14, 1861.
The biblical "curse of Canaan" was a central pillar of the South's defense of slavery. It also invested the Confederacy with a sense of mission to create an ideal slave society, one in which white Christians would take up the task of caring for and uplifting the black race.

tion, and allow them the most unrestricted access to our slaves, that they may teach them the unsearchable riches of Christ?[6]

Boastful declarations such as this, however, masked a real sense of unease in the South. While Southern whites may have seemed "perfectly united" in defending slavery, they were less sanguine about the feelings of the slaves themselves. Southerners professed that at heart, the slaves understood their inferiority and their dependence on their masters' benevolence. They were equally convinced, though, that Northerners were scheming to poison the minds of the slaves by deluding them with dreams of freedom and inciting them to rise in revolt. In 1859, these fears had become horrifyingly real when the abolitionist zealot John Brown attempted to spark a slave uprising at Harpers Ferry in Virginia; now, two years later, Southerners were quick to believe that similar machinations were in the works. As one paper imagined scornfully, the abolitionists, in aiding the North's bloodthirsty work of subjugation, were eager "to send out emissaries to incite our slaves to insubordination, rapine and murder." Rallying under the banner of "Emancipation or Extermination," they would goad these otherwise happy slaves "to apply the knife to the throats and the torch to the dwellings of their masters." This was every Southerner's worst nightmare, and in their anxiety, they had a sense that abolitionist schemers were operating all around them. "We cannot doubt," the New Orleans *Delta* warned, "from evidence constantly accumulating, that combinations with the object of producing a slave insurrection, have already been formed in four or five of the cotton growing states."[7] In reality, there were no organized attempts to foment slave insurrections, but Southerners could not help suspecting the worst.

The war thus seemed to demand that slaveholders think more critically about the loyalty of their slaves and be proactive in telling them the "truth" about what was happening. "Our negroes are anxious to know what all this commotion is about," one slave owner confided to the *Memphis Avalanche*, so it was up to the master class to teach them certain important "facts": that the soldiers of the Union were coming South not to liberate the slaves but to steal them for their own use and enrichment, and that these vicious and tyrannical Yankee "roughs" would treat them much more brutally than their Southern owners did. Slaveholders were expected to be vigilant in impressing these ideas upon their bondsmen and ensuring that they were not led astray by Northern abolitionists. Concerned that many Southern whites were perhaps "at a loss to know how to instruct their servants at this crisis," the *Rome Weekly Courier* published this letter, ostensibly penned by a master (now a soldier in the Confederate army) to his slave Jack, as a template for them to follow:

> My Old Servant Jack:—I am now in Virginia, a long way off from my home and family. . . . Since I left home to go to the war, my mind had been greatly troubled for fear that some of my servants might be led astray by abolitionists, or other mean white men, to run away or do some other bad thing. I heard the other day of a black man in Kingston, Ga., who was persuaded to join in a plot to kill the white people, and it turned out, as it always does, that he was found out and hung. Now I feel it my duty, Jack, to warn you against all people, whether white or black, who will persuade you to kill or steal, or go into any wicked plot of any kind. No matter what promises they hold out to you, do not believe them or trust them. And let me tell you, whether you believe it or not, that the best friends of the black people are their own masters, and those who live in the Slave States. The people of the North pretend that they want to make you free, and some of them may be in earnest, but a greater portion of them really care nothing about the black people. For they too once had negroes, and instead of freeing them sent them down South and sold them, and now they try to ruin us and our property by persuading the servants to run away from us, . . . and when these servants

get to the North they are free only in name, and are, really, a great many of them, poor, miserable, starving creatures. . . .

Now we have been in a quarrel with these Northern people for about forty years about the new lands way out West. These lands belong to us as much as them, but they have all the while been trying to keep us from going there with our servants; and when Lincoln was elected he said that the Southern people should never take their servants to this new country. Now a great many of our folks had already bought land out there, and wanted to go there with their servants to live, so that when we saw that this man Lincoln and the Northern people were determined not to give us our share of the land, we at once made up our minds to leave them, or secede from them, and live to ourselves, and this is what the fight has commenced about. . . . Now, Jack, you can see into the truth of this matter, and can understand what all this drumming and fighting is about, and you must at once see that the South has been greatly imposed upon, and that we are in the right in this business, and the North is in the wrong.

And now that you understand how this thing is, I hope you will take my advice, and go along and attend to your business as a good and faithful servant should do, and don't forget that you are a slave by the appointment of God himself, for the Bible plainly teaches it. If it did not, I for one would have no servants about me. Black people are the descendants of Canaan, the son of Ham, of whom the Lord said "A *servant of servants shall he be unto his Brethren*." The white people are the descendants of Japheth, and the Bible says "Canaan shall be the servant of Japhet." (Gen. IX.). . . . There are other passages in the Bible that teach this doctrine. So you see if you believe these Abolitionists, you must throw away the Bible and deny the truth of God's word. Will you dare believe them in preference to God? And moreover, let me tell you if these Abolitionists were to kill every man in the South, they would be as likely to make slaves of you as to turn you free, and indeed some of them have already been talking of dividing out our lands and negroes among their soldiers. . . . And, of one thing, Jack, you may rest assured, that you are better off now with your Southern Masters, than you ever could be with these people, even of they were to free you. Everybody who has been to the free States and seen how the blacks are treated there knows this to be true. These poor blacks are called free, but they are not treated as equals, and when they get sick there is nobody to pay their Doctors' bills, or to take care of them, as the servants of the South are taken care of, and when they get old and helpless, no one provides for them.—Well, Jack, I think I have said enough to show your danger in these war times, and I have no doubt that you will stay at home, keep out of scrapes, and attend to your business. If any of these scoundrels meddle with you, tell on them, and let them be hung by the neck as they deserve. And now Jack, I have done my duty in explaining the truth to you, and in warning you. If you do not take my advice, you will surely come to an awful end. You may have this letter read to your colored friends and let them all take warning. The war is raging around me, and it is probable I may never see my people again. . . . Remember my last words to you are these: Don't forget that your best friends are the people at the South, and if the South fails in this war, the slaves will be the greatest losers.[8]

The above letter was likely *not* an authentic correspondence between a master and his slave. Enslaved people were largely illiterate, so few had the ability to read a document like this. Nevertheless, it still offers an intriguing glimpse of how white Southerners idealized the institution of slavery and identified a commonality of interest between themselves and their black bondsmen. In this idealistic vision, the war was for the benefit of both races—to free Southern whites from their abolitionist enemies, but also to prevent the slaves from falling under the abolitionists' evil sway. It was hoped that with Confederate independence and the silencing of all abolitionist thought, blacks would grow more docile and accepting of their bondage, and more contented with the care of their owners, who would be able to establish more trusting, symbiotic relations with their slaves. In this way, as the *Rome Weekly Courier* went on to explain in more depth, the war was not just for protecting slavery but also for perfecting it:

> One principle which lies at the foundation of the Southern Confederacy, is the inferiority of the African race; and the consequent right of the whites to hold them as slaves. . . . The relation of master and slave is then one of the most important with which we have to deal, and it is very necessary that all concerned should understand aright its purpose and bearings. The relation has to do with both parties, and . . . a government which should recognize and properly protect it, [is] required not simply to secure the master in his property, but also to secure the slave in all the benefits naturally arising to him, out of a well-ordered, humane and christian system of personal slavery. And the war now going on has as direct [a] reference to the welfare of our slaves, in time and eternity, as to the general prosperity of the South, in all its peculiar interests.
>
> We are not fighting for the opportunity of making the condition of our servants harder, and more oppressive to them, . . . but for that independence and freedom from external interference, which will leave us to manage our servants in the way most fitted to make them more contented and happy than before, and more profitable in their services. . . . We wish to revive the patriarchal character of the institution, so that our servants, while kept in due subjection, shall recognize in their masters their best friends, and enjoy from time to time, such favors and indulgences as will prevent their feeling a want of those indefinite, far-off and uncertain advantages, which some of them are wont to associate with the idea of freedom.
>
> And our first duty to ourselves and our slaves is to make them understand the matter aright. Not by telling them what the North thinks and says about slavery; not by direct efforts to excite their fears of being stolen and sold by Northern soldiers, but by that kind, judicious, impartial treatment of them, which shall attach them more than ever to our own persons, and make them fell free and glad, to come to us with all their cares and vexations, and inform us at once, if any one ventures to approach them on improper subjects, and seeks to loosen their confidence in their masters, and their fidelity to his interests.
>
> It is necessary to keep a close and careful supervision over them, so as to know all about their goings and associates, when not at their regular work; but this should be exercised with as little outward show as possible, and with [an] entire absence of anything likely to make them feel that we doubt their attachment, and fear that they may be plotting to injure us in person and property. . . . Let every one then, who owns or hires slaves, understand his duties and responsibilities, and discharge them in his own station, in the fear of God, and in the spirit of true patriotism. He . . . must begin at his own home, in his own daily life, throughout all his intercourse with his servants, to realise in himself, and in them, that he is a prominent actor in the most beneficent scheme, for promoting the greatest good to the greatest number, which the world has ever seen.[9]

Undeniably, the South had a tremendous interest in slavery. It was the basis of the region's plantation economy and the source of its magnificent wealth. At the same time, slavery was of immense ideological importance to the Confederacy. It was the reason the Southern states had become alienated from the Union, the root cause of secession, and the centerpiece of the new civilization they were aiming to build. In defending slavery, the South believed it was protecting the happiness and prosperity of blacks and whites alike, and establishing a model society—a biracial utopia that would show the world how blacks and whites were meant to live together:

> The present war between the Confederate States and the United States is to determine, in large measure, the future social and political condition of the negro in America. If the United States succeeds in imposing a military despotism on the South, . . . the emancipation of our slaves is inevitable. . . . The South, instead of being the richest, would be the poorest country on the face of the earth. Every branch of industry would be paralyzed. The fountains of our civilization would be frozen at their source. The whole world would feel the shock. In the general reign of poverty and degradation which would ensue, none would suffer so much or so permanently as the poor negro. His development would be indefinitely arrested. His extinction even would be probable.
>
> If, on the other hand, our young republic becomes a great and powerful nation of the earth, the system of African servitude will be placed on a new and durable basis. It will be protected and . . . will contribute more than any other one cause to the final perfection of human society.—By its means the whole world will be subjugated to the controlling brain and heart of the white man. As our own intellectual and moral life expands, it will diffuse its blessings to all around and beneath us. The slavery of the African will become a willing and happy servitude; the mastership of the white man [will become] a wise and generous supervision. A pure Christianity, pervading all society, will link the two races together by the sweet bonds of mutual service and good-will.[10]

By the South's own admission, slavery was the one thing that made its independence desirable and necessary. The Confederacy had arisen from slavery. It seemed to be common sense, then, that if Northerners wanted to wipe out the rebellion, they would have to destroy slavery first. As explained in the *Anglo-African*, a major mouthpiece for the free black community in the North, emancipating the slaves was therefore more than a matter of justice; it was smart strategy for actualizing the Union's military objectives:

> The Union is dissolved; dissolved to destroy that which it was formed to perpetuate—Constitutional Liberty and human rights. . . . If the North wishes to avenge so foul a wrong, if it desires to wipe off a stigma so humiliating, and win back the whole of this fair land as the abiding place of liberty—the heritage of freemen—then let it *strike* the shackles from the slave, proclaim universal liberty, and the victory is won. By so doing, the acknowledged basis of [the South's] incongruous structure is destroyed, and the whole fabric . . . topples down, annihilating Slavery, and removing the only obstacle to the full fruition of a truly Republican Government. We appeal . . . to the conscience of every intelligent American freeman, and, pointing to the Declaration of Independence, confident of an affirmative reply, we ask, is not Slavery the cause of this disunion, and is not Emancipation the remedy?[11]

This kind of logic gave Northern abolitionists, historically a despised and marginalized minority in the North, a compelling new argument to advance their cause. Since the 1830s, the abolitionists had focused on trying to morally reform Southern slaveholders—to help them see the sinfulness of holding men in bondage, and thus convince them to set their slaves free. Now, in the shock of war, abolitionists reached out to Northerners, imploring them to take matters into their own hands and to support putting an end to the South's system of slavery. As described in this public letter, penned by prominent abolitionist Lewis Tappan, they envisioned emancipation as a magical stroke, one that would instantaneously erase the differences between the North and South and allow them to come together once again in peace:

Viewed in the light of Scripture and God's providences, war is the result of sin; and its remedy is repentance and reformation. God, in the present calamitous civil war, has a controversy with the people—with the whole people—North and South. It is not the South alone that is guilty. The North has participated in the guilt. . . . We have sinned in many ways, and especially in our cruel treatment of the Indians and the Negroes. The voice of their blood crieth unto God from the ground. But at the present time we refer particularly to the treatment of the colored man—bond and free—and especially of the enslaved. We have been a slaveholding nation. Slavery has been strengthened and extended by the co-operation of the free and slave States, in spite of the remonstrances and warnings of the abolitionists, who predicted the present state of things, if slavery was permitted to continue. . . .

Slavery is the cause of the present war. Who doubts it? And there can be no permanent peace while slavery exists in this country. There will ever be an "irrepressible conflict" between freedom and slavery. . . . *What then is the remedy?* We unhesitatingly answer, IMMEDIATE AND UNIVERSAL EMANCIPATION. Let the North repent of their sin in conniving at slavery and upholding it, and bring forth works . . . for repentance. There is no safety or lasting peace in any other course. By this glorious achievement we should have the blessing of the God of the oppressed, and thus ensure to ourselves and our posterity a career of prosperity such as this country has never enjoyed, nor any other nation witnessed. . . .

Prosperity would be [but] one of the attendant blessings of emancipation, in which the South would largely partake. Our peace would flow as a river; the people of the north and south would grasp each others' hands in mutual friendship; . . . and, under the benignant smiles of a kind Providence, the civilized world would exclaim: "Behold, how good and how pleasant it is for brethren to dwell together in unity!"[12]

Emancipation was to abolitionists what slavery was to Southerners—an essential building block for a perfect social order. As they saw it, slavery was the primary thing preventing America from actualizing its ideals of freedom and justice and forging bonds of racial harmony between blacks and whites. The following excerpt from the *Liberator*, William Lloyd Garrison's famous antislavery paper, therefore spelled out a wartime mission for the Northern people of moral and political import—the elimination of slavery and the redemption of their torn country:

Eighty-five years ago, the war-cry of "INDEPENDENCE" rang throughout all the American Colonies, and a united people took up arms to sunder their connection forever with the mother country. . . . On the 4th of July, 1776, in justification of their course, they published their world-famous Declaration of Independence, in which they held "these truths to be self-evident:—that all men are created equal; that they are endowed by their Creator with certain inalienable rights; that among these are life, liberty, and the pursuit of happiness." At that time, they held in the galling chains of chattel servitude half a million of slaves! By the standard which they had erected, and by the eternal law of justice, their first duty obviously was to "proclaim liberty throughout all the land to all the inhabitants thereof." Instead of doing this, they went through their seven years' struggle, mingling the clanking of fetters, and the crack of the slave whip, and the groans of their imbruted victims with their cries for liberty and their shouts of victory. It was a revolting spectacle, and a horrible paradox. . . .

Having thus violated its own Heaven attested principles, . . . the nation commenced its guilty career, vainly imagining that all danger was past, that its own oppression would go unwhipt of justice, and that the Union would endure forever. . . . But the illusion is over—the foundation gives way—a tempest of divine fury sweeps over the land—and

> the horrors of civil war are upon us! . . . This is the settlement-day of Almighty God for two centuries of traffic in "slaves and the souls of men"! By slavery the whole land has been defiled; and by slaveholders, in their mad idolatry of that foul system, is civil war precipitated upon the land! In self-defence, those who have hitherto been their accomplices in the North, are compelled to meet them in battle array, each party hot to exterminate the other! Slavery abolished, and how instantaneously would the flames of war be extinguished, the source of all our national troubles dried up, reconciliation everywhere effected, and a true and majestic Union organized, reaching from the Lakes to the Gulf, from the Atlantic to the Pacific, blending together men of all races and climes in one common brotherhood! . . . Men of the North! is it not your mission, in this campaign, to make it possible for a free government and a glorious Union to exist, *by decreeing the extinction of slavery as utterly antagonistical to both?*[13]

Most Republicans in 1861 did not embrace the idea of emancipation. While they were determined to prevent the spread of slavery to new territories in the American West, they believed that the federal government did not have the constitutional right to end slavery in the Southern states where it currently existed. A few Republican papers did endorse it, however—but not necessarily out of a sense of morality or justice to the slaves. Rather, they wielded emancipation like a threat, as a proper penalty that Southerners would have to pay for impudently seceding and rebelling against the Union. Shortly after the eruption of hostilities at Fort Sumter, the *New York Courier & Enquirer* issued this warning to the Upper South states as they contemplated the question of joining the Confederacy:

> Now a word to the border slave States, and especially Virginia, in regard to the punishment of traitors who have arrayed themselves against the government. . . . They have brought upon the country civil war, and cast dishonor upon our flag and the republican institutions it represents; and as surely as there is justice in Heaven, and that man is but the agent of the Almighty in punishing those who perpetrate great crimes against Christianity and civilization, . . . *justice* is destined to fall heavily upon the offender. The punishment of treason is death and the confiscation of the property of the traitor. The death penalty may be evaded; but not so the confiscation. And when the army of the Republic marches into Virginia, let the property of every rebel be at once confiscated by proclamation. A part of this property will of course be negroes. What is to be done with them? Nobody can suppose that our government would consent to traffic in human chattels; and therefore, while land and personal property belonging to the rebels must be sold and the funds paid into the public treasury, the human chattels confiscated to the government, must be permitted to go free and unquestioned. This is not *abolition*. The property of every rebel must be confiscated, including of course, his *slaves*; and being confiscated to the government such property must be sold. Our government cannot sell human beings and put the blood money into the treasury; and therefore, the human "chattels" thus confiscated, must be set free.
>
> Every rebel, then, in Virginia and Maryland, and elsewhere, will readily read their fate. The Union men in the slave States will feel doubly secure in the ability and desire of the general government to protect them; but woe be unto the rebels. No sooner will a conquering army take up its march to Richmond than the shackles which now bind the slaves belonging to the traitors in rebellion, will fall from their limbs, and their freedom become secure.[14]

At the time, this kind of press seemed quite damaging to the Union's objectives. While emancipation might help Northerners win the war, enacting it might mean losing the peace. As the *Harrisburg Patriot & Union* reminded its readers, "We have a greater task

The War not an Abolition Crusade.

It is manifest that upon the proper understanding of the purposes of the North by the people of the South, depends the success of the efforts now making for the restoration of the Union. We have a greater task before us than the subjugation of the South—to gain their good will, and induce them to return to the Union. No man questions the power of the North to conquer the Southern States by beating their armies in the field, by laying waste their country and by putting arms in the hands of their servile population, and inviting them to commence the work of indiscriminate slaughter. But beside being inhuman and diabolical, this would defeat the purposes of the Northern people. It would gain for us the undying hatred of the South, and render the restoration of confidence impossible. The Union could never be re-established by such means.

TOP *Philadelphia Inquirer,* May 16, 1861. To sustain a spirit of unity among Republicans and Democrats, Northern newspapers repeatedly denied that the war would be used as a pretext for destroying the institution of slavery in the South.

LEFT *Harrisburg Patriot & Union*, June 7, 1861. As Northern Democratic papers understood, any attempt to destroy slavery would not only divide the North, but make the task of winning back the affections of the Southern rebels all the more elusive.

before us than the subjugation of the South—to gain their good will, and induce them to return to the Union." Emancipation "would defeat the purposes of the Northern people" by earning them instead "the undying hatred of the South." More than that, though, the specter of emancipation threatened to turn Northern Democrats against the war too. At the start of the conflict, most Democrats had rallied around Lincoln with the understanding that the war effort he headed was for the sole purpose of vindicating the Constitution and preserving the Union. Although outraged that the rebels would attack Fort Sumter and fire upon the American flag, they still agreed that slavery was a state institution that the federal government did not have the constitutional right to touch. Any move by the Lincoln administration to free the slaves would have stirred the ire of these Democratic citizens and perhaps even alienated some of the soldiers in the Union ranks. Those volunteers who were Democrats, warned the *Detroit Free Press*, "go not upon an anti-slavery crusade. They go upon a crusade against rebels. They go to do or die for the Constitution and the Union and the Flag." If the war "shall assume any other character—when it shall cease to be a war in behalf of the constitution—democrats will cease to be soldiers in it."[15] The Democratic press therefore was emphatic in warning abolitionists of the danger they courted in calling for a war against slavery:

> Amidst the generally correct notions that prevail concerning the necessity and purpose of the existing war, it cannot be denied that some very erroneous views as to its object are entertained, and . . . advocated. There are those whose sympathies are with the present military movement, because they hope it is to be converted into a crusade against African

slavery—that our troops are to become a liberating army, to set all the negroes free. . . .

Those who seek to give the present movement such a direction, at least give color and plausibility to the charges . . . made against them—of purposes and acts hostile to the Constitutional rights of the slave States. The only lawful design of the present war is to sustain the Constitutional authority of the Federal government—and that certainly does not comprehend the power to interfere with the relation of master and slave. Those who seek to appropriate the present feeling of loyalty to the government, to a negro crusade, do not less mistake the popular impulse than their own duties as good citizens. We are not to be betrayed, under the patriotic excitement of the present time, into propogandists, seeking by fire and sword . . . to impose unacceptable institutions upon independent States. If the slave States continue this rebellion against the Union and Constitution, and the result of a legitimate exercise of Federal power shall be to break the back of slavery, we shall not regret it. . . . But while preparing military armaments to sustain the Constitution, it is hypocritical and treasonable to avow the design of using them, for a purpose entirely in defiance of that instrument. We trust that the unity and enthusiasm of our people in upholding the legitimate power of the Federal government are not to be marred by the preaching of a negro crusade.[16]

The idea of emancipation was especially threatening to the border states of Kentucky, Missouri, Maryland, and Delaware. Despite staying with the Union, many people in these slave states were still suspicious of Lincoln's intentions and remained sympathetic to the Confederacy. Sensing that citizens in their communities were anxious about the future of slavery, pro-war newspapers such as the *Louisville Journal* worked to put popular fears at rest and affirm that the Union was fighting for the freedoms of white men only:

A great many honest-minded people are deluded . . . into the notion that the freedom of the negro underlies the intentions of the Union-loving and law-abiding people in prosecuting the war for the preservation of the Constitution, the supremacy of the laws, and the security of individual liberty. . . .

The Union people of the United States are contending for the liberty of the white individual precisely on the terms that the men of the American Revolution contended for that birthright against the despotism of England. The Union men and women in the United States are now fighting a despotism in the traitors of the South, as cruel, as pitiless, as destructive, as inhuman as any that England ever exhibited in her warfare upon the individual liberty of the men and women of the colonies. In the revolutionary contest the shadow of the negro never was permitted to darken the path of the great principle—the individual freedom of the white man, nor should the intelligent freemen now, while fighting for the same great principle, permit political demagogues to darken their minds by covering them with the skin of the negro. There is not one deed of the United States in the present or prospective prosecution of the war against the Southern rebellion that shows that the *status* of the negro has any more to do with this war than it had to do with the American Revolution. This *colored* lie of which we have spoken should darken no man's understanding.[17]

Aside from testifying that the Union had no intention of fighting for emancipation, most newspapers tried to say as little as possible about slavery. It was simply too controversial. The times called for unity, and there was no issue more loaded with acrimony and more likely to anger and divide the North than slavery. Still, it proved impossible to totally ignore the topic. While Northerners could attest that the war was not "about slavery"—that they were not waging it with the *conscious* intention of putting an end to the institution—they could not deny that the war really was

The Object.

There is now and then a person who would seem to think the object in view in the present warlike movements of the government, or at least one of the objects, is to put down slavery at the South. What may be the effect on Southern slavery, should an actual conflict of the two sections in arms occur, it is hardly possible to foretell; though should the South be invaded by a powerful army from the North and West, it appears highly probable that the institution of slavery would receive a severe shock, if not a fatal one, on which banner soever victory might perch. There are thousands of slaves possessed of more shrewdness and intelligence than we are disposed to give them credit for; and they would not fail to profit themselves by a war in their midst, to create a servile insurrection. With this, however, we have nothing to do. We still claim the seceded States as members of the Union; and so long as we assert that claim, we are bound to act towards them, whatever may be their conduct, according to our constitutional requirements, and to refrain from interfering with their local institutions. The government therefore in its warlike movements can have no intention of liberating the slaves, any more than of outraging any other right of property. The North will contend for the UNION, the GOVERNMENT, and the LAWS; and leave the subject of slavery to be disposed of by the southern people and by Providence. The people do not take the field as abolitionists, but as Americans battling for the Union.

Providence Post, May 4, 1861.
Legally speaking, most Northerners in 1861 agreed that the federal government did not have the right to actively abolish slavery. The turmoil of war, by its own natural workings, might undermine slavery, but the Lincoln administration could not intentionally meddle with it.

caused by slavery. As acknowledged by the *Chicago Tribune*, a staunch Republican sheet, slavery went hand in hand with secession and was the vaunted "corner stone" of the Confederacy:

> The cause of the civil war which distracts our country, is so plain that a wayfaring man, though a fool, may see it. . . . Slavery alone is the cause of all the trouble. It has no other parentage. . . . The object of the insurrection is to establish a Slave Despotism on the ruins of American Liberty.
>
> They have no disguise as to their purpose down in Dixie. . . . Vice President Stephens, the great orator among the Confederates, is sent forth to proclaim the object of the rebellion. He declares in the face of mankind, that the purpose is to found on the ruins of the Union, a government whose corner stone shall be slavery. He pronounces the ideas of freedom held by Washington, Jefferson, Franklin, Madison, Henry and the other founders of the Union, to be heresies, [which] must be discarded and repudiated, and the new gospel . . . [is] that Capital should own Labor.
>
> Were it not for Slavery the ocean-bound Republic would be profoundly at peace throughout its length and breadth. . . . The proof of this proposition is perfectly overwhelming. Show us a State filled with slaves, and we will show you a State putrid with treason. This rule holds good when applied even to districts and counties. Take a few examples: Delaware is more loyal than any other Slave State, because she has the smallest proportion of slaves. . . . Southern and Eastern Maryland are full of slaves, and as a consequence, those sections are full of traitors. Western Maryland, where a slave can hardly be seen in a day's ride, is almost a unit for the Union. . . . The Slaves of Eastern Virginia are as numerous as the whites, and that country is pestilent with secession. Western Virginia is cursed with but few slaves, and the result is, that the Union has many friends. Western Tennessee is foul with slavery and rotten with treason. Eastern Tennessee is afflicted with but few

bondsmen, and there the Union lamp burns brightly. . . . Ask the question, which is the worst Secession State? and the spontaneous answer is, *South Carolina*, which contains a larger proportion of slaves than any other State. And so we may travel over the whole Republic, and wherever a slave can be pointed out, we will find you a Secessionist not far off. Show us a community free from the baneful presence of bondage, and we will guarantee it to be loyal to the Union. As well dispute that the sun gives light as deny that slavery is the cause of the rebellion.[18]

Even prominent Democrats were attuned to the truth that slavery lay at the heart of the rebellion. Although not eager to push forward with emancipation, the *New York World*—the most widely read Democratic paper in the North—acknowledged that if the proslavery leaders of the rebellion (the "slave power") kept up their resistance, the federal government might eventually, as a last resort, be left with no choice but to enact it as a war measure:

It is impossible not to see that human slavery is the canker-worm which has for so many years gnawed at the heart of our republic. The slave-owner is an aristocrat by the very nature of his life. Even if slavery were *right*, it is impossible that slaveholders could exist peaceably in a republic, founded as ours is upon the will and votes, the industry and intelligence of *the people*. Slavery debases labor, and our slave-owners can find no terms strong enough to express their hatred and contempt for the free laborers of the nation—the "mud-sills of society," as they call them. Democracy maintains the rights and interests of all. But a slave aristocracy must pit its interests against those of the people—it *must* rule—and when the people outvote it, it rebels.

New York Evening Post, April 30, 1861. While most Northern voices tried to downplay the slavery issue, some Republican papers rightly acknowledged that slavery was incompatible with America's founding values and poisonous to the nation's survival as a free and democratic society.

Whether it be deemed a good thing or not, the fact is unmistakable that the northern people are fast learning to hate slavery in a way unfelt before, and that they are beginning to regard their practical relations to it from wholly new points of view. It comes home to every loyal man, with a force not to be resisted, that the sole cause of this most wicked treason the world ever saw is SLAVERY; and, by moral necessity, just . . . as the treason itself is abhorred, in just that proportion do hatred and detestation attach to its cause. The human mind cannot help judging the tree by its fruits. . . .

The treason that has been developing itself since the presidential election [of 1860], in all its hideous proportions, has given the North a new conception of the malignant power of the institution. A year ago it was not believed possible. The threats [of secession] that were made were deemed to be mere bravado. . . . For months after the treason declared itself in positive action, the northern people still remained incredulous. They were confounded and half paralyzed with amazement. The cannon of Sumter awoke them to the actual reality. They realized the monster they had to deal with, and, by a summoning of energy which has no real parallel in all human history, they leaped forth to grapple with it. In this conflict, so unlooked for and so atrociously produced, it is not possible that the northern mind should not get a prodigious impulse on toward the *abolition* of slavery. . . . Slavery has undertaken to destroy the Union. It is this very day straining every muscle to do this. Even the best men are beginning to think it intolerable that there should be such unequal strife—that slavery should aim its deadly blows at the Union, and the Union all the while be compelled to stay its hand from slavery.

> . . . It is too early yet to form any definite judgment upon the expediency of adopting a systematic policy for the overthrow of the institution. . . . But the slave power cannot too well understand that it cannot protract the war it has so impiously provoked, or wage it with the barbarity it so incessantly threatens, without instigating even the most forbearing natures of the North to inquire whether it is not their solemn duty, before the Republic and before God, to use the means in their power to crush [slavery] once and forever. . . . The northern people, in spite of all that has occurred, are not yet abolitionists; but when it once comes to the question whether the Union shall go down or slavery, they will not hesitate. Slavery . . . would be sacrificed without the slightest hesitation before it should be suffered to bring death to the republic, which was made to be immortal.[19]

The Christian press was equally sure that if the rebellion persisted, the Union would be forced to embrace emancipation as a war aim. Perhaps, as the *Evangelist* conjectured, God was overseeing the rebellion for this very purpose—to push Northerners toward realizing that slavery was a monstrosity they must destroy:

> This is *not* a War for the abolition of Slavery. True, Slavery may be the cause of it, [but] . . . the object on our part is not to destroy Slavery. It is to put down treason and rebellion, to sustain the Government, and to enforce the laws. The simple question is, Government against no government; country against no country—order against anarchy; a reign of law against a reign of terror.
>
> But no war ever ends just as was expected at the beginning. Man proposes, but God disposes. In time of war events move rapidly. The position changes from day to day, and what was not thought of yesterday, becomes a military necessity tomorrow. Human passions are wildly excited, and men and institutions are swept away by the destroying flood.
>
> *If* therefore . . . the war goes on for a long time, and especially if it is waged in the fierce and desperate manner in which the Rebels seem disposed to wage it, it will be almost impossible to prevent its turning into a war for the overthrow of Slavery. If the war continues, and the armies of the Government invade the Southern States, it is impossible but that the authority of the master over his slave should be greatly weakened by the mere presence of such bodies on Southern soil. The blacks are not so stupid and ignorant as not to know what the war is for, and they will hail this advance into their country as that of a liberating army. Especially is this likely to be the case if secret emissaries from escaped fugitives at the North or in Canada, should find their way back to their old neighborhoods, and secretly convey information to the negroes on the plantations. We speak of this, not as a war measure to be adopted by the Government, but as one of the inevitable incidents of such a war as the South has so wantonly and wickedly provoked. . . . It may be a matter of humanity, as the speediest means to put an end to this savage warfare, to speak to the millions of Slaves that one word, LIBERTY!
>
> . . . Of course it would be only in the utmost of exigencies of war that such a step would be taken as the forcible Abolition of Slavery. But from present appearances the Rebels seem determined to compel the Government to put forth all its strength, and to resort to the most extreme measures. When this is once begun, who shall say where it will end? War is a terrible avenger of wrongs, and imposes fearful necessities. Hence we believe, if the present Civil War *goes on long*, and is waged with the desperation and bitterness with which it is begun, it will give the death blow to American Slavery. Perhaps such is the will of God. We shudder at the prospect of the sufferings which must be endured before this great revolution shall be achieved. But it may be that a Just God intends that this crime of America

against justice and liberty shall be extinguished in blood.[20]

In this spirit, some Northerners—a small minority—who had never considered themselves "ultraists" or abolitionists suddenly found themselves willing to consider even an immediate assault on slavery. An anonymous writer to the *New York Times* explained his change of heart in this way:

> *To the Editor of the New-York Times:*
>
> You say truly that this war in which we are engaged has for its object simply to put down the rebellion against our nationality. This is the object and the whole of it.
>
> But how are we to *accomplish* this object? Many say, "Gather an immense Army, pay hundreds of millions of money, and go on from battle-field to battle-field, till the treason is stamped out; meanwhile, scrupulously respecting the institution of Slavery. In case it shall be found impossible to succeed in this way, then, as a last resort, decree emancipation." The plan is to do all we can toward crushing the rebellion without harming the peculiar institution; and if, after an immense outlay of money and life, we find that either the Republic or Slavery must die, then Slavery must take the death. . . .
>
> Now, gentlemen, I have never been an ultraist; but I cannot help asking, why not adopt this conclusive measure at the outset? What is this Slavery? What has it done that it should be treated so tenderly, and be marked as the last thing to be thrown overboard in the endeavor to save this laboring ship? Here we are, proposing to sacrifice great commercial and manufacturing interests, hundreds of millions of ready money in the shape of taxes, and tens of thousands of precious lives in an experiment to get along without harming the institution of Slavery by this war. What have these rebels and traitors done that we should be so much more chary of their property than of our own—so much more tender of their investment in human flesh and blood than of the lives of our own sons and brothers? What is there so very precious about this very peculiar institution of our deadly enemies that we should shield it from harm with our own fortunes and bodies up to the last possible minute; that we should dare and sacrifice to the last extremity before consenting to have it perish? . . . Was not this rebellion got up in the interests of Slavery? Are not these men who are stabbing at the public heart, slaveholders, and is it not because they are slaveholders that they are so stabbing? Is not Slavery at this moment the right arm with which treason is working against us? Who . . . make the intrenchments, who drag and manipulate the munitions of war, who furnish the food to support the armies of our enemies, who raise the cotton from which, if at all, our foes must get the sinews of war—who but slaves? The system of American Slavery does not deserve the forbearance and sacrifices we are practicing in its favor. On my conscience, I believe we are acting like fools in this whole matter.[21]

Although the federal government remained unwilling to initiate emancipation, the North was nevertheless making important strides toward ending slavery. At the very least, most Northerners, whether Republican or Democrat, accepted that slavery was the cause of the war and could envision striking against it if the survival of the Union demanded it. That eventuality had not yet arrived, but the friends of emancipation were confident that it was just a matter of time. Northerners could talk all they wanted about the conservatism of their aims—how they only wished to *restore* the Union, and *maintain* the Constitution, and *preserve* their heritage. Those who endorsed emancipation, however, knew that something truly radical was in store, that the North was not simply upholding the Revolution of 1776. Whether they recognized it or not, the Northern people were embarking on an entirely new revolution,

THE WAR AND SLAVERY.

Every Abolitionist must rejoice in the seeming promise given by the signal events that are now transpiring; in the hope for the slave that seems to dawn in the fierce battle-conflict for which the two opposing sections of our country are now marshalling themselves in array. Such a drawing of the lines, there has never been before; on the part of the North, such a measure of unanimity, ardor of enthusiasm, and determination for something. The Northern hosts, now pouring down upon the Slave Border to quell the slaveholders' rebellion against the government, may yet fulfil a purpose higher than their consciousness, or that of those who have summoned them. Slavery may be swept away in the tornado of Northern exasperation and passion. Such an event seems now not unlikely to occur, and every friend of humanity will rejoice that even so the work of God be done, and the very wrath of man made to praise Him.

The Liberator, May 24, 1861.
Although most of their compatriots disavowed any desire to see slavery demolished, abolitionists were avidly hopeful that it would soon be "swept away" in the tumult of war.

one that would broaden the range of freedom in America to include blacks and whites alike. "The Second American Revolution," declared one abolitionist editor, "has begun."

> The Revolution is to consist, simply, in A NATIONAL ABOLITION OF SLAVERY.
>
> We say that the Revolution has begun—not that the [Lincoln] administration has commenced it—or has determined upon it. Most probably it has not yet begun to contemplate it, as a possibility, or even as a consummation to be desired. Neither have the mass of the people yet attained to any definite conception of the change.
>
> But the *thinking* portion of the people are rapidly coming to master the conception of it . . . as a "military necessity" of the present moment, the sine qua non of self-defence, an instrumentality not to be spared. . . . We say, that this Revolution has begun, and is in progress. We say so, because the *Nation* has come into direct physical conflict with the *slaveholders!* . . .
>
> The first shot of the slaveholders at Fort Sumter was the slaveholders' declaration of war against the Federal Government. As such it has rallied the slaveholders of the entire Slave States, to the slaveholder's standard of rebellion, quite as effectually, and with as few exceptions, as it has rallied the non-slaveholders of the Free States against them.
>
> We say it is, on the one part, the slaveholders' war, because it is a war instigated and begun by them, for the protection of the practice of slaveholding and of the system contrived and administered by the slaveholders to the security of the practice.
>
> The Nation, then, that is, the loyal portion of the people, and their Government are, as a *matter-of-*

fact, in a state of war with *the slaveholders*. . . . This is the fact, whether the people and their government are yet aware of it, or no. If they are not, now, they soon will be. They will wake up to find themselves in deadly conflict with the oligarchy of slaveholders and their allies, the white serfs of the South. . . .

We say the Revolution must go on, to its completion—a National Abolition of Slavery—because, we take for granted, that the people of the Free States, when they come to understand their condition, will have the common sense and the sagacity, not to say the moral principle and the justice—to annihilate their sole enemy, the slaveholding oligarchy, by 'proclaiming liberty throughout the land, to all the inhabitants thereof:' thus enlisting the God of battles on their side, and adding to the host of loyal citizens . . . a million of emancipated soldiers, . . . [who are] now panting to fight the battles of liberty and patriotism. . . . What but the insanity of moral blindness can long delay the proclamation, inviting them to share in *the glorious second American Revolution*?[22]

Daily Rutland Herald.

Vol. I.....No 73. RUTLAND VT., TUESDAY MORNING. JULY 23, 1861. PRICE TWO CENT[S] $6.00 PER YEA[R]

(FROM OUR YESTERDAY'S EVENING EDITION.)

LATEST NEWS!

GREAT BATTLE

TERRIBLE FIGHTING.

THE CARNAGE FRIGHTFUL.

FEDERAL TROOPS DEFEATED.

They Retreat in Disorder.

We are not of those who are prone to "cry before they are out of the woods," and we have therefore never encouraged the blatant nonsense of brag which we have been sorry to see pervade the North for the past few weeks, even as it has ever been the marked characteristic of Southern character.

We have never doubted the power of the North over the South in the controversy now pending, and we never felt more sure of this than at the present moment, while the telegraph is every moment bringing us intelligence of disaster upon disaster to our arms at Manassas Junction.

From our account to the hour of going to press this morning, all looked favorable to the success of Gen. McDowell, but from the report which we now publish, it will be seen, that he has experienced not only a defeat, but a most mortifying one.

Of course we cannot, at the present time, stop to reflect upon the effect which this result will have upon the country, or the causes which have led to this untoward result of this our first main march into the enemy's country. Indeed, we are forced to go to press, in order to meet our afternoon trains, before the full story of the disastrous march of Gen. McDowell is fully told, and consequently we shall probably have to continue this tale of evil in our morning edition.

But in the meantime, let us take hope that this is but the dark hour that preceeds the light of a bright and luminous morning.

New York, July 22nd.

The Herald's correspondent says that Manassas Junction is supplied with water from Bull's Run which is now cut off, leaving the traitor country without water.

It is reported that Ellsworth's Zouaves met the Louisiana Zouaves, routed them and took their colors.

Also that the 69th New York stripped to the skin, except pants, pitched into the fight regardless of fatigue or personal safety.

Gen. McDowell's telegraphs (says to the Herald) that the enemy were completely routed from Bull's Run—were retreating towards Manassas, leaving their batteries in possession of the Union forces.

The rebels leaving their dead on the field..

The loss of life on both sides is frightful. The whole forces on both sides were said to be engaged.

Gen. Johnson having joined Beauregard's army, thus swelling the enemy to seventy thousand.

The New York Herald's reporter was on the battlefield. When he left, the rebels were flying in vast numbers.

Lt. Col. Porter, with a flag of truce, was fired on by the rebels while he was endeavoring to obtain the body of Lt. Smith, of the 1st Massachusetts regiment.

The greatest enthusiasm prevails in the Union ranks.

Jeff. Davis is said to be at Manassas.

Col. Cowdin's 1st Massachusetts regiment was fired on by the rebel pickets several times Saturday night while sleeping in the road on their arms. The Massachusetts 1st were in the advance.

The editor of the Times from Centreville 5 30 p. m., dating his dispatch Washington, midnight, says the battle is one of the severest ever fought on this continent. Up to two o'clock our troops had driven the enemy through a distance of two miles, and now have possession of the field of battle.

The enemy fell back from one position on another equally strong and every point was freshly reinforced Their force was certainly double ours. The fire Zouaves were terribly cut up —While drawn up to make an attack they were assailed by a masked battery with strong support on their flank and forced to break. It is stated that both Col. Farnham and Lieut. Col. Cregier were killed. Col. Hunter was wounded in the throat Col. Sleeum of Rhode Island [...] frightful. We were advancing, and taking their masked batteries gradually but surely, and driving the enemy towards Manassas Junction, when the enemy seemed to have been reinforced by Gen. Johnson, who, it is understood, took command and immediately commenced driving us back, when a panic among our troops suddenly occurred, and a regular stampede took place.

It is thought that Gen. McDowell undertook to make a stand at or about Centreville, but the panic was so fearful that the whole army became demoralized, and it was impossible to check them, either at Centreville or at Fairfax Court House.

Gen. McDowell intended to make another stand at Fairfax Court House, but our forces being in full retreat, he could not accomplish the object.

Beyond Fairfax Court House the retreat was kept up until the men reached their regular encampments, a portion of whom returned to them, but a still larger portion coming inside the entrenchments.

A large number of the troops in their retreat fell on the way side from exhaustion, and are scattered along the route all the way from Fairfax Court House.

The road from Bull's Run was strewed with knapsacks, arms, &c. Some of our troops deliberately threw away their guns and appurtenances, the better to facilitate their travel.

Gen. McDowell was in the rear of the retreat exerting himself to rally his men, but only with partial effect. The latter part of the army it is said made their retreat in order. He was completely exhausted, having slept but little for three nights.

His orders on the field did not at all times reach those for whom they were intended It is supposed that the force sent out against our troops consisted, according to a prisoner's statement of about 30 000 men including a large number of cavalry He further says that owing to the reinforcements from Richmond, Strasburg and other points the enemy's effective force was ninety thousand men.

SECOND

EVENING EDITION.

SIX O'CLOCK, P. M.

FURTHER PARTICULARS.

FEDERAL LOSS 3,000!

According to the statement of two fire Zouaves they only have about two hundred men left from the slaughter, while the 69th and other regiments frightfully suffered in killed and wounded. The number cannot now be known. Sherman's, Carlisle's, Griffin's, and the West Point batteries were taken by the enemy and the light siege and thirty two rifle cannon, the latter being too cumbrous to remove.

They were two miles the other side of Centerville; such of the wounded as were brought to the Centerville hospital, were left there after having their wounds properly dressed by Surgeon Frank Hamilton.

The panic was so great that the attempt to rally them to a stand at Centerville, was entirely in vain. If a firm stand had been made there our troops could have been reinforced, and much disaster prevented. Gen. McDowell was thus foiled in his well arranged plans.

It is supposed all the provision trains belonging to the United States government were saved. Some regimental wagons were overturned by accident and had to be abandoned. A large drove of cattle were saved by being driven back in advance of the retreat.

It is supposed here to-day, that Gen Mansfield will take command of the fortifications on the other side of the river, which are able, it is said by military engineers, to hold them against any force the enemy may bring against them. Large rifled cannon and mortars are being rapidly sent over and mounted.

An officer just from Virginia reports that the road from Centerville to the Potomac is strewed with stragglers

The troops are resuming the occupation of the fortifications on the line of the Potomac.

Col. Marston's New Hampshire Regiment reached here this morning. He was wounded. Col. Heintzleman was also wounded in the wrist.

In addition to those reported yesterday, it is said that Col. Wilcox the gallant commander of a brigade, was also killed. Also Capt. McCook, brother of Col McCook of Ohio.

The city this morning is in the most intense excitement. Groups are everywhere gathered inquiring the latest news.

Wagons are continually arriving bringing in dead and wounded.

Soldiers are relating to greedy listeners the deplorable events of last night and this morning. The feeling is awfully distressing.

Both telegraph communication and steamboat communication with Alexandria is suspended to day to the public

The greatest alarm exists throughout the city, especially among the female portion of the population.

The following is an account of the inauguration of the panic which has resulted so disas[trously ...]

Pennsylvania regiment with two guns, the [Garibaldi] Guards and Col. Blenker's 1st Rifle [Regi]ment with its batteries, followed, at some distance, by the DeKalb regiment.

When the courier left, at 4 1-2 o'clock, [it was] in the midst of this excitement. Two masked batteries had been opened by the [enemy] on the left flank, and that portion of the di[vision] had its lines broken and demanded imme[diate] reinforcement.

The right was in good order. The ba[ttery] erected on the hill side directly opposite [the] main battery of the enemy was doing goo[d exe]cution and additional guns were being m[ount]ed

On his arrival at Fairfax Court Hous[e he] was overtaken by a government messenger [who] reported that our army was in full re[treat] towards Centerville.

They were followed by less agitated p[ersons] who state that the report of the retreat was [ow]ing to the fact that the alarm among the te[am]sters had communicated itself to the volun[teers] and even in some instances to the regulars [...] the lines were broken, and that a retirement [of] our forces across Bulls Run was rendered [neces]sary.

Col. Hunter passed at the same time in [a ve]hicle wounded.

Ayre's battery was also reported as lost.

Crowds of carriages and baggage wa[gons] came rushing down the road.

The telegraph offices were closed again[st] private business and in an hour the alarm [had] been communicated all along the road to W[ash]ington.

Washington, July 2[2]

via Philadelphia

Our troops after taking three batteries [and] gaining a great victory, were eventually rep[ulsed] and commenced a retreat on Washington.

The retreat is in good order, with the [rear] well covered by a good column.

Our loss is twenty five hundred to three [thou]sand.

The fortifications around Washington [are] strongly reinforced by fresh troops

A CURIOUS COLLECTION.—A yo[ung] amateur archaeologist named Forglais [has] spent twelve years in forming a co[llec]tion of objects found in the bed of a r[iver] by whose means Paris is always hop[ing] to become a seaport; and in virtue [of] whose waters, it has, from immemo[rial] times, adopted a ship as its armo[rial] bearings. Among the four thousand re[lics] of all periods got together by M. [For]glais are rings, ivories, medals, G[allic] and other coins, a beautiful Roman h[elmet], a curious sword, believed to be tha[t of] Capeluche, weapons and instruments [and] 'curiosities' of every kind. The emp[eror] visited this singular collection be[fore] leaving lower Fontainbleau, and exp[ress]ed his wish that it should not be scat[ter]ed, but should form a part of the omni[um] *gatherum* of the Hotel de Cheny, deve[oted] to the preservation of all manner of [an]tiquities.—*Paris letter N. Y. Eve. P[ost]*.

WENT AWAY AS WISE AS HE CA[ME]—A professional gentleman makin[g a] call, remembered the number of the [resi]dence, but forgot the name of the o[ccu]pants. Ringing the bell, he was ushe[red] into the parlor. Presently the lady [of] the house appeared. After a little p[re]liminary talk, thinking very shrewdly [to] conceal his ignorance and acquire [the] knowledge he wanted, he quietly aske[d,] "Madam, how do you spell your nam[e?]"

"*Our family*," was the reply, "*al[ways] spell it with two L's.*"

A SHARPER.—'Sonny, where's [your] father?'

'Father's dead, sir.'

'Have you any mother?'

'Yes, I had one, but she's got ma[rried] to John Danklin and don't be my mo[ther] any more; 'cause she says she's now [got] enough to do to 'tend to his own yo[ung] 'uns.'

'Smart boy—here's a dime for you.'

'That's ye, sir; its the way I get [my] livin.'

'How?'

'Why, by tellin' big yarns to green[horns] like you at a dime a pop.'

Mr. Braidwood, the Chief of the [Fire] Brigade of London, who was killed in [a] recent fire by the falling of a wall, [was] appointed superintendent of the Lon[don] Fire Brigade on its establishment [in] 1833, and it was through his ability [and] unwearied exertion that the force att[ain]ed the efficiency which now so prom[inently] distinguishes it. On all affecting the s[ecu]rity of the government and other pu[blic] buildings [...]

Part Two Confronting the Enemy

Chapter 4

War and Rumors of War: Manassas, 1861

The war of words between the Union and the Confederacy escalated much more quickly than the clash of arms. After the surrender of Fort Sumter, as editors on the home fronts busily pumped out high-toned articles—about democracy and liberty, tyranny and slavery—to define what was at stake in the conflict, leaders on both sides needed to organize and strategize how exactly to wage and win it. Neither side was really ready for war in April 1861, and it would take time for each to raise and drill troops, requisition supplies, and turn their ultimate objectives into workable plans of action. Consequently, the first major military confrontation of the Civil War did not occur until the end of July, in northern Virginia, about thirty miles southwest of Washington. In Northern parlance, it was the Battle of Bull Run, named for the winding stream around which the fighting occurred, but Southerners called it the Battle of Manassas, after the town closest to the action. The area around Manassas was strategically vital, as it was the junction point for two railroad lines, the Orange & Alexandria and the Manassas Gap, which stretched west and south toward the heart of Virginia. A Union assault on Manassas, if successful, would have opened the way for an attack on the Confederate capital at Richmond.[1]

The strategic importance of northern Virginia made it a natural base of operations for the Confederacy, and Southern papers followed the military buildup there with great interest. "The Confederate troops are fortifying themselves in considerable force at Manassas Gap," a correspondent for the *Greensborough Patriot* observed in early June, shortly after General P. G. T. Beauregard—the hero of Fort Sumter—took command there. Not far away, in Washington, Northern troops were amassing in even greater numbers, and the *Patriot* was quick to surmise that a military showdown was imminent. "Every day brings accessions by the hundreds and thousands to both the opposing armies, and it is hardly probable that they can long remain in such

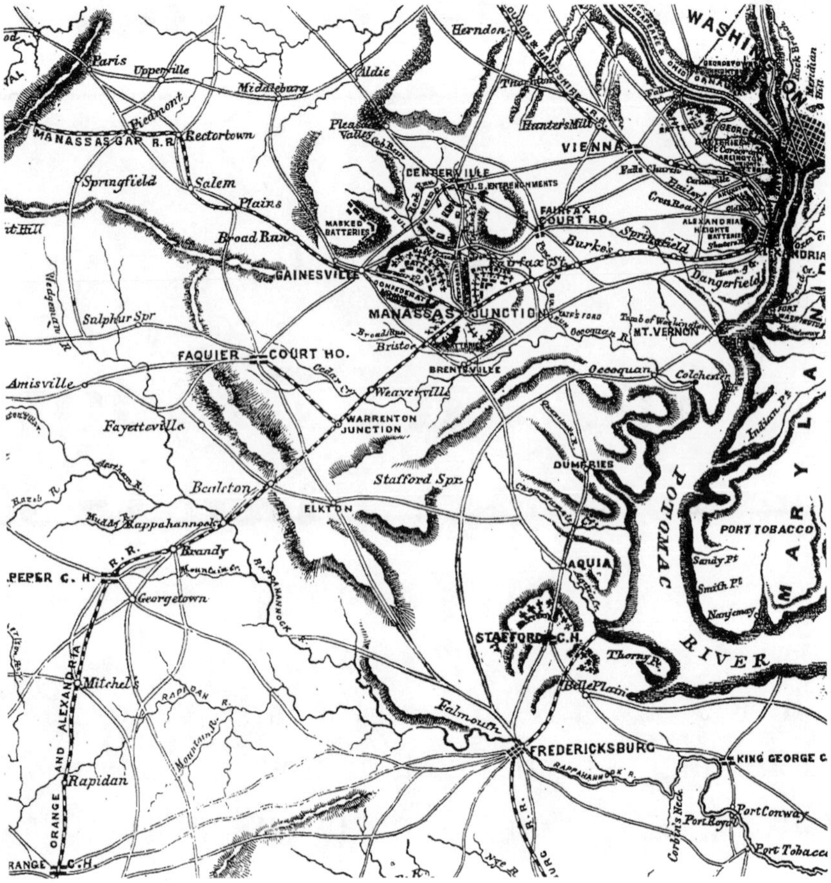

Harper's Weekly, August 10, 1861. Map of northern Virginia, detailing the Confederate position around Manassas Junction.

close proximity, filled as they are with such bitter animosity and hatred, without a conflict," the paper announced expectantly. "Our troops are ready and panting for the conflict, fully determined to conquer or die in the attempt to drive back the invader." Indeed, in the letters they sent home during the summer of 1861, Southern volunteers wrote confidently that they would make quick work of the Yankees. After one or two battles, they believed that the North would be sufficiently whipped and ready to concede the Confederacy's independence.[2]

Northern troops were no less hot for a fight. Certain that Southerners were really lazy and weak-minded creatures, despite their bragging and bluster, they too anticipated a short and decisive war and were excited to get the job finished. Republican newspapers, notably the *New York Tribune* and *Chicago Tribune*, only fanned the war fever with headlines sounding the battle cry "Forward to Richmond!" With Jefferson Davis and the Confederate Congress scheduled to take up residency in Richmond on July 20, Northerners were anxious to capture and control the city before the rebel leaders had the chance to get settled in. Heeding the popular mood, Abraham Lincoln agreed that it was time to make a move into Virginia, and thus instructed General Irvin McDowell, commander of the 30,000 troops in Washington, to plan an attack on the 20,000 soldiers encamped with Beauregard at Manassas.

McDowell doubted whether the men under his charge—mostly novices in the ways of war—were really ready to take the offensive. Indeed, practically from the moment that McDowell led them out of Washington on July 16, their inexperience showed. Weighed down by excessive amounts of provisions and equipment, they moved slowly in the blazing Virginia sun, and as they got thirsty or hungry, some would break away from the column and wander into the woods to collect water and berries. By the time McDowell's men meandered their way to Manassas, Beauregard already had received word of their advance and had secured 11,000 additional troops under General Joseph E. Johnston, thereby eradicating the Union's numerical advantage.

Still, when McDowell launched his attack on the morning of July 21, it went amazingly well. Beauregard had expected McDowell to focus his assault near the railroads south of Bull Run, and the Confederate general therefore had concentrated his forces there. But McDowell surprised him by striking several miles upstream, sending a column of 10,000 Union soldiers against a brigade of only 4,500 Confederates. Hopeful of a Northern triumph, groups of reporters, congressmen, and civilians from Washington had taken carriages out toward the battle zone and spread out picnic lunches a couple of miles from Manassas, to get a better perspective on the action. As they got word of McDowell's surprise attack, they relayed messages back to Washington that made victory seem imminent.

The Confederates held tight, however, as Beauregard and Johnston continued to bring up all the reserves they could find. By late in the afternoon, after almost fourteen hours of fighting on a blisteringly hot day, morale on the Union side began to crack. Sensing his moment, Beauregard organized a counterattack that sent McDowell's troops scattering in a panic. Many abandoned their weapons and threw down shovels, picks, and other munitions in order to lighten their load as they fled the area. The picnickers from Washington suddenly found themselves caught in the chaos, witnesses not to a great Union victory but to a humiliating rout. With around 1,250 men killed or mortally wounded, and another 2,300 non-mortally wounded, the casualties were relatively light compared to future Civil War battles, but they were far more terrible than either side had expected.

For soldiers on both sides, the battle was a transforming experience. Most of them had entered the fray completely green, without any conception of what combat was really like. What they knew of war had come from books and stories. Raised to revere the great accomplishments of their Revolutionary forefathers, they envisioned war as a sublime and gorgeous thing. The actual fighting at Manassas was far more chaotic and gruesome than they had imagined. The meltdown in discipline among the Union troops aside, the whole feel of combat—the deafening discharge of guns, the screams of charging soldiers, the blood of the wounded and dying—lacked the poetic beauty they had expected to find. In a letter to the *Rome Weekly Courier*, one Georgia soldier described just how quickly this single battle at Manassas had altered and hardened his notions of war. "Quite different from all my fancies of great battles," this one lacked any "grandeur of appearance," he wrote.

> Then when the firing commenced, that wonderful, indefinite and superhuman grandeur of movements that my imagination had painted, all faded out, and in its place I had an ugly, dusty, fatiguing and laborious realization of the *actual* in battle. I experienced most fear when the first cannon ball passed over, with a tremendous whizzing, about twenty yards off; and felt the most dread[ful] apprehension, when ordered immediately after, to take a position on a little eminence, in fearful proximity to the place the ball had just passed. After our Regiment had moved forward some 200 or 300 yards, we again came both in range and sight of [the enemy's] celebrated Battery, about three-fourths of a mile from us. Their shell and balls came fearfully near, and as one passed through an apple tree just over my head, a cold chill ran over me, and I suffered from agonizing fear, for probably three or four seconds, but after this, during the entire battle, though I was in almost constant expectation of being killed, yet there was no painful realization of fear, such as would make one hesitate to go wherever duty called. . . . As the dangers really increased, and friends were seen falling

thick upon either side, the *apprehension*, or rather the *fear*, of them became strangely less, and without feeling secure there was a sort of forced resignation to calmly abide whatever consequences should come. . . .

One of the most remarkable mental phenomena, was the sudden and strange drying up of sympathetic feeling for the suffering of the wounded and dying. I could never before look upon even small surgical operations, or persons in extreme pain from any cause, especially when blood was freely flowing, without intense pain and generally more or less faintness. But on this occasion I beheld the most terrible mutilations, the most horrid and ghastly expression of men in the death struggle, men with one arm or a leg shot off, others with the face horribly mutilated, heads shot through and brains lying about, bodies half torn into, and at the hospital, some 50 men with legs or arms just amputated and a half cord of legs and arms, and men in all degrees of pain, from the slight flesh wound to those producing death in a few moments, and viewed all this with far less feeling than I would ordinarily have seen brutes thus mutilated. This obduracy I am truly glad, was only temporary. Only two days after the battle I caught myself avoiding the sight of the amputation of an arm.

I have written thus much of my own feelings, not because they were peculiar, but according to my best knowledge and belief, were nearly the same as those shared by a great majority of all those who were in the heat of the battle, for the first time, on the "glorious 21st."[3]

As this soldier's words suggest, Manassas was for many Americans not only their first experience of actual combat but also their first exposure to suffering and death on a grand scale. Southern newspaper correspondents who lingered with the troops in the aftermath of the fighting tried to give readers at home a realistic sense of its severity through vivid descriptions of the casualties. The roadsides and fords around Manassas were cluttered with dead bodies, and as ghastly as the sight of it all was, the smell was perhaps worse. Having anticipated only light combat, military leaders were unprepared for disposing of so many corpses, and consequently the bodies stayed for days where they fell. In the heat and humidity of the Virginia summer, it did not take long for the odor of rotting flesh to rise to overpowering proportions. It "outstunk any thing we ever smelt," one reporter wrote bluntly. A correspondent from a New Orleans paper put it more delicately. "It was the most terrible scene the eye ever witnessed, more terrible, even, than the mind, thus unaided, can conceive," he remarked a few days after the battle. "Immense numbers of the dead were still lying unburied by the wayside or in the woods, swollen, blackened, and already beginning to decay. In some places so numerous were the dead thus exposed, that the air was foul with their stench. Oh! it was a fearful scene."[4] After surveying the area, a writer for the *Southern Confederacy* made these detailed observations on the condition of the dead and the manner of their burial:

It was a sad sight—the battle field, that day. The enemy's dead lay still scattered in every direction, and the vulture had begun to circle above them. They were well clad, and were larger and stouter than ours. Nearly all of them were lying on their backs, some of them with their legs and arms stretched out to the utmost. Many had their feet drawn up somewhat, while their arms, from the elbows, were raised and the hands rather closed, after the fashion of boxers. . . . Most of them had sandy or red hair and I have observed that this is the predominant color among our own soldiers. Those who were not killed instantly had almost invariably torn open their shirt collars, and loosened their clothing about the waist. There was another mark in addition to this, by which we could tell whether their death was sudden or lingering. It was the color of the face. If the body had time to become cool and quiet before death, the corpse was pale, though not so much so as those who die from disease. Those who were killed instantly, however, and while heated or excited were purple or black in the face. In such cases, the blood being in full circulation, there was not time for it to return to the heart before the body had ceased all its functions. At least, I suppose such is the explanation, and a physician confirms me in it.

Such of the poor wretches as has been buried were placed in the long ditches or trenches sometimes twenty or thirty in the same trench. Of course, it was impossible to procure coffins or boxes for them. They were laid away in the same attitude in which their bodies and limbs had become stiff and rigid—one with his arms and legs stretched out—another bent nearly double—a third with his hands raised, as described above. One poor fellow had died with his arm clasped around a small tree, and others with their hands clasped tightly about their muskets, or such twigs or roots as were in their reach. One was found with his Bible open upon his breast. Some had their hands crossed and the whole body composed after the manner of a corpse. A few were found upon whom there was not the least wound or mark. Whether they had died from sun-stroke, or from exhaustion, or simple fright, it was impossible to say, though probably it was from the first cause.[5]

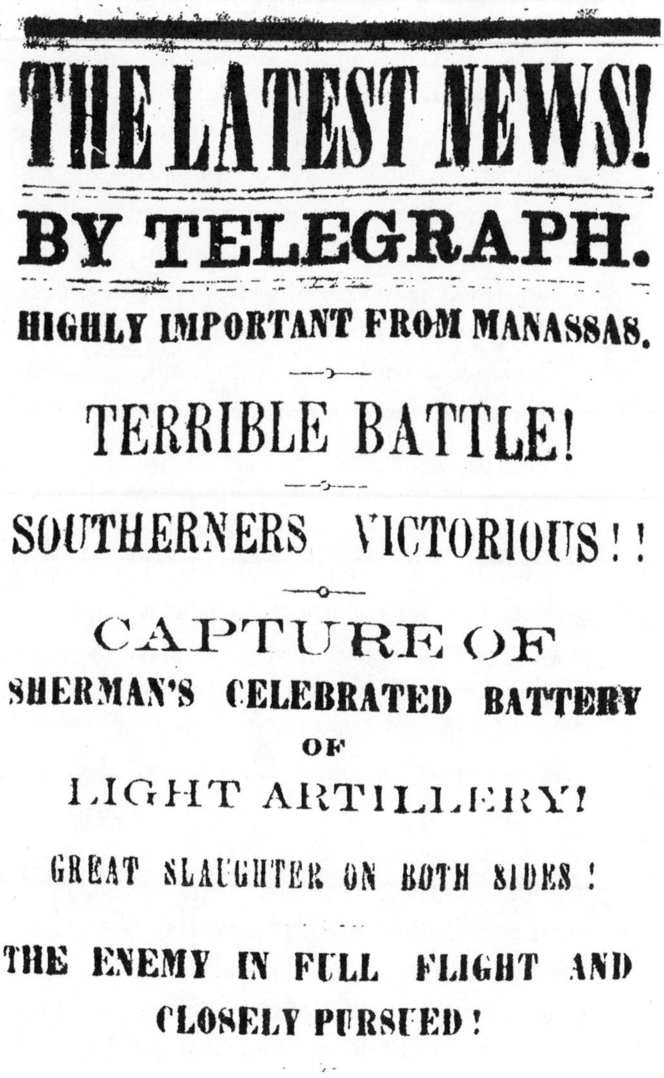
THE LATEST NEWS!

BY TELEGRAPH.

HIGHLY IMPORTANT FROM MANASSAS.

TERRIBLE BATTLE!

SOUTHERNERS VICTORIOUS!!

CAPTURE OF SHERMAN'S CELEBRATED BATTERY OF LIGHT ARTILLERY!

GREAT SLAUGHTER ON BOTH SIDES!

THE ENEMY IN FULL FLIGHT AND CLOSELY PURSUED!

Charleston Courier, July 22, 1861.

Despite the losses of life, for Southerners the sweetness of success made it a euphoric and even sacred day. Since firing the first shots at Fort Sumter, they had reveled in the certainty that God was on their side and would empower them to triumph over their enemies. The victory at Manassas only deepened this conviction—especially as it had occurred on a Sunday. "That we met and defeated" the Northern enemy "on the Lord's Day is another manifest proof that our cause has the sanction of the God of Battles," affirmed the *Charleston Courier*. Southerners interpreted it as a sign from above that the Confederacy was destined to be free. From their pulpits, preachers across the South gave impassioned sermons scorning the Yankees and giving thanks to God for gracing the Confederacy with success. Some of the daily newspapers picked up these inspirational and celebratory missives, as the *Memphis Avalanche* did with this sermon, excerpted below, which was delivered originally in the city's Grace Church:

The 21st of July, 1861, will be a "red letter day" in our national calendar. The contest which then took place at Stone Bridge [Manassas], will not be forgotten. . . . On both sides appeal was made to the "God of battles." To *our* army alone the desired answer was given. The men of the South were animated by a divine impulse. The mercenaries of the North were panic-stricken, and they fled from the little stream to the Potomac river. So that, our enemies themselves being witnesses, God, the Supreme Judge of all the earth, has decided the case against them. And, alas, the record thereof is written in blood. . . .

Previously to the battle of Stone Bridge the most terrible threats were made against the people of the South. Their cities were to be occupied by troops, or reduced to a heap of ashes. Their fields and gardens were to be torn by the wheels of artillery; tramped up by the iron hoofs of cavalry, and despoiled of their beauty by the marchings of thousands of men. The rebels were to be scattered like leaves before an angry wind. Nor should they return to peaceful or contented homes. They must find poverty at their firesides, and see privations in the anxious eyes of mothers and the rags of children. The country along the Mississippi was to be drowned out by cutting the levees, servile insurrections [were] to be encouraged, and the leaders of the revolution hanged. . . .

Such was the programme of those who claim to be civilized and christian! They called it a "holy war!" The Northern troops were on the path of destiny. Their means were ample; their organization perfect. At once splendid and powerful, they dreamed of conquest and reward. The "advance" on the 21st would be a gigantic step in the onward march of subjugation. So confident were they of success, that on God's own day, the churches were deserted, and Senators, Congressmen and ladies followed in the wake of the army to enjoy the anticipated triumph. Well, the struggle came; but the glory was not for them. . . . Awful, indeed, were the scenes of that tremendous day. And yet there was something gorgeous, if not sublime, in its pomp and pageantry. The morn's purple light gleamed on long lines of sharp steel. The little stream glided on with a cold tremor, as if with a presentiment that soon it must be turned into blood. A hundred thousand warriors met there, with plumes and banners waving. The woods and valleys echoed to the sound of trumpet, drum, and bugle-call. . . .

Then followed the deadly conflict—the shout of challenge, and the cheer of defiance, the sulphureous cloud, and the sheet of red flame, the thrust of bayonets and the breaking of ranks, the rush and war of wild excitement. From the terrific fire of guns; from the successive charges of infantry and cavalry, the carnage was horrible. Cut and slashed with sabres or torn with huge balls, the wounded lay, bleeding and in agony. The slain, crushed and mangled, with strong upturned eyes, and streams of gore around them, were massed or clenched together, in ditches, on the road side, everywhere. . . .

Truly we know that God was on our side. Through Him all things worked together for good. By Him our enemies were put to flight. From him came the panic-terror which gave confusion to their minds, and swiftness to their feet. The glory of the [Union] march was changed to the gloom and sorrow of defeat. For Southern arms it was a splendid triumph.[6]

Despite the efforts of preachers to give all the credit to God, it was hard for Southerners to be humble in the face of such a resounding triumph. The newspapers could not help but extol the greatness of Southern manhood and shower glory on the superior prowess of Southern soldiers. As the *Savannah Republican* pointed out, the Union army "was ample in numbers, well officered," and "fought bravely and skillfully." Why then, did the Union go down in defeat? The answer seemed as plain as day:

It was *the superiority of the Southern man over the man of the North*. The latter are wise, brave and strong,

> but we are *wiser*, *braver*, and *stronger!* Here is the grand key that unlocks the terrible mystery of the day, and our enemy cannot learn the fact too soon. As a nation, we are their superiors; and numbers, of which they boast so much, will never turn the scale in their favor. Manassas was a dreadful field but we tell them now, it will be Manassas to the close of this war, even should the battle rage from the Potomac to Bunker Hill and Boston. Physically and morally the Southern man is the highest type of the human race, and he will never be conquered, least of all when defeat involves his self-respect and the ruin of all he holds most dear.
>
> Here is the secret and the lesson. Let our invaders and would be oppressors take both to heart, and cease this unnatural strife which they wage to their own disgrace and destruction.[7]

The *Charleston Mercury* was even headier in the afterglow of victory. Refusing to concede that the Union had fought with any skill or bravery, the *Mercury* bitingly dismissed the Northern people as an emasculated "race" unfit for war and destined for defeat:

> The most disgraceful defeat that we can recall to mind, in modern times, amongst the civilized white race, is that suffered by the Yankee hordes on the 21st, at Manassas. . . . We see it stated in all the Northern papers and stated even in the Virginia papers, that these men fought well and bravely. We have not been able to discover the evidence of any great bravery on their part in the whole transaction. We have carefully scrutinized the record, and we challenge the proof. There were from thirty five thousand men on the [Union] side opposed to fifteen thousand on the other engaged in the conflict—more than two to one. . . . Their arms and equipments were superior to ours in every particular. The fight was very much one of artillery on their side. And their superiority in this respect was even more marked than their vast disproportion in men. For their guns were more than three to one on our side. The fight was an open, fair fight, upon an open, fair field. . . . Every single point was against us in the game of battle. Yet we won the field—as desperate a field as ever men encountered—desperate on account of their overwhelming force of artillery and men. And how, then, was it won? By courage!—nothing but superior courage. It does well for the Yankee to ascribe the defeat to "an unaccountable panic." It is utterly false. A panic they no doubt had; but never could such a panic have arisen, unless they had already been unnerved by the desperate pluck which they had seen our troops exhibit. . . . They were cowed—subdued—terrified. They broke, dispersed, fled, dismayed. Their boasted audacity was curbed. These high hopes of "beauty and booty" were dispelled, and they found they had more stern men to deal with—men holding life light in the balance of honor and liberty. Their craven souls shrunk within them. . . . And they fled like yelping hounds under the lash—insolent curs that would cower under the crack of a driver's buckskin whip. . . . The simple fact is, that this race of sharpers, as a whole, have less fight in them than any white race now on the globe.[8]

The victory at Manassas naturally gave the Confederacy a heightened sense of prestige and power. With it, no one could claim that the Southern people were unprepared or unable to defend their freedom. Eager to build upon this success, some newspapers called excitedly for the South to "strike while the iron is hot" and aggressively pursue the Army of the Potomac until it was annihilated.[9] The fact was, however, that the victorious Confederate forces were badly weakened by the battle and could not continue pressing forward. Nevertheless, the hope remained that the Confederacy might soon secure its independence if the Northern people would simply recognize the strength of the rebellion and give up the fight. In the flush of victory, this did not seem unreasonable. "They have now learned much," the *Richmond Enquirer* promised its readers. "The Southern people are strong, and brave, and cannot be conquered—this fact is now written on the arches of the sky." It was "a question merely of time" before Northerners acknowledged that they could not crush the Confederacy's bid for independence.[10]

In contrast to the joyful boastings that rang throughout the Confederacy, the Northern reaction ranged from outrage to dismay to firm resolve. As some Southerners had hoped, the Union defeat at Manassas emboldened Northern Peace Democrats, who loudly disparaged the war effort as a horrendous waste of American lives and called upon the Northern people to rise in support of a negotiated settlement. The *New York News* thus commanded: "Men of the North, if you are Christians, and you, women of the North, if you have women's hearts, from this hour proclaim yourselves peacemakers, and raise your voices in opposition to this wholesale massacre of your kindred." Convinced that the Union could never be restored by military force, the *News* insisted that the Lincoln administration could win back the seceded states only by extending an olive branch and promising to protect their interest in slavery.

In trying to rally public sentiment against the war, the *News* appealed specifically to the personal interests of women, who were in danger of having their families destroyed by the fighting. Through this anonymous public letter to all the women in America, North and South, the paper urged them to take political action to save both themselves and their country from what seemed to be irredeemable suffering:

> WOMEN OF AMERICA: The gory waves of a cruel war are surging up to our very feet, and threatening to engulf all that we hold dear. Let us break the chain of silence which has bound us; let us throw ourselves between the combatants; let us strive to thrust aside the destroying sword, and implore, from the depths of our bleeding hearts, for peace, peace!
>
> Can we look quietly on and make no effort to save father, husband, brother, son, from the bloody doom of the destroyer's sword? Can we patiently submit to having our hearts and our homes desolated, ourselves made widows, and our children orphans, to gratify the bloodthirsty views of a few politicians? Shall we give all our treasures to be sacrificed upon an altar dedicated to wrong, cruelty and injustice? Forbid it Heaven! Never let the world say that the women of America stood idly, approvingly by and saw those they loved cruelly butchered, and yet raised no hand to save them. . . . Keep silen[t] no longer; tell the world that we at least have no part or lot in this matter; that not with our sanction is brother arrayed against brother; that we cannot, we will not, even with trembling fingers, buckle the armor on our husbands and sons, and bid them on to victory or death.
>
> Let us band ourselves together in a loving sisterhood, knowing no North, no South, and as inhabitants of a common country implore the rulers of this stricken land for peace. Let each county and district, each city and State, send out their petitions; let every woman subscribe her name, and let it go forth as "a memorial of her.". . . Tell the rulers of the land that the sword is dividing the country forever asunder; that soon between the North and South there will flow an awful gulf of blood so wide and deep that it will prove an impassable barrier to reunion.[11]

Such pleadings aside, most Northerners were far from interested in giving up the fight. Nevertheless, they still were stunned by the Union defeat. Much thought and planning had gone into the move on Manassas, and it was inconceivable that the Union armies, well equipped and 30,000 strong, could have failed so disgracefully. All of their presumptions about their own prowess, the South's imbecility, and the imminence of the Confederacy's fall had been turned upside down. The initial reports from the field, which were greatly encouraging and made victory seem so near, only intensified the shock. The *Albany Atlas & Argus*, an organ of the Democratic party, perfectly captured the sense of loss and confusion that overspread the North at this time:

> No one who mingles with the people, can have failed to observe the serious and thoughtful tone of the public mind since the unfortunate battle before Manassas. It amounts to sadness and really casts a gloom over the country. Men no longer speak lightly of the present war, or of the manner of conducting it, or of the time or conditions of its termination. . . .
>
> They ponder—they commune with themselves—they ask themselves questions which they dare not yet ask each other, or utter even in a whisper. Could we read and report their thoughts, we [would] have . . . a record [like] this: "What is to become of the country? Where is all this to end? Have we not been mistaken in our estimate of this whole subject? Have we appreciated it in its whole length and breadth, and in all its far-reaching consequences? . . . Have we not under-estimated the strength of the South—especially its capacity for a strictly defensive warfare? Can we conquer it? Can we crush out this rebellion—especially as promptly as we had expected? Is not the war likely to linger, perhaps, for years? If we beat the Southern States in battle and scatter their armies, so that they can no longer meet us in the field, will that end the war or restore . . . their allegiance as citizens or as States of the Union? Will it not be necessary to garrison the whole South, and for this purpose, will not an immense army on our part continue to be required? May not the expenses of the war be more crushing and longer-continued than we have supposed? How are we to raise money? Can we continue to do it by borrowing, or will not onerous, direct taxes become necessary? Will our people for a long time submit to these burdens, and . . . can we assure them of glorious and beneficent results of the war, which will reward all the trials which it involves? . . . " Such, we have not the least doubt, are the thoughts of multitudes of men at the present time—not expressed, half-fledged, timidly indulged, but yet piercing the heart with sadness and leading our whole people to reflection.[12]

Although alarmed by the defeat, Northerners were hardly paralyzed by it. The day after the battle, Abraham Lincoln signed a bill authorizing the enlistment of 500,000 additional volunteers for a three-year term of service; three days later, he signed another bill calling for 500,000 more. Northern men responded with alacrity, flocking to recruiting offices, and many who had volunteered in April for only three months signed up again for three more years. Meanwhile, the newspapers sought to make sense of what had happened at Manassas. Convinced that the Union had moved prematurely in attacking the Confederates, several papers fumed at "the Tribunes of New York and Chicago," whose command of "Forward to Richmond" seemed, in retrospect, totally wrongheaded and foolish. More generally, though, news editors tried to positively assess what the country could learn from its loss—to find a silver lining in what seemed to be a blatant disaster. First and foremost, they encouraged their readers to take the defeat as a valuable lesson in humility. "We have been too self-confident," one newspaper pointed out. "We needed a reverse to bring us to our bearings." Northerners also had to recognize that while they had exaggerated their own prowess, they were additionally guilty of grossly underestimating the strength and determination of the enemy. Manassas had shown "that the men who are in arms against us are not savages whom a few rounds of shot will send scampering off like a flock of sheep, but our equals in military skill, if not in courage," admonished the *Albany Evening Journal.* "What folly it is, come to think of it, to call American soldiers, South or North, cowards," declared another editor, as if he had just experienced the greatest of revelations. "The truth is, braver men never lived than those who are arrayed against each other in this conflict." Without denigrating the hearty manhood of the

Northern people, the press now at least was willing to concede that Southerners were deadly serious about winning their independence.[13]

If Northerners could find some moral to the story of Manassas, if they could come away with a clearer sense of the sacrifices required for victory, then the battle was not a total loss. It could be a blessing in disguise—a much-needed wake-up call that would strengthen the Union's resolve and make Northerners all the more willing to do whatever was necessary to win. The *Springfield Republican* saw many reasons to be grateful for the setback:

> We now appreciate, as we have never done before, the horrible nature of the rebellion with which we have to deal. We see as we have never seen before that no compromise can touch it. We have wakened fully to the realization of the fact that the North is called upon to join in a gigantic struggle with a baleful power; and that on the results of that struggle hinge the national name, the national existence, and freedom for ourselves and our children. The alternative comes to us, and stares us more sternly in the face than ever before: "Are we to be a nation, or are we to be destroyed?" We see now, most vividly, that we are on the verge of political and national perdition, and that nothing but bravery and devotion and self-sacrifice will save us from disgrace and destruction. It is into these grave convictions that the defeat at Manassas has plunged us, and it is out of these convictions that the nation is rising to-day with strength renewed like the eagle's.
>
> There has probably been no time since the rebellion commenced when soldiers could be enlisted so rapidly as now. A new class of society has been touched. There are men now ready to enlist who have never been ready before. Men with wives and children and dependents burn to burst away, and question themselves as to what is their duty. The calm, cool blood that has not been stirred at all till now, or but feebly, boils and burns. . . . In New York city, there is a rush to the recruiting offices such as there has not been for many days; and that great city, which has behaved so nobly during the whole of this war, is only the more enthusiastic and determined in consequence of our reverses. In every quarter the loyal press fairly throbs with the new life which an unexpected defeat has infused into it.
>
> Nothing can be more obvious to us now than the fact that we needed just this defeat at starting to show us the nature of the work we have in hand, and to teach us how to make the preparations to do it. . . . So there is really nothing in the defeat to give us discouragement, but much to make us stronger. We are among those who believe that God is on our side in this business; and we have no more doubt that He will lead us through it triumphantly, than we have that He has been with us from the beginning. It may be through seas of blood and sorrow; but He will lead us out at last into a large and honorable peace.[14]

While Northerners generally remained faithful that God was still on their side, the outcome at Manassas did make some wonder if the Almighty was perhaps trying to tell them something—to teach them an important lesson about their stance on slavery, in particular. At the start of the war, many Northern newspapers had exclaimed that if the rebellion continued for long, the Union would eventually seek to subdue it by destroying slavery. Now, with the South riding high on victory, some Republican papers started to wonder aloud if God, in giving success and strength to the rebellion, was signaling that the time for enacting emancipation had come. As the *New York Times* cautioned, "There is a divinity shaping the course of this war," and that higher power was not about to allow Northerners to end the war without contending first with the root cause of it. "There is one thing, and only one, at the bottom of this fight,—and that is, the *negro*," the *Times* continued. "If our army had been victorious at Manassas," however, "they would have marched on to Richmond, and ended this war on a false basis," without ever addressing the slavery question. By the "unexpected repulse at Manassas," God was forcing Northerners to continue fighting, and bringing them one step closer to realizing that they could not crush the rebellion until they had crushed slavery first. The *Evangelist*, a paper put out by the Presbyterian Church, seconded this view:

> From the beginning we have predicted that if the war went on, and was waged with fury and bitterness, it would turn into a war for the Abolition of Slavery. Had success at once crowned our arms, doubtless the Government would have observed great forbearance. Feeling strong, it would have been magnanimous. It would have been very tender [with] the persons and property of the rebels. . . .
>
> But the war is fast turning men's minds from these gentle thoughts. We have been wont to speak of the people of the South as "our fellow-citizens," as "our Southern brethren," entitled to the same privileges as ourselves. *So they were*, while loyal to the Government, but not while rebels in arms against it. We are now opening our eyes to the unwelcome fact that they are enemies of the country, and must be dealt with as TRAITORS. This once settled, scruples fast vanish about the mode of conducting the war. We feel bound to use every means in our power to put down a rebellion which is striking at the very life of the Nation.
>
> And now, behold, the means are at hand—means which we have as yet disdained to use, for we have wished to spare those whom we have generously regarded as still our countrymen. We have looked upon it as a paroxysm of madness on the part of the South to rush into War, when it knew it was "fighting over a loaded mine," that mine being four millions of slaves. But she has relied upon the forbearance of the North not to cause that mine to explode.
>
> Nor did we meditate such a thing. But the madmen of the South are driving us to sterner measures. Every battle fought makes the temper of the North more fierce, and God alone knows what the end will be. When hundreds and thousands of our brave young soldiers are brought home from the bloody field; when there is a cry in the land, like the wailing of Egypt, because in every house there is one dead, the question will be asked, Why not make a speedy end of this dreadful business by at once proclaiming freedom to the slaves?
>
> But we hear a faint cry, that such a course would be "illegal and unconstitutional." But can they who are fighting to destroy the Constitution claim its protection? Whatever rights they had before as loyal citizens, they have forfeited by their treason and rebellion. By the laws of every nation in the world traitors in arms forfeit their lives, and they may think the Government very lenient if they lose only a portion of their property.
>
> But in truth this is not a question of laws or constitutions, but of National existence—of the life of the State. The Country and Government must be preserved, whatever else has to be destroyed.[15]

Support for such "sterner measures" developed not only out of frustration over the Union defeat at Manassas but also from feelings of outrage over how the rebels had allegedly conducted themselves there. Within days after the conflict, Northern soldiers began to circulate rumors accusing Southerners of battlefield atrocities: bayoneting and executing wounded and defenseless Union men, firing on field hospitals, mutilating the bodies of the dead, and committing other acts that today would fall under the definition of war crimes. After the war was over, these reports would be dismissed as overwrought and false, but when the stories first emerged, the press quickly picked them up and validated them as truth. The *Cleveland Plain Dealer*, a Democratic organ in the West, issued this summary of rebel misdeeds:

> The barbarities practiced by the rebels at the Battle of Bull's Run are unparalleled. An instance is related

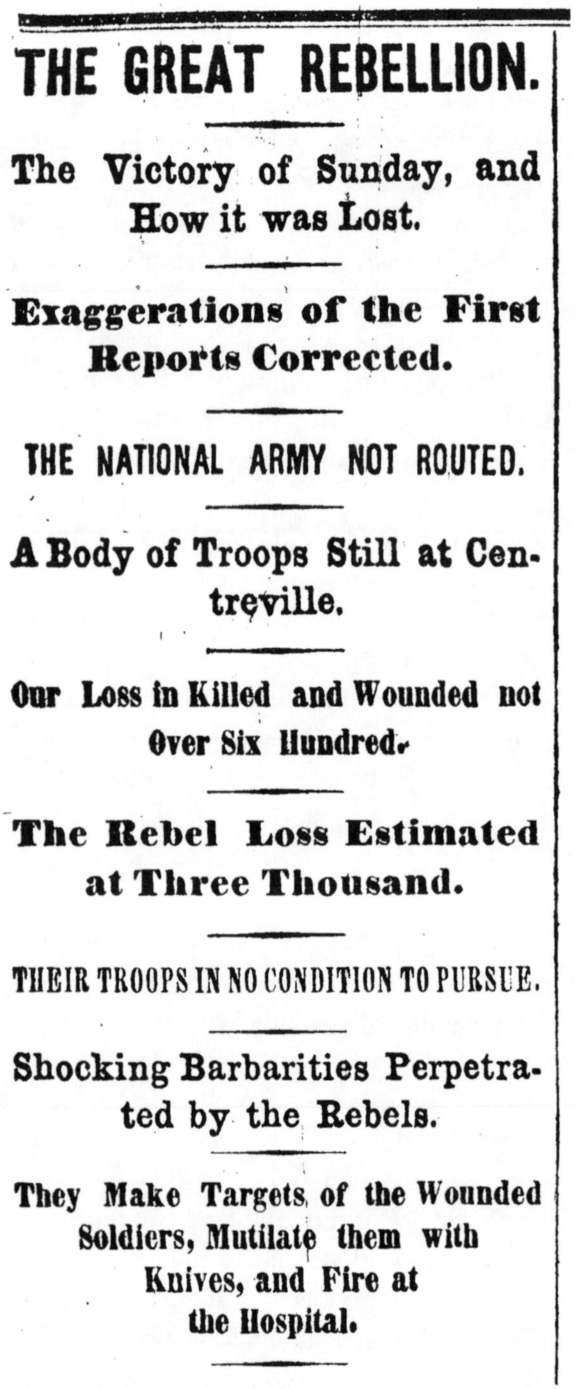

THE GREAT REBELLION.

The Victory of Sunday, and How it was Lost.

Exaggerations of the First Reports Corrected.

THE NATIONAL ARMY NOT ROUTED.

A Body of Troops Still at Centreville.

Our Loss in Killed and Wounded not Over Six Hundred.

The Rebel Loss Estimated at Three Thousand.

THEIR TROOPS IN NO CONDITION TO PURSUE.

Shocking Barbarities Perpetrated by the Rebels.

They Make Targets of the Wounded Soldiers, Mutilate them with Knives, and Fire at the Hospital.

New York Times, July 24, 1861.
In the days after the Battle of Manassas, the Northern press tried to downplay the Union's losses while drawing attention to rumors of atrocities committed by Confederate troops.

> where a private of the First Connecticut regiment found a wounded rebel lying in the sun, and lifted him up and carried him [into the] shade, where he gently layed him and gave him a drink from his canteen. Revived by the drink, the ingrate drew his pistol and shot his benefactor through the heart. Another instance is related of a troop of rebel cavalry deliberately firing upon a number of wounded men, who had been placed together in the shade by their comrades. . . . It is said by Virginians who have come from the battlefield, that these fiends in human shape have taken the bayonets and knives of our wounded and dying soldiers and thrust them into their hearts and left them sticking there, and that some of the Louisiana Zouaves have severed the heads of our dead from their bodies, and amused themselves by kicking them about as footballs. Such barbarities are unworthy of a Christian era.—They are a sample of the boasted chivalry of these worse than fiends.[16]

The coverage given to these barbarities was generally small in scale. Most newspapers, like the *Plain Dealer*, cataloged the accusations vividly but briefly. It was left to a correspondent from the *New York Tribune*, a vehemently antislavery paper, to break the story open with an extended narrative incorporating eyewitness accounts by Union officers:

> Nearly every family in the land which has to mourn the death of a friend is by this time apprised of the fact, and . . . is now devoured with a new anxiety—the eager desire of knowing the exact circumstances of the killing of the dead man, their friend. The press is rapidly laying these individual details before the country. Through the uncertainty that surrounds the fate of some of our men, there begins to loom out in unmistakable proportions a certain barbarous fact, so hideous, so miserably sad, so humiliating to human nature, that heretofore it has been only whispered, even by those who could best attest its truth. I refer

to the *savage and deliberate slaughter of our wounded and helpless men by the Rebel troops. . . .*

To advance backward and give the conclusion before stating the premises, I will say that the proofs are overwhelming and incontrovertible, that our wounded men were *systematically murdered;* that our surgeons were *systematically shot down;* that our ambulances were *systematically blown up by shells;* and that at the last, our hospital, a church dwelling, was charged on by cavalry, who . . . set fire to the building and burned it, and in it scores of wounded and dying men. . . .

Now to [the] authenticated facts.

Lieutenant S.R. Elliott of the 79th Regiment N.Y.S.M. (Highlanders) was standing near Col. Cameron of his regiment, when the latter was struck by a shot and fell mortally wounded. The Lieut. and others instantly rushed to the fallen officer. Lieutenant Elliott, with twelve men of the 5th and 10th Companies of his Regiment, raised the Colonel and started to bear him off the field. No sooner was this group of men discerned by the field telescopes of the enemy, than they were made a target for an entire battery of rifled cannon, and a number of infantry. The shots struck on every side of them, being aimed with great precision, and they were soon covered with dust thrown over them by the flying balls. Finally, a shell thrown by the rifled cannon battery struck in the center of the group, exploded, and killed five men of those who were bearing the dying Colonel. . . .

There was no possibility of mistaking the nature of this group, or their humane errand. The Rebels saw a number of men bearing from the field a wounded officer, and instead of withholding their fire, invariably the practice of a civilized foe, they scientifically took the exact range of the retreating group, and brought a whole battery to bear on them, killing nearly half of them before they had succeeded in placing their dying Colonel in a place of safety.

Colonel Wood, of the 14th New-York Regiment (Brooklyn), being wounded, was placed in an ambulance, and was being carried off the field. The ambulance was fired at persistently by a battery of rifled cannon. A projectile from one of these guns at last took off the top of the ambulance, passed on and killed three men of the Rhode Island Battery, and dismounted their gun. The fire was kept up so unremittingly, that the men in charge of the ambulance were forced to leave it. In this case also the ambulance was made a special target, and was fired at until it was probably destroyed. . . .

Surgeon Barnes of the N.Y. 28th Volunteers . . . went up to the battle-field in the rear of the attacking column, and, as soon as our men began to fall, he took a position with his Assistants under a tree, in a little ravine. The wounded men were brought to him, and he took off his green sash and hung it on the tree to signify that the place was under the charge of a surgeon. The injured men were brought in rapidly, and in 15 minutes he had under his charge nearly 30. As fast as possible he attended to their hurts, and in a short time had been compelled to perform a number of capital operations. He amputated four legs, three arms, a hand, and a foot, and attended to a number of minor injuries. By this time the enemy had discovered the place, and the nature of the business of the men in charge, and began to pour in musket balls, and projectiles from rifled cannon. The place became unsafe for the wounded men, and it was seen to be necessary to remove them. The Surgeon's Assistants and servant had become separated from him, and he had no one to send for ambulances, and was obliged to leave the wounded men and go himself.

It was no easy matter to procure ambulances enough, and it was probably 30 minutes before the Surgeon returned with the necessary assistance. When he returned he found that *every one of those wounded men had been bayoneted, or sabered, and was dead.* They were literally cut to pieces.

Sum up these facts. There were 30 men all dangerously hurt—they had all been cared for by the

> Surgeon—they were lying on the grass in agonies of pain and thirst, with their bandaged stumps of limbs, resting on the little hammocks—with their severed legs and arms scattered about—and, if more could be needed to show the nature of the place, the Surgeon's green sash was flying as a flag in the tree, and the Surgeon's instruments were lying in sight, and yet these 30 helpless men were there and then deliberately butchered.
>
> The Surgeon gathered up his instruments and started to retire to the rear, again to resume his duties. . . . Col. Slocum, of the New-York 2d Regiment, was wounded by a grapeshot through the thigh. The Surgeon went to his assistance, found him, and attempted to dress his wound; but the rifled cannon commenced playing on them, and drove them from the field. They retreated, four men bearing the Colonel. In a short time a halt was made, and again the rifled cannon of the enemy played on them and drove them away. All this time the Colonel was bleeding his life away. From six several positions was Colonel Slocum removed before his wound could be properly dressed, although a tourniquet had at first been applied. At last they took shelter in the Stone Church (Sudley Church), which had been occupied as a hospital. This Church was soon shelled by the enemy. . . .
>
> The shelling, and ultimate burning of this church, is asserted by a crowd of witnesses.
>
> Lieutenant-Colonel Elliott, of the 79th (Highlanders), N.Y., saw the Rebels shelling the building while the hospital flags were flying. He states that the hospital was made a special target for the rifled cannon of the Rebels . . . and that the attempt by them to destroy it, and slaughter our wounded men, was deliberate, and was followed up with the most persistent perseverance. . . .
>
> Every statement in this communication about the treatment of our wounded men by the enemy, was taken by me directly from the lips of the officers, whose names are herein mentioned, and who themselves saw the occurrences.
>
> Not a line is hearsay evidence.[17]

Of course, the entirety of the *Tribune*'s report *was* hearsay. Nevertheless, the atrocity stories had an electrifying effect on public opinion. It proved impossible for Northerners to put these brutal images out of their minds. In response to the public outrage they provoked, the Committee on the Conduct of the War—a congressional body created to investigate war-related problems and controversies—began an inquest to unearth the full extent of the barbarities committed at Manassas. Their findings, which they published in May 1862, confirmed every horrifying detail that the newspapers had reported. According to the witnesses interviewed by members of the committee, the rebels were guilty of much more than just bayoneting wounded men and firing on surgeons and hospitals. They hacked the heads off Union soldiers and sent the skulls home as souvenirs. They collected knucklebones from dead bodies and transformed them into rings and other ghoulish trinkets. They dug up the corpse of an officer from Rhode Island and burned it to ashes. And, as a final insult, they took the bodies of other soldiers they had mutilated and purposely buried them facedown, away from heaven. "The testimony is sickening in its intensity of horror," exclaimed one paper after reading the committee's report. "It is enough to make the blood boil with righteous rage." Giving visual depiction to the reported atrocities, illustrated newspapers in the North presented their readers with macabre cartoons of the bone ornaments and other prizes allegedly collected from the corpses of Union soldiers.[18]

In the summer of 1861, when these atrocity stories first surfaced, a few Democratic newspapers were quick to condemn them as nothing more than overblown fictions designed to inflame the public's hatred of the South. They feared that the reports would only inspire Northerners to escalate the violence by seeking

"The outrages upon the dead will revive the recollections of the cruelties to which savage tribes subject their prisoners. They were buried in many cases naked, with their faces downward. They were left to decay in the open air, *their bones being carried off as trophies*, sometimes, as the testimony proves, to be used as personal adornments, *and one witness deliberately avers that the head of one of our most gallant officers was cut off by a Secessionist, to be turned into a drinking-cup on the occasion of his marriage.*

"Monstrous as this revelation may appear to be, your Committee have been informed that during the last two weeks the skull of a Union soldier has been exhibited in the office of the Sergeant-at-Arms of the House of Representatives which had been converted to such a purpose, and which had been found on the person of one of the rebel prisoners taken in a recent conflict."—*Report of the Congressional Committee on the Conduct of the War.*

THE REBEL LADY'S BOUDOIR.

LADY (reads)—"*My dearest wife, I hope you have received all the little relics I have sent you from time to time. I am about to add something to your collection which I feel sure will please you—a baby-rattle for our little pet, made out of the ribs of a Yankee drummer-boy,*" &c., &c.

Frank Leslie's Illustrated Newspaper, May 17, 1862.

The impact of the 1862 report by the Committee on the Conduct of the War is vividly—and grotesquely—captured in this cartoon, entitled "The Rebel Lady's Boudoir." The female figure in the center, seemingly a woman of the slaveholding class, sits in a room lavishly decorated with treasures manufactured from the body parts of Union soldiers: tables with skeletal legs and feet; walls adorned with bone ornaments; bowls made from skulls. While her young child plays with one of the many skulls scattered across the room, the woman peruses a letter from her husband, a soldier in the Confederate army. It reads: *"My dear wife, I hope you have received all the little relics I have sent you from time to time. I am about to add something to your collection which I feel sure will please you—a baby rattle for our little pet, made out of the ribs of a Yankee drummer-boy," &c. &c.* The caption also cites a portion of the committee's report, detailing the rumored desecration of Union dead at Manassas.

Some Specimens of "Secesh" Industry—intended for the London Exhibition of 1862, but unfortunately intercepted by the "*Paper Blockade.*"

Harper's Weekly, June 7, 1862

This rendering of "secesh industry" provides a catalog of the goods allegedly crafted by the Confederates after Manassas: a goblet made from a Yankee skull, a jawbone paperweight, a reading desk formed by the entire skeleton of "one of Lincoln's hired Minions," a fur woven from the scalps and beards of Union men, a necklace and head wreath sporting Yankee teeth, a bread basket fashioned from rib bones, and a bell handle made from the delicate remains of a hand, wrist, and arm.

SLAVERY.—The present slaveholders rebellion, as it has been aptly termed, presents for the solution of the people of the North the fate of the institution of slavery. We entered upon the war to defend our flag, to save our government, with no thought but a restoration of government to its former basis. Though the insurrection was the fruit of slavery, we entered the war with no intention of eradicating that evil. It has been the purpose of the North and now is, to preserve an protect the institution as it has been hitherto preserved and protected. In view, however, of the magnitude of the struggle, the vindictiveness of the insurrectionists, and the future peace and prosperity of the country, the question of abolishing slavery, driving the pest from our shores forever, is worthy of serious attention.

Hampshire Gazette & Northampton Courier,
July 23, 1861.
Sure that slavery was the cause of the rebellion, and that the evils of slavery predisposed the rebels to commit atrocities at Manassas, more Northerners began to look favorably upon the idea of abolishing the institution altogether.

vengeance. They were not wrong in this. The South's euphoria and the North's embarrassment over the military outcome of the battle at Manassas were fleeting. Northern wrathfulness over the reported barbarities was far more enduring. For Republicans, who had entered the war already hostile toward slavery, the rumors carried special meaning. Confident that the cruelties of slavery had accustomed Southerners to such savage behavior, they became all the more determined to see slavery destroyed and the Confederacy's master class—the "slave power"—stripped of its wealth and influence. As the *Springfield Republican* avowed after reading the report of the Committee on the Conduct of the War:

> Ever since the battle of Bull Run there have been vague reports of indignities heaped on the bodies of dead Union soldiers, and outrages committed on the wounded and prisoners. It was difficult to believe these stories; we could not imagine how a people professing to be civilized, could do such horrible things as were reported, even to an enemy. But the recent report of the congressional committee establishes beyond a doubt, on the testimony of unimpeachable witnesses, . . . that the rebels have committed outrages that should put a native of the Feejee Islands to the blush. Henceforth it is a matter of history; and when the record of the war is written, it will tell not only of the base treason and ingratitude of the leaders of the rebellion, . . . but of many an outrage practiced during the struggle, which exceed in horror the excesses of the sepoys of India, or the barbarities of the North American Indians. . . .
>
> These monstrous revelations of inhuman deeds, of concerted systems of mutilation and desecration, can but arouse the deep vengeance of the North against the authors of this rebellion. It is difficult to read these accounts without crying out for a war of extermination against the South. We can hardly believe these men were once our brothers, or that they belong to the same race, country or age. But we have not in the past, and cannot in the future, return outrage for outrage. Our motive in conducting the war is the noblest that a nation could have, and our actions should accord with our principles. But this conduct of the rebels should spur us up to new activity and a new zeal in the work of crushing out the rebellion. And let us remember that slavery is the source and fountain of all this evil, and see to it that the slave power dies with the rebellion. No nation except a nation of slaveholders could be

guilty of such barbarism as has been witnessed since the war commenced, and it is our duty to provide that the scenes of this rebellion shall never be acted over again in this country.[19]

As a military event, the Battle of Manassas was far less monumental or death-dealing than others that would come later in the war. Psychologically, however, it was tremendous in its consequences. Victory took Southerners to new heights of confidence and strengthened their conviction that the Confederacy was destined for independence. Northerners, on the other hand, came away with a deeper sense of resolve not only to defeat the rebels but also to punish them severely for their allegedly atrocious battlefield behavior. In part, these mental shifts were natural responses to news of the Confederate victory. But they also were shaped by the stories and editorials that appeared in the newspapers, which gave Northern and Southern readers food for thought in contemplating the battle and judging its significance. Particularly for the North, the press coverage of Manassas made it an unforgettable experience, one that would color its attitude toward the enemy for the duration of the conflict.

The Daily Delta.

VOL. XVII. NEW ORLEANS, THURSDAY, MAY 29, 1862. NO. 143.

THE DAILY DELTA

From Yesterday Evening's Edition.

"Evacuation About Played Out."—This is what the Memphis Avalanche says in reply to those who propose to evacuate that city on the approach of the Federal army. It says the Confederates have but little more territory to spare for this operation. It has that look, rather. After evacuating Bowling Green, and Nashville, and Columbus, and Yorktown, and Norfolk, and New Orleans, and a score of places of less note, the game of evacuation may well be considered about played out. Richmond, Memphis, Mobile, Savannah and Charleston are now exposed to the same depleting process, and what port or city of refuge will then remain where the grand evacuating armies of the rebellion can make "their last stand?" There will be one. They can fall back to the original starting point of their peripatetic Government, their first capital, Montgomery, Ala., and on the spot where the misbegotten thing was born, bury out of sight the foul remains of the rebellion.

FOREIGN AFFAIRS.

Our European advices come down to May 7. The distress existing in the manufacturing districts of France and England is of a very serious character, and that neither government could devise any home means for its relief. Our advices allege that in France it had become even dangerous to the throne, and would be more aggravated in this direction daily unless the capitalists could receive a supply of cotton and the export trade to the United States be improved.

Under these circumstances it is generally conceded that Napoleon has made some overtures to the British Cabinet, asking its support in a scheme for putting an end to the rebellion in this country. The writers all connect the late visit of M. Mercier, the French Minister in Washington, to Richmond, with this subject. The Paris Patrie of the 4th instant asserts that that gentleman had a long interview with Jefferson Davis, and that President Lincoln was well aware of the political character of his mission, but the journalist does not intimate under what form the intervention offer is to be presented.

The Edinburg Scotsman, however, says that the Emperor will soon address a remonstrance to both the Northern and Southern Governments on the duration and effects of the war. This remonstrance, it is said, will be designedly offensive to our Government, should hostilities be continued after its reception; and that then the Emperor will propose that a vote be taken by States on the question of final separation or re-union, the vote to be conducted on his favorite Italian plan of "universal suffrage."

England, it is said, will not join the Emperor in any such scheme.

Forty deaths from destitution have been reported by the Irish Coroners from one district of that island. The cases were submitted to the House of Commons by Mr. Maguire, M. P. A Spitalfields (England) weaver has just died from starvation. The report of the case is melancholy. He worked independently and manfully at his loom, the earnings of himself and his wife being only one dollar and a quarter a week, until he sank with hunger and died in a few minutes. His family had sold and pawned all their clothing sooner than go to the poorhouse. All this suffering is attributed in England to the war in America, and the working people were becoming greatly agitated on the subject.

LATER FROM EUROPE.

The steamship Great Eastern, Captain Walter Payton, which left Milford on the afternoon of the 7th instant, arrived at New York at 1 o'clock on the 17th, with passengers. Her news is two days later.

The London Times, of the 5th inst., in an editorial on American affairs, says:

Sooner or later the Federal taxes must be actually collected, and then will come the test of public failure. So long as the Federals are not absolutely winners, they are losers; whereas, so long as the Confederates are not actually subdued, they may regard themselves as winning. These are conditions which counterbalance the superiority of the North in its resources and magnitude of its armies.

A dispatch from Madrid of May 4, says:

According to advices received here from Havana to the 8th of April, Juarez had ordered Generals Piquon, Uniyez and Negrete to be shot. The Spanish Government is about to send a reinforcement of four thousand soldiers to Havana as a precautionary measure.

Accounts from Cherbourg state that the French iron-plated frigate Couronne had arrived there after an excellent passage from Belleisle. During the passage her eight fires were lighted, and she performed the one hundred marine leagues in twenty-five hours, with a heavy sea running from the west, which considerably impeded her speed. The Couronne is now lying alongside the iron-plated frigate Normandie, whose first trial has been so successful. The two frigates are shortly to make a trial trip together, in order that their relative capacity may be compared.

The London Critic says:

Mr. Geo. Hamilton, editor of the London American, has resigned his office in order to give his attention exclusively to American law and agency business in London. The editorial conduct of the London American will hereafter be under the sole direction of Mr. A. W. Bostwick, who has had the practical management of that department during the past year, when Mr. Hamilton was away on a visit to the United States.

The number of season ticket holders at the Great Exhibition on Saturday, the 3d inst., was estimated at 12,000.

Gen. Guyon will shortly be nominated a Senator of France.

HIGHLY IMPORTANT NEWS.

New Orleans Again Open to the World.

President Lincoln's Proclamation.

The Latest War Intelligence.

Arrival of the Ocean Queen, with New York Dates to the 18th May.

The steamship Ocean Queen, with provisions for the army, and dispatches for General Butler, arrived this morning, with New York dates to the 18th of May. The steamer Connecticut, with a full mail, and the great steamer Constitution, with troops, are in the river.

The latest news from Gen. McClellan's army is that he is pushing on as fast as practicable. General Wool was in Norfolk on the 17th, and is about to move his headquarters from Fortress Monroe to that city.

A dispatch was received at the War Department on the 17th, from Col. David Campbell, of the Fifth Cavalry, dated at Williamsburg, and endorsed by Gen. McClellan, to the effect that on Friday our whole fleet of iron gunboats—the Monitor, Galena, Naugatuck, Aroostook and Port Royal—were repulsed from Fort Darling, on the James river, seven miles below Richmond. This intelligence came from Lieut. Morris, of the Port Royal, who sent to Williamsburg for assistance to bury the dead. The 100 pound gun of the Naugatuck exploded at the first fire. Seventeen were buried on shore, and it is said that a number of wounded are on board the boats, some of which have returned to Jamestown Island, near Williamsburg.

The only news from Gen. Banks's division is contained in a dispatch from Brig. Gen. Geary, received at the War Department, dated from Rectortown on Friday, to the effect that a portion of a company of infantry belonging to his command had a skirmish with a large body of rebel cavalry, numbering from three hundred to six hundred, at Linden, in which the Union troops were overpowered. Gen. Geary says that Gen. Shields also had a skirmish with the same party.

The dispatch from Commander Davis, of the Mississippi gunboat squadron, to the Navy Department, furnishes another evidence of the daring and efficiency of our river navy. Eight iron clad rebel steamers, four of them fitted with rams, advanced up the river at Fort Wright on the 10th inst., and made an unexpected attack on Capt. Davis's flotilla; but the vigor with which his men met the enemy was too much for them. Two of the rebel boats were disabled almost at the opening of the conflict and drifted down the river, while a 50-pound rifle shot, fired by Com. Walke, went through the boilers of another and put her *hors du combat*. The result was that the rebels withdrew their boats very hastily to a point below the fort.

Gen. Pope's division has advanced to within three miles of Corinth. Deserters say that disaffection exists to an alarming extent among the Tennessee and Missouri regiments in Beauregard's army, who are contending that they have nothing to fight for, as their States are already restored to the Union.

A portion of the celebrated Jeff. Thompson's guerrilla band has been captured near Bloomfield, Mo. The captives number 100, half of whom gave themselves up voluntarily.

The President has issued his important proclamation declaring the ports of Beaufort, Port Royal and New Orleans open for commercial intercourse after the 1st of June, except for the export and import of goods contraband of war, and of information calculated to give aid and comfort to the enemy. Secretary Chase has also issued a circular, based upon the President's proclamation, defining the mode of obtaining licenses from the collectors of customs, under which vessels can enter and sell from these ports. We give Mr. Chase's paper in full:

Treasury Department, May 12, 1862.

First—To vessels clearing from foreign ports and destined to ports opened by the proclamation of the President of the United States of this date—namely, Beaufort, in North Carolina, Port Royal, in South Carolina, and New Orleans, in Louisiana. Licenses will be granted by Consuls of the United States upon satisfactory evidence that the vessels so licensed will convey no persons, property or information contraband of war either to or from said ports, which licenses shall be exhibited to the Collector of the port to which said vessels may be respectively bound, immediately on arrival, and, if required, to any officer in charge of the blockade; and, on leaving either of the said ports, every vessel will be required to have a clearance from the Collector of the Customs, according to law, showing that there has been no violation of the conditions of the license. Any violation of the said conditions will involve the forfeiture and condemnation of the vessel and cargo, and the exclusion of all parties concerned from any further privilege of entering the United States during the war for any purpose whatever.

... May, 1862, opening the ports of Beaufort, N. C., Port Royal, S. C., and New Orleans, La., with the regulations of the Secretary of the Treasury governing the trade with the said ports. In view of the said proclamation, and in pursuance of the regulations referred to, you are hereby authorized to grant clearance and license to vessels to proceed to any of said ports under the following restrictions.

Before granting any such clearance and license, you will require the master of such vessel to exhibit to you a manifest or descriptive statement of his cargo and a list of the passengers and crew, and to verify the same by his oath or solemn affirmation, and you will fully satisfy yourself that said vessel is intended in good faith for a lawful trade, and will in no wise directly or indirectly violate the provisions of the aforesaid proclamation and the regulations referred to.

You will insert in such clearance the following:

Master of the ——, of ——, having exhibited to me a manifest or descriptive statement of his cargo, and a list of the passengers and crew, and having verified the same by his oath or solemn affirmation; and I having satisfied myself that the said vessel is intended in good faith for a lawful trade; now, therefore, by the authority of the Secretary of the Treasury, and in pursuance of a proclamation of the President of the United States, and the regulations of the Secretary of the Treasury, issued May 12, 1862, permission is granted to the said vessel to proceed to the port of ——, in the State of ——, and to leave said port for any lawful destination on the conditions hereinafter mentioned to wit: That the said vessel will convey no persons, property, or information contraband of war, either to or from said port, and that the clearance or license shall be exhibited to the Collector of Customs at the said port of ——, immediately on arrival, and, if required, to any officer in charge of the blockade, and, that the master and all persons concerned in the management and control of the vessel shall faithfully comply with the revenue laws and regulations of the United States, and with the conditions of this clearance and license.

The violation of any of the conditions of this clearance will involve the condemnation and forfeiture of the vessel and cargo, and the exclusion of all parties concerned from any further privileges of participating in the trade thus opened by proclamation of the President of the United States. The officers of vessels-of-war and all other persons will respect the clearance and license, and permit the said vessel to proceed on her lawful voyage unmolested, while prosecuting the same in conformity with its conditions. In all clearances given prior to the 1st of June you will insert the further proviso that the vessels so cleared shall not enter any of the said ports previous to the 1st of June, on penalty of forfeiture of the vessel and cargo.

I am, very respectfully, your obedient servant,
S. P. Chase,
Secretary of the Treasury.

The proclamation of Gen. Hunter, declaring all the slaves in Georgia, Florida and South Carolina free, has made a great sensation in Washington. The New York Herald says "President Lincoln has expressed the utmost dissatisfaction and indignation at the course of Gen. Hunter, while at least four members of the Cabinet sustain that General. The President, however, is reported to be determined to meet the issue thus forced upon him in the spirit which has governed him all through the war; and, whether supported by his Cabinet or not, will act consistently with his previously expressed opinions and intentions. It is confidently stated that Gen. Hunter will be recalled, and his proclamation will be ignored forthwith."

The following order has been issued by the President, thanking Gen. Wool for the capture of Norfolk:

Washington, May 16, 1862.

The skillful and gallant movements of Major General John E. Wool and the forces under his command, which resulted in the surrender of Norfolk and the evacuation of the strong batteries erected by the rebels on Sewell's Point and Craney Island, and the destruction of the rebel iron-clad steamer Merrimac, are regarded by the President as among the most important successes of the present war. He therefore orders that his thanks as Commander-in-Chief of the army and navy be communicated by the War Department to Major General John E. Wool and the officers and soldiers of his command, for their gallantry and good conduct in the brilliant operations mentioned.

By order of the President.
Made at the city of Norfolk, on the 11th day of May, 1862.
Edwin M. Stanton, Secretary of War.

The Senate has confirmed the nomination of Brevet Major General Wool to be Major General of the army, for gallant conduct on the 10th of May, in taking the city of Norfolk, and for other gallant services.

A dispatch to the War Department from Gen. Mitchel, dated at his headquarters, Huntsville, Ala., contains the encouraging intelligence that a portion of his force, under Gen. Negley and Col. Little, had driven the rebels across the Tennessee river, taken possession of Rogersville, captured a portion of the ferry boats, and, having proceeded to Shoal creek, seized the bridge and ferry below the mouth of that stream. Gen. Mitchel continues to say: "No more troops will enter from that region, and we have now upon this side of the river twelve or fifteen hundred cavalry of the enemy, in bands of three or four hundred, whom we will endeavor to hunt down, destroy or capture. The gunboat which I have extemporized will be ready for service to-day, and I will soon be able to pay my respects to the enemy on the eastern side of the region under my command."

We have the proceedings of the great Union meeting held by the citizens of Tennessee in the Hall of Representatives at Nashville, on the 12th inst. and succeeding days. Addresses were made by Gov. Johnson and others. There were loud cries for "Polk!" Polk!" and Col. Wm. H. Polk, of Columbia, brother of ex-President Polk, came before the Convention. He said:

Fellow Citizens—As the hour is approaching that is usually devoted to dining, and as you have already been listening to several interesting speeches, I propose that we now adjourn until after dinner.

Cries of "No!" "No!"

Col. Polk. Then you prefer dining on patriotism. (Laughter and cheers.) Col. P. proceeded to say that a year ago he did not know whether it would be a year or ten years before he could again address an audience in Tennessee. He cleaved to be in Nashville when the State was stampeded out of the Union. The time has come, said Col. P., when one or the other must be put down; when the loyal or disloyal must triumph. There is no half-way in the matter. Our heel must be put upon the necks of the enemy, or their heel will be put upon our necks. We must keep them down until they ask forgiveness for their transgressions of the father who has given them all they have possessed. They must go down. (Voice—"to the bottom of the ocean.") Aye, and deeper than that, (pointing below,) if Satan will take them. (Laughter.)

NEWS FROM GENERAL BANKS' CORPS.

Skirmish With the Enemy's Cavalry at Rectortown.

Washington, May 17, 1862.

The following is extracted from a dispatch to the Secretary of War by Colonel John W. Geary, dated

Rectortown, Va., May 16, 1862.—A company of infantry of my command was yesterday ordered to Linden, to remain stationed there. A detachment of seventeen men, guard to the company wagon, reached there a short time before the main body of the company, which was on a train. They were attacked by a body of cavalry, variously estimated at from three to six hundred, coming upon them from four directions. Our men resisted them, keeping up a sharp fire under shelter of the depot, which was riddled with bullets. My men were overpowered. One was killed and fourteen taken prisoners, three of whom were wounded, when the enemy hastily retired, under fire and with some loss. I have been informed that a portion of General Shields' command had a skirmish with them.

John W. Geary, Brig.-Gen. Commanding.

DISPATCH FROM GEN. M'CLELLAN.

Camp, Nineteen Miles from Williamsburg, May 11, 1862.

Hon. E. M. Stanton, Secretary of War:

Without waiting for further official reports, which have not yet reached me, I wish to bear testimony to the splendid conduct of Hooker's and Kearney's divisions, under command of Gen. Heintzelman, in the battle of Williamsburg. Their bearing was worthy of veterans. Hooker's division for hours gallantly withstood the attack of greatly superior numbers, with very heavy loss. Kearney's arrived in time to restore the fortunes of the day, and came most gallantly into action.

I shall probably have occasion to call attention to other commands, and do not wish to do injustice to them by mentioning them now. If I had had the full information I now have in regard to the troops above named when I first telegraphed, they would have been specially mentioned and commended. I spoke only of what I knew at the time, and I shall rejoice to do full justice to all engaged.

Geo B McClellan,
Major General Commanding.

SOUTHERN NEWS.

Chicago, May 17.—A special dispatch from Cairo says:

The steamer Shingiss, with forty Memphis refugees, has arrived. They report that hundreds of others are making their way North as best they can.

Governor Morton and Adjutant General Noble, of Indiana, arrived to day.

Cairo, May 17.—The steamer Diligent, from Hickman, brought up a second load of refugees from Memphis and other points South to-day. All tell the same story of hardships endured in traveling on foot through the woods and swamps, and subsisting on such provisions as could be carried in their pockets. The party is almost entirely composed of men in the prime of life. They bring Memphis papers of the 13th inst.

We learn from the telegraphic columns of these papers that Pensacola was evacuated on the 12th. On the morning of that day the batteries of Santa Rosa Island, together with the fleet, commenced shelling the works, but no response was made. After a short but vigorous cannonade a flag of truce was sent ashore to discover the cause. No enemy whatever was found. The Union troops were to take possession the following day. No mention is made of the direction taken by the rebels.

The evacuation of Yorktown and Norfolk are pronounced strategical movements, by no means indicating a rebel defeat. Williamsburg is claimed as a rebel victory. According to their accounts the Yankees were repulsed with great loss.

Refugees say that officers from Corinth, who are frequently in Memphis, complain bitterly of the loss the Southern cause sustained by the delay of General Halleck in making an attack upon them. Beauregard has been ready for a week. Every day that passes weakens him. He has received all the reinforcements that it is possible for him to procure except raw levies, while sickness rages throughout his camp to an alarming extent.

Beauregard has placed an imperative embargo on letter writing from his camp. No soldier is permitted to send any written communication to his friends.

The whole country from one hundred miles below Corinth has been swept to obtain supplies for the rebel army, and is now nearly exhausted. Serious embarrassments from this cause are anticipated.

Arrangements have been effected between Gen. Halleck and Beauregard for an exchange of surgeons. One hundred and fourteen prisoners were sent on by Beauregard to day under a flag of truce, borne by Col. Pegram, of the Army of Western Virginia. Not only these prisoners, but others have been confined at Columbus, Mississippi. Some of them were taken in Missouri last summer. Before leaving Corinth, one of them was recognized by one of Price's men as a member of the Twenty fifth Illinois, paroled at Lexington, and Beauregard ordered him to be heavily ironed.

The Union people in Memphis are reported sorely dispirited at the delay of our fleets. Many, in anticipation of their arrival, have been emboldened to the utterance of Union sentiments, which got them into serious trouble.

Speaking of the fall of Norfolk, the Memphis Avalanche of the 13th inst. says:

"But worse than all, the Virginia, on which we so confidently rested, was burned at Craney Island on Saturday night. Such is the tenor of the brief but painful intelligence flashed over the wires."

There were three cases of yellow fever at New Orleans at last accounts—two at the Charity Hospital and one in the French Hospital.

The Avalanche says it has been formally decided that Savannah is never to be surrendered.

The Provost Marshal of Memphis has received instructions from the military authorities to take Confederate notes as currency, and to arrest as disloyal all persons who refuse to receive them in ordinary business transactions.

Flour was quoted at $20, $21 and $22; bacon, 30c. for sides and hams; sugar, 6c.; molasses, 25c.; of cotton and tobacco no sales, receipts or shipments; corn, $1 40; oats, $1 25.

"Notwithstanding the Federal progress," says the Avalanche, "we feel all confidence that Magruder will get to Richmond some time before McClellan." Advances it thinks our real and best security. It urges money holders to invest in real estate.

NEWS FROM WASHINGTON.

REPORTS FROM GENS. HALLECK AND M'CLELLAN'S ARMY.

Washington, May 17, 1862.—Advices from General Halleck's army, dated yesterday, and from General McClellan's army, dated to-day, have been received at the War Department. The former was in close proximity to the enemy, but no engagement had taken place. The latter was concentrating and bringing up supplies preparatory to a movement.

MEETING OF THE CABINET—REPORTS RELATIVE TO THE ...

... of the policy enunciated at the beginning of the war and has maintained ever since, however beset by those who have tried every means in their power to turn him from the line of conduct he prescribed for the administration.

EXECUTION OF THE FUGITIVE SLAVE LAW.

Since yesterday eight or ten fugitive slaves have been returned to their claimants. It is estimated that there were in Washington recently about a thousand slaves, principally from Prince George's, Maryland, adjoining the District. At least forty slaveholders from that county were at the Court-house to-day, filing their petitions for reclamation. The runaways—in some cases as many as twenty one—are claimed by a single person. In several instances, after the Court had issued the necessary writs, the Marshal and his deputies were unable to find the fugitives, who, having, by some means, been informed of the judicial process, removed beyond the reach of arrest.

INTERESTING STATEMENTS OF REBEL PRISONERS.

The rebel prisoners who are here express astonishment at the treatment they receive. They say that they are themselves heartily tired of the war. They enlisted for one year, and at the expiration of their term of service they expected to be discharged; but this was refused. They were not even permitted to change the arm of service they had adopted, and were compelled to return to duty under menace of being shot without even being allowed a court martial. They have a poor opinion of the North Carolina regiments, which are said to have been always ready to shun the post of danger, and to accept special duty in the rear whenever a battle was regarded as imminent. These regiments were esteemed the pets of the rebel leaders to the cost of the rest of the rebel army. While in the rebel service they were permitted to read no news from the North. They were told that the Yankees would give no quarter in battle, and thought that they would suffer less to die on the field than to fall into the hands of the Federals. Some of them contrast their comfortable quarters here, as prisoners, with those assigned to the Federal prisoners in Richmond, and draw from this fact alone conclusions far from favorable to the rebel leaders. Many of these prisoners have signified their willingness to take the oath of allegiance. It is probable they will be released on this condition.

Flag Raising.—The Customhouse was yesterday adorned with a new American flag. "Long may it wave over the home of the free and the land of the brave." It was raised at 8 o'clock, in presence of General Butler and his staff, (who saluted it uncovered) and Colonel Birge's 13th Connecticut volunteers—the finest regiment in the city. We had a salvo of artillery from Thompson's 1st Maine battery, and Col. Jones's band discoursed sweet music.

COMMERCIAL INTELLIGENCE.

NEW YORK MARKET.

Friday, May 16—6 P. M.

Breadstuffs—Flour—The market was steady, with a fair demand from the trade. State brands, though unchanged in prices, were firm. The sales footed up about 18 000 bbls., closing within the range of the following quotations:

Superfine State	$4 40@$4 60
Extra State	4 70@ 4 80
Superfine Western	4 40@ 4 60
Common to choice extra Western	4 65@ 5 25
Canadian	4 70@ 5 25
Southern mixed to good superfine	5 00@ 5 60
Extra do.	5 70@ 6 75
Good to choice family do.	6 75@ 7 25
Rye Flour	3 00@ 4 10
Corn Meal, Jersey and Brandywine	2 80@ 3 15

Canadian flour was in fair request, with sales of 1,600 bbls., closing within the range of the above quotations. Southern flour was without material change in quotations, closing at our figures, while the sales embraced about 1,200 bbls. Rye flour was in fair demand at our quotations. Corn meal was firm at our figures, with sales of 600 bbls. Wheat was irregular; common grades were heavy and lower, while prime to choice lots were not plenty and firmly held. The sales embraced about 75,000 bushels, at $1 05@$1 08 for Chicago spring, $1 04@$1 06 for Canada, $1 05@$1 11 for Milwaukee club, $1 14@$1 18 for red State, $1 38 for choice white Michigan, in store, and $1 35 for fair white Kentucky. Barley was quiet and heavy. Barley malt was in moderate request, with sales of 700 bushels at 94c. per 34 lbs. Oats were more active and in good demand, at 38@40c. for Canadian and Western, and at 41@41½c. for State. Corn was firm and in fair demand, with sales of about 50,000 bushels at 52@52½c., in store, for Western mixed, and at 53@53½c. for do., delivered, and 55c. for Jersey yellow.

Coffee.—The market was steady, and sales limited at unchanged prices.

Cotton.—The market was firmer and more active, with sales of 1109 bales, closing stiff on the basis of 27½@28c.

Freights.—Rates were somewhat less buoyant and active. To Liverpool 13,000 bushels of corn, in bulk, were engaged at 8½d.; 23,000 bushels of wheat at 9d., in bulk; 3,300 bbls. flour at 2s 10½d., and 700 boxes bacon at 35s. Lard was at 33s. 6d. To London 1500 bbls. flour at 3s. 3d. per British vessel. To Gloucester a British vessel was taken up, to load with 21,000 bushels wheat, at 17d. @ 60 pounds.

Provisions.—Pork—The market was heavy and lower. The sales embraced about 950 bbls. at $12 50 a $12 62½ for mess, closing at the inside figure, and $9 75 a $9 87½ for prime, and at $12 for thin. Beef was quiet and less buoyant, sales of 300 bbls. were made at $11 50 a $13 for plain mess, and $14 50 a $15 for extra do. Lard was heavy, while the sales embraced about 800 bbls. and tierces at 8c. a 8¾c. Cut meats were steady and in fair demand, while sales of 150 packages at 4½ a 4¾c. for shoulders, and 5c. a 5¾c. for hams. Bacon was steady, with sales of 150 boxes at 6¾c. for short ribbed middles. New yellow State butter was in steady request at 16c a 17c., while do. at 11c. a 14c.; Ohio was in limited supply and prices measurably nominal. Old prime State cheese was at 5c., and new do. at 7c. a 8½c.; Ohio was scarce and nominal.

LIVERPOOL COTTON MARKET.

Liverpool, May 5, 1862.

The demand for cotton to day has been moderate only, and the sales do not exceed 5,000 bales, including 300 on speculation and for export. Prices steady.

THE LATEST.

Liverpool, May 6—P. M.

Cotton.—Sales, 4 000 bales. Market dull and unchanged.

Flour declined 6d. Wheat irregular and easier. Corn quiet and steady. Beef had a declining tendency. Pork heavy. Lard quiet and steady.

London, May 6—P. M.

Consols 93¼@94. American securities quiet and steady.

French Experiences in Richmond.—A New York paper has quite a list of anecdotes in connection with the late visit of the French Minister to Richmond, among which we find the following:

The French Minister and several officers, who have just returned from Richmond, are extremely cautious in speaking about what they learned during their visit. Upon two points, however, they freely talk—the confidence and the poverty of the rebels. All with whom they came in contact, high and low, declared that of eventual success there was no doubt. They had won one great victory at Shiloh, and were sure of winning one at Yorktown.

CITY ITEMS.

The Crevasse.—The apprehension which prevailed for several days past on account of the ... in the "Garden District," seems to-day to ... allayed. There was "a mighty rush of wa... it had to yield at last to the superior str... muscle of the large number of men who we... work by the military and civic authorities. ... is also believed to be receding, and we trus... the present the danger of crevasses is over. ... Surveyor, meantime, reports that he is en... strengthening the levees wherever they give ... weakness.

Madame Rumor.—For several hours this m... firing of a salute, in honor of the elevation of t... States flag to a more conspicuous position ... Custom House, gave rise to a great variety of ... some very preposterous, of course, and ... cudgeled by paid labor from shallow pates. ... ferred that a naval engagement was taking p... by; some had it that it was the new Collect... Port had arrived; but the whole affair soon ... smoke.

Inquest.—Coroner Beach yesterday held a... over the body of Thomas U. Laster, who w... dead in the Fourth District Station-house on ... last. The testimony in the case showed th... was under arrest, and while being taken to the ... he stabbed the policeman (Wilkinson) sever... S. Sparkman, to save Wilkinson, struck Last... head with a stick; and the verdict of the ... that the death of Laster resulted from that bl...

Drowned.—A soldier named Bates, of the ... Hampshire Regiment, was accidentally drown... New Canal, near the Half-way House, yester... noon. He had a companion, a shoemaker of ... who was also drowned at the same time.

Provost Marshal's Office, May 28

The following persons, applicants for pos... the Police, are requested to assemble at the ... House of the Second District, Jackson Squar... day, 29th inst., at 9 o'clock A. M.

Jonas H. French, Provost M...

Adler Edward	Koster Michael
Ahrens Williams	Kolmar D R
Abbe John	Lanch Joseph
Adams P August	Loyd Thomas
Alcain Manuel	Linehan Denis
Alyon A	Lux Jacob
Ajellolo Francis	Lay Joseph
Allen Alexander	Lardito J
Borone Samuel	Michel Charles
Braun Joseph	Moulton William
Bierme Ferdinand	Murphy David
Buckly Daniel	Miller Conrad
Bligin Thomas	Marsel J W
Brandlon Charles	Bertrand Peter
Borgia Thomas	Mass George
Babylon Anthony	McCarthy John
Bose August	Monigal David
Coyf C	Nicholas John
Lartigue F A, Sergeant	Orr John
Rodrigues E A, Day Police	O'Neale John
Connor James	Piotrowske John
Carr A	Paris Theodore
Champ F	Sweet E
Cassidy L	Sirs W
Castelli John	Schlolf Hugo
Couvret Frederick	Palet Pire
Carberg Daniel	Brew Davis
Daterman John	Pirviera Vincent
Didway John W	Perrault Hypolite
Drus Alexandre	Quegley Martin
Dereche Joseph	Riffer Frank
Bos H L	Rittenger Daniel
Dreasel W G	Scanlon T T
Dunn Michel	Saunders Charles
Dominick A	Sheridan Patrick
Easton Frank	Strohan John
Evans Michael	Sullivan John
Flangnan Thomas	Thilson A
Finn J A	Voery Henry
Frank Simons	Wilson W
Gunter Aloys	Welp Bernard
Gotta Williams	Walsh John
Goodman B	Walsh Thomas
Grawley S W	Pelissier Louis J, corporal.
Grimsale Conrad	Wagner V
Gallagher John A	Weddell John M
Halnroth H	Wilken Louis
Kunger William	Welch Conrad
Hayes F	Yalba Julius
Haslan William C	Gonzales A
Hoon Mathies	Gonzales L A, night...
Holton Peter	Bertin E O, 1st Lieu... Second District.
Hasifelts A	ma...
Kutchen Andrew	
Kolp Louis	

Headquarters Military Commandant's O...
New Orleans, May 27, 186...

General Orders No. 5.

I—The undersigned, having been assigned ... duty of Assistant Military Commandant of the ... New Orleans, directs that hereafter the mor... ports of the several corps composing the milita... of this city be sent in as early as 8 o'clock A. M.

II—The Medical Director at St. James Hosp... cause a consolidated report of the sick under hi... to be made daily at these headquarters, to be ... at 9 o'clock A. M.

III—Commanders of camps, posts or picket ... will cause a most thorough and perfect police ... quarters and grounds. This duty has bee... neglected in more than one case. Lime ca... nished for the use of sinks on the proper requi...

IV—No requisition will be entertained unle... out according to the prescribed form and requi... of the regulations.

Requisitions for ordnance, commissary and q... master's stores and hospital supplies, are each r... to be made out separately.

V—Hereafter colonels and commanders of se... corps will give the countersign to all sentinels o... posted after tattoo. All enlisted men found ... quarters after tattoo will be arrested and retain... the next morning, when the old officer of the d... see that they are sent with a written memoran... their offenses to their several regiments.

Company officers will not be allowed to ... their company or quarters during the day fo... than one hour, except with the written consent ... commanders. Commanders only, of regime... corps, are authorized to sign such passes.

All officers found away from their quarte... tattoo, without a written pass from the proper ... ity, will be arrested by the patrols and sent t... quarters in arrest. The officer commanding ... will each morning make a statement of the c... stances attending the arrest, &c.

VI—At least one commissioned officer to eac... pany throughout the command will at all times b... their company.

By order. Col. N. A. M. Dudley,
Assistant Military Command...
Edwin Ilsley, A. A. A. General.

MARINE INTELLIGENC...

PORT OF NEW ORLEANS.

Office of the Daily Delta, Thursday Morning, May 29, 1...

CLEARED YESTERDAY.

Ship E W Farley, Nichols, for Boston.

ARRIVED YESTERDAY.

VESSELS FROM SEA.

U S steamship ... from New York 18th ins... Nichols ... Mdse ...

U S steamer Mississippi, ... from Key West ...

Chapter 5

Occupied and Dishonored: New Orleans, 1862

In May 1862, as Northerners fumed over the official report on the barbarities at Manassas, they were also basking in the news of a plum Union victory—the capture of the Confederacy's premier city, New Orleans. It was the capstone event in a spring offensive that saw the Union take important strides toward accomplishing one of its main strategic objectives, regaining control over the Mississippi River. Along with maintaining the coastal blockade, commanding the river was an essential part of the Union's "anaconda plan," by which it hoped to surround and strangle the Confederacy into submission.[1]

The fall of New Orleans was several months in the making and demonstrated the military wisdom of Abraham Lincoln in pursuing simultaneous operations on multiple fronts. Through carefully coordinated assaults that combined land forces with naval power, the Union captured Forts Henry and Donelson in northern Tennessee in February 1862, and then proceeded to move upon Nashville, which became the first Southern state capital to surrender. Six weeks later, the Union started making its long-awaited inroads down the Mississippi River by seizing Island No. 10, a Confederate garrison situated near the adjoining corners of Missouri, Tennessee, and Kentucky. With this string of victories, the Union reasserted control over much of Tennessee and stood poised to take on Memphis.

Faced with the crisis in Tennessee, the Confederacy had to make a choice on how to distribute and utilize its limited military resources. Strengthening the defenses at Memphis required transferring forces away from New Orleans and possibly leaving that vital port vulnerable to the enemy. Yet it was a decision that Jefferson Davis did not hesitate to make. The president left New Orleans with only 3,000 militiamen and a dozen small gunboats to protect it, banking all of his faith on the notion that Forts St. Philip and Jackson, which guarded the mouth of the Mississippi River, were

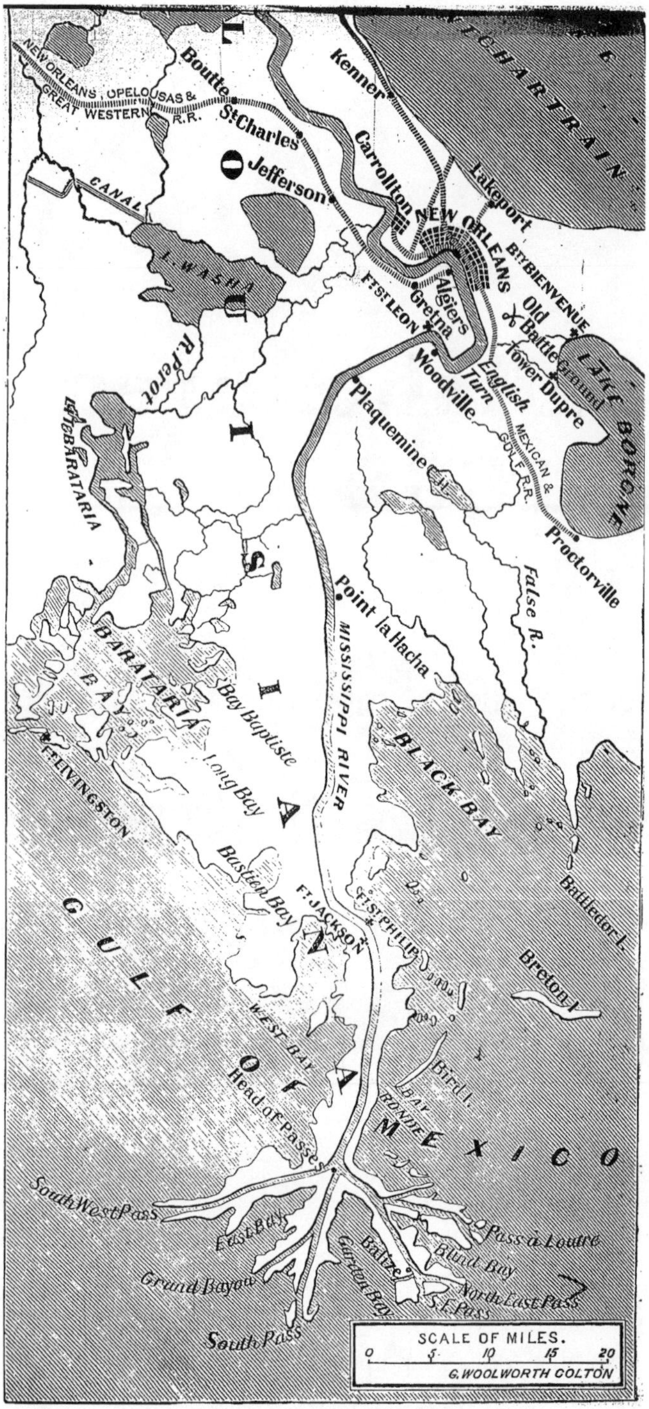

Frank Leslie's Illustrated Newspaper, May 10, 1862. Map of New Orleans and the mouth of the Mississippi River, showing the position of Forts Jackson and St. Philip.

impregnable and would blow any approaching Yankee fleet out of the water.

This was the kind of strategic opportunity and military challenge that appealed to Admiral David Farragut, a lifelong man of the sea and a veteran of both the War of 1812 and the Mexican War. Farragut's plan was to use overwhelming firepower to exploit the Confederacy's thinned defenses. After leaving the East Coast with a fleet of over forty vessels, and with transports carrying 15,000 troops under General Benjamin F. Butler, Farragut neared the Louisiana forts by mid-April and proceeded to shell them with mortar fire for a week. Frustrated by the slowness and inconclusiveness of this mortar assault, Farragut changed tactics and on April 24 elected to run the gauntlet. On his orders, two Union gunboats smashed a gap through a defensive boom that blocked passage beyond the forts, enabling the other vessels to slip through. Although the gunners at Forts St. Philip and Jackson succeeded in sinking one ship, Farragut managed to get the rest of his fleet past them and then steamed his way toward New Orleans, demolishing and dispersing the small convoy of Confederate gunboats along the way.

New Orleans was practically defenseless at this point—dependent as it was on its 3,000 militia troops—so the city was in no position to resist Farragut. In fact, the head of military operations in New Orleans, General Mansfield Lovell, promptly evacuated his soldiers from the city in order to save it from being shelled and possibly destroyed. But the civilians there showed their defiance in other ways. As the Yankees approached, state officials authorized the burning of 15,000 bales of cotton that had been stocked along the levee, determined to prevent such valuable goods from falling into enemy hands. And when Farragut demanded a formal surrender, including the raising of the Stars and Stripes over the mint building, customs house, and city hall, Mayor John T. Monroe refused. He would not make any move that would stain either himself or his community with dishonor. The city council finally did agree to surrender to the Union, but insisted that they yielded "to physical force alone" and still maintained their allegiance to the Confederacy.

This attitude of accepting the situation at hand, while still maintaining the honor of New Orleans and its inhabitants, was exuded by the city papers as well. For the sake of self-interest, they actively encouraged their readers to refrain from doing anything to anger or annoy the Federals, but at the same time, they clearly expected that by being gracious in defeat, they would earn the Union's respect and mercy. Under the circumstances, "defiant language, manifestations of resentment, gratuitous insults offered the Federal soldiers, are not merely uncalled for, but are decidedly wrong and highly imprudent," the *New Orleans Bee* cautioned. "If we desire the respect of our foes, we must show that we deserve it." Similarly, the *New Orleans Crescent* wrote:

> A wise, prudential, dignified bearing in our adversity should be maintained by every one who has truly our good at heart, and no word or act should be committed whereby in the future we may suffer reproach, or tend to the disparagement of the general interest. That events of the day or hour have been of an excitable nature, is past dispute; yet nothing is gained by passion, and still less by persevering in an injudicious course. The city of New Orleans, after a gallant resistance, . . . has succumbed to the sway of the conqueror, and it now only remains for us to demean ourselves with becoming pride and dignity, and thus entitle us to that magnanimity which should ever characterize the truly brave and powerful.
>
> We . . . earnestly solicit our people to strive, with their utmost powers of persuasion, . . . to the maintenance of the of the public tranquility, and the preservation of our dearly-cherished honor and welfare. Let this be done, and we stand forth to the world as heretofore, a people proverbial for all that is truly great and noble.[2]

Outside of New Orleans, others throughout the Confederacy also struggled to maintain their composure. After a spring filled with so many reverses, the ebullience that had overtaken the country in the wake of its victory at Manassas was long gone. Southern papers readily conceded that the loss of New Orleans was a particularly depressing blow; however, they were equally determined that the public not become riddled by anxieties or paralyzed by despair. Calling the city's capture "a great calamity" and "the heaviest blow that has yet fallen upon the country," the *Wilmington Journal* nevertheless insisted that it was "no just cause for despondency," so long as "the people are true to themselves" and prepare for a longer, harder struggle.[3] If Southerners required any motivation to remain vigorously committed to the war, they needed only to recall the devastating consequences of defeat. The theme of "beauty and booty"—which the press had trumpeted so forcefully in the spring of 1861—remained just as pertinent and powerful one year later in reminding Southerners of why they were fighting. In the words of the *Richmond Enquirer*:

> If any of our people are growing faint-hearted and beginning to hesitate between their duty as patriots and the cravings of their animal natures, perhaps a few well-timed reflections as to the personal results of subjugation will recruit their flagging zeal.
>
> Their property will be confiscated to help pay the Yankee war debt, and they and their families will be rendered penniless and homeless. This will be a certain result of subjugation.
>
> Many will be restrained of their liberty and all will be deprived of arms and subjected to military domination and police espionage.
>
> Their families will be liable to insult, maltreatment and every form of oppression.
>
> The most reckless, unruly and profligate brutes will be poured from the great cities of the North into our midst, to indulge their grossest passions. Lust, rapine and murder will riot with impunity.
>
> The negro will be encouraged to insubordination, insolence, plunder and violence and will be protected in them by the Yankee soldiers.

Our little children will grow up under the taunts and kicks and cuffs of the children of the Yankee families that will come in swarms to take possession of our farms and houses.

The Yankee, as the conqueror and the dominant race, will assume the administration of government, State and municipal—will occupy all offices and positions of trust and honor, will make and execute laws, will hold a privileged place in society. . . . Our people will be tabooed, proscribed and degraded—our men made to do the base and menial work of vulgar masters, and our women to play the parts of maids and drudges to the painted and impure jades who will be their mistresses.

These will be some of the certain results of subjugation. Who would consent to submit to such a state of things? Better death than such misery and degradation! Welcome any sacrifice in preference to this! Let us resolve anew, cost what it may of blood, treasure and privation, to defeat and drive back our boastful and rapacious enemies, to preserve our liberties and to establish our independence on enduring foundations. Inspired by our patriotism, we only need to be patient, courageous and self-denying, and the victory will surely be ours.[4]

The Southern press was determined that their readers not forget that victory ultimately was a matter not just of arms but of *will*. Southerners would be subjugated only when they *allowed* themselves to submit. Until then, the Yankee enemy could occupy their cities and attempt to impose its lordly rule upon them, but it would never succeed in really winning them back to the Union:

The fall of New Orleans has not astonished us, but it hangs heavily on our almost drooping spirits. It has inflicted a stunning blow on the Confederacy. . . . But, looking at the darkest side which the picture can possibly present, does it afford any pretext to despair of the Confederacy? Was the successful defence of New Orleans essential to the safety of the Republic or the ultimate triumph of our arms? By no means. It may increase our difficulties, dangers, and privations; it may lead to the sacrifice of more of our noble sons on the blazing altars of our country; but what are all these in view of the only alternative of liberty or slavery which the case presents? "Subjugation is an impossibility." Let these words be cut in letters of brass and nailed on the lintels and door posts of every man's house in the land. Between honor and dishonor, liberty and slavery, life and death, freemen will accept no alternative. Our houses may be pillaged and given to the flames; our property may be wrested from us by mobs of thieves and bands of ruffians, but our honor and the rights of freemen can never be lost, but will survive all our sufferings.

In the fall of New Orleans we yet perceive one blessing. It offers a new incentive to a yet wilder and fiercer resistance than we have yet made to the foe. We must unite our energies. From the seaboard to the centre, from the centre to the mountains, from every hill and valley, from the point of Cape Henry to the mouth of the Rio Grande we must all assemble, take counsel of each other, and determine, by the honor of freemen, by the valor of soldiers, by the blood of our sons already slain, and the chastity of our daughters already violated, that we will achieve our independence.[5]

In summoning this kind of unsinkable resolve, newspaper editors pointedly reminded their readers of the military crises their own forefathers had overcome during the American Revolution. Throughout the spring of 1862, as one Confederate stronghold after another surrendered to Union control, they published hopeful articles detailing how George Washington had rallied his troops to defeat the British, even after suffering the loss of key cities on the Atlantic seaboard. Southerners, who saw themselves as fighting the same battle for freedom that the Revolutionary generation had waged, needed to remain faithful that they too would eventually enjoy the same glories earned by their ancestors:

> The capture of the Crescent City by the Yankees involves a serious loss to the Southern Confederacy. It cuts off an extensive depot of supplies for our army, and curtails our facilities for the manufacture of arms and ammunition. It virtually gives the enemy the control of the Mississippi river, and deprives us of our supplies of sugar and molasses. In short, it is a severe blow to the Confederacy, and an immense advantage for the enemy. But admitting all this, it does not signify that the Confederacy is about to be conquered, or that the rebellion, as our foes are pleased to style our efforts for independence, is about to be crushed. We have time and again asserted that the capture of our seaboard cities . . . would not involve the conquest of the South . . . ; and we need only refer to the history of the American Revolution to sustain this assertion. It is true, the loss of those cities is a sad disaster—deplorable occurrences—but not sufficiently so to cause us to "despair of the Republic."
>
> When New York, Philadelphia, Charleston, Savannah and Augusta were in the hands of the British, our fathers did not succumb to the terrible power of their enemies; but with an unswerving faith in the justice of their cause, they gained fresh ardor, and pursued the struggle for independence with renewed energy and an unfaltering devotion. Shall we prove ourselves unworthy sons of such noble sires? Shall we, with resources so much superior to theirs, falter for one moment in the defence of our liberties and of our nationality? Shall we despond and be cast down because we have met with reverses here and there? Shall we, the freemen of the South, become the hewers of wood and the drawers of water for a despotic and implacable foe? No! the patriotism of the people, refined in the crucible of adversity, must, like pure gold, shine the brighter; their high resolves must be renewed upon the altar of their country's independence, their willingness to bear suffering, to give all and risk all for the Confederacy, must be reaffirmed and made apparent by their acts of patriotism and devotion to the cause.
>
> Away, then, with despondency—with despair—it is a disgrace to freemen—to men struggling to be free.—They know but one resolve, but one shibboleth, and that one is: "Victory or death."[6]

In striving to drive away all overarching anxieties and despondency, the papers were particularly strident in warning civilians living in New Orleans and other Union-occupied areas not to take the oath of allegiance to the United States. As the Union successfully reestablished control over different parts of the Confederacy, it still was unknown whether the federal government would actually try to enforce laws related to treason—laws that established it as a crime punishable by death and that made rebel property liable to confiscation. Benjamin Butler, the commander of the Union's occupying forces in New Orleans, hoped to capitalize on popular fears of reprisal by promising that all Southerners who took the oath would have their lives and their property protected. Those who refused, however, would be treated as enemies. The incentives for taking the oath were therefore tremendous, and the leading voices in the Confederacy worried that at least some citizens—perhaps just out of fear—would take the bait. Even if Southerners uttered the oath disingenuously, it would still give the appearance that their unity was cracking, and would only encourage the Union to continue in its efforts to subdue them. The Southern people, warned the *Memphis Appeal*, could not allow themselves to look divided:

> Firmness of principle and unanimity of sentiment among our people is what we now need more than at any previous period. Particularly is this the case in cities and districts that may be captured or overrun by the ruthless Vandals who seek our subjugation. . . .

> If . . . our whole people are true to themselves, their oaths, their consciences, and duty, they will embarrass and foil the nefarious designs of the enemy, at the same time that they secure his respect. But if any give way, if ever so small a number submit to the demand that they should declare their allegiance to the conqueror, they will stimulate and encourage the Federal authorities to persecute and outrage those who cannot in conscience and honor make such submission.
>
> If we are unanimous, if the whole people stand together, if one sentiment and will prevail, there is little danger of the United States achieving anything valuable or encouraging by overrunning a portion of our country or occupying our cities. It was thus, the people of Moscow and of Madrid bore themselves when their cities were occupied by two hundred thousand French soldiers. Napoleon said he could "conquer their armies, but not their affections."
>
> So let it be with us, even should the fortunes of war possibly prevail against us in the field. The consequences of any attempt to divide our people, or create factions, or excite animosities would be deplorable, indeed, and we may well say that nothing could so add to the horrors and humiliation of the enemy's presence in our midst as a want of loyalty, resolution, FIRMNESS AND UNANIMITY.[7]

Remaining true to the Confederacy in their hearts, however, was not sufficient; Southern men also had to be ready to defend it with their lives by joining the army. In summoning the country's manpower reserves, the Confederacy had help from a newly minted conscription act, which had been passed by the Confederate Congress only two weeks prior to the fall of New Orleans. The Confederacy's conscription bill was the first national draft ever imposed on American soil, and unlike today, when military draft policies are an accepted part of American life, it was an enormously controversial step. Southerners claimed to be fighting for liberty—for freedom from oppression and for the rights of states to determine their own destinies. A national draft contradicted all of this. It stripped states of their control over local militia units and military resources; even more fundamentally, it divested the Southern people of their freedom of thought and action. Every previous American war had been fought by volunteers—by men who chose of their own free will to go into battle. Now, Southerners were to be *coerced* into military service. The basic provision of the new law was unambiguous: all white men between the ages of eighteen and thirty-five, as well as all of those who had previously enlisted as volunteers, were drafted into the army for three years.[8] Some groups were exempted, including state and national government officials, workers in war industries, foreign citizens, and those who were medically unfit to serve. Southern men also were able to avoid military service by securing a substitute from among one of the exempted groups. Nevertheless, the conscription act still promised to press hundreds of thousands more men into fighting for the Confederacy's survival.

Although the act provoked some anger and indignation, most newspapers supported it, if only grudgingly. Given the capture of New Orleans and the other advances made by the Union along the Mississippi, it was difficult to deny that the Confederacy now needed the service of every man able (but perhaps not exactly willing) to defend it. In Memphis—which was the Union's next target—the city's *Avalanche* threw itself completely behind the conscription law and admonished all Southern men of military age to submit cheerfully to it. With the Union "anaconda" coiling itself around the Mississippi River, there was no time to lose:

> What is our duty now? The huge serpent has wound along through the interior [with] his glittering coils, and is even now gliding over hill and through dark ravine, to sting us to death. . . . We should all be of one heart in this crisis. No cavilings and carpings about the propriety or expediency of this or that

measure, should divert our attention from our stern and solemn duty. We should be ready for any sacrifice. It is our country that is perilled—our common mother. We all owe her our allegiance. We must protect her with a rampart of hearts, all glowing with ardor in her sacred cause. The young, who by the law of conscription, even though they have seen service, must again endure hardships and privations and dangers, should not murmur. The greater glory [will be] theirs when the foe has been baffled of his prey. . . .

Those who have not been to the wars must buckle on their armor, for our country now needs all her sons. Those exempt by law must not stand aloof. They must be ready wherever their country "most needs a soldier."

Let us look hopefully forward. If there be doubters with craven hearts, who would desert their country's banner in her perilous night-time, let them shake with coward tremors for the great future.[9]

The Southern press hoped not only that conscription would enable the Southern states to better defend themselves, but that by adding so many new troops to the ranks, it would empower them to take a more aggressive posture against the enemy. In the wake of the fiasco at New Orleans, some Southerners had begun to question the wisdom of allowing the war to be fought on Southern soil, amid Southern cities and civilians. Objectively, the Confederacy's best chance for success was to stay on the defensive—to lure the Union deep into Confederate territory, exhaust its resources, and slowly grind down the will of its people to keep fighting. But as recent events showed, that strategy also meant that Southern cities and fortresses were likely to fall into Union hands. Desperate to halt the Union's progress, and mindful of the growing public concern over losses like New Orleans, the *Savannah Republican* demanded that the Confederacy adopt a new strategy—a quick, sharp offensive into Union territory that would help Northerners realize the terrible costs of continuing the war:

Our system of defensive warfare has squandered the means, wasted the energies, poured out the blood, and well nigh brought to ruin as gallant a people as the sun of heaven has ever shone upon. There is nothing more palpable—more terribly true—than the proposition: we must change our policy, or consent to come under the yoke of the oppressor—at least expose all our cities, and a large portion of the Confederate territory, to Abolition vassalage, and plunder for many months, if not years, to come. The government owes it to the people, to the spirit of liberty, to inaugurate a change, and at once.

This war must be brought to a close. There is but one way of doing it. . . . The enemy must be whipped—he must feel the hardships, the devastation and the terrors of war in his own borders—or there is no peace for the South. If simply driven back, he may still harass us for years. . . . He has already possession of much of our territory, and, holding it, will starve out the rest—let us give up the whole, and let him take possession if he will. Let it be evacuated by our own armies, for he can do us but little more harm than he has already done; and let those armies, by forced marches, bend their course northward, and thus make the enemy's territory the theater of our future strife. . . . Our legions once in Ohio and Pennsylvania, not a Yankee would be left in the South in a week after the movement; and when the enemy overtakes us, we shall have, at least, a fair field to meet him in and no gunboats to annoy and impede our progress.

Yankee homes and firesides might be desolated with fire and sword, as they have desolated ours; their grand capitals and commercial emporiums might be set upon and made to feel what it is to face the terrors of bayonets and cannon; their fair domains, groaning with the wealth of the earth, might, likewise, be razed or turned out to the beasts of the field; their ships might be made to keep aloof from their accustomed ports, and thus teach them the comforts of a blockade; in fine, every fiber of the political body of the North might be made to quiver and throb under the destructive blight of an unjust war, provoked and ruthlessly carried on by themselves. In the consternation that would ensue, we would discover the germ of peace.[10]

Even more than clamoring for an offensive strike, the press demanded that there be no more surrenders. At the start of the war, many voices in the South had proclaimed that it was better to die in defense of liberty than to submit to tyranny. Yet, Southern strategy, and in some cases, Southern military commanders, had failed to live up to that vow. Besides the Union victories in Tennessee, Fort Macon in North Carolina and Fort Pulaski in Georgia both surrendered shortly before New Orleans, and then afterward Forts St. Philip and Jackson yielded as well, making the entire spring campaign extremely costly to the Confederacy. From the perspective of many observers at home, it was now time for Southern men to prove that they were ready to make the ultimate sacrifice. "Rather than submit, let our armies perish," the *Richmond Whig* contended. "What is patriotism, if it cannot dare or die for the freedom of the State?"[11] To encourage soldiers toward this lofty sense of selflessness, several papers published letters from women who flatly demanded it. Disgusted by the recent rash of surrenders by the Confederacy, one female patriot offered these thoughts to the editor of the *Augusta Chronicle & Sentinel*:

Mr. Editor: . . . I have a heavy stake in this war—those nearest and dearest to me, are in the army—one has already given his life [as] a sacrifice. I have always felt that to a people resolved, as I have thought we Southern people were resolved, to die, rather than submit, defeat was almost an impossibility, [and] subjugation, an entire one. Things, however, are now looking dark and weary to me. Conquered by a superior force we possibly might be, . . . but it seems to me that even though conquered we should never submit; that we should die game; that nothing but brute force should wrench our guns from our hands; that we should rather, with a shout of triumph, throw the torch into the magazine which would involve all in a common ruin, than live to yield it up of our own accord. That even in death we should defy our hated enemies, proclaiming with our last breath, our freedom and defiance.

But now, if I read aright, no such heroic feeling animates our bosoms. If we are not subdued, it is something very like it. . . . Fort Donelson, after a noble resistance by the men, was surrendered by the *Generals!* Nashville, the capitol of Tennessee, offered herself through her Mayor to the not conqueror, for, as nobody resisted they were spared the trouble of conquest. . . . No. 10 "surrenders"—immense public stores, cannon, etc., fall into the enemy's hands. Pulaski "surrenders," and a quantity of powder and other ammunitions is left to be used to batter down the houses of the surrendering garrison in old Savannah. Fort Macon "surrenders"—and another heavy loss there. . . .

New Orleans heaps disgrace upon disgrace. With Fort Jackson, garrisoned by men who battled nobly in its defence, still in our possession (although that too has since surrendered,) New Orleans is evacuated by troops placed there for its protection, and the Mayor of our great Southern city writes a letter to the enemy, who demands the surrender of the city—tells him that Gen. Lovell has withdrawn his troops out of regard to the lives of the women and children; adds, the people of New Orleans are a "sensitive people;" and prays him to "spare their susceptibilities!" Countrymen and women, what shall we do? . . . What are our Generals placed in command for? To surrender our cities at the appearance of the enemy, "out of regard to the women and children," or to defend them with their lives? . . . There is not a woman, nor a child—for as the women, so are the children—who would not scorn Gen. Lovell for his tender care for their "susceptibilities." Better die—yes, die,—and far, far, rather would we die, pierced with Yankee bullets than live to be subjected to Yankee outrages. Yes, die. Oh, friends! Men and women of the South! remember, if we are not successful in this war, a fate worse than death is before us. Remember, death to the brave is nothing—disgrace is every thing. . . . Friends, we will conquer, if but true to ourselves; and we must conquer; we must be true; we must be self-sacrificing; we must not count our lives dear to us; our women must set the example, and teach their husbands and sons that a dead hero is dearer than a living coward. Our men must swear rather to die at their posts than yield them up. Our generals must be taught that Southern women and children are made of sterner stuff than General Lovell attributed to those of New Orleans, and would rather perish in the flames of their burning homes than live the vassals of the hated Yankee. "Conquer or Die," must be our war cry. Thus, and thus only, shall we wipe out the disgrace which the surrender of Nashville and New Orleans have brought upon us. Thus, and thus only, shall we conquer. Thus, and thus only, shall we ever be free.[12]

To some extent, the North found this "conquer or die" attitude amusing. People on the Southern home front might say such things, but the men in the Confederate armies—those who actually would have to *do* them—clearly were not so irrational. And there was no reason to doubt that if their military protectors surrendered, southern civilians would follow in tow. When push came to shove, no one really would choose death over submission. As the *New York Times* observed:

The rebels are very fond of saying that they may be *beaten*, but they cannot be *subjugated*. They may lose all their cities, have all their armies defeated, and be driven from every important military position,—and yet, they say, no progress will have been made toward the conquest of the South. They can retire to the mountains, and there protract the contest indefinitely. . . .

Now, all this *may* be true. It depends in some degree, certainly, on the spirit and temper of the Southern people. . . . But that is a point to be tested. They cannot expect us to take it for granted, or to take their word for it, and stop the war on their assurance that victory will do us no good. *We must try it, and see*. Thus far the Southern men of war do not act as bravely as they talk. They fight well enough in the field, but they do not "die in the last ditch," nor fight "till the last man falls," nor do any of the desperate things which they have threatened so loudly in advance. On the contrary, they act very much like other sensible men under similar circumstances. When they are beaten, they surrender. When they cannot hold a position, they leave it. They are not madmen, nor fools. They have not lost their powers of reasoning. . . . There is a great deal of human nature left in these Southerners, after all.

Seeing all these things, we cannot help believing that, when the Southern armies are thoroughly beaten, the Southern rebellion will be crushed. We do not believe that the inhabitants will flee to the mountains, or take refuge in the swamps, or do anything of the kind. When they do, it will be time enough to consider what is to be done about it. . . . But we don't anticipate any such necessity. If the Southern armies now in the field are fairly and finally beaten, and driven into the Gulf States, our troops will hold the frontier; our ships will hold every seaport; our gunboats on the Mississippi will bound the rebellion on the West, our ships in the Gulf and Altantic on the South and East, and our line of bayonets on the North. The rebellion and all who abet it will be *shut up* within that iron chain. . . . There will be but one way open to it, and that is *surrender*.[13]

As a key step toward encircling and suffocating the rebellion, Northerners naturally greeted the capture of New Orleans as their greatest victory yet, and

Republicans and Democrats alike were quick to cheer it. Despite the anti-Union sentiments articulated publicly by the South, Northern papers remained optimistic that by acting generously toward the people of New Orleans, the old bonds between the North and South could be restored. The *Harrisburg Patriot & Union* thus declared earnestly:

> The cheering news from New Orleans diffused general joy throughout the country. Not that a city had fallen—that lives had been lost and property destroyed—but that a position had been achieved which was an important step toward the end. All that tends to the termination of this contest—to restore the Government to its legitimate sphere of action—subdue rebellion and conquer peace—will be hailed with thanksgiving by loyal hearts, though won at any cost. No sacrifice is too great to preserve our country—its Constitution, its Boundaries, its Liberties; hence the victories that will accomplish this, although they come to us through blood, and while the ear is filled with the groans of the wounded and dying, they will be welcomed,—but only as the sad necessity through which our redemption must be obtained. The proud Crescent [New Orleans] has not been humiliated, but elevated, by a return to the glorious banner which has floated over her in all her days of honor and prosperity. . . . And now may we not hope the evil spirit has been exorcised from her bosom and henceforward she will find peace, through love and obedience, in her father's house? The mighty river which bears her wealth and strength will soon hold no enemy upon its banks to the benign Government which stretches forth its arm to protect and save. Let this be realized—let the people at the South realize that the armies under the old starry flag come to bless, not to oppress, and anarchy, hatred and misery will soon give place to order, confidence and plenty, and Heaven's smile will be upon us again as a united and fraternal people.[14]

One of the ways in which the Union sought to "bless" New Orleans was by lifting the Union blockade on it. Certainly, this was a decision that redounded greatly to the benefit of the Northern economy. Farmers in the northwestern states were anxious to regain full access to the Mississippi River for shipping their produce, and merchants throughout the North looked forward to enjoying whatever supplies of cotton, sugar, and molasses New Orleans could now offer them. But reviving the local economy of New Orleans was also essential for pacifying the public mood there. As the Democratic *New York World* pointed out, "nothing expedites the return of the old Union feeling like the resumption of the old business relations." Once Southern consumers had access to goods that had previously been denied to them by the blockade, they would come to appreciate the occupation of their city and welcome reunion. This kind of economic diplomacy, the *World* conjectured, might even undermine public support for the rebellion throughout the South:

> In acquiring New Orleans, the great mart of southern commerce is in our hands. In all probability, there is a large amount of marketable produce in the city still undestroyed. Its people are in most urgent want of a thousand commodities and articles from which the blockade has excluded them. . . . It is very certain, then, that the removal of the blockade of New Orleans by the government would very speedily lead to an active reciprocal trade between that city and those of the North. The commercial connections once re-established, the old political associations would gather strength every day. And all Louisiana, which is immediately dependent upon New Orleans, . . . would feel the same influence. In fact there could be no more effectual means of breaking down the rebellious spirit of the whole planting and trading interests of the confederacy. Mobile and Savannah and Charleston would never, for any length of time, quietly endure the reports of a thriving business in New Orleans while they them-

selves were suffering the last extremities. Nor would the cotton and rice planters remain content to see their own crops given to the flames, or rust with mould, while the sugar planters [of Louisiana] were again on the tide of high prosperity. . . . Remove the blockade, and the change which would follow would strongly impel them to secure the same advantage. We have in New Orleans a fulcrum by which we may soon upset the whole confederate concern, if we manage [it] wisely.[15]

Actually, Unionist sentiment in New Orleans was rare and did not improve with time. Northerners had entered the war believing that the rebellion was an act of "terrorism"—the work of a small cabal of slaveholders, who had manipulated or coerced the Southern masses into supporting them. There was some hope in the North, then, that when the Union took possession of New Orleans, citizens who had been cowed into silence by the rebellion would suddenly emerge to welcome them. For the most part, though, Northerners were disappointed with what they found. While some New Orleans residents seemed friendly, very few took the oath of allegiance, and most seemed downright hostile. One news correspondent in the city reported:

> I have failed to notice any general manifestation of Union sentiment, though instances of individual loyalty have frequently come under my observation. Men of respectability and wealth have visited the federal ships by stealth, going off in the evening when the levee is deserted. Union ladies have sent congratulatory letters to the officers, and not unfrequently we have seen them on the levee at nightfall, slyly waving their handkerchiefs at the officers on the federal vessels. Passing along the street, one is occasionally greeted with a smile of friendliness, but oftener the haughty curl of the lip and the flashing eye betray the malignant spirit which rankles within. The lady who should be seen conversing with a federal officer would be tabooed in the aristocratic circles of New Orleans, and the man suspected of entertaining Union sentiments, is looked upon with suspicion, and hunted by the bloodhounds of the rebellion. While Unionism rests under this ban, the manifestation of disloyalty is open, bold and defiant. We see and hear it everywhere. Elegantly dressed ladies stand on the levee as we pass in boats, and cover their finely chiseled features with their hands, looking at us through their delicate and gem-bedecked fingers. One draws her veil over her face in token of her contempt, and [another] in deep mourning, whose brother, perhaps, has fallen a victim to federal bullets in an unholy cause, turns her back upon you until you have passed, when, womanly curiosity overcoming her anger, she glances over her shoulder to get a sight of a real "live Yankee." All are bitter and crestfallen, and months of federal rule, stern yet mild, must elapse before the Union sentiment will develop itself to any great extent in this city.[16]

The insolence of the people of New Orleans toward their Union occupiers became legendary, particularly the spitefulness of the women. With galling regularity, they snubbed Union soldiers and officers in public, turning their faces away in disgust, spraying epithets at them, and even emptying chamber pots from second-story windows onto their heads. Incensed by such actions and determined to put an end to them, General Butler, as the head of the military government in New Orleans, made a move that subsequently rendered him infamous and detested throughout the South. On May 15, he issued General Orders No. 28, authorizing that "any female" who "by word, gesture, or movement," should "insult or show contempt for any officer or soldier of the United States," would be "treated as a woman of the town plying her avocation"—in other words, treated like a prostitute. What exactly this meant was unclear. Later, Butler would claim that his "Woman Order" was harmless, intended only to remind the gentlemen under his command that the "she-adders

BUTLER'S ORDERS.

The following is the entirety of Butler's Order to the ladies of New O.leans:

NOTICE.—*Headquarters Department of the Gulf, New Orleans,* May 15th, 1862.—General Orders, No. 28.—As the officers and soldiers of the United States have been subject to repeated insults, from the women calling themselves ladies of New Orleans, in return for the most scrupulous non interference and courtesy on our part, it is ordered that, hereafter, when any female shall, by word, gesture or movement, insult or show contempt for any officer or soldier of the United States, she shall be regarded and held liable to be treated as a woman of the town plying her avocation.

TOP *Macon Telegraph,* May 21, 1862. Benjamin Butler's infamous "Woman Order," with its implicit threat to the honor of Southern women, made him universally detested throughout the Confederacy.

BOTTOM *Frank Leslie's Illustrated Newspaper,* May 18, 1861. Portrait of Benjamin Butler.

THE LADIES OF NEW ORLEANS before GENERAL BUTLER'S Proclamation.
After GENERAL BUTLER'S Proclamation.

Harper's Weekly, July 12, 1862.
In support of Butler, this Northern cartoon shows the women of New Orleans before the Woman Order, spitting in the faces of the Union soldiers around them, and then after the order, acting with genteel respect and restraint.

of New Orleans" were not worth their attention or time. Others saw the order in a more sinister light, as a threat to imprison, or perhaps assault, any woman in New Orleans who seemed to act rudely. Even some Union newspapers spoke out angrily against it. Butler's order "is a disgraceful one," the *Louisville Journal* proclaimed. While it might be important to clamp down on public insults against Union soldiers, this had to be done with "vigor but not vulgarity." The *New York Times* agreed and recommended that Butler be "dismissed from the army" for embarrassing the Union and committing "an infamous outrage upon the morality and decency of the country."[17]

There were several Northern papers however, that applauded Butler and maintained that the threat of imprisonment was just what the women of New Orleans deserved for their obnoxious and aggressive behavior:

The order of Gen. Butler in relation to the women who insult our soldiers in New Orleans has been sharply criticized. A gentleman just returned from that city, where he has resided ever since the war broke out, says we can have no conception of the indignities our brave fellows are compelled to suffer at the hands of these fiends in petticoats. All sense of shame and decency appears to have departed out of them. They rival the most degraded of street-walkers, not only in ribaldry, but in obscenity. Women who have been regarded as the pattern of refinement and good breeding, indulge in language toward our officers and men which no decent journalist would dare put into print. Presuming upon the privileges of the sex, they not only assail them with the tongue, but with more material weapons. Buckets of slops are emptied upon them as they pass; decayed oranges and rotten eggs are hurled at them;

BUTLER, THE BEAST, AT WORK.

Southern Illustrated News, April 30, 1864. In Southern eyes, the Woman Order transformed Benjamin Butler into "Beast Butler." He is pictured here as a hyena scavenging among the graves of General Albert Sidney Johnston and Lieutenant Colonel Charles Dreux, fallen Confederate officers buried in New Orleans.

> and every insult that a depraved fancy can invent, is offered to the hated Federals.
>
> The forbearance of our troops, this gentleman says, is wonderful. They endure the jibes and persecutions of these unsexed wretches with a philosophy that nothing can overthrow. But the nuisance was fast becoming intolerable. The offenders were presuming upon the chivalry of troops to commit physical assaults. Something like the order of Gen. Butler became imperative. If women, pretending to be decent, imitated the *conduct* of "women of the town," it was proper that something like the same punishment should be meted out to them.[18]

The Southern response was unanimously fierce. Certain from the very start of the war that the North was fighting for "beauty and booty," they read Butler's order as giving his soldiers a license to commit indiscriminate rape. In their eyes the women of New Orleans were not merely to be jailed for making insults; rather, whenever a Union man felt slighted by one of them, he would have the liberty to treat her literally like a prostitute—to use her for his own sexual gratification. "She may be perfectly innocent of having treated any Yankee with disrespect," the *Richmond Dispatch* exclaimed, yet if accused of giving insult, she is "liable to be made the victim of any Yankee soldier's brutal passions."[19] Consequently, the Woman Order became for the South what the alleged atrocities at Manassas were for the North—proof of the enemy's utter barbarity.

The South's culture of honor made Butler's order particularly offensive. According to the code of Southern honor, female chastity was sacred; any woman who lost it was "ruined" and "fallen." As one Alabama paper affirmed, "If there is one thing from which a Southern woman shrinks as from the deadliest viper, it is [the] thought of dishonor." The dictates of honor also required that men protect their women by responding to such threats with violent retribution.

Southern newspapers therefore abounded with demands for vengeance. Some of these were personalized and directed specifically at Benjamin Butler—"Beast" Butler now, in Southern parlance. "Butler should be assassinated," one Georgia paper commanded. "Some one should brave certain death to accomplish this end."[20] It was a sentiment that others in the Confederacy clearly shared. One Southerner, styling himself as Brutus to Butler's despotic Caesar, sent this suggestion to his local paper, to help hasten the Union general's demise:

> To the Editor of the Mississippian:—As the modern Nero, the brutal, beastly and sanguinary savage, Gen. B.F. Butler, has by virtue of his general order No. 28, dated at New Orleans on the 15th of May, violated the principles of warfare, and as he proposes to outrage the chastity of the women of the South who, by the misfortunes of war, fall into his hands, it is our plain duty to rid our country and the world of the horrid, hideous monster by any means that can be commanded. When a man turns to be an enemy of the human race he forfeits his right to a habitation upon the face of the world; and he who relieves the world of such an unnatural creature is entitled to a monument in the memory of mankind.
>
> Let there be a purse of $10,000 made up and offered for the head of this man Butler, or to any one who will take his life by any means whatever. If the person who kills him should lose his own life by doing so, let the money go to his heirs, or to whoever he may designate. I would suggest that this money be made up in sums of not less than $100.
>
> BRUTUS.[21]

The *Mississippian* embraced this as a wonderful idea. Surprised that "such a festering, loathsome reptile" as Butler had not already been hunted down by the outraged people of New Orleans, the paper was eager to see the general meet his doom, and even pledged to contribute "a small sum" toward the reward money. "Money is no object," the paper declared, "in the removal of a nuisance or monster that stinks in the nostrils of all honorable people." Beyond targeting Butler, the South hoped his Woman Order would stiffen the resolve of its men to fight even more devotedly and valiantly to expel the Yankees from their soil. In this way, the order became a propaganda coup for the Confederacy. Several newspapers published the following appeal—ostensibly penned by the ladies of New Orleans collectively—to the soldiers of the Confederacy, begging for their protection and imploring them to never again surrender defenseless women into the hands of the enemy:

> *An Appeal to Every Southern Soldier—*
>
> We turn to you in mute agony! Behold our wrongs! Fathers! husbands! brothers! sons! we know these bitter, burning wrongs will be fully avenged—*never* did Southern women appeal in vain for protection from insult. But, for the sakes of our sisters throughout the South, with tears we implore you not to surrender your cities, "in consideration of the defenceless women and children."—Do not leave your women to the mercy of this merciless foe! Would it not have been better for New Orleans to have been laid in ruins, and we buried beneath the mass, than that we should be subjected to these untold sufferings? Is life so priceless a boon that, for the preservation of it, *no* sacrifice is too great? Ah no! ah no! Rather let us die with you, oh our Fathers! Rather, like Virginius, plunge your own swords into our breasts, saying "This is all we can give our daughters!"
>
> THE DAUGHTERS OF NEW ORLEANS.
>
> New Orleans, May 24, 1862.[22]

As portrayed in the Southern press, the soldiers of the Confederacy were fighting for more than just victory. They were fighting to protect themselves from being subjected to Yankee tyranny, and fighting to save the women they loved from being attacked,

An Appeal from the Daughters of New Orleans.

We need not commend to the attention of our readers the following simple, touching, beautiful, appeal of the lovely daughters of New Orleans. We could add nothing to its melting pathos. "Every soldier of the South" who reads it, will pant for an opportunity to avenge the wrongs and insults so touchingly portrayed.

AN APPEAL TO EVERY SOUTHERN SOLDIER.

We turn to you in mute agony! Behold our wrongs! Fathers! husbands! brothers! sons! we know these bitter, burning wrongs will be fully avenged—*never* did Southern woman appeal in vain for protection from insult! But, for the sakes of our sisters throughout the South, with tears we implore you not to surrender your cities, "in consideration of the defenceless women and children." Do not leave your women to the mercy of this merciless foe! Would it not have been better for New Orleans to have been laid in ruins, and we buried beneath the mass, than that we should be subjected to these untold sufferings? Is life so priceless a boon that, for the preservation of it, *no* sacrifice is too great? Ah no! ah no! Rather let us die with you, oh our Fathers! Rather, like Virginius, plunge your own swords into our breasts, saying "This is all we can give our daughters!"

THE DAUGHTERS OF NEW ORLEANS.
New Orleans, May 24, 1862.

Charleston Mercury, June 11, 1862.
This public message from "The Daughters of New Orleans," appealing to the sense of honor and duty among Southern men, epitomizes the Confederate response to the Woman Order.

abused, and ruined, for the dangers confronting the women of New Orleans were certain to befall the ladies of every city or hamlet that the enemy should penetrate and occupy. "Grasp, then, your arms with renewed resolution," the *Richmond Whig* exclaimed. There was no greater duty or sacrifice than defending "the mother that bore, the wife that loves, or the sister that cherishes you."[23] This message was especially pertinent for areas of the Confederacy that were imminently in danger of invasion. As Admiral Farragut's forces proceeded up the Mississippi River to contend with the Confederate stronghold at Vicksburg, the Reverend W. W. Lord preached these words to the citizens and soldiers there, warning them of the dire fate that awaited them should they ever fall into Union hands:

> Until this proclamation [the Woman Order] was issued, my fellow citizens and soldiers, there may have been some doubt as to the ultimate intentions of the invaders from the North, in case they should once get possession of that fair domain, the coveted land of the sun—the rich and beautiful South. . . . Whether they intended merely to reduce us to a state of political subordination, . . . or whether they proposed to seize our property and take charge of our domestic institutions, has hitherto been an open question. . . . The question, so far as this proclamation bears upon it, may be considered to have been decided. More than political subordination is intended. More than confiscation and seizure of property; more than the *abolition* of slavery is designed. Slavery is *ordained*, but it is for us. For negro slavery abolished, white slavery is to be established. Such slavery as that to which Russia has reduced Poland—nay worse—such enslavement as was perhaps never before exercised or attempted; a slavery of body and soul for which there is no parallel; and this imposed not only upon their own race, their own blood and color, but upon the women—the matrons and daughters—the most respectable and respected—the LADIES of that race. . . .

History furnishes no example of such infamy; language has no words to express the depth of degradation to which the tame submission to such a threat would sink a people!

Consider the letter of the proclamation, the spirit, or the effect, and it . . . seems incredible. It threatens legal prostitution to every woman of the South, whose dark eye should even involuntarily flash at the sight of a foreign hireling parading the symbols of tyranny . . . in the streets of a Southern city, before the very door of her hitherto sacred dwelling.

Hard always is the lot of the conquered. But was there ever a daughter of Ireland legally prostituted to the English soldier—were it even an Irish peasant girl—because her eye flashed or her bosom swelled, at the sight of the hereditary tyrant? . . .

What motives then, my countrymen, are wanting to make us the bravest of soldiers and most inflexible of patriots? Our interests and our manly honor were in the cause before. The honor of our women is now in it. . . . With the memory of this last great wrong and insult burning in your minds you will go into the battle of Vicksburg. With "guns to the right of us, guns to the left of us,". . . we have here an opportunity to strike a blow which will make the dark eyes of Southern women flash . . . with pride and joy, to hear that their honor has been vindicated.[24]

The loss of New Orleans was for the Confederacy a terrible blow to its political sovereignty and its military effort. But like the defeat at Manssas for the Union, the psychological fallout was no less significant. Butler's Woman Order not only earned him the personal enmity of the South but also affirmed the absolute savageness of the North in the minds of the Southern people. If, for the North, capturing New Orleans was a momentous step forward in conquering the rebellion, for the South, Butler's rule made the notion of reunion seem all the more unthinkable.

Boston Evening Transcript.

HENRY W. DUTTON & SON, PROPRIETORS, TRANSCRIPT BUILDING, 90 & 92 WASHINGTON STREET.......SEVEN DOLLARS PER ANNUM.........SINGLE COPIES THREE CENTS

VOL. XXXV. | BOSTON, FRIDAY EVENING, JANUARY 2, 1863. | NO. 10,030.

PRESIDENT LINCOLN'S PROCLAMATION.

EMANCIPATION OF THE SLAVES IN THE REBELLIOUS STATES.

BY THE PRESIDENT OF THE UNITED STATES OF AMERICA.

A PROCLAMATION.

WASHINGTON, Jan. 1863.

Whereas, on the 22d day of September, in the year of our Lord 1862, a Proclamation was issued by the President of the United States, containing, among other things, the following, to wit:

That on the 1st day of January, in the year of our Lord 1863, all persons held as slaves within any State or designated part of a State, the people whereof shall then be in rebellion against the United States, shall be then, thenceforth and forever free, and the Executive Government of the United States, including the military and naval authority thereof, will recognise and maintain the freedom of such persons, and will do no act or acts to repress such persons or any of them in any effort they may make for their actual freedom; that the Executive will on the first day of January aforesaid, by proclamation, designate the States and parts of States, if any, in which the people therein respectively shall then be in rebellion against the United States; and the fact that any State or the people thereof shall on that day be in good faith represented in the Congress of the United States, by members chosen thereto at elections wherein a majority of the qualified voters of such State shall have participated—shall, in the absence of strong countervailing testimony, be deemed conclusive evidence that such State and the people thereof are not then in rebellion against the United States.

Now, therefore, I, ABRAHAM LINCOLN, President of the United States, by virtue of the power in me vested, as Commander-in-Chief of the Army and Navy of the United States, in time of actual armed rebellion against the authority and government of the United States, and as a fit and necessary war measure, do, on this first day of January, in the year of our Lord one thousand eight hundred and sixty-three, and in accordance with my purpose so to do, publicly proclaimed for the full period of one hundred days from the day above mentioned, order and designate as the States and parts of States wherein the people thereof respectively are this day in rebellion against the United States, the following, to wit: Arkansas, Texas, Louisiana, except the parishes of St. Bernard, Plaquemines, Jefferson, St. John, St. Charles, St. James, Ascension, Assumption, Terrebonne, Lafourche, St. Mary, St. Martin and Orleans, including the city of New Orleans; Mississippi, Alabama, Florida, Georgia, South Carolina, North Carolina, and Virginia, except the forty-eight counties designated as West Virginia, and also the counties of Berkley, Accomac, Northampton, Elizabeth City, York, Princess Ann and Norfolk, including the cities of Norfolk and Portsmouth, and which excepted parts are for the present left precisely as if this proclamation were not issued.

And by virtue of the power and for the purpose aforesaid I do order and declare that all persons held as slaves within said designated States and parts of States, are and henceforward shall be free, and that the Executive Government of the United States, including the military and naval authorities thereof, will recognise and maintain the freedom of said persons; and I hereby enjoin upon the people so declared to be free to abstain from all violence, unless in necessary self defense. And I recommend to them in all cases when allowed to labor faithfully for reasonable wages, and I further declare and make known that such persons of suitable condition will be received into the armed service of the United States, to garrison forts, positions, stations and other places, and to man vessels of all sorts in said service. And upon this act, sincerely believed to be an act of justice, warranted by the Constitution upon military necessity, I invoke the considerate judgment of mankind and the gracious favor of Almighty God.

In witness whereof, I have hereunto set my hand, and caused the seal of the United States to be affixed.

Done at the city of Washington, this first day of January, in the year of our Lord one thousand eight hundred and sixty-three, and of the Independence of the United States of America the eighty-seventh.

(Signed) ABRAHAM LINCOLN.

By the President.

WM. H. SEWARD, Secretary of State.

NEW BOOKS. A very pretty little story, a very elegant poem, is Stoddard's "King's Bell," just published by Carleton, of New York. 'Tis full of pleasant incident and beautiful description; it abounds in passages of great beauty, eloquence and power; its verse has now the sonorous ring of Dryden, then the dainty beauty of Leigh Hunt, and anon the music and exquisite modulation ... is abundantly fulfilled in "The King's Bell," which is, we think, worthy a place beside Leigh Hunt's "Story of Rimini" and Keat's "Eve of St. Agnes." All admirers of Stoddard, all lovers of poetry, should read "The King's Bell." The work is gotten up in a neat and attractive style—for a New York book.

A very dainty little volume, of most exquisite versicles, is Carleton's edition of Aldrich's Poems in "blue and gold." The little tome,—

Of not too large a grasp
For Queen Titania's dainty hand to clasp.

contains some of the prettiest, daintiest, most graceful little poems ever written by an American bard. They are full of the most brilliant fancy and the most poetical conceits. Many of them are

Musical as brooks that run
O'er yellow shallows in the sun.

If Bryant is the American Wordsworth, and Saxe the American Hood, Aldrich is the American Herrick. Indeed there are songs and madrigals in this delectable "little book" that are not unworthy of him who sang so divinely of "Blossoms," "Daffodils" and Roses.

IMPORTANT PROCLAMATION OF GENERAL BANKS.

HEADQUARTERS DEPARTMENT OF THE GULF,
New Orleans, Dec. 24, 1862.

To the People of Louisiana: In order to correct public misapprehension and misrepresentation; for the instruction of the troops of this department, and the information of all parties in interest, official publication is herewith made of the proclamation by the President of the United States, relating to the subject of emancipation. In the examination of this document it will be observed:

I. That it is the declaration of a purpose only—the full execution of which is contingent upon an official designation by the President, to be made on the 1st day of January next, of the States and parts of States, if any, which are to be affected by its provisions:

II. That the fact that any State is represented in good faith in the Congress of the United States, is conclusive evidence, in the absence of strong countervailing testimony, that such State, and the people thereof, are not in rebellion against the United States.

III. That the State of Louisiana has not yet been designated by the president as in rebellion, nor any part thereof, and that it has complied with all the conditions of the proclamation respecting representation:

IV. That pecuniary aid to States not in rebellion, which may hereafter provide for immediate or gradual emancipation; the colonization of persons of African descent elsewhere, and the compensation of all citizens who have remained loyal, "for all losses by acts of the United States, including slaves," are among the chief recommendations of this important paper.

It is manifest that the changes suggested therein, and which may hereafter be established, do not take effect within this State on the first of January proximo, nor at any precise period which can now be designated, and I call upon all persons, of whatever estate, condition or degree, soldiers, citizens or slaves, to observe this material and important fact, and to govern themselves accordingly. All unusual public demonstrations, of whatever character, will be for the present suspended. Provost marshals, officers and soldiers are enjoined to prevent any disturbance of the public peace. The slaves are advised to remain upon their plantations until their privileges shall have been definitely established. They may rest assured that whatever benefit the government intends will be secured to them, but no man can be allowed in the present condition of affairs to take the law into his own hands. If they seek the protection of the government they should wait its pleasure.

Part Three The Emancipation Proclamation

Chapter 6

Emancipation in Northern Eyes

Even before issuing his infamous Woman Order, Benjamin Butler had already gained notoriety for his policies bearing on the most crucial question of the war—emancipation. When hostilities first erupted in 1861, newspapers in the North, both Republican and Democrat alike, had affirmed that while the war was about slavery, the Union had no intention of attempting to undermine or overthrow the institution. In order to calm the fears and encourage the loyalty of citizens in the slave states, it seemed imperative to assure them that the North was not aiming to revolutionize the labor system of the South or uproot the racial order there. To this end, whenever runaway slaves were found behind Union lines, Union officers actually were required to help return them to their rightful owners. Butler, however—then serving at Fortress Monroe in Virginia—had different ideas. In May, just a few weeks into the war, when three slaves who had been employed as military laborers by the Confederacy fled by canoe from their encampment and arrived at Fortress Monroe, Butler welcomed them. Using the Southern idea that slaves were property, he declared that these men were "contraband" goods, no different from any other matériel that aided the Confederate war effort, and thus liable to confiscation. The War Department, following Butler's lead, endorsed his contraband policy, and a couple of months later Congress passed a confiscation act, which made it fully legal for the Union army to seize slaves who were being used as military workers by the rebels. These were important but limited steps against slavery—initial strikes in what would eventually evolve into an all-out assault to destroy it completely.

The question of emancipation was enormously volatile, for it was not just about ending slavery; it entailed changes that, if pushed far enough, promised to revolutionize the nature of race relations in America. It was impossible to think about emancipation without opening up a host of other questions that at the time were confounding and frightening. If slavery ended, would the slaves then become citizens? Would they gain voting rights? Were they to be integrated fully into American society? Most Northerners were not prepared to answer these questions in the affirmative, and consequently they were loath to endorse a policy of wholesale emancipation.

Even Abraham Lincoln, despite his belief that slavery was morally evil and that undercutting it would help subdue the rebellion, hesitated to make emancipation a Union war aim. For Lincoln, though, the racial arguments against it were less compelling than the political ones. When the war broke out in 1861, an edict of emancipation would have been disastrous to the Union cause. Not only were the people of the free states opposed to such a policy, but it would have alienated the border slave states, whose loyalty to the Union was desperately needed but tenuous. Emancipation also contradicted the Union's "limited-war" strategy—its hope of quelling the rebellion without wreaking so much havoc as to make reunion difficult or impossible. Lincoln's public position on emancipation could never be delinked from his primary goal of saving the Union.

Despite his initial reservations, in the summer of 1862 Lincoln privately began composing a plan for enacting emancipation by presidential proclamation. By that point, the loyalty of the four border slave states seemed secure. Moreover, support within the Republican party for emancipation had grown—in part a reflection of the public's frustration with fighting a limited war and its desire instead for a "hard war" that would hit the rebellion more forcefully. As part of this hard war mentality, the Republican-dominated Congress in July 1862 passed a second confiscation act, authorizing that all slaves of disloyal masters would be freed if they came into Union hands, regardless of whether they had been used by the Confederacy for military labor. In addition to helping the Union win the struggle at home, Lincoln also knew that, diplomatically, freeing the slaves would generate more sympathy for the country abroad. As a practical matter of war policy, then, emancipation now made sense, and under the war powers clause of the Constitution, Lincoln believed he had the legal right to enact it.

Lincoln had fleshed out his Emancipation Proclamation by mid-July, but at the urging of his secretary of state, William H. Seward, he chose to wait for a Union military victory before issuing it. He wanted it to be seen as a reflection of the Union's strength, not as a desperate act of weakness. As fate would have it, it would be a lengthy delay—a full two months, until the Battle of Antietam on September 17, when the Army of the Potomac succeeded in driving Robert E. Lee's Army of Northern Virginia out of Maryland and back behind Confederate lines. Five days later, Lincoln issued his Preliminary Emancipation Proclamation, announcing that on the first day of January in 1863, all slaves residing in areas "in rebellion" against the United States would be declared free and that all representatives of federal authority, both civil and military, would work to promote and protect their liberation. The "in rebellion" clause was a crucial one, for it meant that slaves in the loyal border states, as well as those in the parts of the Confederacy that were under Union control, were excluded. At the time, critics chided Lincoln for this—for his proclamation only applied to areas where he had no authority to enforce it. Nevertheless, in promising eventual freedom to the slaves in rebel territory, Northerners knew that Lincoln had just made a revolutionary step, one that some of them still could not accept. The response from the press was bitterly, angrily divided, revealing just how far apart Northerners remained in their thinking about the place of slavery in the war and in American life more generally.

For those in the abolitionist camp, who had been agitating against slavery for decades, Lincoln's proclamation offered them a tremendous feeling of vindication. Before the Civil War, they had been a despised minority in the North—vilified and often threatened for harboring radical views on universal black freedom. And in 1861, when they argued that emancipation should be enacted to help end the war more quickly, they had been ignored. Now their position on slavery had gone from marginal to mainstream, and they could hardly wait to see it go into effect. The *Liberator* exclaimed:

> The twenty-second of September, 1862, will henceforth be a memorable day in this Nation's history, if our National life is yet to continue. After seventeen months' waiting for the event, we at last hear the President speak the word which, had it been spoken at first, would have commanded the sympathy and applause of the world, and cut short the life of the Rebellion with a comparatively small loss of life and treasure. But a foolish people and Government . . . [had] chosen to go in the path of bloodshed, death, terrible suffering, and grinding debt, only to learn at this late hour the simple truth which the Anti-Slavery people have long been urging upon them. Pray God it may not be too late!
>
> But now that the word Freedom is spoken, why, we ask, is the great Act of Justice delayed for three months longer? The postponement to January next is much to be regretted. . . . The three months' delay will afford opportunity to the enemies of the Great Measure, North and South, but particularly at the North, to concoct plans to strangle it if possible, to postpone and cripple it at any rate. That they will be busy at this work, no one can doubt for an instant. All the energy and craft these people possess, find scope only in plans to circumvent justice and human liberty, and strengthen the power and dominion of slavery. . . . Let them be closely watched.[2]

So splendid a vision has hardly shone upon the world since the day of the Messiah. From the date of this Proclamation begins the history of the republic as our fathers designed to have it—the home of freedom, the asylum of the oppressed, the seat of justice, the land of equal rights under the law, where each man, however humble, shall be entitled to life, liberty, and the pursuit of happiness. Let no one think to stay the glorious reformation. Every day's events are hastening its triumph, and whosoever shall place himself in its way, it will grind him to powder.—*Chicago Tribune.*

The Liberator, October 3, 1862.
For Northerners who had been clamoring for the abolition of slavery, Lincoln's Preliminary Emancipation Proclamation was a glorious and thrilling turn of events, one that fulfilled America's destined role as the asylum of freedom for all people.

What the *Liberator* said was true. The Preliminary Emancipation Proclamation turned many of Lincoln's Democratic supporters into disillusioned, resentful opponents who were determined to reverse his policy. Promised by the president in 1861 that the war was not to be fought for abolition, they felt betrayed by his sudden change of heart, and denied that he had any legal leg to stand on. "We demand to be informed whence the President derives his power to issue any such proclamation," the *New York World* fumed. "The Constitution confers on the Federal Government no power to change the domestic institutions of the States," but "this policy makes changes of the most violent and sweeping character." As riled as the *World* was, its indignation paled in comparison to that of the *Louisville Journal.* Situated in the slave state of Kentucky, the *Journal* felt the threat of emancipation very directly. Even though the proclamation did not apply to Kentucky or any other of the loyal slave states, it was difficult to imagine that slavery could survive anywhere once it had been demolished in the South. Beyond any interest it had in slavery, though, the paper also agreed that the proclamation was unconstitutional and criminal. While careful to emphasize its unfaltering devotion to the Union, the *Journal* angrily withdrew its support from Lincoln, and with an eye on the upcoming 1862 congressional elections, it called upon the masses to show their disapproval by voting Democrats into office:

The Deed is Done !--The Dictator presumes to Speak !--The Negro in the Ascendant!

Crisis, January 7, 1863.
As far as the Copperheads were concerned, the Emancipation Proclamation was not only utterly illegal but also gravely threatening to the privileged place of whites in American society.

> Kentucky cannot and will not acquiesce in this measure. Never! As little will she allow it to chill her devotion to the cause thus cruelly imperilled anew. The government our fathers framed is one thing, and a thing above price; Abraham Lincoln, the temporary occupant of the Executive chair, is another thing, and a thing of comparatively little worth. . . . What Abraham Lincoln as President does or fails to do, may exalt or lower our estimate of himself, but not of the great and beneficent government of which he is but the temporary servant. The temple is not the less sacred and precious because the priest lays an unlawful sacrifice upon the altar. The loyalty of Kentucky is not to be shaken by any mad act of the President. . . .
>
> The President has fixed the first day of next January as the time for his proclamation to go into effect. Before that time the North will be called upon to elect members of Congress and the new Congress will assemble. We believe the proclamation will strike the people of the North in general with amazement and abhorrence. We know it. We appeal to them to manifest their righteous detestation by returning to Congress none but the avowed and zealous adversaries of this measure. Let the revocation of the proclamation be made the overshadowing issue; let the voice of the people at the polls, followed by the voice of their representatives in Congress, be heard in such tones of remonstrance and of condemnation, that the President, aroused to a sense of his tremendous error, shall not hesitate to withdraw the measure. The vital interests of the country demand that the proclamation shall be revoked [and] the sooner the better.[3]

As in Kentucky, Democratic newspapers throughout the North fixated upon emancipation and made it the central campaign issue. In agitating against emancipation, editors appealed to the most visceral prejudices and interests of their readers. They spoke in particular to the economic concerns of white men, who feared that Southern slaves, once freed, would flood northward, settle in their communities, and compete against them for jobs. Even before the war, Indiana and Illinois already had established laws to prevent free blacks from immigrating there. Now, in response to Lincoln's proclamation, anxieties over black immigration and labor competition intensified. The Democratic press in Ohio, eager to reverse Lincoln's decision on emancipation, called on voters to recognize their economic interests and unseat all Republican incumbents from power:

> Workingmen, remember that the President's Negro Proclamation, if it can be enforced, will bring hundreds and thousands of negroes into Ohio to compete with the white laboring men. They can not go to Indiana, for that State has a statute excluding them from her borders; they can not go to Illinois, for the people of that State, at their last election, by a majority of 160,000, declared against their immigration there. So [too] with several other of the Northern States. Abolitionized Ohio stands with open doors to receive them. They will come here "in force," and steal or seek employment at greatly reduced wages, thus forcing white men to work cheaper or be "ratted" out of their situations by "de born equals" of the Abolitionists. Already you have seen white laboring men discharged, and negroes,

who would work cheaper, hired in their places. If the Abolition policy is carried out, these things will be of no uncommon occurrence. Mechanics and workingmen, as one of you, with interests and feelings akin to yours, we appeal to you to vote against this Abolition party that would ruin you and yours for the purpose of elevating the negro. As you value the Union and desire its restoration; as you cherish the old Constitution which our fathers gave us; as you prize the blood-bought liberties wrested from tyrant hands through the blood and fire of the Revolution, and transmitted to your keeping, we beseech you to labor and vote against Abolitionism. It is your only means of preserving those glorious heritages.[4]

For the *Weekly Caucasian*, a Copperhead journal published in New York City, the economic threat of black competition paled in comparison to the social disorder that emancipation was certain to create. In the eyes of its opponents, emancipation meant more than just the freeing of the slaves. It implied racial equality. In reality, this was an overblown notion. Even before the war, free blacks generally were segregated from whites and possessed only limited rights and opportunities. There was no logical reason to presume that ending slavery would lead to the eradication of all racial barriers. Nevertheless, the Emancipation Proclamation tapped racial fears that went beyond the rational. Its Democratic critics worried that blacks now would be welcomed fully into American society, given voting privileges and other citizenship rights, and permitted to intermingle—even intermarry—with whites. In blurring the lines between the races, many Democrats believed emancipation would drag down American society. Race mixing would degrade the superior blood of whites and infuse all of the stereotyped failings of the black race—indolence, imbecility, brutishness—into white society. It thus imperiled American civilization itself, for how, they asked, could America survive as a free country if its people devolved into a mass of lazy, depraved mongrels? As the *Caucasian* explained:

There are eight millions of white citizens in the South in juxtaposition with four millions of negroes. They are all alike human, but *specifically* different, just as in all other groups, families or forms of being. Why this is so, or why the Almighty Creator has seen fit to thus ordain things, to make the Caucasian a different and superior being to the negro, we are not permitted to know any more than we are permitted to know why the hound is different and superior to the bulldog, or the eagle to the owl, or the lion to the tiger, or the shad to the catfish, or indeed, why *species* or specific creations exist at all. We only know, and can only know, that they do exist, and always must exist, each after its kind, generation after generation, century after century. . . . And we know, moreover, that the Creator has endowed us with abundant capacities to investigate the *facts* that surround us, to comprehend these facts, . . . and when we do so, and conform to them, we are happy, while, on the contrary, if we stultify or abuse these gifts of God and blindly beat our brains against the Eternal order, then we are punished, and always must be punished. . . . For example:—We have on this continent and adjacent islands thirty millions of white men, twelve millions of negroes, and about the same number of aboriginals or Indians. Now, were all of these . . . universally intermingled and amalgamated together, what would be the result? Is it not obvious to the most unreflecting mind that such a state of things would involve the total ruin of society as well as Republican liberty? Or even this:—If we were to amalgamate universally with the negroes in our midst, . . . is it not obvious, absolutely certain, that it would debauch and demoralize our blood, our system, our liberty, and imperil, if not altogether overthrow, our civilization? . . . What a stupendous and awful delusion has therefore gotten possession of the northern mind! Within the last fifteen months the lives of two hundred thousand northern citizens have been sacrificed, as many more morally or physically disabled, and two thousand

THE ISSUE ON MONDAY
Let no one vote the Republican Ticket unless he can "swallow the whole Negro."

Cleveland Plain Dealer, April 4, 1863.
Emancipation became the central issue in the 1862 and 1863 state elections. This illustration from a newspaper in Ohio illustrates how Democrats appealed to the visceral racial prejudices of voters.

millions of treasure expended for what? . . . Why, it is a conflict over the negro—to defend or to change his status—to preserve or to "abolish slavery." It is represented every day that the South secedes to preserve "slavery"—withdraws from the Union to defend slavery and render it perpetual. This, of course, is so. . . . The South does secede to "save slavery," to render it perpetual, to remove it beyond the influences that seek its destruction. . . . What, then, is "slavery?" Should it be defended, or should it be destroyed? This brings us back to the beginning of this article. The negro, as observed, is specifically different and inferior, and the white man different and superior. These relations, fixed eternally by the hand of God in the organism of nature, are embodied by the human law, and this embodiment is called "slavery." The subordinate negro instinctively submits to the will of the superior white man, and the latter protects him, guides him and cares for all his wants. This relation . . . is the most perfect and most beneficent social condition in Christendom. We can only get at truth by contrast and comparison, and we must compare the negro of the South with his African condition or status. Will the wildest and most unreasoning among us, venture to say that the idle, non-producing, snake-worshipping African heathen is in a more desirable condition than the useful, progressive Christian negro of America?

There is the whole question. . . . As regards the white citizenship of the South, it is not an open question. . . . The South, these eight millions of people, are fighting for "slavery," to defend the *status quo*, the social order, the existing social relations, in short, to defend society, and all that is sacred and valuable in human existence. This is charged every day, and everywhere, and it is true: the South fights to defend "slavery"—the subordination of the negro—the supremacy of the white man—the natural relations of the races on this Continent—and if defeated, its defenders beaten down, "slavery" overthrown, and the negro distorted into the *status* of the white man, then liberty and Republican institutions, and civilization itself, will be overthrown.[5]

Equally appalled by the "social revolution" that the Republican plan for "Negro emancipation and elevation" portended, the *Harrisburg Patriot & Union* painted the approaching congressional elections as a strictly "black and white" matter, or rather, as a matter of black versus white:

> The present contest is a contest between the white and black races for supremacy. President Lincoln and the Abolitionists have made it so. The white race is represented by the Democratic party—the black race by the Abolition-Republican party. The fact can no longer be disguised. The simple question to be decided is, whether the white man shall maintain his *status* of superiority, or be sunk to the level of the negro. Equality of races is demanded by the Abolitionists; they claim that, socially, civilly and politically, the black man should be the equal of the white. The Democrats deny and oppose this. It is a fair and square fight between the Caucasian and the African, and the issue of the contest will be decided at the ballot box. The question is referred to the people—to the white people. They must determine it one way or the other—in favor of the negro, if they elect Abolitionists; in favor of the white man, if they elect Democrats. Draw the line at once—make the mark distinct—let the only question asked between this [moment] and the election be, "Are you White?" or, "Are you Black?"[6]

Many voters cast their ballots just as these Democratic sheets had hoped. After the election, the congressional delegations of six states—the stretch from New York to Illinois—now had Democratic majorities, and in all, the party picked up an additional thirty-four congressional seats. Republican editors were aghast at the virulence of the Democratic opposition. They could not understand how anyone could question the utility and justifiability of enacting emancipation. The Confederacy was fighting for slavery and was using slave labor to support its military effort. So why should the Union hesitate any longer in resorting to emancipation in self-defense? As the *Rutland Herald* recalled:

> At an early period in the present rebellion, Vice President Stephens of Georgia, one of the ablest, most fearless and outspoken men of the South, in a speech . . . declared the object and purpose of the war against the Union. He said that the government of the United States was founded upon a false theory of human rights,—namely, the political equality of all men. He said that such a system of government is incompatible with the interests and the social system of the Southern States.—He declared in substance that the rebellion is a struggle against the democratic principle of government,—against the great and sublime principle enunciated by Thomas Jefferson in the Declaration of Independence that "all men are created free and equal.". . . Insisting that the compulsory servitude of the African race to the Anglo Saxon, as it exists at the South, is the normal condition of society, . . . he claimed that a government should be established in which the system of negro slavery should be made the chief corner stone. . . .
>
> It results as a corollary that slavery is the great enemy to the constitution and the Union. It is slavery which is demanding the life blood of the nation. It is slavery which insolently clutches at the throat of Freedom and cries: "Your life or mine!" It is slavery which says "Eternal war upon the right of non-slaveholding whites to have a voice in government!"
>
> Notwithstanding the defiant front of slavery, and notwithstanding the rivers of blood which have been shed by our fathers, sons, and brothers, in resisting its frantic attempts to destroy the government, with what amazing regard has it been treated by the Northern people, and by the President. . . . We have all along besought the slaveholders to return to their allegiance and save their cherished institution. We have fondly but vainly hoped that the mad frenzy of the rebels would subside, and so have refrained to do that which might exasperate them. But all in vain! . . . There is no hope of reconciliation while slavery exists. . . . We must, there-

Harper's Weekly,
October 11, 1862.
The cartoon entitled "Lincoln's Last Warning" exemplifies the utilitarian way in which many Northern Republicans, by 1862, had come to regard emancipation. In issuing the Preliminary Emancipation Proclamation, Lincoln was simply preparing to chop down the main prop of the rebellion.

LINCOLN'S LAST WARNING.
"Now, if you don't come down, I'll cut the Tree *from under you.*"

fore, accept the issue. There is no escape. It is thrust upon us. . . .

Yet even in this condition of things, with what reluctance does the President join issue with the despoilers of Freedom. He has issued his proclamation of emancipation, but behold, even now, it is accompanied with a provision of amnesty and pardon if the rebels will desist and lay down their arms. . . . What ground for sympathy can the rebels claim to have if they refuse to accept this last offer of the olive branch of peace? If they will persist in forcing the issue upon the nation, after so much leniency has been shown them, and is still shown them, who shall hold Abraham Lincoln responsible if slavery goes down in blood?

. . . What, then, is the duty of the northern people? Is it to denounce the President, to denounce the proclamation, and foment strife and discord? Such a course is just what the rebels anxiously desire, and nothing could be devised whereby they could be more effectually aided in their hellish purpose of destroying the national life. It is the grand mission of the northern people between this and January next, to unite the northern masses in earnest, and religious support of the new policy, upon which the government will then enter. Since the cry of slavery is "Down with the Constitution and free Government," let our war cry by "Down with slavery, now and forever!" It is the only open and declared foe of our Union, and the Union must be preserved.[7]

Contrary to the Democrats' worst fears, this support for emancipation as a war measure did not translate into a belief in racial equality. In order to help allay any anxieties about racial integration, Republican papers were careful to affirm that emancipation would not jeopardize the supremacy of whites in American society. In this way, their views were remarkably similar to those of their Democratic rivals. When considering the hostility of Democrats toward the equalization of blacks and whites, the *New York Evening Post* asserted bluntly:

> We, too, say, America for white men. We believe that this country, great and free, was destined by Providence to be the open asylum for the oppressed millions of Europe. We believe that one of the principal offices of our free and fertile country, in the Divine scheme, was to offer to the teeming populations of Europe homes, liberty, prosperity, a secure place for themselves and their children. Our free states have been thus open; but from the southern states the white emigrant seeking liberty and comfort in America, has always been turned away. It is only the barbarous black emigrant from Africa, who has found a welcome home there. Shall the free states, too, be closed against white workingmen? or shall not rather the whole continent be thrown open to the Germans, the Irishmen, the Norwegians, the white workingmen of Europe who have so greatly helped to build up the wealth of the free states, and who are ready to enter the South also, whenever they are permitted? America for white men—certainly—Texas as well as Minnesota, Florida as well as Iowa, Virginia as well as New York.
>
> As the Indians were crowded westward, and out of our bounds, by the irresistible advance of the white man, so will the blacks be, whenever that powerful protective system with which the slaveholders have guarded them is removed. It is the destiny of the free white workingmen of this country to possess it; the efforts of the slaveholders have hitherto robbed them of one half of it—the richest, fairest half—and devoted it to blacks. It is the slaveholders who have preserved the negro race from decline amongst us; it is the slaveholders who have increased the blacks from seven hundred thousand in 1790 to four millions in 1860. It is the slaveholders and slave-breeders, who have crowded the "poor whites"—the free white workingmen—from every southern state into the free states. It is the slaveholders and slave-breeders who bar the way now, as they have always done, and by their selfish system close one half of this continent against the free white workingmen of America. If, in our cities and in our eastern states, white men find themselves overcrowded, find it hard to live, let them remember that they suffer and toil at [a] disadvantage, because the slaveholders . . . hold Virginia, and all the South, and close against them, by their system, the most fertile part of the Union.[8]

Even if blacks were not totally pushed out of the way, it was hoped that emancipation would at least rid the North of them. In response to Democrats who feared a sudden influx of free blacks, Republican papers countered that the opposite was actually true. Emancipation, they argued, would not bring the South's "negro problem" northward and place thousands of unwanted blacks into direct competition with white workers. The slaves "*will not run away from freedom*," affirmed the *Harrisburg Telegraph*. Slaves yearned to come north only because that was where they could find freedom. If emancipation was enforced in the Southern states, though, the liberated slaves would stay there, close to the friends and family they had always known, and in the warm tropical climate that American whites presumed those of African descent preferred. For these very same reasons, blacks in the North would move South too. "*Thus the practical results of this policy will be to drain the north of its negro population*," exclaimed the *Telegraph* reassuringly. Touting similar hopes, the *Troy Times* wrote:

The Democratic leaders and newspapers . . . declare that the President's proclamation, if carried out, will result in a negro equality, and impoverish white labor by negro competition. Any one may see that the design of this is to foment opposition to the Government in the prosecution of the war, and to give aid and comfort to the rebels. There is no truth or logic in the assumptions put forth. If every slave in the rebel States is emancipated under the President's proclamation, white labor at the North will be benefited rather than injured. . . . On the contrary, with freedom assured to the blacks as proposed, the colored people of the North would naturally join their brethren at the South, where, as teachers, leaders and colaborers, they would best promote their material prosperity and social welfare. The demand for negro labor exists at the South. . . . In the natural order of things, the negroes will remain where their labor is wanted, in their own sunny clime, while thousands of the race here will join them under the guaranty that they have rights which white men and all others are bound to respect. . . . They are not going where they are not wanted, when the cherished home of their fathers, relieved from oppression, and inviting them to labor, is open to them, with compensation for their toil instead of slavery and despotic ownership, as a reward for industry. The laws of nature and climate, home attachments and self-interest, and the demands of labor, all contribute to make the emancipated South the home for black men. Many of them have hitherto fled Northward to escape oppression. Slavery abolished, these fugitives would return, and others of their race [would] accompany them. Emancipation, instead of bringing negro labor in competition with the industry of white people, would relieve the latter of a good share of the small competition of this sort it now experiences, while at the same time an element of aristocracy, wrong and despotism,—the active and wicked element of the present rebellion—would be finally extirpated and the Union, reestablished on the basis of liberty, [would] afford us henceforth peace and prosperity.[9]

Others within the Republican ranks articulated more charitable notions on how this southward migration would proceed. Optimistic that the postemancipation South would be a land of opportunity, they hoped to see blacks leave the North so they might find new avenues for professional success and advancement there. In this spirit, the *Anglo-African* published the following editorial, which had appeared originally in the *Springfield Republican*:

> Great opportunities are about to open before the free colored people of this country—chances for usefulness, wealth and position, such as have been denied to their race through many weary ages of injustice and contempt. Do they begin to comprehend the future that awaits them? Four million of their race, born in slavery, are about to be transformed into freemen. They are to begin a new life, in which they will come into possession of their own persons, their own physical and mental powers, and will be thrown upon their own resources for self-direction and support. Their long degradation has rendered most of them mere children in intellect—a nation of vigorous animals, who are to be trained to intelligent manhood. . . .
>
> Who [are] so well fitted to be the teachers and guides of their emancipated brethren as the intelligent and Christian colored men and women of the free States, and especially of New England, who have grown up in our schools and Churches, and who in real culture and character are very much above the average white men of the slave States? Many white people will doubtless be found . . . to enter the opening field of the South from motives of philanthropy. But the colored people of the North have besides the sympathy that comes from race and blood, and will naturally be attracted southward just as soon as the freedom of their race is established.

THE NEW MAP OF THE UNITED STATES.

Topographical View of President Lincoln's Emancipation Proclamation—The Slave Territory and the New Free Territory of the Union.

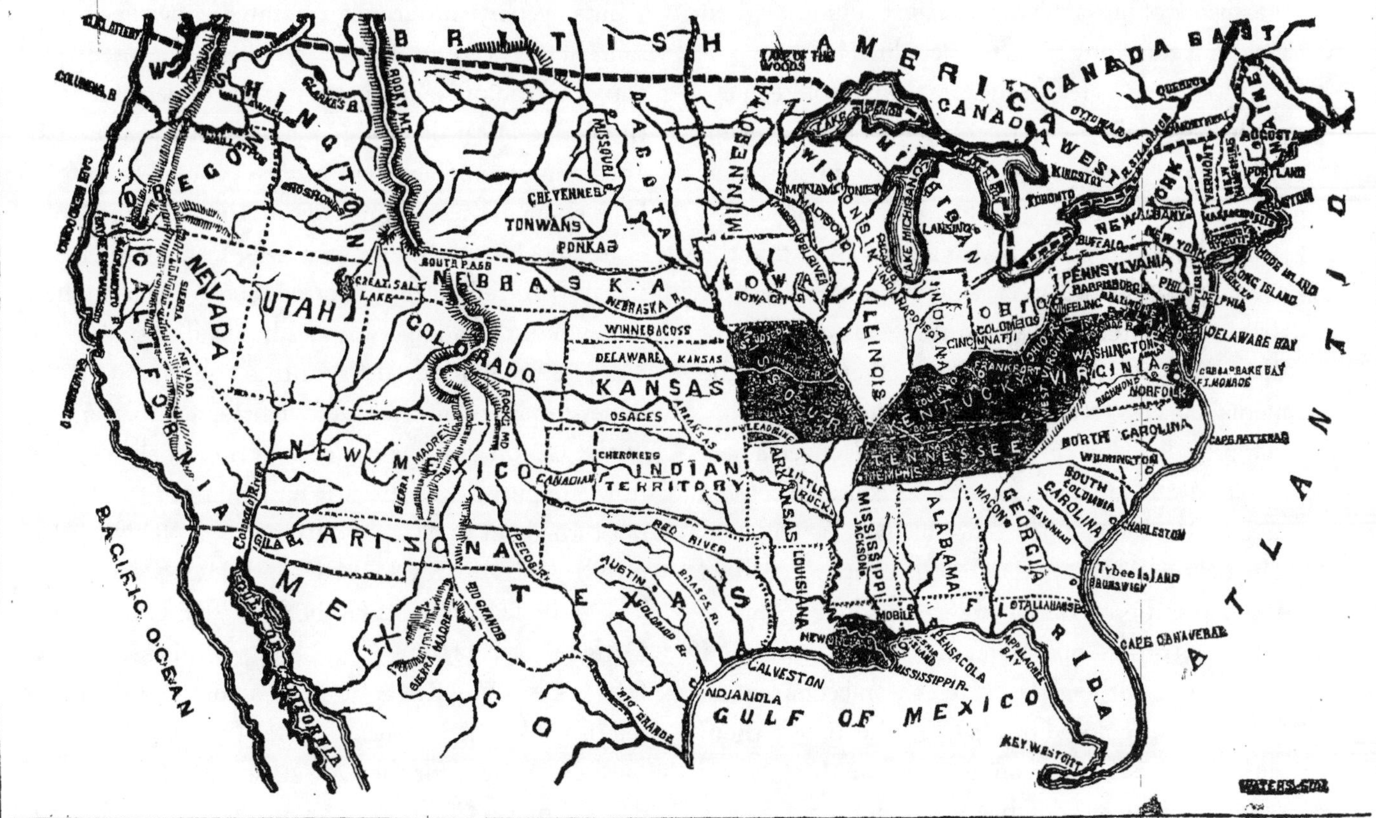

NOTE.

The Slave States are in Black; the Old Free States in White; the New Free States in White.

New York Herald, January 4, 1863.
As pictured by the *New York Herald*, Lincoln's Emancipation Proclamation promised to redraw the American map, leaving only narrow strips of slave territory in the border states, Tennessee, West Virginia, and southern Louisiana.

They will be the most acceptable instructors of their emancipated brethren. And to them will be offered not only opportunities for philanthropic effort, but for enterprise and skilled labor. The rude cabins of the slaves are to give place to the neat cottages of the free laborers, and thousands of school houses are to be built for the education of the negro children. And there are young men and women of color, trained in our public schools, who are competent to [do] this great work of lifting up the degraded millions of their race, and educating them from civilized life.

It would be a great thing for our free colored people if they could rise to the grandeur of this conception, and prepare to undertake the mission that Providence is just about to offer to them. Our colored people have complained, with good reason, that the avenues to influence and position were closed against them in the free States, and that the education of their children only made them discontented with the menial pursuits to which the negro is limited by popular prejudice. But this is to be true no longer. There is to be a demand for the services of educated colored men and women, which is not likely to be half met. The next half century is to be one of unprecedented activity and progress among the colored people of this country, and talent and industry will gain their just rewards, without respect to race and complexion. Let no smart colored boy lay aside his books, then, with the idea that he can never be anything better than a barber, a boot black or a waiter. He may become a lawyer, a preacher, an educator, and win his way to fortune and distinction at the same time that he does invaluable service to his race.[10]

In the first few months after Lincoln issued his Preliminary Emancipation Proclamation, everything was uncertain. Would blacks soon flood northward or stay to seek new opportunities in the sunny South? Would whites benefit from emancipation or be dragged down by it? Would emancipation spell the beginning of a new era for black advancement or do nothing to narrow the racial divide? Even after the proclamation went into effect on January 1, 1863, the freedom of the slaves remained only speculative. The proclamation applied only to areas in rebellion—areas not under Union control, where it could not be enforced. Therefore, emancipation continued to follow in the paths of the Union armies. Where they asserted their control, slaves would seek freedom behind their lines and offer themselves as laborers, cooks, and scouts. When the armies retreated, however, these same slaves were in danger of being recaptured. The actual spread of emancipation was thus dependent on the cooperation of Union soldiers. In the winter of 1863, however, they were no less divided than folks back home in their feelings toward the proclamation.

To give force to their own views, Democratic newspapers printed letters they received from soldiers denouncing emancipation as a betrayal of their trust. They had volunteered for military service with the understanding that they were fighting for the survival of the Union, not for the destruction of slavery, but now the purpose of the war had changed totally. "It has turned out to be an abolition war, AND NINETY-NINE SOLDIERS OUT OF ONE HUNDRED SAY THAT IF THE ABOLITIONISTS ARE GOING TO CARRY ON THE WAR, THEY WILL HAVE TO GET A NEW ARMY," ranted a soldier in a letter published by the *Providence Post*. "They say they came out here to fight for the Union, and not for a pack of d——d niggers." Another admitted, "*I am sick of this war*—so sick that I do not care upon what terms it is settled." The final Emancipation Proclamation, coming as it did on the heels of a terrible Union defeat at Fredericksburg in December 1862, also made it seem as if Lincoln and Congress were more concerned with freeing the slaves than seeing to the success of the soldiers. One soldier therefore painted this bleak and cynical picture to the *Cleveland Plain Dealer*:

ED. PLAIN DEALER:—I do not write these lines particularly for publication; I simply wish to express my humble opinion in regard to this (called by four-fifths of the army) "nigger war." I have written many letters since I have been in the army to my friends and parents, but this is the first wherein I have made one complaint, and I have been in it for over fifteen months.

Within the last month there has been a great change in the feelings of the soldiers of this army. After the first of January we were to have a *noble* object to fight for, one *worthy* of Christians. For my part, "I can't see it" from where I stand. We did not come to fight for the nigger, and what is more, we *won't* do it. . . . When I came into this war we were fighting for the Union, but now we are fighting for too much. I tell you that it is not because we can not whip the South that this war has continued so long, but because those dirty Abolitionists at Washington are spending all their time thinking of the nigger, instead of looking to the poor soldier, and having them ready for work when they are wanted. . . .

The soldiers look to the honest Democrats of the North to put a stop to this bloody, unholy war. Throw out the nigger, and our Union will be restored. But continue to make him the object of this war, and the Southern ranks will be swelled with *Northern volunteers*. Those *dogs* at Washington will not take warning from the numerous complaints that are made daily by the soldiers of this army. But the people should . . . root out this corrupt Administration that holds the wires and ropes of our Government, before it is too late. Our country is trembling on the brink of ruin. Stand silently by, ye who can save it, and the crash will soon come, as true as there is a God in Heaven.[11]

Not all of the men in blue felt outraged by emancipation, however. The following letter, written by a Massachusetts soldier to the *Hampshire Gazette & Northampton Courier*, reveals many interesting things. His recounting of events around his post in Louisiana details the way in which the army both stifled and advanced emancipation, the determination of blacks to aid the Union and secure their own freedom, as well as his personal support not only for emancipation but also for the enlistment of blacks for military service:

We have had a great doings to-day. Somebody in the night went a bee hunting, and this morning we lived on honey, having all we could eat. A negro had been around our quarters for a day or two, telling us that there was a planter over the bayou who had several hundred chickens and lots of eggs, butter, &c., and promised to lead us over to where they were. His object was to get his wife who was still over there. By the way, I ought to tell you that it is not allowed to let any one, black or white, over the bayou without a pass from the Col. The reason given is that there is nothing for the blacks to eat here if they do come, and nothing for them to do. I am not satisfied with the course pursued, but have nothing to do about it. I think they ought to be received every one of them, and protected; and it is galling to me to see crowds of poor slaves sitting on the other side of the bayou, looking longingly over to us and no friendly hand is permitted to be extended to them. But I trust it will not be so long. A party of our company headed by the orderly, got a pass today, and under the guide of the negro, went over the bayou to see what they could find. They had good success, and brought back eighty chickens, twenty doz. eggs, a lot of butter, four turkies, two guns, nuts, etc. The negro brought his wife to the bayou but the guard would not let her pass, so she had to remain [on] the other side. However, he managed to smuggle her over during the night. I met him the next morning and said to him, "You have got your wife, have you?" Yes, said he, thank the Lord, and thank you and all the rest who have helped me. He was glad enough I assure you. . . .

I presume you would like me to give my views of slavery from actual contact with it, and also my general impressions concerning the war. With regard to slavery I hate it worse than ever. I believe the slaves are abundantly able to take care of themselves, and would demonstrate their ability if they had the chance. There is more shrewdness, more intelligence than I expected to find among them. The desire among them to be free is universal. They are the only class that exhibit the least signs of joy at our presence, while the whites meet you with sullen looks or averted faces, testifying in a manner not to be mistaken, their hatred toward us. The blacks manifest their joy in every way they can. They flock to us in crowds. They do the menial work around the cook houses with alacrity. They say God bless you with look and words; they scour our guns, steal for us,—that is, they get sugar, sweet potatoes, milk, &c. and bring [them] into our mess. One woman told me she had prayed for 30 years for this time to come. I do not believe there is a single slave in Iberville Parish who does not hope and expect to be free, and who does not look upon us as friends. The men say they are ready to enlist and fight with us this war to the bitter end. And I believe our government can get all the additional troops she will need from the blacks, by a proper course of treatment. They will undoubtedly need to be taken and drilled by white officers for some time, in order to give them confidence in themselves; but when that is obtained I believe they will fight like heroes. I think the sooner [the] government begins in this direction the better. I believe also that there is nothing that will so weaken the rebellion as freeing the slaves. I judge so by some conversation I have had with the planters themselves. They do dread losing their slaves above all things. I give it as my opinion, that the President's proclamation, faithfully carried out, will end the rebellion before 1863 passes by.[12]

Direct contact with slaves was indeed very influential in shaping the attitudes of some Northerners toward emancipation. In addition to witnessing the yearning for freedom among the slaves, they had their eyes opened to the realities of slavery, particularly with regard to its sheer brutality. Slaves who came behind Union lines talked openly about the severity of plantation discipline and had the physical scars to prove it. Certainly, the Northern public was already well acquainted with the cruelty of slave owners, especially through abolitionist literature such as *Uncle Tom's Cabin*, but actually seeing the marks left by the whip on the bodies of runaway slaves made a more stunning and indelible impression. A correspondent for the *New York Times*, riding on the Union gunboat *Lafayette* along Louisiana's Black River in the summer of 1863, received a firsthand education of this kind from two male slaves and their wives, who had taken refuge aboard the boat after escaping from the Gillespie family plantation in Catahoula Parish:

The treatment of the slaves, they say, has been growing worse and worse for the last six or seven years. . . . Flogging with a leather strap on the naked body is common; also, paddling the body with a hand-saw until the skin is a mass of blisters, and then breaking the blisters with the teeth of the saw. They have "very often" seen slaves stretched out upon the ground with hands and feet held down by fellow slaves, or lashed to stakes driven into the ground for "burning." Handfuls of dry corn husks are then lighted, and the burning embers are whipped off with a stick so as to fall in showers of live sparks upon the naked back. This is continued until the victim is covered with blisters. If, in his writhings of torture the slave gets his hands free to brush off the fire, the burning brand is applied to them.

Another method of punishment, which is inflicted for the higher order of crimes, such as running away, or other refractory conduct, is to dig a hole in the ground large enough for the slave to squat or lie down in. The victim is then stripped naked and placed in the hole, and a covering or grating of green sticks is laid over the opening. Upon this a quick fire is built, and the live embers sifted through upon the naked flesh of the slave, until his body is blistered and swollen almost to bursting. With just enough life to enable him to crawl, the slave is then allowed to recover from his wounds if he can, or to end his sufferings by death.

. . . "Charley Sloo" and "Overton," two hands, were both murdered by these cruel tortures.— "Sloo" was whipped to death, dying under the infliction, or soon after punishment. "Overton" was laid naked upon his face and burned as above described, so that the cords of his legs and the muscles of the back refused longer to perform their office. He was, nevertheless forced into the field to labor, but being crippled, was unable to move quick enough to suit "Jeems" [the widow Gillespie's son, James]; so one day, in a fit of passion, he struck him on the head with a heavy stick and killed him.

. . . There was a middle-aged [slave] woman in the family, named Margaret, who had a nursing child. Mrs. Gillespie ordered Margaret to wean the child. The babe was weakly, and Margaret did not wish to do so. Mrs. G. told her that she would examine her breast, the next Monday, and, if she found any milk in it, she would punish her severely. Monday came round, and on that day Margaret's [stint] was to spin eighteen "broaches"—spools— but she did not finish it. At night the promised examination took place, and the breast of Margaret gave but too convincing proof that, in obedience to the yearnings of a mother's heart, she had spurned the threat of the inhuman mistress. Mrs. G. then ordered the handsaw, the leather strap, and a wash bowl of water. The woman was laid upon her face, her clothes stripped up to around her neck, and "Becky" and "Jane" were called to hold her hands and feet. Mrs. Gillespie then paddled her with the handsaw, sitting composedly in a chair over her victim. After striking some one hundred blows she changed to the use of the leather strap, which she would dip into the wash bowl in order to give it greater power of torture. Under this infliction the screams of the woman died away into a faint moan, but the "sound of the whip" continued until nearly 11 o'clock. "Jane" was then ordered to bring the hot tongs, the woman was turned over upon her back, and Mrs. Gillespie attempted to grasp the woman's nipples with the heated implement. The writhings of the mother, however, foiled her purpose; but between the breasts the skin and flesh were horribly burned. . . .

Margaret was a long time in recovering from her wounds. Rose Ann, who was [a] child's nurse, was sent upon one occasion to find and bring home a little boy named Tommy. . . . Mrs. G. accused Rose of not trying to find the boy at first. She ordered her hands to be crossed and tied over her head; she was placed upon her back on the floor, her hands secured to the balusters and her feet to the extension table. In this position her person was exposed, the poker heated in the stove, and to make the punishment the more humiliating as well as most acute, the hot instrument was applied to *the most tender part of her body*. She then gave her fifty lashes and let her loose. This horrible idiosyncracy seemed to be a favorite method of torture with the widow. America, who saw and related these facts to the writer, in the presence of several of her fellow slaves, suffered a similar punishment on the plantation only a few months since. She is a seamstress, and had by mistake sewed in two sleeves of Mrs. G's daughter's dress the wrong way. For this offense she was laid upon a board upon a ladder, her hands and feet secured, and a leather strap and buckle tightly fastened around her stomach and going under the ladder. Having previously placed the tongs in the fire, she ordered them brought and began pinching and burning her about the thighs, abdomen, and other parts, until they were baked and stiff. This species of refined torture seemed to be a favorite one with her. On another occasion "America" said she was whipped with a new "yellow cowhide" until her flesh ceased to feel the blows. Mrs. G. then brought a bottle of "No. 6," and with a small sponge wet the lacerated parts with the fiery liquid, causing the most intense torture she ever experienced. Edmund,

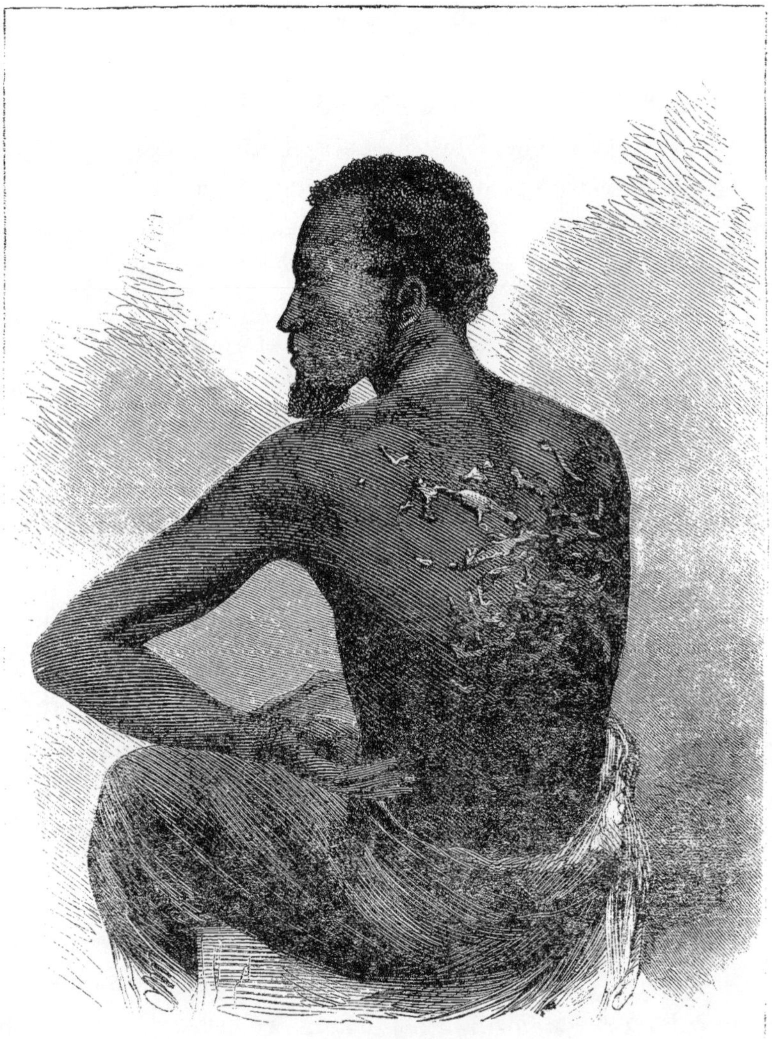

Harper's Weekly, July 4, 1863. Stripped of his shirt, an escaped slave named Gordon displays the terrible lacerations covering his back and bears testimony to the true brutality of slavery. The published version of this picture, and the original photograph from which it was taken, became one of the most famous images of the Civil War.
(© Applewood Books, Inc. Reproduced by permission of Applewood Books and harpersweekly.com)

Essex, and the rest assert that it was a very common thing to see a slave carried by force to the bedroom or the shedroom of Madame for punishment. She would order him to undress, and with her own hands apply the lash until she became exhausted. . . .

If any one, upon reading this record of horrors, says he does not believe it, I have only to reply—*I do*. The simple earnestness of these men and women, fresh from the prison-house of bondage which their tyrants have unintentionally thrown wide open by their wicked rebellion; the particularity of times, persons and places; *their readiness to exhibit the scars upon their own persons*—all attest to the sincerity and truth of their statements.

It is not presumed or asserted that these *extreme* punishments are inflicted every day, even on Louisiana plantations, or every week or month. They are horrible episodes in the negro's experience, which have made but too vivid an impression upon the slave's being, and which he cannot forget. What could more fully exhibit the natural fruits of a bad system, or illustrate its pernicious influence upon even the gentle nature of woman. Let it be accursed, and let it die with the slaveholders' rebellion.[13]

As this narrative suggests, the Republican press depicted slavery as not only physically brutal, but sexually perverse. The idea of the widow Gillespie or any other woman standing, whip in hand, over the naked black body of a slave, contradicted all notions of female decency. Generally speaking, though, the newspapers were much more intrigued by the sex crimes of male slaveholders than by the improprieties of their wives. Southern men were notorious for having illicit liaisons with their slaves, sometimes fathering children in the process. For decades, abolitionists had called attention to this kind of sexual depravity, and now, at the dawn of emancipation, Republican papers pointed to it in defense of Lincoln's policy. In January 1863, as Benjamin Butler was preparing to be transferred from his post in New Orleans, he and his staff conducted an interview with the *Atlantic Monthly*, in which they related stories of Southern aristocrats having sex with their slaves, keeping any resulting offspring in bondage, and—most shockingly—sexually abusing their mixed-race daughters. Butler's testimony struck a particularly deep chord with a woman named Mary Clarke from Troy, New York, who had served as a governess on a South Carolina plantation before the war. After reading his comments, she felt compelled to write a letter to her local paper, describing the sexual crimes of slaveholders against their own white daughters, as well as the necessity of doing away with the slaveholding culture that fostered such behavior:

> *Mr. Editor*: . . . Some of those horrible things related by Gen. Butler . . . I know to be *facts*. I once resided in South Carolina; returned to my Northern home but two years before the present Rebellion. I was governess for six years in the family of the son of ex-Gov. Richardson. While there, I was told by Col. Richardson's own white daughters all I know of the degradation occasioned by Slavery. I desired to tell its most degrading features to those whom I have so often heard advocating a continuance of negro slavery; but I dared not, for the facts seemed too indelicate for a female to publish. But, Sir, these are remarkable times; and should I hold my peace, even the very stones would cry out; for *Slavery is a wrong* to the planter's slave and to the planter's daughters. It is time our Northern men, and women, too, should know what Slavery is; that they may gird themselves and prepare for a great effort to put away this mighty evil from our land.
>
> Slavery demoralizes all that comes within its influence. It is a deadly upas. . . . What Gen. Butler said, he said truthfully, of the utter demoralization of the Southern people, resulting from Slavery. . . . I wish to strengthen his testimony by my own. I wish to state that it is the custom of the South Carolina aristocracy for fathers to have criminal intercourse with their own daughters. Col. Richardson had four beautiful daughters, two of whom yielded to his hellish persuasions. The third daughter had for four years refused to listen to the base propositions of her father. He hunted her from room to room, until in very anguish of spirit she came to my room, and hid her face in my lap, and told me all her awful trial. I could not believe the child; but she told me it was true—that her father would give her no peace. He seemed determined to gratify his hellish lust. He would come to her bedside when she was suffering from sick headache, and attempt to take improper liberties with her person. She begged me to come and sit with her in her room whenever she was confined to her bed, because she was afraid of her own father, who had ruined two of her sisters. She said that one day her cousin Camilla came to visit there. She told her cousin how her father had behaved for the four years past toward her, hoping her cousin Camilla would strengthen her. But Camilla had been ruined by her own father, years before, when she was young, and dared not be woman enough to refuse her father anything he might wish. Her advice to her cousin Mary was this—"Die before you yield."
>
> This is the effect of the institution of Slavery. Shall we not strengthen our worthy President in its abolition? Yes, say all the mothers and daughters

> who read these horrid facts; root out the deadly upas, Slavery. Some may say they cannot see how Slavery is responsible for these family evils of which Gen. Butler speaks, and of which I affirm. The secret is just here: from very infancy the planters' sons are gratified in everything they desire. I could tell you some startling facts of the boyhood of these planters' sons—facts communicated by Col. Richardson's own white daughters—but I forbear. From youth to manhood they go on, gratifying every lust, simply because the institution of human bondage puts it in their power to do so; when they become fathers of black and white children all must be sacrificed to their overgrown lust. Shall not the prayers of the fair daughters of South Carolina be heeded? Shall not the evil, Slavery, be rooted from our land? Let the North awake and be earnest in this matter. . . . Lay aside party spirit, and listen to the cries of the abused daughters of South Carolina, and rush to their rescue.[14]

It cannot be forgotten that although many Northerners by 1863 had come to hate slavery and to sympathize with the slaves, their underlying racism persisted all the same. Stereotypes about black imbecility and bestiality were so ingrained in American culture that they seemed impossible to break, regardless of what happened to the institution of slavery. As one antislavery man wrote in a letter to the *Liberator*, "for so long has the black man been called a brute, that few of us are untainted by prejudice against color." While he personally was determined that this attitude "must and can be overcome" with time and conscious effort, not everyone within the Republican camp felt similarly. In fact, Northerners generally endorsed the Emancipation Proclamation on the ground that while it aimed to destroy slavery, it did not—and would not—give blacks an equal place in America. "It does not seek the equalization of the races," one paper wrote definitively. "It does not propose to elevate the negro to the eminence of the white man, or degrade the white man to the level of the negro. It simply proposes to rescue this government from the destruction of rebellion." As the *New York Times* elaborated, Republicans and Democrats—and Northerners and Southerners more generally—did not differ fundamentally in believing that whites and blacks were inherently different and unequal:

> That any portion of the Republican party, or any but a very small and insignificant portion of the people of the North believe the negro race to be the equal of the white race, . . . we totally deny. . . . It is not about negro inequality that we differ with the South or with the Democrats. There is nothing within knowledge so well established, as that some races are inferior to others, morally, intellectually and physically. One might as well deny that some men [are] more eloquent, or more clever, or handsomer, or stronger than others, as to deny this. Where we part company . . . is in drawing inferences from this patent truth. They hold that where a body of weak, ill-favored, stupid men are dwelling alongside a [body of] stronger, better-looking, abler and more energetic ones, it is the right of the latter to rob, beat and sell the former. This is the great "truth" on which the Confederacy is founded. It is, too, the great "truth" on which the social organization of all the Slave States rests. . . .
>
> We . . . hold that the sound republican theory of human rights and human duties makes physical weakness and mental or moral deficiency titles to pity and protection, and not invitations to fraud and violence; that the more helpless and inferior a man is by nature, the more carefully should the laws of a democratic commonwealth enforce his claim to his wages, his wife, his children, and his own body. We do not advocate, because we do not believe in, negro equality. We would not, if we could, give negroes a share in the Government. But we heartily indorse . . . that they are entitled to protection, not

only none the less, but all the more because they are inferior.[15]

This seemingly unshakable belief in black inferiority carried enormous consequences, and ultimately dictated the terms under which emancipation would proceed. The slaves were to be freed from their old masters but not necessarily empowered with rights, protected from physical abuse but not shielded from discrimination, prevented from aiding the South but not necessarily welcomed to the North. Undeniably, the Emancipation Proclamation, in devoting the Union to the destruction of slavery, was a revolutionary step. But it was a revolution that would have definite limits.

DAILY Macon Telegraph

By JOSEPH CLISBY. | THURSDAY MORNING, OCTOBER 9, 1862. | No. 829

HARRY MACARTHY,

Assisted by Miss Lottie Estelle, gave their second Concert at Ralston's Hall to a full audience, who were highly entertained, not only by the numerous characters impersonated, but by the excellent singing of the songs. "It is my Country's call," by Harry Macarthy, was received with almost unbounded applause.

This evening they give a Benefit to the Ladies' Soldier's Relief Society, and we bespeak to those who patronize the benevolent object, one of the richest entertainments of the season.

FROM CORINTH.

The news from Corinth does not read right and suggests the suspicion that our arms may have suffered a reverse. The telegram, however, is very vague and unsatisfactory, and further news may bring us out all right.

P. S.—Since the foregoing the news leaves no question that our troops have sustained a severe defeat.

The Herald of the 4th says the fight had commenced in Kentucky.

Rev. Henry Ward Beecher on the Proclamation.

The New York Herald, of Tuesday, gives Rev. Mr. Beecher a complimentary notice, as follows:

The mountebank Beecher, who has turned his church in Brooklyn into a theatre where applause is given to his points by the audience, just as it is to Forrest, or Miss Bateman, or any other theatrical star, appeared on the boards at Plymouth church on Sunday evening, when he derided the Constitution as a mere "sheepskin parchment," of no account, and said "we are going to have the Union as it never was but as it was meant to be. The Union as it was meant to be, and not as it was is to be our doctrine, because the Union as it was, was a monstrous outrage on your rights and mine." In this he declared himself to be the mouthpiece of millions, like Greely a short time ago, and applause resounded from all parts of the house. After ridiculing the *Union* and the Constitution he next assails things still more sacred. He exhibits the Divine Being in the light of a tax-gatherer, who "is out now and will have a good time." Let us quote the whole passage: "The North, too, was suffering to an extent to which she had winked at slavery for the sake of commerce. When the North had paid two thousand millions of taxes (and only just begun) he thought that the Lord would get back pretty much all the North made out of slavery. God is the great tax-gatherer. He is out now, and He will have a good time." (Great laughter.)

The character of the audience may be judged from their laughter at such horrible profanity. Unfortunate sheep who follow such a shepherd. He alluded to the very general wish of the people to have twenty leading Abolitionists hanged. He said if it would do any good he had no objection to be the first. Just let him try. By following the example of Judas he may induce Greely and Garrison, and Phillips, and sixteen others, to go and do likewise; and with twenty of the leading Abolitionists swinging all in a row, from a sour apple tree, there will be some chance of our arms being speedily successful in restoring the rebellious South to the Union, when we can perform the same service for the leading Secessionists, when we catch them, that Beecher volunteers to do for himself.

The reverend mountebank closed his sermon with the following prediction of the result of the proclamation:

We shall see a glorious nation, a restored Constitution. We shall see a liberty in whose bright day Georgia and Massachusetts will shake hands that never shall be separated again. There is love to be raked open yet.—Now there is the fierceness of hatred; but there shall come concord, fellowship, and union; and when this comes we shall have a Union that no foreign influence can break, and no home trouble shall ever mar again.

GEN. TAYLORS' PLANTATION PLUNDERED.—The Montpelier Journal contains a letter from a soldier of the Vermont 8th, dated Camp Allemand, August 29th, in which he states that on the previous Thursday, the property of General Richard Taylor, a son of old General Taylor (by whom it was bequeated to him,) was confiscated, the son being now in the Rebel army. The slaves, 150 in number, were all declared emancipated, while the plantation was plundered by the Union soldiers. According to the writer:

"It is one of the most splendid plantations that I ever saw. There are on it 700 acres of sugar cane, which must rot upon the ground if the Government does not harvest it. I wish you could have seen the soldiers plunder this plantation. After the stock was driven off, the boys began by ordering the slaves to bring out everything there was to eat and drink. They brought out hundreds of bottles of wine, eggs, preserved figs and peaches, turkeys, chickens and honey, in any quantity.

I brought away a large camp kettle and frying pans that belonged to old General Taylor, and also many of his private papers. I have one letter of his own hand writing, and many from Secretary Marcy—some from General Scott and, some from the traitor Floyd. I

THE EMANCIPATION PROCLAMATION.

The New York Albion (English organ) has the following comments of Lincoln's atrocious proclamation:

This is general emancipation held in *terrorem* over the South, if it does not return to its allegiance before New Year's day, with a broad hint to the negroes that they are at liberty to cut their master's or mistresses' throats, if there be any hesitation about the matter.

As for Europe, it is a ludicrous delusion to imagine that any sentimental effect will be produced by the tardy adoption of a sliding scale principle. It does not need the sarcasm of a Times, or the malignity of a Saturday Review, to point out the hollowness of a policy that is made contingent on dates. If the South be beaten and submit in 98 days, Slavery is the law of the land; if the operation requires 90 days to effect it thoroughly, emancipation takes its place! Again, if from the sentimentality of Exeter Hall you turn to the interested views predominant at the Tulleries, what follows? Is intervention rendered less probable, inasmuch as, to difficulty in procuring Cotton, might succeed a total cessation in producing it? Is the universal confusion, which would ensue upon sudden emancipation, and the consequent abandonment of all hopes of a supply, a very tempting prospect for those who are looking anxiously for the hour when peace—not anarchy—shall be proclaimed? Never believe it.

We still hold that nothing can or will induce British intervention; but if Great Britain were ruled and moved to action by the principles attributed to her by most American writers of to-day, the receipt of President Lincoln's emancipation edict would be the signal for an abandonment of neutrality.

The Washington correspondent of a New York paper, says:

As there is much inquiry in regard to the position of the different members of the Cabinet on the emancipation proclamation, it is proper to state that at a Cabinet meeting on Tuesday the question of its approval was not submitted by the President, he having made up his mind to the act, and being desirous only of consultation on two or three of its clauses, but it is known that Secretary Chase has from the first been a most decided advocate of the measure, in which he has been moderately sustained by Secretaries Welles and Bates. Secretary Stanton has long favored any measure that will strike slavery, though not specially advocating this proclamation. Secretary Blair continues bitter in his opposition to the last, as of late was Secretary Smith. Secretary Seward has all along been known to be unfavorable to the act, though not as out spoken in his opposition as Secretary Blair.

From our Army in Northern Virginia.

There seems to be a general impression that our own forces and those of the enemy in the vicinity of the Potomac, are on the eve of a determined collision. This impression is strengthened by the statements gathered from passengers who came down on the Central train from Staunton yesterday afternoon. From these we learn that on Thursday last the enemy, in considerable force, advanced from Harper's Ferry as far as Charleston, shelling that place from a point about one mile and a half east of the town. Ascertaining that the town was unoccupied by our forces, they moved up and took possession.

On Wednesday evening our cavalry pickets at Martinsburg fell back, and reported the advance of a column of the enemy on the Williamsport road.

The force of the enemy in and around Harper's Ferry is said to be very heavy. The division commanded by Gen. Geary occupies the Loudoun Heights. It is supposed that their main force has crossed, or intends to cross at the Ferry. The force which reached Charlestown Tuesday is believed to be the advance of their army.

From all accounts the condition of our army is excellent. The barefooted have been recently shod by large arrivals of shoes, and the commissariat is now abundantly supplied. The stragglers have all been gathered up, and the whole army is in buoyant spirits and confidently anticipating another brilliant triumph.—*Richmond Dispatch.*

SUNDRIES.

100 WEAVING SLEYS,
10 Bushels Shoe Pegs,
50 Pounds Shoe Thread,
Shoe Pincers, Peg Cutters,
500 Shoe Lasts,
Cotton Plow Lines,
Toilet Soap,
Georgia made Buckets, for sale by
oct 8 N. WEED.

IN STORE,

500 POUNDS Choice Country Hams,
500 " " Sides,
200 " " Shoulders,
250 " " Lard,
40 yds Handsome Jeans,
25 bbls. Fresh Family Flour,
oct 8 J. W. FEARS.

LOST—REWARD.

LOST between Wilder's shop and the Bank of Middle Georgia, on that side of the street yesterday evening, a Lady's Gold Breast Pin with a green bow to it, and the pin containing hair. The finder will be liberally rewarded upon leaving the pin at R. C. Wilder & Co's. shop. (oct 8—2t)

Pay Your Taxes.

THE BOOKS are now open for the payment of CITY TAXES for the year 1862. The books will close the 1st of November next, after which time Execution will issue against all defaulters.

Trunk Lost—$10 Reward.

LOST at the Passenger Depot in Macon, Saturday night last, a Large Black Leather Trunk marked in paint "Ira Harris, Natick, Mass." The finder will receive the above reward on leaving the Trunk with Mr. Brown, at the Brown House, Macon.
Macon, Oct. 7th—d2w* IRA HARRIS.

$15 REWARD.

LOST OR STOLEN between the Passenger Depot and the Bridge, a Silver Double Cased Watch, with a Star cut on the case, the finder will receive the above reward by leaving it at this Office.
oct 7—d3t* WM. H. BROXTON.

Pensacola and Georgia Railroad

EIGHT PER CENT BONDS FOR SALE.—$20,000—Twenty Thousand Dollars Pensacola and Georgia Railroad 8 per cent Bonds. Interest payable in Charleston, S. C., July and January, and Bond redeemable 1870, secured by 2nd Mortgage of Road, and first Mortgage on 280,000 Acres of land—in Bonds of $500 each.
Apply to H. H. DE LEON,
oct 7—d2w* Columbia, S. C.

Book, Job and Fancy Printing!

HAVING bought out the Establishment of JOHN L. JENKINS & CO.,

SAMUEL BOYKIN

Respectfully informs his friends and the public generally, that he is now prepared with experienced workmen to execute all kinds of

JOB AND FANCY PRINTING,

SUCH AS

Minutes, Pamphlets, Bill-Heads, Programmes, Circulars, Posters, Labels, Blanks, Hand-Bills, Railroad Tickets, Hotel Registers, Bye-Laws, Constitutions, Addresses, Catalogues, Notes, Freight Lists, Receipts and Books, and all kinds

OF LETTER PRESS PRINTING.

Orders executed with neatness and dispatch for CASH. Office next door to Ross & Coleman, Cotton Avenue, Macon, Ga. [oct 6—d3t*

ON TROUP HILL.

A VERY desirable building lot, on Troup Hill for SALE. For particulars enquire of
S. B. BURR, Macon Daily Telegraph Office.
oct 6—d3t

$20 REWARD,

LOST by a Lady this morning, at market, a small Buck-skin Port-monie containing Seventy Dollars in Confederate Notes, two or three Postage stamps and some small change. The finder can have the above reward by leaving it at this Office.
Macon, Oct. 4th, 1862. (oct 6 d3t)

Notice to Debtors and Creditors.

ALL persons indebted to the estate of Chas Schneider late of Houston county, deceased, are requested to make immediate payment to the undersigned, and those having demands to render them in terms of the law. HENRY S. DAVIS,
Administrator.
Schley county, Ga., Oct. 6—d1w*

Removal.

HAVING removed my Studio from Washington Block, to the Room above C. T. Ward's Carriage Repository opposite the Floyd House, I respectly inform my patrons and the public that I am prepared to attend to all business entrusted to my care with my endeavors to please all. CHARLES BERUFF,
oct 4—dtf Portrait Painter

For Sale.

BY T. T. & A. H. WYCHE, the best and heavest variety of Seed Oats, Wheat, Barley and Rye. The Oats grown from these Seed will not rust as stated by Mr. Brown, of Wilkerson county. Provisions of all kinds bought and sold.
oct 4—tf

J P Harvey & Co,

HAVE removed their Store to the next door above Freeman & English, where they will be glad to see all their old and many new customers.
oct 4—1w

Copartnership.

I HAVE this day associated with me Mr. George Burdick in the Produce & Commission Business, and will continue the same at the old stand, next door to Hardeman & Sparks' Warehouse. Thankful for past favors, I would respectfully solicit a generous share of publicic patronage to the new Firm.
W. M. DUNN.
Macon, Oct. 1, 1862. oct 4—tf

Sundries.

4000 LBS. Prime Bacon Sides and Hams,
12 Sacks Rye,
150 Sacks Family Flour,
25 Sacks Fine do.
200 Boxes Tobacco, all grades,
5 Bbls. Extra Syrup,
In store and for sale by
oct 4—tf DUNN & BURDICK.

Wanted to Hire.

A NEGRO GIRL for a nurse, from 12 to 15 years old.
oct 4—1w* N. S. PRUDDEN.

Seed Wheat.

1000 BUSHELS OF SEED WHEAT
for sale by T. C. NISBET,
oct 4—d1m Macon Flour Mills.

Tinners Wanted.

FIVE or Six good Tinners can get employment by applying immediately. Good wages paid.
RICHARDSON & FAULKNER.
Atlanta, Sept. 29—1m*

Clinch County Lands FOR SALE!

Lot Number	316—490	Acres.	
"	"	352—490	"
"	"	278—490	"
"	"	353—490	"
"	"	314—490	"
"	"	279—490	"
"	"	*344—490	"

Nearly all of the above Lots lying on or near Suwannee River. *Lot No. 344 partly improved.
PETER J. WILLIAMS,
oct 5—d1m* Macon, Ga.

Just Received,

150 Sacks Liverpool and Virginia Salt,
11 Bales 8oz. Osnaburgs,
6 Hhds. N. O. Sugar,
2 Bags Black Grain Pepper,
12 Barrels pure Corn Whiskey,
5 " " Rye,
10 " Peach Brandy,
10 " Assorted Wines,
150 Boxes assorted grades Tobacco.
For sale by HARRIS & DENSE.
oct. 3d—d1w.

LIVERY SALE.

WILL be sold before the Court House door, in the town of Forsyth, on the first Tuesday in December next, all the Horses, Mules, Buggies, Coaches, Hacks, Harness and other appurtenances belonging to the Livery Stable of the undersigned, unless privately sold before that time. Terms cash. S. H. STONE.
sep 20—d2m

For Rent.

TWO Stores on Cherry street, several Stores under Floyd House and Rooms up stairs, Cherry street.
T. C. DEMPSEY,
oct 2—tf or J. T. WILKINSON.

Tax Notice.

THE Books of the Tax Collector are now open for the payment of State and County Tax, for the year 1862, and I hope all will come forward at once and pay their taxes, as the money is needed, and as the time for paying will necessarily be short, as I have been in bad health and have not been able to open the books as soon as I otherwise would have done.

The books will be closed on the first of November, and as I wish to issue no executions against any, I trust tax payors will save me the necessity by settling in time. Judge H. H. Howard is duly authorised to attend to the business for me until I get able, which I hope will be in a few days.

Office next door to Little & Smith's Harness Store, Cherry street. J. P. SIMS, T. R. & C.
oct 9—

NOTICE.

THE FIRM of L. P. STRONG & SONS is dissolved by the death of the Senior Partner. All those indebted to the Firm will please call at the old stand and settle; all having accounts against the Firm will present them for payment. EDGAR P. STRONG,
FORESTER W. STRONG,
oct 9—d1m* Surviving Partners.

Vineville Property for Sale.

BY order of the Ordinary of Houston county, I will sell on the first Tuesday in November next, before the Court House door in Macon, Bibb county, the House and Lot in Vineville, belonging to the Estate of Benjamin Bryan, late of Houston county, deceased. The lot contains fifty acres, more or less, and is the most beautiful and desirable lot in Vineville. It adjoins W. A. Huff, R. P. Ously and Troutman.
N. L. BRYAN, Adm'r.
oct 1—d1m* on Estate of Benj. Bryan.

$50 Reward.

RANAWAY on the night of the 27th of September last, my negro man JOHN, about 60 years of age, bald-headed, large whiskers, dark complexion, very heavy set and very stout for his age. I will give Fifty Dollars for proof to convict any white man engaged in assisting said negro off, or $25 for said negro lodged in any safe Jail so that I can get him. He once belonged to the estate of Benjamin May, of Bibb county.
oct 1—tf G. J. BLAKE.

Fresh Arrival.

200 BBLS. Fresh Ground Flour,
100 Sacks do do.
100 Reams Wrapping Papper.
50 Hhds. N. O. Sugar,
50 Tierces Rice,
20 Bags Choice Grain Pepper,
20 " " Chickory,
5 " " Coffee,
20 Baskets and Boxes Champaigne,
10 Bales Cotton Yarns,
10 " Sheeting and Shirting,
5 " Drills,
10 Cases Imported Brandy, &c., &c.
All in store and for sale by
oct 1—tf PRITCHETT & WILLIAMSON.

House and Lot for Sale.

IN a good neighborhood and convenient to the business part of the city.
For particulars enquire for me at J. W. Fear's store, Third Street. N. COATES.
oct 1—1m*

For Sale.

IN STORE AND TO ARRIVE,
20 Barrels Peach Brandy,
10 Barrels Corn Whiskey,
10 Barrels Rye Whiskey,
25 Barrels Flour,
15 Bushels Apples.
oct 1—1w* JOHN G. GILMER.

POST OFFICE, Macon, Ga., Oct. 1, 1862.

IN consequence of the change of Schedule on the Macon & Western Rail Road, office and mails will, from and after this day, close at 5 P. M.
oct 1 WASHINGTON POE, P. M.

NOTICE.

SIXTY DAYS after date application will be made to the Court of Ordinary of Wilcox county to sell all the land belonging to the estate of James D. Gibbs, late deceased. ALLEN GIBBS, Sen., Adm'r.
Per J. W. MASHBURN,
oct 1 Ordinary.

For Ladies and Children.

Just received a lot of

CONGRESS GAITORS

& CHILDREN'S SHOES.

Several Gross of German Matches, (Paper Boxes,) and Common do. JOHN C. SCHREINER & SON.
sep 30—tf

PATENT AGENCY.

HAVING been employed, for several years previous to the war, in the Patent Office at Washington, the undersigned feels authorized to offer his services to Inventors wishing to secure Patents for the Confederate States.

PETITIONS, SPECIFICATIONS, DRAWINGS & MODELS,

required by the Patent Office before Patents can be granted, will be promptly executed on due notice. Information or advice applied for in person or by mail, will be given free of charge. (Postage stamps must be enclosed to pre pay the answers by mail.)
CHAS. MALLON, Pat. Agent,
sept 30—d6m Marine Bank, Macon, Ga.

NEW ARRIVAL!

Just received from Charleston a lot of

ENGLISH TOOTH BRUSHES,

Extra Fine Windsor Soap,

Ivory, Horn and Rubber Combs.

Letter and Note Paper, Envelopes, &c.

sep 23—tf JOHN C. SCHREINER & SON.

Shingles Wanted

AT THE C. S. ARMORY, MACON, GA.

75,000 best quality Pine Shingles, for which the market price will be paid on delivery.
Apply to Mr. J. Fuse, Master Builder, on the premises. JAMES H. BURTON,
sept 27—tf Superintendent.

To Rent.

A PLANTATION in Putnam County, containing

Lee County Plantation for Sale.

I WILL sell my Plantation in Lee county, six miles East of Starkville and nine miles from S. W. R. R., containing 1515 acres; 800 cleared, mostly fresh and in a fine state of cultivation. The improvements are new and suited to the place, well watered and healthy, range for Stock good, &c.

Mr. Ray, my overseer on the place, will show the land to any one wishing to purchase.

For further information address me at Macon, Ga.
sep 30—d1m STEPHEN WOODWARD.

Strayed or Stolen

FROM the premises of Dr. M. S. Thomson on the night of the 27th, two Mare Mules. One is a dark rone about 15 hands high, 4 years old; the other is a mouse colored, about 14 hands high, 6 years old, and has a britchung mark on the rump.

I will pay a liberal reward and expenses for their delivery to me at M. Stubblefield's Stable.
sept 30—tf M. R. FREEMAN.

Planters House,

CHERRY STREET, MACON, GEORGIA,

IS NOW open for the reception of Boarders Will accommodate by the day, week or month.
Transient customers $2,00 per day.
aug 20—tf

TO RENT.

ROOMS suitable for a Dwelling. Apply to
oct 7—dtf MRS. A. BULKLEY, Cherry St.

For Sale in Store,

45 BBLS. Virginia Rock Salt,
200 Sacks reboiled Virginia Salt, equal to Liverpool. [oct 7] J. W. FEARS.

Carpenters Wanted.

15 CARPENTERS—white or negro—can find employment and good wages at the C. S. Armory, Macon, if application be made immediately.
Apply to Mr. J. Fuse, Master Builder on the premises. JAS. H. BURTON, Sup't.
sep 24—tf

OFFICE OF THE MILLEDGEVILLE R. R. CO.,
Augusta, Sept. 23d, 1862.

THE Annual Meeting of the Stockholders of this Company will be held at this office in the city of Augusta, on the first Monday of October, (6th day,) 1862, at 10 o'clock, A. M., at which time an election will be held for Directors for the ensuing year, and the general interests of the Company considered
W. MILO OLIN,
sept 24—tf Secretary & Treasurer.

Administrator's Sale.

WILL be sold in the town of Talbotton, Talbot county, Georgia, at the Store House of Joshua P. Strickland, deceased, on Saturday the 11th day of October next within the legal hours of sale the entire Stock of Goods in Store of said deceased, consisting of a good and well assorted Stock of Drugs and Medicines and such other articles as are usually kept by Druggists.

Also a good assortment of Miscellaneous and School Books. The whole to be sold together unless it shall be found necessary to sell in lots on the day of sale.

Terms made known on the day of sale.

A complete Inventory of the whole stock can be seen at the Ordinary's Office. CYRUS ROBINSON,
sep 24—dtd* Administrator

Another Rose Wood Piano for Sale

ONE of Light, Bradbury & Co's best—almost new—in perfect repair. Call soon, and examine. All applications from the country must contain Stamp for reply to insure attention. Price, including boxing, store and cover, (the latter a little damaged,) $500,00.
sept 23—tf J. W. BURKE, Ag't.

MAPS OF THE SEAT OF WAR

IN VIRGINIA & MARYLAND.

A FEW—colored—and containing all the principal localities in the two States. Price 50 cents—by mail 60 cents. J. W. BURKE, Agent.
sep 23—tf

Land for Sale!

THE subscriber offers for sale a Plantation of 1200 acres on the Macon & B. R. R. in Twiggs county. This Land lies between Flat Creek and Savage Creek, and includes a great deal of very rich Swamp Land. 600 acres are in a good state of cultivation; 450 Upland and 150 River Bottom. The improvements consist of an excellent Dwelling House, good Negro Cabins and all necessary outbuildings.

Persons wishing a nice place, blessed with a great many conveniences, would do well to call on me. The terms can be known by addressing me at Marion, Twiggs county, or by application on the premises where I live.
sep 11—d1m* G. W. BRYAN.

Wanted.

NEGRO LABORERS to work in the city.
Apply to R. L. STROHECKER.
sep 24—tf

NOTICE.

WE expect holders of Cotton in our Ware Houses to come forward and pay up their Storage promptly to first of September inst. From that date begins a new commercial year, and our first month's storage will, as usual, be 50 cents per bale. Come up and settle or we will sell cotton enough to pay ourselves.
H. J. COOK,
Albany, Sept. 20—1m* SIMS & RUST.

BARLEY.

50 BUSHELS prime heavy seed Barley for sale by
sep13tf BOWDRE & ANDERSON.

Stolen

ON the night of the 11th inst., a light yellow bay Horse, about 15 hands high, seven or eight years old, one white hind foot, blemish in the left eye, sight of the eye not injured, black main and tail. The above described horse was stolen from the stable of T. N. Killen in Fort Valley. I will give a liberal reward to any one who will deliver me the horse in Fort Valley or for information sufficient that I may get him.
sep13tf* J. N. KILLEN.

DR. NATHAN BOZEMAN,

(LATE OF NEW ORLEANS,)

WOULD respectfully inform his medical friends in Georgia that he will spend the month of October, and perhaps November, in Macon, and will be pleased to take charge of any cases requiring surgical treatment that they may entrust to his care. The "Woman's Hospital" which he has established and conducted for several years in New Orleans, is for the present closed.—Persons in the State having applied for admission into that institution, will now have an opportunity of being treated near their homes.

Letters addressed to the care of Dr. Wm. F. Holt, Macon, will receive prompt attention.
sep 16—d1m

☞ Augusta Constitutionalist and Columbus Sun, will please publish one month and forward bill to this office.

DeBow's Review

FOR MAY—AUGUST, 1862, just received and for sale at the Book Depository. Price 50 cents.
sep 22—tf J. W. BURKE, Agent.

NOTICE.

THE 50th (Col. Jack Brown's Regiment,) left for Virginia under orders on the 17th inst., absentees from

Wanted.

TWENTY GOOD MACHINISTS for employ at "Georgia Armory," Milledgeville.
LACHLAN H. McINTOSH
July 10—tf Chief of Ordnance, State of Geo

Letter and Note Paper.

AN ELEGANT LOT just received and for sale
sep 9—tf J. W. BURKE, Ag

City Marshal's Sale.

WILL be sold before the Court House Door, city Macon, Bibb county, on the first Tuesday in November next, within the legal hours of sale, the following one half of undivided interest in part of lot No seven, square No. (40) forty, in the city of Macon, fronting 33 feet on Cherry street and running back the alley, being Store occupied by Thomas T. W Levied on as the property of James Melcher to sa a city Tax fi. fa. for 1861 and 1862, in favor of the M and Council of the city of Macon vs. said Melch Amount of tax $17 and costs.
sep 12 GEO. D. LAWRENCE, Mars

FOR SALE!

CHAIRS,
SOFAS,
BUREAUS,
BEADSTEADS,
&C.,

FINE AND COMMON COFFI

READY MADE.

By GRENVILLE WO
sep 8—tf

For the Little Ones.

A LARGE lot of Alabaster Dolls—Doll Heads, B &c., Balls, Tin Toys, China Setts, &c., &c.
aug 25—tf J. W. BURKE, Ag

Jailor's Advertisement of a Runaway Slave.

STATE OF GEORGIA, DOUGHERTY COUNT Brought to jail in said county, by Murdock J a runaway slave who says his name is BILL, and he belongs to one Colson, of Pulaski county, in State. Said slave is about six feet high, of dark plexion, and weighs about one hundred and sixty supposed to be about fifty years old. The own said slave is hereby notified to come forward, pay ges, prove property and take him away, otherwi will be sold according to law. J. H. BROWN
aug 22—oaw-ly Dep.

To Pattern Makers.

WANTED at the C. S. Armory, Macon, Ga., se good Pattern Makers, to whom constant and good wages will be given.
Apply to the undersigned. J. H. BURTON
aug 7—tf Superinten

Uniforms.

75 ROSWELL Jeans Uniform Frock Coats, some three months ago for a company an called for. They are 33 per cent. cheaper than the now be manufactured. For sale by
July 9—tf E. WINSH

TO RENT.

2 STORES on Second Street, one formerly occ by Landauer & Bro., as clothing Store. Also Damour's well known Millinery Store, an old lished house of 28 years standing. Also four R 3 formerly occupied by Dr. McDonald as Den rooms. Mrs. Damour offers her entire stock of nery and Fancy Goods for sale at a reduced price sons wishing to purchase would do well to call a amine.

Possession given 1st of October. Apply at
MRS. A. DAMOUR'S
aug 15—tf Millinery Store, Mulbery Str

TO RENT.

THE CITY HOTEL, at present occupied by Mrs. ris on Court House Square, containing 14 R Possession on the 1st of October.
aug 2—tf J. HOLLINGSWOR

A Liberal Reward

WILL be paid for a common Memorandum which I lost yesterday morning, if left at my Size 5⅛ by 3⅛ inches. T. H. BOLSHA
aug 5—tf

The Georgia Academy FOR THE BLIND

THE next Term of this Institution commenc the first day of September. Blind person such as, for want of sufficient sight, cannot be edu in the ordinary schools, of good health and mind, between the ages of 8 and 25, are proper su to become pupils. The indigent of this State a ceived free of charge for board and tuition. The of Instruction embraces all the branches of a co English Education, with Music and some branc handicraft. The Institution is well supplied w the facilities of instruction and with ample acco dations for a large school. Information in reg the existence of blind youths in this State is ea solicited and also applications for their admiss the institution. Address W. D. WILLIAM
Principal, Mac

☞ Papers in this State friendly to the Instit will please copy.
July 22—tf

CHOICE DRESS SILK

HANDSOME DELAINES!

Poplins, Mourning Dress Goods, White and Red nels, Irish Linen, Bleached Homespun, Silk Cotton Hose, White and Black; a fine select of Ribbons, Zephirwool, Knitting Needles Tooth Brushes, Perfumes, Coates' best Spool Cotton, Linen Cambric Handkerchief, beautiful Embroideries, Silk and Kid Gloves, Superior Shawls, Ladies Undervests.

Also, a good assortment of

HATS AND BONNETS, FEATHERS,

For sale at the lowest market prices.
aug 30—tf MRS. F. DES

Works on Baptism

THE following works on Baptism, defending the Baptist view of the subject, may be found Depository, to which the public attention is in
Theodius Walton, a Reply to Theodosia
Summers on Baptism,
Baker on Baptism,
Fairchild on Baptism,
Proselytors Defeated,
Reasons for not Joining the Baptist Chur
Baptismal Demonstrations,
Apostolic Baptism, by Taylor.
Doctrine of Baptisms, By Armstrong.
Baptist Controversy, by Reneau.
aug 26—tf J. W. BURKE, A

GENERAL HOSPITAL,
Macon, Ga., August 18th, 18

NOTICE is hereby given to Conscripts and a lies interested, that all examinations, and ness relating thereto, are conducted ONLY at the ling Office, Washington Block, opposite the House. It is impossible for me to give any att whatever, to such, at the Hospital.

Chapter 7

Emancipation in Southern Eyes

As in the North, the Emancipation Proclamation elicited a spate of intense emotions and reactions among whites in the South: fear, insecurity, and suspicion, mixed with indignation and contempt. Almost instinctively, white Southerners read the proclamation as a clarion call for blacks to rise in rebellion and ruthlessly overturn the Confederacy's slave-based civilization. For years, they had feared that the slaves—either of their own accord or with the help of Northern abolitionists—would attempt such a racial revolution. Now, in announcing that his government and his armies would no longer do anything to prevent the slaves from achieving their freedom, Lincoln was, in Southern eyes, giving the signal for the bloodletting to begin. "It is an invitation to murder, and rape, and spoilation," wailed the *Charleston Courier*. "No scheme more atrociously wicked ever entered the mind of man." Lincoln's "fiendish proclamation," another paper agreed, was designed specifically "to incite servile insurrection in the Southern States and thus consign our women and children to indiscriminate butchery." A correspondent to the *Greensborough Patriot*, adding to the consensus, condemned Lincoln's "sweeping proclamation" as "an open declaration of an intention to foster a servile war in our midst." It was proof positive that the Union was fighting not just to "restore the Union" or merely to "crush the rebellion" but rather to initiate the wholesale "*extermination*" of the Southern people.[1] Amid the anxieties of the moment, suspicions ran high, as Southern planters were left to wonder what their slaves were really thinking, and perhaps plotting. Shortly after Lincoln announced his Preliminary Emancipation Proclamation in September 1862, the Atlanta *Southern Confederacy* issued this cautionary report about a possible slave uprising, which was quickly reprinted and circulated in newspapers across the state of Georgia:

> We learned yesterday that the citizens residing in and around Palmetto have been considerably

MASKS AND FACES.

King Abraham before and after issuing the EMANCIPATION PROCLAMATION.

Southern Illustrated News, November 8, 1862.
In the Southern mind, the Emancipation Proclamation exemplified the true wickedness of Abraham Lincoln, depicted here in the shape of a devil who only masquerades as a man.

excited for a few days owing to the confessions of a negro man belonging to the Beavers' estate in Campbell county. It appears that he was implicated in stealing some leather, and under the lash revealed, or pretended to reveal, the existence of a plan being on foot to raise and organize several negro companies, which . . . were to make their way to the Yankees, in response to Lincoln's proclamation. He seemed to be pretty well posted as to the proclamation declaring emancipation, and the time it was to take effect, &c. He told a great many things—some of which were probably true, and many not; but he told enough to show that our people should be on their guard. Lincoln intended the proclamation to excite insurrection among us. There are some vicious negroes among us the same as there are some vicious white people or vicious horses; and the whole negro race is weak-minded and easily led away by having their passions wrought upon by incendiaries and emissaries from the North. No doubt we shall have such vile characters sent among us for that express purpose. Let our people be on the alert.

We have often insisted that all kinds of public negro gatherings, such as balls, Sunday gatherings, and night meetings, should be suspended. We still advise slave owners to keep their slaves at home as much as possible, and out of bad company. Proper vigilance in this matter may be *wise*.[2]

Despite the horrors that emancipation evoked in the minds of whites, there remained a hope that if nothing else, the proclamation would at least make Southerners all the more determined to win their independence. As this editorial from the *Richmond Examiner* declared expectantly, if there was anyone in the Confederacy who held any lingering love for the old Union, the proclamation would surely crush it out forever:

The most startling political crime, the most stupid political blunder, yet known in American history, has now been consummated.—The promised proclamation of Abraham Lincoln to decree the abolition of negro slavery, in all the States of the late Union not yet subjugated by the arms of the United States, is laid before the reader this morning.

It is difficult to decide whether wickedness or folly predominates in this extraordinary document. . . . The pretense that slavery is abolished as an act of justice to the negro, will provoke a smile if the hypocritical falsehood did not excite disgust. In Maryland, Missouri, Tennessee and Kentucky, and those portions of Virginia and Louisiana now in possession of his armies, the institution of slavery is left in its full force. Yet these are the portions of the late Union in which this violator of human and divine laws possesses the power—the actual, practical power—of destroying the relation between master and slave. If sympathy for the slave and justice to the negro were the least of his motives, he would take especial care and pains that his proclamation should be fully applied to those districts where he has the means of executing its provisions. But he directs it only to those portions of the Southern Confederacy still inhabited by free citizens, where his armies have never been, and where his proclamation can take effect only in the bloody scenes of foreign conquest or servile insurrection.

To produce this last named effect—servile insurrection—is the real, sole purpose of this proclamation. . . . No other translation of this paper will be given to it either in Europe or America. That it will fail to accomplish this vile end, and be void and entirely without effect in the Southern Confederacy, unless our armies should be not only beaten, but destroyed, are truths which need not be explained or argued before our readers. So far from being a cause for alarm, this proclamation is a subject of congratulation to the friends of the Southern cause. It exposes the true character of the enemy, beyond the possibility of misconception. . . . Its effect on the people of the South will be most salutary. It shuts the door of retreat and repentance on the weak and timid. Those who would turn back in their path, if there are any, have now no longer that miserable chance. Even submission now cannot procure mercy. The deed is done, and the Southern people have only to choose between victory and death.[3]

The Black Flag.

The recent fiendish proclamation of the Washington despot, intended as it evidently is to incite servile insurrection in the Southern States and thus consign our women and children to indiscriminate butchery, has evoked an earnest indignation throughout the Confederacy which looks strongly to the erection of the black flag. Not that any body supposes any mischief will be sustained beyond the Federal lines; but the document, however harmless in its effect, betrays a depth of depravity which finds no parallel in the history of the world since the dawn of Christianity. The *spirit* it embodies could not be more savage and cruel, if it had emanated from a conclave of demons in the bottomless pit. A nation of people who can calmly acquiesce in such a policy from their authorities, have reached the last degree of which depravity itself is capable.

South-Western Baptist, October 16, 1862.
Across the Confederacy, the Emancipation Proclamation elicited calls for raising the "black flag"—the pirate's symbol of death. Convinced that the proclamation invited slaves to arise in revolt and massacre their masters, the Southern press insisted that retaliation was the only proper response.

As far as the newspapers were concerned, it was not enough for the Southern people to come together in rebuking and resisting the enemy. The Confederate government had to take official, retaliatory action and make the Yankees pay a heavy price for fomenting a race war in their midst. Since the time Union soldiers first set foot on Confederate soil, the question of retaliation had been discussed constantly in the Southern press, but especially so as the Union shifted tactics from limited war to hard war. In August 1862, Jefferson Davis had issued a public statement on the subject of retaliation, promising vengeance on Union officers for acts perpetrated against Southern civilians, but he stopped short of requisitioning retaliatory raids against noncombatants in the North. Now, in the wake of the Emancipation Proclamation, Southerners openly questioned the wisdom of maintaining such restraint. When the *Memphis Appeal* published a demand for "a more general and effectual retaliation" to protect and vindicate the "self-respect" of the Southern people, it met with rousing approval from one reader. From his perspective at least, the desire to see Northern homesteads desolated had become a prevalent and ardent one:

> All say raise the black flag—send one hundred thousand cavalry, such as Texas, Arkansas and other southwestern States can instantly furnish, into the grain growing territory of the enemy, and let them, torch in hand, burn corn, wheat, flour, bacon, hay, and every combustible thing upon which man or beast can subsist; let them furthermore kill every horse, mule, ox, or other beast useful in transporting supplies for the enemy; nay, let them spare no beast, no machinery or supplies that will either directly or indirectly aid the enemy to prosecute this infernal war. . . .
>
> The high tone of the President's [Jefferson Davis's] message has gone before the Yankees as pearls before swine. No responsive throb of honor beats in their pulses. He says that "we cannot make war upon unarmed men, nor upon private property," etc. These sentiments show well the high moral worth of our President, and every Southern man would say amen! if the enemy were to pursue the same policy; but in the present attitude of affairs the President must instantly recede from the high ground he has taken, or he will inflict an unmeasurable injury upon the people of his own government. "An eye for an eye" and "a tooth for a tooth" has always been the law of war amongst the most enlightened nations, and any ruler that does not give his people the full advantage of this standard robs them of their natural right of self defense; and when this means of self defense is taken from a people contending with three times their number, this injury is increased beyond endurance—it is ruin.
>
> Is the private property of the enemy better than our private property that it should be sacredly protected, and ours destroyed; should he be allowed in peace to cultivate his fields . . . when our houses are in flames, our wives and children screaming for protection, our property of every description destroyed, and when even our slaves, who are our hereditary friends, are invoked at midnight to butcher our wives who in childhood were the playmates of their wives, and are yet the best friends their wives ever had; and when these slaves whose children are the playmates of our children are invoked to destroy our children with the knife and with fire? Under these circumstances can the President hesitate to adopt any means of defense that will be most likely to thwart the enemy? In cold blood the enemy is shooting and killing men in the South that never bore arms against him. Must this be borne unavenged?—justice says never![4]

In keeping with what appeared to be the popular will, the Confederate Congress took up the issue of retaliation in October 1862 and passed a resolution vowing to support Jefferson Davis in whatever measures he might propose in response to Lincoln's proclamation. Consequently, as the proclamation went into effect in January, the Southern press clamored loudly for Davis to take a decisive and defiant stand—at least against Union troops caught on Southern soil. The individual Southern states already had their own laws regulating slavery, and inciting a slave insurrection was a crime of the highest order. "The punishment for such a felony, by the laws of all our Sates, is *death by hanging*," one paper remarked pointedly.[5] As the *Mississippian* made clear, Davis was expected to honor the letter of the law on this issue:

> According to the best information which we can get from the North, Abraham Lincoln will probably issue his proclamation to-day . . . by which our slaves are declared free, and invited to rise up in servile insurrection, to kill their masters and all the white women and children of the South. . . .
>
> What does Lincoln expect to gain by such a proclamation? His first idea was perhaps to frighten the slave States back to their bondage. He is, however, thoroughly convinced that this was a vain hope. Does he think the destruction of the institution of slavery would restore a Union? He knows full well that it would make wider and deeper the gulf that separates the two sections. . . .
>
> What, then, does he hope to gain by it? Simply our destruction—to inaugurate upon us those horrors which make the soul sick to contemplate. . . . It is the act of a grovelling, vengeful assassin, who, through envy and hatred, having provoked quarrels with a brother, . . . betakes himself in the dead hour of night to the dark paths of crime, waylays and stabs his unsuspecting brother in the back.
>
> A Government actuated by such a spirit throws itself beyond the pale of civilization; and the minions engaged in fighting the battles of such a government are not proper subjects for the mildness of civilized warfare. We must acquiesce in the grand necessity upon us, and avert from our people those horrors which the diabolical venom of our inveterate foes would inflict upon *us* by turning them *upon their own heads!*… The duty of the [Confederate] government is clear. The people who have periled all, and given thousands of lives for the disenthralment of their country, have a right to look to the government for protection. There is only one effective way for the government to give the protection needed, and that is RETALIATION.
>
> The last Congress wisely left the subject of Lincoln's proclamation and retaliation with the President to be dealt with as exigencies arose. . . . Let him then issue his [own] proclamation declaring that all commissioned officers in Lincoln's insurrectionary army shall be treated as felons and be held amenable to the laws of the States on the subject of tampering with slaves. Let this be done promptly, and let all the commissioned officers which fall into our hands be consigned at once to felon's prisons and be tried by the courts of our several States.—This

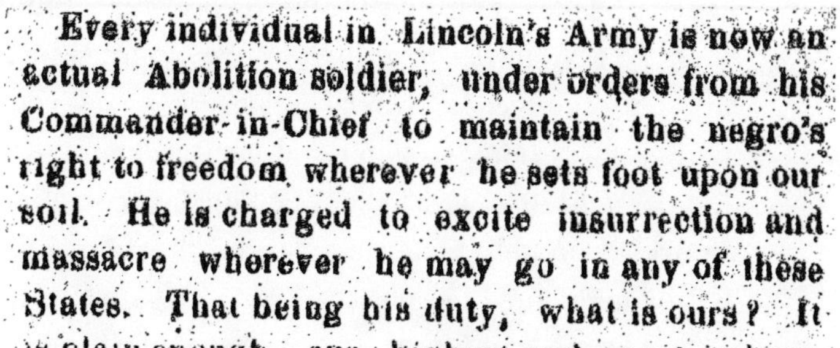
Every individual in Lincoln's Army is now an actual Abolition soldier, under orders from his Commander-in-Chief to maintain the negro's right to freedom wherever he sets foot upon our soil. He is charged to excite insurrection and massacre wherever he may go in any of these States. That being his duty, what is ours? It is plain enough—our highest and most solemn duty is to see to it, that he meets the punishment which our laws ordain. The intention, design and motive of the North have been proclaimed to all the world. Nothing now remains for Lincoln's soldiers to do, to consummate the *felony* of attempting to excite insurrection but *the act*, and that consists in coming upon, or remaining on, any part of the soil within the jurisdiction of any of the Confederate States. This alone now constitutes the felonious act; the intent is already made known, and after the proclamation, no Northern soldier comes upon our soil but with the intention manifested in that proclamation. The punishment for such a felony, by the laws of all our States, is *death by hanging*. Let the law be enforced whenever the guilty party is taken.

Augusta Constitutionalist, January 16, 1863.
The demands for retaliation invoked Southern laws that made inciting insurrection a capital crime, one deserving of death by hanging.

course will be fully justified by every sentiment of justice. . . . If we must continue the war under Lincoln's infamous and demoniac proclamation, let it be continued in the spirit of that proclamation. Let there be no more child's play.[6]

Equally outraged, the *Natchez Daily Courier* agreed that the time for "play" was over. Southerners had to take swift action for their self-defense:

> So far as the South is concerned, the Lincoln Emancipation Proclamation needs very little discussion. . . . This is not the time for discussion; it is the hour for action. If a man in your own country sets fire to your residence, thereby endangering lives, you hang him. If he is an aider and abetter, you hang him, or put him out of the way. If Lincoln's commissioned scoundrels come among us for the same diabolical and murderous purposes, *why, hang them, and string them to the first tree*, that those whom they would endeavor to corrupt may witness their horrible fate. The day has passed for argument; the hour has come for quick retribution on the heads of the invaders. The Union question, the right of secession, and all other debatable matters shrink into insignificance, when the fiendish enemy is commissioned, with sword and torch to murder our people and destroy our homes!
>
> We say, hang all their Commissioned Officers! and let their uncouth bodies die and rot as high as Haman's did!
>
> They first attempted to starve us to death, by means of the blockade; their next move was to ruin us by stealing our property; and now Lincoln, throwing himself into Abolition arms, seeks to encourage murder and rapine in our own families. The hour for ACTION has arrived. Let our people strengthen our armies. Give a new and powerful impetus to our cause. Drive back and destroy the invading foe, and take no officers as prisoners, except to hang them by the neck until they are dead, DEAD, DEAD![7]

Officially at least, Jefferson Davis met the expectations of the press perfectly. In a message to the Confederate Congress on January 12, 1863, he publicly lambasted the Emancipation Proclamation and promised that captured Union officers would be given over to state authorities for prosecution on the capital charges of inciting servile insurrection. In practice, though, the policy was never systematically enforced. Although the threat of reprisal was empowering in theory, the Confederacy could ill afford to provoke even sterner counterretaliatory measures from the Union. Davis's stance on retaliation was more for home consumption. The Southern people needed to feel that he stood ready to defend them.

Indeed, while denouncing the enemy, the press was also very mindful of the need to mollify Southern public opinion. For behind the calls for united action and renewed determination against the Yankees lay a lingering fear that Lincoln's new policy might actually divide Southerners along class lines and alienate poorer whites from the war. Emancipation drew attention to the fact that the war was about slavery—that the slaveholding class had special property interests at stake that other, ordinary Southerners did not share. Only one-quarter of all Southern whites owned any slaves, and the wealthiest planters, who possessed fifty slaves or more, constituted a mere 1 percent of the South's white population. Lincoln's proclamation thus implied that the common people of the Confederacy were sacrificing themselves in a "rich man's war." As one paper wondered aloud: "Perhaps, the Proclamation aims to create the impression at the South, that the war is simply a war for and against slavery" and thereby to incite "a separation in feeling and action, between slaveholders and 'non-slaveholding whites.'"[8] Traditionally, race had always trumped class as the main line of social division in the South. In the face of black slavery, whites felt a common brotherhood that belied the status differences between them. The leading men in the Confederacy wanted to make sure it stayed that way. The press therefore carefully counted the ways in which ordinary whites benefited from slavery. In the interest of affirming the economic interest of the masses in preserving it, the *Richmond Whig* published this excerpt from a sermon preached by the Reverend J. D. Renfroe, chaplain of the Tenth Alabama Regiment, to the soldiers under his charge:

> I contend . . . that the poor of the country have more reason to desire Southern independence than the rich. I speak it, too, as the representative of the poor. I am a poor man myself, and . . . I urge, most earnestly, that I have more interest in the war—more at stake—than any rich man can have. The rich man's property is at stake, while the freedom of my children and children's children is involved in the issue. I never owned a slave in my life, and yet I contend that I have more interest in the institution of slavery than the man who owns five hundred. Abolish the institution of slavery, and your children and my children must take the place of the institution. Abolish that institution—as is the design of our enemies—and in less than a half century the poor of the land must become the carriage drivers, body-servants, waiting maids and tenants of the rich. You may say that the poor would never submit to this. How would they avoid it? The capital of the rich would be converted into land; they would own the land of the entire country. The poor man has to live somewhere, and he must have something upon which to subsist—he cannot live on the air. Sheer necessity would drive him to gladly accept the tenancy and employment of the rich. I ask you, soldiers, to contemplate first the subjugation of your country, and the abolition of slavery, and then look down through a few generations, and behold your worthy offspring grinding in a factory, scouring a tavern, tilling the soil of the wealthy, and blacking the boots of the dandy; and then tell me whether the poor have anything to fight for? See your posterity in cruel bondage—see them reduced to an equality with the negro man and woman, and then remember that those whom they serve are the proud descendants of the very people who subjugated your country, and overthrew your Government; and then tell me if this is not pre-eminently a poor man's war?
>
> In our country, color is the distinction of classes—the only real distinction. Here the rich man and the poor man and their families are equals in every important respect. The poor . . . are as free and independent as the rich. . . . This is not true of any free State on the face of the earth—I mean any State where domestic slavery does not exist. With them the grades of society are controlled by the weight of the purse. Examine any nation in any age of the world where the existence of the institution is not allowed, and the poor of the land are the slaves of the rich. It is so in the North; it is so in Europe. . . . And here it will be so when the "free labor" fanaticism shall have ruined our land.
>
> Another thought: it is a matter of very great importance to the poor of any country that the value of labor be kept at the highest price possible. It is the constant interest of the laboring man to use every fair and honorable means to keep the price of labor up. In the South the poor have the co-operation of the rich in estimating the worth of labor, because it is also the interest of the rich that the price of a day, or a week, or a month's work, stands at the highest possible figure. The rich man wants the highest estimate placed upon the labor of his servants, and the poor man desires a similar estimate to be fixed for his labor; thus they co-operate to keep up the price of labor. . . . With us, all classes conspire for the constant increase of the value of labor—because it is their interest to do so. But remove the institution of African slavery, and will this be true any longer? No, verily; at once it becomes the interest of every rich man to put the price of labor down to the lowest figure. He owns the land, he owns the factories, he holds the property and the money of the country, and he must have his tenants, his laborers and his hired servants. Then the rich conspire to reduce the

> price of labor in all its departments, and the poor man must work at the prices established for him by the rich; I say *must*, because he must eat; and if he eat, he must work; and if he work, he must work at the rich man's price, though it be but a penny a day. . . . The institution of slavery constitutes the reason why labor is worth so much more in the South than anywhere else on the globe.[9]

Adding to the argument for white solidarity, the *Charleston Mercury* cautioned that emancipation was more than just a threat to the economic status of common citizens. It also exposed them to horrific social problems that no white man could countenance. As the *Mercury* warned, the proclamation would upend the rigid racial order that *all* Southerners enjoyed. Eventually, the free intermingling of whites and blacks would spark either a genocidal power struggle between them or—what was deemed equally disastrous—the intermarriage and melding of the races into a degraded, mongrelized mass:

> We believe that there is not in the world a more harmonious population than the white population of the Southern States. Every white man feels and knows that the negro is not of his race, that one race is the superior race, and that he is one of the superior race. . . . With the same privileges and rights, his affinities are with his race. All his aspirations, his security, his interests, are bound up in their destiny. Nor is he left to speculation to know the fate of white men in a community of liberated negroes. . . .
>
> Suppose the object of Northern Abolitionists then accomplished, and the four millions of slaves liberated at the South—what becomes of the poorer whites? The rich—the sagacious—will leave the country. None will remain, but those who are unable to leave it, or who do not realize the fearful terrors of their condition. A strife will arise between the white men who remain in the South and the negroes, compared with which the atrocities and crimes of ordinary wars are peace itself. The midnight glare of the incendiary's torch will illuminate the country from one end to another; while pillage, violence, murder, poisons and rape will fill the air with the demonic revelry of all the bad passions of an ignorant, semi-barbarous race, urged to madness by the licentious teachings of our Northern brethren. A war of races—a war of extermination—must arise. . . . Or, possibly, suppose no antagonism between the two races—and harmony and identification takes place—amalgamation must be the result. There is no portion of our people who contemplate such a fate with as much horror as our white non-slaveholders—because they are the people who will be exposed to it in the wreck of our institutions. With the continuance of these institutions, not only their industrial occupations, but their political and social station—their domestic safety—the purity of their homes—is identified. And the white man of the South is as proud as the haughtiest aristocrat that walks Wall street or lives in a Fifth Avenue palace with his wife and children. The consequence is, that there are no people in the South who abhor Abolitionists more than the non-slaveholders of the South, or who are more ready to resist their machinations. With them, it is not only the patriotic hatred of a public foe who would involve the country in convulsion and ruin, but it is also the hatred of a social, personal enemy—the Black Republican—who would force upon them the alternative either of the most terrible degradation and barbarism, or of slaughtering the negro, or being slaughtered by him, in a war of extermination.
>
> The people of the North cannot, or will not, understand this state of things. They gloat with secret joy at the anticipations of conflicts among the citizens of the South, by which their fiendish policy will be consummated. . . . Our people—slaveholders and non-slaveholders—they . . . are one in sympathy, interest and feelings. They have equal rights and privileges—one fate. They will stand together in

defence of their liberties and institutions, and will yet exist at the South [as] a powerful and prosperous confederation of commonwealths, controlling the welfare and destiny of other nations, but controlled by none.[10]

If the newspapers offer any indication, the Emancipation Proclamation did nothing to shake the Confederacy's devotion to slavery. Now that the institution was officially under attack, Southern newspapers frankly affirmed—as they had at the start of the war—that slavery was the heart of the Confederate nation and the motivation behind its bid for independence. Regardless of the other political questions or military events that helped precipitate the outbreak of the Civil War, "negro slavery was the *cause* of it," avowed one Georgia paper. "But for this, there would have been no occasion . . . for the disintegration of the Union in 1861" and the establishment of a separate Southern nation. "The Confederate Government was created as a necessity for the protection of the right to property in slaves." More than just a matter of fact, the central place of slavery in Southern society remained a point of pride. At the beginning of the conflict, Southern newspapers had declared that the Confederacy had a great destiny to fulfill in vindicating the rightfulness of slavery. The proclamation only made the Confederacy all the more committed to proving that emancipationism—which not only the Northern states but also the European nations had endorsed in the nineteenth century—was wrong. "The establishment of this Confederacy is verily a distinct reaction against the whole course of the mistaken civilization of the age," the *Richmond Examiner* explained forthrightly. "For 'Liberty, Equality, Fraternity,' we have deliberately substituted Slavery, Subordination and Government." While Northerners evidently would have blacks and whites mingling together as equals, the South remained wedded to the belief "that there were slave races born to serve, master races born to govern." As the *Examiner* reverently envisioned, the Confederacy was "a God-sent missionary to the nations" of the world, "with great truths to preach" on the proper place of blacks in a white-dominated society.[11]

Buoyed by the belief that they were doing God's work in defending slavery, Southerners looked imploringly to Him for refuge and strength. If God was truly on their side, and if emancipation interfered with His plan for the black race, then certainly the Almighty would come to the rescue and shield both the Confederate nation and slavery from destruction. In this spirit, the *Charleston Courier* issued the following "prayer for the times," affirming the absolute righteousness of slavery and beseeching God to give His aid to the Southern people in their holy mission to protect it:

> O, God, we adore thee as the high and mighty ruler and judge of all mankind; the creator of our bodies, the inspirer of our minds, the preserver of our lives, the source of all our mercies, and the sovereign disposer of all things that affect the time and manner of our birth, our condition in society and our natural rights, privileges and responsibilities. Thou hast so ordained human government . . . as to make it necessary and wise that there shall be rulers and subjects, masters and servants, rich and poor, and that these inequalities of condition and diversities of rank should be permanent and inevitable. From the beginning hitherto Thou hast also, O righteous God, associated the institution of slavery as an organic form of involuntary labor with Thy Church and people, thereby securing for slaves religious teaching and provision for their temporal wants, and to the world the benefit of service not otherwise attainable. . . .
>
> By Thy holy, wise and powerful providence, O Lord, Thou hast introduced slavery into these Southern States. . . . Thou hast brought this people among us and hast multiplied and blessed them, and by their labor, their social progress, their spiritual attainments and their conversion to God, thou hast ordained out of their mouth[s] praise to Thy great

name. . . . And now, O Lord, it is time for Thee to work, for . . . we are persecuted, defamed and overwhelmed with all the miseries brought upon us by malicious and merciless enemies, who neither regard God [nor] man. But Thou, O Lord, beholdest from heaven the rage and madness of this people. . . . And as Thou hast commanded that from such men we should withdraw ourselves, we now invoke Thine omnipotent arm for our protection. Thou hast seen, O Lord, all their past perfidy, perjury and oppression, and Thou hast heard their loud boastings, and arrogant and God-defying proclamations for our destruction, and the ruin of the slaves whom Thou hast given us. . . . Thou hast heard, O Lord, the raging of their people, who gnash upon us with their teeth, and would devour us as their prey.

Oh Thou that sittest in the heavens, laugh at them. Speak to them in Thy wrath, and vex them in Thy sore displeasure. . . . Preserve us from all fear of them, and deliver us, O Lord our God, out of their hands. . . . Having driven us to the Red Sea of blood, may they be engulphed beneath its overwhelming waters, that all the kingdoms of this earth may know that Thou art the Lord, and Thou only. Blow with Thy wind and cause the sea to cover them, and let them sink as lead in the mighty waters. . . . And in the greatness of Thine excellency overthrow them that have risen up against Thee. Oh Thou art glorious in holiness, fearful in praises, a God doing wonders, in Thy mercy lead forth Thy people, our wives and our little ones, our men servants and our maid servants, and guide us in Thy strength to Thy holy habitation. Bring us in and plant us in the mountain of thine inheritance; in the place, O Lord, which Thou hast made for us to dwell in, . . . free from the despotic interpretations and enforcements of men.

Establish us, therefore, O God, as a Confederacy of States, and build us up on that rock of eternal truth against which the gates of hell shall not prevail. . . . Look down upon us especially as a slaveholding Confederacy . . . and make slavery a blessing to ourselves, to our slaves, and to the world at large. . . . Preserve our slaves from the fanatical machinations of our enemies who would delude and destroy them, and under the promise of liberty reduce them to poverty, barbarism and exile from the Christian home and happiness of their fathers. Imbue their minds with confidence in their masters, and with a spirit of cheerful and loving obedience. May they remain loyal and true notwithstanding all the temptations with which they are assailed. Secure to them their present religious advantages, and dispose our hearts to be more faithful to their souls and render unto them things just and equal.

May the issue of this war signally prove that this battle is the Lord's. . . . May atheistic blasphemy and blind fanaticism be openly rebuked . . . and the wisdom, equity and mercy of Thy providential dealings towards this people, be gloriously established in the sight of our enemies, and before all nations throughout all generations; and may glory rest on our land.[12]

Despite such earnest displays of faith in the divine nature of slavery, the new policy of emancipation compelled God-fearing Southerners to question why He would allow the institution—*His* institution—to be undermined and threatened with destruction. If God sanctioned the subordination of blacks to whites, why would He tolerate Lincoln's attempts to separate and alienate the slaves from their masters? Certain that slavery itself was right, Southerners began to consider the possibility that the problem was with themselves. God was using emancipation to punish them for *abusing* slavery, for taking the labor of their slaves without giving back the humane, Christian care that God expected them to provide. In this vein, the *Columbus Sun* avowed:

Has God any interest in this struggle? Is there any principle involved in it, that concerns the interest of His church? We answer each of these queries without any hesitation in the affirmative. The question involved in this war is African slavery. Whatever we may say, whatever our enemies may say, that is the issue. This institution undoubtedly concerns the interest of the church. He has settled the legality of it in His word for His followers. He intends by this struggle to settle it before the world. It is not necessary to discuss the subject of slavery here. We believe God intends to put his seal to it and that He will do [so] by our deliverance. No reasonable man can doubt that our subjugation (which is impossible) would result in the abolition of slavery. This would entail ruin upon ourselves and our slaves, and such ruin as the world has rarely witnessed. Now the church of God has much at stake in this conflict, and if we are but faithful to our trust and firm in our purposes, all will be well. This war is only a chastisement. We have sinned. We have abused the institution of slavery, that was intended to be a blessing to us and to the slave. We have not consulted his interest and welfare as we should have done. God intends by this war to correct this matter.[13]

In addition to questioning the morality of excessive punishments, Southerners concerned by the abuses of slavery pointed specifically to two problems. One was the slighting of the slaves' moral education. In order to prevent their slaves from falling under the sway of abolitionist literature, many planters forbade them to learn how to read—a rule that also prevented them from studying the Bible and fully appreciating God's word. The second related to the destruction of slave families. When selling their slaves for profit, masters routinely separated parents from children and husbands from wives, in complete disregard of biblical laws on the sanctity of marriage and family. Records from interstate slave sales conducted in the South during the nineteenth century reveal that one-quarter of them entailed breaking up a first marriage, while half tore apart a nuclear family, often by severing young children from their mothers and fathers.[14] For decades, Southern politicians and ideologues had been defending slavery as a beneficent institution ordained by God to bring barbarous blacks under the civilizing influence of white Christian masters. However, these abuses suggested that the South was failing to live up to God's expectations.

The belief that God was now chastising the South for abusing slavery fueled a religious movement to transform it into a more humane and thoroughly Christian institution. Certainly, interest in improving slavery was not new. The notion that the Confederacy should fashion itself into a more perfect biracial society—one characterized by ties of Christian goodwill between white masters and black slaves—had been articulated in the press at the start of the war. But only after the Emancipation Proclamation did the idea gain real momentum. This reformist impulse, which was especially strong in Georgia and Alabama, started within the Episcopal Church but eventually garnered the support of Baptists and Presbyterians as well.[15] It is important to remember that although the churches critiqued the manner in which slaves were treated, they never went so far as to call into question the rightfulness of slavery itself. They simply aimed to please God by making slavery better. For the sake of winning His approval and help, they wanted Southerners to stop viewing their slaves solely as economic investments, loved only for their profit value. Such avariciousness or "greed of gain," warned the *Christian Index*, was the Confederacy's "Great National Sin" and the cause of its present suffering:

> Heaven knows, this is a general and particular sin of our people. . . . O how we gloried in the *negro*, the source of our wealth!—And oh, how we enthroned *Cotton*, the symbol of our monetary power, as *King*. . . . The one great thought of the nation was to own "land and negroes" and "raise cotton." Far too forgetful of God, we ranged ourselves under the banner of Mammon, forgetful that we "cannot serve God and mammon.". . . Is not this covetousness—the "love of money," which "is the root of all evil?" And what evils have followed?

RELIGIOUS DUTIES OF MASTERS TO SLAVES.

The Protestant and Catholic clergy of the Confederacy are calling attention to the duty of enforcing the sanctity of the marriage relation among slaves. The Baptist Convention of Georgia has adopted an emphatic resolution upon this subject. The *Southern Churchman* quotes various religious authorities, setting forth the sinfulness of any neglect by masters of this Christian duty; among them Bishop Verot, (Roman Catholic Bishop of Savannah,) who says: "Slavery, to become a permanent institution of the South, must be made to conform to the law of God; a Southern Confederacy will never thrive unless it rests upon morality and order; the Supreme Arbiter of Nations will not bless with stability and prosperity a state of things which would be a flagrant violation of His holy commandments.

Richmond Dispatch, January 30, 1865.
Although the Emancipation Proclamation did nothing to weaken the Confederacy's devotion to slavery, it did make the country's religious leaders more committed to reforming the abuses of slavery, so as to win God's approval for preserving the institution.

Why, great and foremost beyond all others, . . . we neglect our moral duties to our slaves.

Short-sighted man! Vainly will he ever contend against the will of [the] Deity!

God, doubtless, placed the black man in our midst for some grand special purpose, and we have sought to turn him solely to our own selfish advantage, regardless, in a great degree, of his moral rights and the inscrutable decrees of Providence.

What christian slaveholder can lay his hand over his heart and say he has done his *whole duty* to his slaves? Have we not slighted their moral and religious education? . . . Have we not failed, by legislation, to protect them in their marriage relation? Have we not inflicted untold distress in separating families? We rightly claim divine sanction for the institution; but have we not, in the sight of heaven, abused that institution? And may it not be that, in the sight of God these heaven-reaching sins, growing primarily out of *avarice or covetousness*, are the cause of our present sufferings? Can we, as a sensible people, shut our eyes to the great fact that slavery is the cause of this war, and that God . . . seems to be depriving us of those very beings, whom we so conscientiously believe He has placed here in accordance with the righteousness of his own moral government? Because of conviction or prejudice, shall we, *after all*, . . . blindly shut our eyes to what may be *"our great national sin?"* Does not the finger of Providence seem unmistakably to be pointing at this dependent race, and indicating that in some way or other, in our duty towards that race, we are guilty of a sin for which He is afflicting us, and seeking to bring us into the line of march with his own grand Providence?[16]

Eager that changes be instituted quickly, leaders of the Methodist Episcopal Church in Alabama created a special Committee on the Duties of Masters and Slaves and issued this report in the *Southern Christian Advocate*, affirming both the need for slavery reform and their hope that the planter class would cooperate in enacting it:

> The . . . lawfulness of the relation of master and servant will not be questioned by any in our community. . . . But with what prerogatives does this relation endow the master? Does it give him the absolute proprietorship of his slaves? No sensible man imagines that it does. "All souls are mine," says Jehovah. The master and the slave are alike His property. By His providence, He has given the master the right to control the labor of his servants. In view of the responsibilities involved in this relation, the master enjoys the *usufruct* of his servants—nothing more. He may compel them to labor, according to their ability, for a reasonable portion of time, allowing leisure for their meals, which, with their clothing and other necessaries, should be plentiful and good—and for recreation and repose. The Committee are happy to believe that there are but few masters in the Confederate States who do not recognize the justness and importance of these views. It is believed that the opinion is very generally entertained, that man as well as beast can do more work in six days than in seven. Hence on economical grounds, servants are allowed the weekly day of rest. Sound policy, as well as humanity, induces masters to pay attention to the physical wants of their servants—to be moderate in exacting labors and enforcing penalties—to take care of their humble dependents in childhood, sickness, and old age. But have the slaves no higher and more imperative claims than these? Are they not moral, accountable, immortal beings, as well as their masters? Have not both parties one and the same Maker and Redeemer—the same origin, duty, and destiny? And, is it not the bounden duty of masters to see that their servants are provided with the means of grace, the ordinances of Christianity? Is it not as much the duty of a master to secure the blessings of the Gospel to his servants, as it is the duty of a father to supply them to his children? And will God hold him guiltless if, while he controls the time and labor of his servants, he is unconcerned whether they are Christians or heathens? The Committee are deeply pained to be assured that after all the efforts of our Church and other Churches, there are many plantations, from which the minister of Christ has never received a call or on which he has never found a welcome. In these dark places the negroes live in ignorance, superstition, and sin, but little removed from the deplorable condition of their kindred race in Africa. The Committee hold that it is the duty of a master to give his personal and vigilant attention to this matter. He must not devolve the responsibility upon overseers, even though the latter may be (which is not always the case,) humane and pious men. The master must see that his servants receive the best religious instruction and culture he can secure. . . . The souls for whom Christ died, must not be allowed to live and die without a knowledge of their Redeemer.
>
> The golden rule applies to this relation as well as to all others; and the Committee believe that this principle is generally recognized. They regret, however, to believe that in many instances it is practically ignored. In most, if not in all of our States, there are laws forbidding the separation of parents and young children. . . . Ought not the conjugal rights of slaves to be held equally sacred? Does not the Scripture law of marriage apply to them as well to the Caucasian and other races? No one will defend promiscuous and illicit intercourse among slaves. No one will deny that negroes, as well as those of a superior race, are entitled to enter wedlock, or that the sanctity of this relation is guarded in their case as well as in that of others by the Divine prohibition, "What God hath joined together let no man put asunder." Providential circumstances, sometimes indeed, make separation inevitable—this is the lot of humanity. But there are [often] needless separations—separations that might be prevented, if the

authority of God and the rights of the slaves were as much consulted as the temporary convenience and worldly gains of their masters. The Committee respectfully submit that masters and overseers should do all in their power to promote purity among the slaves, encouraging holy matrimony and fostering the domestic relations.

The Committee, despite the abolition revolution that is menacing our country, see no reason to believe that Divine Providence intends to abolish the institution of slavery among us, if we are careful to use it so as not abusing it. They deny that there is necessarily any evil in this more than in other human institutions. Let the abuses be corrected and prevented, and there does not seem to be any reason to hope or fear its abolition. It has done more, with the aid of Christianity, to elevate the most inferior and degraded race of men, than any other instrumentality or agency yet employed for this purpose. Indeed, it seems to be the only lever which can raise them to the proper dignity of humanity. It is the means which Providence has overruled for their civilization, and through it hundreds of thousands of them have been called to take rank among the kings and priests of Jesus Christ. The Committee firmly believe, that were it abolished, both races would suffer by the abolition, but incalculably the greater sufferers would be the inferior and dependent race. To prevent this catastrophe, let its abuses be corrected and prevented, and its power for usefulness be more developed on the principles of our holy religion.[17]

According to the men who ran the Southern press, the slavery question was a matter of faith. By honoring the South's Christian beliefs and making slavery conform to the values of compassion and chastity that lay at the heart of their religion, they expected that the institution would survive the Union's efforts to destroy it. And fundamentally, they saw no reason to doubt that slavery was a holy institution that Southerners were meant to embrace and sustain. Even if almost every other nation in the Western Hemisphere had eschewed slavery, and even if God had allowed the North to enact emancipation, the Confederacy had to stand firm in the knowledge that slavery was right:

If there had ever, during this war, been any doubt as to the true issue between the North and the South, that doubt has been dispelled by the late message and proclamation of President Lincoln. Slavery is the only issue. The United States is fighting against the Confederate States for slavery. The result of the contest depends upon the righteousness of our cause. If slavery be not of God, then we are fighting against Him, and our cause will fail; if it be of God, then our enemies are fighting against Him and we for Him and Truth: and 'if God be for us who can be against us?'

But the civilized world says that slavery is wrong, and has inaugurated against it a crusade of the most fearful and determined character. The moral sentiment of christendom, except for the South, has for years brought to bear its mightiest engines to crush out the institution, and now the sword has been unsheathed in the name of humanity and freedom, of philanthropy and the Bible, to drink the blood of the pro-slavery South, or to liberate the last African held in bondage. Are not these combined circumstances enough to shake the confidence of the South in the scriptural propriety of her long cherished institution? Can the civilized world all be wrong, and the South right? Is it presumptuous for us to stand out thus against mankind? But the student of the Bible, and of the history of the past, is not thus intimidated. Planting himself upon the revelations of heaven, he does not fear what man can do. Who that has read the early struggles of the christian religion, as it passed through the fires of persecution, does not know that every institution of heaven has met with the most deadly opposition from man? [Christianity] was called 'the most detestable superstition,' as slavery is called the 'sum of all vil-

> lainies.'. . . The disciples of Christ were considered the enemies of mankind and were punished accordingly. No nation would befriend them. Persecution in its most horrid forms met them wherever they went. . . . But were the christian heroes and martyrs of that age discouraged? Did they conclude, because all the world was against them, therefore they were wrong?—Christianity lived and triumphed because it was of God; and so slavery, and the South with it, will live and triumph because it is of God.[18]

The movement for slavery reform did not produce any general changes in the workings of the slave system in the South. Its importance rests not in what it achieved but in what it symbolized—namely, an unyielding commitment to preserving the institution, and establishing it on an unshakable, holy foundation. Reform, as envisioned by the Southerners who supported it, would make blacks more contented with their lot, reduce points of strain between masters and slaves, and promote a spirit of mutual goodwill between them. In this way, the threat of emancipation made Southerners all the more wedded to protecting and perfecting slavery, and to making the Confederacy the glorious biracial community that they felt God wanted it to be. It would be a biracial harmony based on rigid hierarchy, of course, not equality. As this editorial from the *Mississippian* proclaimed, the South would never willingly participate in the kind of mongrelized "Union of Colors" that the Emancipation Proclamation portended:

> It is for a union of colors that the war is now being waged and to this end will every energy of the North be brought to bear. We have no objection to such a government at the North. We shall not meddle with their own affairs. They can love and pamper the nigger as much as they please. They can put him in their halls of Congress, in every position of trust and profit, make a companion of him in the family circle, and finally permit him to marry into their own families. . . . If their taste is for amalgamation, and [if] their ideas [are] for equality, irrespective of color or decency, we are willing that they should remain so. Let them go on with their "union of colors." We are building up a government here on a far different plan—a government that will command the obeisance and homage of the world—a government having for its object the improving and fostering of the negro race in that state [of slavery in] which God intended they should always remain—a government wherein freedom will exist as it was intended by our forefathers, and whose peace, happiness, and prosperity will ever reign. This is the object of the stupendous work in which we are engaged. Let us push on with it vigorously, and we will soon have a fabric that will far outshine the embryo "union of colors" of the North—a union disgraceful to its founders—a stigma upon the country and injurious even to the negro for whose freedom the North has seen fit to destroy a government, the like of which her people will never enjoy again. They may have their "union of colors," but our soil will not be included in it.[19]

The Anglo-African.

"MAN MUST BE FREE!—IF NOT THROUGH LAW, WHY, THEN, ABOVE THE LAW."

VOL. III. NO. 5. WHOLE NO. 109. NEW YORK, SEPTEMBER 5, 1863. PRICE, FIVE CENT[S]

The Anglo-African.

PUBLISHED WEEKLY, ON SATURDAY,

AT TWO DOLLARS PER ANNUM; OR, FIVE CENTS PER COPY, PAYABLE ON DELIVERY.

ROBERT HAMILTON, PUBLISHER,

No. 50 Beekman St., New York.

AN ADDRESS

TO THE EXECUTIVE COMMITTEE OF MERCHANTS FOR THE RELIEF OF COLORED PEOPLE.

J. D. McKenzie, Chairman.

Edward Cromwell,	Geo. C Collins,
J. S. Schultz,	A. R. Wetmore,
Jona. Sturges, Treas.,	J. R. Colllins.

Presented by Colored Ministers and Laymen, New York, Aug. 22, 1863.

GENTLEMEN: We have learned that you have decided this day to bring to a close the general distribution of the funds so liberally contributed by the merchants of New York and others for the relief of the colored sufferers of the late riots, which have recently disgraced our city.

We cannot in justice to our feelings permit your benevolent labors to terminate, even partially, without offering some expression of our sincere gratitude to the Universal Father for inspiring your hearts with that spirit of kindness of which we have been the recipients during the severe trials and persecutions through which we have passed.

When in the pursuit of our peaceful and laudable occupations we have fallen among thieves, who stripped us of our raiment and had wounded us, leaving many of us half-dead, you had compassion on us. You bound up our wounds and poured in the oil and wine of Christian kindness, and took care of us. You hastened to express your sympathy for those whose fathers, husbands, sons and brothers had been tortured and murdered. You also comforted the aching hearts of our widowed sisters and soothed the sorrows of orphan children.

We were hungry and you fed us. We were thirsty and you gave us drink. We were made as strangers in our own homes and you kindly took us in. We were naked and you clothed us. We were sick and you visited us. We were in prison and you came unto us.

Gentlemen, this generation of our people will not, cannot forget the dreadful scenes to which we allude, nor will they forget the noble and spontaneous exhibition of charity which they excited. The former will be referred to as one of the darkest chapters of our history in the Empire State, and the latter will be remembered as a bright and glorious page in the records of the past.

In the light of public opinion we feel ourselves to be among the least in this our native land, and we therefore earnestly pray that in the last great day the King may say to you and to all who have befriended us, "Inasmuch as ye have done it unto one of the least of these my brethren ye have done it unto me; come ye blessed of my Father, inherit the kingdom prepared for you from the foundation of the world."

But as great as has been the benefit that we have recived from your friendly and unlooked for charity, they yet form but the smaller portion of the ground of our gratitude and pleasure. We have learned by your treatment of us in these days of our mental and moral affliction, that you cherished for us a kindly and humane feeling of which we had no knowledge. You did not hesitate to come forward to our relief amid the threatened destruction of your own lives and property. You obeyed the noblest dictates of the human heart, and by your generous moral courage you rolled back the tide of violence that had well nigh swept us away.

This ever memorable and magnanimous exhibition of heroism has had the effect to enlarge in our bosoms the sentiment of undying regard and esteem for you and yours. In time of war or peace, in prosperity or adversity, you and our great State and our beloved country may count us among your faithful friends, and the proffer of our labors and our lives shall be our pleasure and our pride.

If in your temporary labors of Christian philanthropy, you have been induced to look forward to our future destiny in this our native land, and to ask what is the best thing we can do for the colored people? This is our answer. Protect us in our endeavors to obtain an honest living. Suffer no one to hinder us in any department of well directed industry, give us a fair and open field and let us work our own destiny, and we ask no more.

We cannot conclude without expressing our gratification at the manner in which the arduous and preplexing duties of your office have been conducted. We shall never forget the Christian and gentlemanly bearing of your esteemed Secretary, Mr. Vincent Colyer, who on all occasions impressed even the humblest with the belief that he knew and felt that he was dealing with a heart-broken and a crushed people.

We also acknowledge the uniform kindness of man's inalienable rights, for the preservation of the American Union, and for the reign of that righteousness in the hearts of the people, that saves from reproach and exalteth the nation.

Signed,

Rev. H. H. Garnet,	Mr. John Peterson,
" Chas. B. Ray,	" Chas. L. Reason,
" Clinton Leonard,	" Peter S. Porter,
" John Cary,	" Stephen N. Geer,
" Henry M. Wilson,	" John R. Porter,
" Sampson Talbot,	" John L. Hudson,
" Rich'd Wilson,	" Aaron F. Potter,
" Isaac Colman,	" T. S. W. Titus,
" John T. Raymond,	" Wm. O. H. Curtis,

And many others.

COLORED MEN OF CALIFORNIA.

From the Pacific Appeal.

NO. IV.

DR. E. R. JOHNSON.

This gentleman is, perhaps, the best educated colored man of his age in California. He was born in New Bedford, Mass., of Puritanic and Quaker origin, claiming descendants from the Indian, African and Caucasian races. His father, Richard Johnson, fought in the Revolutionary war, was captured by the British, and was confined, we believe, in the American bastile, the New York Sugar-house: he is favorably noticed in William C. Nell's work, "The Colored Heroes of the Revolution." Like most all the New Bedford men, Richard Johnson was a whaler; they take to the water as naturally as a duck, it is their destiny, and at the close of the war the young soldier of the Revolution pursued the avocation of his ancestors; he followed the sea many years, filling with honor and profit every position on shipboard, from cabin boy to captain. On retiring from that arduous profession, he established a mercantile business in New Bedford, which he continued until his death, and to which his sons succeeded.

Ezra Rothschild Johnson is now between 45 and 50 years of age; he received an Academic education in New Bedford, where he obtained all the educational advantages for which the New England seminaries are so renowned. After finishing his course of studies, he was apprenticed to Mr. James Forten, the well-known sail-maker of Philadelphia, with whom he continued his friendly relations during the life of that gentleman.

Dr. Johnson has led an eventful stirring life. During the disastrous riots of 1834, when the colored people of New York, Philadelphia, and other places were mobbed, their house pillaged, their property destroyed, their churches and public buildings burned and their lives endangered, the residence of Mr. Forten was threatened by an infuriated mob, eager for spoil, and anxious to inflict injury on such a prominent and patriotic colored man; the apprentice of Mr. Forten volunteered to defend his home and family. Young Johnson, throwing aside the Quaker principles in which he had been educated by a loving and pious mother, armed himself with all the ardor of his revolutionary sire, to protect from ravage and devastation the family and property of his master.

On the expiration of his term of apprenticeship, he returned to New Bedford, where he opened a sail loft and continued in that business several years, after which he joined his father in the mercantile business.

His first public essay was in 1837, when he delivered an address before the Young Men's Wilberforce Debating Society, a literary institution of New Bedford, composed of colored men. He has always been an ardent supporter of the political principles of the Liberty party; he was their candidate for Senator to the General Assembly of Massachusetts, in 1840, and received the entire support of that party. The African Colonization Society, during its palmiest days, found in him a strenuous opposer in the press and on the platform, and all schemes of Colonization or expatriation have always received his hearty denunciation.

He was among the first emigrants to California who crossed the Isthmus. He left New York in 1849, and arrived here after a tedious passage of nearly four months. Dr. Johnson always had a penchant for the study of medicine; he had pursued it as a recreation, and during his first residence in California ('49 to '51), he made the knowledge he had obtained available. Prior to leaving New York, he had shipped a cargo of goods, via Cape Horn, and while waiting their arrival here, he followed his original occupation of sail-making, and also practiced medicine. When his goods arrived he engaged in mercantile business.

He soon turned his attention to land speculation, and is probably the oldest owner of real estate among the colored people of this city. He purchased land in 1849 which be still owns.

Fearless when battling for rights and the maintenance of principles, he advocated the freedom of the slave, the universal rights of mankind, and the enfranchisement of his race, before large religious assemblages in the early days of San Francisco. During his first residence in California he made many friends, among whom were the late James King of William, Charles D. Cushman, Esq., now deputy collector of this port, and others; those who are living he retains their friendship until the present day.

He only remained in this country about two years, and returned home in 1851. He was the first colored person who obtained a cabin passage from this port; it was through the introduction of Gen. McDougall, now U. S. Senator, to Captain Pearson, then commanding the steamer Oregon. On the Isthmus, he was translator for his fellow-passengers in transactions by his residence in foreign climes. The infamous Fugitive Slave bill had recently become a law. New Bedford and Nantucket were well known as places of refuge for fugitives from Southern bondage—they had received an hospitable welcome in those places; the sea-girt, iron-bound shores of New England offered them an asylum from the thraldom they had so long endured; many of them had acquired property, had reared families, and were respected for their industry and upright conduct; fears were entertained that attempts would be made to enforce the law in those places; to drag from their homes and families those who had sought refuge in their midst from tyranny and oppression. A public meeting was held in New Bedford, on which occasion Dr. Johnson offered resolutions which called upon colored persons to oppose the enforcement of that odious enactment, to arm themselves, and if assailed by the slave-catchers, to shoot them down; if the courts did not decide it was justifiable homicide, it was better to suffer imprisonment, or even death itself, than endure the horrors of slavery on a cotton or sugar plantation. The resolutions were so bold and emphatic, assuming so much defiance, that they caused considerable consternation, but, being ably supported by the Doctor and others, they were finally adopted. In 1860, he was elected by acclamation a member of the N. B. Lyceum, a literary institution which had previously refused to sell colored person tickets of admission to their lectures. When the war broke out he presided at a public meeting of the colored citizens of New Bedford, held in the City Hall, at which resolutions were passed, offering their services to the Governor.

After an absence of ten years he returned to this country in 1861. He was treated with great respect, and on the ship from Panama, the ship's surgeon being absent, he prescribed for several of the passengers. Since his return here, he has applied himself to the practice of his profession.

As a writer, Dr. Johnson is terse and vigorous, as his contributions to the columns of *The Appeal* and other periodicals evince. During his first residence in this city he was the Californian correspondent for the New Bedford *Standard*; he has also contributed to *The Aliened American*, *Frederick Douglass's Paper*, THE ANGLO-AFRICAN, *The Liberator*, and other journals. The Doctor is not a graceful writer; he abounds more in strength of thought and originality of his ideas than in beauty of expression, or poetic diction: he is an eloquent speaker, as those who have heard him at Hays's Park, Tucker's Hall, and other places in this city will testify.

His complexion shows his unmixed origin; he is of large frame, but not robust: of a billious, nervous temperament, easy manners, and of quiet gentlemanly bearing, a calm logical reasoner, and a good talker.

He is a loving husband and a fond father: he was an affectionate, dutiful son: he often in his public speeches refers to his mother, who was an exemplary woman, and a consistent practical Christian, and it is to her counsel and training that he owes his present position in life. C.

July 15, 1863.

ABOUT OUR CINCINNATI LETTERS.

MR EDITOR: The colored people of Cincinnati feel no little pride in having as able and truthful a chronicler of current events as the gentleman that writes from this point to your excellent and ever-welcome paper. His letters in regard to the school exhibitions, schools, and boards of trustees, are so very impartial and correct, that he has had showered upon him, and justly too, the encomiums of the residents of both districts, which anyone familiar with the antecedents of the schools will inform you is no easy task. A few more strokes of the writer's pen in that direction will remove the jealousies, rivalries and antipathies heretofore existing, and blend these refractory districts into an harmonious unity, the completion of which will add new laurels to the chaplet of this great writer, who, like great commanders, sometimes changes his base.

If the person whom many of your readers here suspect is "L'Occident," surely no one can or will accuse him of having a superabundance of modesty, natural or acquired. I forget that modesty is not an essential requisite for incognito writers. As there is no law against self-praise or libel, we should at least not allow our self-esteem to warp our approbativeness in cases of this kind.

L'Occident tells with the gravity of a certain unmentionable beast, whose name I shall not introduce here, although many of us know him full well, we are not always in the mood to recognize and do the agreeable to our more "kind than kin"—that there is a difference of opinion among the friends of the school. Marvellous! Will the gentleman be kind enough to inform us at what period during the existence of the schools there has not been a difference of opinion among its friends? we have no doubt if the schools had a voice they would long since have cried "God save us from our friends." "Why not discuss the differences through the columns of THE ANGLO?" Certainly, gentlemen, if it is anything calculated to most excellent fancy, but since he has been dubbed what he aspired to, D.D., with the well-earned affix of A. S. S., his buoyancy has returned and added inspiration to aspiration.

I am glad to see so many of our home-made young ladies on the list of teachers for the coming year. This looks like business. Most people think "the fool that goes to Rome, excels the fool that stays at home." I intend to say something of the vanity of the gentleman who nominated and labored with the utmost urbanity to elect himself. "A man may smile and smile and be a villain still." A friend tells me it was an act of charity on the part of said person, it is the more conspicuous as it stands alone. *Absit Invidia*—farewell, ye mighty.

EASTERN DISTRICT.

NEGROES AS SOLDIERS.

THE evidence which has come before the Commission, bearing on the capacity of the negro as a soldier induces them to recommend that the government should bring into the field, as early as possible, two hundred thousand colored troops, or upward. They recommend them as alike advantageous to the cause of the Union and to the race to which these troops belong.

Colored troops, taking a pride in their position, exhibit great neatness and care of their persons, uniforms, arms and equipments, and in the police of their camps. Usually skillful cooks and providers, they exhibit resources in taking care of themselves in camp.

The religious sentiment strongly characterizing the African race may, in the case of the colored soldier, be successfully appealed to by leaders who share it as a powerful element of enthusiasm. If the officers feel, and impart to their men the feeling, that they are fighting in the cause of God and liberty, the Commission believe that no part of the army may be more relied on than the colored regiments. But with these people more than with a more independent race, success depends upon sympathy between their officers and them. Thus, how important soever the proper choice of officers in all cases, the Commission think it to be more important in the case of colored than of white troops: deeming it probable that colored troops badly officered might be liable to give way more readily than badly officered regiments of the more self-reliant white race. Colored soldiers criticize their officers very sharply. There is as much difference in the standing of the officers in colored as in white regiments.

A distinguished general officer expressed to the Commission the opinion that, in case of alarm, negroes, accustomed to stand together against master and overseer, are disposed to segregate—to run to each other—while whites disperse—"each for himself, and God for us all."

Negroes have proved themselves especially daring and serviceable as spies; and the organization of colored guides, in connection with each army corps, is recommended.

If one hundred thousand negroes be employed in military services other than actual warfare, and if 200,000 or more be mustered in as soldiers, we shall require the military services of at least 300,000 blacks. But this number of able-bodied men represent a population of a million and a half, being one-half of all the colored people in the insurrectionary States.

To reach this number there is needed, beside military successes, a strict enforcement of the orders issued by the government that the colored refugees be treated with humanity. Upon such treatment it depends, in a great measure whether we can have the full military advantage which, in this contest, we ought to have, from the aid of the negro race, and whether the military resources of the South, shall be sapped by disintegration of her labor-system.

Examples are given in which, in spite of the efforts of provost-marshals, negro refugees have been plundered by our pickets as they entered the Union lines; and it is recommended that such offenses be severly punished, so that, independently of their inherent criminality, their practical effect is to discourage the emigration of those whom as soldiers we desire to enlist. A general order on the subject is recommended.

The Commission also recommend, as to all property brought in by negro refugees, that when taken by the Quartermaster for the public service, it be paid for, as other property of loyal men is paid for, to the refugee if he makes no demand on the government for support for himself, or family; otherwise, that the proceeds go into the Fredmen's Fund.

While refugees should not be exempted from draft, if draft be necessary, the Commission expresses the opinion, founded on actual observation and testimony, that if men of the proper stamp are selected as negro superintendents, these can, and will procure the voluntary enlistment of a much larger proportion of negroes than is called for by the draft. Most of the freedmen can be made to understand, by a proper appeal, that only by proving their manhood as soldiers—only through a baptism of blood—can they obtain, in this generation, such a change in public opinion as will insure to their race respect and decent treatment, in its social relations with whites.

It has been found in practice that it is easy, by judicious treatment, to create among these people a state of public opinion such that pains be taken to make this widely and officially known.—*Report of Am. Freedmen's Inquiry Commission to Secretary of War.*

A SUGGESTION.

MR. EDITOR: I see by the proceedings of the Poughkeepsie Convention, held July 16th, that there was a State Central Committee appointed for New York. As some time has elapsed since the Convention was held, would it not be well for the Chairman of that Committee to call the State Committee together for some definite action? Now or never is the time for the colored man to take his stand as a man, for the war has begun and now let every colored man help to finish the job. OLD GUARD OF TROY.

IN MEMORIAM.

RESOLUTIONS adopted at a meeting of Company F, 7th Regiment, N. Y. N. G., held Aug. 16, 1863:

Whereas, ROBERT G. SHAW, formerly a member of this organization, fell at the head of his regiment, the 54th Massachusetts, in the attack on Fort Wagner on Morris Island, South Carolina, on the 18th day of July, 1863; and, Whereas, Upon the intelligence of his death, the services of this company, as an escort at his funeral, were offered, and were declined, because his remains could not be procured,

Resolved, That while, to his family and near friends, we tender earnest sympathy in their bereavement, and ask that we, his former comrades, may in some manner show their grief; yet we rejoice with them in the proud recollection that he fell a martyr to the cause of Freedom, and died that the Republic might live.

Resolved, That although the hearts of his enemies were hardened, so that we cannot render at his grave the last tokens of regard and respect, according to our strong desire; yet we feel that when his spirit went to its reward with those of his faithful men, it was meet that his dust should rest with theirs, beneath the very spot where the heroic act of his self-sacrifice was consummated, and that the State for whose redemption his life was given should be forever honored by his sepulchre.

The Free South of Aug. 22d, states: A collection was taken on Sunday morning in the Baptist Church of Beaufort, in aid of the fund for the proposed monument to the late Col. ROBERT G. SHAW. Sixty dollars was contributed. The colored people seem to take a great interest in this effort to honor Col. SHAW's memory, and we learn that a large sum has already been promised by the different colored regiments. There are now six regiments of colored men in this department, and a little energy is all that is required to raise a monument honorable alike to the noble dead and to the donors.

COLORED REGIMENT OF OHIO.

On the 4th day of this month a large number of colored people of this State met in Convention at Xenia. Many of the most distinguished and influential men among them were in attendance. The proceedings of the Convention were in all respects harmonious. At 12 o'clock on the day the Convention met, a procession, said to be a mile long, formed in the County Fair Grounds (where the Convention held its sittings) and marched to the depot to meet John M. Langston, Esq., who was to address the meeting in the afternoon on "The Hour and the Duty of Colored men to the Government." On account of sickness, Mr. Langston did not speak until the following afternoon. He was listened to with marked attention for over two hours. And as he spoke of the duty of the colored men of Ohio to come forward and fill up the regiment now rendezvousing at Camp Delaware, he was heard with demonstrations of the liveliest interest. The following preamble and resolutions adopted at this meeting utter in unmistakable terms the sentiment of the colored men of Ohio as to their duty towards the government, and their determination to meet it:

Whereas, We, the colored citizens of Ohio, this day assembled at Xenia, in view of what has already been done by the President of the United States and the General government in behalf of the Africo-American, have unshaken and increasing confidence in Abraham Lincoln, our President, in his Administration, and the General government; therefore,

Resolved, That we stand as ever on the side of the government, and pledge to it "our lives, our property and sacred honor," in its efforts to subdue the rebellion of the slave oligarchy of the country, in its determination to emancipate the slaves of all rebels, to establish freedom in the District of Columbia and the national Territories, to welcome Hayti and Liberia to the great family of nations, to recognize the citizenship of the native born colored American, and to protect the colored soldiers, who, taking the American musket and bayonet, have gone forth at the call of their country to *do* and *die* for the government and the Union.

Resolved That we are proud of the heroic conduct of the colored soldiers who fought at Milliken's Bend and Morris Island, vindicating as they did, by their noble and manly behavior, their claim to the admiration and respect of their countrymen.

Resolved, That it is the duty of the colored people of Ohio to fill up at once, by volunteering, the notable colored regiment now being formed at Camp Delaware as far as they have been appointed, ar[e] satisfied with everything connected wi[th] treatment in camp.—*Columbus (O.) City August 25th.*

CALIFORNIA ITEMS.

(*Compiled from The Pacific Appeal.*)

The nett proceeds of the Masonic Re[...] Festival, held June 24th, for the benefit [...] A. M. E. Church, was $220.

In the District Court of Shasta Co[...] June term, Joseph J. Pindell was gra[nted a] decree of divorce from his wife, Anne Pindell.

Quite a crowd of respectable persons [...] in attendance at the wedding of Mr. [...] Persons and Miss E. Phillips on Tuesday [...] 21st, at the First Baptist church, Dupo[nt ...] San Francisco.

DEADLY ASSAULT.—Thos. Fitzgerald w[as ar]rested, on Tuesday last, on a charge of [...] with a deadly weapon. It is said that [...] cut Richard Dalton, Steward of the P[...] Jonathan, with a bowie-knife. The [...] such offences now is very severe. M[...]ton, though cut and otherwise bruised se[...] we are glad to learn, is able to be at h[is vo]cation.

July 30th, the Ladies' Accumulatin[g] Beneficial Society gave a pic-nic at Al[...] The day being cool and cloudy, there we[re not] as many present as there would have [been if] the day had been warm and pleasant. [...] those who live across the Bay, togethe[r with] those who went over from the city, a ve[ry ...] company was made up at the Grove, [...] seemed to enjoy themselves.

At a meeting held in Shasta, July 11, [...] lation to a call for the formation of [...] regiments, the following resolutions wer[e unan]imously adopted:

Resolved, That we hail the call with [...] are, and will hold ourselves in readi[ness to] respond to any requisition made upon [us by] the government.

Resolved, That appreciating the many [...] granted to us by the State of Californ[ia ...] the recognition of our manhood and [...] ship by the General government, we w[ould be] recreant to our duty as men should we [not be] warm in the glorious work."

The Appeal of August 1st says: "[...] day last, after an impressive sermon [...] Rev. Thomas Howell, Pastor of the [...] Church, the proceeds of the lecture d[elivered] by the Rev. T. Starr King, on the 21[st ...] amounting to $178.60, was presented [to Mr.] Howell, on behalf of the congregatio[n. The] presentation was made by Dr. E. R. J[ohnson] accompanied by an appropriate addre[ss to] him, which was pathetically responde[d to by] Mr. Howell, who thanked the members [and] friends generally for their efforts in re[...] their timely aid in his behalf. Am[ong the] female members, Mrs. Geo. M. Wyb[...] credited with being the most active in [getting] up the benefit for the Pastor."

AN INTERVIEW WITH THE PRES[IDENT] OF THE UNITED STATES

THE American Baptist Missionary [Conven]tion, now holding its twenty-third an[nual ses]sions with the First Colored Baptist [...] appointed a Committee to wait on the P[resident] to ask him what protection missionari[es ...] have on Southern soil, etc. The Co[mmittee] having waited on the President reporte[d to the] Convention as follows:

Your Committee, in compliance w[ith your] wishes, have waited on the Presiden[t of the] United States, and beg leave to sub[mit the] following report:

The Chairman of the Committee (Re[v. Leon]ard A. Grimes) introduced the Commit[tee, who] were cordially received by the Presiden[t. The] Chairman stated the object of the vis[it in the] following words:

Mr. President: We, the Committee a[ppointed] by the American Baptist Missionary [Conven]tion, now in session with the First [...] Baptist Church, Washington, D. C., d[esire to] know what protection we might have [...] toward sending missionaries on Sout[hern ...] to promulgate the Gospel of Christ w[ithin the] lines of the military forces of the Unite[d States.]

The President then made some in[...] remarks, after which he presented the C[ommittee] with the following letter:

EXECUTIVE MANS[ION,]
WASHINGTON, D. C., August 21, [...]

To whom it may concern:

To-day I am called upon by a Com[mittee of] Colored Ministers of the Gospel, who [express] a wish to go within our military l[ines and] minister to their brethren there. Th[e object] is a worthy one, and I shall be gla[d for all] facilities to be afforded them which ma[y not be] inconsistent with or a hindrance to our [military] operations. A. L[INCOLN.]

COMMITTEE.

Leonard A. Grimes, Boston, Mass[...]
Sampson White, Philadelphia, Penn[...]
Samuel Madden, Washington.
Edmund Kelly, New Bedford, Mass[...]
Noah Davis, Baltimore, Maryland.
William Williams, Baltimore, Mary[land.]
William E. Walker, Trenton, New [Jersey.]
Albert Boulden, Washington.
William J. Walker, Fredericksburg[...]
Collen Williams, Georgetown, D[istrict of] Columbia.

Chapter 8

Blacks in Union Blue

The name given to Lincoln's new policy—the Emancipation Proclamation—really understates its scope and impact. Beyond declaring an end to slavery in all areas of the South still in rebellion and disavowing any Union responsibility to protect the institution, it also contained a clause supporting the enlistment of blacks for military service. The decision to welcome blacks into the army ranks was, in part, based on brute necessity. By the end of 1862, the North was having difficulty drumming up new recruits; the supply of white volunteers seemed well near exhausted. Blacks were one segment of the population that still teemed with men eager to enlist. And as it was, many were already aiding the Union cause. Up until this time, the Union—like the Confederacy—had been employing black laborers for the army, despite denying them the chance to participate militarily. Blacks who contributed to the war effort before 1863 served primarily as teamsters, construction workers, pioneers, and ditchdiggers. In a couple of limited areas, including New Orleans, regiments of free black soldiers were organized under federal authority, but without any intention of actually using them for combat purposes. Nevertheless, the mere existence of these black troops, and the essential services provided by those who did manual labor for the armies, helped pave the way for the more than 180,000 black men who eventually fought for the Union.[1]

In important ways, the decision to enlist blacks as soldiers was the most revolutionary aspect of the Emancipation Proclamation. The use of black troops did not just undermine the institution of slavery; it actively challenged the racial prejudices and stereotypes on which slavery and black subordination rested. Popular thinking in the North and South alike characterized blacks as lazy, cowardly, immature, and even imbecilic—not the stuff of which soldiers are made. Even most Republicans who endorsed emancipation and believed that blacks ought to be given the opportunity to fight for the Union still doubted that they could

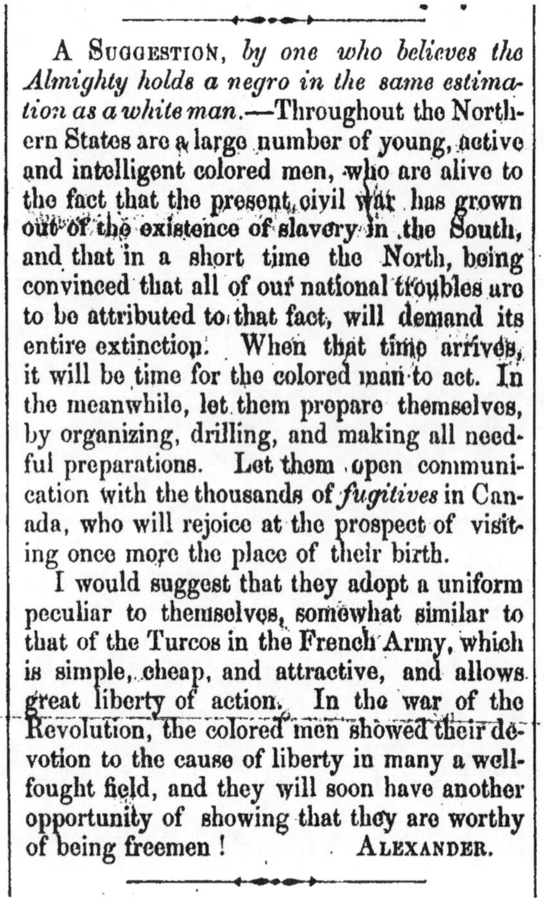

A SUGGESTION, *by one who believes the Almighty holds a negro in the same estimation as a white man.*—Throughout the Northern States are a large number of young, active and intelligent colored men, who are alive to the fact that the present civil war has grown out of the existence of slavery in the South, and that in a short time the North, being convinced that all of our national troubles are to be attributed to that fact, will demand its entire extinction. When that time arrives, it will be time for the colored man to act. In the meanwhile, let them prepare themselves, by organizing, drilling, and making all needful preparations. Let them open communication with the thousands of *fugitives* in Canada, who will rejoice at the prospect of visiting once more the place of their birth.

I would suggest that they adopt a uniform peculiar to themselves, somewhat similar to that of the Turcos in the French Army, which is simple, cheap, and attractive, and allows great liberty of action. In the war of the Revolution, the colored men showed their devotion to the cause of liberty in many a well-fought field, and they will soon have another opportunity of showing that they are worthy of being freemen ! ALEXANDER.

Anglo-African, April 27, 1861.
In 1861, the Union refused to accept black men into its army ranks. But free black's and their allies in the North remained hopeful that the opportunity for military service would come eventually, and actively considered how to prepare for duty.

make acceptable soldiers. As the *Troy Times*, an otherwise avid supporter of Lincoln's policies, confessed: "We do not believe that, if the President and Congress issue to them an invitation, the negroes North and South will rush in large numbers to join our armies. They are not a military race." While the *Times* was willing to concede that some brave men "might" be found among the free blacks of the North, newly freed slaves from the South were utterly incapable of doing a soldier's work. "Long subjection has taught them the meekness of inferiority," the paper explained. Many of them were physically strong, but slavery had reduced them intellectually and spiritually "to the condition of unthinking brutes."[2] Military service afforded blacks an opportunity to shatter these humiliating presumptions, which justified denying them an equal place in America. Moreover, it seemed to give them a clear stake in society—something that emancipation alone did not do. While the enactment of emancipation offered the promise of freedom to the slaves, the act of fighting for the country would allow all blacks, slave and free, to lay claim to the same rights and protections that white soldiers and citizens already possessed.

The rules of military service, however, also carried their own injustices. Whereas white soldiers were paid $13 a month, black troops received only $10, and in June 1863, Secretary of War Edwin Stanton would reduce their pay by an additional $3 for clothing expenses. Moreover, the new black regiments were to be officered by whites, thereby placing a strict ceiling on how far a black soldier could advance in the ranks.[3] Despite these limitations, though, the potential benefits of military service seemed tremendous. With the doubting eyes of Northern whites upon them, leading men within the Northern free black community were eager to make a good showing. In hopes of drawing volunteers into the newly created black regiments, the famous orator Frederick Douglass, issued this "word to colored men" in the columns of the *Anglo-African*:

> The broad eye of the nation is fixed upon the black man. They are half in doubt as to whether his conduct in this crisis will refute or confirm their allegations against the colored race. They stand to applaud, or to hurl the bolt of condemnation. Which shall it be, my brave and strong-hearted brothers? The decision of our destiny is now, as never before, in our own hands. We may lay here low in the dust, despised and spit upon by every passer-by; or we may, like brave men, rise and unlock to ourselves the golden gates of a glorious future. Depend upon it, we have no time to lose. To hold

back is to invite infamy upon ourselves and upon our children. All the negro-hating vermin of the land may crawl all over us, if our courage quails at this hour. He is whipped oftenest who is whipped easiest. As with individuals, so with nations and classes. It has been the fashion in this country—even in some of our Northern cities—to assault and mob colored citizens, for no other reason than the ease with which it could be done. We have it in our power to do something towards changing this cowardly fashion. When it is once found that black men can give blows as well as take them, men will find more congenial employment than pounding them. The black man, in arms to fight for the freedom of his race and the safety and security of the country, will give his countrymen a higher and better revelation of his character. The case stands thus: We have asked the nation for a chance to fight the rebels—to fight against slavery and fight for freedom. Well, the chance is now given us. We must improve it, or sink deeper than ever in the pit of social and political degradation, from which we have been struggling for years to extricate ourselves. When the nationality of the United States is set in safety, in part by your hands, the whole world would cry shame upon any attempt to denationalize you.

To fight for the Government in this tremendous war is, then, to fight for nationality and for a place with all other classes of our fellow-citizens. I know that Congress has been pleased to say, in deference to prevailing prejudice, that colored men shall not rise higher than company officers. They might as well have passed a law that black men shall not be brave; that they shall not learn to read; that they shall not shoot straight, and that they shall not grow taller than five feet nine inches and a half. The law is even more absurd than mean. Enter the army and deserve promotion, and you will be sure to get it in the end. To say that you will not go into the army until you can be a Colonel or a General, is about as wise as to say you won't go into the water until you shall learn how to swim. . . . Once let colored men be made captains of companies, and demonstrate their capacity for such captaincy, and I will risk their upward progress. The great thing to be done first of all is, to get an eagle on your button and a musket on your shoulder. . . .

Do not flatter yourselves that the colored troops of the South can do our work. They cannot do it, no matter how brave and enduring they may prove themselves to be. The fact that they make better soldiers than we will be quoted against us. Their good behavior will be set to the credit of slavery, and we shall be told that while slavery elevates the character of the colored man to the level of the soldier, freedom debases him to the level of a spiritless coward. There is no mistake about it, colored men of the North; we shall either go up, or we shall go down, precisely as we ourselves shall determine in view of the demands of this hour. The day that sees the fifty-fourth regiment of Massachusetts march down Broadway, composed of well-drilled, well-uniformed, well-armed, well-appointed colored soldiers, under the ample folds of the Star Spangled Banner . . . will be the proudest and happiest day for the colored race ever witnessed in the United States. After that spectacle, colored men and women in New York will walk among their country-men and women without asking pardon for having been born.[4]

Even among Northern editors who in theory supported the raising of black troops, there were those whose racial pride still rankled at the idea. On a practical level, they admitted that the supply of white volunteers was nearly exhausted and that the North had no choice but to reinforce the armies with black manpower. And since Southerners were already using slaves for digging trenches, building forts, and other heavy labor, why should Northerners refrain from utilizing blacks to their own advantage, whether as laborers or as soldiers? Moreover, it seemed like poetic justice to have blacks—particularly former slaves—take a hand in putting down a rebellion organized by slaveholders specifically for the preservation of slavery. "It would be a righteous retribution," the *Albany Evening Journal* declared; in fact, "the moral of this war will not be perfect until something of this kind shall happen." Still, the notion of having blacks fighting side by side with whites was instinctively disconcerting. Even though the *Journal* was convinced that black soldiers would never fight as well as white men, the paper was honest enough to also admit, "It would be exceedingly mortifying if they should."[5]

Union soldiers tended to be much less divided in their feelings. Most saw no justice whatsoever in being forced to serve alongside blacks. A white soldier in the Massachusetts Fifty-second, writing in February 1863 to the *Hampshire Gazette & Northampton Courier* from his

RECRUITS
FOR MASSACHUSETTS REGIMENTS
—o—

All able-bodied colored men desirous of going South to assist in suppressing the rebellion and rescuing the slave, can do so by joining the Massachusetts Regiments. Recruits are wanted at Wm Roberts, No. 17 Worth st., Johnson & Wilson, 81 Wooster st., John V. Givens, 154 East 10th st., and Thomas E. Garribrance, 55 West Broadway.

Anglo-African, July 4, 1863.
As with the recruiting of white volunteers, efforts to enroll blacks in the Union army relied on newspapers to advertise how and where to enlist. But unlike those for their white counterparts, recruitment signs for blacks appealed specifically to their interest in "rescuing the slave" from bondage—a motive that many Northern whites still were not prepared to embrace.

A QUEER RENCONTRE.

SLAVE CATCHER (who has strayed into a Federal camp)—"*You arn't seen a boy o' mine named Cæsar, have you?* (Aside.) *Darn'd if it arn't the black nigger himself.*"
COLORED SENTRY—"*Who goes dare—advance and gib de countersign.* (Aside.) *Golly, if dat arn't my old massa.*" (Sensation.)

Frank Leslie's Illustrated Newspaper, March 7, 1863.
As depicted in this cartoon, the enlistment of escaped slaves into the Union army presented the interesting possibility that these new black soldiers might again come face-to-face with the white Southerners who previously held them in bondage.

camp in Baton Rouge, described the attitudes of his fellow men toward the Third Louisiana Native Guards, a black regiment composed largely of former slaves. The Third Native Guard had actually been organized in 1862, after the federal occupation of New Orleans. Benjamin Butler had welcomed them under his command and even allowed the regiment to maintain black captains and lieutenants. By 1863, however, Butler had been transferred out of New Orleans, and his replacement, General Nathaniel Banks, quickly began ridding the regiment of its black officers. When the following letter was written, the Third Louisiana Native Guards was headed by a mix of black and white officers, but the men of the Massachusetts Fifty-second found the entire regiment—blacks and whites alike—to be a disgrace:

> The principal event of the past few days, in camp, has been the arrival of a negro regiment. I never realized before that the prejudice against the negro soldiers was so intense. It pervades every regiment, from every state, and exists in officers and privates alike. . . . Some of the captains of this regiment are blacks, and their lieutenants, whites. This is considered a great degradation to the latter. I do not see how this regiment could remain here, and take an equal position with the other regiments, without great irritation and even serious trouble. The colored soldiers are often insulted and their officers subjected to gross indignities. Already have collisions occurred. I judge that the number of soldiers here who would be willing to have the blacks take position alongside with them, as soldiers, is very small, it might almost be stated as insignificant. You may say this prejudice is all wrong, that the black man ought to be allowed to fight, that he *can* fight as well as the white man, that we need every man we can put into the field, &c. Grant that this is so, what then? Is the prejudice removed? Is it any the less intense? Can the white soldier be compelled to take a position repugnant to his feelings, and still be a reliable soldier for the government which has forced him into such a position? For myself, I have no objection to the negro's trying his hand at fighting, and hope he may yet have a favorable chance to show his qualities; but if, under the state of feeling which exists, twenty white men, upon whom we have a right to rely, and upon whom we *must* rely, are thereby disaffected, . . . ought I, as a practical man, looking to the maintenance of the Union in its full integrity as my sole object, to insist upon my plan? These are the reflections which many entertain, who seek the perpetuity of the Union, regardless of slavery or the condition of the slaves themselves.[6]

Despite the evident hostility of white troops, those blacks who enlisted believed that they had an obligation to stay in the army and prove the manhood and worth of the black race. When the wife of Menomine L. Maimi, a black soldier from New England, wrote to him and recommended that he resign his post in protest against some ill-treatment he had received, he issued an impassioned response, explaining his unflinching determination to stay put. It was a firm but loving rebuke, which was reproduced for the public by the *Anglo-African*:

> My Dear Wife:
>
> . . . Do you know or think what the end of this war is to decide? It is to decide whether we are to have freedom to all or slavery to all. If the Southern Confederacy succeeds, then you may bid farewell to all liberty thereafter. . . . If our government succeeds, then your and our race will be free. The government has torn down the only barrier that existed against us as a people. When slavery passes away, the prejudices that belonged to it must follow. The government calls for the colored man's help and, if he is not a fool, he will give it.
>
> The present is different from the Revolutionary war, for that was to decide between a king and a part of his subjects, who had fled . . . to a new land. He claimed even there to still hold them and sought by

cruel and unjust taxation to subdue these people. They then rebelled; and after a long and bloody war won their independence and established a free government of their own. It was intended to be free to all, even to the few slaves who were in the land. . . . The Constitution of the United States was such that it allowed each State to make its own laws, as long as they did not infringe upon the laws of the general government. Some of the Northern States in a few years set their slaves free. The other States would have followed their example, but they were in a warmer climate and . . . soon found out that some parts of this country would grow cotton, rice, sugar and indigo. They had to decide who should cultivate these plants that would produce so much wealth. They considered the climate and came to the decision that the white man could not stand it and the attendant fevers, and so they must have some other race of people besides the pale-face, for he was only fit to rule in that line of business. . . . They cast their eyes . . . upon the black man. . . . They denied that God made the black man a man at all, and brought their most learned judges and doctors of the gospel and laws to attempt to prove . . . that the sons of Africa were not even human. They tried to convince the world that the black man sprang . . . from the loins of monkeys and apes . . . and [that] it was but right to buy and steal the children of apes or monkies and to enslave them.

How do you fancy, wife, the idea of being part ape or monkey? . . . You will say that you are not part ape if you are part black; the slaveholders say that you are and all those who have the least drop of African blood in their veins are the same. So my wife is part baboon, and her husband is a gorilla of the masculine gender, a kind of monkey nearly as large as a man, a black man, of course. It is said that his hand, which is the foot of him, . . . is very powerful. He hides in trees and reaches down from his perch with his hind legs, of which the foot is formed like the human hand, except the thumb, which is longer and stronger than his fingers, and seizes a man by his throat and lifts him from the ground, chokes him to death, throws his body down and afterwards stamps on it. . . . Such is the history of one part of our ancestors, according to the learned slave-holding traitors. They had better look sharp after that long stout thumb, for I assure them, that if once it clasps their lying throats, it shall never unclasp until their bodies are beneath its feet. What better can they expect from the monkey? They are now about [to be] caught in their own trap: the monkies are on the way to their doors, . . . with loud-mouthed cannons, &c., sending forth fire, smoke, and death.

They shall see these gentle monkies, that they thought they had so fast in chains and fetters, coming on a long visit to them, with rifle, saber, and all the terrible trappings of war. Not one at a time, . . . but by thousands, and if that don't suffice, by millions. Like Pharaoh's lice, we shall be found in all [the enemy's] palaces; will be his terror and torment; he shall yet wish he had never heard of us. We will never forsake him, until he repents in sack-cloth and ashes [for] his crime of taking from us our manhood and reducing us to the brute creation. We will accept nothing but . . . our rights and liberties. He shall give up his monkeyizing, his demoniac, infernal plan of ruining our country and destroying our race. The black man shall yet hold up his head and be a man; not a poor, despised brute. But his own good hands must help strike the blows and gain the victory through blood, before the American slavery-taught white man can believe that the poor, oppressed slave and the down-trodden black man is his true friend and brother-man. . . .

Now, . . . I know that it was your wifely anger at the mean treatment which your dearly beloved husband has suffered at the hands of some of his fellow-soldiers, that made you speak so quick and without forethought, bidding me [to] desert my flag and leave my country to fall into the hands of its worst enemies. You did not speak such words as those on the day when I stood before you with the uniform of a volunteer, the uniform of a freeman on. You told me at the door, with a smile on your face, but a tear in your eye, that if I thought it was my duty to go to what was then a white man's war, to "go, and may God bless you!". . .

You have never doubted my true and faithful love for you; it is still the same, or else I would come running home like a little cur that some large dog had badly frightened, and leave you to become a slave to those wretches who hate us. For if these Southern demons conquer, then you, with your Indian and Negro blood mixed in your veins, must bow down to them and become their slave or perhaps some white man's mistress; not an honored wife, loved and respected by her husband, but a mere plaything, to be cast aside as soon as he discovers a fresh victim to administer to his beastly lusts, and bear more monkeys for him to sell to others, to be used in the same way. . . .

I do not blame you altogether for what you said about returning home, as it was cowardly [of] me to complain to you. . . . But I want you to remember hereafter, that you are a soldier's wife, a warrior's bride—one who has not a single drop of cowardly blood in his veins, and who will not desert his flag, or country, or his brother in bonds, not even for his dearly beloved wife, the friend of his bosom. . . . If I return at all, let me come back to your arms a free man, of a free country and a free flag, and my brothers free, or else let me rest in death on the battle field, with my face to the slaveholders, a continual reproach and curse unto him, as long as the world shall stand or a slaveholder breathe.[7]

The racial hostility of white soldiers toward black recruits was generally viewed by the press as something natural and ineradicable. Only the most radically pro-emancipation journals lamented or disparaged it. When one of them—the *New York Tribune*—decried the prejudice against black soldiers as "wicked," the *Detroit Free Press* quickly chimed in with this retort:

The prejudice of our white soldiers against the niggers may be "wicked"—though we deny that it is—but it is certainly *their* prejudice, and we do not see how it is to be rooted out in time to make the two races act harmoniously during the present war. Our troops are volunteers; they went willingly into an army composed of whites, at a time when it was not the policy of the administration to put them on equality with niggers. They would never have enlisted to be the "brothers" of the sable abolition deities. That was not what they bargained for. . . .

The prejudice of race, whether "wicked" or not, is certainly deep-seated in the nature of man. Experience teaches that it is one of the most difficult prejudices to eradicate. Why shall this nation, in this critical period of its history, essay an experiment so onerous and so uncertain?

We have the facts: first, that a large party in the North is irrevocably opposed to the nigger schemes of the administration; second, that the mass of the army consider themselves degraded by forcing them into military companionship with the blacks. The soldiers may be . . . driven to serve in the same army with the niggers. No doubt the abolitionists would prefer to see a few thousand white soldiers flogged every day rather than relinquish a single black regiment; but the great party at the North cannot be shot, nor flogged, and will never stir an inch from their present opposition to the abolition schemes.

What, then, shall the administration do?

We answer, return to the policy of a white man's war. Nothing short of this can save the country.[8]

The Copperheads—the most conservative and proslavery wing of the Democratic party—were even more extreme in their disgust. Firm in the belief that blacks were uncivilized and animalistic, one of them exclaimed that their use as soldiers was "a disgrace to

WHAT ARMING NEGROES HAS DONE.

The History of the San Domingo Massacre.

Crisis, March 18, 1863.
Copperhead papers published histories of the slave uprising in Saint-Domingue (San Domingo) to remind Northerners of the horrific dangers they allegedly courted by enlisting blacks for military service.

the Government." "The negro is a barbarian," and thus utterly incapable of understanding the rules of civilized warfare. "His method of making war is by the destruction and massacre of women and children, as well as men, by the perpetration of atrocities that makes humanity shudder."[9] For the Copperheads, this fear of bloodthirsty, rampaging blacks was embodied in the memory of Saint-Domingue (Haiti today), the French Caribbean colony that was the site of a shocking revolution by slaves and free blacks at the end of the eighteenth century. In an effort to remind their white countrymen of the dangers they courted in placing weapons in the hands of newly freed slaves, several Copperhead papers published an extended narrative, excerpted below, recounting the unrestrained violence that erupted around the sugar plantations of Cap (Cape) Haitien in 1791, which made the country's name synonymous with "race war" in the American imagination:

> It was on the morning of the 23rd of August, 1791, just before day, that a general alarm and consternation spread throughout the town of the Cape. The inhabitants were called from their beds by persons who reported that all the negro slaves in several neighboring parishes had revolted, and were at that moment carrying death and desolation over the adjoining large and beautiful plain to the north. . . . The rebellion first broke out on a plantation called *Noe*, in the parish of Acul, nine miles only from the city. Twelve or fourteen of the ring leaders, about the middle of the night, proceeded to the refinery, or sugar house, and seized on a young man, the refiner's apprentice, dragged him to the front of the dwelling house, and there hewed him to pieces with their cutlasses; his screams brought out the overseer, whom they instantly shot. The rebels now found their way to the apartment of the refiner, and massacred him in his bed. . . .
>
> The revolters (consisting now of all the slaves belonging to that plantation) proceeded to the house of a Mr. Clement, by whose negroes they were immediately joined, and both he and his refiner were massacred. The murderer of Mr. Clement was his own postillion (coachman), a man to whom he had always shown great kindness. The other white people of this estate contrived to make their escape.
>
> At this juncture, the negroes on the plantation of M. Faville, a few miles distant, likewise rose and murdered five white persons, one of whom (the attorney of the estate) had a wife and three daughters. These unfortunate women, while imploring for mercy [from] the savages, on their knees, beheld their husband and father murdered before their faces. For themselves, they were devoted to *a more horrid fate*, and were carried away captives by the assassins.
>
> The approach of daylight served only to discover sights of horror. It was now apparent that the negroes of all the estates in the plain acted in concert, and a general massacre of the whites took place in every quarter. On some few estates, indeed, the lives of the women were spared, but they were reserved only to gratify the brutal appetites of the ruffians; and it is shocking to relate, *that many of them suffered violation on the dead bodies of their husbands and fathers.*
>
> In the town itself, the general belief for some time was that the revolt was . . . but a sudden and partial insurrection only. The largest sugar plantation on the plains was that of Mons. Gallifet, situated about eight miles from the town, the negroes belonging to which had always been treated with such kindness

and liberality. . . . Mons. Odeluc, the attorney or agent for this plantation, . . . being fully persuaded that the negroes belonging to it would remain firm in their obedience, determined to repair thither to encourage them in opposing the insurgents, to which end he desired the assistance of a few soldiers, which was granted him. He proceeded accordingly, but, on approaching the estate, to his surprise and grief, he found all the negroes in arms on the side of the rebels, and (horrid to tell) THEIR STANDARD WAS THE BODY OF A WHITE INFANT WHICH THEY HAD RECENTLY IMPALED ON A STAKE! Mons. Odeluc had advanced too far to retreat undiscovered, and both he and his friend that accompanied him, with most of the soldiers, were killed without mercy. Two or [three] of the patrol escaped by flight, and conveyed the dreadful tidings to the inhabitants of the town.

By this time, all or most of the white persons had been found on several plantations, being massacred or forced to seek their safety in flight, [and] the ruffians exchanged the sword for the torch. The buildings and canefields were everywhere set on fire, and the conflagrations, which were visible from the town in a thousand different quarters, furnished a prospect more shocking and reflections more dismal than fancy can paint or powers of man can describe. . . .

These two districts therefore—the whole of the rich and extensive plain of the Cape—together with the contiguous mountains, were now wholly abandoned to the ravages of the enemy, and the cruelties which they exercised on such of the miserable whites as fell into their hands cannot be remembered without horror, nor reported in terms strong enough to convey a proper idea of their atrocity.

They seized Mr. Blen, an officer of the police, and having NAILED HIM ALIVE to one of the gates of his plantation, chopped off his limbs one by one with an ax.

A poor man named Robert, a carpenter by trade, endeavoring to conceal himself from the notice of the rebels, was discovered in his hiding place. The savages declared that *he should die in the way of his occupation*. Accordingly they bound him between two boards, and deliberately *sawed him asunder*. . . .

All the white and even the mulatto children, whose fathers had not joined in the revolt, were murdered without exception, *frequently before the eyes or clinging to the bosoms of their mothers*. Young women of all ranks were first violated by a whole troop of barbarians, and then generally put to death. Some of them were indeed reserved for the further gratification of the lust of the savages, and others had their eyes scooped out with a knife. . . .

To detail the various conflicts, skirmishes, massacres, and scenes of slaughter, which this exterminating war produced, should offer a disgusting and frightful picture—a combination of terrors, wherein we should behold cruelties unexampled in the annals of mankind. . . . Are the people of the United States prepared for such horrid scenes of devastation, atrocities and bloodshed in their midst?[10]

This reactionary fear of a brutal race war plagued Southern minds as well. Despite the South's repeated declarations that blacks were at their happiest when enslaved under white authority, the memory of attempted slave uprisings—particularly Nat Turner's bloody rebellion in Southampton, Virginia, in 1831—illustrated for Southerners what would inevitably happen when blacks got weapons in their hands. As efforts to organize black regiments in the North got under way, the *Richmond Examiner* therefore warned its readers of an imminent bloodbath. "War upon the South by means of negroes, means nothing short of war to extermination," it declared starkly. "They invoke the blacks to the work of blood and rapine. They seek to spread abroad the flames of insurrection."[11] Determined to fight fire with fire and shore up the South's racial order, the Confederate Congress responded by authorizing the execution of any black soldiers captured in combat.

A good chance to get Negroes.

We see that Lincoln's Congress is about to procure one hundred regiments of negroes (from Liberia we suppose) to help his own white slaves whip the Southern "Rebels" Here will be a good chance for poor men to make a fortune at short notice. Cuffee will not fight. He has'nt got the "widgunce"—"he can't stand the fish sar". He may run but it is more probable he will surrender, without firing a round. If Lincoln gets his black regiments in the field it will kill "Konscript" dead as a door nail. Instead of dodging the Conscript officers, there will be a general rush into the army by everybody to get a nigger. If old Abe had tried his best, he could'nt have hit on a better plan to fill up our decimated regiments. One hundred thousand negroes to be had just for catching! What a bait for the boys that will be. We like the idea prime, and hope old Abe and his Congress will give his new levies a good outfit, before he sends them into the field, as negroes are not valuable property just now unless they are well *endorsed on the back,* and footed up right.

"It is thought by many among us that the Confederates should seek chiefly to capture, not slay, the negro soldiers, in order to return them to slavery, both the free negroes of the North and the escaped slaves. But it is the fortune of war that much evil must be done that good may come, and it is impossible, in the heat of conflict, to discriminate. The death of an able-bodied negro is certainly a loss and an evil, but a soldier is not to stop to estimate a negro's value when he meets him in battle, for if he devotes himself to capturing negroes Yankee bullets are all the time threatening him. Besides, it is a matter of doubt whether it would be to our interest to keep these negro soldiers, whether Northern freedmen or Southern slaves, for use as slaves in the future. There are perhaps many of them, seduced or forced from their owners, who might become useful and docile slaves again. But the large majority, including all the free negroes of the North, are a desperate, worthless set of diseased, mind polluted wretches, who could scarcely become again useful and desirable servants among us; and even those who are better inclined have become debauched, and lost value, by contact with the Yankees. On the whole, the Confederates should, and they certainly will, kill all indiscriminately that they can, Yankees, Dutch, negroes, or what not, whom they meet in battle; but if any negroes are captured, it would be better than hanging to sell them to Cuba or Brazil."

AN ILLUSTRATION OF THE NEW YANKEE DOCTRINE ABOUT THE DARKEY.

CORPORAL —— MASS. REGIMENT.—Cuffee, advancing rapidly to the rear during an engagement, to Yankee officer, who tries to stop him—*loq.*— "No, sah! can't go back dar—dis chile too '*motional* for dat sorter thing."

TOP LEFT *Confederate Union,* December 30, 1862. With astonishing delight, this Southern editorial saw the Union's use of black soldiers as an opportunity for Confederates to "get Negroes" for their own use and enrichment.

TOP RIGHT *Southern Confederacy,* as reprinted in the *Washington Intelligencer,* June 27, 1863. Believing that captured black soldiers were too valuable to be killed, some Southern papers recommended that they be used as slaves in the Confederacy or sold to plantation owners in Cuba or Brazil.

LEFT *Southern Illustrated News,* November 21, 1863. Southerners liked to believe that blacks did not have the strength of character to be good soldiers and that they would fight only when coerced by their white officers. In this Southern cartoon, a terrified black recruit attempts to run from battle; when confronted by his commanding officer to return to the fight, he exclaims in pidgin English: "No, sah! I can't go back dar—dis chile too *'motional* for dat sorter thing."

Not all Southern newspapers agreed with this policy. In fact, some approached the Union's decision to employ black troops quite sanguinely. Instead of condemning it as a prelude to race war and calling for the execution of any armed blacks caught in their midst, they saw it as an opportunity to capture (or, in the case of recently emancipated slaves, recapture) more blacks for plantation labor. According to the headline of one Georgia newspaper, the introduction of black troops into the Union army represented a "good chance to get Negroes"—particularly for those who did not currently own any. "One hundred thousand negroes to be had for catching!" it announced excitedly. The paper seemed to imagine a sort of free-for-all in which ordinary Southerners would have the opportunity to suddenly catapult to slaveholder status. Many editors, if not exactly enthusiastic about Lincoln's attempt to bring blacks into the army, at least agreed that those who were caught were "too valuable to be killed." Although the dastardly white officers who led them might be shot or hung, "the negroes will be captured for laborers" and sold to masters either in the Southern states or abroad.[12] In an enterprising fashion, the *Augusta Chronicle & Sentinel* laid out this plan for putting captured blacks to good use:

> One among the most important measures that needs to be put into operation immediately is the disposition to be made of negroes captured with arms in their hands. These negroes are much needed to work on fortifications and perform the labor now being performed by the slaves who have remained faithful, and whose masters are needing them to work in the fields and prepare food for our soldiers. They could be so secured with ball and chain, or with chains in pairs, that they could not escape. At the close of the war, they could either be bought by the Government and kept employed on the public works, or sold to the sugar planters of Cuba. . . . In this way negroes who are taken, who have learned bad manners [from] the Northern Abolitionists, could be made serviceable during the war, and after the war is over, could be disposed of in a sure way, and be put in a position where there would be no chance for them to be troublesome to us. If this plan was adopted, most of the free negroes of the North would be deterred from enlisting in the army of the Abolitionists, and what few did enlist, if captured, could be made useful and profitable to the Confederacy.[13]

The *Savannah Republican* took a more charitable view of the situation. Believing that Northerners had seduced the contented slaves of the South to run away and that they were forcing them against their will into the Union army, the *Republican* imagined that these new recruits were now languishing under the cruel authority of their white officers. The paper therefore looked forward to the day when these runaway slaves would desert the Union cause and return to their rightful place on the plantations of their former masters:

> It is reasonable to assume that by desertion, captures in war, and possibly by the voluntary surrender of them by the Yankee government, very many, if not a majority of these slaves . . . will again fall into our hands. We have testimony entirely reliable that a very large proportion . . . would gladly return to their owners to-day were they allowed to do so. . . . Should the enemy land and seek to give us battle with their black regiments in front—as they propose to place them there to stop the bullets aimed at their own infamous heads—they will drop their guns and run after the first round, or desert in a body to the Confederate side. We have not a shadow of a doubt on this point.
>
> The question then arises: What is to be done with this betrayed and unfortunate race when they come again into our possession? . . . We differ from very many whom we have heard express opinions on the subject. Some think they would prove the most dangerous members in our community of blacks, and

that they should suffer death in coming again into our hands. Severe punishment would, perhaps, be meted out by others, whilst a third class, prompted by a most ungenerous philosophy, would sell them away into distant parts, as if safety was not equally dear to every community.

Our views differ widely from all to which we have referred. We would decide this moral question, not by the promptings of passion, but from the dictates of justice and enlightened philanthropy. Even should rigid justice demand severity, it is always safest and best to lean to the side of mercy. We have never regarded the negro so much to blame in this matter. He is a weak, credulous being, and we should deal with him as such. He knows and feels the superiority of the white man. He admires his better judgment, and is accustomed to look up to him for counsel and direction. It is this confiding spirit that has made the negro the ready victim of his worst enemy—the Abolitionist. For a long series of years his mind has been poisoned by the basest of deceptions and lies. Attractive visions of freedom, luxury, and idleness have been systematically held up to his untutored and unsuspecting mind . . . to seduce him from his lawful allegiance. He has been taught by wicked men to believe that he was by nature as good as his white master, [and] that in the hands of his Abolition friend he would become rich, independent, and in all respects, the equal of those to whom he has been accustomed to submit. Is it strange that such a creature should have fallen into the snare thus ingeniously laid for him, and especially when . . . his master has not taken the pains to enlighten and guard him against the wiles of the tempter? We think not. On the contrary, we, ourselves, are much to blame for keeping him in the dark as regards the truth. But he has at last found it, elaborated from the crucible of bitter experience. He has followed the advice of the Abolitionists, and instead of realizing his grand dreams of power and importance, he finds himself plunged in ruin. . . .

Such is the conviction of the absconded slaves of the South. They remain with the Abolitionists, work for them, take up the weapons of war, only through compulsion. They have awoke[n] from their fatal dream, only to sigh for the happy and contented homes they have left behind them. They have been deceived and betrayed to their ruin, and they know it. The freedom of the African in the hands of the Abolitionists is no longer a picture of fancy—he has met and realized the dread reality. We regard the . . . association of the two races, under the circumstances, as the most fortunate thing that could have happened for the South. It has opened the eyes of the slave, and taught him a philosophy which nothing but experience could impart. It will make him happy and contented with his lot in life, for it has satisfied him and disarmed his fanatical sympathizers. He will be a better negro from what he has passed through, and adhere to his position in the social scale with contentment and pleasure. His return to the old plantation he will consider a deliverance from the worst of bondage, and he will come back both repentant and loyal.

It is clearly therefore the policy and duty of the masters of the South to receive their fugitive slaves with kindness, and extend a christian forgiveness for the errors of the past. They need not even a lecture, for they have the dear-bought lessons of experience to prompt them ever hereafter to loyalty and duty. We would tell the w[a]nderer: Return and sin no more.[14]

In actuality, Southerners often were vicious in their treatment of the Union's black troops, and atrocities against them—including the execution of wounded and surrendered black soldiers and the sale of black captives into slavery—did occur.[15] In part for this very reason, the real conduct of black troops in combat was far different from how most Southerners and Northerners had envisioned it. They were neither poor nor timid fighters, but rather demonstrated tremendous grit and valor. Although blacks did participate in sev-

Frank Leslie's Illustrated Newspaper, June 27, 1863.
Although not an accurate depiction of the fighting at Port Hudson, this illustration perfectly captures the great admiration many Northern whites came to feel toward the Union's black soldiers.

eral small-scale skirmishes against Confederate troops and guerrilla fighters in the winter and spring of 1863, the first serious test of their abilities came in May of that year, at Port Hudson, Louisiana. At the time, Port Hudson was one of two Confederate bastions on the Mississippi River—the other being Vicksburg—that had not yet been captured by the Union. Making an assault on Port Hudson was no small undertaking, as the 6,000 Confederate troops who occupied it had erected formidable defenses. By orders of the U.S. War Department, the challenge of seizing it fell to Major General Nathaniel Banks, whose command included over 1,000 black soldiers of the First and Third Louisiana Native Guards.

On the morning of May 27, 1863, the attack began. The initial advance was made by a regiment of white troops, but when their charge failed to penetrate the Confederate defenses, the First and Third Louisiana Native Guards filled the breach. As they came within two hundred yards of the fortifications, they endured a decimating shower of canister and rifle fire. Lifted by their own inner reserves of courage and determination, they continued to move forward, but after several charges were still not able to make a breakthrough. Recognizing the futility of continuing with the operation, Banks ordered a retreat. The black regiments paid a steep price for their gallantry, suffering nearly two hundred casualties.

Militarily, the assault was a failure, but the black troops succeeded in wiping away the doubts harbored by Northern whites about their courage under fire. Although Copperheads back home would never acknowledge their bravery, other Democrats joined with Republicans in lauding it before the Northern people. The blacks "fought with the desperation of tigers," displaying a level of intrepidness that "raised them very much in my opinion as soldiers," wrote a correspondent for the *New York Herald*. The *New York Times* and *Chicago Tribune* published a report by none other than General Banks himself, giving an official assessment of events at Port Hudson. "Their conduct was heroic," he affirmed of the Native Guards. "Whatever doubt may have existed before as to the efficiency of organizations of this character, the history of this day proves conclusively . . . that the Government will find in this class of troops effective supporters and defenders."[16]

Surprised and excited now by the prospect for utilizing blacks militarily against the Confederacy, the *New*

THE BLACK FLAG.—In the recent battle of Port Hudson it is said the black flag was raised defiantly to the breeze by the Confederates. This was justifiable under the circumstances. Let it be understood that the black flag is to wave in every battle in which the negroes are made the tools of the cowardly Abolitionists, and let there be no officer in command of a black regiment or company taken prisoner, unless it be for the purpose of giving him a more merited death by hanging.

NEGRO TROOPS IN LOUISIANA. The following paragraphs are from a letter written by an officer of high rank in Louisiana:

HEADQUARTERS OF BRIG. GEN. ULLMANN,
New Orleans, June 6th, 1863.

As to the negro, he is enthusiastic to enlist. I am astonished by their intelligence and comprehensive knowledge of their position. They appreciate the deep stake they have in our success, and know that if we fail it is "all up" with them. They are *in earnest* far more than we. They know that if taken by the rebels they will be tortured and hung. That is why they fought *so splendidly* at the assault on the 27th inst. on Port Hudson. All agree that never did men fight with more dauntless courage. Their praise, is constantly more and more spoken by unwilling lips. It is surprising how readily they take to the drill. Their camps are models of neatness and order. I feel every confidence in the complete success of the colored troops. We have had occasion in the whole command to punish but *one colored man*. We have the best opportunity ever afforded of verifying some facts which have always been doubted at the North. Every man presenting himself to be recruited strips to the skin, to be surveyed by the surgeon. We do not accept one-half that offer. On Tuesday, out of 82 only 33 were accepted. I have directed my surgeons to keep accurate lists of the causes of rejection. They report to me that not *one in fifteen* is free from marks of severe lashing. More than one half are rejected because of disability arising from lashing with whips and the biting of dogs on their calves and thighs. It is frightful. Hundreds of them have welts on their backs as large as one of your largest fingers. I intend to have these memoranda collected and published with certificates of Surgeons.

TOP *Richmond Whig,* June 20, 1863.
Instead of denying rumors of brutality against black soldiers, the Southern press openly justified raising the "black flag" against them.

RIGHT *Boston Evening Transcript,* June 16, 1863.
The courageous bearing of black troops amazed many white observers, as did the scars that they bore from their years in slavery. In this document, a white officer comments that among eighty-two former slaves who attempted to join his regiment, only thirty-three of them were acceptable—the rest were so disfigured and injured as to be unfit for service.

York Times looked hopefully toward the final triumph of the Union:

> This . . . settles the question that the negro race can fight with great prowess. Those black soldiers had never before been in any severe engagement. They were comparatively new troops, and were yet subjected to the most awful ordeal that even veterans ever have to experience—the charging upon fortifications through the crash of belching batteries. The men, white or black, who will not flinch from that, will flinch from nothing. It is no longer possible to doubt the bravery and steadiness of the colored race, when rightly led.
>
> As to the controllability of the black regiments, so that they can be kept strictly to the limits of civilized warfare, Gen. Banks reports nothing specifically; but his broad terms cover the point. They never could be "effectual supporters and defenders" if they fought in the wild Indian style, with unrestrained barbarity. They went into the conflict with terrible earnestness; but . . . were as obedient to rule as any soldiers on the ground. Probably they went in and held on with the greater desperation, under the consciousness of what might befall them if taken prisoners—but desperation, no matter what it springs from, is every soldier's privilege, so long as it adheres to honorable warfare.
>
> Neither is there any intimation that the cooperation of black troops at all demoralized the white. The fact that the white never did better fighting is proof positive . . . that the original prejudice against forming black regiments, and putting them upon active service, had nearly or quite died out.
>
> The remaining military inquiry, whether the exigencies of the war could call for black help, has been

settled . . . , and no genuine friend of the war can longer object to it.

Well, what is to come of it? We suspect the rebels have studied this point more than we. The fierceness with which the Confederate Congress and Executive have declared that the laws of war shall not be observed toward black soldiers, or toward white officers commanding them, and that every one taken in arms shall be summarily hung, unmistakably shows that they greatly dread this new resort. They would never so trample upon the settled principles of war, and defy the opinion of all civilization, unless they believed their very fate depended on it. They have among them three millions of black men . . . within their present military limits. These three millions cannot be made to fight for them, and they know it. They never would dare to expose a black regiment against ours in battle, for it would surely desert in a body, if it did not turn its arms against them on the spot. But those of them who can get the opportunity are willing to fight for us, and can fight, as is now proved with great effectiveness. . . . It is the realization of this that nerves the Confederate authorities to such desperate measures to arrest our thus turning their former slaves to account. But they will fail. . . .

There is no possible escape of the rebels from utter overthrow but timely submission. It has been plain enough from the beginning to all clear observers. It is now more plain than ever in the light of the recent demonstrations of the practicability of raising effective armies from the black population of the South. This seals and confirms what before was sufficiently assured. There is no salvation but in a return to allegiance. That fact—the Confederates may rely on it—is as fixed as destiny.[17]

This assessment by the *Times* was only partially right. As it expected, black soldiers would indeed continue to make important contributions to the ultimate success of the Union. But its projections regarding the future course of the Confederacy were totally wrongheaded. For one thing, the rebels had no intention of putting down their weapons and making "a return to allegiance." Moreover, not all Southerners would have agreed with the *Times* on the impossibility of arming the slaves to fight for the Confederacy. Although most Southern papers derided or despised the employment of black troops by the Union, some voices in the Deep South found it impossible to be so dismissive.[18] Exasperated by the onslaught of the Union armies, and confronted by the evident heroism of black soldiers, they began demanding that the Confederacy try to utilize its slaves for its own military advantage. The *Columbus Sun*, brazenly confident that the slaves could be transformed easily into effective Confederate soldiers, proposed this plan for using them in a massive retaliatory assault against the Union:

That remarkable freak of nature, the President of the Yankee nation, despairing of uniting the territory of the once United States under one government, except by exterminating the eight millions of freemen whom he is pleased to call "rebels," issued a proclamation more than twelve months since in which he declared all the slaves in the seceded States to be free, and offered them bounties to take up arms against their masters. This proclamation was sustained by the Yankee Congress . . . , and officers in the Yankee army were detailed to South Carolina, Louisiana, Mississippi, and other localities over-run by the enemy, to enlist negroes in the military service, to organize them, place arms in their hands, and give them all the means necessary to execute the bloody work which had been assigned to them. . . . Not satisfied with this, negro regiments, composed of the worst types of the African race, who are generally fugitives from their lawful owners in the South, have been raised in the North, and . . . turned loose upon us with the promise that "Beauty and Booty" is to be the reward of their hellish work. In short, . . . the Yankee government and people have inaugurated an indiscriminate slaughter of our people, sparing neither age nor sex, and with the avowed purpose of *extermination*. . . .

Now how long shall this unequal contest continue? How long shall our brave, high souled, chivalrous men be permitted to stand up in an unequal contest with savages and fiends incarnate. . . ? Is there no limit to human forbearance, beyond which it should turn to vengeance? And have we not the means of vengeance abundantly in our hands? Suppose our Government should arm 100,000 or 250,000 negroes and march them North—tell them that the New York banks are full of gold, that Yankeedom is full of booty, and that they may have a good time generally when they reach New York or Philadelphia, and we will wager our head *that they will reach New York*—leaving a track of fire and blood through Washington and Pittsburg. The panic in Yankeedom would be fearful. When the news reached New York and Boston that Gen. Lee had been reinforced by 100,000 negroes, and that he was driving them North to be turned loose upon Yankee cities, what power on earth could keep men in the Yankee army, under military discipline, with such a calamity threatening their homes? . . . Our enemies should begin to think of these things, and our people would do well to prepare themselves for emergencies. We are fighting now for self-preservation, . . . and whenever it shall become *necessary* to employ such desperate means to defend our lives and the honor of our families, they should, and *will* be employed.[19]

Others went even further. So determined was the *Mississippian* to beat back the enemy that it endorsed not only arming male slaves but also emancipating them, regardless of how such a move might undermine the whole system of slavery:

This knotty subject is exciting comment in nearly all of the newspapers of the Confederacy, and thoughtful men throughout the country are giving it their serious attention. It seems to us, [that] there should be no difficulty as to its solution. We must either employ the negroes ourselves, or the enemy will employ them against us. . . . They must be taught to know that this is peculiarly the country of the black man—that in no other is the climate and soil so well adapted to his nature and capacity. He must further be taught that it is his duty, as well as the white man's, to defend his home with arms, if need be.

We are aware that there are persons who shudder at the bare idea of placing arms in the hands of negroes, and who are not willing to trust them under any circumstances. The negro, however, is proverbial for his faithfulness under kind treatment. He is an affectionate, grateful being, and we are persuaded that the fears of such persons are groundless.

There are in the slaveholding States four millions of negroes, and out of this number at least six hundred thousand able-bodied men capable of bearing arms can be found. Lincoln proposes to free and arm them against us. There are already fifty thousand of them in arms in the Federal ranks. Lincoln's scheme has worked well so far, and if not checkmated, will most assuredly be carried out. The Confederate Government must adopt a counter policy. It must thwart the enemy in the gigantic scheme, at all hazards, and if nothing else will do it—if the negroes cannot be made effective and trustworthy to the Southern cause in [any] other way, we solemnly believe it is the duty of this Government to forestall Lincoln and proceed at once to take steps for the emancipation or liberation of the negroes itself. Let them be declared free, placed in the ranks, and told to fight for their homes and country.

We are fully sensible of the grave importance of the question, but the inexorable logic of events has forced it upon us. We must deal with it, then, not with fear and trembling—not as timid, time-serving men—but with a boldness, a promptness and a determination which the exigency requires, and which should ever characterize the action of a people resolved to sacrifice everything for liberty. It is true, that such a step would revolutionize our whole industrial system—that it would, to a great extent, impoverish the country and be a dire calamity to both the negro and the white race of this and the Old World; but better this than the loss of the negroes, the country and liberty.

If Lincoln succeeds in arming our slaves against us, he will also succeed in making them our masters. He will reverse the social order of things in the South. Whereas, if he is checkmated in time, our liberties will remain intact; the land will be ours, and the industrial system of the country still controlled by Southern men.

Such action on the part of our Government would place our people in a purer and better light before the world. It would disabuse the European mind of a grave error in regard to the cause of our separation. It would prove to them that there were higher and holier motives which actuated our people than the mere love of property. It would show that although slavery is one of the principles that we started out to fight for, yet it falls far short of being the chief one; that for the sake of our liberty we are capable of any personal sacrifice; that we regard the emancipation of slaves and the consequent loss of property as an evil infinitely less than the subjugation and enslavement of ourselves; that it is *not* a war exclusively for the privilege of holding negroes in bondage. It would prove to our own soldiers, three fourths of whom never owned a negro, that it is not "the rich man's war and the poor man's fight;" but a war for the most sacred of all principles, for the dearest of all rights—the right to govern ourselves. It would show them that the rich man who owned slaves was not willing to jeopardize the precious liberty of the country by his eagerness to hold on to his slaves, but that he was ready to give them up and sacrifice his interest in them whenever the cause demanded it. It would lend a new impetus, a new enthusiasm, a new and powerful strength, to the cause, and place our success beyond a peradventure. It would at once remove all the odium which attaches to us on account of slavery, and bring speedy recognition, and if necessary, intervention.

We sincerely trust that the Southern people will be found willing to make any and every sacrifice which the establishment of our independence may require. Let it never be said that to preserve slavery we were willing to wear the chains of bondage ourselves—that the very avarice which prompted us to hold on to the negro for the sake of money invested in him, riveted upon us shackles more galling and bitter than ever a people yet endured. Let not slavery prove a barrier to our independence. If it be found in the way—if it proves an insurmountable object to the achievement of our liberty and separate nationality, away with it! Let it perish![20]

Wholesale emancipation was an obviously extreme and revolutionary step for anyone in the Confederacy to consider—further evidence of just how monumental the Union's decision to enlist black troops truly was. In essence, what the *Mississippian* was saying was that the Confederacy might have to compromise the position it had taken in 1861 when the war began. At that time, the Southern press had asserted that the Confederacy was fighting for liberty—to protect the individual rights of all Southern white men, including their right to own slaves. But by 1863, with the Union penetrating deeply into the Mississippi Valley, it had become clear that the Confederacy might need to revise its goals and sacrifice some freedoms in order to secure others. To defeat the Yankees and ensure their own personal safety and national independence, Southerners might have to scuttle slavery. The suggestion did not signify a lack of commitment to the institution, just a lack of confidence in the ability of Southerners to achieve all that they had desired initially. It was symptomatic of a growing sense of panic and desperation that would continue to gnaw, with increasing torment, at the core of the new southern nation.

Montgomery Daily Advertiser.

VOLUME XIV. MONTGOMERY, ALA., WEDNESDAY MORNING, DECEMBER 10, 1862. NUMBER 241.

The Daily Advertiser.

TERMS OF SUBSCRIPTION

Daily Advertiser, per annum..................$.. 8

Weekly Advertiser, per annum.................. 3 00

NOTICE.—Positively no subscriber is received or continued without cash in advance.

Tuesday Evening, December 9, 1862.

[COMMUNICATED.]

MR. EDITOR:—In your paper of the 2d instant appears a communication signed "An old member of the Legislature," in which the writer passionately urges the necessity for the present Legislature to make magistrates, constables, clerks, deputy sheriffs, and notaries, subject to the Conscript law. Now, sir, this question was sprung in our Congress by some member but it had not been discussed far before they discovered that they had found a mare's nest. I am sure that your correspondent had not maturely considered this matter. If he had examined the Code of Alabama, and the various acts of the Legislature since its adoption, he would have found that the duties of clerks and magistrates, and especially of magistrates, are multifarious and important. Now, I will admit that some of the officers mentioned by your correspondent might well be spared from the country, and would probably do the country more good in the army than they would at home, especially those who have been elected since the passage of the Conscript law, for the purpose of avoiding it, but the idea of vacating the commissions of clerks and magistrates who had been elected in good faith before the passage of the Conscript law, and who have given bond and taken an oath for the faithful discharge of their duties, is preposterous in the extreme. Although this matter was brought before the Legislature in the early part of its session for the consideration of its members, I did not suppose that any person seriously contemplated the passage of any such measure until my eyes fell upon the communication of your correspondent. He seems not only earnest but enthusiastic about the matter, and calls upon you as "a watchman upon the public tower," to thunder forth your appeals to have the "humble magistrate" dethroned, and his commission and that of other officers, torn to atoms, in order that the country may be saved! He certainly imagines that a large army can be raised from the magistrates of Alabama. Now sir, I have taken some trouble to ascertain the number of magistrates in the State. Supposing that each county has its quota of magistrates according to the number of beats, there would be about 350 magistrates in the State. Your correspondent says that "in many of the beats in this county, (this county) and I have no doubt it is so everywhere, there has not been a magistrate for years." Suppose, then, that "it is so everywhere," and that half the beats throughout the State have no magistrates, that would reduce the number to 175. It is reasonable to calculate that at least half that number are not subject to conscription, either from infirmity or age, (I have reference to the number as it stood before the enactment of the Conscript law,) and that would reduce the number to about 87. I do not imagine that our Legislature would be guilty of such a gross violation of the rights of individuals, and bring upon the State the disorder and confusion that would result from such a measure.

But your correspondent says that these offices that were heretofore vacant are now filled with conscripts. Very well! Then if his object be to get at those who have shielded themselves behind the office to avoid the conscript, I have no serious issue with him, but certainly it would be an act of great injustice, to make a general sweep and hold those elected in good faith, before the passage of the conscript law, amenable for the acts of the others. I will not argue the unconstitutionality of the measure, that must be apparent to all, but is it policy? Among the many duties imposed upon magistrates, is that of enforcing the patrol law, and keeping a proper subordination among slaves, which we all agree is very essential at this time. In many counties they are charged with the very important duty of keeping in order the public roads, appointing overseers, apportioning hands, &c. Your correspondent says, "The Legislature did well when they made the militia officers liable to the conscript." So we all say, because they put them where they properly belong, but it is quite different with civil officers. This is no time, Mr. Editor, to reorganize the magistrates' courts; they are indispensable to the country. In many sections they are the only convenient tribunals to which the soldier's wife can appeal for or the matter and examine the law carefully, he will have more respect for the office of Magistrate than he has shown in his communication.

CONSTITUTION.

More Yankee Lying.

The Richmond *Examiner* publishes an abstract of a report made by an investigating committee of the Washington Congress which exceeds in mendacity all the Yankee falsehoods which have been issued by their commanders and propagated by their press. It professes to recount "rebel barbarities." The purpose is evident. It is intended to divert attention from their own barbarities, deceive the European world, and throw dust in the eyes of the Northern people. The *Examiner* says:

According to this report the quantity of Southern *bijouterie* manufactured from the bones of dead Yankees is astonishing, and the number of skeletons worked up in the jewellers' shops would be sufficient to supply every family in the Southern Confederacy with these popular trinkets.

We are told in the official text of this Yankee investigation, that it is the regular practice of the Confederate soldiers to ransack battle fields, and collect Yankee bones, which after being worked into pleasing shapes, are displayed for sale in the bazaars of the South. After the first battle of Manassas, we are assured that "the rebels commenced digging bodies two or three days after they were buried, for the purpose, at first, of obtaining the buttons off their uniforms, and that afterwards they disinterred them to get their bones. They had taken rails and pushed the ends down in the centre under the middle of bodies and seized them up." In the narrations of the testimony embodied in the committees' report, we are informed that Mrs. Pierce Butler, who lives near that place said she had seen the rebels boiling portions of the bodies of the dead Yankees in order to obtain their bones as relics. They could not wait for them to decay. She said that she had seen drum sticks made of "Yankee shin-bones," as they called them. Mrs. Butler also stated that she had seen a skull that one of the New Orleans artillery had, which, he said, he was going to send home and have mounted, and that he intended to drink a brandy punch out of it the day he was married.

But the recital of the "barbarities of the rebels" does not stop with these pictures of the bloody bones and the witches cauldron. It appears that Gov. Sprague, of Rhode Island, was called to the witness' stand by the Committee. This respectable witness furnishes a fresh dish of horrors. He had visited the battle field of Manassas to recover the body of an officer, and must, as we imagine, have been very much nonplussed in his search, for the flesh and bones of the Yankee "Colonel" to find that the corpse had been "dug up by the rebels, by some men of a Georgia regiment, his head cut off, and his body taken to a ravine thirty or forty yards below, and there burnt." The Governor's search was only repaid by "a shirt" and "a blanket with the hair upon it," which figurative relics were duly consigned to a rosewood coffin and buried with military honors. The Governor also complains, in his testimony, that on opening the "ditches" where the Yankees were buried, he found them "filled with soldiers, all buried with their faces downward."

There are similar falsehoods narrated in this document, but they will fail of the intended effect as regards foreign nations, at least. Yankee representations of every kind are estimated at their just standard of veracity all over Europe.

General Lee.

The army correspondent of the Savannah *Republican* furnishes that paper with the following sketch of Gen. Lee:

As was remarked in a former letter, the Confederacy is fortunate in having such a man as Gen. Lee in its service. He is still in the prime and vigor of physical and intellectual manhood, being about forty five years of age. He is six feet in height; weighs about one hundred and ninety pounds; is erect, well formed and of imposing appearance; has clear, bright, being quit black eyes, dark grey hair and a heavy gray beard. He is exceedingly plain in his dress, and one looks at his costume in vain for those insignia of rank for which most officers show such a weakness. He wears an unassuming black felt hat, with a narrow strip of gold lace around it, and a plain brigadier's coat with three stars on the collar, but without the usual braiding on the sleeves. He travels and sleeps in an ambulance when the army's in motion, and occupies a tent when it is stationary, and not the largest and best house in the neighborhood, as is the custom of some officers. In a few words, he cares but little for appearances, though one of the handsomest men in the Confederacy, and is content to take the same fare his soldiers receive.

In character and personal deportment, he is all that the most ardent patriot can desire. Grave and dignified, he is yet modest and painfully distrustful of his abilities. The descendant of a gallant officer of the elder revolution, the husband of the granddaughter (by adoption) of Gen. Washington, the inheritor of a large estate, and the trusted leader of a great and victorious army, he is nevertheless accessible to the humblest and most ragged soldier in the ranks, courteous to his officers, just and kind to the citizen, and withal and above all, a meek and humble Christian.

Tanning.

We are indebted to Mr. William Crutchfield, of Goochland Court House, for the following details and receipt for tanning leather. If, in any particular, not perfectly intelligible, Mr. C. will take great pleasure in affording any additional information.

The true mode for farmers to adopt, is for each neighborhood, consisting of from three to six, to combine, construct the vats and divide the labor among themselves.—They will make as good leather as they now get, if not better, and they will get double the quantity they now receive from the tanners:

TANNING LEATHER.—Pure water vat six feet square, four feet deep. Lime water vat—same.

Vat for bark four feet wide, four deep, and eight long. Soak hides till soft in pure water—from five to seven days—then flesh on beam.

Beam for breaking the hides six feet long—a log, two feet diameter, split in two—underneath hollowed out for prop, to raise or depress. In the process of breaking, use a knife two feet long with shanks for handles—knife little rounding.

As soon as flesh is taken off, (one hand will flesh a dozen a day,) the hides are put in the lime vat—weak solution—one bushel lime—first slacked. The vat not quite full of water. Hides to be taken out every other day to air, and replaced smooth—plunge or stir vat every time the hides are drawn. An iron hook, like ice hooks, to draw the hides.

As soon as hair will slip, throw hides over beam, hair side up and rub with fleshing knife. The hair off, the hides are put back in vat of pure water, and to remain there a day or two—then throw across the beam again, and with smooth fleshing knife, work on all the lime and remaining flesh. One hand will flesh 50 hides a day.

The process of bating may be omitted in tanning coarse leather.

Take the hides as clean as possible to the bark vat. At first one bushel of bark, pounded or ground—the weak solution to continue two days—and gradually strengthened by addition of bark, say one bushel daily. Keep it in two weeks; handling and strengthening liquor.

Then clean out vat, taking out all the bark. Throw in pounded bark—put down one hide—cover that inch thick with bark and so on, each hide. Let in water and let it remain a month. Again clean out vat, reverse hides and repeat operation—and let this remain a month. Again clean out vat and repeat operation, and remain another month.

[Chestnut oak bark the best—though the Spanish or black oak good.]

After three months, the hide being tanned, is taken out and hung upon poles. This is sole leather without further labor.

That intended for upper leather, half dry, is oiled on the grain or hair side with a mop. It averages [illegible], and grease heavily on flesh side, one pound tallow and one half pound train oil to a side mixed. This mixture is prepared thus: melt the tallow slowly and take same quantity of oil mixed and stirred in—after it becomes cool, is ready for use. Then hang hides in shade till dry.—*Richmond Whig.*

Georgia Legislature.

Wednesday, 3d.—The Senate passed the House bill making all males, white and black, between 18 and 60, subject to road duty; also the bill to authorize the issue of $1,000,000 in change bills by the State.

The House laid the "Woman's bill" on the table—yeas 85, nays 43; also the bill to appropriate $200,000 to remove the women and children of Savannah from the city in case of an attack.

Thursday, 4th.—In the Senate, Mr. Vason, from a select committee, reported a bill to prevent monopoly and extortion, and to put in force the laws of England on that subject.

The Senate laid on the table the resolution in reference to the Conscript law, State rights, &c., that has for some time been under discussion.

The bill to suspend the computation of compound interest against executors, administrators, &c., was passed.

The House, after some debate, passed a resolution instructing the Governor to collect the sum of $600,000 or $800,000 due the State Road by the Confederate Government. An amendment instructing him to take pay in 8 per cent. bonds was rejected.

A bill to increase the salaries and daily wages of employes of the State Road, passed.

The bill to enlarge the militia by including all between 16 and 18 and all over 45 years of age, was laid on the table for the present.

☞ We can appreciate the feelings which induced brother Morse of the Augusta *Chronicle & Sentinel,* to pen the following paragraph:

GRATUITOUS ADVICE.—If you have anything to communicate upon any subject, no matter whether it is of any earthly interest or not, rush into an editor's sanctum when he is deep in the contemplation of half sheet exchanges, or deeper still in a metaphysical leader for the next morning's issue, and just "unbosom" freely to him. Tell him all your griefs and disquietudes, and be as verbose about it as you please—everybody knows the editor has nothing to do but listen, *auribus erectis.*

Beautiful Engraving.

We are indebted to Messrs. Keatinge & Ball [illegible]

ADJ'T & INSPECTOR GENERAL'S OFFICE,
RICHMOND, Nov. 27th, 1862.

General Orders No. 96.

Commandants of conscripts will cause the following order to be published for at least seven times in a sufficient number of newspapers in each State of the Confederacy to ensure its reaching every part of the country.

I. All commissioned officers and enlisted men who are now absent from their commands from any other cause than actual disability, or duty under orders from the Secretary of War, or from their department commanders, will return to their commands without delay.

II. Commissioned officers failing to comply with the provisions of the foregoing paragraph within a reasonable length of time, in no case to exceed twenty days after the publication of this order, shall be dropped from the rolls of the army in disgrace, and their names will be furnished to the commandant of conscripts for enrollment in the ranks.

III. All enlisted men who shall fail to comply with the provisions of paragraph I, of this order, within a reasonable length of time, shall be considered as deserters, and treated accordingly, their names to be furnished to the commandant of conscripts in their State, for publication, or such other action as may be deemed most efficacious.

IV. In order to ensure the efficient co-operation of all concerned to carry this order into immediate effect, Department Commanders are directed to require from the commanding officer of each separate command in their Departments a prompt report of the names of all commissioned officers and enlisted men now absent from their commands. These reports must state in each case the cause of absence, and any regiment, battalion or company commander who shall neglect to furnish such a report, or who shall knowingly be guilty of concealing any case of unauthorized absence, shall, on conviction thereof, be summarily dismissed.

V. Under the provisions of the 2d clause of paragraph I, of General Orders No. 82, commissioned officers and privates, who are incapable of bearing arms in consequence of wounds received in battle, but who are otherwise fit for service, are required, if not otherwise assigned, to report to the nearest commandant of conscripts in their respective States, who will, if they are fitted for such duty, assign them to the collection of stragglers and the enforcement of the provisions of the order, with full power to call upon the nearest military authority for such assistance as may be necessary thereto.

VI. Officers of the Quartermaster's Department, charged with payment of troops, are hereby directed not to pay any commissioned officer, non-commissioned officer or private who does not furnish satisfactory evidence that he is not liable to the penalties described in the foregoing order. Any disbursing officer who shall make payment in violation of this order shall be liable on his bond for the amount of such payment.

By order.

(Signed) S. COOPER,
Adj't. and Inspector General.

dec 9d7t

MANUFACTURERS' CONVENTION AT GREENSBORO'.—We learn that 18 cotton and woolen establishments were represented in the Convention held in Greensborough on Wednesday last, and that the result is highly favorable. The 18 present, with 6 at Fayetteville that have already complied with the law in this respect, agreed to work hereafter according to the terms of the exemption act. Cotton yarns will, therefore, hereafter be sold by the factories at from $2 75 to $3 75 per bunch, according to quality, and cloth at from 30 to 35 cents per yard.—*Raleigh Standard.*

☞ It is rumored, but not credited, that the militia Brigadier General Shields has organized an armed force, said to be two thousand strong, in Cocke county, to resist the enforcement of the Conscript Act. Col. Thomas, of the Confederate service, has sent here (so it is rumored on the streets) for additional troops, in order that he may enforce the law and disperse Shields' band of tories. We believe this story to be an exaggeration, but it was current and credited on yesterday afternoon.—*Knoxville Register.*

YANKEE FINANCIAL SCHEME.—The New York *Journal of Commerce* has submitted to the Yankee Government at Washington, a financial scheme which proposes that Congress shall authorize the issue of coupon bonds, to any amount less than two thousand millions of dollars, in various sums, ranging from twenty-five to five thousand dollars, bearing interest at the rate of four and a half per cent. per annum; which bonds shall be a legal tender in payment of dues to the Government and the debts of corporate bodies and individuals.

More of Butler.

One would suppose Butler to be satisfied with the hanging of Mumford for "desecrating" the Stars and Stripes. We learn, however, that his detectives are at work to discover every man who was connected with the affair, and that he promises to hang them, if they fall into his hands. A gentleman who was a party to it arrived in this city the other day, glad enough to escape from the threatened doom.—*Mobile Tribune.*

Part Four Points of Crisis

Chapter 9

If We Are Subjugated We Will Do It Ourselves

Southerners never deluded themselves about the grave disparities that existed between themselves and their enemy. Behind the bluster of the Confederacy's determination to vindicate its "rights" lay the knowledge that the Union had more manpower, more railroads, more factories and industrial capital, and a more powerful army and navy. The South's hopes for victory rested not on the vastness of its military resources—for they could never match those of the North—but rather on the unity of its people. If Southerners stuck together, if they made common and wholehearted sacrifices, if they never gave up, they would eventually wear down the will of the Northern people to continue fighting. The realities of war, however, fanned and fueled bitter tensions between the rich and the poor in the Confederacy that, by 1863, threatened to tear the new nation apart.

In the heady days after the fall of Fort Sumter, it was difficult for Southerners to imagine that their spirit of unity and martial zeal would ever dissipate. The newspapers had welcomed the onset of war in 1861 in part because they assumed it would lift the Southern people to a higher level of virtue, that it would force them to lose their narrow-minded selfishness and become more patriotic and self-sacrificing. The war, after all, was for the good of everyone in the South. In the Southern mind, Confederate independence was essential because the "tyrannical" government in Washington sought to divest Southerners of all their rights—to take over their lands, invade their homes, seize their property, brutalize their families, and force them back into the Union as second-class citizens. In theory, at least, the war was a common struggle in which every citizen's most cherished possessions and privileges were at stake.

Still, there was a general understanding that some Southerners—those of the slaveholding class—had more to lose than others. Although slave-owning families were a minority in the South, they controlled over 90 percent of the region's wealth. Their substantial investments in land and slaves gave them a special interest in seeing the Confederacy succeed, and slaveholders were therefore expected to devote themselves completely to the war effort. Moreover, since these men had been at the forefront of the secession movement, it seemed only right that they should also be generous in defending their country's independence.

In the opening weeks of the war, when the entire South seemed zealous for a good fight, slaveholders and nonslaveholders alike participated in the popular rush to enlist for military service. Indeed, over the course of the conflict, the percentage of slaveholders within the Confederate ranks closely paralleled their proportion within Southern society. Just as slaveholding families constituted only one-quarter of the entire Southern population, it is estimated that they accounted for one-third of the soldiers who fought for the Confederacy's independence.[1] Nevertheless, most of the army consisted of common citizens—men who had no economic investment in slavery and who had played only a small part in pushing the Southern states to secede. Perhaps because slaveholders were a minority in the army, the perception grew quickly that they were not sufficiently involved in the war and that too many of them were shirking their primary patriotic duty. The Confederate general Sterling Price, a slaveholder and one of the largest landowners in Missouri, gave legitimacy to this view in a speech he delivered at the end of 1861, to pressure more men to enlist in the Confederate ranks. In his speech, Price pointed out to his fellow citizens, "Boys and small property holders have, in the main, fought for the protection of your property." And, he explained, when the common people of the South started asking, "Where are the men for whom we are fighting?" he would have no good answer to give until more of them put their lives on the line by joining the army.[2] Price was not alone in feeling that some men in the South were not doing enough to support the war, as this 1862 editorial on "Who have fought our Battles" makes clear:

Every man, woman and child in the Southern Confederacy has an interest in the present war and its results, and of course they have a right to know by whom it has been carried on. The renowned Gen. Sterling Price, of Missouri, in his late celebrated and forcible proclamation, very properly and truthfully declared that "the boys and small property holders have fought the battles of the country thus far." As a general thing the truth of this assertion cannot be successfully controverted. "The boys and the small property holders," so far as our observation has extended, with a few exceptions, have hitherto fought our battles and achieved our victories. . . .

In looking around us we see many men in the prime of life who, on account of their riches, refuse to enter the ranks of our armies. They say they have too much to attend to at home to fight for their property and country; but we often see them engaged in persuading "the boys and small property holders" to leave all for the war and the army. Others think, and we are sorry to say it, that they are too rich and high born to enter our armies as common soldiers. It gives us no pleasure thus to write, but believing these things to be so, we believe it our duty to place them before our readers.

Now, we say to the rich that it is in vain to endeavor to shirk or avoid the just responsibilities, for the time is coming . . . when they will have to meet and stand up to them. "The boys and small property holders" have done and are doing their duty; and we predict that if this war continues twelve months longer, the rich will have to meet the stern realities of the case, and instead of its being the "boys and small property holders" war, it will be turned into the rich man's war.

During the war of 1812, while Gen. [Andrew] Jackson was pushing on the defenses of New Orleans, day and night, for the protection of that city, a wealthy citizen approached the General and remonstrated against the employment of his property by the authorities for the public defense. The

> General asked him if he was a property holder. He stated that he possessed a large property in the city. The General had a musket placed in his hands and ordered him into ranks, stating at the same time that he knew no one who was under greater obligations to defend the city. Our rich men should learn from this anecdote....
>
> In conclusion, we must be permitted to say that the declaration of Gen. Price is strictly in accordance with the facts of the case. We are in the midst of one of the most sanguinary wars of modern times. . . . If a man has much property he has the greater inducement to fight for. It is one of the great ends of government to protect his property, but in order to enable it to do this he must come to the support of the government in war as well as in peace.[3]

The press expected that the Confederate Conscription Act, passed in April 1862, would help redress this perceived inequity between the services rendered by the rich and the poor. Although many groups were exempted from the draft, the scope of it was sweeping, and laid the burden of defending the nation on all men of military age, regardless of wealth or status. As one paper put it, "The law was passed with . . . the design of placing the rich and poor side by side in a revolution equally for the good of both." More than just a matter of military necessity, it was thus "an act of justice," one that would guarantee that no single class in the Confederacy would make greater sacrifices than any other.[4]

However, instead of solidifying a spirit of social harmony in the South, the implementation of conscription only exacerbated social tensions. In October 1862, in response to unremitting pressure from slaveholders, the Confederate Congress added a new statute exempting one white man for every twenty slaves he owned or managed. The government justified this so-called Twenty Negro Law on the ground that efficient slave management was essential for ensuring that the Confederacy produced enough food to feed its armies. In the eyes of its critics, though, the law was a blatant act of favoritism toward the rich that contradicted the ethic of equality that the Confederacy was supposed to embody. "The war is waged, not alone for negro property, but for Constitutional liberty and the defence of our homes," the *North Carolina Weekly Standard* noted disapprovingly. "It is a common cause, and it is as much the duty of one class to fight for it as another. Political equality is the cornerstone of our government; but what justice, or what political equality can there be in providing that one portion of our people shall be subject to military duty, while another portion [is] exempt, because they may happen to own a certain species of property?"[5] The law seemed all the more egregious and unfair because instead of growing corn and grains to help feed the soldiers and their families, some planters in North Carolina used their exemption as an opportunity to continue cultivating tobacco for their own enrichment. One citizen, writing to the editor of the *Standard*, spoke out angrily against such self-serving behavior:

> Mr. Editor:—I wish to call the attention of our legislators, and of the people generally, to the consideration of a subject in which we are all concerned. It is well known that Congress passed an exemption act exempting certain persons therein named from "military service;" and among [them], owners of twenty negroes. The question arises, why were the owners of twenty negroes exempted from "military service?" The object in view was undoubtedly of a two-fold nature. First, as expressed in the act, "to secure the proper police of the country," and secondly, by securing said "proper police," to enable the owners of slaves to raise food for the sustenance of those who are shielding their necks from the iron hoof of Yankee despotism.
>
> Notwithstanding the laudable designs of Congress in exempting certain owners of slaves from military service, some planters will be found inconsiderate enough, lured by the high prices of tobacco, to bend

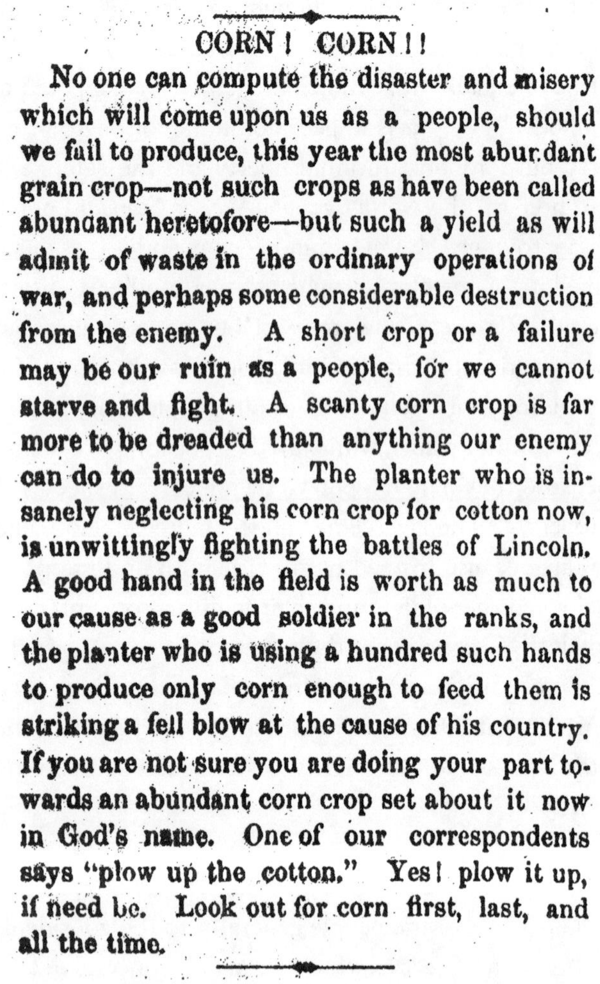

CORN! CORN!!

No one can compute the disaster and misery which will come upon us as a people, should we fail to produce, this year the most abundant grain crop—not such crops as have been called abundant heretofore—but such a yield as will admit of waste in the ordinary operations of war, and perhaps some considerable destruction from the enemy. A short crop or a failure may be our ruin as a people, for we cannot starve and fight. A scanty corn crop is far more to be dreaded than anything our enemy can do to injure us. The planter who is insanely neglecting his corn crop for cotton now, is unwittingly fighting the battles of Lincoln. A good hand in the field is worth as much to our cause as a good soldier in the ranks, and the planter who is using a hundred such hands to produce only corn enough to feed them is striking a fell blow at the cause of his country. If you are not sure you are doing your part towards an abundant corn crop set about it now in God's name. One of our correspondents says "plow up the cotton." Yes! plow it up, if need be. Look out for corn first, last, and all the time.

Macon Telegraph, May 4, 1861.
The wartime need for food supplies in the Confederacy dethroned "King Cotton" and gave new impetus to the cultivation of corn and other edible crops.

their energies to its culture! Such ought not to be the case. The Confederacy needs the aid and sympathy of all her sons for the support of her armies. . . . If conscripts are required by law . . . to leave their homes, their wives and little ones, and enter the service, is it requiring too much at the hands of exempts to do something for their support and comfort while defending our institutions? . . .

It does seem to me that planters who are exempted from military service—staying at home enjoying the company of their wives and "prattling innocents," might afford to raise food, at *remunerative prices*, for the sustenance of those who have left their once cheerful firesides, and periled life, property, and everything in defence of their country.—With what degree of spirit can one in the service nerve his arm for the conflict, when he knows and feels that his neighbor, who is exempt because he owns twenty slaves, is raising tobacco at high prices, leaving *his* wife and children naked and hungry around him? But let him *feel* that his wife and little ones have "bread enough and to spare," he can meet the foe with unflinching firmness, and unwavering attachment to his country, and feels like if he falls in her defence, that he will fall in defence of those who will mourn his loss and appreciate his services by providing for the "loved ones at home."

In conclusion, I must say this is no time to be bending all of one's energies to the culture of the "filthy weed," leaving the wants of the country unsupplied. The exigencies of the times demand something at the hands of all who are able to contribute to the glorious cause in which we are engaged. And I am clearly of [the] opinion that it is wrong to exempt *unscrupulous curmudgeons* from military service, and turn them loose, *unchecked*, upon the country, to go to and fro, like prowling "wolves in sheep's clothing," with their coffers filled with the proceeds of their high priced tobacco, cheating the wives and widows of those who have entered service of their country, out of everything they can.[6]

In actuality, most planters *did* heed the nation's need for food crops and reallocated their lands for the production of corn, wheat, sorghum, beans, sweet potatoes, and field peas, the last of which served not only as a staple of the Southern diet but also as fodder for maintaining beef cattle and hogs. However, compliance in forsaking cash crops was far from perfect, particularly when it came to cotton, the most resplendent jewel in the South's agricultural crown. The enormous wealth of the Southern states was built primarily on cotton. Even in the late 1850s, as the rest of the United States slipped into an economic depression, Southerners had continued to thrive on their cotton exports to textile manufacturers in the North and in England. During the war, though, the South had no legitimate reason to produce any more cotton than was needed for home consumption. The Union had established a blockade on all Southern ports to prevent overseas trade, and the Confederacy itself—in order to coerce England into intervening in its defense—had placed an embargo on its cotton crop. Nevertheless, for some planters, the lure of cotton remained intoxicating, and they continued to pour their energies into its cultivation, either in hopes of partaking in illegal trading with Northern or European merchants or simply in anticipation of the time when the war would be over and normal economic ties with the outside world could be resumed. Southern planters harvested almost 4.5 million bales of cotton in 1861—only a 10 percent decrease from the previous year's record yield. Although the cotton crop declined more dramatically over time, the 7 million bales produced during the war far outstripped what the Confederacy could use. Given the food needs of the moment, such excessive cotton raising was a dangerous habit that the newspapers tried tirelessly to dissuade.[7] In an attempt to rally the patriotism of the planters and fully wean them from their infatuation with cotton, one Southerner, in a letter to the *Columbus Sun*, made this impassioned appeal:

> Planters of the South! our young men, our children, have gone forth from our midst to endure the heat and cold, to peril life and limb, and place their broad breasts as a shield between you and the insolent foe who is bent upon our moral, social, political and *personal* destruction. When those children turn their eyes to you from the cold and damp of a comfortless camp, or from the dust and blood of a dearly-bought victory, and ask for bread, . . . will you give them cotton?
>
> What commentary will the future historian make in recording the fate of our section, if he writes that our new Confederacy, which sprung into existence under such happy auspices, . . . failed *because its soldiers did not have bread to eat?* What, the South, into whose teeming lap nature's God has cast his most bounteous gifts, not able to raise bread for its hungry soldiers! Oh shame! . . .
>
> Planters of the South! We have lost nearly all of our grain growing country. The best portions for that purpose [in] Arkansas, Mississippi, Tennessee, Virginia and North Carolina, are now either in the hands of the enemy, or every blade of grass [is] trodden under foot by the swaying and contending armies. To whom then shall we look for food for our soldiers and their suffering families? I answer, *to you* and you *alone*. To those of you who are exempted from the conscript act as overseers of slaves, I would say it is your sacred duty to plant corn and raise meat. This is what the government left you at home to do; and when it calls on you for the result of your labors to feed its starving armies, will you exhibit your piles of cotton? Can our worn and hungry soldiers eat it? Do all that you can in the way of raising [this] provision, and then it will be a hard matter to feed our immense armies and those of us at home. . . . Think of that you who are at home preparing to plant cotton, while your brothers and sons are fighting your battles without meat to eat, and then go and plant your cotton. . . . Plant cotton, farmers, and our government will perish before it is fully grown, from starvation. . . . But plant corn and peas and potatoes, and raise hogs and cattle and everything else that man can eat, and another Spring will bring peace and quiet, and prosperity and independence to our troubled country.[8]

Between their exemption from military service and the refusal of some of them to forsake cash crops for food crops, members of the slaveholding class gave ordinary Southerners good reason to be suspicious, irritated, and resentful. But these feelings were inflamed all the more by the misdeeds of merchants, who sought to manipulate the wartime economy for their own enrichment. The isolation of the Confederacy from its normal trading ties with Northern and European suppliers created opportunities for merchant middlemen to drive up prices by engaging in the twin evils of "speculation" (buying up goods to create a monopoly) and "extortion" (withholding those hoarded goods from the market to create scarcity). From the very start of the war, newspapers had anticipated these kinds of abuses and tried to counsel retailers against squeezing exorbitant profits from their war-torn country. The following public address, issued originally in a Virginia newspaper just three weeks into the war, was republished in several others as far away as Alabama and Georgia:

> We hope that no man in the present crisis of affairs will take advantage of the necessities of the people by advancing the price of their goods, wares and merchandise. . . . A merchant who has bought bacon at 10 cents and sells it at 20, coffee at 14 and sells it at 25, flour at 5 and sells it at 10, is an enemy of his race and country. No patriot will do it. Every friend of humanity will execrate it. Our merchants should sell every thing they have on hand at their usual prices. . . . Otherwise the poor of our town and country will be unable to live at all, especially when we have a hundred thousand volunteers in the field. Every dollar extorted from the necessities of the people is just so much aid and comfort to the enemy.[9]

Such appeals to patriotism were ignored, however, as price gouging quickly became a national problem. Before the end of 1861, prices in Tennessee had risen so dramatically that the governor went before the state legislature to request legal intervention, as common food items and other basic products were now "beyond the reach of the more indigent classes of society." As the *Memphis Avalanche* noted in the spring of 1862, "There is not an article of merchandise that has not been raised in price, from fifty to more than a hundred per cent." It was the same story in many other Southern communities, and by 1863, some basic items had become generally unaffordable, and others were impossible to find. The *Rome Weekly Courier* reported in January of that year that bacon, butter, corn, and sweet potatoes were no longer available, while the small quantities of flour on the market sold for an outlandish $40 per barrel. In Richmond, which experienced the most astronomical rise in prices, the cost of bacon had increased eightfold over its prewar cost, butter was seven times more expensive, and the price of cornmeal had quadrupled.[10]

The burden was especially great on soldiers' families. The men in gray were paid a fixed income of $11 a month, which became increasingly worthless in the galloping inflation of the times. With conscription,

***The Results of Extortion and Speculation.*—The state of affairs brought about by the speculating and extortion practiced upon the public cannot be better illustrated than by the following grocery bill for one week for a small family, in which the prices before the war and those of the present are compared:**

1860		1863.	
Bacon, 10 lbs at 12½c....	$1.25	Bacon, 10 lbs at $1.....	$10 00
Flour, 30 lbs at 5c.......	1.50	Flour, 30 lbs at 12½......	8 75
Sugar, 5 lbs at 8c........	40	Sugar, 5 lbs at $1.15....	5 75
Coffee, 4 lbs at 12½c......	50	Coffee, 4 lbs at $5......	20 00
Tea, (green,) ¼ lb at $1..	50	Tea, (green,) ¼ lb at $16	8 00
Lard, 4 lbs at 12½c......	50	Lard, 4 lbs at $1........	4 00
Butter, 3 lbs at 25c......	75	Butter, 3 lbs at $1.75....	5 25
Meal, 1 pk at 25c........	25	Meal, 1 pk at $1........	1 00
Candles, 2 lbs at 15c.....	30	Candles, 2 lbs at $1.25.	2 50
Soap, 5 lbs at 10c.......	50	Soap, 5 lbs at $1.10.....	5 50
Pepper and Salt (about).	10	Pepper and Salt (about).	2 50
Total....................	$6 55	Total................	$68 25

So much we owe the speculators, who have staid at home to prey upon the necessities of their fellow citizens.

Richmond Dispatch, January 29, 1863.
Extortion and speculation contributed to overwhelming inflation in the Confederacy. This table compares the 1860 and 1863 prices for one week's worth of household goods for a small family in Richmond. As calculated here, prices rose more than tenfold, from $6.55 to $68.25.

most of the Confederacy's young men were now in the army, leaving hundreds of thousands of families dependent on these meager military wages. Moreover, while the South was an agricultural society with abundant lands, the prospects for self-sufficient farming were poor in wartime. Military engagements not only resulted in scorched fields, downed fences, and slaughtered livestock, but also forced Southerners to flee the countryside and seek refuge in urban areas. Consequently, increasing numbers of civilians became dependent on buying whatever they needed from local merchants, who were more likely to hoard their goods than to sell them. Between the vicissitudes of war and the avariciousness of individual merchants, scarcity reigned, and it did not take long before the press began to fret openly about the possibility of famine. As one Mississippi paper observed, "The unheard of prices asked for provisions of almost every kind . . . are fast reducing a large class of our population to the condition of paupers." The dwindling supply and rocketing cost of cornmeal and flour for bread—the staple of even a starvation diet—were especially worrisome. "Shall we have bread, or must we starve," asked a Georgia editor, issuing a refrain that had become all too common.[11] The most frustrating thing was the knowledge that the food Southerners desperately needed was being produced; it simply was not being made available to them at prices most of them could afford. Amid the many economic problems faced by the Confederacy—the blockade, the property damage, the disruption of normal transportation lines—Southerners at least hoped that those who had food supplies would be generous toward their countrymen and keep their prices at a reasonable level. The penchant for extortion was exasperating, and in the eyes of the Southern press, it painted a bleak picture for the Confederacy's future:

> The rage to run up prices is going to ruin us if anything does. It is impossible to overrate the degree of uncertainty, insecurity and alarm felt by the masses of the people from this cause alone.—The fact that everything, corn, fodder, and news papers excepted, have within the past year run up from three to twenty and thirty [times], opens the gloomiest prospect for the future.—Where is this thing to end? If it has traveled thus far what is to hinder its going twice, three times, five times, or twenty times as far in the next year? Who, then, can live? . . . What then is before us if things go on only for six months, in the future, as they have gone for six or eight months past? Plainly ruin! We see little chance of escape from this conclusion, and there is some comfort in the thought that the money makers who will have brought on the catastrophe will at least perish with the rest. . . .
>
> It is plain that this, and not the Yankee armies, is the real problem of Southern independence, liberty and security. If, as but seems too probable, our people prefer heaping up gains in Treasury notes, to their own self-preservation from a cruel, licentious, rapacious and remorseless foe, the great God himself will and must say to such a people, 'Thy money perish with thee!' God is not going to work miracles in our behalf; and if we choose to prey upon each other, instead of standing by, assisting, and encouraging each other to withstand the common enemy, we must abide the awful consequences. Then shall repentance come—but too late. . . . Heaven pity us, unless we wake up to some sense, reason and duty upon this subject![12]

Proposed solutions to the extortion problem varied. The *Religious Herald*, defining extortion as "moral treason," called upon the churches to combat it by excommunicating any members found guilty of wartime profiteering. Most papers, secular and religious, hoped at the very least that public opinion could be used to shame extortioners into showing more mercy toward consumers by reducing their prices. Some went further and asked the national government to forcibly seize hoarded goods and redistribute them. Others called for state officials to intervene and create price caps.[13]

Despite these suggestions, though, the Confederacy never did find a satisfactory way of saving civilians from poverty. In fact, the problem only seemed to spread more widely over time. While it was the mercantile class that was often associated with extortion, planters in the countryside started to engage in it as well. Rather than retaining their surplus stocks of food and making them available to poorer people in their towns, many either withheld them from the market, to push prices even higher, or sold them to merchants who could pay for them but who did nothing to make the goods accessible to ordinary consumers. The miserliness of these country "gentlemen," declared the *Augusta Chronicle & Sentinel*, was egregious and maddening:

> If there is one on earth whose generous soul should expand with all the generous glow of kindness and philanthropy, it is the Southern planter. Blessed with a soil adapted to the grains for the use of man and beast—with servants at his beck and call—living in ease and comfort, and dependent alone upon his own exertions and his God that giveth the increase. Can it be possible that such a man, so situated and so blessed, can, at a time like this, when our whole fair land is . . . convulsed with the awful and heart rending ravages of war, turn a deaf ear to the pressing wants of his government and his people.
>
> Can such a man, thus surrounded with all the good things in life, assist in pulling down the temple of liberty, which the noble soldier is now erecting for the South, at the peril of his life? Can it be possible that the Southern planter, the synonym of nobility and benevolence, can hear the accounts of the desperate battles, the heroic deaths and the hairbreadth escapes of his gallant countrymen, and then turn away and ingloriously revel amidst his comforts and wealth, and extort upon his government and his people, for the necessaries of life, which God, in his goodness, has given him. From an early attachment to the cultivation of the soil, and from the high estimate always placed upon the character of the Southern planter, it pains and grieves me publicly to state that many, very many have been found wanting, when the times which try men's souls have come upon us. The mercantile mania for wealth has penetrated the peaceful shades and calm retirement of the country, and many a man whom all have regarded as a good and generous hearted citizen . . . has now his granaries filled to overflowing, which he has avariciously closed until he gets his price, and, like the Jew, his pound of flesh also. I blush for my country, when I witness its destruction by our own people.[14]

Others in the South did more than just blush. They got angry. The exemption of planters from conscription had been tough to accept. Their devotion to cotton had been worrisome. Now their attempt to keep whatever food they had off the market, in anticipation of higher prices, added unbearable insult to injury. The *Houston Weekly Telegraph*, appalled by such behavior, publicly warned the slaveholding class of the wrath it was courting:

> We tell cotton planters one thing right here. It is no easy matter to keep down public clamor against the want of patriotism exhibited by many of them. They are looked upon by men that out vote them three to one, as the spoiled and petted children of the republic. They are regarded as fattening on the blood and flesh of the brave soldiers who are fighting, bleeding, dying, to defend them and their property. They must come out of their shells and share their good things with the families of their defenders, or they will be made to do it despite of law, gospel and every other peaceful principle. They must assist the families of soldiers in planting their crops, and feeding their little ones. They must volunteer to support those who have volunteered to fight for them or they will see trouble.
>
> The last thing we would do would be to encourage any unlawfulness, or any antagonism between

Recipe to Get Rid of Extortioners.—Chain them to a stake, as above; pile their ill-gotten gains around them, and any passer-by will fire the mass. This will have the happy effect, both of ridding the community of their presence, and at the same time reducing the circulating medium.

Southern Illustrated News, September 19, 1863.
Incensed by the greed of extortioners, the creator of this Southern cartoon offers a recipe for getting rid of them: "Chain them to a stake, as above; pile their ill-gotten gains around them, and any passer-by will fire the mass. This will have the happy effect, both of ridding the community of their presence, and at the same time reducing the circulating medium" of Confederate dollars.

> classes of society. . . . But that antagonism is rising now, and it is encouraged by the nabob who despises and neglects his poorer neighbor. The way to avoid it is to remove the cause, and the way to do this is to share with all, the asperities and sacrifices of this war, which is for the freedom of all.[15]

Merchants and planters who kept goods off the market not only consigned families to privation; they also made it difficult for the Confederate government to procure supplies for the soldiers. Food rations, as well as leather for shoes and cloth for shirts, uniforms, and blankets, were increasingly unattainable. By 1863, soldiers were subsisting on half rations consisting mostly of cornmeal, which they then tried to supplement with whatever they could find around their camps. Sometimes this meant catching fish or stealing chickens; more often, though, they had to make do with rats, which were plentiful and easily killed with a shovel.[16] Clothing was even harder to come by. With the government unable to outfit them with anything new, soldiers had only the shirts on their backs, and when their shoes fell apart, there was nothing to replace them. In August 1862, when Confederate forces under Stonewall Jackson fought their way to victory in a second battle at Manassas, their achievement was overshadowed by their evident destitution. As the *Columbus Sun* reported:

> Army correspondents and others, familiar with the condition of our army, represent some of our regiments as being in a desperate condition for clothes. In the late battle of Manassas, one hundred men of the 20th Georgia regiment are said to have went into the action, and actually stormed a battery *barefooted.* A correspondent, who was an eye witness of the scene, says that the macadamized road over which our poor fellows charged, was profusely marked with the blood from bruise[d], bare feet of whole regiments. Only think of our soldiers going

THE FOOD QUESTION DOWN SOUTH.

JEFF DAVIS. "See! see! the beautiful Boots just come to me from the dear ladies of Baltimore!"

BEAUREGARD. "Ha! Boots? Boots? When shall we eat them? Now?"

Harper's Weekly, May 9, 1863. The scarcity of food not only devastated families on the home front, but affected soldiers as well, forcing them to subsist on half rations consisting largely of corn bread. In this mocking Northern cartoon, a barefoot Jefferson Davis holds out a new shipment of boots to General P. G. T. Beauregard, who exclaims hungrily, "Ha! Boots? Boots? When shall we eat them? Now?"

barefooted, charging over the flinty surface of a macadamized road, marking their course with their blood, while thousands of sleek speculators, who have been industriously buying up all the leather in the country, and creating other monopolies calculated to drive the destitute families of these poor barefooted soldiers to privation and want, are wearing their $20 calf skin boots and resting at night on the downy beds of ease! Is there no remedy for this monstrous evil? Must our soldiers continue to battle for our country's freedom half-naked, while thousands of able-bodied young men are permitted to remain at home, it would seem, for the express purpose of oppressing their indigent families? Is ours a speculator's government, or is it a government of the people? Why are vampires and bloodsuckers protected in their infamous villainy, whilst those who stand a living wall between us and our enemies are permitted to go barefooted and their families allowed to suffer for the common necessaries of life?[17]

The problem of procuring provisions for the army only worsened the plight of civilians at home. In March 1863, in order to make it easier to raise military supplies, the Confederacy enacted an impressment law, authorizing government agents to seize goods from civilians, who were supposed to receive just compensation in return. The law backfired, however. It only made extortioners go to greater lengths to keep their caches hidden from the public, away from impressment officers and needy consumers alike.

Consequently, for many ordinary Southerners, the Civil War devolved into an exhausting struggle for personal survival. At the start of the conflict, the notion of sacrificing for Southern independence seemed like a noble thing. In reality, it was painful and ultimately demoralizing. In a letter to his local paper, one North

Carolinian frankly admitted, "It may not be generally known, but it is true, the extortion of the times is stirring up a spirit in a certain class of perfect indifference" to the war. "He who does not see it or hear it, mixes not with those who are ground down and pulverized by the fell hand of extortion." While terrible in and of itself, the impoverishment of the home front particularly upset the newspapers when they considered how it would affect army morale. The soldiers might be willing to endure their own lack of supplies and provisions. But it was difficult to imagine that they would have the heart to keep fighting if they knew their families were on the verge of starvation. The Confederate government was deluding itself, warned one paper, if it believed it could keep the troops contented "while these men *were receiving eleven dollars per month for services, and their families paying two dollars per bushel for corn meal, thirty dollars per barrel for flour, fifty dollars per bushel for salt, ten dollars per pair of shoes* and similar prices for all other necessities of life!" Even the most ardent patriotism was bound to flag in the face of such conditions. As a writer to the *Rome Weekly Courier* envisioned, "When our brave and true men, shall hear that their wives and little ones are actually suffering for bread, they will naturally become restless and dissatisfied, and mutiny in our army will result, as naturally and as certainly as gravitation."[18]

This was not an exaggerated or baseless concern. The emotional strain placed on the women of the Confederacy was enormous, and in letters to their fathers, husbands, brothers, and sons in the army, they wrote despairingly of the starvation conditions they were facing at home. Even without the women necessarily intending it, their words had a chilling effect on the fighting spirit of soldiers. The men of the South had been ushered into the army for the defense of their firesides and the protection of their wives and children. Now, for these same exact reasons, more and more men felt compelled to return home, to aid their struggling families. By the spring of 1863, 140,000 of the almost 500,000 soldiers in the Confederate army were absent

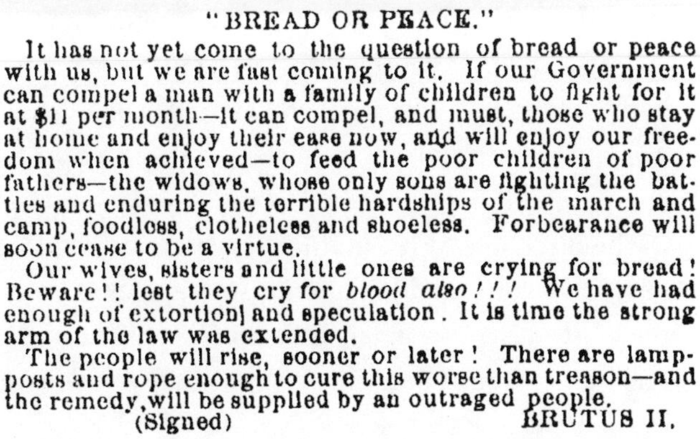
"BREAD OR PEACE."

It has not yet come to the question of bread or peace with us, but we are fast coming to it. If our Government can compel a man with a family of children to fight for it at $11 per month—it can compel, and must, those who stay at home and enjoy their ease now, and will enjoy our freedom when achieved—to feed the poor children of poor fathers—the widows, whose only sons are fighting the battles and enduring the terrible hardships of the march and camp, foodless, clotheless and shoeless. Forbearance will soon cease to be a virtue.

Our wives, sisters and little ones are crying for bread! Beware!! lest they cry for *blood also!!!* We have had enough of extortion] and speculation. It is time the strong arm of the law was extended.

The people will rise, sooner or later! There are lamp-posts and rope enough to cure this worse than treason—and the remedy, will be supplied by an outraged people.

(Signed) BRUTUS II.

Albany Evening Journal,
April 23, 1863.
As even basic necessities such as bread became impossible to obtain, public anger against extortioners and resentment against the Confederate government burned fiercely. This handbill, which reportedly was posted throughout the city of Mobile, Alabama, in April 1863, suggests the desperation and fury felt by ordinary citizens struggling to survive in the Confederacy.

from the ranks. A portion of this group consisted of men on furlough or sick leave, but the overwhelming majority were deserters.[19] And it was widely understood that despairing letters from home were the proximate cause of the problem.

While the papers had no sympathy with the extortioners who were helping to drive Southern families into dire poverty, they were no less hard on Southern women for actually giving in to despair. They therefore reached out to their female readers to chastise them for writing gloomy, griping letters to their men, as this story, written by a correspondent to the *Selma Morning Reporter*, illustrates:

> A few weeks ago a soldier was tried and convicted of the crime of desertion, and sentenced to be shot. He was taken to the place of execution, and the preparations being soon completed, at the word "fire" he fell a bloody corpse at the hands of his brave comrades. I was curious to know why he deserted, and I learned that his wife was the cause. He received a

letter from her full of complaints. Looking alone upon the dark side of the picture, she had magnified her troubles and sufferings, and earnestly entreated her husband to return home. He became restless, discontented, unhappy. He ceased to take any interest in the discharge of his military duties, and thought only of how he could get home.—His solemn oath never to desert troubled him much, and he well knew the crime of desertion had become so frequent in the army it would be punished with death. In this state of perplexity he drew his wife's letter from his bosom and read it again, and shutting his eyes to the consequences, he *deserted!* and for this crime he suffered a bloody and ignominious death.

His wife is now a widow. Tortured with the thought that her husband was brought to an untimely end by her own imprudence, she knows no peace of mind. True, she had been deprived of many of the comforts of life, and had many sore trials, and anxiously desired the return of her husband, but now she feels that she had exaggerated her trials and sufferings, and she would give the world to recall that fatal letter which tempted her husband from his duty. But it is too late; it cannot be recalled, and the grief and agony of this heart-broken woman are inexpressible. She inconsiderately brought her husband to a dishonorable death and refuses to be comforted.

Wives! mothers! beware what you write to your sons and husbands in the army. A thoughtless and imprudent letter may lead to discontent, desertion and death. Our soldiers have toils and hardships and trials enough of their own to bear, do not burden them with the history of your troubles and complaints. They cannot aid you; it does no good; it may do much harm. When you write say nothing, I beseech you, which may embitter their thoughts, weaken their arms, depress their courage, or tempt them from the path of patriotic duty to death and dishonor. Encourage them, cheer their hearts, fire their souls, arouse their patriotism, but do not disturb and harass their minds with unavailing murmurs and complaints.[20]

However, instead of becoming more pliant, some women took more aggressive action in order to save themselves and their children from starvation. The plight of families on the home front was so horrendous that in some communities, bands of women took to the streets in "bread riots," to seize the goods that they could no longer afford to buy. The most famous of these erupted in the capital city of Richmond on April 2, 1863, when a crowd of women, some armed with knives and hatchets, marched down Cary and Main Streets, breaking into stores and emptying the shelves of their stock. Even after Governor John Letcher ordered the crowd to disperse and threatened to deploy the city guard against them, the rioters remained defiant and undeterred, until Jefferson Davis himself emerged from his executive mansion to ask the crowd to go home. With their president standing before them, backed up by troops with loaded guns, the women finally relented, although by no means contentedly. The Richmond riot was only one of several uprisings that occurred in the spring of 1863. Atlanta, Milledgeville, Macon, and Columbus in Georgia, as well as Salisbury, Raleigh, and Greensborough in North Carolina, experienced similar outbursts as women went after food, calico and muslin cloth, bonnets, thread, and other goods that in 1861 had been abundant and cheap. While some of these uprising were easily quelled, others required a more forcible response, as the *Greensborough Patriot* observed of the riot that occurred there:

We feel it to be a disagreeable duty to note a little affair which took place in the streets of Greensborough on Wednesday of last week. . . . Early in the morning it was reported that some thirty or forty women were three or four miles west of town, on their way to Greensboro', to break into the stores here and help themselves to whatever their fancy might suggest. Some of our staid citizens immediately went out to meet them, to reason with them, and if possible to ascertain their designs, and particularly their necessities, so that if they were really suffering for the necessaries of life, that proper means might be taken to relieve their necessities. But before the return of the messengers sent West, some twenty women, armed with axes, hatchets, pistols, bowie knives, and sword canes, made their appearance from the East, and soon commenced battering down Mr. Willard's store door. At this juncture a Magistrate present ordered them arrested and disarmed. . . .

These women were taken inside the jail lot enclosure . . . and there guarded until it was ascertained that the company from the West had turned back, when they were released.

This affair has deeply mortified the friends of the soldiers and their families. . . . We would fondly hope that this will be the last frolic of the kind that will be attempted; for we can assure all concerned that there is a determination by the substantial citizens and Magistrates of at least Guilford county, to put down all such proceedings at all hazards. The civil laws of the land must be respected and obeyed; otherwise society would soon fall into disorganization and anarchy—a most dangerous state of affairs for any community. . . .

That there are men in the county who are withholding their provisions from market, refusing to sell at the present prices, with the hope that before harvest prices will rise still higher, we have no doubt; nor have we any doubt that there are speculators watching and trying to buy up what provisions can be purchased, and thus secure a monopoly of the trade and secure whatever price they please; and further, we are also satisfied that there are scattered all through the country persons who have a surplus of provisions, who, [upon] hearing that these speculators and extortioners will pay a little more than the current price for provisions, forthwith sell the surplus to them, although their neighbors my be suffering for something to live upon. All this is wrong—heinously wrong; and all such persons should receive equally the scorn and contempt of the generous and humane. For all such acts, we have nothing but condemnation. Such conduct has been one of the main causes of the present *mania* for female raids.[21]

If the newspapers were unsympathetic to women who sent "gloomy letters" to their men in the army, they were downright hostile and scornful toward those who took the law into their own hands. Some papers were so scandalized by the riots that they denied that true Southern women had organized them, attributing them instead to prostitutes, criminals, foreigners, or Yankee spies interested in plundering and defaming the Confederacy.[22] Others could admit the truth—that the rioters consisted "mostly of soldiers' wives"—but they were no less appalled to see them create public disturbances in wartime.[23] In the eyes of the men who ran the presses, women who acted so aggressively unsexed themselves. They were dangerous "Amazons" and "viragos" that could not be tolerated. According to the *Vicksburg Whig*, writing shortly after the Richmond riot, they deserved nothing less than harsh and swift punishment:

> Now . . . it is to be hoped in the future we will hear of no more Amazonian bands making assaults upon stores and helping themselves to whatever articles of provisions or clothing they may select. Such conduct is decidedly unbecoming [to] our Southern ladies and exhibits altogether, we think, too much virago. Aside from this such acts have a bad tendency—a tendency towards disorganization—and an infringement upon the rights of men engaged in a legitimate trade. We are [loath] to be compelled to condemn any act of the ladies of the South for since the beginning of the war, they have exhibited a spirit of devotedness to the cause which stands without parallel. But when they strike a direct blow at

BAKERY
SOWING AND REAPING.
SOUTHERN WOMEN HOUNDING THEIR MEN ON TO REBELLION.
SOUTHERN WOMEN FEELING THE EFFECTS OF REBELLION, AND CREATING BREAD RIOTS.

Frank Leslie's Illustrated Newspaper, May 23, 1863.
Northerners had little sympathy with the plight of Southern women. One Northern illustrator derisively depicted their hardships in a cartoon entitled "Sowing and Reaping." On the left, well-dressed Southern women in 1861 are seen "hounding their men on to rebellion," while on the right, they are shown two years later, clad in rags and engaging in a bread riot.

the existence of society—when they force merchants to declare dividends on the stock for sale in their favor—when they enter private houses and carry away *vi et armis*, family provisions—we say the time has come for public condemnation, and such punishment by the laws of the land as has been provided for all rioters. If women will go so far as to aim a blow at our commercial honor, which should remain untarnished, their sex should not save them from punishment. We hope steps will be taken to prevent any [more] of these female riots which are productive of no good, but on the other hand are fraught with wide spreading mischief.[24]

The riots were a dreadful embarrassment to the Confederacy. Jefferson Davis was particularly concerned over how the North would perceive them, and after the Richmond riot he asked newspaper editors in the city not to make any reports about it. Not ones to pass up a good story, however, they ignored him and discussed it freely. Northern papers that got wind of the bread riots responded just as Davis had feared—with feelings of satisfaction. As the *New York Times* recalled, "Every one remembers how the Southern women stimulated the war fever in its early stages"—"how their faces beamed with joy" after the Confederate victory at Fort Sumter. Their current suffering was therefore of their own making, the *Times* concluded, and rather than regret it, the Union could, if it acted quickly, take full advantage of it:

> In spite of all the efforts of Confederate journals . . . to conceal the fact, or deprive it of importance, no doubt remains that very serious *bread riots* have taken place in Richmond and other Southern towns. In these riots the women have been the leaders, and that fact alone proves that absolute hunger must have been the cause of them. Women do not get up street riots, break open provision shops, and pillage bakeries and flour stores from political sympathies, nor from resentment against high prices. When their children are in peril of starvation, they become capable of anything. Nothing short of that extremity can have provoked the demonstrations admitted by the rebel papers to have taken place in Richmond, in Raleigh, in Salisbury and many other Southern towns.
>
> In each of these cases the rioters were women—"mostly soldiers' wives," say the North Carolina papers, that give account of the latest transactions. And these papers . . . candidly admit that the women were prompted by hunger, their spirit sharpened, perhaps, by "hatred against speculators." The women armed themselves with hatchets and axes, broke open stores that were not willingly opened for them, and took barrels of salt, flour and molasses, which they had hauled to the market-house, and divided equally between those who needed it. This was a real hunger-riot, and no cloak for indiscriminate robbery, as pretended at Richmond. . . .
>
> We do not wish nor expect to create hopes of advantage over the rebellion by the mere representation of scarcity of provisions in the South. The best reliance—as it is, indeed, the only one—that a wise and powerful Government should have, is the arm of military power delivering irresistible blows upon the enemy in the field. But it is certainly sound policy to consider the physical condition of the enemy we are contending with, and to take advantage of any moment of weakness and exhaustion that may come upon him. That time with the rebels we surely believe is *now*. We have cumulative evidence that a scarcity of food never before paralleled exists in the South. . . . This is the time, then, to press our armies upon the enemy, and still further disturb and disorganize his agriculture. Two months hence it may be too late. He may have then harvested his crops and passed the point of famine.[25]

If the Union continued to apply pressure from the outside, agreed the *New York Tribune*, the Confederacy was certain to crumble under the weight of its own internal problems:

> That the main Rebel armies have been on half rations for weeks is well known. . . . That there have been serious Bread Riots in Richmond, Savannah, Petersburg, and perhaps other Rebel cities, is not denied. That they have been partially successful in compelling gratuitous distributions of bread, is admitted. True, it is said that the ringleaders were not famishing; but their followers clearly were. . . . They were mainly the wives of conscripts serving in the Rebel armies, whose entire wages, if promptly paid, can do little for their families, when flour is worth $40 to $110 per barrel, meat of all kinds 50 cents to $1.25 per pound, the coarsest and poorest fabrics sell at prices hitherto unheard of, and shoes are worth $20 to $30 per pair. Of couse, famine is very general. . . . The large slaveholders can grow enough for themselves and their dependents; but how are the families of the "Poor Whites" to find bread? Above all, how are the enormous demands of their armies to be supplied? Even half rations for Half a Million men form an appalling aggregate: a quarter of a pound of meat to each man requiring over six hundred barrels per day. How is even this to be extracted from a people who have little or nothing to spare?

We shall doubtless have disasters and backsets yet; but it does seem that the Rebellion, if vigorously and skillfully pressed, cannot hold out much longer, and that scarcity of Food will powerfully contribute to its collapse and overthrow.[26]

The riots did nothing to improve the way in which the Confederacy dealt with the massive numbers of Southerners who were now mired in poverty. Ignored by public officials, destitute Southerners also found little support among their compatriots. Wealthy individuals who had stockpiles of goods continued to hold on to them, as Southerners sought only to take care of themselves and their own immediate families. Under the straitened conditions of the times, there was little room for charity. For all of their demonstrations of unity at the start of the war, by 1863 all goodwill among the Southern people seemed to have disappeared. As accounts in the newspapers describe, the war had produced a palpable shift in the way Southerners had come to regard human suffering. The following article, although not written in response to the riots themselves, offers an intriguing perspective on the emotional toll that the war was taking on the Southern psyche:

> The events of the past two or three years have caused a great change in the feelings of the people of this country on the subject of human life. It is undeniable that the popular estimate of its value is not what it was at the commencement of the war. Then the announcement of the sudden death of a dozen or more persons by accident or otherwise would have filled all hearts with sympathy, and the intelligence that one or two hundred had perished by shipwreck, flood or fire, would have been followed by an outburst of horror from the entire population. . . . We all remember the excitement in the country consequent on the reception of the news of our losses in the first battles of the war. Every man and woman felt as though they had been personally bereaved, and the voice of mourning was heard throughout the land.
>
> All this has changed. Familiarity with blood and death has created an apparent indifference on the part of the people, and they now read of engagements in which ten, fifty or a hundred soldiers are killed and wounded, almost without emotion. They peruse accounts of battles in which, may be, five hundred are killed or disabled, and lay the paper down with the complacent remark, perhaps, that it could not have been very much of a conflict as our loss was *only* five hundred. There is nothing strange in this, and it cannot be taken as an indication that the people are naturally regardless of the lives of their fellow men, but their constant association amid scenes of suffering and death, has . . . led them to look upon the destruction of their fellows as matters of course.[27]

The war was indeed atomizing Confederate society and forcing individuals to scramble and compete among themselves for survival. The Southern people, instead of "fighting a common enemy who is invading our soil, have turned to fighting each other," one paper lamented. "*Gouging* is the word. We are fighting each other harder than we have ever fought the enemy." The change in attitude was impossible to deny. "People get more and more disobliging and unaccommodating every day," agreed the *Richmond Whig*. "Scarcely anything is done for kindness," and the "little that is done," it claimed, "is done grudgingly. 'Every man for himself' . . . is the motto. Here and there may be found noble exceptions, but, as a general thing, the aim of every human being now is to take care of Number One." Under such circumstances, the chances of the Confederacy holding itself together long enough to win the war seemed dangerously slim. "It is a common remark, that, if the war continues much longer, we shall all be subjugated, not by force of arms, but by our own selfishness," the *Whig* concluded somberly. This dread of national suicide echoed throughout the Confederacy in 1863. One man, writing to the editor of the *Carolina Spartan*, offered this plain-spoken response to the weighty question, "Will we achieve our independence?":

Mr. Editor: Just now the above question strikes us with peculiar force, and assumes quite an important aspect. For on the assumption that we *will* achieve our Independence are based our fondest hopes and brightest anticipations, in reference to the future history of our beloved country. We must choose one of three things, we must either fight and suffer on until final victory shall have crowned our efforts with peace, independence and glory, or we must willingly and ingloriously submit to the Lincoln despotism, or we must be subjugated by the brute force of our wicked enemy. Which of these three results are we going to choose? Are we as individuals and as a people determined to sacrifice everything if need be, rather than be slaves? Or have many of us determined to make money by this cruel war, and hoard up for ourselves fortunes at the risk of plunging ourselves and our entire country into inextricable ruin? Indeed, I am sorry that so many of us have so far gone crazy after the "*almighty dollar*,". . . that we can ask any kind of a price for our fabrics or products, except a reasonable one. Or we can do even worse, by closing our barns, or other places of trade and absolutely refusing to sell anything for Confederate money. . . . O, my fellow citizens, where are we drifting to? Have we lost all fellow feeling? Have we lost sight of the dearest and most sacred interests of our beloved country? Have we forgotten that ours is a common cause, that we are mutually and *individually* interested in this great contest for freedom? Have we stopped our ears against the groans of the suffering and dying patriot soldier, the cries for bread that come up from the poor and destitute, and the sighs and sobs of all the afflicted ones of our land? . . .

Let us my fellow citizens wake up, and arise in the majesty and true dignity of man's nobler nature, to the magnitude of the present occasion. Are we *men*? Let us then show ourselves to be worthy of this appellation, by the exhibition of a virtuous, noble and self-sacrificing spirit of true patriotism and devotion to our country. If we do this we are safe. If every man, woman and child throughout our country is ready to do and suffer everything rather than be subjugated, our cause will inevitably triumph. . . .

I am no alarmist nor am I a desponding croaker, yet if selfishness and a spirit of extortion continue to reign throughout our country, I awfully fear that we will be subjugated and brought under the foulest despotism and into the most servile state of slavery that has ever existed. If we are subjugated we will do it ourselves. We will be self-murderers.[28]

The Philadelphia Inquirer.

CIRCULATION OVER 60,000. | PHILADELPHIA, FRIDAY, JUNE 19, 1863. | PRICE TWO CENTS

THE REBEL INVASION

THE WAR ON OUR BORDERS

CONFLICTING REPORTS FROM CHAMBERSBURG.

Reported Advance on Hancock, Md.

The Battle at Winchester, Va.

SAFETY OF A LARGE PORTION OF GEN. MILROY'S MISSING TROOPS.

A FIGHT AT POINT OF ROCKS.

CAPTURE AND DESTRUCTION OF A RAILROAD TRAIN.

LATEST FROM VICKSBURG

The Rebel Batteries Silent

REBEL OFFENSIVE MOVEMENTS IN TENNESSEE.

Interesting from Port Royal.

NEWS FROM GEN. KEYES' DIVISION.

A Skirmish Near Aldie, Va., and Capture of Eighty Rebels.

Admiral Foote Dangerously Sick.

THE INVASION OF PENNSYLVANIA.

From a gentleman who left Chambersburg yesterday (Thursday), we obtain the following interesting and authentic statement, respecting the Rebel raid into Pennsylvania:—

The Number Engaged in the Foray.

The Rebels, under JENKINS, nine hundred and fifty strong, entered Chambersburg on Monday evening, and left it on Wednesday afternoon at one o'clock. They were composed of cavalry and mounted infantry. They are also reported to have had two pieces of our artillery captured at Martinsburg, which they did not bring into the town. They seem to have been drawn as far as Chambersburg in their attempts to capture the wagon train which escaped from Martinsburg.

Jenkins' Precautionary Measures.

Immediately upon taking possession of the town JENKINS threw out pickets as far as Scotland, a distance of five miles from Chambersburg, where the railroad bridge, a substantial wooden structure, some eighty feet long, was destroyed by them. He also established a chain of expresses between himself and General RHODES at Williamsport. Scouting parties of considerable force were sent out in the direction of Shippensburg.

He Orders the Surrender of Government Property.

Having taken these precautions, JENKINS issued an order requiring the citizens to produce all the Government arms in their possession by ten o'clock on Tuesday morning, under threat of searching the houses of all who did not produce a musket. About eight hundred Government muskets were brought in by the citizens, which were broken and burned by the Rebels before leaving on Wednesday. A storehouse was fired by them, but the flames were extinguished by the citizens.

He Helps Himself to Drugs and Patent Medicines.

The contents of the drug stores of Mr. NIXON and Mr. MILLER were packed up and removed. Everything in the way of a beaver was seized upon, while the shining silk dress hat was passed by in contempt. Everthing in the millinery line was also gathered up. Where payment was made it was generally in Confederate paper. Occasionally a greenback was offered.

A Skirmish with our Scouting Cavalry.

Harrisburg than Scotland, as mentioned above, with the exception of a scouting party of 30 to 50, which rode around Shippensburg on Tuesday night. And the force above named has been the only one which has, up to Wednesday night, been within the borders of Pennsylvania.

THE WAR ON THE PENNSYLVANIA BORDER.

Reported Advance of the Rebels on Hancock, Maryland.

MCCONNELSBURG, FULTON COUNTY, PA., June 17.—Stragglers from the late fight bring information up to 6 o'clock, P. M., yesterday, from below. They report that eight thousand Rebels crossed at Williamsport, and marched on Hancock, at which point 1600 of General MILROY's force had been collected.

These men, being in a state of demoralization, without officers or organization, fled at the reported advance of the Rebels, and are now scattered through all parts of the country.

[This would seem to account for a large portion of the 2000 reported as lost by General MILROY.]

Matters in Harrisburg.

HARRISBURG, June 18.—It is believed that there are now no Rebel troops in this State.

The cavalry force, under JENKINS, was at Hagerstown last night.

There is no evidence of any infantry force having been with him.

While at Chambersburg the Rebels cleaned out all the drug stores, paying in Confederate scrip.

Troops are rapidly arriving at Harrisburg. The State authorities are making them as comfortable as possible.

On leaving Chambersburg the Rebels took with them a number of the most prominent farmers in that section of the valley.

Despatch from Governor Curtis.

The following despatch, addressed to Colonel WM. B. THOMAS and A. G. CATTELL, was received yesterday:—

"HARRISBURG, June 18.—Please have your men mustered for the present emergency, and I will, as Governor of the State, determine the matter and return them to their homes at the earliest date consistent with the safety of the border. There should be no hesitation on the part of the men. Send them here at once, so that an organization can be perfected. (Signed) "A. G. CURTIN,
"Governor of Pennsylvania."

Defense of the Pennsylvania Railroad.

ALTOONA, June 18.—The Pennsylvania Railroad Company is acting with its characteristic energy in the present crisis, and the line of the road, an especial object of the Rebel movement, will be defended at all hazards, come what may. In the Department of State Defenses, Professor COPPEE is giving renewed evidence of his skill and efficiency. For nearly a week he has been engaged in superintending the construction of barricades at important points, and the works erected testify to his capacity, evincing a strategic engineering ability deserving the thanks of every loyal citizen.

Correspondence with General Cameron.

The following despatch was sent to General CAMERON by a citizen of Philadelphia:—

PHILADELPHIA, June 17, 1863.—Hon. SIMON CAMERON, Harrisburg, Pa.:—It is reported that you advised taking the command of the State troops from General COUCH and giving it to either Generals FRANKLIN or MCCLELLAN. Is this true? If not, will you authorize me to contradict it?

Reply of General Cameron.

HARRISBURG, June 18.—Your telegram of yesterday was handed to me late last night. I authorize you to say that I made no such proposition.
SIMON CAMERON.

CONFLICTING REPORTS FROM CHAMBERSBURG.

Rebels at Greencastle—Cannonading Heard.

HARRISBURG, June 18.—The reports from the border line have been very conflicting during the day. The following is the latest report from the operator at Chambersburg, dated 6 P. M.:—"The latest scout just in, reports being eight miles from here and saw no Rebels, and heard of none being at Greencastle."

Another scout confirms the report of a body of 200 being at Greencastle at noon, and dividing—one portion going towards Waynesboro' and the other towards Mercersburg, supposed to be after horses.

Heavy cannonading is heard at Greencastle, in the direction of Harper's Ferry.

A misunderstanding exists here among a number of citizens arrived for the protection of the State. The authorities are receiving troops for six months or the emergency, and the time of service under this call cannot exceed one or two months, at the furthest.

A large number left for their homes to-day, having refused to enlist for fear of being held for the six months. There is probably no fear of such an emergency arising. There are no Rebels now in the State, except thieving parties operating along the border.

The stores were opened to-day, and the city has assumed its usual appearance. A number of citizens who fled during the stampede are now returning. The city is filled with soldiers, and drunkenness is

OUR HARRISBURG LETTER.

Special Correspondence of the Inquirer.

HARRISBURG, June 17, 1863.

The work on the intrenchments and other fortifications is still going on bravely. For all practical purposes, Harrisburg is now well fortified. Heavy artillery has been planted in the works, and all the fords and bridges along the Susquehanna are well fortified.

Troops are pouring into the Capital from all points in the State. The sight of these noble and patriotic responses on the part of the people of the old Commonwealth of Pennsylvania is inspiring.

The scenes this morning at Camp Curtin were quite animating. The martial sounds of the fife and drum, the assembling of masses, and the scenes of camp life, have become so familiar to the eyes of Americans that their recitation can serve only to recall reminiscences of similar popular responses in the past.

Of the many thousands who have arrived here from points in the interior of the State, I have been able to obtain but a brief list, as follows:—

One-hundred-and-twenty-seventh Regiment (Col. JENNINGS), Harrisburg, 1000 men.

First Pennsylvania Militia (Colonel R. A. LAMBERTON), Harrisburg, 1000 men.

Captain William H. Connechan, Bradford, 105 men.
Captain J. M. Gregory, Lehigh, 70 men.
Captain J. H. Holion, Lehigh, 70 men.
Captain J. M. Broomall, Delaware, 71 men.
Captain G. T. Waters, Northampton, 58 men.
Captain William R. Ash, Chester, 100 men.
Captain J. G. Eicholtz, Chester, 53 men.
Captain J. B. Davis, Northumberland, 50 men.
Captain John McClay, Northumberland, 71 men.
Captain William Steel, Chester, 50 men.
Captain W. McVeigh, Chester, 60 men.
Captain W. M. Hinkson, Chester, 45 men.
Captain W. C. Dickey, Chester, 48 men.
Captain E. F. James, Chester, 68 men.
Captain George B. Thomas, Chester, 57 men.
Captain Charles Roberts, Chester, 40 men.
Captain R. D. Townsend, Chester, 16 men.
Captain A. Ricketts, Luzerne, 56 men.
Captain R. F. Clark, Columbia, 90 men.
Captain J. B. Granters, Bradford, 71 men.
Captain J. D. Jenkins, Chester, 82 men.
Captain James Dickson, Luzerne, 40 men.
Captain H. Bloss, Northampton, 85 men.
Captain J. F. Ramsey, Mentour, 78 men.
Captain J. M. Scott, New Jersey, 46 men.
Captain D. A. Smith, Schuylkill, 105 men.
Captain T. J. Sleppy, Columbia, 81 men.
Captain Wm. B. Mann, Philadelphia, 101 men.
Spencer Miller's Battery.

District Attorney MANN, of Philadelphia, it will be seen, is here, with a full company. His company was the first to reach Harrisburg from Philadelphia.

A number of Philadelphia regiments are expected to arrive here this evening.

The Berks county men are completely organized under their late Colonel, MATHEWS. They are looking fine and "spoiling for a fight." They are anxious for another sight of the old enemy.

The following order was posted around town this morning:—

"HARRISBURG, June 17, 1863.

"The following order has been made by Major-General COUCH, commanding the Department of the Susquehanna:—

"HEAD-QUARTERS, DEPARTMENT OF THE SUSQUEHANNA, HARRISBURG, June, 17, 1863.

"SPECIAL ORDER No. 6.—Captain DODGE, Chief Mustering Officer, will, at nine o'clock A. M., on the 18th instant, commence to muster the troops here assembled, under the proclamation of the President of the United States, and the call of His Excellency Governor CURTIN, and will continue to muster from day to day, until all are mustered. The term of service will be six months, unless sooner discharged, or *during the existing emergency*. By command of
"Major-General D. N. COUCH.
"ROBERT LE ROY, Captain and A. A. G.

"The volunteer militia who are willing to peril themselves for the defense of public and private property in this Department will assemble, those in Camp Curtin at Camp Curtin, and all others on Capitol Hill, on to-morrow (Thursday) morning, when they will be sworn in at once and furnished with all the necessary equipments, prior to being regularly organized into regiments.

"The people of Pennsylvania, who have testified by their presence here their willingness to bear arms to drive the Rebels from our State and protect it from invasion, will readily notice the propriety of this order and their duty to act in obedience to it.

"They are called into service by the United States Government for the purpose of protecting the State, and are placed under the command of a general officer for that duty.

"To enjoy all the benefits of that Government they should be mustered into its service, that service only to continue *during the exigencies of the emergency* for which they were called, and no one can desire to return to his home until all the people of Pennsylvania and the soil of our State is safe from the Rebels.
A. L. RUSSELL,
"Adjutant-General of Pennsylvania."

At least nine-tenths of the troops who have already responded, are men who have been engaged in all the hard fighting during the nine months' service. Great enthusiasm prevails among the militia, and their marches through the streets are characterized by cheering and other patriotic demonstrations.

Rebel prisoners, captured in the vicinity of Shippensburg and Carlisle, while scouting or stupidly straggling away from the main body, are daily brought into town. There are now over a dozen under guard in Camp Curtin, who have been thus caught.

FROM MURFREESBORO', TENN.

Rebel Offensive Movements.

MURFREESBORO', June 18.—BRAGG has undoubtedly received reinforcements of three brigades, viz:—BATES', CLAYTON'S and CHURCHILL'S. These, with BROWN'S Brigade of MCCORMICK'S Division, left behind, form a new division of STEWART HARDEE'S Corps. BRAGG has now eighteen brigades of infantry

soldiers were killed, and several passengers wounded. The boat was attempting to land for cotton claimed by three passengers, who were evidently in collusion with the Rebels. They were arrested and brought here.

Chaplain EATON, Superintendent of the contrabands here, is making arrangements to withdraw to a safe place the large number of negroes which have been collected here.

General OSTERHAUS holds Black River bridge without interruption.

The Paymasters will begin to pay the troops immediately.

The prospects of the siege look brighter and brighter, and no fears are entertained for the result.

FROM HARPER'S FERRY.

Fight at the Point of Rocks—Destruction of a Train of Cars—Return of General Milroy.

From the Baltimore American.

Capture and Destruction of a Train of Cars.

About nine o'clock last night a body of Rebel cavalry crossed the Potomac near the Point of Rocks, and moved upon that place, at which there was no force of defense, except Captain MEANS' irregular local cavalry. All these were captured, including the Captain himself, without the least engagement, so far as we could learn. There were between twenty and thirty in all.

Simultaneously another body of the enemy, mounted, crossed the river higher up, and attacked Major COLE'S Cavalry at Catoctin Station, about seven or eight miles east of Harper's Ferry. A fight ensued, but with what result has not yet been ascertained.

About the same time a part of the enemy's cavalry charged upon a military train and succeeded in its capture. It consisted of one first-class locomotive and about twenty-three cars, returning from Harper's Ferry to Baltimore, after having carried provisions to supply the garrison during the day. Fortunately this was the last train of a convoy of five, the others having just preceded it in safety, and all reached Baltimore. Of the captured train were several cars loaded with produce that was being rescued from danger from the vicinity of Harper's Ferry, also, some fifteen passengers, who took advantage of the train either to escape, or else business connected with the army required them to come down the road. Several of them were sutlers, and perhaps one or two subordinate Federal officers. These are said to have been all carried off to Virginia, with two of the four railroad men who were in charge of the train.

Soon as the passengers were arrested, the train was burned entirely by the enemy, who carried burning coals from the furnace and laid them upon the floors of the cars. These consisted of fifteen empty horse cars, one flat car laden with iron, one or two laden with flour, and three or four empty stock cars. This train was first attacked at a point beyond Catoctin by the force which appeared at that place, but succeeded in escaping. On reaching the Point of Rocks, however, it was again attacked with such a force as obliged it to stop. Efforts were made to destroy the locomotive, but it is believed to have been but slightly damaged.

The firemen and brakemen of the train succeeded in escaping, but the engine men and conductor are believed to be among the prisoners.

Thus far, in the present campaign, this seems to have been the first railroad property destroyed. Neither the tracks nor bridges of the Company have been damaged, but the telegraph lines of the road were cut by the enemy in several places. Upon the enemy making his first appearance, the Company's telegraphic operator at the Point of Rocks bravely held his position, and remained at his post while the destruction was going on, but was finally forced to leave.

After the perpetration of these mischiefs the enemy moved off, but it is said watched the road in the vicinity during the night, in the hope that other trains or detachments of troops would fall into their clutches.

It is believed that the two detachments of the enemy numbered in all not over four hundred men, and were commanded by Major or Colonel WHITE, of a somewhat noted guerrilla or irregular mounted corps.

Excitement at Frederick.

Yesterday there was considerable nervousness exhibited at Frederick and points west of it, on account of a report to the effect that a detachment of Rebels were actually seen near the line of the Baltimore and Ohio Railroad, and about forty miles from this city. The basis of this report is as follows:—During the attack made by the enemy upon the command of General MILROY, a Captain and eight men of one of the companies succeeded in making their escape.

They made a forced march through Jefferson and Loudon counties, and passed through to Maryland, and thence along the border of Montgomery county. Their appearance at the point above alluded to, and their repeated inquiries for the latest military news, gave rise to the suspicion that they were Rebels, and hence the rumors. They have since arrived in this city.

General MILROY and the members of his staff who left here yesterday afternoon in a special train, proceeded as far as Monocacy, but upon hearing of the disasters then in progress at the Point of Rocks, returned to this city.

There were also rumors in Frederick last evening of the appearance of the enemy in considerable force at the old South Mountain battle-ground, which added to the excitement. There were no Rebels at Frederick this morning, however.

Departure of General Milroy.

General MILROY this morning received information (whether correct or not is not ascertained) that 2500 of his late force, consisting of 1500 infantry and 1000 cavalry, had succeeded in reaching Cumberland, Maryland, last night. The General, who had a narrow escape from being captured on a train on the Baltimore and Ohio Railroad yesterday, immediately took the eight o'clock train of the Northern Central Railway this morning with his Staff, and proceeded to Harrisburg with the view of joining them.

Capt. Alexander's Battery.

We are gratified in being able to announce the arrival of Lieuts. ALEXANDER, LEARY and HALL, of

city is occupied by a detachment of JENKINS' ... ry. BOYD, the former editor of the *Free* ... paper which was suppressed by the Gover... and the editor sent South, returned with the ... He took possession of the office of the *Hera*... Union paper, and had commenced the re-issu... *Free Press*. The Rebels, it is understood, o... purpose to remain in Maryland. Perhaps som... parties may have something to say on that sub...

LATER FROM VICKSBURG.

The Rebel Batteries Silent.

HEAD-QUARTERS, WALNUT HILLS, VICK... June 13.—A ride along the lines develo... change in the position. The enemy's batte... silent on all sides, only a few riflemen firin... bombardment is maintained with continuou... and we have more guns in position.

Deserters coming into our lines, to-day, rep... men and line officers discontented, and on... vented from deserting by the hope that they ... honorably surrendered in a few days.

General BLAIR's reconnoissance revealed ... of the enemy within thirty miles. Every usef... is destroyed for fifty miles around. General ... ENRIDGE is said to be at Jackson. Our positi... is equal to 100,000 men.

June 14.—Nothing of importance has tra... within the last twenty-four hours.

June 15.—Our batteries have slacked, ... enemy rarely replies. The Rebels are believe... erecting an interior line of works, for the pu... falling back. About one hundred of the Re... reported to be killed and wounded daily, ... sharp-shooters. Our wounded are well taken... in field hospitals. The health and morale of t... is good.

FROM WASHINGT...

Special Despatches to the Inquirer.

WASHINGTON, June 18,

Rebels at Point of Rocks.

On Tuesday a force of Rebels crossed the ... at Point of Rocks and cut the telegraph w... returned to the other side. In the best in... quarters it is believed that no Rebels are ... Maryland east of the South Mountain range.

The Twenty-eighth New Jersey

The Twenty-eighth Regiment New Jersey ... teers arrived here to-day on their way home.

From the Army of the Potomac—A ... mish—Rebels Captured.

Information has officially reached here of ... skirmish yesterday, at or near Aldie, betwe... of our cavalry forces and those of the enem... latter were forced to retire. Eight officer... tween sixty and seventy men, it is report... captured by our troops. Aldie is in Loudon ... ten miles southward of Leesburg, and in ... between the Bull Run and Katistin Mountain...

Superintendent of Iron-Clads.

Chief Engineer J. W. KING has been or... superintend the construction of all iron-clad... building west of the Alleghenies.

[BY THE ASSOCIATED PRESS.]

The Two Great Opposing Armi...

WASHINGTON, June 17—By Mail.—The ... of the several corps of the Army of the Pot... known in this city to-night, information ... southern side of the Potomac having been ... up to 12 o'clock. Were the facts in this co... publicly stated, however, they would be rep... nothing more than might be expected unde... cumstances.

The whereabouts of General LEE himse... known—at least not publicly—and there is ... much solicitude everywhere to discover so... concerning him. Whatever may be his ... keeps them very secret, and anything said... ing them would be mere matter of speculati...

From Port Royal.

An officer with BANKS' army, relates, in ... letter, an incident which occurred during a te... truce at Port Hudson, on the 27th of ... availed himself of the opportunity thus afford... to the rebel works as close as he could to ge... view of them, when he saw a regiment of ... throw down their arms, and heard them g... cheers and say "We surrender!" The rebe... at once approached them, and, with drawn ... and pistols, overpowered and controlled t... compelled them to take up their arms an... their position.

The same officer, at a truce entered into ... for the purpose of looking after the dead an... ed, while riding as near to the rebel lines a... get, was hailed by a rebel officer within ... with the question whether he did not think, ... flection, that he was coming nearer than w... proper. Our officer replied in the negativ... we had had men wounded and killed as ne... enemy as he himself then was. A convers... ensued, in which the rebel officer spoke of ... MAN charge of the preceding day, and rema... "inside" they regarded it as the finest thi... war. Our officer did not belong to SHERM... vision.

War Rumors from Washingto...

No general alarm exists in Washington ... quence of the proximity of the enemy. ... sons, however, not of our resident populati... day turned their United States notes into ... left the city for their homes.

It is reported that General LEE is near A... don county, but of this there is no certaint... seems to be no doubt, however, that so... forces are in that direction.

Up to last night nothing of stirring imp... scarcely anything has been heard from the...

Official Report of the Destruction ... ton, S. C.

The Navy Department has received the

Chapter 10

We Are Now in the Great Crisis of the War

The Southern press was correct in proclaiming that economic problems on the Confederate home front carried significant consequences for soldiers in the field. Not only did the shortages of food sharply affect army morale, but they also at times impacted military planning. In June 1863—in part as an effort to relieve Southern civilians from the burden of feeding his troops—General Robert E. Lee made an unexpected offensive move into Pennsylvania, where his men could forage on Northern farms and raid Northern supplies. It was a maneuver that would eventually culminate in the famed Battle of Gettysburg.

As Lee made his foray into Union territory, another crucial showdown was already unfolding in the western theater of the war, at Vicksburg, a strategically vital hill town built atop a two-hundred-foot bluff along the Mississippi River. From the very start of the war, one of the Union's primary objectives had been to take control of the river and thus sever the Confederacy in two. Union forces had taken important strides toward accomplishing this goal in the spring of 1862 by seizing Forts Henry and Donelson in Tennessee, capturing Memphis, and occupying New Orleans. Since that time, the Federals had progressively expanded their hold over the river's course, so that by mid-1863 the Union controlled the entirety of it, with the exception of Vicksburg on the Mississippi side and Port Hudson on the Louisiana side.[1]

Because Vicksburg sat on such high terrain and was surrounded by swampland and dense forests, it was a tough nut to crack. In the summer of 1862, after capturing New Orleans, Admiral David Farragut's fleet had continued upriver and tried, unsuccessfully, to compel Vicksburg's surrender. Then, in December of that year, General Ulysses S. Grant had attempted to take it in a land invasion, before Confederate cavalry cut his supply lines and forced him to retreat. With little Vicksburg still standing defiantly after two attempted assaults, Southerners began to regard it as their

Gibraltar—their unsinkable fortress that would save the Mississippi River, and ultimately the entire Confederacy, from completely falling into Union hands. "It is now being universally admitted that Vicksburg is the key to the Confederacy," declared one Mississippi paper. "It is, perhaps, not saying too much," affirmed another, "that upon the gallant defence of Vicksburg, and the holding [of] that point against all the assaults of the enemy, the success of our revolution has turned." Specifically because the Southern people regarded Vicksburg with such reverence, defending it was of tremendous political importance for the Confederacy. If it fell, discontent and despondency on the home front—already brewing hotly—might boil over uncontrollably.[2]

Given all that was at stake, emotions ran high on both sides when in April 1863, Grant initiated yet another attempt to capture Vicksburg. In an incredibly daring move, Grant set out to march his troops southward, along the west bank of the Mississippi, to a point below Vicksburg, where they were to meet up with Union gunboats that would ferry them across the river for a land campaign against the Confederate stronghold. Grant's success in implementing his plan stands as one of the most incredible military feats of the war. The area around Vicksburg was heavily defended by forces under the command of General John C. Pemberton, but Grant orchestrated diversionary raids that enabled him to move his troops across the river on April 30, precisely as he had envisioned. Then, over the next seventeen days, Grant executed a campaign in which his army marched 180 miles and destroyed the Mississippi capital at Jackson, inflicting significant casualties on Pemberton's troops along the way. Without resting, Grant continued to pursue the Confederates, compelling Pemberton and his remaining forces to hole up in Vicksburg. This set the stage for a final showdown. After two failed attempts at taking the town by direct assault, Grant and his troops proceeded to dig a system of trenches, from which they planned to bombard Vickburg until the soldiers and civilians sequestered there surrendered.

Between Lee's invasion of Pennsylvania and Grant's determined attempt to take Vicksburg, the turning point of the war seemed to be at hand. If either the Union or the Confederacy emerged triumphant on both fronts, the military balance would tip decisively in favor of the victor; perhaps the whole war would be brought to an end. The weight of the moment seemed enormous. In Cincinnati, which was perched north of Vicksburg and due west of Gettysburg, the *Cincinnati Gazette* was transfixed by events on both fronts. "At no time since the breaking out of the war has the military situation presented an aspect of greater importance than at the present hour," the paper declared gravely. "It would seem, so far as human vision can penetrate, . . . that we are now in the great crisis of the war, and that the events of the next few weeks may decide the fate of the rebellion."[3]

Naturally, Northerners looked to the situation in Pennsylvania with tremendous concern. Lee's decision to cross the border had surprised them completely, and while his ultimate intentions remained a mystery, they feared the worst. Rumors flew wildly that Lee hoped to destroy the state capital at Harrisburg, perhaps as a precursor to marching on Philadelphia, and then—anything seemed possible—maybe an attack on New York, or maybe a daring southward plunge toward Washington. There was no telling what the illustrious Confederate general might try. In central Pennsylvania, where the threat was most imminent, the citizens ran scared. A news correspondent in Harrisburg reported that "a perfect panic prevailed" there, as "hundreds if not thousands of people" prepared to escape the city before the Southern troops arrived. The hysteria continued throughout the last two weeks of June, as Confederate soldiers made their way into Franklin County, Pennsylvania, stationing themselves primarily around Chambersburg. Along the way, they seized much-needed supplies of food, clothing, hats, boots, medicines, and horses, destroyed the Caledonia Iron Works, and were spotted "running down little darkies"—some of whom were captured and sold into slavery.[4] As word of the hardships suffered by Northerners filtered southward, newspaper editors in the Confederacy responded with unabashed glee. "Most pleasant, unspeakably delightful, are all these reports of the sensation caused throughout Yankeedoodledom by Gen. Lee's advance into Pennsylvania," cooed the *Charleston Courier*.[5] Southern soldiers on the scene, however, were more ambivalent, as this letter, written by a soldier from Georgia to the *Savannah Republican*, recounts:

Editor Savannah Republican:

. . . It is no longer a myth, we are among the Dutch of Pennsylvania. The country surpasses in improvement and evidences of comfort anything I ever saw in my life! Every spot of it almost is under the most thorough cultivation and plenty—even superabundance—is everywhere. . . . For two days now that we have traveled into their country, we have passed one long succession of golden wheat fields, excepting where portions were devoted to hay-making, which were the finest prospects of the kind I have seen yet. The people are circumscribed . . . in their intelligence, and know little of the war or its ravages, being a simple minded set of dupes to the Washington dynasty. Their surprise and consternation knew no bounds when they found out that the "ragged rebels" were actually in their midst, living and moving monsters among their granaries and fowl houses. "Mine Got" was on every tongue, expressing the hopeless despair which weighed down every Dutch heart. The old women went into fits and the old men rocked themselves out of their wits in the old ancestral rocking chairs, despairing of another day of existence. . . . Their surprise was great when they were not hurt, nor any ferocious demonstrations of appetite made on their actual personages. They grew tame wonderfully fast . . . in the country, but our reception in Chambersburg, which is quite a large and flourishing city, was very different indeed. There seemed to be a superabundance of venom, the offspring of an education from the miserable abolition sheets and anti-slavery speeches which had been ding-donged into them from time immemorial. Such long faced men I never saw, and the features of the women would have made vinegar ashamed of itself for sourness. Some wreathed their pretty lips in ugly scorn and turned up their noses as if everything they saw before them was offensive to their olfactory organism. . . .

[Lieutenant General Richard S.] Ewell has preceded us and got most of the good things that lay in the path of the conqueror—such as shoes and clothing generally, but an abundance of provisions is found everywhere. From the number of fowls that

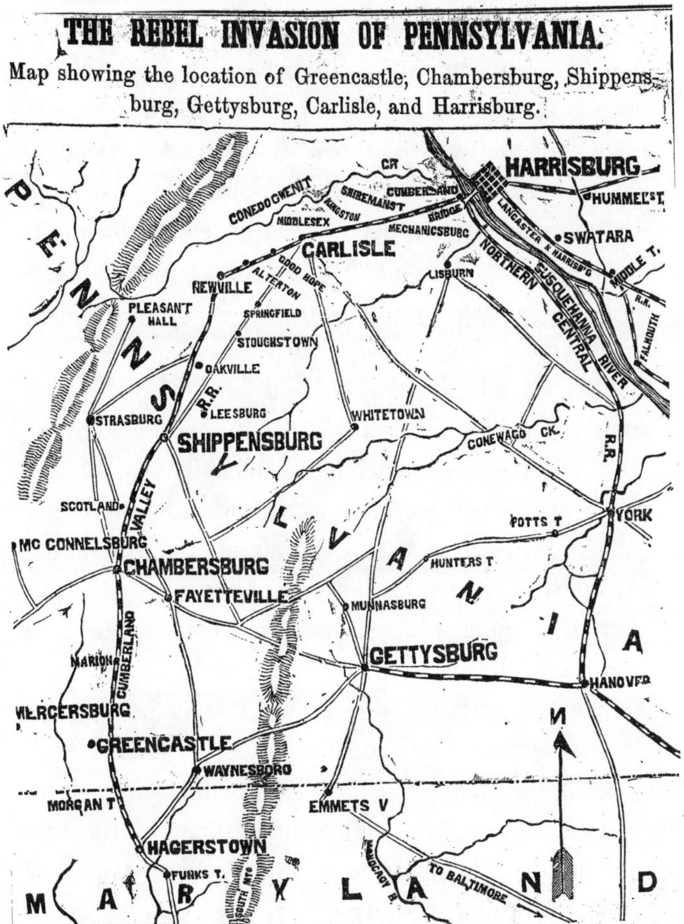

LEFT *Philadelphia Inquirer,* June 27, 1863.
Map of central Pennsylvania, including the roads around Gettysburg.

The precept, "thou shalt love thy neighbor as thyself", belongs not to the international code—it was only designed, by its Divine author, to regulate the conduct of individuals, not of nations, towards each other. Policy and *humanity* both require that a cruel and vindictive war should be met with stern and uncompromising retribution. This is the only way, in which such a war can be brought to a close. Let the enemy sup full of the horrors he inflicts, and he will cease to inflict them. Practice towards him humanity and chivalry, while he is outraging civilization by worse than Indian barbarities, and he will only be encouraged to persevere in cruelty and crime. We trust, then, that the sober second thought will induce the accomplished LEE, should he successfully invade the enemy's country, to wage war, even as it has been waged against us, sparing neither public nor private property, but ravaging and destroying in every direction, and imitating the enemy in all but his unmanly and cowardly warfare of *cruelty* and *insult* to women and children.

Charleston Courier, June 25, 1863.
As Lee's men tramped through Pennsylvania, Southern papers clamored for them to exact vengeance against Northern civilians, as a matter of justice.

have made their appearance in camp to-day I am disposed to think our men have been interfering with the roosts. This would be a just retaliation for the same thing committed by their troops in our country. However, there is something so disgraceful and low in this kind of robbery and vandalism over the helpless that I cannot but applaud Gen. Lee's strong efforts to suppress it. Only such things as are really necessary for our progress and supply [are] allowed to be taken, and then our currency is offered at their market price for them to refuse or take as they think proper.—But many of the farmers have eluded our search for horses, having fled with them to the mountains to hide. Detachments will be sent after them. Some of the gentlefolks raise quite a storm about the Quartermaster's ears when he comes with the news that, "I must have your horse, sir." Just about then the rebels are spoken of in very unpleasant Dutch terms. But the good humored Quartermaster takes the animal jocosely, hands him the Confederate money and gallops away. . . . Our resentment grows very strong when we think of how much vandalism has been practiced in Virginia, but when it comes to practic[ing] it upon defenseless women, children and old men, a true Southern soldier cannot find heart to do it. I fear there are some in our ranks who have been unmerciful, but it cannot be discovered who they are or they would be punished. Orders are very strict and read every day to [the] troops against vandalism.[6]

Indeed, as this soldier suggests, the invasion could have been much more destructive and terrorizing than it was. Lee's army showed relative restraint in its operations in Pennsylvania—in large part because of the strict controls exerted by Lee himself. Shortly after the first of his men moved into Pennsylvania, Lee issued General Orders Number 72, which forbade them from destroying private property or seizing goods from civilians without paying for them. He also issued General Orders Number 73, prohibiting his soldiers from engaging in vengeful retaliatory strikes against noncombatants. Lee's religious beliefs and gentlemanly ideals could not countenance acts of lawless violence. In his mind, Northern soldiers might behave like barbarians, but Southerners were of a higher order and Lee expected them to act with appropriate and honorable decorum. Moreover, he did not want to do anything to alienate Copperheads in the region from continuing with their calls for peace.

By and large, the Confederates who came through Pennsylvania obeyed Lee's directive. Observers back home, however, lamented it. So many times in the past, the Southern press had called out for retaliation against the enemy—an aggressive move into Pennsylvania or Ohio that would strike true sorrow into the hearts of the Northern people—and now, with Lee's army standing on Northern soil, they ached to see it happen. Still smarting from the effects of the Emancipation Proclamation, the *Richmond Dispatch* offered these opinions on how Lee ought to make Northerners pay for the Confederacy's lost slave property:

> Their armies, with their approval, have stolen 500,000 negroes from the South, valued at $500,000,000 at the commencement of the war. They have no negroes to steal, but they have towns and manufactories to burn, and every one of them should be reduced to ashes. Property is property. There is no reason why once species of it should be exempt from the laws of war more than another.—Were our troops to burn Harrisburg, the loss to the enemy would not counterbalance the loss we have sustained in the article of negroes alone. We say, then, make the whole Pennsylvania Valley an astonishment to future generations. . . . It was said that "no blade of grass grew where the horse of Atilla had once set his foot." Let the Confederate army imitate the leader of the Huns in this particular. The Valley of Pennsylvania ought to become a sea of flame. . . . Nothing should be left that man could eat, or sleep upon, or shelter himself, or procure food with. All this might be turned into a desert, and yet the balance of destruction would be against us. The whole city of Philadelphia if burnt to the ground would not pay for the negroes they have carried off. We are opposed to plundering—it ruins the discipline of an army. . . . But we would have every house gutted, and the contents set on fire. Thus only can we get even with this villainous foe, who has no compunctions of conscience, no regard for the laws of war, no respect for the usages of civilized society; no belief in the truths of Revelation, no fears of punishment in another world, no reverence for God, and no mercy for his fellow man.[7]

VICKSBURG SURRENDERED!

ANOTHER VICTORY AND RENEWED REJOICING.

THE GIBRALTAR IN OUR POSSESSION JULY FOURTH.

New York World, July 8, 1863.

The Southern press had little time to begrudge Lee's treatment of Northern civilians, however, as military events soon overtook their attention. In the West, Grant's siege slowly but effectively devastated Vicksburg. For forty-seven days straight, Union artillery and gunboats kept the town under fire, driving civilians to take refuge in caves that had been dug into the bluffs, where they subsisted on whatever food they could find—dogs, cats, mules, and even rats. The Confederate troops there, weakened by starvation and sickness, and incapable of driving away Grant's forces, eventually had no choice but to concede defeat. On July 4, Pemberton and the soldiers under his charge surrendered to Grant. Five days later, the Union captured Port Hudson and finally took control of the Mississippi River. Vicksburg paid a heavy price for its efforts at resistance; the landscape was as wrecked as the troops that had attempted to defend it. Previously a symbol of Southern defiance, Vicksburg now betokened the South's desolation. Northerners who entered the town witnessed an awful scene:

> It is difficult to describe the condition of the city after undergoing a siege and constant bombardment lasting forty-seven days and nights, and an intermittent bombardment for more than a year. The citizens insist that the damage is trifling, and from what they

say I suppose the loss of life has been much smaller than could have been reasonably expected. But nearly every house in the city has been perforated by conical and round shot shells. The pillars of piazzas are knocked down, and doors and windows smashed, floors torn up, and damage done in every shape and form. I found no house in the city that had escaped unscathed, though it is said that there are some. The streets are barricaded by breastworks and rifle-pits intended to guard against an attack from the river, and in some places they are covered with grass and weeds. The business houses all have a musty, dusty, deserted look. Wherever you go in any direction, you have to guard your steps against holes dug in the ground by our shells. At every available place a cave has been dug. In these caves the women and children were saved at night. During the day time they took the chances for successful dodging, and most of the ladies rather pride themselves upon their expertness in getting out of the way of shells as if it were quite a ladylike accomplishment.

Vicksburg [had] been a really handsome place. The public buildings were good, the residences well surrounded with beautiful, well-kept shrubbery, the site of the town high and rolling, and on every hand were evidences of the existence at one time of wealth, taste and general prosperity. It is now pre-eminently war-worn—some degree and kind of devastation marks every thing you see.[8]

While the physical destruction of Vicksburg was massive, it practically paled in comparison to the 50,000 casualties suffered at Gettysburg. The fighting erupted on July 1, as a division of Confederate soldiers approached Gettysburg on a mission to seize a supply of shoes that were reportedly being stored there. What they found instead were two brigades of Union cavalry, which had hurried to the town in anticipation of the Confederates' arrival. The fighting around Gettysburg escalated quickly, as reinforcements from both sides poured into the area, and initially it went poorly for

NEAR VICKSBURGH, Saturday, July 4.

Vicksburgh has capitulated. Yesterday Gen. GRANT received the following letter:

GEN. PEMBERTON TO GEN. GRANT.

HEADQUARTERS, VICKSBURGH, July 3.

Maj.-Gen. Grant, Commanding United States Forces:

GENERAL: I have the honor to propose to you an armistice for — hours, with a view to arranging terms for the capitulation of Vicksburgh. To this end, if agreeable to you, I will appoint three Commissioners to meet a like number to be named by yourself, at such place and hour to-day as you may find convenient. I make this proposition to save the further effusion of blood, which must otherwise be shed to a frightful extent, feeling myself fully able to maintain my position for a yet indefinite period. This communication will be handed you under flag of truce by Maj.-Gen. JAMES BOWEN.

Very respectfully, your obedient servant,

J. C. PEMBERTON.

To this Gen. GRANT replied as follows:

GEN. GRANT TO GEN. PEMBERTON.

HEADQUARTERS DEPARTMENT OF TENNESSEE,
IN THE FIELD, NEAR VICKSBURGH, July 3, 1863.

Lieut.-Gen. J. C. Pemberton, Commanding Confederate Forces, &c.:

GENERAL: Your note of this date, just received, proposes an armistice of several hours for the purpose of arranging terms of capitulation through commissioners to be appointed, &c. The effusion of blood you propose stopping by this course, can be ended at any time you may choose, by an unconditional surrender of the city and garrison. Men who have shown so much endurance and courage as those now in Vicksburgh, will always challenge the respect of an adversary, and, I can assure you, will be treated with all the respect due them as prisoners of war. I do not favor the proposition of appointing commissioners to arrange terms of capitulation, because I have no other terms than those indicated above.

I am, General, very respectfully,

Your obedient servant,

U. S. GRANT, Maj.-Gen.

New York Times, July 15, 1863.
The correspondence between Generals Grant and Pemberton, in negotiating the surrender of Vicksburg.

the Union. By the end of the first day, the men in blue—regiments in General George Meade's army—had been forced to retreat south of the town, but they established a formidable defensive position on the hills along Cemetery Ridge. The following day, Lee commanded a series of uncoordinated and ultimately unsuccessful assaults that left both armies badly bloodied. There were already 35,000 casualties as the second day of fighting came to close. The most stunning losses, however, came on July 3. That afternoon, after a two-hour barrage of Confederate artillery fire that did nothing to weaken the Union's line of defense, nine brigades under the command of General George Pickett executed an uphill, headlong charge. It was an incredibly daring but ultimately horrendous move. While Union artillery heaped shot and shell upon the Confederates as they initiated the charge, infantry fire mowed down those who made it within close range. Of the 14,000 men who started with Pickett, only half made it back alive. The failure of Pickett's charge effectively ended the Gettysburg campaign and sent Lee's army retreating toward Maryland.

Those present at the scene found it almost impossible to convey to readers at home the extent of the carnage. A correspondent from the *New York Times*, after surveying the battle zone, tried to give a sense of the sheer number of dead bodies. The field upon which Pickett's men had rushed "was literally covered with dead and wounded," he reported. "Where our musketry and artillery took effect they lay in swaths, as if mown down by a scythe." This certainly was not the first major battle of the conflict, but it did seem to be the most terrible one yet. As the *Times* correspondent concluded: "This field presented a horrible sight—such as has never yet been witnessed during the war. Not less than one thousand dead and wounded laid in a *space of less than four acres* in extent." A soldier from the Massachusetts Thirty-seventh Regiment added these vivid observations from the field in a letter to the *Hampshire Gazette & Northampton Courier*:

> *Messrs. Editors*: . . . The battle of Gettysburg may be pronounced one of the severest of the war, and we rejoice in its success, as also in the taking of Vicksburg and Port Hudson, but while we think of the victory and advantage derived, we cannot forget that hundreds and thousands of hearts and households are made sad and desolate through its fearful cost. God only can know all the sorrow and bereavement that a battle occasions; it was a sad sight to pass over the battle field and see friend and foe lay side by side in the array of death. They had died from wounds of all descriptions, some with a severed arm or shattered leg, others with head half blown off or partially severed, the brains strewn in every direction. In one place lay seven dead in the space of a square rod, and in some places [it] could be plainly seen where a line of battle stood by its row of dead. Dead horses lay around in large numbers; but who can describe such a scene. I noticed one poor fellow of whom I will make mention, he lay in a garden near an old house, and had been struck by a piece of shell on the forehead, the skull cracked and the brains protruding. He had lost the sight of both eyes and the face was covered with dried and clotted blood; he was held in a sitting position by a comrade, unable to speak, but at times showed that he was conscious by a nod of the head to questions that were asked him; he lived but a few hours; was of the first corps. Another was shot in the bowels and lingered in great agony till morning and died. In looking around the battle field, I heard a low moan that came from a thicket. I at once approached the spot, and found that a rebel soldier had crawled behind a rock, in a shady place, and was entirely helpless. He wished to be turned over and have his canteen filled with water, as he was very thirsty and had been without water for a long time. As soon as possible I had him taken to the hospital; he was shot in the side, the ball remaining there, but you are familiar with many such incidents as described in letters, and yet the one-half cannot be told.
>
> During the two days of the 5th and 6th we followed on after the retreating army to Emmetsburg, distance some 20 miles. On the way every barn we

THE REBELLION RECEIVES ITS DEATH STROKE.

REBELS COMPLETLY ROUTED.

Rebel Generals Longstreet and Hill Wounded and in Our Possession.

Rebels Defeated at all Points.

THE VICTORY COMPLETE

THE DECISIVE BATTLE OF THE WAR FOUGHT.

The Enemy's Loss Terrific

THE BRAVERY OF OUR TROOPS BEYOND DESCRIPTION.

Harrisburg Telegraph, July 6, 1863.
The failure of Lee's Gettysburg campaign prompted some Northerners to believe that the end of the rebellion was at hand.

came to was filled with the enemy's wounded, all the barns and houses for miles around were used as hospitals, which showed that their loss was fearful. Some of them were a scaly looking set, though there were others that appeared smart and intelligent, and all were unanimous in wishing to have the war close. They gave much credit to the fighting qualities of our army, and we must certainly do so toward them, as they fight with a zeal and earnestness worthy of a better cause.[9]

As this soldier's words illustrate, one of the interesting psychological features of the war was that those who fought it came to feel a certain kinship with the enemy. Even though they belonged to different sides, they respected their common valor and shared an understanding of the horrors of war that the average civilian would never quite obtain. In stark contrast to the solemn reflections of those at the scene, the response of Northerners at home was utterly joyous. Between the feelings of relief occasioned by Lee's retreat and the euphoria of finally capturing Vicksburg, Northerners generally were in a frenzied and celebratory mood. Many even thought that the Confederacy would soon capitulate. The *New York Evening Post* captured the feel of the city in this way:

> The great news of today fills the city with gladness. The cheering still continues, as successive crowds gather about the bulletin boards and flock into the offices of the newspapers to hear the confirmation of the tidings from Vicksburg. In the crowd which thronged the street in front of the Evening Post office this afternoon, there were so many amusing incidents. Men fell to shaking each other's hands with extreme violence. Others slapped their neighbors on the back, and said "Isn't it glorious!" Others again, wild with enthusiasm, tossed their hats into the air and shouted; and one old gentleman, unable to contain himself, mounted our doorstep and delivered the following brief but pithy speech: "Gentlemen! . . . I don't know how you feel—but *I am just as happy as I can be!*" This seemed to be the universal feeling. Three or four men were seen in the street this afternoon ardently embracing each other in the exuberance of their joy. So far as we could ascertain the tribe of copperheads was invisible.[10]

The Copperheads may have *seemed* invisible in the post-victory euphoria, but they remained no less active or vocal than before. If anything, they saw the Union's wave of success as an occasion for speaking out all the more fervently in favor of peace. As they saw it, the fact that Robert E. Lee, after two years of fighting, still had the power to invade the Union and engage its troops in the bloodiest combat yet was hardly reason to celebrate. Even in the face of the Union's recent victories, they pointed to the fierce, horrible—and seemingly unending—conflict as a sign that the war was not ultimately winnable:

> The festal demonstrations which have signalled the butcheries of Gettysburg, and the booming of guns over the fall of Vicksburg, cannot divert the people from their intense convictions that blows are no salve for wounded friendship. With a strong conception of the truth, dawning upon them tardily, but irresistibly, they feel that while there has been a fearful addition to the hundreds of thousands of our slain, nothing has been accomplished toward a reconstruction of the Union. A battle has been fought; a stronghold has surrendered; but there have been bloody fields before now in this struggle, and cities and fortresses have succumbed. Neither then nor now, has one hope of reconciliation been engendered out of the blood of the fallen; and amid the shell battered walls of Vicksburg . . . our armies have overcome only so much material strength, but nothing of the spirit of the South.
>
> . . . The graves that this day sadden the hill-sides of Pennsylvania are but so many mounds added to the barriers between the North and South. They promise nothing but augmented hate and bitterness. The obstinacy with which Vicksburg was defended, and the terrible loss of life which it cost us . . . to protect the soil of one of our most populous States, are but evidences of our incompetency to subjugate a foe that has so much vitality and force, and so much willingness to suffer in its cause. The events which are now the themes of public interest, in place of being made the occasion for congratulation, should be accepted as the unimpeachable proofs of the utter hopelessness of a reconstruction by force of arms.
>
> If there is a Peace man in the North who has hitherto remained passive, let the blood that reeks up from the soil of Pennsylvania appeal to him. What better arguments for Peace can there be that those pitiless dispatches that briefly announce the killing and maiming of our countrymen to the extent of fifty thousand? How many more such sacrifices of our best and bravest shall we consent to offer at the shrine of Abolitionism? . . . We have in this heart-sickening record of suffering and carnage, a fresh incentive to fearless, energetic action. . . . We call upon the Democracy to advance the Peace standard loftier now than ever, for never before did Christian duty, patriotism, reason, and every worthy attribute of man so imperatively call for their vigorous opposition to this fiendish appetite for human blood. . . . Now, when war is most hideous is the time for Peace to be most earnestly invoked.[11]

For the moment at least, such words of caution carried little effect. Northerners certainly looked forward to peace. But just having reaped two hard-fought victories, they were positive that it would be a peace earned by the defeat and surrender of the rebels, not by weak-kneed negotiations with them. The Northern press was especially heartened by the auspicious fact that the successes at Gettysburg and Vicksburg—as well as another victory at Helena, Arkansas—happened on the Fourth of July. It seemed to be a sign that the cause of the Union was destined to triumph in the end?

> It is not easy to speak coolly and reflectingly of the recent splendid triumphs of the Union arms. . . . The first day or two after hearing the news must be given up to unrestrained exultation. Patriotic emotions cannot be repressed in times like these. Bells will be rung, salutes will be fired, and there will be spontaneous meetings, processions, illuminations and fireworks. . . . The impulse of the hour is to rejoice over the rout of the invaders from Pennsylvania, over the surrender of the rebel army at Vicksburg, and over

the brightening prospect of a full restoration of the Union [for] which we are fighting this war. . . .

It is a coincidence that one cannot help regarding as peculiarly auspicious, that Grant took Vicksburg, Meade occupied Gettyburg and Prentiss repulsed an attack on Helena on the 4th of July. That memorable day, and the principles consecrated on it, have been repudiated by the rebels. But the Union men cherish the principles of the 4th of July more warmly than ever, and doubtless they fought on that day with a peculiar sense of the sacredness of their cause and of the duty that was before them. Is it any wonder that the rebel soldiers, conscious that they were fighting against the flag they had so often honored on the 4th of July, should have been defeated? The American people will have greater reason than ever for celebrating the anniversary of their independence, now that it has been consecrated anew by glorious victories.[12]

Whereas the Copperheads invoked the humanitarian strains of Christianity to advocate for peace, other pro-war voices in the North detected a different religious message in the Union's recent victories. For the *Evangelist*, the glory of the moment was literally of divine proportions, suffused with evidence of God's goodwill toward the Union war effort:

How strange and sudden are the contrasts in human life, in the fortunes of men and nations—the changes from grief to gladness, or back from joy to sorrow, and from triumph to despair. The human spirit is often cast into the depths, yet scarcely has she begun to sing her De Profundis, when she is raised up again, and begins to sing her song of triumph. Never was this truth more strikingly illustrated than in the events of the past week. One week ago the country was in the extreme of depression and gloom. A tremendous Rebel invasion had brought the war to our very doors. A large section of Pennsylvania was occupied by the enemy, its capital was threatened, Philadelphia, Baltimore, and Washington, were all in danger.

But the week has passed, and how changed the scene! The mighty host of the invader has been swept away; a series of great battles has been fought in swift succession; the force of the enemy has been utterly broken, and his legions that but a few days ago advanced so haughtily to Northern conquest, have been overwhelmed with utter defeat. A change of fortune so sudden and so complete, may well lead us to pause, and ask the reasons for this altered state.

In looking for the causes of this . . . startling change, we award full praise to the skill of our leaders and the discipline and courage of our soldiers. Heroic men! . . . No soldiers of Napoleon or of Wellington ever stood the shock of battle with greater firmness, or more willingly made the sacrifice of their lives. All honor to these brave soldiers of liberty. . . .

But, above all the wisdom, the skill, and the courage of man, do we recognize the interposition of a Higher Power. There is something in the very swiftness and suddenness of this overthrow, that inevitably suggests a stroke of Divine vengeance. . . . Truly it is God who hath given us the victory. He it is who hath raised us up out of the depths, who hath gone forth before our armies, and inspired them with courage for the decisive hour. "Not unto us, not unto us, O Lord, but unto Thy name be the glory." May we acknowledge our Great Deliverer![13]

While most Northerners reveled in the Union's victories, Southern newspapers grappled with feelings of despondency. The fall of Vicksburg—the Confederate Gibraltar—was especially hard to take. As the *Richmond Dispatch* freely admitted, "Our heart and hope was with it." Some papers tried to maintain a brave countenance in the face of defeat, but it was difficult to deny that the public mood was sinking. "Our reverses have come so rapidly and unexpectedly that some of our people appear ready to give up the contest in despair," one paper reported from Georgia.[14] Indeed, the defeats at Gettysburg and Vicksburg gave force and focus to a growing peace movement centered in North Carolina. That state had been one of the last to secede, and now, as the tide of the war seemed to turn decisively against the Confederacy, the *North Carolina Standard* led the way in calling into question the wisdom of continuing to resist the Union. The *Standard* was not an advocate of peace at any price. Rather, it hoped that through negotiations, an agreement could be arranged that would preserve the South's slave-based social system, as well as the lives and dignity of the Southern people. It was a vain hope, really. Why should Northerners agree to such liberal truce terms when they had just won two crucial and grueling victories? Still, the *Standard* reminded its readers that they held their destiny in their own hands, and if they wanted peace, they simply needed to band together and demand it:

> It is a great crime, especially at a time like this, to conceal the truth from the people. We intend to tell them the truth as far as we know it, let the consequences be what they may.
>
> From the beginning of the war to the present the enemy has slowly but surely gained upon us. . . . Vicksburg has fallen, as we feared many months ago it would. Port Hudson has fallen. Charleston, Mobile, and Savannah will probably go next. Gen. Lee is attempting to retire from Maryland with his spoils, but no substantial victory has crowned his arms. We are weaker to-day than when he crossed the Potomac into Maryland. . . . Our fighting population is pretty well exhausted. Every body knows this. . . . On the contrary, our enemies, flushed with triumph, have a large army in the field, and their President has just called for three hundred thousand more. He will get them. The movement on Pennsylvania by Gen. Lee, and the fall of Vicksburg and Port Hudson, have hushed all clamors for peace in the North, and have banded the people there as one man for the prosecution of the war. . . . The war, then, will go on. One side or the other must *conquer*. Will five millions of [Southern] whites conquer twenty millions of the same race? Will they conquer a peace on the very soil of these twenty millions? . . . Northern troops are not cowards,—they fight nearly as well as Southern troops. We cannot achieve signal victories over them on their own soil.
>
> What then? If the worst is destined to overtake us, would it not be wise and prudent to take less than the worst, provided we could do so compatibly with honor? . . .
>
> It is time to consult reason and common sense, and to discard prejudice and passion. Our people must look at and act upon things as they are, and not as they would have them. They must remember *that they are sovereign*—that they are the masters of those who administer the government—that the government was established by *them*, for *their* benefit; and they must not be afraid to utter their opinions freely and boldly. If they want continued, wasting, bloody war, let them say so; if they want peace, let them say so, and let them state the terms on which they would have it. That peace cannot be attained by fighting merely is now apparent to all. . . .
>
> We spoke just now of the worst befalling our people as the result of this war. What *is* the worst? It would be the condition of provincial dependence on the federal government, each State being ruled by a [Northern] military Governor . . . , and the emancipation and arming of our slaves in our midst. That would be the worst. If the war continues is it not likely that this will happen? . . . What then? Must we rush on to our doom? Must the sword still wave, and the strong arm of physical force still exert itself, and no effort be made by mental and moral means to close the war? Why, North-American savages sometimes bury the tomahawk and meet together to smoke the pipe of peace. Are we of the North and South—Christians as we profess to be—more savage than the savages?[15]

For the Standard.

PUBLIC MEETING IN CHATHAM COUNTY.

At a meeting of the citizens of Lick Creek District, Chatham county, July 29, 1863; on motion of William Dickens, Esq., Dr. Pleasant Pattishall was called to the chair, and J P. Badders appointed secretary.

The chairman then stated the object of the meeting, after which the following preamble and resolutions were unanimously adopted:

WHEREAS, The time has arrived that every true friend of liberty should exercise the right, which is guaranteed under the Constitution of North-Carolina, to express his opinions with regard to the public good; and whereas, we are fully of the opinion that the condition of our people is such as to demand every lover of life and liberty to be willing to adopt some method, and to put forth some effort to stop this wicked and bloody war; therefore,

Resolved, That we are opposed to the continuance of this unholy war to the destruction of our lives and property.

Resolved, That we are in favor of any peace that will secure our rights, and which will not tend to enslave us.

Resolved, That we will resist the appointment of any man from another State for the purpose of collecting tythes from the citizens of this State, over the head of her own sons.

Resolved, That we agree to abide by a majority of the voters of North-Carolina in any plan that may be devised in Convention assembled, or otherwise.

Resolved, That we heartily endorse and approve the course pursued by W. W. Holden, Editor of the Raleigh *Standard*, relative to the peace question.

Resolved, That we hereby pledge our lives, our sacred honor, and our property, for the maintenance of any honorable effort that will secure the people of this State a speedy peace.

Resolved, That the proceedings of this meeting be sent to the Editor of the Raleigh *Standard* for publication.

Resolved further, That we recommend that similar meetings be held in all the districts of Chatham county.

On motion, the meeting adjourned.

PLEASANT PATTISHALL, Chm'n.

J. P. BADDERS, Sec'y

North Carolina Weekly Standard, August 12, 1863. In response to editorials by W. W. Holden of the *North Carolina Standard,* which advocated peace negotiations, several counties in North Carolina organized public meetings where they passed resolutions condemning the war and seconding Holden's pleas for peace.

In the weeks following this call for peace negotiations, public representatives in counties across the state of North Carolina began passing resolutions (which the *Standard* then published) advocating that Northerners and Southerners come together "as brethren, to put a stop to the present cruel, savage and unchristian war"—"this disastrous war"—"this unnatural and bloody war"—"this wicked war"—"this unholy war." Echoing the *Standard*'s own sentiments, they asserted that it was the democratic right of the Southern people to demand an end to the devastation, chaos, and horrendous wasting of human lives. Meanwhile, along the Mississippi, Southerners fearful that the Yankees would follow up their victory at Vicksburg with a triumphant sweep through the entire region joined the growing chorus in favor of negotiations. Again, these were not calls for the unconditional surrender of the Confederacy; nevertheless, the high-toned spirit of unity that had swept over the South in 1861 was clearly cracking.[16]

Meanwhile, Southern supporters of the war looked to the press to give the country direction and hope in this time of adversity. As one Southerner wrote in a letter to the *Augusta Constitutionalist*, "I call upon the editors of our Confederacy, the class, who more than any other, control the feelings and the energies of the people, to look our danger fully in the face . . . and advocate the measures necessary in this trying hour." It was the duty of the newspapers to serve as war propagandists and to stir the public to take immediate and concerted action in defense of the Confederacy.[17] The masses had to be made to understand that although the momentum of the war had tipped in favor of the Union, they were the makers of their own fates. If they allowed themselves to become paralyzed by fear and demoralized by the military reverses they had suffered, then the Confederacy surely would be crushed. But if they resolved to sacrifice everything for freedom—if they each made a personal commitment to never give up the fight—then the Confederacy would eventually triumph. Even though Union troops might succeed in occupying the entire country, the Confederacy could still win its independence, so long as the will of the people remained unbroken:

> The Southern people had flattered themselves that with Vicksburg holding out against the enemy, and

Gen. Lee marching in triumph beyond the border, the war would soon be closed. But Vicksburg has fallen, Gen. Lee has been driven back across the Potomac, and our people are gloomy and desponding. Hope has been deferred, and the popular heart has grown very sick. We ourself . . . will not seek to disguise the fact that our own feelings have participated in the general depression.

When, a few weeks ago, we read that our army under Gen. Lee had crossed the Potomac, we trembled for the consequences—literally and truly, we trembled. It is an unmanly confession, perhaps, but our nerves were altogether unstrung. The act of invading the enemy's territory, with the disparity between our numerical strengths, was one so pregnant with dire consequences that we, for one, were entirely unmanned in its contemplation. The stake which depended upon the cast of the die was altogether too overwhelming for us to contemplate the throw with equanimity. Some of our worst fears have been realized—thank God, not our worst ones—for we did fear the total destruction of Lee's army. Let us, with devout hearts, be truly grateful to Almighty God that that noble army again pitches its tents upon Southern soil.

The consequence of the fall of Vicksburg, and the failure of Gen. Lee's plans, is an indefinite postponement of any idea of peace. We believe that we shall yet reach an acknowledgement of our independence, but it will be through long years of blood and toil. In the mean time, let us look our difficulties coolly in the face, and see what they are, and what it is we have to contend against. . . .

Not only has Vicksburg fallen, and Gen. Lee failed in his invasive policy, but Jackson [the capital of Mississippi] has followed in the wake of its sister by the river, and the enemy is closely pressing upon Charleston. Suppose Charleston falls, and then Savannah—there is no need then of yielding the fight. . . . Should the enemy occupy all of our territory, the Southern people should determine never to have any part nor lot in the yankee government. They might, for awhile, drive us to the polls at the point of the bayonet, and force us to vote for candidates of their dictation, but it would be a costly government that had to keep a guard of gendarmes at every ballot box.

Even if the enemy succeeds in conquering us, and occupying all our territory, what will they do with us then? To rule us, after they conquer us, will then be their trouble. . . . Shall we unite with the yankees any further than they can force us to do it? No! if they conquer us, let us hate them, hold ourselves aloof from them, and pray for a foreign war in which we may become the allies of the yankee enemy, and strike another blow for freedom, at least from him. The cause need not be lost even if we are temporarily conquered.[18]

"*Let us hate them.*" It is common to assume that people instinctively hate what they fear, that hate is driven by fear. The hope of the Southern press, however, was that hate would drive away all fears. After two years of war, and two years' worth of newspaper editorials about the war, Southerners had to know that the consequences of defeat would be dreadful. Not only did giving up the fight mean giving up slavery, it meant giving up their lands and homes, their honor, their pride, their freedom—their reasons for living—to Yankee masters who would lord it over them with an iron fist. "Have we seriously contemplated the humiliation and disgrace—the endless and unutterable infamy of subjugation and slavery—at the hands of the fiends in human shape who come to take our homes from us," one paper asked of its patrons. "Better to die in a moment covered with glory," rushing headlong toward the "bloody gates" of martyrdom, "than to linger like cowards."[19] As the fortunes of the Confederacy faltered, the Southern people still had to maintain their honor and protect themselves from humiliation at all costs. Southerners had long spoken of the war as a matter of "do or die," and now, explained the *Montgomery Mail*, it was time to show that these were not empty words:

> The fortune of war for this week, is against us. What then? . . . Shall our proud banners droop, or our faith fail, or our trust in a just providence grow feeble? God forbid! All that we have already done, and vowed to do; all our past, all our future, call on us, pledge us, compel us to read in all that has befallen but [one] lesson—that we must repair our faults, reinforce our strength where it is weak, redouble our efforts, and use all our resources so as to present a stern front of resistance to the base and brutal foe who wages so persistent a war for our destruction. We have to remember that by our acts of secession and our defiance of all consequences, we are simply bound to make good that secession, or die. We have to remember that we Confederates have always loudly professed towards these Yankees, not hatred and defiance only, but ineffable scorn and disdain also; and that if we suffer our country now to be subdued by a race we despise so much, it were better for us we had never been born. Those who die in stern resistance will then be the only fortunate and happy Confederates. . . . Thrice; indeed, and four times blessed, will be the dead, whose eyes will never behold the degradation of their country; and ten thousand times accursed the unhappy man condemned to live on and beget vassals to Yankee lords!
>
> It may be needless to urge this topic. . . . We boast that we have in our veins that good blood which will not sink, but rises higher for every blow. Now is the time to show it.—The army we have raised, the Government we have created, have never failed us yet; let us not fail them now. Let them be maintained and strengthened by every man able to bear arms. . . . The spirit that should live and burn in every bosom this day, is a haughty disdain of life, either for ourselves or those who are dearest to us, unless that life be crowned with the wreath of glory and of freedom. With such a spirit, animating such a people, we are sure of our ultimate triumph, and shall think it cheap, purchased with best blood.[20]

Moreover, as the *Memphis Appeal* pointed out, the people of the Confederacy had a blood debt to account for, comprising the tens of thousands of men who had already died in the country's defense. Their memory and their honor were now at stake in the outcome:

> Two hundred thousands of our finest young men have lost life or limb in this war. They shed their blood, they risked and lost their lives, under the impression that they were doing an honorable and rightful thing—that they were fighting for their country! Their fathers, their wives, their children, are proud to say, my son was killed at Gettysburg, my husband fell at Richmond, my father, my brother, my uncle was one of the brave men who bled for the land in the great war. But what were all these persons if the Union never has been dissolved—if the Confederacy is an illegal combination—if its "so called" laws have no authority? There is no uncertainty—they were criminals, traitors. Their graves are dishonorable graves. They did not fight for their country. THEY FOUGHT AGAINST THEIR COUNTRY. They lifted up parricidal and sacrilegious hands against that thing which every good man is bound to protect. They did not kill enemies, but committed murder on their fellow-citizens. Their names must be disgraced; their memory a memory of shame to all their posterity, friends and relations. Is there any man so mean and poor of heart as to be willing to reward the friend, the son, the father, the cousin, who has fought for him and his, with that ignominy? Perish all things; perish altogether, rather than so desert, so betray, the generous and the unfortunate.[21]

As far as most editors were concerned, the only way to deal with the recent defeats was for Southern men to grab their guns and throw all hesitation to the winds.

The Confederacy needed to mobilize all available manpower into the army to have any chance of turning the tide of the war. Yet, as the nation was facing its greatest crisis yet, many men of military age still were not in the ranks. Some of them had secured exemptions from military service or had hired substitutes, in keeping with the Confederacy's conscription laws. Others, however, were simply absent without leave. This had been a problem for the Confederacy even before the summer of 1863, but the number of deserters only continued to climb, and by the end of the year, around 33 percent of the troops were AWOL.[22] In an effort to stem the tide, Lee made a public address to deserters from the Army of Northern Virginia, ordering them to return to their posts. Jefferson Davis also issued the following proclamation of amnesty to wayward soldiers. By the president's request, newspapers across the Confederacy printed it for twenty-one consecutive days:

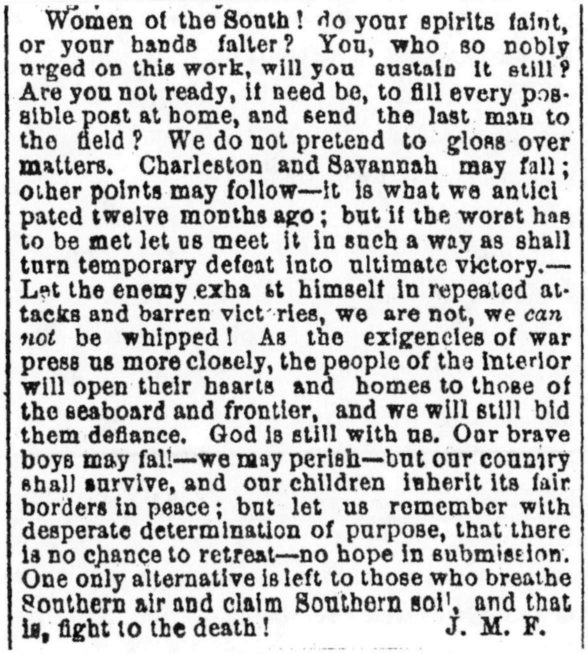
Women of the South! do your spirits faint, or your hands falter? You, who so nobly urged on this work, will you sustain it still? Are you not ready, if need be, to fill every possible post at home, and send the last man to the field? We do not pretend to gloss over matters. Charleston and Savannah may fall; other points may follow—it is what we antici pated twelve months ago; but if the worst has to be met let us meet it in such a way as shall turn temporary defeat into ultimate victory.—Let the enemy exha st himself in repeated attacks and barren vict ries, we are not, we *can not* be whipped! As the exigencies of war press us more closely, the people of the interior will open their hearts and homes to those of the seaboard and frontier, and we will still bid them defiance. God is still with us. Our brave boys may fall—we may perish—but our country shall survive, and our children inherit its fair borders in peace; but let us remember with desperate determination of purpose, that there is no chance to retreat—no hope in submission. One only alternative is left to those who breathe Southern air and claim Southern soil, and that is, fight to the death! J. M. F.

Savannah Republican, July 19, 1863.
In the main, the Southern press responded to the setbacks at Vicksburg and Gettysburg with calls for greater resolve and continued sacrifices. Many of these appeals were made directly to Southern women, who were expected to be cheerful in the face of defeat and ready to see their men "fight to the death."

> After more than two years of warfare scarcely equalled in the number, magnitude, and fearful carnage of its battles; . . . your enemies continue a struggle in which our final triumph must be inevitable. Unduly elated with their recent successes, they imagine that temporary reverses can quell your spirit or shake your determination, and they are now gathering heavy masses for a general invasion, in the vain hope that by a desperate effort, success may at length be reached.
>
> You know too well, my countrymen, what they mean by success. Their malignant rage aims at nothing less than the extermination of yourselves, your wives and children. They seek to destroy what they cannot plunder. They propose as the spoils of victory that your homes shall be partitioned among the wretches whose atrocious cruelties have stamped infamy on their government. They design to incite servile insurrection and light the fires of incendiarism whenever they can reach your homes. . . .
>
> Fellow citizens, no alternative is left to you but victory, or subjugation, slavery and the utter ruin of yourselves, your families and your country. The victory is within your reach. You need but stretch forth your hands to grasp it. . . . The men now absent from their posts would, if present in the field, suffice . . . to secure us victory in the struggle now impending.
>
> I call on you, then, my countrymen, to hasten to your camps, in obedience to the dictates of honor and of duty, and summon those who have absented themselves without leave . . . to repair without delay to their respective commands, and I do hereby declare that I grant a general pardon and amnesty to all officers and men within the Confederacy, now absent without leave, who shall, with the least possible delay, return to their proper posts of duty. . . .
>
> Finally, I conjure my country women—the wives,

> sisters and daughters of the Confederacy—to use their all powerful influence in aid of this call . . . and to take care that none who owe service in the field shall be sheltered at home from the disgrace of having deserted their duty to their families, to their country, and to their God.[23]

This final appeal to the women of the Confederacy was one that the newspapers strongly seconded. It was well known that men were able to desert the army because women were welcoming them home and even hiding them from conscript officers when necessary. In hopes of rallying women to honor their patriotic duty, the *Richmond Enquirer* addressed them urgently, assuring them not only of the precarious state of the country but also of the painful degradation they would suffer if the Confederacy were ever totally overrun:

> The President appeals to the women of the Confederacy, and with good reason; for not even the men have so deep and dread[ful] an interest in this affair as they have. Men can at least fight to the last, and die, and have done with it. Even the cowards can at least fly to other countries, change their shameful names, spend their vile gains, and "peep about to find themselves dishonorable graves." But the women can neither fight nor fly. They must follow the fortunes of the country; and if it be subdued by that Yankee nation, must only bow their proud heads to their destiny and take the fate to which the men *will have left them*. Many may be employed as governesses to teach small Yankees; many, owing to their experience in ruling negro households, may get service as housekeepers, in their own houses, to superintend their own slaves for their new [Yankee] mistresses. Some may be fancied, as concubines, by Yankee dry goods merchants who have turned brigadiers or quartermasters.
>
> We do assure the women of the Confederate States that in these pictures is no color of exaggeration. The President, who never exaggerates, states plainly what the enemy's success in this war means: "Their malignant rage aims at nothing less than the extermination of yourselves, your wives and children.—They seek to destroy what they cannot plunder. They propose, as the spoils of victory, that your homes shall be partitioned among the wretches whose atrocious cruelties have stamped infamy on their government. . . . No alternative is left to you but victory—or subjugation, and utter ruin." Just so; this is precisely the alternative; there is no middle ground to rest upon. Either we go up and our enemies *down*, or *vise versa*. No wonder an appeal is made, then, to the women to aid in this crisis. None have so momentous an interest; and none, as we firmly believe, wield so much power. They can do more for us this day than the President with all his conscript guards, . . . or General Lee with his appeals to the stragglers. *They* know those stragglers, one by one, and where they are to be found. They, the mothers and the sisters, may, if they will, be a conscript guard impossible to be evaded. They know whose furloughs are out, whose wounds are healed, who are lingering idly about home . . . boasting of the perils they have *passed*, philandering and making love, while far away on some northern field the bronzed veterans of the old army are dressing their thinned ranks to face the storm of battle. . . .
>
> Will not the women help us, then, to set every man in his place? Will they not refuse so much as to speak to any one who evades his duty? We all know that they, by combining together, can drive all stragglers at once to the field; they can make existence intolerable to those who stay; but to those who go, and do the *devoir* of gallant gentlemen, they can promise paradise. . . . If our soldiers do their duty now they can save the country and make it the proudest nation upon earth; *if not*, better for them they had never been born![24]

In the thoroughly Christian South, human effort remained only part of the equation for achieving victory. The rest—the better part, really—was in God's hands. Despite the shattering defeats at Gettysburg and Vicksburg, the Southern papers insisted that God remained on the Confederacy's side. They would not allow their readers to become demoralized by the notion that He had deserted them. "It is impossible to believe that God ever intended that this fair domain and this Christian people, should be the prey of worse than vandal barbarism and savage cruelty and oppression," counseled one observer of events. It was true that God had allowed the Confederacy to suffer these terrible reverses, but that did not change the fact that He was ready to come to the nation's defense. The Southern people simply had to show that they were *deserving* of His blessing. In papers secular and religious, editors blasted Southerners for their "accursed greed for gold"—the Mammon-worshiping, extortionist practices that drove up prices and caused the Confederacy so much economic and emotional distress. Southerners had to turn away from such unholy dealings and give themselves to God. Devout and continual prayer, argued the *Christian Index*, would reach God's ear and win for the Confederacy the strong arm of His protection:

> The war in which we have been engaged for more than two years, is no ordinary one. It has taxed us to the utmost in men and means. Most extraordinary exertions have to be used, and extraordinary self-denial has to be practiced in order to obtain success.—And with all this, we have again and again failed to accomplish what we desired.
>
> In a war of such magnitude, it will not do to fold our hands, and wait for the Lord to help us. We must strain every nerve and make use of every means, God has given us. And what are the means? Guns, powder, men, horses, food, brains and bayonets—Doubtless these are among the means that have to be used in extraordinary measure for this no ordinary war. But are these the only means to be used? Is not prayer just as much a means of success as shot and shell? Now if shot and shell have to be used abundantly, should not prayer be used in the same way? . . . Does not this war as much demand extraordinary praying, as extraordinary shelling? We think there can be no difference of opinion upon such a point. . . . We therefore suggest to our readers, that they go by themselves once in every day and plead with God for their country; and plead *earnestly*; that God, for his dear Son Jesus Christ's sake, would vouchsafe us deliverance from our enemies. . . . We will not succeed unless God be on our side. He will be on our side if we ask him—if we ask him aright—both as to spirit and to zeal. This is no ordinary war and no ordinary means will carry us through it. Our soldiers have to exercise no ordinary self-denial. Should we not be willing to do the same, in praying for our country?[25]

In the moral calculus of the Confederacy, military defeat was no reason for despondency. The losses at Gettysburg and Vicksburg, while hurtful, did not have to be totally ruinous. If the Southern people approached these setbacks not only manfully but faithfully, they could regain the upper hand. They had to stand firm in their conviction that the Yankees, in their evilness, could never be blessed with ultimate success. As one newspaper was quick to avow, "We are confident their joy will shortly be turned into sorrow, their mirth into sadness. *The triumphing of the wicked is short*."[26] Indeed, as these lines were being written, Northerners were already learning just how ephemeral the sweet taste of victory could be.

The World

MORNING COURIER AND NEW-YORK ENQUIRER.

Vol. III. No. 959. Cour. & Enq'r. 3... | NEW-YORK: WEDNESDAY, JULY 15, 1863. | PRICE THREE CENTS.

THE RIOT

New-York City Declared in a State of Insurrection.

PROCLAMATION BY GOV. SEYMOUR.

Law to be Maintained in New-York by the Governor of New-York.

Second Day of the Armed Opposition to the Conscription.

Terrible Scenes in the Metropolis.

MOBS ALL OVER.

The Military and Police Using Fire-arms.

Gallantry of the Police and Rage of the Mob.

SPEECH OF GOVERNOR SEYMOUR.

CONTINUOUS CONFLAGRATIONS.

Schools, Private Residences, Hotels, Stores, and Station Houses Burned or Sacked.

Gen. Sandford's Pickets Driven.

The Riot Raging Late Last Night.

Five Thousand Troops in the City and many more to Arrive To-day.

&c., &c., &c.

PROCLAMATIONS OF GOV. SEYMOUR.

Whereas, It is manifest that combinations for forcible resistance to the laws of the State of New-York and the execution of civil and criminal process exist in the city and county of New-York, whereby the peace and safety of the city, and the lives and property of its inhabitants, are endangered; and

Whereas, The power of the said city and county has been exerted, and is not sufficient to enable the officers of the said city and county to maintain the laws of the state and execute the legal process of its officers; and

Whereas, Application has been made to me by the sheriff of the city and county of New-York, to declare the said city and county to be in a state of insurrection;

Now therefore I, HORATIO SEYMOUR, Governor of the State of New-York, and Commander-in-chief of the forces of the same, do in its name, and by its authority, issue this proclamation, in accordance with the statute in such cases made and provided, and do hereby declare the city and county of New-York to be in a state of insurrection, and give notice to all persons that the means provided by the laws of this state for the maintenance of law and order will be employed to whatever degree may be necessary, and that all persons who shall, after the publication of this proclamation, "resist, or aid or assist in resisting, any force ordered out by the governor to quell or suppress such insurrection," will

every citizen will be properly guarded and defended by the chief magistrate of the state.

I do therefore call upon all persons engaged in these riotous proceedings to retire to their homes and employments, declaring to them that unless they do so at once, I shall use all the power necessary to restore the peace and order of the city. I also call upon all well-disposed persons not enrolled for the preservation of order to pursue their ordinary avocations.

Let all citizens stand firmly by the constituted authorities, sustaining law and order in the city, and ready to answer any such demand as circumstances may render necessary for me to make upon their services; and they may rely upon a rigid enforcement of the laws of this state against all who violate them.

HORATIO SEYMOUR, Governor.

New-York, July 14, 1863.

NOTICE.

FOR THE PURPOSE OF PERFECTING A CITIZENS' ORGANIZATION.

All citizens are requested to assemble immediately at the following places, when they will be enrolled under the direction of the persons hereinafter mentioned, viz.:

City Assembly Rooms.—General Ward B. Burnett.

Seventh Regiment Armory.—General Abram Duryea, Major S. R. Pinckney, Colonel John W. Avery.

Central Market Drill-Rooms.—Colonel John O. McGregor, Charles G. Cornell, Captain John D. Ottiwell.

Room N. E. corner Thirty-second street and Broadway.—Colonel J. Mansfield Davis, Captain R. Smedberg, Fourteenth Regiment U. S. A.

City Hall.—Colonel Robert B. Shannon, Captain I. Rynders, Captain T. S. Murphy.

No. 220 Third street.—Captain H. Sowur, F. Repper.

By order of HORATIO SEYMOUR, Governor.

Josiah T. Miller, Inspector-General.

The city yesterday morning was gloomy and warlike. Business was to a great extent suspended, crowds of men with anxious and excited looks filled the streets, squads of policemen and soldiers marched hither and thither toward scenes of violence with weapons ready for use. Anxious knots of people gathered at corners, and nothing was talked of but the draft and the riot. Such omnibuses and cars as commenced running in the morning were crowded, but before noon all cars and stages in the city had stopped their trips and gave place to hacks and a very few carts. Broadway was deserted by the gay throng that usually promenades there in the afternoon—they had given place to a continuous march of police, of military, of citizens, of ominous-looking men with ragged clothes, bronzed faces, and hard hands, moving to the aid of the rioters. Hundreds, from the general suspension of business, were led to the scene of disorder who might otherwise have been still better employed. The laborers on all new buildings, in large manufacturing establishments, the stevedores and other laborers along the docks all left off work, being in many instances compelled to do so by the mob. In some cases, in upper parts of the city, they would command persons to come from their doors to join their ranks, under threat of having their houses burned in the evening. Everywhere, almost the whole middle and laboring classes turned out in aid of the rioters. Other citizens merely looked on, as a general thing with more apparent curiosity than indignation. Eating-houses and saloons where negroes had been employed were closed, or white men had been substituted as waiters. Crowds gathered around the bulletins of newspapers, and no one thought of the fate of Meade's or Lee's army, and all news out of town had utterly lost its interest. The newsboys were selling extras with a rapidity unequaled in any previous time of excitement. They used sometimes the phraseology that they have been accustomed to since the war, only changing the name of the place, as "Terrible battle in the Fourteenth ward!" Others took up the cry, "Hor-r-rible riot in the Second avenue!" About dark a number of newboys were running through the Park and down Chatham street, shouting frantically, "Extra-a-a! Capture of Horace Greeley!" But rumors passed from lip to lip faster than extras could be printed; and every person, coming from whatever part of the city he might, had his budget of incidents or startling events to narrate. The riot seemed extended to every part of the city.

The fire-bells were ringing at very frequent intervals from early morning until late in the night, and the cheers and cries of firemen were heard through all the streets as the "boys" drew their machines in every direction to the rescue of life and property. All the ordinary noises of the business life and activity of the great city gave place to an unnatural quiet, frequently disturbed by appalling sounds of riot and disorder. The taking of life and the destruction of buildings far exceeded that of the day before. In several places fights occurred between the mob and the militia, resulting in many killed. The events of the day are given in detail below.

SPECIAL MEETING CALLED OF BOARD OF ALDERMEN.

The Board of Aldermen have issued a call for a special meeting, to be held to-day, the 15th instant, at 11 o'clock A. M., of which the following is a copy:

NEW-YORK, July 14, 1863.

David T. Valentine, Esq., Clerk of the Common Council:

SIR: You will please notify the members of the Board of Aldermen to meet in special session in the Chamber of the Board, City Hall, on Wednesday, the 15th day of July instant, at 11 o'clock A. M., for the purpose of transacting such public business as may come before the Board.

JOHN HARDY, Alderman, 11th District.
LEWIS R. RYERS, Alderman, 9th Dist.
CHAS. H. HALL, Alderman, 4th Dist.
JOHN FOX, Alderman, 1st Dist.
GEO. A. JEREMIAH, Alderman, 10th Dist.
JOHN D. OTTIWELL, Alderman, 14th Dist.
CHARLES J. CHIPP, Alderman, 7th Dist.
JOHN T. HENRY, Alderman, 3d Dist.

SALE OF AMMUNITION FORBIDDEN.

Mayor Opdyke has issued the following enjoinment:

MAYOR'S OFFICE, NEW-YORK, July 14, 1863.

It is highly important to the peace of the city and the suppression of the existing riot, that the rioters shall not be allowed to furnish themselves with arms

tained at headquarters the regulars under his command. Upon hearing of the outbreak General Brown sent Lieutenant Wood with a company of regulars from Fort Lafayette and a company of marines to the scene of action. They marched along Houston street to the Bowery and down the Bowery to Grand and Pitt street, where they found the rioters in full force. The crowd then rushed toward the soldiers, whom Lieutenant Wood at once drew up in *quasi* line of battle. One of the ringleaders attempted to speak to the commanding officer, but was waved aside. This was the signal for a shower of stones. In response the soldiers were ordered to fire over the heads of the people, which only made matters worse, and the lieutenant was compelled to order the troops to fire in earnest. The first volley killed twelve men and two children, and wounded seventeen others. Seeing that preparations were making for another volley, the mob fled in all directions.

ANOTHER ACCOUNT.

There is another account of this disturbance which is more explicit even than the one just recited. A couple of companies of marines were coming up Delancey street from the ferry, when, as they reached the corner of Pitt street, they met a large procession of men, headed by a banner bearing the inscription, "NO DRAFT." The marines filed three abreast, when the leader stepped up to the lieutenant in command, saying:

"Let us pass, sir."

"You cannot pass here," was the laconic reply.

Nothing daunted the leader called to his adherents to come on, and started to advance in spite of the marines, when the latter were ordered to fire. The leader seemed to think the order all bombast, for he turned his back to the muskets, regardless of his fate. "Ready," "Aim," "Fire!" rang along the lines of the little company, and the stalwart rioter fell pierced with half a dozen balls. Eight others were also shot dead, and several were wounded, including two women and one or two children. Upon this the mob hastily dispersed, leaving the marines in possession of the field.

AT THE ARSENAL.

On Monday night the streets in the vicinity of the arsenal, corner of Seventh avenue and Thirty-fifth street, were quite quiet and deserted. Pickets were thrown out in every direction. Inside of the arsenal everything betokened vigorous preparations for the morrow. Commissary-General James A. Farwell, immediately on his arrival, commenced distributing arms and ammunition to the volunteers who had come to assist in the city's defense.

But little sleep was enjoyed on Monday night. At an early hour yesterday morning, the commissary-general, assisted by his brother, Colonel William R. Farrell, served out breakfast. The rations had been obtained with great difficulty from the different parts of the city, and were eagerly devoured by the garrison.

A FIGHT.

During the morning information was received that a number of people had congregated in the Sixteenth ward. Captain Phillips and Lieutenant Demorest were instantly started off with a company of twenty-five volunteer citizens to disperse the crowd. They were stoned from Thirty fifth to Twenty-seventh streets. Bricks and every other available missile flew around fast and thick. On reaching Twenty-seventh street, one of the volunteers was struck in the head with a brickbat; he instantly fell to the rear. Captain Phillips then ordered his men to charge, which they did, and the crowd dispersed in every direction.

THE GARRISON AT THE ARSENAL

was composed of Company A, Eleventh Regiment New-York Volunteers, Captain A. B. Sage; Company K, Eleventh Regiment New-York Volunteers, Captain John Canty, and one or two other companies.

THE EXCITEMENT IN THE VICINITY.

Around and in the arsenal yesterday all was excitement and commotion. The streets were blockaded with the militia. Several 32-pounder howitzers were placed on all the streets leading to it. People were not allowed to pass through any of the streets in the vicinity, and residents found it extremely difficult to reach their homes. All day drunken individuals and some isolated rioters were arrested by the guard and imprisoned in the arsenal. Occasionally one of them would throw out insulting remarks to the guard, and in many cases attempted to force a passage through the street. Such characters were cared for. No carriages were allowed to pass. Business in this section, as well as in other parts of the city, was suspended.

On every corner in the vicinity there was a throng of laboring men, boys, and women, some counselling violence at once; others discussing their power to do anything, and many allowing their judgment to be overcome by frequent potations of ardent spirits.

Drs. J. W. Powell and H. S. Gilbert are in attendance at the hospital.

FEARFUL COLLISION IN SECOND AVENUE.

Several hundred of the rioters assembled at the corner of Second avenue and Twenty-second street at about noon, and stood in groups discussing the incidents of the previous day, and talking about the best means of putting themselves on a footing to resist the draft and overcome the police and any forces that might be brought against them. In nearly each crowd there seemed to be one or two individuals of better appearance and apparel than the rest, who incited those surrounding them to take forcible measures, and expressed full sympathy with such movements; but when requested to become leaders, as they frequently were, they modestly declined, disclaiming the proper qualifications for the position. It was noticeable that these individuals who were so zealous in urging others to acts of violence, were nowhere to be seen when these scenes were being enacted, and sedulously avoided any chance of coming in collision with those deputed to disperse the rioters. The crowds in the vicinity grew larger and larger. The factories and shops in the neighborhood were visited and threats were made to sack and burn each establishment unless they were closed, and the workmen turned out and joined the forces of the rioters. Nearly every place of business and workshop was therefore closed, and the men who did not take an active part with the mob stood looking on at the street corners. It was known that there were some four or five hundred carbines in the Union Steam Works building, on the corner of Twenty-third street and Second avenue, which were saved from the arsenal on the opposite side of the street and secreted there, when the arsenal was burned by the mob on the day previous. It was de-

possession of the ground around the Union Steam Works, and remained there till the crowd seemed to have entirely dispered.

THE RIOTERS REASSEMBLE.

Soon after the police force marched away, the mob, largely augmented in numbers, again took full possession of the building, and having armed themselves, shouted defiance to soldiers and policemen. The Eighteenth ward police again attempted to drive them off, but were themselves forced back, and many of them badly hurt.

COLLISION WITH THE MILITARY AND POLICE.

At half-past two a large force of police and enrolled citizens under Capt. Helme, accompanied by a detachment of regulars under Capt. Franklin, which had been hurriedly dispatched thither, arrived in the vicinity, and were so placed as to take the factory by storm and disarm the mob at all hazards. The force was divided in squads so as to come forward from all directions toward the building. The mob there were busily preparing themselves for a desperate resistance, and the surrounding streets were filled with an excited crowd. The police and military came briskly forward, and were received in many places with a storm of stones, brick and shot. The regulars fired at the crowd in each instance where they did not immediately disperse, and volleys were discharged down First and Second avenues, as well as along Twenty-second street. The policemen also made liberal use of their revolvers. The streets were entirely cleared in a few moments, and the building containing the arms was again taken possession of. The police behaved with great gallantry, and their charge upon the rioters, who had armed themselves with carbines, was so impetuous that they met with but little opposition, the mob throwing away their guns and making the best use of their legs to get away, screaming and howling with pain, as the clubs were playing with terrible force upon them. A large number of the rioters were killed and wounded, and many citizens who had taken no part in the acts of violence, as well as a number of women and children, were shot in the streets. Some of them were struck half a mile away from the scene of the riot. Four young girls were shot in Twenty-second street, and a fine-looking little boy, who was alone in First avenue, near Twentieth street, was shot through the shoulder. An intelligent-appearing and well-dressed young man, while walking up First avenue near Nineteenth street, was shot in the left breast, the ball passing through the body. He was taken into a dwelling house near by and every attention paid him, but he soon became insensible, and survived but a short time. His name was Williams, and he was a resident of Brooklyn.

THE CARBINES TAKEN POSSESSION OF.

After the police had scattered the mob they took possession of the carbines, each man having one, and a wagon was loaded with the remainder, which they took along. The police and the military then marched down Fourth avenue, the regulars bringing up the rear. As they came opposite Tompkin's Market a number of the members of the Seventh Regiment who were in the armory made their appearance, and great cheering followed. The soldiers cheered for "law and order" and the New-York police, and the police cheered for the Seventh Regiment. The police then proceeded to the headquarters in Mulberry street.

SCENES AFTER THE CONFLICT.

The police having departed from the locality of the riot large crowds again assembled in the streets, and from every window women again looked out. The dead bodies of the killed were to be seen being borne away by their friends, the blood trickling on the pavement. Pools of blood would be met at frequent intervals, and in a large number of the houses lay the wounded writhing in pain.

Crowds were congregated at every corner, excitedly, though not loudly expressing each his determination to avenge the death of their friends, and urging some concerted measures for organization and the procurement of arms. One man mounted an awning and harangued with much volubility the crowd below, urging vengeance for the murder (as he called it) of the women and children who had been killed. They had not fought aright. They should go upon the house-tops and hurl bricks from the chimneys upon those who opposed them. "All we want is a leader," said he, "and then we will go to victory or the devil." He was vehemently cheered by the crowd, and they unanimously affirmed that he was a fit one for a leader. He consented to assume command, and, jumping down, called upon all to follow him and punish the aristocrats of Fifth avenue. He proceeded up Twenty-second street, but the crowd were not enthusiastic to follow, and his adherents comprised two or three dozen boys and six or eight men. He stopped, and his lieutenant reproached the halting crowd for their want of spirit. Harangues were made to each of the several crowds in the vicinity, and it was finally determined to meet last evening at 9 o'clock, and determine upon their course of action.

A FEMALE EXHORTER.

A middle-aged Irish woman addressed a large crowd at the corner of Twenty-first street and Second avenue, expressing in strong terms her contempt of the behavior of the mob when attacked by the police. After such an exhibition of cowardliness they ought to be ashamed ever again to show their heads. There were as many of them with carbines in their hands as there were of the police, she said, but instead of bravely defending themselves they threw down their weapons and with abject whines allowed themselves to be pummelled and struck to the ground.

MAYOR OPDYKE'S HOUSE SACKED.

There was a report in the forenoon that the mob had sacked and burned Mayor Opdyke's house, number 79 Fifth avenue. Happily the rumor was somewhat exaggerated. The facts are these: At about ten and a half o'clock the crowd proceeded to his residence and made a formal attack upon it, with the evident intention of demolishing the building. Half an hour later the juvenile portions of the mob scampered into the house and began to appropriate whatever they could lay their hands on. At this juncture a number of gentlemen living in the neighborhood, armed with heavy bludgeons, rushed into the house and drove out the boys. The mob then set up the cry of "Sack the house," "Burn it to the ground," but the aforesaid gentlemen appeared so determined to resist any attempt at further violence that the rioters stood aloof. Just then a body of some 150 po-

Stoltz, of the Seventeenth New-York Volunteers, was shot in the neck and right cheek by an officer for cowardice.

The wounded were removed to the arsenal, where hey were properly cared for.

HE BECOMES ALARMED.

General Sandford immediately sent the following dispatch to the police headquarters:

Police Commissioners, 300 Mulberry street, under Brig. Gen. Brown:

Send me two hundred policemen if you can: if not, send me as many of the troops as possible. We are attacked. My pickets driven in.

C. W. SANDFORD, Major-General.

RIOT IN THIRTY-FOURTH STREET.

Early yesterday morning there was a large gathering in the vicinity of Second avenue and Thirty-fourth street, who soon commenced cutting the telegraph poles, breaking the wires, and making other riotous demonstrations. A force of 300 policemen were therefore sent from headquarters under Inspector Carpenter to disperse the mob and protect property in the neighborhood. Before the police arrived, the mob having been informed that Colonel H. F. O'Brien, of the Eleventh regiment, whose residence was not far distant, had tendered his services and those of his command for the suppression of the riot, immediately proceeded to his residence, and notifying the family to leave, sacked the house, completely destroying the furniture and all movable articles therein. The police having marched from the headquarters to the Bowery, went to Thirty-second street in the Third avenue cars. The track at this point having been obstructed, they marched up the avenue in solid file, the crowd on either side of the street quietly looking on as they proceeded. When they had passed Thirty-fourth street, the rioters suddenly closed in upon them on all sides, and a shower of missiles was hurled at them, the women on the house-tops and at the windows actively doing their part in aid of the mob below. The suddenness of the attack caused the officers for a moment to waver, but they soon rallied, fired their revolvers upon the masses around them, and then made a furious charge, quickly driving the rioters into the houses and around the street corners. In a very few moments all the streets were cleared, and the police marched several blocks without meeting any opposition. Soon after a detachment of the Eleventh Regiment, under Colonel O'Brien, arrived, bringing a couple of field pieces. The two forces joined, again marched through the streets where the mob had assembled, but encountered no opposition. Several of the rioters were shot in the first dispersion, and several of the policemen were badly hurt by being struck on the head with stones.

REPORTED HANGING OF COLONEL O'BRIEN.

It is stated that Colonel O'Brien was subsequently caught by the enraged mob, and after being horribly beaten, was hung to a lamp-post on the corner of Thirty-fourth street and Second avenue.

THE RIOT IN AVENUE A.

After the rioters had been dispersed in the vicinity of Second avenue and Twenty second street many of them proceeded toward Tompkins Square, halting at every hardware store and breaking into them for the purpose of securing ammunition. Several stores were thus broken open in Avenue A, between Sixth and Tenth streets, and the contents scattered along the street or carried away.

THE MOB IN FORTY-SEVENTH STREET.

About 3 o'clock P. M., yesterday, upwards of one hundred and fifty rioters made their appearance in front of Dr. Ward's house, No 24 West Forty-seventh street, and commenced sacking the house. Captain Walling with fifty-six policemen were marching from police headquarters up Broadway to the Twentieth Precinct station-house. Hearing of the affair on Forty-seventh street, they hastened to the spot. They were followed by a company of soldiers. The rioters were armed with clubs and every dangerous weapon conceivable. The appearance of the policemen and soldiers did not in the least tend to stop their outrages, but they seemed to act still more desperately. A brisk conflict ensued, in which all the weapons in the crowd were used without the least reserve. Soon the policemen got the better of them and they ran in all directions, the policemen and soldiers pursuing. One of the soldiers who was fatigued and completely worn out fell to the ground and was picked up by the mob and inhumanly beaten. He was taken to the hospital.

WOUNDED RIOTERS.

It was perfectly shocking to see the wounded rioters in the streets. They indeed were desperate in all their actions and insulting and threatening in their language.

In every street they might be seen reeling to and fro, their faces covered with clotted blood, their clothes torn, and everything about their appearance disgusting and absolutely sickening to behold.

They acted rudely toward women in many instances.

JUVENILE RIOTERS.

In Rivington street, near Clinton, a number of boys entered a small frame tenement, whose inmates were obnoxious to them, and after throwing the furniture into the street proceeded to tear down the house. The building was soon completely dismantled, nothing but the bare frame remaining. The materials were piled in the street and set on fire. A large crowd was collected around, but no attempt was made to prevent the boys from accomplishing their purpose.

ROW ON A FERRY BOAT.

On one of the boats of the Union Ferry Company, coming from Brooklyn about eleven o'clock yesterday, were two groups of men. One party, intelligent in appearance though poorly clad, stood by the railing near the ladies cabin, while the others, who were talking about the riot, were but a few feet off. One of these vehemently spoke of the necessity of crushing the rioters, and presently read an editorial in the *Times* of Monday, headed, "CRUSH THE MOB." The emphasis given by the reader was plainly intended for the ears of his more Democratic neighbors, who listened quietly for a few moments, and then said, "Well, now gentlemen, do you believe all that? Would you dare to crush a mob like that, anyway?"

"Certainly I would," replied the reader, "and devilish glad to do it."

"Well, take that, now—and that, and that," said the aroused workman, as, suiting the action to the word, he gave the foolish diatribe blow after blow with his horny fist.

The friends of the two men soon separated them and kept them apart the rest of the trip, and when the boat arrived at the slip the assailed party was not

THE WORLD.

The DAILY WORLD, published every morn[ing and] evening (Sundays excepted), price THREE CENT[S] ... ed at EIGHT DOLLARS a year; served by ... EIGHTEEN CENTS per week.

The SEMI-WEEKLY WORLD, published T... and Fridays, THREE DOLLARS a year; two co... one address for FIVE DOLLARS.

The WEEKLY WORLD, Two DOLLARS a year ... copies FIVE DOLLARS; five copies EIGHT D... Any person who will send us a Club of TEN subs... at $1.50 each, shall receive an extra copy for him... may retain One Dollar as his compensation. Th... Weekly and Weekly sent to Clergymen at the ... club rates. Specimen numbers forwarded on appl...

TERMS—Cash, invariably in advance.

All letters should be addressed to THE WO... PARK ROW, New-York City.

VICKSBUR[G]

Complete and Graphic Accoun[t of] the Siege and Surrender.

HISTORY OF PRECEDING CAMPAI[GNS]

The Failure Last Summer--The At[tack] in December--The Canal Efforts--The Mississippi Struggle.

&c., &c., &c.

LAST DAY OF THE S[IEGE]

Parley Between Gens. G[rant] and Pemberton.

OUR ENTRY INTO VICKSB[URG]

Thrilling Scenes in the Streets and [on the] Wharves--Singing by the Troops--Amazement of the People.

THE FRUITS OF THE VICT[ORY]

Appearance of Vicksburg and [its] Fortifications.

HORRORS OF THE BOMBARD[MENT]

The Prisoners—Their Appearance [and] History.

The Diary of a Citizen of the Beleag[uered] Stronghold.

[FROM OUR SPECIAL CORRESPONDENT.]

LATE HEADQUARTERS OF LIEUTENANT-GEN[E]RAL PEMBERTON, IN THE CITY OF VICKSBURG, Anniversary Day, July 4.

I.—A SPLENDID VICTORY.

Vicksburg has fallen! After forty-seven d[ays of] steady siege, the stronghold has succumbed! W[e are] now in peaceable possession of the place; the e[nemy] as prisoners of war, are being paroled; his colo[rs], guns, his stores, are left in our hands! As an e[arnest] of the good things to follow, fifty steamers lie [...] at the landing, and a few days will doubtless se[e] after fleet floating grandly on their peaceful mi[ssion] from Cairo to New Orleans!

So great—so proud an event comes opportun[ely on] the glorious anniversary of our national inde[pend]ence. The rush of bombs is exchanged for the [...] of rockets; the flare of heavy guns for the fl[...] Roman candles, and the crackle of musketry tur[ns to] the sputter of Chinese crackers and pyrotechnic [...]ities.

They who were yesterday taking deadly ai[m at] each other are now fraternizing over common [...]forts, and the din and war of battle is lost in th[e] laugh of merriment, and the hum of anxious co[ngrat]ulation.

It is, indeed, a "glorious victory"—not w[ithout] the attendant woes of war. Six thousand s[ick] huddled and crowded in the narrow limits. [...] every house is a hospital. Soldier and civilia[n] glad to be relieved from the terrible ordeal that [has] long hovered over them. Exhausted, weary, [...] and soiled, the garrison rests at last in securi[ty and] shade, while the victors, flushed with no more [than] brightening enthusiasm, greet their vanquished [...] becomes brave men to a brave but fallen enemy. [...] too, are glad to cease the labor, the danger, the [watch] and ward over the place, happy in the fact th[at the] reward of all our endeavors and hopes is ri[chly] commensurate with the toil.

THE FOURTH OF JULY.

The day is celebrated with all the internal w[...] at least that marks it as one of the most illustr[ious in] all history. Our brave Army of the Southwe[st has] this day consummated a victory more glorio[us and] more pregnant than any which has thus far b[lessed] our arms. The names of General Grant and h[is] adjutors are again in all mouths. The praises [of] soldiers and sailors are being spoken in uns[tinted] terms. The fatigues, hardships, perils, and tr[ials of] the campaign are at an end. Twenty-seven tho[usand] prisoners, among which are nineteen general of[ficers], a hundred and twenty cannon, and standa[rds in]numerable, are among the substantial trophies o[f vic]tory.

II.—THE SIEGE OF VICKSBURG.

It was on the 18th day of May that our fleet, [under] Admiral Farragut, after his capture of New Or[leans,] first made his appearance before Vicksburg. [The] confederates had foreseen the danger to their w[estern] territory from the loss of New Orleans, and [made] haste to fortify some point higher up. Vicksbu[rg, be]ing accessible by railway, offered the best faci[lities,] besides being situated on a point naturally s[trong.] At that time we held Baton Rouge on the one e[nd, and] menaced Fort Pillow at the other end of the [river.] At that time there were five heavy guns mo[unted.] Farragut made a demand for the city, when the [mayor] made his famous reply that "Mississippians c[...]

Chapter 11

A Perfect Reign of Terror

Throughout the week of July 13, 1863, the joyous celebrations occasioned by the victories at Gettysburg and Vicksburg were suddenly shattered by the outbreak of horrific mob violence in New York City. It was the most destructive riot in American history; by the time it ended, 105 people were dead, and many homes and workplaces had been reduced to rubble.

Unlike the riots that had erupted in the Confederacy, events in New York were not a reaction against grinding inflation and impoverishment. Class tensions and economic hardships did play some role in sparking the violence, but other problems—including festering feelings of outrage against emancipation—were involved as well. As the newspapers of the time detail, the riots betokened deep divisions in the North over how the war was being waged, despite the successes that had recently graced its arms.[1]

The direct cause of the New York City riot was the attempt by the Lincoln government to implement a national draft. By the end of 1862, the Union had essentially tapped out its reserves of men willing to volunteer for military service. Although Northerners had been eager to enlist in 1861, as the actual horrors of war became evident, those men remaining on the home front felt little enthusiasm for joining the action. While attracting new recruits became more challenging, the Union also experienced high rates of desertion from its ranks. Some of these deserters were bounty-jumpers—men who abandoned their posts only to enlist again, collecting each time the cash bounty that was paid to every new volunteer. Others left the army for less enterprising reasons, because of fear, hunger, combat fatigue, family concerns, or general hatred of military life. Either way, the results were staggering. Within the Army of the Potomac alone, around one-quarter of the soldiers were absent without leave at the start of 1863.[2] With the rebellion still raging and recruitment efforts sagging, Congress in March 1863 passed the Act for Enrolling and Calling Out the

National Forces, which made all men between the ages of twenty and thirty-five, as well as unmarried men ages thirty-five to forty-five, liable for military service. Unlike conscription in the Confederacy, the Union draft was a lottery. Every congressional district in the country had a quota; if sufficient numbers of volunteers could not be found to fill it, men listed on the draft rolls were to be selected for service randomly. Those unfortunate enough to be drafted could gain an exemption in one of two ways—by hiring someone else as a substitute or by paying a $300 commutation fee.

The response of the Northern public, like that of the Confederacy when it instituted its first national draft, was far from favorable. While Republicans generally accepted it as a necessary war measure, Democrats were intensely critical, even outraged by it. As a matter of principle, they recoiled from the very idea of conscription, which they regarded as a relic of European despotism. Only tyrannical, autocratic governments forced their citizens into military service. A free country such as the United States was supposed to fight its battles with the voluntary support of its people. This discomfort with the draft was particularly strident in light of the Emancipation Proclamation. Those who were to be conscripted would be fighting not just for the Union but for black freedom as well—a war goal that not all Northerners endorsed. The draft seemed all the more despotic because it overrode the rights of states to control their militias, and thus placed an incredible amount of power into the hands of the federal government. But on top of all these objections, Democrats also angrily disapproved of the $300 commutation clause. Although not an enormous sum today, in the Civil War era it was beyond the means of practically every working-class family. The draft law thus seemed to serve the interests of wealthy men at the expense of their less fortunate countrymen. As the *Detroit Free Press* criticized:

> This is a discrimination in favor of the rich and against the poor, which is both unjust and impolitic. When the national forces are called out there should be no favoritism shown between the different classes which compose the State. All should be called upon to defend the government, the rich and the poor, the high and the low—all alike. If a man has wealth he has more interest in protecting the government than the day laborer, who lives from hand to mouth. . . . There is no good reason why one man should be exempt and another compelled to perform military duty, simply because one happens to have temporarily more money than another. If there is to be discrimination of this kind, the poor—those whose families will be likely to suffer by their absence from home—should be the favored class. Those who are able to pay the three hundred dollars are able to support their families during their absence, but the hardship and wrong of the law, as it now is, falls upon the poor—those who are not blessed with a surplus of this world's goods. . . . We hope the next Congress will alter this section so as to compel every able-bodied man drafted, to go to the war, whatever his rank or pecuniary condition. If he has wealth, he has more reason to fight for its protection than the man who has nothing.[3]

The commutation clause was not ever amended or repealed. Nevertheless, preparations for the draft, which was set to begin in New York on Saturday, July 11, proceeded without much difficulty. The calm in New York was deceiving, however. The state's newly elected Democratic governor, Horatio Seymour, had promised to fill New York's quota through volunteers, leaving many to hope that a draft would not be necessary at all. It also was rumored that the New York state courts might rule that the federal conscription act was unconstitutional and thus unenforceable. When neither of these possibilities came to pass, the draft went into effect—again, without incident initially. Republicans in New York City welcomed it with loud cheers. They saw it as a wholesome sign of the nation's power to defend itself, both in the current crisis and in all wars to come. The *New York Times* declared:

It is a matter of prime concern that it should now be settled, once and for all, whether this Government is or is not strong enough to *compel* military service in its defence. More than any other one thing, this will determine our durability as a Republic and our formidableness as a nation. Once establish that not only the property, but the personal military service of every ablebodied citizen is at the command of the national authorities . . . and both successful rebellion and successful invasion are at once made impossible for all time to come. From that time it will be set down as a known fact that the United States is the most solidly based Government on the face of the earth.

The standing reproach against the Republican form of government hitherto has been, that its superior freedom was obtained at the expense of its security. . . . In fact, up to the last year, the . . . general notion was that Conscription was a feature that belonged exclusively to despotic Governments. . . . But as the war lingered on without result, the Government gradually braced itself up to the responsibility of demanding, under the mild name of a National Enrollment bill, what was in reality nothing less than a Conscription law on the European model. Congress, after deliberations, framed and passed such a law. The great practical question now to be determined is whether such a law can be sustained or not; in other words, whether this American Republic has or has not the plenary power for its own defence which is possessed by a European monarchy.

. . . The world will now have a better chance to judge . . . what the real strength of this Republic is. And unless we [are] greatly mistake[n], it will be seen that an overwhelming majority of the people will stand by the Government in this exercise of the mightiest of its powers; and will show a proud satisfaction in demonstrating that freemen are as capable as subjects and serfs of abiding any needful requirements for the national safety. No people on the face of the earth have such reason to submit to the extremest sacrifices for the salvation of their Government. . . . The Government is the people's Government, and the people will never consent that their Government shall suffer in a critical hour for the want of a power which is not [denied to] even the worst Government when its existence is threatened. When it is once understood that our national authority has the right, under the Constitution, to every dollar and every right arm in the country for its protection, . . . this Republic will command a respect, both at home and abroad, far beyond any ever accorded to it before. It will be a new and priceless security against all future rebellion and wanton foreign attack.[4]

The *Times* need only have read the columns of the local Democratic papers to see that its hopes for a seamless implementation of the draft might be disappointed. On the same day that this *Times* article appeared, the *New York News* issued a public call to the working-class men of the city, inciting them to rise and denounce conscription as an assault on their personal freedom. As the *News* emphasized—and as the rioters themselves would soon demonstrate—its opposition to the draft was wrapped up in its virulent racism against blacks and its determination to never support a war fought for the emancipation of slaves:

Only a few among the workingmen of this city who may be conscripted into the ranks of the Abolition army will march to the field with the proud consciousness that they are the soldiers of a Republic about to do battle for Republican institutions. The very fact that a power exists that can drive them from their homes to the slaughter pen will teach them that they are no longer free agents, but that an earthly will, superior to their own, controls their movements and points out to them the path that they must tread, even [though] it lead to present death.

For the first time in our history, Conscription has stalked among us, like the *avant-courier* of a confirmed despotism. Conscription, that does not dare invade a cottager's dwelling in monarchical Great Britain, steps arrogantly upon our Republican soil and draws lots for its victims from among the sons of industry, leaving the rich man to his luxurious repose. Conscription, the familiar tool of Emperors, who cannot trust the patriotism of their subjects, is now about to teach us our rudiments in subordination to a military government. It is a stranger upon our soil. Heretofore we have fought our battles without its aid. . . . Even in the infancy of this republic, when its cradle was being rocked amid the elements of strife, and patriots nursed it with their blood, . . . it disdained to call a forced and unwilling soldier to its rescue. Without wealth, without experience, without numbers, for eight long years it struggled for independence without counting one conscript among its defenders. But now, rolling in affluence, standing upon a level with the first empires of the world, . . . it introduces this foreign nuisance upon the soil to make soldiers for an abolition crusade.

. . . It is a strange perversion of the laws of self-preservation which would compel the white laborer to leave his family destitute and unprotected while he goes forth to free the negro, who, being free, will compete with him in labor. Let the laboring population assemble peaceably in mass meeting, and express their views upon the subject. . . . If they would avoid Conscription, let them speak in opposition to that which has given birth to Conscription. Let them protest against the continuance of the War. Let them swell the cry for Peace that is already ascending from all parts of the North. Let them make it a necessity with the Administration to give up its insane Emancipation scheme. Let them insist that in place of the Conscription of white men to serve the blacks, we shall have Negotiation, Compromise, and Peace.[5]

The intentions of the men who started the riot were much more limited than those of the *News* or other Copperhead organs. They did not aim to bring the war to an end; they merely wanted to shut down what they perceived to be an unfair law. Over the weekend of July 11, working-class folks congregated in their homes and in neighborhood saloons to discuss how exactly to respond. By the time Monday rolled around, promising the resumption of the draft, they were ready to act. The riot began in the city's Ninth District. During the six o'clock hour on Monday morning, workers from the railroads, docks, machine shops, iron foundries, and construction sites began banding together, and with signs proclaiming "No Draft," they marched toward the site of the conscription lottery at Third Avenue and Forty-seventh Street. While en route, they cut telegraph lines, felled telegraph poles, committed petty thefts, and attacked police officers, including Superintendent John A. Kennedy, whom they beat to pulp.

Regardless of the agitation surrounding them, officials at the Ninth District office continued with the draft lottery anyway. It came to an abrupt halt, however, shortly after a unit of firefighters from the Black Joke Engine Company arrived on the scene. One of their men had already been drafted in Saturday's lottery, and now the company sought to bring down the entire enterprise by busting into the District Office, smashing the lottery wheel, and—in a most ironic act—setting the building on fire. Still, these rioters on Monday morning clearly had no intention of fomenting a large-scale revolt. When the draft was suspended at eleven-thirty, they simmered down, and as the fire from the district office began spreading to neighboring buildings, the Black Joke men helped put it out. The rioting, however, quickly began to rage beyond their control.

Beginning on Monday afternoon, and continuing throughout the next several days of violence, the composition of the rioters began to change. The mob of Monday morning had been quite mixed. It included Irish Catholic as well as German and native-born

Protestant laboring-class men who worked in a variety of industries. Some were skilled craftsmen—carpenters, masons, and the like—while others were industrial laborers, dockhands, and unskilled construction workers. Once the draft had been shut down, many of the skilled workers, who tended to be native-born or German, removed themselves from the mob, while the remaining and swelling crowd—which became largely Irish and now included women and children—started settling other scores. In venting their anger against the government, they attacked policemen as well as other icons of Republican authority like the offices of the *New York Tribune*, which they tried to burn down. Wealthy men who looked like they might be Republicans were stalked and attacked in the streets, and their houses were invaded, ransacked, and set on fire. James Gibbons and his wife, Abby Hopper Gibbons, well-known abolitionists and friends of the *Tribune* editor Horace Greeley, saw their home ravaged. In a public letter to the *Tribune*, James Gibbons detailed the wrecking of his property:

> *To the Editor of The N.Y. Tribune,*
>
> SIR: It is impossible to answer separately the letters of inquiry received by the different members of my family relative to the extent of damage suffered by the sack of our dwelling-house on the 14 inst. You will therefore oblige me by inserting the following summary:
>
> No person was in the house at the time of the assault. Seeing no appearance of the mob in the immediate vicinity, I had walked over to Broadway to get an evening paper. On my return homeward, in about 40 minutes, I found that the house had been broken open, fired in several places, and was already half sacked. It was in the hands of a thousand thieves. I passed in and up stairs to see whether anything could be done to clear them out, but found it impossible, and retired. The lower doors and windows were all broken in, and all the interior rooms and closet doors, with two or three exceptions.

THE GREAT DRAFT RIOT

Tremendous Uprising Against the Draft in this City.

THE LABORING POPULATION IN ONE VAST MOB.

A CARNIVAL OF FIRE AND BLOOD

Conflagrations all over the City.

Wanton Destruction of Private Property.

ATTACK UPON THE TRIBUNE OFFICE

Mr. Horace Greeley's Adventures to Escape the Mob.

FURIOUS ATTACK UPON THE NEGROES.

Great Numbers of them Beaten and Killed.

New York World, July 14, 1863.

Everything was carried off—beds, bedding, all the bureau drawers and the lighter bureaus, tables, and even the grate pans and last kitchen pot. Of 2,500 volumes, the accumulation of thirty years, not a single book was left in the house. Of the furniture that was too heavy to carry off, one small piece only was left unmutilated by axes. Nearly all the glass and much of the sash work were destroyed. The stair banisters and marble mantles were chopped down. All the gas fixtures were twisted off, and most of the water faucets. The Croton pipe was pounded up in the cellar to cut off the water, that the fire might not be extinguished; and but for the neighbors, who at the peril of life brought in buckets from their own houses, the place would have been burned. A piano was broken into fragments, and even sliding doors pulled out and their panels split. The lower parts of several heavy bureaus, and portions of several bedsteads and tables, were left in the house, and nothing more. . . .

J. S. Gibbons[6]

THE REIGN OF THE RABBLE.

Continuation of the Riot---The Mob Increased in Numbers.

DEMONSTRATIONS IN THE UPPER WARDS

Encounters Between the Mob, the Metropolitans and the Military.

Large Numbers of the Rioters Killed.

COLONEL O'BRIEN MURDERED AND HUNG.

Streets Barricaded, Buildings Burned, Stores Sacked, and Private Dwellings Plundered.

New York Times, July 15, 1863.
In the eyes of Republican onlookers, the riot was a repulsive instance of mob rule that had to be squelched, not an expression of legitimate grievances that should be heeded.

As horrible as the looting became, the rioters directed their most vicious attacks against the city's black community. Many of the Irishmen in the mob were furious over emancipation and anxious to protect themselves from competition with black laborers. Through violence and intimidation, they demonstrated just how deeply they resented the city's black population. On Monday evening, a group of rioters razed the Colored Orphans Asylum and began randomly assaulting black men and boys they encountered in the downtown waterfront area. The draft riot thus morphed into a race riot, with horrendous consequences to its victims, many of whom either sought refuge at police stations or fled Manhattan altogether. The *New York Herald* offered this account of the "reign of terror" that prevailed against the city's black residents:

The negroes of this city are certainly in a very unfortunate condition—that is, those who are left behind. Since Monday night large numbers have departed for more congenial residences. Hundreds have gone to Brooklyn, and many more to New Jersey, while all trains and steamboats leading to the interior have been overrun with the flying blacks. A perfect reign of terror exists in the quarters of these helpless people, and if the troubles which now agitate our city continue during the week it is believed that not a single negro will remain within the metropolitan limits.

It is sad to see the fear with which the few negroes left go upon the street in order to procure the bare necessities of life. One of our reporters, yesterday, while walking through Sullivan street—a great negro quarter—noticed this particularly. Now and then a woman would steal carefully through an alley, and gazing up and down the street before venturing in full view, would run at full speed to the neighboring grocery. Some of the storekeepers said that they preferred to take articles of food to the colored people, as it was positively dangerous to allow them to remain for any length of time within their buildings. This feeling is general everywhere in New York, and the police are utterly powerless to protect the blacks, as the events of Monday and yesterday fully demonstrated. Men, women and children stealthily wend their way to the [police] station houses every night, to seek protection, being positively afraid to sleep in their own dwellings. Last night, in one station, twenty eight colored women and quite as many children sought protection from the fury of the multitude. In many cases, they were followed by crowds, and some of them [were] severely beaten.

The Fourth ward has been the scene, probably, of more destruction of negro residences than any other. There are, or were, a number of colored men's boarding houses in Roosevelt street, and these were nearly all destroyed early yesterday morning. Two of them, [at the] corner of Roosevelt and Batavia streets, were kept by a black named Beverly. The crowd, once determined upon their destruction, soon gathered in large numbers about the neighborhood. A few of them finally entered and beat a colored man who was found there. The rest, a dozen in all, had expected the coming storm and fled. In a few moments everything of value in the house was destroyed, and the building was fired. It soon burned to the ground. A German kept a store next door, but as it was frequented by colored people, it met the same fate, much to the anguish of its Teuton owner. The crowd distributed its contents, as victors do the spoils.

In Roosevelt street, near by, was a negro barber shop, and the crowd, now swelled to several thousand, scattered its contents about the street, and then applied the torch. It was not long before the shaving saloon had disappeared. It is unnecessary to say that the owners made no attempt to save their property. . . .

Last night a negro was caught in Oliver street. An infuriated crowd began to beat him. He struck out in self defence, and getting clear, ran way. The throng followed him to the pier foot of Oliver street, and succeeded in getting him upon it. He was driven to the end of the pier and forced into the East river. It is supposed that he was drowned, as his injuries must have disabled him so that he could not swim. No one made an effort to save him. . . .

The Twenty-eighth precinct, in Greenwich street, has also been the scene of much disorder. It was in this district that the negro was hung on Monday night. Yesterday morning a black man, named John Williams, was pursued by the crowd and knocked down upon the sidewalk. While in an insensible condition he was beaten so severely that he cannot possibly survive. He now lies in an extremely critical condition at the City Hospital. . . .

Taken together, the day has been a severe one for the blacks. It ends, for some time at least, their residence in this city. They must seek peace elsewhere, for in the present excited state of public feeling, there is no ease for them in New York. It is estimated that upwards of one hundred and fifty negroes have been killed or badly injured.[7]

In the weeks following the riot, details began to emerge about the specific identities of the victims. One was William M. Powell, a professional seaman whose son and namesake—a graduate of the Pennsylvania

Harper's Weekly,
August 1, 1863.
In an expression of sympathy with New York City's black community, *Harper's Weekly* depicted an assault by Irish rioters on a well-dressed and defenseless black man and his child. The portrayal of Irishmen here, with their bulbous noses and grotesque faces, reflects the disdainful attitudes that many Northerners held toward them—the working-class Irish were viewed as a lesser and semisavage breed.

HOW TO ESCAPE THE DRAFT.

College of Medicine—was now one of only a handful of black physicians serving in the Union army. In a letter to the *Anglo-African*, Powell described his narrow escape from the mob, as well as his frustration that his family's loyalty to the Union was rewarded with such viciousness:

> Mr. Editor: With a sorrowful heart I write you a narrative of the outrages perpetrated upon myself and family by a lawless, infuriated New York mob. On the afternoon of the 13th inst., my house, No. 2 Dover street, was invaded by a mob of half-grown boys. . . . But the God that succored Hagar in her flight came to my relief in the person of a little deformed, despised Israelite, who, *Samaritan-like*, took my poor helpless daughter under his protection in his house, where I presume she now is, until friends send her to me. He also supplied me with a long rope. I then took a survey of the premises, and fortunately found a way to escape, and though pitchy dark, I took *soundings* with the rope to see if it would touch the next roof, after which I took a clove-hitch around the clothes line, which was fastened to the wall by pulleys, and which led from one roof to the other, over the space of about one hundred feet. In this manner I managed to lower my family down on to the next roof, and from one roof to another, until I landed them in a neighbor's yard. We were secreted in our friend's cellar till 11 p.m., when we were taken in charge by the police and locked up in the Station-House for safety. In this dismal place we found upwards of *seventy* men, women

and children—some with broken limbs—bruised and beaten from head to foot. We stayed in this place for twenty-four hours, when the police escorted us to the New Haven boat at 11 p.m. Thus we escaped from an infuriated mob, leaving our invalid daughter in New York, in the hands of kind friends.

All my personal property, to the amount of $3,000, has been destroyed and scattered to the four winds, which, "like the baseless fabric of a vision, leaves not a wreck behind," except our lives, and so the Lord be praised.

As a devoted loyal Unionist, I have done all I could to perpetuate and uphold the integrity of this free government. As an evidence of this devotedness, my oldest son is now serving my country as a Surgeon in the U.S. army, and myself had just received a commission in the naval service. What more could I do? What further evidence was wanting to prove my allegiance in the exigencies of our unfortunate country? I am now an old man, stripped of everything which I once possessed, of all the comforts of life, but I thank God that he has yet spared my life, which I am ready to yield in the defence of my country.[8]

The *Anglo-African* also published the personal stories of several other black New Yorkers who were not so fortunate as to escape the rioting alive. One of these was Abraham Franklin, a defenseless and crippled coachman who was snatched from his home, dragged through the streets, and then hung from a lamppost, where the rioters continued to mutilate his body. When Franklin's corpse was finally taken down, a sixteen-year-old Irish boy named Patrick Butler paraded it about, by the genitals, while the crowd around him cheered. The accounts are all sadly ironic. Many Northern whites had resisted emancipation because they believed blacks to be inherently barbarous and disposed to bloodthirsty violence. As the following article illustrates, however, the white mobs in New York were actually the ones giving themselves over to their worst instincts:

"Mother! they may kill the body, but they cannot touch the soul"—was the language used by poor Abraham Franklin, as he was borne from the presence of his mother by the barbarous mob on the morning of the 14th ult. This young man, aged 23, had been an invalid for about two years, and was a confirmed consumptive. When the mob broke into the house they found him in bed. They bore him into the street and there, although he had not raised a finger against them, indeed was not able to do so, they *beat him to death, hanged him to a lamp-post, cut his pantaloons off at the knees, cut bits of flesh out of his legs, and afterward set fire to him!* All this was done beneath the eyes of his widowed mother. Such an exhibition of bloodthirstiness is without parallel in the history of crime. Patrick Butler and George Glass, both Irishmen, the latter 53 years of age, have been arrested for the murder of Mr. Franklin.

On the evening of the 13th a portion of the mob attacked a colored man about the neighborhood of Bleeker and Cornelia streets. The man fired on the mob and shot two of them. He then ran into a house in the latter street, and thus made his escape. When the mob found they were balked of their game, they pounced upon a colored man by the name of William Jones, who resided at 88 King street, a woodsawyer by occupation,—hung him to a lamp-post, and then set fire to him. . . .

On the 16th Mr. Nathaniel Jackson, residing in the upper part of the city, was conveying a load of swill to his pigs on Long Island, when on arriving at the 34th street ferry he was beaten by the mob, who, before life was extinct, threw him into the river and he was drowned.

On the 14th an industrious and respectable colored man of 63 years, while returning from his daily avocation, was caught by the mob on the corner of

Frank Leslie's Illustrated Newspaper, August 1, 1863.
An artist's rendition of the killing of Colonel O'Brien.

Oak and Chambers sts., and beaten so terribly that he died from his wounds on the 27th ult. His name was Peter Huston.

The colored man found near the grain elevator above South Ferry, Brooklyn, last week, was on the 29th identified by his relatives residing in New-York, as Samuel Johnson. They stated that he was employed in a store in New-York, and resided in Williamsburg; that on the evening of the fourth day of the riot, on his way home, he was met at the ferry by a body of rioters, attacked and beaten and thrown overboard; that while in the water he raised up his hands and cried out: "for God's sake, save my life," when he sunk and was seen no more. The head of [the] deceased presented evidence of having been beaten with clubs, but as there was no direct testimony when the inquest was held; a verdict of found drowned, was rendered.[9]

In addition to pitting whites against blacks, the spiraling violence also included deadly confrontations between civilians and soldiers. The most notorious of these was the murder of Colonel Henry O'Brien of the Eleventh New York Volunteers. On July 13, the first day of the riot, O'Brien had tried to restore order by firing his howitzer into the mob of people on Second Avenue, killing a woman and her child. From that point, he was a marked man. On Monday evening, O'Brien's house was destroyed, and then on Tuesday, a crowd directly confronted him, initiating an orgy of retribution that lasted for *six hours* and left O'Brien's tortured corpse unrecognizable. One eyewitness account described the mob's attack on O'Brien with these words:

> He was immediately surrounded, and one of the men came behind, and, striking him a heavy blow

on the back of the head, staggered him. The crowd then immediately surrounded and beat him in a most shocking manner. After having been terribly beaten his almost inanimate body was taken up in the strong arms of the crowd and hurried to the first lamp-post, where it was strung up by a rope. After a few minutes the body was taken down, he being still alive, and thrown like so much rubbish in the street.

The body lay in the middle of the street, within a few yards of the corner of 34th st. Nature shudders at the appalling scenes which here took place. The body was mutilated in such a manner that it was utterly impossible to recognize it. The head was nearly one mass of gore, while the clothes were also saturated with the crimson fluid of life. A crowd of some three hundred persons wounded the prostrate figure. These men looked upon the terrible sight with the greatest coolness, and some even smiled at the gay object. Our reporter walked leisurely among the crowd which surrounded the body, and in company with the rest gazed upon the extended mass of flesh which was once the corpulent form of Col. H. F. O'Brien. Notwithstanding the fearful process which the soldier had gone through, he was yet breathing with evident strength. The eyes were closed, but there was a very apparent twitching of the eyelids, while the lips were now and again convulsed, as if in the most intense agony.

After lying for somewhat of an hour in this position several of the crowd took hold of the body by the legs, and dragged it from side to side [in] the street. This operation was [repeated] several times, when the crowd once again left the body lying in its original position. . . . Now and then the head would be raised from the ground, while a foot from one of the crowd would dash the already mangled mass again to the earth. This conduct was carried on for some time, and when our reporter left the body was still lying in the street, the last spark of existence having taken flight.[10]

The social, racial, political, and purely emotional motivations of the rioters made for a volatile mix. In this one sweep of violence, working-class New Yorkers vented a tangle of anxieties that related not just to the war but to their own sense of right as free white citizens. One man who had participated in the riots on Monday explained his reasons to the *New York Times* in this way:

MONDAY AT NIGHT—UP TOWN

To the Editor of the New-York Times:

You will, no doubt, be hard on us rioters tomorrow morning, but that 300-dollar law has made us nobodies, vagabonds and cast-outs of society, for whom nobody cares when we must go to war and be shot down. We are the poor rabble, and the rich rabble is our enemy by this law. Therefore we will give our enemy battle right here, and ask no quarter. Although we got hard fists, and are dirty without, we have soft hearts, and have clean consciences within, and that's the reason we love our wives and children more than the rich, because we got not much besides them, and we will not go and leave them at home to starve. Until that draft law is repealed, I for one am willing to knock down more such rum-hole politicians as KENNEDY. Why don't they let the nigger kill the slave-driving race and take possession of the South, as it belongs to them.

A POOR MAN BUT A MAN
FOR ALL THAT[11]

In the end, city officials indeed gave the rioters "no quarter." The violence continued for five days and was quelled only after Union troops that had fought at Gettysburg were brought into the city to restore order by military force. It was a disturbing turn of events; two weeks after these soldiers had successfully resisted Lee's invading forces, they were on the streets of New York City, fighting their own people.

Although the New York riots stand as the most stunning and extreme example of wartime violence on the Northern home front, it was not the only city that experienced public disturbances in response to the draft. In Boston, a man charged with the unenviable responsibility of delivering notices to drafted men was attacked and beaten by a mob, which then marched on the local artillery armory and peppered it with stones, until the police successfully dispersed it. Rioters in Troy, New York, set fire to the offices of the town's Republican newspaper, the *Times*, destroying it completely. Small demonstrations occurred in Newark, Jersey City, Brooklyn, and Staten Island as well. Those who supported the war—whether Republican or Democrat in sympathy—flatly condemned all of these outbursts as outrageous threats to the stability of the country. Segments of the Northern public might feel that the conscription act was oppressive and unjust, but it was a matter of law and therefore they believed it had to be obeyed. In the eyes of its advocates, resisting the draft was equivalent to resisting the government and promoting anarchy. Lawlessness put the whole fabric of American government in jeopardy—and, by extension, put all democratic rights and liberties at risk. The *Hampshire Gazette & Northampton Courier* explained:

> We all equally owe allegiance to our government; it is the stability of government that gives value to our property; it is the consciousness that the laws are to be enforced and crime punished, that gives security to life; it is the unity of the nation that gives us the blessings of religion, education and prosperity. Let it be understood or even implied that government is powerless and law will become ineffective, property insecure, and might instead of right will prevail. . . . If government falls, we fall. If there is no central controlling power, then "every man for himself," becomes the rule and anarchy will prevail.
>
> This government, that has conferred so much upon us at so little cost to ourselves, is in danger. No, not the government alone, it is ourselves, every individual citizen of the republic that is threatened. It is our own property, our own security, our own life that is menaced, for if rebellion succeeds, the protecting hand of government will be withdrawn and individual, no less than national ruin will follow. To protect itself, to protect us, government has ordered a draft. If we are men, patriotic, self-sacrificing, we shall respond to it. The act has been termed "conscription," and connected with that term is the odious tyranny of European systems, which compells a certain portion of its people to serve in the army, for the pleasure or the ambition of their rulers. The word as generally used, is not applicable to the present case. . . . There is nothing odious in the term; nothing tyrannical in the law. Those who are rioting against the law are men who are willing to receive all the benefits government can bestow but are unwilling to make any sacrifice to sustain the government that has protected them and given them safe and wholesome laws to live under. . . .
>
> Government must and will enforce the draft. Rioting in New York or Massachusetts cannot prevent it. Now is the time for the strong arm of government to show itself, resistless and overpowering. If necessary, the fight will be maintained both in the northern and in the southern states. We will put down rebellion at home and then march to put it down in the southern states.[12]

In this vein, Republicans blasted the riots as not just wicked but unpatriotic. In wartime, being a true American meant respecting governmental authority and the rule of law. Anything less, declared the *New York Times*, was simply treason:

> It has heretofore been the boast of this country that liberty, regulated by law, was the principle which governed its citizens. The most perfect freedom to every man in every relation of life—freedom of person, of speech and in the pursuit of happiness, has been our glory, while the universally upheld governance of law has been the safety both of ourselves

and of our liberty. The dominance of the mob strikes at the root of this great and special American principle. It reverts us back to semi-barbarism, and throws us forward into despotism. A mob is un-American, anti-American. Every grievance can here be remedied, every wrong can be righted by *law*, which has its power in the rule of the people and "its fountain in the bosom of God." It will be a dark day for the liberties of America, for its honor, its greatness, its power, its glory, when the excrescence of European despotism fastens itself upon our free institutions and society. Every man who prides himself [an] American must use his determined efforts to drive back this black and deadly tide of human depravity.[13]

Although many Democratic papers agreed with those in the Republican camp that rioting was dangerous and unlawful, Republicans blamed the Copperhead wing of the Democratic party for fomenting the violence by their constant sniping against Lincoln and his war policies. Looking in retrospect, Republican organs saw the riots as part of a larger plot by the Copperheads and their Confederate allies to weaken the Union and distract it from prosecuting the war:

It is a mistake to treat the outbreak in the city of New York as a sudden ebullition of momentary excitement. . . . It is no ordinary street row—no mere mob arising from a temporary uneasiness among the masses of the people on the subject of the draft. It is a deliberate effort, got up by copperhead leaders, to weaken the hands of the national Executive, to oppose the measures necessary for the vigorous prosecution of the war, and to nullify the acts of Congress.

New York city, at the commencement of the war, was a thoroughly loyal community. Rebel sentiments found no favor there. The national flag, the emblem of the national authority, was everywhere demanded of institutions, establishments, or persons suspected of disloyalty. The people made it a perilous thing for newspapers to preach disloyalty, and no man dared brave the overwhelming Union sentiment by giving vent to expressions of sympathy for the rebellion, or, what is equivalent, opposition to the war. . . . Regiment after regiment was raised with the utmost promptitude and sent to the war. Money was freely subscribed for patriotic objects. The theatres echoed with the applause of patriotic Union sentiments. . . . The rebellion received neither sympathy nor quarter in New York.

But by insidious approaches, . . . rebel agents in New York have done their work well and faithfully. They have succeeded in their object. They have debauched the public sentiment of the city. . . . They have kept up a perpetual agitation in favor of peace and against war; they have identified the struggle with abolition; they have exaggerated all the losses of our armies to inflame the public mind with indignation at what they have termed useless waste of blood. . . . It is a fact that the Democratic party of New York city, which was thoroughly loyal during the first year of the war, has been gradually drawn away from this affection for the Union by the efforts of the rank copperheads. . . . No part of the rebellion has been more skillfully executed than this, and the result has been, as we now see, that the great city of New York has lapsed into the hands of the enemy.[14]

The Copperheads, in turn, insisted that the problem was not their rebelliousness but rather the criminal behavior of the Republican administration in Washington. On so many occasions during the war, they believed the president had overstepped the strict bounds of his authority—in calling up the troops after the Fort Sumter attack, for instance, and in enacting emancipation. Now the Copperheads pointed to the draft as one more example of Lincoln's own disregard for constitutional law. Not only did conscription negate an individual's right to withhold his support from the war, but it violated the legal rights of states to control the raising of militias. As the virulently anti-Lincoln sheet the *Caucasian* pointed out, the rioters in New York were simply following Lincoln's lead in disregarding the dictates of the law:

> For two years, a wicked and reckless administration has been setting at naught and defying the laws of this State. . . . In all and every respect, its acts have been lawless, riotous, illegal and revolutionary. Finally, to cap the climax of its iniquitous proceedings, it passed a conscription act, by which it was proposed to drag from their homes just as many men as it might demand. "All the property and all the lives of all citizens," said the *Daily Times* of Monday last, "must be at the command of the Government." On Saturday, the conscription took place in the 9th Congressional District of this city. On Sunday morning, the fatal list appeared in the papers. Families were terror-stricken. Wives and children crowded around their husbands and fathers, weeping and wailing as if all were lost. It is said that pen cannot describe the anguish of these poor defenseless, wretched people, on that gloomy Sunday. The men were rendered desperate by the sorrow and lamentations of their families. Money, the price of life for the rich, they had not—but brave hearts and strong hands they had; and without organization, without leaders and without system, they sallied forth, as savage as tigers, with the words of Spartacus on their lips: "If fight we must, we will fight for ourselves; if slaughter we must, we will slaughter our oppressors."
>
> Thus originated the terrible riot which has swept over our city, for three days past, and which has made the entire town cow down under its fearful ravages, as the stately forest is sometimes forced to bend before the shock of the whirlwind.
>
> Now, no one can condemn lawless proceedings more than we do. We have been condemning them, for two years past, with all our might and main. We have striven to impress upon Mr. Lincoln and his party the imperative necessity of obeying the laws; but they would not listen. We have warned them that, unless history were a falsehood, their disregard of laws and constitutions would come back to them with fearful vengeance. . . . After the fall of Vicksburgh and the defeat of Gen. Lee, they no doubt felt strong enough to do anything. But how fatally they were mistaken. . . .
>
> Now, there are a few facts, in the present controversy between Mr. Lincoln and the People, which deserve to be kept in mind constantly. *The people of this city have determined not to be dragged from their homes by a Federal Conscription Act.*
>
> . . . What, then, is to be done? Why, evidently, it is the duty of Mr. Lincoln to withdraw the draft. It is unconstitutional. . . . The Constitution of the United States gives Congress power "to provide for *calling forth* the militia," but nowhere authorizes it to *create* a militia, as this bill aims to. . . . The Constitution allows Congress "To provide for *calling forth* the militia *to suppress insurrection and repel invasion*," but by this so-called law of Congress every man, between twenty and forty-five years of age, is liable to perform military duty whenever called out *by the President!*
>
> . . . If the Conscription Act is Constitutional, then there are no more *States*. The United States Government becomes a Consolidated Nationality—a primal Sovereign Power. The power to *command* the services of the citizen is the *test* of sovereignty. The moment it is conceded to the Federal Agency, that moment the States are but provinces or counties, and Governors, instead of being vested with powers co-ordinate with the President, are reduced to the positions of Mayors and Supervisors. The question, then, is no ordinary one, for it involves nothing more nor less than the proposition whether the State of New York shall live or die! . . . Let Mr. Lincoln stop *his* riotous proceedings. . . . Let the laws everywhere be

obeyed by everybody—high and low, rich and poor, President and People. In this way we can have peace, quiet and social safety. Our country has been great, happy and prosperous, for years and years. It is only since Mr. Lincoln introduced the agencies of brute force, to govern us, that desolation and anguish have fallen upon our people. The lawless proceedings in our city, this week, have already inflicted sorrow and misery upon hundreds of our people. Blood runs down our streets like water. Deeply, bitterly do we lament it, and sorrowfully do we point to it as another crimson leaf to be added to the pages of history attesting, as in all times past, that revolutions beget counter-revolutions, and that laws violated on one side are sure to be violated on the other.[15]

The ultimate goal of the Copperhead press, though, remained what it had been since the start of the war: to bring about an immediate end to the fighting. The riots gave them yet another platform from which to drum up popular support for peace. The *New York News* thus declared:

> In place of giving way to their passions, and brooding over means of vengeance for their grievances, let the workingmen of this city apply their energies to the propagation of peace sentiment. The enforcement of peace will prevent the enforcement of the draft. Peace can be enforced by the firm and emphatic expression of the popular will. The Administration, however fanatical and headstrong it may be, cannot long resist the pressure of the public feeling. The workingmen will best consult their interests by . . . turning their attention to the cause of conscription, this unnatural war. Remove the cause and the effect will remove itself. In place of talking turbulence and riot, let the populace talk peace. In place of gathering for purposes of violence and incendiarism, let them quietly assemble to discuss the necessity of immediate peace. Peace is the panacea for their ills.[16]

For those in the North who supported the war, the persistence and vehemence of peace sentiment was certainly frustrating, but at the moment, they were also concerned with how observers in the Confederacy would interpret the outbreak of such awful rioting in the nation's premier city. Having just lost major battles at Vicksburg and Gettysburg, the rebels needed something like this to rejuvenate their belief that they could still win the war. "The riots will give the greatest satisfaction and hope to the people and rulers of the southern confederacy," the *New York World* surmised. "They will see in them the signs of social revolution; they will interpret them as meaning opposition to the war for the Union; they will hope for their continuance here, their spread over the country, and the consequent paralysis of the nation's arm. For this reason, therefore, in common with every true patriot, we regard the riots with profound regret."[17] Indeed, the *World* was not wrong. Newspapers in the Confederacy, when they got wind of the violence, were overjoyed by it. The *Charleston Courier* gushed:

> We derive abundant encouragement from these open and successful manifestations of hostility to the draft. They are worth as much to us as a signal victory. If the people of the North set their faces against the war, and resolve firmly that they will fight no longer, we may safely conclude that the end of the conflict is not far distant.
>
> These furious outbreaks possess the greater significance inasmuch as the enforcement of the draft was attempted after the battles of Gettysburg and after the fall of Vicksburg. They would not have so clearly evinced the real feelings with which the masses regard the war, had they occurred on the heels of a crushing Federal defeat. They might have been expected, and we would have supposed that the opposition was owing to a firm belief that the attempts to conquer and subdue the South would result in sure and disgraceful failure. But that order [to initiate the draft] from the Despot did not go

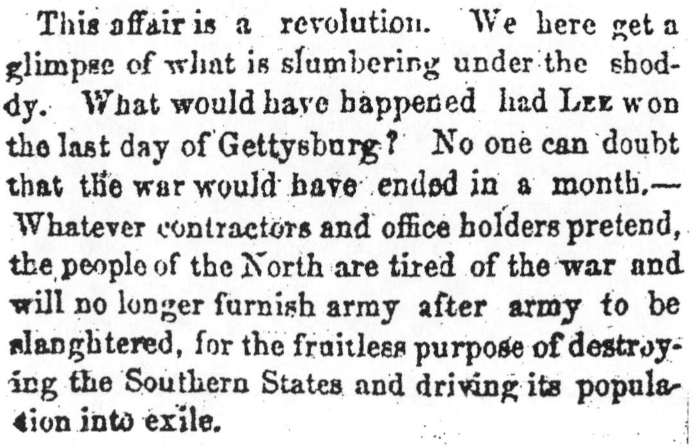
This affair is a revolution. We here get a glimpse of what is slumbering under the shoddy. What would have happened had LEE won the last day of Gettysburg? No one can doubt that the war would have ended in a month.—Whatever contractors and office holders pretend, the people of the North are tired of the war and will no longer furnish army after army to be slaughtered, for the fruitless purpose of destroying the Southern States and driving its population into exile.

Richmond Examiner, July 18, 1863.
Southerners saw the riots as a ray of hope, signaling that the North was on the verge of internal collapse.

> forth to the people when they were downhearted by reason of more blood vainly shed. It was issued at a time when the whole nation was rejoicing over great successes. That such demonstrations were made when the public mind was in such a frame gives assurance that the people, the fighting men of the Yankee nation, are tired and sick of the war . . . and that they are resolved to resist to the utmost that attempt to force them into the ranks. . . .
>
> The feeling that found so terrible an expression in New York City prevails in equal intensity in Hartford, Springfield and Newark. Four States have already caught the epidemic; and the West will shortly speak out in like manner, while the movement extends itself to all parts of Lincolndom. The sounds we have heard are but the mutterings of the storm which is about to burst with frightful fury. Let the enrolling officers proceed with their work. Let the military disperse the mob with muskets and cannon, and insist upon the enforcement of the draft. Let the people remain firm in their opposition. That discord gratifies us greatly. The hand of an avenging God is in it all. We cannot sack their cities. They will do it themselves. With their own hands they will inflict upon themselves those frightful woes their base soldiery have poured out upon us. . . . The war has put us in a savage mood, and nothing delights us so greatly as to hear of Yankees burning, destroying and killing Yankee buildings, Yankee property, and Yankee men.[18]

The glee of Southern onlookers reflected more than a lack of sympathy. As the *Richmond Enqurier* articulated, there was also an active hope that the North was on the verge of imploding:

> Riot, murder and conflagration have begun in New York. It is a world's wonder that this good work did not commence long ago; and this excellent outbreak may be the opening scene of the inevitable revolution which is to tear to pieces that most rotten society, and leave the Northern half of the old American Union a desert of blood-soaked ashes. We bid it good speed. . . . The news is cheering to us, indeed, because it portends the breaking down of the whole structure of Yankee society. Yet, the process may be long; and in the meantime, the desperate energy of their war for conquest for the Confederacy may grow more furious for a season.
>
> No matter; we can at least now see to the end of it. This one insurrection may be suppressed for the moment, but it will be the parent of other and still worse convulsions. We have but to persevere in our determined resistance, gird ourselves to the task of winning our independence more sternly than ever, . . . and we shall see the giant, but hollow bulk of the Yankee nation bursting into

fragments and rushing down into perdition in flames and blood. Amen.[19]

One Southern newspaper, however—the *Greensborough Patriot*—offered a more balanced view. Perhaps since North Carolina was the center of the Confederacy's own peace movement, the editor there was reluctant to bask too luxuriantly in New York's troubles. Actually, anyone who read the papers in the Confederacy knew that feelings of outrage and disillusionment with the war were hardly unique to the North. As the *Patriot* rightly observed, "it is useless to disguise the fact that the masses of the people North and South . . . are becoming sick and tired of the quarrel." It was true. But how exactly this dissent would play out—whether it would stifle the ability of either the Union or the Confederacy to sustain the struggle—was still anyone's guess.[20]

THE NEW YORK HERALD.

WHOLE NO. 10,343. NEW YORK, THURSDAY, DECEMBER 22, 1864. PRICE FOUR CENTS.

SHERMAN.

The Gallop Through Georgia.

Forty-two Counties of the Rebel Empire State Laid Waste.

The State Capital Formally Surrendered to Ten Scouts, who Stampede Two Hundred Rebel Soldiers.

THE COUNTRY STRIPPED OF EVERYTHING

All the Railways Destroyed and Iron Burned.

THE BATTLE OF GRISWOLDVILLE.

Walcott Almost Annihilates Three Rebel Brigades with One and Captures the Rebel Commander.

Sherman Subsists on the Fat of the Land and Does Not Lose a Wagon or Gun.

The Spoils of the Campaign 4,000 Prisoners, 15,000 Horses, 10,000 Negroes, Thirty Pieces of Artillery, &c.

MILLIONS WORTH OF COTTON BURNED.

Sherman's Total Loss Only Fifteen Hundred.

STORMING OF FORT McALLISTER.

The Garrison and Twenty-four Guns Captured.

THE FLEET GOES UP TO THE NEW BASE.

The Siege of Savannah Opened.

MUTINY OF THE PEOPLE OF SAVANNAH!

They are Ready to Give Up—Warehouses Thrown Open and All Told to Help Themselves,

&c., &c., &c.

The United States steam transport Fulton, Capt. Wotton, from Port Royal on the 18th, via Fortress Monroe on the 20th inst., arrived at this port yesterday morning.

The Fulton touched at Fortress Monroe to land Lieutenant Colonel O. E. Babcock, bearer of despatches from Gen. Sherman to the War Department. Also Colonel A. H. Markland, General Sherman's mail agent.

Savannah was still in possession of the rebels. Its surrender had not been demanded by Gen. Sherman up to the time of the sailing of the Fulton.

Among the passengers per Fulton are Col. W. Gurney, One Hundred and Twenty-seventh New York Volunteers, nineteen other officers of lesser grade, who were wounded in the late battle at Pocotaligo, South Carolina, and our correspondents who accompanied General Sherman in his

SHERMAN'S TRIUMPHANT MARCH.

Routes of the Army from Atlanta to the Atlantic----The Investment of Savannah.

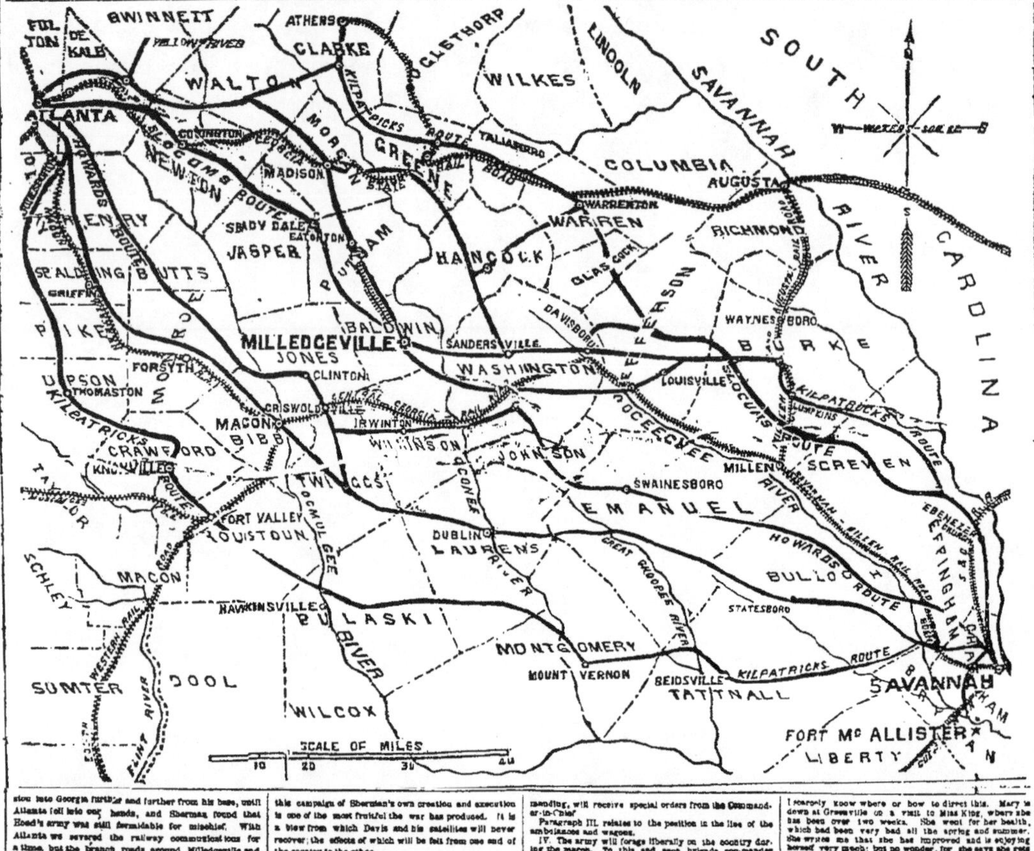

sion into Georgia further and further from his base, until Atlanta fell into our hands, and Sherman found that Hood's army was still formidable for mischief. With Atlanta we severed the railway communications for a time, but the branch roads around Milledgeville and Macon still enabled the enemy to draw supplies from Florida, Southern Georgia, Alabama and Mississippi, for the subsistence of their armies, while it gave us one hundred and forty miles more of railway to guard against raids upon our flanks and guerilla depredations in the rear.

The further pursuit of Hood, consequently, seemed freight with danger and perplexity, and Sherman seems to have studied well the problem how to shorten his line of supplies, and at the same time hold Chattanooga, the key to Tennessee. The campaign of the summer had ended, Hood's army being not less than thirty thousand, while the draft had very largely swelled Sherman's ranks. It was then that the great genius of the man solved the question; and this campaign was created and worked out upon the map. The moment he could draw Hood away from his front, beyond the reach of railway communication with the rebel base of supplies, Sherman saw that by dividing his large army he could with the one wing keep Hood employed and by bold and rapid movements strike the coast and open up a new line of supplies, via some of the large rivers, from which he could operate against the interior of Georgia, Alabama and the Carolinas.

I have the best authority for saying that the subsequent advance to the coast was of Sherman's own conception, submitted and explained by him to General Grant and the War Department, and by them heartily approved.

With the subsequent movement of Hood to Sherman's rear, the cutting of his communications, the apparent tardiness of Sherman in pursuit, and the escape of Hood into Northern Alabama, the reader is familiar, and at the time, no doubt, felt like censuring Sherman for not showing more determination and energy against inferior numbers. But they must now see that this was a part of Sherman's well matured plan.

While Hood was boldly pushing away from his base Sherman was gathering all his strength for a desperate blow that was destined to break the outer shell of the rebellion and expose its vitals.

PREPARATIONS FOR THE MARCH.

Sending the Fourth and Twenty-third corps to Thomas as a nucleus for a new command, a new army was organized under that well tried general, and then Sherman bade the North good bye, destroyed the railroad from Atlanta to Chattanooga, refitted his army at Atlanta and cut loose—destination, the coast; object, a new base.

Loading his wagons with sixteen days rations for a march of over three hundred miles through an enemy's country, he first divides his command into four columns, marches via the Augusta and Atlanta Railway, destroys it in his march as well as the road to Macon. While his right wing threatens Macon the left occupies the capital of the State and lays waste the railways, cotton mills, foundries and machine shops. In his march he subsists his

this campaign of Sherman's own creation and execution is one of the most fruitful the war has produced. It is a blow from which Davis and his satellites will never recover; the effects of which will be felt from one end of the country to the other.

But there is still another effect it will have. It demonstrates to European Powers the weakness of the rebels and the power of the national government to cope with armed treason and rebellion.

But to the detailed narrative, which opens with

THE CONCENTRATION OF THE ARMY.

On the 11th the army was located as follows:—The Twentieth corps at Atlanta, the Fifteenth and Seventeenth corps at Powder Spring road, on the Chattahoochee river, and the Fourteenth corps at Kingston, Ga. Sherman's headquarters were at the latter place.

On the morning of the 12th the army commenced concentrating around Atlanta. The Fourteenth corps, Brevet Major General Davis commanding, remained at Kingston to cover the shipment north of the government property and rolling stock of the railway, and at noon of that day the Third brigade of the First division, Colonel H. A. Hambright, Seventy-ninth Pennsylvania, commanding, who, by the way, was the first commandant at Kingston, moved out, and the place was evacuated. Notwithstanding that the Colonel took every precaution to prevent a wanton destruction of the place, the negroes, who brought up the rear, fired several buildings, which were consumed. The corps reached Cartersville at night, and, after provisioning the troops, the public property was destroyed, and on the following day (the 13th) Big Shanty was reached, and the troops bivouacked for the night. Next day the corps reached the Chattahoochee river, and on the 15th Atlanta.

CHATTANOOGA RAILWAY DESTROYED.

The railway was torn up from Chattanooga to Atlanta, and all the bridges laid in ashes, as well as every building that could be of benefit to the enemy. The straggling negroes and cavalry destroyed quite a number of uninhabited houses, and, I regret to say, three or four churches.

On the 14th and 15th, the Fifteenth and Seventeenth corps, under General Howard, marched to a camp one mile south of Atlanta, to which point Slocum, commanding the left wing, moved on the morning of the 15th, leaving the city entirely empty, except a few citizens, who remained scattered over the city, preferring to dwell in the city until the return to its ruins of their disloyal friends than to accept of free transportation to the land of "Yankee mudsills" and "Puritanical abolitionists." The afternoon was spent in emptying the storehouses of clothing, commissary supplies, &c., and their transfer to the persons of the troops of the Fourteenth corps.

During the entire day Atlanta presented a very busy appearance, every street of importance being blockaded by wagon trains and mounted officers and men. Quite a number of houses were fired during the day, and regular detailed parties from the Twentieth corps destroyed all the public buildings of value to the enemy.

GENERAL SHERMAN'S ORDERS TO HIS TROOPS.

After the men had bivouacked for the night the follow-

manding, will receive special orders from the Commander-in-Chief.

Paragraph III. relates to the position in the line of the ambulances and wagons.

IV. The army will forage liberally on the country during the march. To this end each brigade commander will organize a good and efficient foraging party, under command of one or more discreet officers, who will gather near the route travelled corn or forage of any kind, meat of any kind, vegetables, corn meal, or whatever is needed by the command; aiming at all times to keep in the wagons at least ten days' provisions for the command and three days' forage. Soldiers must not enter the dwellings of the inhabitants, or commit any trespass, but during a halt or in a camp they may be permitted to gather turnips, potatoes and other vegetables, and to drive in stock in sight of their camp. To regular foraging parties must be entrusted the gathering of provisions and forage at any distance from the road travelled.

V. To army corps commanders alone is entrusted the power to destroy mills, houses, cotton gins, &c., and for them this general principle is laid down:—In districts and neighborhoods where the army is unmolested no destruction of such property should be permitted; but should guerillas or bushwhackers molest our march, or should the inhabitants burn bridges, obstruct roads, or otherwise manifest local hostility, then army commanders should order and enforce a devastation more or less relentless, according to the measure of such hostility.

VI. As for horses, mules, wagons, &c., belonging to the inhabitants, the cavalry and artillery may appropriate freely and without limit, discriminating, however, between the rich, who are generally hostile, and the poor, or industrious, usually neutral or friendly. Foraging parties may also take mules or horses to replace the jaded animals of their trains, or to serve as pack mules for the regiments or brigades. In all foraging, of whatever kind, the parties will refrain from abusive or threatening language, and may, when the officers in command think proper, give certificates of the fact, but no receipts and they will endeavor to leave each family a reasonable portion for their maintenance. * * * *

By order of Major General W. T. SHERMAN.
L. M. DAYTON, A. D. C.

ATLANTA ON FIRE.

"Now negress night came solemn down" upon the city, and as the flames spread from the public buildings and the depot that had been fired the whole heavens became illuminated by the lurid glare, while the unexploded shells in the dwellings and storehouses became heated, and as they exploded in rapid succession one almost imagined that the scenes of August last, when one hundred thousand heroes confronted the rebel stronghold, were being re-enacted.

Standing upon an eminence overlooking the doomed city, I had an excellent view of the conflagration, and never had I beheld so grand a sight. As night waned the gentle breeze carried the destroying element from house to house, and block to block, until one-half of the rebel city was in flames, the glare of which was so bright that the soldiers a mile distant read their last letters from home by the light. Next morning I rode over the city among the ruins, where nothing remained to tell the tale but tottering walls and blackened chimneys, that, like gravestones, stood there as monuments of departed glory.

ON THE WAR TRACK AGAIN.

On the morning of the 16th, at daylight, the whole army once more took up the line of march—the Seventeenth corps on the McDonough road, the Fourteenth on the Augusta road (running parallel with the railroad), with the Twentieth on the left and the Fifteenth on the right flanks. I accompanied the column of the Fourteenth corps, which passed out through the

I scarcely know where or how to direct this. Mary is down at Greenville on a visit to Miss King, where she has been over two weeks. She went for her health, which had been very bad all the spring and summer. She writes me that she has improved and is enjoying herself very much; but no wonder, for she says she gets so well fed, that no one at Greenville seems to feel the war, but live in full and plenty, as they did before, though Margaret King always did live well; but she has plenty of money and nothing to do with it but support herself.

We had a terrible alarm the night the raiders were expected in Montgomery. This is the most excitable family the world ever produced, from the Judge down to the smallest negro child in the lot. Words of mine would fail to give you an idea of the time we had. Sufficient to say that the Judge snatched up his papers and money, flew down to the cars to take care of his own precious self, leaving orders that we all should follow at the first alarm bell, &c. Such a scene of confusion I never saw, and, without stopping to reflect, I jumped out of bed and commenced gathering together my clothes, for I was determined to try and save them, as I never expected to get any more, and where to get trunks or boxes to pack in I knew not. So I was up the whole night long, flying here and there, half dressed, and six o'clock came in the morning before I even sat down. Of course my servants were of no use whatever, and the Judge's, whom he thinks paragons, were in open rebellion. What influence they would have had on Dolly when the time came to leave I cannot tell. Fortunately they were not tried, as the vandals did not get here; but when the excitement was over, and I had time to reflect, I thought how foolish it was in me to worry about running away any more, especially with Judge Jordan, for, in any great danger, he is a broken reed to lean upon—self is No. 1, and I have resolved hereafter to just stay where I am, and only regret that I was induced by the entreaties of the Judge to leave my all in Pensacola, not that I would have taken the Yankee oath. Selfish motives were at the bottom with the Judge. I hope I may do him injustice. The day after the alarm I was taken with a violent, nervous pain in my head, which seemed to get worse daily for about ten days, until I suppose the climax came, and then such excruciating pains run down the back of my head and neck that I was senseless for a short time. A powerful remedy was administered—opiates and quiet—and in a few days I was myself again. In any great alarm, or excitement or rumor, I seem composed and do all that I can; but afterwards the reaction comes and prostrates me. But after this I think I shall have to stand my ground and take the Yanks as I find them. Now, I have reserved the bonne bouche for the last. On Monday, greatly to my surprise, a letter came from the post office, directed to Mary. It was so like your handwriting, though from Wilmington post office, that I was sure it was from you, and, while breaking the seal, wondered how you came to be there. Just think! it was a blockade letter from dear Peyton, written ever since the 20th of January—only seven months since. He had just arrived at Panama and found in the post office there two letters from Mary and one from you, dated, I think he said, 22d of July. It seems he has been in New York for the last two years. His health had been wretched, and after seeking and travelling about to various places in search of a climate to suit him, found that New York was the only place. His intention was to come into Dixie, but could not succeed, and after the fall of Vicksburg had to give up. Some of his good friends tried hard to get him in Fort Lafayette, but failed. His pecuniary matters are as usual, but it takes all he can raise to pay travelling expenses. He expected to meet his agent at Panama, but as he was not there he should go to Nicaragua, from thence to California, or perhaps accompany his agent to Europe; but would write and let us know; that we must write to him and direct our letters as we used to, to his agent in New York, and he would forward them to him, no matter in what part of the world he was. I have lost and forgotten his direction. I know it was a Mr. [illegible], Wall street, but what were the initials of the Christian name or the number of Mr. [illegible] I have forgotten. Do you remember? If so write and let me know, though if I write I don't see how we can get a letter to him, and as

shoulder shift, the State and national floating in the mixed Southern breeze, a[…] nicely paved streets resounding to the tread of […] diers of the Union, presented an imposing appe[…] not soon to be obliterated from the memories of […] bellious sympathizers with Davis and the Devi[…] column encamped at eleven o'clock A. M. near Al[…] river, distant ten miles north of Social Circle, and […] for the day.

FORAGING PARTIES

were sent out in the afternoon, and at night retu[…] camp with a large amount of fine stock, grain and […] tables.

THE RIGHT WING.

To-night (16th) Howard's (right) wing is encam[…] Jackson, and has met no enemy. Slocum, on the […] parallel with Howard, and has had no fighting.

SHERMAN'S HEADQUARTERS.

General Sherman makes his headquarters […] Thomas' veteran corps, now commanded by B[…] General Jeff. C. Davis.

SHERMAN TASTES SORGHUM.

Many little incidents occur daily that go to […] leader like Sherman can make himself familiar w[…] soldiers, and still retain their confidence and […] thorough discipline. A colonel commanding a re[…] who witnessed it, informs me that to-day a num[…] soldiers who were filling their canteens from a m[…] barrel, near Sherman's headquarters, were qu[…] over the division of the syrup, when Sherman pa[…] cooly crowded in among them, and dipping his […] it put it to his lips, remarking, "Don't crowd, […] there is enough for all."

A PLANTATION SCENE.

About six miles south of Covington we stru[…] plantation of [illegible], who is a Massachuse[…] and owns over two hundred negroes. The plant[…] one of the most extensive in Central Georgia […] production of cotton and cereals of all descr[…] As the column moved past the Third brigade […] division band struck up a quick step, when t[…] village of negro huts the dusky sons o[…] swarmed forth in large numbers and rushed […] fences. A rich scene followed. The negroes—m[…] men and children—struck off into a dance, […] themselves round and twisting themselves into gr[…] shapes that called forth peals of laughter from […] dlery, while shouts of "Glory be to de Lord, de L[…] hab come!" "Won't we go long wil[…]" "Ise off to glory!" "Bress de Lord!" […] heard on all sides. They followed the troops fo[…] mile, making the air resound with their exclama[…] gladness, until driven back to the rear.

ANOTHER REBEL ATTACK.

On the 19th the column moved at daylight, […] division leading, Baird next and Carlin covering […] The column took the Sandtown road, and when […] three miles, were fired upon by a few rebel sco[…] retreated.

WET WEATHER AND BAD ROADS.

Up to this time we had beautiful […] but at daylight the roads were found […] impassable from the rain that had fallen […] rents during the night. Nevertheless, nine mi[…] made through a pouring rain, and we encamped […] o'clock in the evening three miles south of Sh[…]

On the 20th the command moved at the usu[…] rain still falling, and the roads in a horrible co[…] About noon we arrived at Shady Dale, the plant[…] an old man named Matthew Whitfield, who own[…] the whole of Putnam county, and an abundance […] and crops. There we found

ANOTHER VILLAGE OF NEGROES,

who worked the large plantation upon which Wh[…] field resided, and where another scene […] that enacted at Harris greeted the men […] twenty five women followed the column a m[…] were driven back by the staff officers. […] all the male negroes went with the army volo[…] At night the command encamped near Eatonton, […] the morning of the 21st resumed their march, […]

MUDDIER CREEK

before night closed in upon them and rendered m[…] over muddy roads and swollen rivers too dangerous […] attempted. The country through which we pass[…] the garden of Georgia, the plantations furnish[…] abundance of everything necessary for the subsis[…] man and beast, which was very generally appro[…] by the foraging parties, who obtained so much […] and meal that the commissary wagons were no[…] upon to disgorge a portion of their hard tack and […]

THE ARMY TRAINS

had become thoroughly rejuvenated by the sec[…] of hundreds of fine mules captured from the wea[…] bims who had hidden them in the woods whe[…] were found by the aid of the negroes. Some of th[…] horses I have seen in the South, were also impress[…] the United States service.

[illegible]

Among the blooded stock captured was Genera[…] Cobb's celebrated pacing mare, that cost $2,0[…] was found in a swamp near Milledgeville, by […] Walter Furns, Company I, Twenty-first [illegible], who […] twelve days after, was captured while foraging […] murdered. He was acting as orderly and when h[…] panions dug open his grave they found that the[…] had cut his throat after shooting him through the […]

THE APPROACH TO MILLEDGEVILLE.

The rain cleared off on the 20th, and the col[…] winds came down the good spirits to aid the […] march of the victors by drying up the roads a[…] ing the faithful friend of the sun [illegible] […] bracing wind and warm sun were balm to the […] veterans, whose clothes for four days had been d[…] with Georgia rains and mud, and as they w[…] Milledgeville—the capital of the State—where w[…] the ordinance of secession, increased speed was […] discernable in the movement of the men.

At twelve o'clock noon, Davis' advance reach[…] Baird's division, encamped in the city, and by d[…] woods and shrubbery around the city were lit[…] by the camp fires of Sherman's grand army […] vaders."

But let me here dwell a moment upon the

OPERATIONS OF THE TWENTIETH CORPS,

which formed the left, and moved from Atlant[…] road parallel with Davis' route, through Decatur, […] son, Eatonton, &c. General Williams, of Michigan, […] manded the corps, Jackson the First, Geary, of P[…] vania, the second, and Ward, of Kentucky, th[…] divisions. The corps made excellent time from […] to Milledgeville, encountering no enemy nor ever […] a shot, except at venturesome rebels and cavalry […] strayed too near foraging parties.

[illegible]

Part Five The Confederacy Undone

Chapter 12

Smashing Things to the Sea, and Onward

Although the riots that erupted in New York during the summer of 1863 were successfully squelched, the anger, disgust, and frustration that gave rise to them only continued to fester. The revolutionary nature of Lincoln's war policies, particularly with regard to slavery, gave the Democratic opposition a steady base of supporters who railed against his leadership and recoiled from fighting a war for emancipation. The dreary military situation in the spring of 1864 only increased the stridency of Lincoln's detractors. Things were particularly distressing in the eastern theater. In an effort to finally defeat the Army of Northern Virginia, Ulysses S. Grant—who had been transferred east after his extraordinary triumph at Vicksburg—engaged Lee's army in a series of battles in Virginia that produced enormous numbers of casualties, but no significant results. Between battles in the Wilderness, at Spotsylvania, and at Cold Harbor, Grant lost 60,000 of his men before settling into a siege at Petersburg—an unremitting and painfully slow struggle that had no foreseeable end. Already exhausted by the war, many Northerners longed for peace and doubted Lincoln's ability to bring the fighting to a successful termination. The malaise that hung over the North was especially portentous, for it was an election year. Come November, voters would have the opportunity to change their leaders, and consequently, to alter the whole course of the war.

The lack of faith in Lincoln's leadership showed even with his own party. In the summer of 1864, a faction of disillusioned Republicans held a convention separate from the rest of the party, where they nominated the esteemed general John C. Frémont for president. The main wing of the Republican party—renaming itself the Union party—stood by Lincoln and endorsed him for reelection. But between the unpopularity of his policies and the frustrating downturn in the Union's military fortunes, even Lincoln himself doubted that he would win a second term in office. Lincoln's Democratic opponent was George B. McClellan, the Union general who early in the war had been Lincoln's choice to head the Army of the Potomac, but who had since been replaced in the president's good graces by the more successful Grant. Although McClellan claimed to support the war effort, the campaign platform for the Democrats had been written by leaders of the Copperhead wing of the party. It was therefore a peace platform, one that flatly characterized the war as "four years of failure," and called for an immediate cessation of hostilities, to be followed by negotiations for restoring the Union. The Democratic platform was really a pipe dream. Jefferson Davis had publicly vowed to continue fighting until the South had won its freedom. As far as he was concerned, there would be no negotiations for reunion—only for recognition of Confederate nationhood. A victory for McClellan, followed by a cease-fire and negotiations, would only jeopardize the Union cause. Quite literally, then, the survival of the Union seemed to rest on Lincoln's reelection. For that to happen, though, the president needed a military victory to revive the public's confidence in him.[1]

Lincoln's saving grace came not from Grant in the east but from General William Tecumseh Sherman in the west. While the political organizations at home were hammering out their campaigns for the 1864 election, Sherman was in Tennessee, pushing his way toward Atlanta—a railroad hub and major manufacturing, transportation, and supply point. Since the fall of Vicksburg, Atlanta had deservedly taken up the mantle as the new symbol of Confederate strength and resistance. Valuable in and of itself, Atlanta's strategic importance also lay in the fact that its capture would open up central Georgia, the breadbasket of the South, to invasion. Therefore, as eagerly as the Union sought to control the city, the Confederacy could not afford to lose it. But at the end of August, after outmaneuvering the defensive line established by General John Bell Hood, Sherman successfully seized control of the roads and rail lines leading into Atlanta. Although Hood attempted to push Sherman back, his resistance was too little too late, and the Confederates were forced to evacuate the city and consign it to Union occupation. Atlanta's capture was a momentous achievement, one that revived the North's confidence in Lincoln and ensured his electoral victory in November. It also ushered in the final phase of what was already a tremendously destructive war.

Sherman's success in Atlanta leveled a heavy blow to the Confederacy, and privately, at least, some Southerners were "plunged into despondency" over it. "Neither the fall of Vicksburg, nor the repulse at Gettysburg, produced so painful an impression here as the loss of Atlanta," one observer in western Georgia conceded. In the interest of shoring up morale, the press presented a public face of defiance, as with this editorial from the *Augusta Chronicle & Sentinel*:

> We have suffered a great disaster. We can not conceal from ourselves the magnitude of the loss we have sustained in the fall of Atlanta. But it is not irreparable. If the administration and people be true to themselves, we can rise above this fresh misfortune, and hurl back the foe from the important position he has gained.
>
> It is from just such disasters that nations have risen with renewed vigor and determination, to expel an invading enemy and save themselves from conquest and subjugation. . . . It was after the capture of Madrid, and the conquest of Spain by the armies of Napoleon, that the rekindled energies of patriotism of the Spaniards . . . expelled the Gallic conqueror from their soil. It was after Cornwallis had overrun the Carolinas, that he was compelled to surrender [at Yorktown]. History is full of such examples of a people startled from their lethargy by some crushing defeat, or mighty calamity, to the successful defence of their liberties and nationality.
>
> This is the moral which we would deduce from the signal calamity we now deplore—that our

Government and people should redouble their determination and efforts to expel the enemy, who has pressed into the very heart of our territory, with the haughty bearing and reckless hardihood of a conqueror. Whether he shall be permitted to stay, to entrench himself in the heart of our land, and cover it with desolation and ruin is the question which the people and administration of the South are now called upon to decide for themselves and posterity. Who can doubt their decision. Where is the craven heart that is ready to surrender country and liberty to a detested and ruthless foe under the paralyzing influence of dastardly fear or ignoble despair?

We can drive Sherman from Georgia if we will, notwithstanding the fall of Atlanta.[2]

In Sherman's mind, victory for the Union could not be secured until this spirit of defiance was crushed out of the Southern psyche. As he himself put it, he wanted to break the will of the Southern people—to "demonstrate the vulnerability of the South, and make its inhabitants feel that war and individual ruin are synonymous terms." It was a blueprint for what today is called "total war," a mode of warfare in which traditional distinctions between combatants and noncombatants no longer apply. Therefore, instead of pursuing Hood's army, which had retreated westward, Sherman turned his attention to the east and envisioned marching through the heart of Georgia, "smashing things to the sea"—destroying the granaries, farms, livestock, and other productive resources of the state—before moving northward to join forces with Grant. The goal was psychological, to frighten and intimidate the common people of the Confederacy into ceasing their support for the rebellion.[3]

In November, Sherman put his plan into motion. After exiling the civilian population of Atlanta, he ordered the city torched, and promptly set out on his famous March to the Sea. Telling the story of the march through newspaper accounts is a rather one-sided affair, for while driving through Georgia, Sherman was cut off from his normal lines of communication with the North. Northern newspapers actually had to rely on *Southern* accounts of Sherman's actions and whereabouts in order to keep their readers informed. The relative lack of Northern commentary on the march is more than balanced by the wealth of attention devoted to it in the Southern press, which published not only impassioned editorials but also private letters from citizens chronicling its effects.

By any account, the March to the Sea was awesome in its power of devastation. Divided into two wings, Sherman's army of 60,000 men cut a path of destruction that was sixty miles wide and extended through three hundred miles of Georgia's territory. Contrary to what many people presume, while the havoc wrought by Sherman's troops was fearsome, it was *not* indiscriminate. They sought specifically to ruin Georgia's productive capacity. While seizing food and supplies for themselves from the farms, stores, and stockyards of civilians, they destroyed what they did not take, setting fire to granaries, killing farm animals, breaking agricultural equipment, and ripping up fences, bridges, rail lines, and other basic infrastructure. But after leaving Atlanta, Sherman's men did not methodically demolish private homes.[4] Although they certainly entered them to rummage through cupboards and closets, the soldiers typically stopped short of decimating them. Only Southerners who attempted to resist and impede Sherman, or who were rebels of prominence, were likely to have their homes put to the torch. Even so, in Southern eyes, the destruction was still unremitting and merciless. In December, after Sherman rolled through the town of Eatonton, the *Countryman* published this letter from a local woman to her sister, detailing both the restrained behavior of Union troops, and the vitriolic emotions they nevertheless inspired:

Dear Sister:—I have been thinking, ever since our visit from the blue-coat scoundrels, I would write

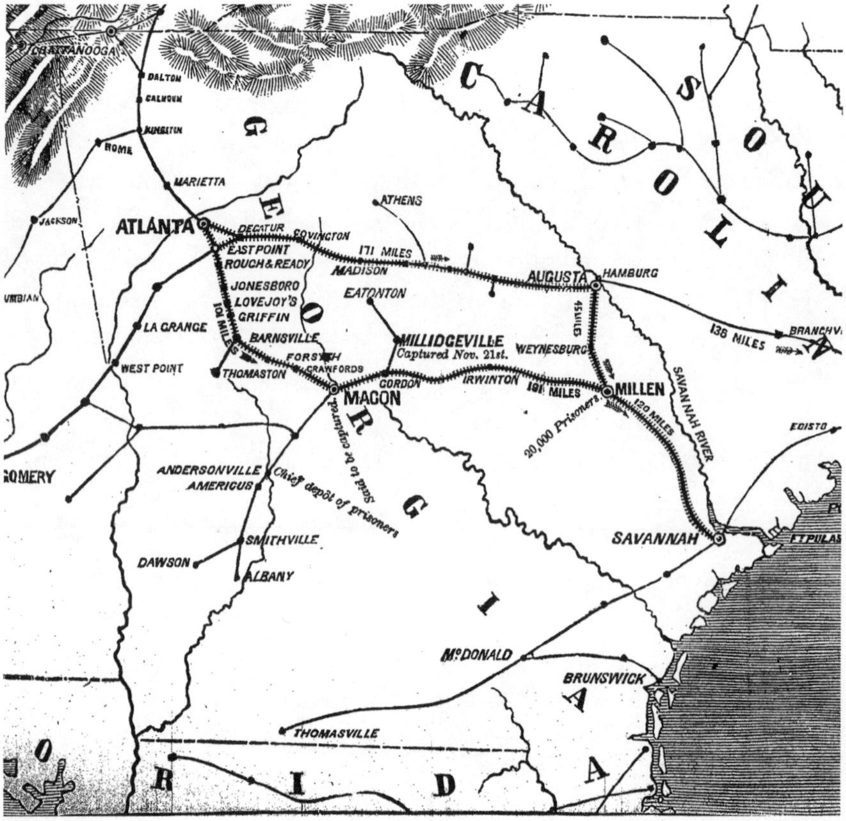

Frank Leslie's Illustrated Newspaper, December 10, 1864. A map of Sherman's March to the Sea, which cut a swath of destruction through Georgia as much as sixty miles wide.

you, but first one thing, and then another, has prevented: for it does seem as if I will never get straight again.

You ask me to tell you all about the raid. Why, sister, it would take several quivers of paper to record all the yankees' deeds of meanness: but they did not trouble me much, except coming near eating me out of house, and home. But few came in the house, and they did no damage. But they stole Mr. M.'s buggy, besides all my turkeys, and chickens. They left me one hen, out of two dozens, and not a rooster, out of four. You well know how much I hated to see my pretty white turkeys go. They were very fat—in good Christmas order. I had five, but, alas, for human plans, these times!

Two of pa's negroes went off—George, and Duane. Our other negroes behaved splendidly. They were offered every inducement to go. . . . All of uncle J.'s negroes left, but one. That was a little negro girl about ten. Aunt L. gave all her money, jewelry, and watch to old Joe [a slave], to take care of, and he marched off with them. I feel very sorry for her.

You never saw such a complete wreck as pa's store was. There was not a five cents' worth left in it. He saved a few of his goods, such as dresses, &c., by carrying them up to the house. . . . I can't tell you half I wish to tell you: but will reserve the rest until I see you, which I hope will be soon. . . . I thought I had a hatred of the yankees enough, ALL my life: but I knew nothing about hating them, until I saw them.[5]

This experience was shared by many well-to-do families in central Georgia. Until Sherman's arrival, these Southerners had managed to avoid the crushing destitution that afflicted their less fortunate countrymen. Sherman's army, however, quickly reduced them from relative luxury to poverty in what seemed like one brutal stroke. Southern civilians certainly had suffered from the war before, but never in such a systematic way. Without any exaggeration, the *Augusta Chronicle & Sentinel* could rightly assert that "Sherman's audacious march though the heart of our territory, has given a new aspect to the war. . . . It is no longer a mere frontier war, to be waged by our armies in the field. It is brought to every man's door. Its threatening cloud darkens every man's habitation. We are called to grapple with the foe in our own homes, and by our own hearths."[6] By direct consequence, Union troops came into regular contact with Southern women. For Southerners, this kind of warfare—these images of heartless Union soldiers intruding upon private homes and threatening their female inhabitants—embodied the horrendous "beauty and booty" policies that they had feared since the start of the conflict. In 1861, the Southern press had envisioned that the Union invasion of the Confederacy would be characterized not just by wanton destruction but by indiscriminate rape. Now, with Sherman's men ransacking the countryside, accusations of sexual violence flew.

Whether rape actually occurred during Sherman's march is an open question, one that historians of the Civil War have not systematically studied, although sex crime cases certainly do appear within the Union's courts martial records.[7] According to Southern newspaper accounts, however, they occurred repeatedly in Georgia. In a letter to the *Columbus Enquirer*, for instance, one correspondent angrily recounted the plight of a seventeen-year-old girl who had become a "victim of the hellish appetites" of Yankee soldiers. "Three of them, in broad daylight" and directly in view of her aged parents, "outraged her!" A reporter for the *Augusta Constitutionalist*, writing from the state capital at Milledgeville, testified that at least six or seven ladies there had suffered "the last extremity"—rape—while others had been "stripped of their garments" and then compelled to entertain the troops by playing piano.[8] Another eyewitness to events in Milledgeville added these details, which the *Augusta Register* publi-

From Georgia.—We find in the Georgia papers some history of the horrors of Sherman's march through that State. In a long letter, written from Milledgeville after the Yankees had left, and written in a calm, dispassionate style, without any attempt at exaggeration, we find the following terrible paragraph:

"The most dreadful thing was their violence towards the ladies. *At least six or seven suffered the last extremity.* One young girl became crazed in consequence, and has been sent to the asylum. Other ladies were stripped of their garments, and, in such a plight, compelled to play the piano; and, in the event of a refusal, switched unmercifully. Let Georgians remember these things in the day of battle!"

Richmond Dispatch, December 7, 1864.
Accusations of rape followed in Sherman's path. Newspapers published them in hopes of rousing Southern men to higher levels of exertion in defending their families—and the Confederacy—from ravishment and dishonor.

cized with a demand for vengeance and the defense of their honor:

> A gentleman arrived in this city yesterday evening who left Milledgeville on Tuesday morning. He says the State House, Executive Mansion and Milledgeville Hotel, have not been burned. The depot, Penitentiary and Arsenal were all the buildings that were burned. They burn all granaries and cotton they find in the country, and kill or carry off every living thing that could possibly serve for food. The country is left a barren waste. Many families that one week ago were comparatively wealthy have not now the means of sustenance.
>
> But the most hellish deeds that the infernal demons committed remain to be told. We are informed that the incarnate devils ravished some of the nicest ladies in the town. We pen the paragraph with horror. Our blood runs cold as we write. We would forbear doing so, but we wish our people to know the destiny that awaits them if the villains are allowed to continue their invasion of the country. One of their unfortunate victims was, we learn, consigned to the asylum on Monday. Her reason tottered beneath the load of wounded honor, and the poor victim is ruined forever. How long! oh, how long is our country to be insulted by these savages? In the name of justice and humanity we urge our people to vindicate their honor. We have a heavy score against our foemen; blood will scarcely obliterate the record. There have been deeds committed by these God forsaken wretches, that should cause the heavens to peal the thunder cry of vengeance, and the earth to open and swallow the wretches. . . . But the earth would spew out such wretches; the sea would disgorge them. Hell is scarce fit to domicile them.
>
> To our armies we would say write on your battle-flags, in broad, black letters, AVENGE THE HONOR OF OUR WOMEN! Let it be emblazoned before the eye of every soldier, and in the hour of conflict let it be the battle-cry that goads our men on to deeds of valor which will crush out the foe, and leave not a vestige of them save a great stench in the land. At the sight of those words the guilty hounds who have ruined our homes and despoiled our women of their honor, will quail and sink as before a mighty whirlwind, and the righteous indignation of an outraged people will overwhelm them. Then thunder it over the land until the rocks shall echo back the sound and the hills reverberate the echo and every heart be filled with the fires of vengeance.[9]

Behind these strident remarks lay an understanding that at the very moment that the safety and sanctity of their homes were so imperiled, there were tens of thousands of military-age men lurking about the Confederacy, not engaged in the fighting at all. Some of these men were stragglers who had avoided conscription entirely. But others had deserted. In November 1864, in a public speech, Jefferson Davis made the embarrassing admission that two-thirds of all enlisted soldiers were now absent from the ranks, without leave. Desperate to rouse these absentees to action, the *Macon Telegraph* issued this stark picture of "The Dishonoring of Southern Women," to remind them not only of their duty as citizens but of their responsibilities as men:

> It is fully time that every Southern man, who loves his estate, or liberty or honor, should open his eyes, clearly and broadly, to the probable results of the war. Among these results, is the subjecting of our wives, daughters and sisters, to the brutal lusts of an infidel, coarse, and fiendish horde. . . . Let us look at the avowed policy of our enemy. No compromise, but war until the rebellion *is crushed*. *That* is to be crushed out, by force in the field—by military occupation of our territory—by garrisoning our cities and towns—by hanging, or executing our leaders, civil and military—by freeing our slaves—by confiscating our lands and parceling them out to their Dutch and

New England free laborers—by leaving the freed slaves upon the soil, to be merged into the white race, by miscegenation. . . . How else? *By insulting and ravishing our women.*

Is this an overdrawn picture? Does any sane man question that subjugation is to be accomplished by each, and all of these means? . . . How has the programme of subjugation been worked out in the conduct of the war? . . . The Federal States claiming to be Christian, and boasting a civilization higher and purer, than any that history records, have, whenever their armies have occupied our territory, destroyed provisions and turned the women and children out to starve—from kitchen to garret, they have plundered the homes of the rich and the poor, they have consumed the dwellings of the people with fire—ravaged plantations with fierce and wanton devastation. . . . To this catalogue of atrocities, there remains to be added one other specification. In numerous well authenticated cases, they have ravished our women. Not content with insult, in word and act—with entering chambers—plucking jewelry from the person, and robbing wardrobes; they have murdered the life element of female character.

The mothers of children and the innocent maidens have been made the victims of their beastly lusts. . . . If these things do not arouse the spirit and intensity the energies of Southern men, they deserve the hissing and scorn of the civilized world. Southern ladies are the noblest type of womanhood. None equal them in beauty—none approach them in delicacy and refinement, and they are unrivalled in the sweet graces of wife, sister and mother. These are they who are subject to this vile pollution. . . . If men hold any trust that is holy it is female honor. We boast of our chivalry. Where is it? Dormant or dead? If indeed our country is subjugated, every process of humiliation which Yankee ingenuity, stimulated by revenge, can devise, will be resorted to to degrade the Southern race and break down its spirit. . . . Beast Butler presided over the enormities of New Orleans . . . and Sherman . . . led the columns which baptised the fairest portions of Georgia and Mississippi with the fire of almost remediless ruin. He (Sherman) drove out with remorseless universality, the inhabitants of Atlanta; witnessed, in person, the burning of four thousand homes, and in a moral, if not a literal sense, sowed its soil with salt. The tears he caused to be shed in that one city, would make saline the waters of all its fountains. Who can tell the agony of women during his terrible reign? Who shall record her wrongs? . . . Before God, and in the assize of reason and common sense, he is responsible for the outrages upon honor, decency, and the usages of war, committed by his soldiers.

Let us not hug to our bosoms the unmanly reflection, that *my* wife, *my* daughter is not the victim of lustful violence; for before the flowers of another spring shall open; *our* families may be visited with a similar cause. Besides, the cause of one such victim, is the cause of the Confederacy. . . . It is the imploring cry for protection, not of one poor sufferer, but of the sex. The alternative left us, is *final ruin, social, political, and monetary*, or, *Independence won by fighting*. He who does not see this, is blind indeed. *What then is to be done?* Let the soil be cultivated and the offices filled by the old men and the disabled soldiers; and every other man hasten to the Front, and meet the foe with souls of fire, and hearts of steel, and hands of iron. . . . Perish we may, but it is sweet and becoming, to die for home, altars and female security.[10]

Despite the stridency with which the Southern press attempted to inspire and rally their readers, the state of affairs in the Confederacy only became more unsettling. The havoc wreaked by Sherman's troops was only one part of the problem. On top of that, there was a more general breakdown of law and order, and an upsurge in violence that pitted Southerners against each other. Throughout the countryside, renegades—mostly deserters from the Confederate army—were suddenly appearing with alarming frequency, holding civilians at gunpoint and stealing whatever valuables they could get their hands on. As the Confederate authorities were already preoccupied with Sherman, there was no attempt to crack down on these marauders. In the closing days of 1864, the *Augusta Chronicle & Sentinel* reported that incidents of robbery, assault, and murder had "fearfully multiplied" to such an extent that people were now walking the streets armed for self-protection. Everywhere, it seemed, "outrages and violence are rapidly on the increase," pushing the South toward "a condition of universal insecurity" and "domestic anarchy." This was not just a problem in Georgia. The situation in the western part of North Carolina was similarly "deplorable in the extreme," noted the *Raleigh Confederate*. "Bands of deserters and murderers [have] been organized for depredation upon the peaceful inhabitants, and they well nigh have possession of the country." One man, in a letter to the *Confederate*, wrote imploringly but angrily for some sort of relief:

> MESSRS. EDITORS:—One of the most important matters for the consideration and action of this Legislature, is the condition of that portion of the State immediately contiguous to the Blue Ridge mountains. I do not think I exaggerate the State of things existing there, when I say that over a very large extent of territory in the locality referred to, life and property are almost as insecure as within the enemy's lines. Robberies and murders of the most atrocious kind are daily and nightly perpetrated, and from the disordered state of the country, the offenders go unwhipt of justice. A remedy of some sort ought to be devised by this Legislature. If it cannot do all that the people of the district referred to desire, it ought at least to exhaust all its power to suppress the outrages which have occurred so frequently, of late, in the western part of the State. The lawless perpetrators of these offences are composed in the main of deserters from our own army; but there are besides these many bad men infesting our mountains who have deserted both armies and who are now living as outlaws against both Governments. Is it too much to ask of the Legislature, to adopt some severe and decisive measures to rid the country of these wretches? Can any man, be he friend or foe to the Confederate cause, sympathize with those who subsist by indiscriminate murder and rapine? Is the Legislature powerless to act in such an exigency? If it is, then it must confess its incompetency to secure to the people the peaceful enjoyment of their property and lives.[11]

Indeed, neither the state governments nor the national government in Richmond were able to adequately defend the common people. While lawlessness in the countryside continued to spiral unabated, Sherman's march across Georgia was an unstoppable success. By the end of December, he had reached Savannah, which capitulated without resistance. After presenting the city to Lincoln as his "Christmas gift," Sherman set his sights northward, and prepared to head into the Carolinas. The march sapped the morale of many civilians in the Confederacy. Exhausted by the war and sickened by the inability of their leaders to counter Sherman, communities not only in Georgia but in other states now vulnerable to attack succumbed to despondency and defeatism. In North Carolina, the situation seemed especially dire. On January 15, 1865, a Union assault led by General Alfred Terry captured Fort Fisher, at the mouth of the Cape Fear River, twenty miles from Wilmington. With Sherman poised to join him, the *Raleigh Progress* frantically called upon the state legislature to do something bold—to sue for a separate peace with the Union that might spare North Carolina from being demolished and abolitionized:

> Sherman is in motion, and, according to refugees from Savannah, has a force of 80,000 men. Nor is his army a loose mob, prowling on the country to oppress friend as well as foe,—it is an army of disci-

SANTA CLAUS SHERMAN PUTTING SAVANNAH INTO UNCLE SAM'S STOCKING.

Frank Leslie's Illustrated Newspaper, January 14, 1865.
Sherman is pictured here as Santa Claus, stuffing the city of Savannah, which surrendered on December 21, 1864, into Uncle Sam's stocking as a Christmas gift.

pline, vigor, action. With Savannah and Beaufort, S.C., as a base he moves north with the sun, and already Charleston and Columbia begin to feel the oppression. But will he come to Columbia, with those 80,000 men? Yes, if he wants to do so he will, and even farther into the bowels of the land.

Terry is on our own coast—has Fort Fisher, at the mouth of Cape Fear, and will soon, we think, have Wilmington. He probably has 20,000 to 40,000 men. Suppose they combine their forces, Terry and Sherman; we must set them down at not less than about one hundred and twenty thousand men. And they will move on with the sun, and before the orb that lights the world shall stand erect in the heavens, it is more than probable that the Federal flag will fly over Charleston, Wilmington, Columbia and Raleigh! Yes, Raleigh too! . . .

What then? Sherman will in all human probability be here with the spring, and . . . if we have no armies to meet [his] armies why continue the unequal contest? If there be those in our Legislature who believe there is no salvation for the people of North Carolina but in an appeal for their rights under the old constitution, let them speak out, for the time has come to discuss those questions. And if there be those who believe that the only way to save us from abolition, negro equality, servile insurrections, and a general upheaving of society, [is] a restoration of the old government, under the constitution of our old fathers, let them present their plans—the people will listen. . . . If we are subjugated, or so near to it that a protraction of the unequal contest can end in nothing else, whey continue the war?—This is a question for our Governor and Legislature to answer to the people of North Carolina. The people of the country, not only here in North Carolina but throughout the whole South, begin to see the state and condition to which the war has brought them, . . . and the popular voice is loud and constant for peace!

We say, candidly, to our friends in the Legislature, that we believe this to be *their* last chance. Do something now or you may never have another opportunity. And take the bull by the horns and do something practical. What is to be done must be done quickly, for it is not thought that Sherman will give you more than sixty or ninety days to work in. The people want peace, regardless of Jeff Davis and Abe Lincoln. Give them peace, and protection for person and property, and they care very little about boundary lines or who may be President.[12]

Not everyone had been cowed into submission, however. Among soldiers in the field—those who continued to risk their lives, even as so many others deserted or avoided military service—the faintheartedness of people at home was both enraging and demoralizing. As a soldier from the Fifty-third Regiment of Alabama Cavalry explained in a letter to the *Columbus Sun*, it seemed far more honorable to fight to the last, than to tamely submit to Lincoln and his abolitionist scheme for "negro equality":

Mr. Editor:—We but seldom see a newspaper, situated as we are in the piney woods of Scriven county, Georgia, with our railroads cut off, and no mail facilities. We know but little of what is transpiring in our little Confederacy, except as it is brought [to] us by wounded and furloughed soldiers returning to their commands—and I must confess the accounts given are anything but cheering. Immediately upon the heel of our reverses comes the disheartening intelligence that nothing is thought of or talked of at home but a Reconstruction of the old Union. Are the sacrifices which our soldiers are making and have made in vain? . . . Do our citizens value their property above liberty and independence? I believe not. Certainly the accounts we receive are incorrect. They will never consent again to live with a people who have disregarded every constitutional obligation, who have invaded our country, stolen our property, murdered our citizens, and who have perpetrated acts, the base mention of which would cause a demon to blush. . . .

Give us but the spirit of our illustrious sires of '76; give us but a spirit to resist tyranny in every shape: give us but a spirit to rise above these reverses, and a determination to conquer or die. . . . I know not what others may prefer, [but] we in the army had rather die freemen, than live slaves. We will never sheath our swords nor stack our arms until the independence of our country is established. We have followed the dear old Flag of our Country, for four years, through many a bloody and hard fought battle, and it shall never trail ingloriously in the dust. We fling it to the breeze, and "swear with it, to live by it to die."

The people at home may Reconstruct if they wish, for themselves, but *not for us*. . . . What terms have the Lincoln dynasty ever proposed, which an honorable man could accept? Such that the wolf offers the lamb. Nothing but humiliation and degradation, and an elevation of the negro race upon an equality with ourselves. This is Lincoln's ultimatum. Are we prepared to accept such terms? For the army, I answer, never, *no, never*.[13]

The troops resented the peace sentiment of civilians and decried the impact it had on the fighting power of the Confederacy. They knew all too well that Sherman alone was not responsible for the dramatic rise in desertions from the army at the end of 1864. The disaffection of the common people and their willingness (and in some cases, their eagerness) to pursue a negotiated peace, which they continued to convey in letters to friends and loved ones in the army, were equally to blame.[14] In the eyes of soldiers who were still in for the fight, the people at home were doing more than just abandoning them. They were betraying the memory of those who already had sacrificed their lives for the Confederacy. In a letter to his father in Macon, Georgia, a soldier wrote passionately about this blood debt that everyone in the Confederacy was responsible for honoring:

> Dear Father: . . . I am, of course, tired of this unnatural war, and would like, above all things, to be restored once again to my family; but I will never return unless I can do so with a clear conscience. Come what may I am willing to make sacrifices of my property, and the separation from my wife and friends; but we have gone too far to retrace our steps or even look back. I have been from home nearly four years, and if necessary, let me remain four years longer, so we but accomplish the ends we are determined to gain. I can never give my consent to live peaceably with the Yankee race, unless held down by armed power: for the memory of my dear brother is still fresh in my mind, as well as of other members of our family, and I would prove recreant to them who cry aloud for vengeance, and by their examples before they fell, exhort[ing] us to continue the struggle "until the last armed foe expires."
>
> The people at home, who have escaped the dangers and struggles of this contest, owe it to the brave soldiers and gallant dead to contribute all in their power to assist them in protecting their homes and firesides, wives and children, and all that they hold dear and sacred. We can still have peaceful homes and firesides, . . . if we but do our duty. The most of our desertions from the army are caused from the tenor of the letters the men receive from home. I hear that Georgians are continually deserting the army of Virginia. . . . I trust for the sake of the many gallant and noble dead whose bones whiten the soil of Virginia, Tennessee and many other States, that our people at home will remain true to the trust

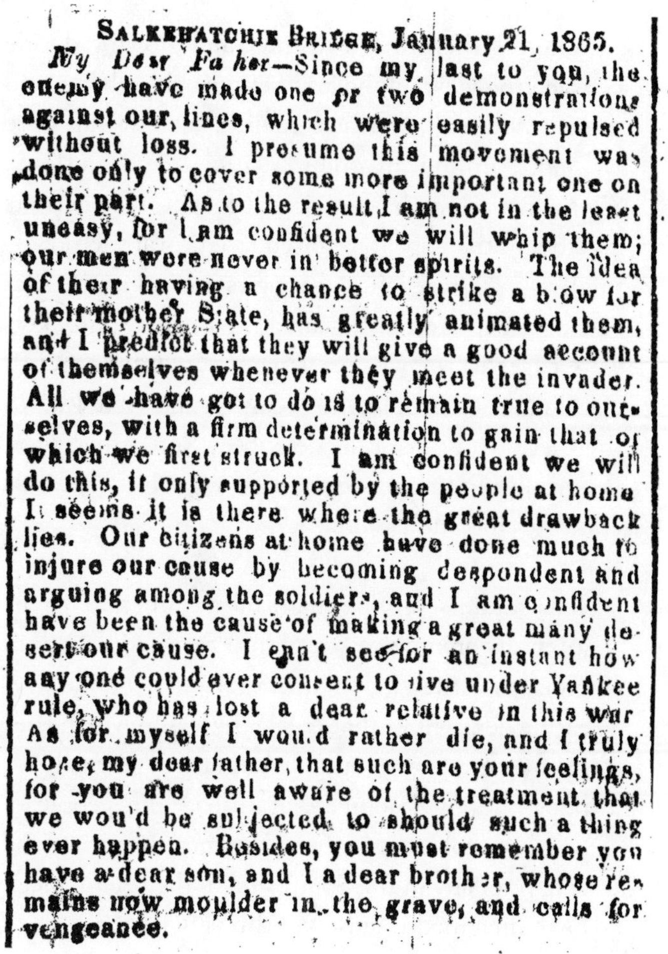

SALKEHATCHIE BRIDGE, January 21, 1865.

My Dear Father—Since my last to you, the enemy have made one or two demonstrations against our lines, which were easily repulsed without loss. I presume this movement was done only to cover some more important one on their part. As to the result I am not in the least uneasy, for I am confident we will whip them; our men were never in better spirits. The idea of their having a chance to strike a blow for their mother State, has greatly animated them, and I predict that they will give a good account of themselves whenever they meet the invader. All we have got to do is to remain true to ourselves, with a firm determination to gain that for which we first struck. I am confident we will do this, if only supported by the people at home. It seems it is there where the great drawback lies. Our citizens at home have done much to injure our cause by becoming despondent and arguing among the soldiers, and I am confident have been the cause of making a great many desert our cause. I can't see for an instant how any one could ever consent to live under Yankee rule, who has lost a dear relative in this war. As for myself I would rather die, and I truly hope, my dear father, that such are your feelings, for you are well aware of the treatment that we would be subjected to should such a thing ever happen. Besides, you must remember you have a dear son, and I a dear brother, whose remains now moulder in the grave, and calls for vengeance.

Charleston Courier, January 31, 1865.
Sherman's march psychologically demoralized many civilians and prompted a surge in desertions from the Confederate army. At the same time, though, it enlivened the patriotism of those Southern men who stayed in the ranks and who continued to fight not only for Confederate independence but also to vindicate the sacrifices made by those who had died in the conflict.

> reposed in them, and never falter as long as they can lift a hand or contribute a mite for their deliverance. Will they do it? I hope so—trust so.[15]

Whereas there was a distinct and growing divide between the views of the Southern people at home and those in the army, Northern soldiers and civilians were far more united in their attitudes and outlook. Sherman's triumphant march brought Northerners together in the hope that the end to the war was now—finally—within reach. After news arrived of the successful occupation of Savannah, Northern onlookers were eager to see what Sherman would do in South Carolina, the birthplace of secession and civil war. As the *Cleveland Plain Dealer* described, Northerners were practically panting to see the state suffer bitterly for its crimes against the Union:

> The soldiers of Sherman's army are said to be intensely anxious to be led into South Carolina, in order that they may teach a few facts to the fire-eating denizens of that cradle of treason which they have probably not yet quite sufficiently learned. We hope they will soon be gratified. The people of South Carolina have been the most insulting and defiant of any in the South, and in their self-conceit have imagined themselves the very *ne plus ultra* of Southern chivalry and gallantry. No men are better qualified to silence their boastings and bring them to the dust than the gallant soldiers of Sherman. Moreover, they could with good heart punish them as they justly deserve. South Carolina was the birthplace of rebellion; she passed the first ordinance of secession, and by her example and instigation drew the other Southern States into the same web; on her soil was fired the first gun and fought the first battle of the war. Not only Sherman's soldiers, but the whole North, would rejoice at her downfall—her utter annihilation if possible—for upon her head should of right be heaped the retribution that belongs to the rebellion she inaugurated. She deserves no mercy, no quarter. . . . Let her suffer to the full penalty of her misdeeds, and the army of Sherman is fully qualified to perform the office.[16]

While Northerners detested the entire state of South Carolina, they reserved the brunt of their spite for Charleston, the precise meeting place of South Carolina's secession convention and the base of operations from which the first shots of the war had been fired at Fort Sumter. In the Northern mind, Charleston was the heart of the rebellion, and consequently, they wanted it to be obliterated. The following editorial from the *Harrisburg Telegraph*, featuring quotes from soldiers under Sherman's command, reveals not only the harsh attitudes of the men at the front but also the fundamental agreement of the people at home that Charleston's total destruction would be richly deserved:

> Marching with General Sherman, are several Harrisburgers. These men . . . have lately written to their friends and ourselves . . . that the ruling purpose of the hardy heroes . . . is, after Charleston, S.C. has been captured, to demolish that nest of traitors, and mark the spot where it now stands with a heap of embers and ashes. These correspondents write that among the men in the corps to which they are attached, the feeling is unanimous that Charleston must be destroyed—must be, to quote the language of one of these letters, "*wiped out, given as a burnt offering to freedom and the Union, before both can be considered safe from the wiles of traitors.*" Another of the correspondents writes, "*The army is unanimous for the destruction of Charleston. Our companions in arms do not want to pillage the accursed city, where treason was first hatched. It does not contain an article worthy of becoming a trophy in the hands of a brave man. Its destruction will therefore become complete, and when the army leaves it the soldiers will shake its ashes from their feet, fearful to bear even such a vestige of its foul existence to any of the territory of the country.*" From another of these letters we quote:

"The army is resolved on the complete destruction of Charleston; and I am satisfied that there is no power lodged in man to save that city from its doom. Gen. Sherman, even if he desired, could not save the city, unless he changes the course of his army, and marches around instead of into Charleston. The capture of Charleston by the army will be equal to blotting the name of the city from the map of the Union, as in that event this hell-hole of treason will be utterly destroyed."

There is something so startling in the harmony of these statements, that we could not refrain from thus laying them before our readers. Nor is it strange that the soldiers under Sherman's lead should feel this bitter resentment towards Charleston. In that city, the evils of treason and rebellion were hatched. . . . Justice, therefore, seems to demand the utter destruction of that city. Its imperious arrogance should be humbled—its bloody villainies should be adequately punished by levelling its structures to the earth, and tearing up its very foundations.[17]

In the end, Charleston would be spared the ruination that many in the North had wished upon it. Sherman's route, instead of veering toward the Atlantic coast, went directly through the heart of the state. Along the way, Sherman's men showed little restraint, setting fire to entire towns as they headed toward the capital at Columbia, which took the beating that had been envisioned for Charleston. When two of Sherman's units occupied the city on February 17, chaos and looting immediately ensued. By evening, Columbia was engulfed in flames that would eventually consume over half of it. The origin of the fires remains unclear. Southerners were quick to point fingers at the Union soldiers, although it may be that rebel cavalrymen started it by setting fire to bales of cotton as they evacuated, to prevent the North from taking possession of them. Regardless of how the conflagration began, though, Sherman's men undeniably had a hand in helping to fan the flames. Columbia fared far worse than most of the places in Georgia through which Sherman had passed—and worse than the North Carolina towns toward which he then headed. If Northerners felt any regrets about the unusually harsh treatment of South Carolina, the newspapers show no evidence of it. Even afterward, when the North had the chance to reflect, it was only to congratulate Sherman on a job well done. The *New York Herald* explained:

South Carolina is honestly hated by the whole North as the prime mover of secession, the head and front of the attempt to destroy our government—the proudest spirit in the Southern oligarchy, that in its contemptible pride had the impudence to look upon longer association with the better people of the North as beneath her, and that, in the blind, mad purpose to get rid of that association, cared not what ruin might ensue. Hence the Northern people can see her cities burn with much less concern than they would feel if those terrible blows fell upon any other people. We have patience with Sherman's men when we reflect where they are. . . . When soldiers burn cities it is ordinarily a bad sign for the discipline of the army of which they form a part; but in the present case we know that the burning of the cities and farms is not an evidence that the discipline is looser, but simply that the men, in the real spirit of the people, feel the unconquerable national hate for that pestilent people who have caused all this trouble. Why should they withhold their hands? South Carolina never withheld hers so long as it was perfectly safe to strike. Will they turn this rich farmer out of his house and home, burn all that he has and make him a starveling outcast? Certainly. Here are ten thousand men from Illinois and Indiana, as many from New York and Maine, and he has turned every one of these out of house and home. For his fault, for the gratification of his mad and ignorant political passion, they have been compelled to abandon all the comforts of home, as he must now. . . . They can never hope to inflict upon him a tithe of the wretchedness he has caused them;

SHERMAN.

COLUMBIA OURS!

Occupation of the Capital of South Carolina.

Beauregard Officially Announces that Sherman Reached the City on February 17.

CHARLESTON IS BEING EVACUATED.

The Rebels Admit that the Occupation of Columbia Necessitates the Fall of Charleston.

New York Herald, February 19, 1865.

> but what little they can do they will, and so they burn. Through Georgia the army was manageable. . . . So soon as it touched the North Carolina line it was again a disciplined force; but in all the space in between, across the whole of South Carolina, it was a scourge, inflicting the wild and passionate vengeance of the people who sent it.[18]

Although Northern soldiers were less bitter in their attitude toward North Carolina, they by no means lost momentum. As described in the following letter, written by a woman in Fayetteville after Sherman's men had moved through the town, they remained as exacting of civilian property there as they had been in their march through Georgia:

> Sherman has gone, and terrible has been the storm that has swept over us with his coming and going. My head is dizzy, my heart is sick, at what I have seen and felt in the last four days. I feel like I had just awakened from a dream of impossible horrors—a nightmare. I can hardly realize that what has transpired around us was indeed reality. . . . Squad after squad unceasingly came and went and tramped though the halls and rooms of our house, day and night during the entire stay of the army.
>
> Safe-guards were placed around some houses, but that very guard would ransack the house and premises with a more merciless exactness, if possible, than any others. At our house they killed every chicken, goose, turkey, cow, calf, and every living thing, even to our pet dog. They carried off our wagons, carriage and horses, and broke up our buggy, wheel-barrow, garden implements, axes, hatchets, hammers, saws, &c, and burned the fences. Our smoke-house and pantry, that a few days ago were well stored with bacon, lard, flour, dried fruit, meal, pickles, preserves, etc., now contain nothing whatever except a few pounds of meal and flour and five pounds of bacon. They took from old men, women and children alike, every garment of wearing apparel save

what we had on, not even sparing the napkins of infants! Blankets, sheets, quilts, &c., such as it did not suit them to take away, they tore to pieces before our eyes. After destroying everything we had, and taking from us every morsel of food, save the pittance I have mentioned, one of these barbarians had to add insult to injury, by asking me "what you (I) would live upon now." I replied, "Upon patriotism; I will exist upon the love of my country as long as life will last, and then I will die as firm in that love as the everlasting hills."

"Oh," says he, "but we shall soon subjugate the rebellion, and you will have no country to love."

"Never!" I interrupted; "never! you and your blood-handed countrymen may make the whole of this beautiful land one vast graveyard, but its people will never be subjugated. Every man, woman and child of us will sleep quietly in honorable graves, but we will never live dishonorable lives." And he turned and left me with a fiendish chuckle.[19]

As this woman's story suggests, not all Southern civilians shrank in the face of Sherman's march. To say that *all* Southern civilians lost their will to fight would overstate the case. Instead of growing despondent, some of them became all the more defiant and angry.[20] Importantly, this sense of indignation was suffused by abiding feelings of patriotic love for the Confederacy. For these Southerners, the Confederacy remained the repository of all their hopes and affections—an attitude that comes through clearly in this letter, written by a Texas woman to her cousin, and later published in the *Galveston Tri-Weekly News* as a model of the high-toned spirit of sacrifice that all Southerners were still expected to demonstrate:

Dear Cousin:—The reports of disasters that have lately befallen our cause, render me apprehensive that Texas may yet be the dark and bloody field of this fearful struggle, but if I could only animate every Southern man with the spirit that glows in my own bosom, the prospect, so far from striking terror to their souls, would only arouse them to yet more desperate exertion.

. . . Should our infuriated foe succeed in destroying the spirit of liberty among us, I trust it will not be until I shall have no further need of more land than will afford *me a grave*. God grant that our flag, baptised as it has been in the holy baptism of patriotic blood, may yet wave triumphant. I will not despair though our own loved Lone Star State may yet be dyed in the gore of her patriotic sons. The fiery current of war may leave her prairies and hillsides a blackened waste; our women and children may be driven to the slow torture of starvation, but never will this true heart quail beneath any or all the accumulated miseries which our enemies may heap upon us. Still will it ever beat true to that cause in which my noble-hearted husband sacrificed his precious life.

How can any one, even for a moment, think of the suicidal measure of reconstruction, whilst we are still in possession of our honor, our liberties and our *grave yards*? There is scarcely one of us who has not some dear friend, a husband, father, son or brother, now resting in the cold earth; and shall we surrender their last habitations into the hands of their *murderers*, that they may exult and upbraid their memories over their cold ashes?

I have suffered much, and am prepared to suffer more; I can endure any and every hardship, make every sacrifice for the South. . . . Dear Cousin, forgive me, I write just as I feel, and every other thought is absorbed in the one. *My country is now my earthly idol.* I love the South. I love her institutions. . . . Under her bright skies, I have passed the happiest days of my life. My loved ones sleep beneath her sod; my dear husband died for her. . . .

I have little to lose in a pecuniary sense, but my dear husband left me an honored *name* and a *country*, rich legacies which I will defend with my life. I cannot shoulder a rifle and go to the field, but I

> can and do try to animate and encourage my male friends to maintain the fight in this most righteous cause by every means in my power, believing it to be the most glorious struggle in which a nation ever unsheathed a sword.[21]

It was relatively easy for civilians in Texas—far from Sherman's operations—to maintain their devotion to the Confederacy. Southerners residing along the eastern seaboard, who had to deal directly with the threat of invasion, were much more likely to succumb to fear and exhaustion. Sherman and his total war tactics really pushed the Southern people to emotional extremes, toward greater heights of Confederate patriotism or deeper depths of disillusionment. As fate would have it, on the very same day that the *Galveston Tri-Weekly News* published the above letter, the *Raleigh Confederate* published another letter of a much different stripe. According to the *Confederate*, it was written by a woman living in the path of Sherman's advancing army who was trying to reach her beau—a Confederate soldier—to encourage him to desert and seek refuge on enemy soil. The *Confederate* printed the letter in order to condemn such treasonous plottings and to admonish women about writing gloomy, dispiriting letters to the soldiers. "These letters are now common," the paper lamented. "They are part of a system by which our good and brave soldiers are to be seduced from their duty." The *Confederate*, by exposing and disgracing this practice, hoped to discourage it entirely. Reading the letter takes some patience, as it was written with tremendous haste, without standard punctuation. However, it is an intriguing document, one that acknowledges the frantic despair felt by at least some Southerners that were sitting in Sherman's way:

> Mr. Care, My ever remembered friend:
>
> I received your very kind letter yesterday. I had certainly come upon the conclusion, that you had forgotten your friend, or, perhaps, you had something of more importance to occupy your leisure hours. I havent nothing of interest to communicate—indeed my mind is so mixed up I am at a loss to know what to write. This is a day of great trouble and a great many have to participate in them. I think it a true saing that the darkest hour is just before dawn. The general opinion of the people is that Sherman will be through here in less than three weeks you spoke of your troubles and privations I know a soldiers life is a hard one. I hope this war will soon close so that the soldiers will be permitted to return to their dear ones at home and have peace gloreous peace, in our once happy country. I am going to tell you something if you will promise me you will not repeat it. I heard that you and some others of your company had crossed the lines. I did sincerely hope that it was so, not that I wanted you to leave and never to return, no indeed, but there is a probability of returning if you were there, but life is uncertain in this poor confederacy now do not let any one know that I have written this to you if some of them knew it they would not recognize me as a Southern Lady. Burrell Johnson is in Indianna his wife is going to him soon. I have a notion of emigrating with her she is very anxious for me to go with her. You say you cannot write your centiments. why not I will assure you I will not expose them. I am a good hand to keep a secret. You must tell me in your next, but I will not insist fearing you will think I am too *official*.—Emily's husband is in Yankeedom she will go to him when she hears from him again. . . . You must excuse this mixed up letter it is so badly written I dont reacon you can read it it is most time for the mail so I must close you must not think hard of me for what I have said I dont often express my opinions except to those I can confide the mail is here I must close.
>
> From your true friend,
> Lou A V*******[22]

As the Southern press recognized, this kind of breakdown in home front morale made it difficult to stem the tide of army desertions. Desperate to remind female readers of their responsibility for sustaining the momentum of the war, the *Army Argus & Crisis* issued this anxious appeal "To the Women of Alabama and Mississippi":

> We write under a deep sense of responsibility. The fate of our country is suspended on the events of a few short months. By virtue of prompt, earnest, faithful effort, we may be redeemed from a fate worse than death, and our country may be blessed with peace and free Government. If we sleep, or if we meanly and ignobly refuse to listen to the calls of our struggling, bleeding land, we may plunge into a yawning abyss of degradation, ruin, and misery, and fall like the darkened star to rise no more. In this fearful issue, no class of human beings have so much at stake as the women of the South. There are truths—there are threatened evils which we are not permitted to describe, but which all good and well informed ladies can imagine for themselves.
>
> It may be asked, what of all this? And what can the *women* do for the country? We answer, before God, we believe they can do more than all the men—more than all the armies of the South can do, if these armies are left wholly without your aid. Come, honored daughters of this land, come, and let us reason together for one moment. You ask, do we want your jewelry and plate to redeem the currency? No, no! . . . What we want is infinitely more precious than jewelry. What we want is not the redemption of the currency, but the redemption of our homes, our fair fields, our altars and temples!
>
> In different ages of the world heroic and patriotic women have sacrificed at the shrine of their country's safety and honor. The mothers of ancient Israel, of Sparta, and of Rome have left an immortal record of what true womanhood can do for their own land in the hour of its peril.
>
> Come, then, women of these great Commonwealths, rise to the grandeur and dignity of this time

We may be called upon to suffer much; we may be forced to endure great trials; we may be almost drowned in a sea of misfortunes; but as long as our proud spirits quail not; as long as we remain defiant and threatening; as long as we bear up under our calamities and resist the invaders, we are unconquered and unconquerable. Let us, then, proudly lift ourselves in our disdain of disaster, cast haughtily from us all weak and vain despondency, and determine that, come what will, we never will give o'er the contest 'till our enemies recognize our independence. Unmistakable evidences of such a spirit on our part, sooner than marshalled hosts and bannered array—sooner than victories and bloodshed—will gain us triumph to our cause; for our enemies, themselves convinced that subjugation, even if Europe permitted it, is an impossibility, will soon weary of the hopeless contest and make terms of peace with us on the basis of our independence.

Away, then, with doubts and fears! Away with despondency! Away with all wavering and hesitation! Away with that drivelling spirit that asks "if we have not got enough"! Away with all poltroonery and cowardice and money-loving selfishness! The independence of our country deserves every sacrifice we can make: upon its altars let us lay ourselves, our property, our comfort, our *all*—a holocaust to freedom and to honor!

Christian Index, February 2, 1865.
Even in the face of Sherman's unstoppable momentum, many Confederate newspapers called upon the Southern people to continue fighting and to sacrifice everything they had, including their lives, in "a holocaust to freedom and to honor."

of peril, and leave on the pages of our history a proud and glorious record of the spirit and deeds of Southern women.

Know then, that more than one-third of the whole number of soldiers whose names are on the rolls are not in the army with their brethren, ready to defend you, and to beat back the foe; but they are absent without leave, loafing, skulking, or hiding from duty! Know, further, that this state of things would be impossible, *if public opinion at home did not tolerate this shameless desertion of duty*. Never would these straggling soldiers remain a single week at home, in the criminal desertion of their flag, *if the women of the country would take the matter in hand.*

For this purpose it is only necessary for you to exert that simple *moral influence* with which Providence has invested you. The way to exert this power is plain. Let the principal, and elderly ladies of each community assemble, and give expression in some suitable and becoming form to an earnest appeal to every absent soldier, and to each skulker from duty, to repair at once to the army. Call upon these truant men to go forth in your defence. And then resolve, and make the resolution public, that you will not recognize, nor receive into your social circles, any man who is improperly absent from his command, or who evades the proper service to his country.

Let this be done generally, and 40,000 soldiers will be added to our ranks! Let that number increase our forces, and we are redeemed! Your country will be free! . . .

O will you not do this much! It may save your children from manacles, your old men from slaughter, your homes from desolation, your daughters from violence, your country from ruin! Will you not do only this much! . . . Will Columbus, Miss., or Montgomery, or Selma, or Aberdeen, or Tuscaloosa, or Mobile, Jackson, or Demopolis, have the spirit to set the example? . . . Will they—O will they only aid their endangered country in this simple mode!

If they do not, history may record that their influence was thus invoked, and *they refused to exert it!*[23]

Whether individual Southerners remained vehemently supportive of the war or were demoralized by it, the central fact remained the same: Sherman had just marched through the heart of the South triumphantly, and virtually unopposed. For most Northern observers, the meaning of this was unmistakable. As one Philadelphia paper announced, the ultimate crumbling of the Confederacy was just a matter of time—and a matter of sweet justice as well:

Do we not see on every hand the unmistakable proofs of rebel exhaustion? Everywhere upon the field of combat, save in Virginia alone, their energy seems spent, and incapable of re-invigoration. They could not save Georgia, whence came so much materiel of war, from scathing desolation; they could not protect South Carolina, nor save her metropolis or capital. And now we see Sherman advancing his victorious legions through North Carolina itself, still meeting no powerful enemy, and threatening to reach Virginia in regular progression. . . . It is equally improbable that anywhere within the realm of rebeldom there are sufficient means to stay the loyal armies, already far outnumbering the insurgents and receiving daily accessions from the northern States. The infusion into the dying confederacy of a vitality and strength equal to a hopeful renewal of the combat seems almost as unlikely as the resurrection from their graves of the countless hosts of rash and desperate men who flocked at first to the banners of rebellion, and have verified the declaration that those who take the sword shall perish by the sword.[24]

Not everyone in the North was so convinced, though. The *New York News*, that main organ of Copperhead thought, remained as disparaging of the Union cause as it always had been. Convinced that the surrender of Atlanta, Savannah, Columbia, Charleston, Wilmington, Raleigh, and so many other points in between were part of a grand plan by the Confederacy to lure Sherman into one final, decisive showdown, the *News* counseled its readers not to be so quick to imagine that the rebellion was over. "We warn the people that these visions of Southern submission are false and empty," the paper asserted ominously. "The South is not conquered," and would not ever be conquered. "Having ventured so far, and lost so much, they will stake all, and bide the issue."[25] Indeed, the war was pushing some Southerners to the brink of embarking on a new, last-ditch policy to save themselves—one that in 1861 would have been unthinkable.

THE COUNTRYMAN.

By J. A. TURNER. —"INDEPENDENT IN EVERYTHING—NEUTRAL IN NOTHING"— $5 for Three Months.

VOL. XX. TURNWOLD (NEAR EATONTON) GA., TUESDAY, JANUARY 17, 1865. NO 3.

Negro Soldiers.

We have got to abandon this war, or put negro soldiers in our army—one or the other.

Nothing is certain, as mortals know it. When we (that is mankind—not we editorially, specially, though it includes us generally) affirm a thing, dogmatically, or otherwise, we mean that, according to the lights before us, or according to the superior probabilities, the proposition we lay down is true. At least this is what all ought to mean, though most people haven't sense enough to see it so.

Then, according to the lights before us, the editor of The Countryman, and according to the superior probabilities, as they present themselves to our view, we have got to abandon this war, or put negro soldiers in our army—one or the other.

Death, disease, and the camp, make a constant drain, and, for the last four years, have made a continual draft, upon our white population. So they have upon the white population of the north. But the north has the world from which to supply its loss, and instead of its population having decreased, during the war, it has actually gone on increasing.

Not only do we lose from disease, and the killed in battle, but our kid-gloved gentry—many of whom were most active in raising the storm, but whose white livers now desert the ship in a manner the most heartless, and cowardly—many of these able-bodied men—run the blockade, and seek safety, not only in European, but in yankee cities.—These are the drains that deprive us of our resources for making soldiers.

And how do we supply the desideratum? Why, not even by marrying, and the natural increase of population. Our young men are all sent to the army, and our girls pine, at home, in single-blessedness.

And right here we are going to say, in our "choice Georgian dialect," that marrying ought to go on. Our girls and boys ought to marry, even if the latter come home from the army only once in twelve months, to see their wives. If mankind are foolish enough to wage war—a thing we have been opposed to, all our life—they ought to go on marrying, and giving in marriage, so as to supply the victims for gun-powder, and the bayonet. So far as our limited mind can take a proper view of the subject, it is a great pity anyone ever married, or that a child was ever born. But Adam and Eve adopted both the habit, and the co-habit which produced multiplication of the human family, and their sinful descendants have followed their example, with wonderful tenacity, down to the present time. If their example could be disregarded, the world over, we would not object to it, but rather approve of it. But as the balance of the world avail themselves of the advantages, as well as disadvantages of marrying, we only insist that our own people shall no longer abandon the institution. Our population must be kept up, by some means or other.

But we want more soldiers, now, if we are going to continue this war, and cannot wait eighteen or twenty years for them. We have but one source left us, from which to draw reinforcements for our army: and that is our negro population.

But negroes won't fight, say some.—The contrary has been demonstrated, by the yankees. The number of our own men, slain by negro troops, shows the contrary. The southern people once thought yankees wouldn't fight. Our men, in congress, had been accustomed to insult, and sometimes beat yankees, with impunity; and we concluded that because northern men wouldn't fight duels, therefore they wouldn't fight at all. We know, now, even yankees can be made to fight, in crowds, especially where they have the advantage in numbers, with several rear lines, to crowd the front line forward. The truth is, soldiers are nothing but machines, put up for the purpose of shooting, and being shot at. Discipline will make soldiers of negroes, and even of yankees—though we believe, now, as much as ever we did in our lives, that neither of the races has any very great natural appetite for being shot at.

But if you put negroes in the field, as soldiers, you withdraw them from the field of labor, and thus our country will suffer.—If we could have our choice, the negro would always remain in the cotton, or corn field. But we can't have our choice. It is not a question of our preference, but a hard, dire necessity is upon us. If we don't put our negroes in the camp, the yankees will, as they are doing every day. And instead of our availing ourselves of the only source of reinforcements now left us, we will voluntarily, and foolishly, turn over that source, also, to our foe, who has all the balance of the resources of the world at his command.

But it is not constitutional, to put negroes in the army.—The constitution! When did anybody pay any attention to it? Why it is no longer heard of, nor thought of, except when Joe Brown wishes to violate it himself, or quarrel with Jeff Davis because he won't allow him a monopoly in its violation.

But you take away our property, when you take away our negroes to put them in the army.—Your property, heh! You give your sons to be killed by the yankees, but you can't bear to have your property killed. Is not Abraham Lincoln taking away your property, every day, to put it in his army? And can't you let Jeff Davis have a little of it to put in his?

But you destroy the institution of slavery, by putting negroes in the army.—Well, is not Abraham Lincoln destroying that institution, every day of his life? And if he is not whipped, will he not cut it up, root and branch? If you don't put negroes in the army, slavery is certainly destroyed. If you do put them in the army, it can but be destroyed, any way. But if we succeed in whipping Lincoln, by the aid of our negroes, slavery will not be destroyed. The women and children will remain in bondage, even if the men are all killed. And the negro women will go on raising children, even after a part of the men are put in the army. And, then, if we succeed in achieving our independence, Africa is still full of negroes, granting that a great part of ours are destroyed. The "civilized world," after this war, can't blockade all the African ports, nor all the southern ports. And such will be the demand for slave labor, our independence once achieved, that you will find the very yankee soldiers—the very same marines—the very northern vessels now engaged in fighting us, bringing us negroes, from the slave coast of Guinea.

But negroes, once in the army, will never do to make corn-field slaves of, any more.—Admit that they will not (which we do not admit) then keep them for soldiers, either for our standing army, as a peace establishment, or to push our conquests out west, and south, in Mexico, Central America, and so on—notwithstanding our good friend Maximilian—whom the yankees will be glad to aid us in crushing.

We are in favor, therefore, of putting our negroes in the army, and doing it immediately, and as fast as they can be disciplined. By doing so, we can add from 200,000 to 400,000 able-bodied men to our ranks. And, with this additional force, can not only soon drive back the enemy to his own borders, but can pursue his shattered and retreating columns, into the heart of his own territory. And if the negro must have the promise of freedom, and plunder, in order to make him fight, give him the incentive of freedom, at the north, where he can not only be "free," but "equal:" and give him richer fields of plunder than he can find at the exhausted south. Give him the fat store-houses of northern villages, and cities: and thus will we turn, and press to the lips of our foe, the bitter draught he has prepared for ours. We repeat, we have got to do this, or abandon this fight. Let us present to the north, at once, the alternative of letting slavery alone, in our midst, or of having it in all its power, terror, and "barbarism," turned loose upon its own homes, and firesides. Let Boston, and New York, and Philadelphia, be made to quake to their centres, in anticipation of the tread of a column of 300,000 negroes, marching upon their firesides, next July. But, at the same time, let us hold aloft, also, the olive branch, and say to them, let us alone, and we will not trouble you.

VALUE OF A BAR OF IRON.—"A bar of iron, originally valued at $5, is worth, when worked into horse shoes, $10 50; into needles, $355; into penknife blades, $3,285; into shirt buttons, $29,480; into balance springs of watches, $250,000. 31 lbs. of iron have been made into wire upwards of 111 miles in length, and so fine was the fabric, that part of it was converted, in lieu of horse hair, into a barrister's wig."

Chapter 13

We Must Employ Slavery If We Expect to Perpetuate Slavery

At the end of 1864, with the Confederacy facing desperate times, it was forced to consider the most desperate of measures—the arming of its slaves. The idea certainly was not new. A year earlier, as the Union began to effectively use black soldiers (many of them former slaves) against the Confederacy, several newspapers in the Deep South had voiced their approval for bringing them into the army, even if slavery itself might perish in the process. Those suggestions had met with little serious discussion, however, and the idea might have languished entirely if the fate of the Confederacy had not become so obviously imperiled. Particularly after Sherman's stunning occupation of Atlanta, it was hard to deny that the Confederacy was in immediate need of help from everyone, whether black or white, willing to come to its defense. As one Alabama man confessed in a letter to the *Mobile Tribune*, "Up to the fall of Atlanta," the proposition for turning the slaves into soldiers "would have been by me indignantly spur[n]ed," as it had been by most Southerners. "But alas! the change," he exclaimed. "Now, I concur fully, not only in the propriety, but, necessity of arming our negroes to preserve us and them from the horrors of Yankee rule." Convinced that blacks and whites still shared a common interest in seeing the Confederacy survive, this concerned Southerner declared that it was now "the first duty" of the government to conscript "all able bodied negro men between the ages of 18 and 45" into the army.[1]

The *Richmond Enquirer*, one of the most widely read and respected newspapers in the Confederacy, endorsed this idea wholeheartedly, but with an even more provocative twist. The *Enquirer* not only called on Congress to purchase and equip 250,000 slaves for combat, but recommended that the government also "present them with their freedom" and ensure them the "privilege" of remaining in the South as free men after the war, in exchange for their military service.[2] It was an incredible suggestion that called into question what Southerners were fighting for. In 1861, the Southern press had been clear what the war was about. The Southern states were seeking more than just freedom from the Union. They specifically wanted freedom from abolitionism, and the right to preserve and cultivate their cherished institution of slavery. Slavery was sacred—literally a holy institution that could not be questioned or touched. Now the *Enquirer* was endorsing a policy that tugged at the very cornerstone of the Confederacy.

Observing this turn of events from the outside, the *New York Times* was incredulous:

> We confess that this development takes us by surprise. Few who knew the South in her old days of pride and chivalry—few who knew the unutterable contempt entertained by the dominant race for the humanity of the negro, could believe that anything whatever could ever reduce her to the adoption of such a policy as this, or even to its discussion.
>
> Of all the signs of the fearful [straits] of the Southern Confederacy, of all the proofs of the desperation of the rebel fortunes, this is by far the most striking and conclusive.
>
> Moreover, it furnishes ground of justification [for] our own Government in its policy of using, militarily, the negro element of the South, as an aid in operating upon the rebellion. When our Government first proposed to use the negroes as soldiers, it was furiously denounced, on several grave grounds, both by the rebels and Copperheads. It was said to be atrociously cruel to arm an inferior against a superior race, as the former would indulge in general massacre, rape and arson. It was said to be against the law of nations, placed on the same level with well-poisoning, and . . . last, [but] not least, it was pronounced a "mean Yankee trick." No brave people, they declared, with a particle of self-respect, would consent to owe anything, not even the preservation of its Government, to a race which, from time immemorial, had been hewers of wood and drawers of water, for anybody who chose to catch and flog them.
>
> We beg of the Southern chivalry to remember now their own doctrines, and to respect them. Let them consider for a moment what the consequences will be in case the Confederacy should be saved by the instrumentality of black soldiers. If the blacks should succeed in winning Southern independence, after the whites have tried and failed, it will be *de facto*, as well as *de jure*, a negro Republic. The negroes will carry off all the honors of the struggle, and will by every rule of law and justice be entitled to all the rewards of victory. . . . Under these circumstances the gift of freedom to the slaves will be a ridiculous farce. They will laugh in the faces of the chevaliers, at the mere mention of such a thing. To inform an army of 500,000 men who have been called into service as the last hope of a desperate cause, that they shall not be *paddled* any more on the bare back, that they shall not be robbed of their wages, that their mothers shall not be treated as cows nor their children as calves, would be simply a piece of wasteful and ridiculous excess. Whenever there is that number of able-bodied blacks under arms in the South, it will be wholly unnecessary to pass any act or make any appropriation toward bestowing their freedom on them.
>
> Moreover, if they secure the triumph of the Confederacy, it will be by doing what the 6,000,000 of Southern whites have failed to do—conquering the North. Any body of men who succeed in doing this, will be inevitably masters of the situation afterward. The country they have saved will be theirs, by the laws of war, and every other law. The legitimate Government at Richmond will be a black government. . . .

There is also another consideration which ought not to be overlooked. Suppose, after the blacks are armed and drilled, and in the field, they should take it into their heads to choose which side they would fight on—what then? Suppose that this great host, after having discovered the secret of their strength, should remember their "paddlings" and "larrupings," remember their scar[r]ed backs and stolen wives and children, and should for once find the savage instinct of hate hitherto kept down by the iron yoke of plantation discipline, swelling up within, and should . . . mutiny here under our eyes—what then? Three or four years ago there would have been plenty of people to tell us that the "love" of the slaves for their owners would prevent anything of that kind. But now we know better. The war has rudely unveiled the secrets of the prison-house. There is no telling what the future may bring forth, but it would certainly be one of the strangest and most striking events in history, and one bearing the strongest marks of providential retribution, if the final blow to the accursed Confederacy should come from the hands of its own slaves, armed and disciplined by itself.[3]

I am emancipating the slaves and compelling them to fight against the South, in order to weaken the South, says Lincoln; and we will emancipate the slaves and run the risk of their fighting for us, in order to strengthen the South, say the authors of the proposition. Between the two slavery will be utterly destroyed and the Southern country St. Domingoized. It is bad policy to blow up the ship with the hope of saving the crew. If the proposition to arm the slaves should be adopted by Congress, the two sections will soon be vieing with each other in the work of emancipation.

North Carolina Weekly Standard, November 16, 1864. The irony of the Confederate debate on emancipation confounded some Southerners. If the Southern states agreed to the arming and freeing of their slaves, they would voluntarily do what they had gone to war against the North to prevent—the destruction of slavery.

Members of the Southern press indeed were very aware of the absurdity—and the apparent dangers—of arming the slaves. The *Enquirer's* suggestion, particularly its support for freeing those slaves taken into the army, provoked some angry responses from Southerners who, despite events in Georgia, could not see any justification for such a drastic move. As they rightly understood, once a large number of male slaves gained their freedom, it would be difficult to keep their wives, children, and parents in chains. The whole institution of slavery would fall to pieces. To allow that to happen, explained one North Carolina paper, was tantamount to abandoning the whole purpose of the war. "In the commencement we proclaimed to the world that we were fighting for the right to manage our own domestic affairs in our own way, which included the right to own and hold slaves," it emphasized; "but now, if the advice of those who want to raise an army of negroes be followed, we are to do to ourselves what we went to war to keep the North from doing."[4] The proposal to enlist and free the slaves thus forced Southerners to clarify what exactly the war was about. Those who condemned the idea acknowledged that in their eyes, the Confederacy was created to protect the right of Southerners to own slaves, and nothing could be allowed to imperil that right. The *Lynchburg Virginian* exclaimed:

It is painful to reflect how soon the landmarks of great principles are lost amid the throes of revolution. For forty years the people of the South have been fiercely battling against the mad schemes of the abolitionists to destroy the institution of domestic slavery. We have uniformly contended that negroes were property, and that slavery was a local institution with which no power under the sun could interfere, save the sovereign States themselves in their individual capacity. For this great principle of the right of the States to regulate their domestic institutions to suit themselves, we went to war with the North, and for nearly four years we have maintained the dreadful conflict with unexampled success. Just at the moment when all the gigantic schemes of the enemy to subjugate us have failed . . . it is gravely proposed by respectable though chimerical journals in the South to ignore all of our past cardinal principles, surrender the great question for which we went to war, and do for ourselves precisely what Lincoln and the abolitionists proposed to do for us without war—*abolish slavery!*

This is the naked proposition of those who advocate the conscription of our slaves as soldiers. They propose to conscript "all the able bodied negroes of the country, between the ages of 18 and 45, respectively," arm and equip them and put them in the field as soldiers, along with our white men. As an inducement to make these negroes faithful to our cause, they are to be given their freedom, and permitted to live amongst us after the war as freemen. The result of such a proposition, if successful, cannot be mistaken by a blind man or an idiot. It will convert the sovereign States of the Confederacy into free negro colonies, with all the social and political evils which attend the amalgamation of adverse races. If our negro men are made free, then justice and sound policy would require that their wives and children should be permitted to enjoy freedom along with their husbands and fathers. . . . Whether this be just or not, it is very certain that our slaves once made freemen, and trained in the skill of arms, and the hardships of the camp and the dangers of the battle-field, would not only insist on their own freedom, but on the freedom of their entire race. Nay, more. They would insist, and have the right to insist at the point of a bayonet, upon enjoying all the civil, social and political rights enjoyed by their former masters, on the ground that they had suffered equally the dangers and responsibilities of the struggle. The horrible result would be either the amalgamation of the black and white races in the South, with all its attendant shame and ruin, or a dreadful civil war of extermination between the white men and the black! Can such consequences be contemplated by the Southern mind without a shudder for the result? And yet this is the certain end . . . , for we hold it to be impossible that we can escape these calamitious consequences with half a million of negroes trained to the use of arms and suddenly elevated to the rights and notions of freemen. . . .

But supposing the question to be fraught with none of these terrible social and political evils, it is perfectly clear to our mind that armed negroes would be a source of perpetual danger and weakness to the South in this struggle, instead of strength. When we shall have armed them what security have we that they will not desert us and join the enemy in a body? Reasoning from all natural principles and from observation, they would certainly do so. It would be folly for them to fight for their proffered liberty, when by simply walking into the camps of the enemy, they could be *ipso facto* free by Lincoln's proclamation. Place our negroes in the field as soldiers, and they would surrender every position which they might be placed to defend, for it is idle to talk to sensible men about the fidelity of slaves. That is a subject which will do to amuse the brains of romancers, but the experience of this war as well as the teaching of common sense have shown that not one negro in a thousand will refuse to accept the proffered boon of freedom tendered by the Yankees when he can do so with impunity. To arm the slaves is to arm a powerful foe in our own midst![5]

The plan for arming the slaves not only seemed illogical; it contradicted all of the racial assumptions upon which slavery rested. The institution was based on the notion that blacks were incapable of taking care of themselves—that they could not be trusted with any authority. Moreover, it presumed that blacks and whites could not exist together as equals. Allowing slaves to serve alongside whites in the army negated these ideas and raised the status of blacks in society. Consequently, as one Southerner noted in a letter to the *Macon Telegraph & Confederate*, the proposal insulted the white pride of those soldiers who remained in the ranks:

> As a question of principle, this thing of negro soldiers for the Southern army is monstrous. It is a virtual abandonment of the long contested question, not only of the equality of races, but of the negro's capacity for self-government and for freedom; for if the negro is worthy to *fight* for liberty, he is worthy of liberty itself; and if he is worthy to be free, he must, of necessity, be accorded [the] capacity for self-government. There is no escaping these conclusions, and the friends of negro recruits for our Southern army, either have failed to analyse the scheme in all its bearings, or they are prepared to abandon principles which lay at the foundation of this defensive war. Have they been *whipped* into the latter alternative?
>
> But aside from principle, what would be the effect of introducing negroes into the ranks of our army, as a measure of policy? Are our brave boys who have borne the brunt of battle for four years, going to open their arms to the embrace of negro compatriots, think you? With a knowledge that thousands upon thousands of able-bodied whites have remained at home through evasion of the conscript law, . . . will they feel complimented, after four years of hard service, with the assurance, not that their white fellow-citizens are to come to their aid, but that *negroes*, the menial laborers, the slaves whom they were wont to govern and direct at home—are to be sent to occupy the position of their *equals* in the Southern army! Shame on those who would this day insult the intelligence, the patriotism and the honor of our gallant soldiers. The writer of this is a soldier, but if he could bring to life the noble son who fell defending his country's flag . . . and replace . . . his own crippled limb, not another drop of his family blood should be shed in a cause which could so degenerate from the high moral principle which first inaugurated this defensive war.[6]

Contrary to this Southerner's contention, opinion in the army actually was divided on the issue. Certainly some agreed that it was an outrage and an embarrassment to call upon the slaves for help and to treat them as if they held an equal stake in Southern society. "No," wrote one indignant soldier to the *Richmond Enquirer*; "there are stout arms and brave hearts enough amongst the white men of our Confederacy to fight her battles and win her independence without resorting to so low and execrable means as that of conscripting and arming the poor ignorant negro." Even if the slaves could perhaps be molded into effective fighters, racial pride forbade it. Such a move, this soldier explained, would "tarnish our fame" and "stain our manhood." However, the *Enquirer* also received supportive letters from the army. Those who endorsed the arming of the slaves were concerned less about the principle of white supremacy and more about the realities of the situation at hand. The simple fact was that while the Confederacy was hesitating to bring its slaves into the ranks, the Union was openly welcoming them into theirs and using them to help subdue the rebellion. Therefore, as another soldier prudently pointed out, "would it not be better for our Government to arm two hundred thousand negroes than allow the country to be overrun by the enemy, and have the negro turned against us?"[7] Supporters at home agreed with this logic completely. Necessity required that the Confederacy finally tap this reserve of black manpower, rather than allow Northerners to use it to their own advantage. The *Army Argus & Crisis*, a paper from Mobile, Alabama, explained:

We are in a struggle for existence, as truly as that involved in the fable of the infant Hercules, who strangled the serpent coiled around him to destroy. If beaten at last in this conflict, there is absolutely nothing left on this continent for which a high-souled Southerner would desire to live!

Lincoln recently admitted that without the aid of the 200,000 negro soldiers, already stolen from Southern men and armed against them, *it would be impossible for the Yankees to conquer us, or to hold the territory already occupied by Yankee troops*. If this be true, then with two hundred thousand negro troops on our side, the conquest of the South would become impossible, and the effort would be given up.

In this great conflict, the Yankee . . . has constantly insisted that because 20,000,000 were numerically greater and [embodied] more potential than 6,000,000, therefore the South must be conquered; and hence he has persisted in the fell purpose, uninfluenced by any motive, or any consideration, but deadly hate and the thirst for plunder. Now, if that materialist shall see that the South will bring up her great "reserved power," and meet the invader with the aid of our armed slaves, it will appal his cold, calculating soul, and his hopes of conquest would fade and die.

But the objection is to making a negro a soldier—a free soldier. Do we not forget that he is already made a soldier—a free soldier, *against us*, and that our sons and brothers have to meet them in the deadly breach? But the danger—the negro would not be loyal. Give that negro the same inducements to fight for his home, . . . and it contradicts all human experience to say he would not be true.

But what shall we do with so many free negroes after the war is over? *What shall we do with all of them free if we are crushed?* But it will involve so great a loss to the industrial interests. *Everything you have on earth is at stake, and if beaten, all is lost.* But our people have such a strong repugnance to freeing the slaves, and thus promoting their *status*. But the Yankee will use the negro to utterly destroy you and your children, if you do not use the negro to crush the invader and drive him from our soil.

We are in a death struggle, and rather than let the hated thieves and murderers dominate this land, we would rather see the Confederacy sunk in a lake of bitumen and become a Dead Sea forever! But the army will oppose this measure. The army is composed of the ablest and best of the land, and when these men give the subject a little reflection, they will not only favor the proposed increase of force, but they will *demand* it. Shall these men fight a foe numerically superior, composed of Yankees, foreigners and negroes, and be overborne at last, because we refuse to make negroes fight negroes?

But the most important result of all would be, we should thus frighten, appal, and drive back the insolent foe. If in the judgment of those who survey the whole field, . . . this measure is necessary to our final success, and our speedy success, what good man, what patriot will oppose it? Let no human effort be spared to save the State, and preserve to our children the priceless heritage of freedom, safety and happy homes.[8]

Jefferson Davis, in a presidential message to the Confederate Congress in November 1864, agreed in principle with these ideas. Although he denied that the Confederacy was currently in such a desperate state as to require the arming of its slaves, Davis asserted that in the future, if the situation were to worsen, and "the alternate ever be presented of subjugation or of the employment of the slave as a soldier, there seems no reason to doubt what should then be our decision." For the time being, though, the president only aspired to have the government employ up to 40,000 slaves as military engineers and laborers. The really stunning part of Davis's message, however, came not so much with his recommendations of how slaves could be used by the Confederacy, but rather in how they were to be treated. For in order to make slaves willing contributors to the Confederate cause, he declared that those who aided the country militarily should be given their freedom at the end of the war, "as a reward for faithful service." Taken together, Davis's message to Congress offered official sanction not only for enlisting tens of thousands of slaves, but for emancipating them.[9]

Most Southerners found it impossible to embrace these views. The sticking point was not so much the notion of using the slaves as soldiers, but rather the proposal that they be given their freedom—as a *reward*, no less—as if slavery were a bad thing from which blacks were to be delivered. Davis's logic was confounding, even to those Southerners who wanted to arm the slaves. "I believe that it is generally conceded that the white male population of the country has been so much exhausted that the negro's services must be invoked," acknowledged a citizen of Tuskegee, Alabama, in a letter to the editor of the *Columbus Sun*. "On what terms or ground to put them in the army is the great question. *If we free him*; would this not be giving him his freedom in lieu of his services, and would this not be a confession that his condition when free is better than when a slave?" As this Southerner knew, such a suggestion was completely "antagonistic to the views and teachings of this country which prevailed when the States seceded and the war began." For years, Southerners had defended slavery on the ground that it benefited blacks by placing them under the protective care of good, Christian masters. Moreover, according to popular opinion, blacks were innately barbarous and immature and could not handle freedom. "But now the President of the Confederate States opens quite another view of the matter," the *Richmond Whig* reported scornfully. "According to his message, it is a rich reward for faithful service to turn a negro wild. Slavery, then, in the eyes of Mr. Davis, keeps the negro out of something which he has the capacity to enjoy." And if that was indeed what the president was saying, "then slavery is originally, radically, incurably wrong and sinful, and the sum of all barbarism."[10] Southerners who truly believed that slavery was a holy institution, therefore, had to stand behind their beliefs and rebuke any attempt to entice slaves into the army with the promise of freedom. In this vein, the *Charleston Mercury* declared:

> The African is of an inferior race, whose normal condition is slavery. Prone to barbarism, and incapable of any other state than that of pupilage, he is at his best estate as the slave of the enlightened white man of this country. All history, experience, and the closest observation and research for truth have brought the people of these States to this conclusion; and it constitutes, in a moral point of view, the rock of their defence. But if the slavery of the Confederate States be not the best condition for the negroes amongst us—if they are fit for freedom, and manumission be a desirable improvement in their political *status*—an improvement which they may obtain as a reward for service—then the justification heretofore set up for holding them as slaves is false and unfounded. . . .
>
> We would owe an apology to our readers for these stale remarks, but for the extraordinary suggestion in the President's message to which these remarks are pertinent. The purchase of forty thousand male slaves by the Confederate Government . . . might possibly be judicious if properly managed, but to emancipate them afterwards, would not merely disturb the *status* of our negro population, but would go a great way to justify the arguments and views of the abolitionists, while it would give the lie to our professions and surrender the strength of our position. We cannot believe that a policy so inconsistent, unsound and suicidal can meet the sanction of any respectable body of Southern men.[11]

Most advocates for arming the slaves actually agreed with the *Mercury* on this point, and believed that it was wrong of Davis to talk of emancipation as a "reward" for military service. At the same time, though, they understood that the slaves themselves would consider it a boon, and if that is what it took to win their assistance, then many were willing to pay that price. Freeing them was simply a matter of necessity—an undesirable but unavoidable step for drawing more men into the army. "Let us here note the fact," one newspaper assured its readers, "that emancipation would not be tendered as a right, nor as proof of our conviction of the impropriety and sinfulness of the institution, but only as a medium to insure the fidelity and good conduct of those to whom it is administered."[12] Moreover, as supporters of the measure were quick to add, *only* those slaves who joined the army would be emancipated; all others would remain in bondage. And if the Confederacy, with the help of its black soldiers, could win the war, then it would be able to retain and rebuild the institution once the fighting had ended. Firm in the faith that the slaves would be much more useful to the Confederacy as soldiers than as mere laborers, the *Countryman* issued this confident assessment of how blacks could actually be used to *save* and *perpetuate* slavery:

> We have got to abandon this war, or put negro soldiers in our army—one or the other . . .
>
> But negroes won't fight, say some.—The contrary has been demonstrated, by the yankees. The number of our own men, slain by the negro troops, shows the contrary. The southern people once thought yankees wouldn't fight. . . . The truth is, soldiers are nothing but machines, put up for the purpose of being shot at. Discipline will make soldiers of negroes, and even of yankees—though we believe, now, as much as ever we did in our lives, that neither of the races has any very great natural appetite for being shot at.
>
> But if you put negroes in the field, as soldiers, you withdraw them from the field of labor, and thus our country will suffer.—If we could have our choice, the negro would always remain in the cotton, or corn field. But we can't have our choice. It is not a question of our preference, but a hard, dire necessity is upon us. If we don't put our negroes in the camp, the yankees will, as they are doing every day. And instead of our availing ourselves of the only source of reinforcements now left us, we will voluntarily, and foolishly, turn over that source, also, to our foe, who has all the balance of the resources of the world at his command. . . .
>
> But you take away our property, when you take away our negroes to put them in the army.—Your property, heh! You give your sons to be killed by the yankees, but you can't bear to have your property killed. Is not Abraham Lincoln taking away your property, every day, to put it in his army? And can't you let Jeff Davis have a little of it to put in his?
>
> But you destroy the institution of slavery, by putting negroes in the army.—Well, is not Abraham Lincoln destroying that institution, every day of his life? And if he is not whipped, will he not cut it up, root and branch? If you don't put negroes in the army, slavery is certainly destroyed. . . . But if we succeed in whipping Lincoln, by the aid of our negroes, slavery will not be destroyed. The women and children will remain in bondage, even if the men are all killed. And the negro women will go on raising children, even after a part of the men are put in the army. And, then, if we succeed in achieving our independence, Africa is still full of negroes. . . . The "civilized world," after this war, can't blockade all the African ports, nor all the southern ports. And such will be the demand for slave labor, our independence once achieved, that you will find . . . the very same northern vessels now engaged in fighting us, bringing us negroes, from the slave coast of Guinea. . . .
>
> We are in favor, therefore, of putting our negroes in the army, and doing it immediately, and as fast as they can be disciplined. By doing so, we can add from 200,000 to 400,000 able-bodied men to our ranks. And, with this additional force, [we] can not only drive back the enemy to his own borders, but can pursue his shattered and retreating columns, into the heart of his own territory. And if the negro

must have the promise of freedom, and plunder, in order to make him fight, give him the incentive of freedom, at the north, where he can not only be "free," but "equal:" and give him richer fields of plunder than he can find at the exhausted south. Give him the fat store-houses of northern villages, and cities: and thus will we turn, and then press to the lips of our foe, the bitter draught he has prepared for ours. We repeat, we have got to do this, or abandon this fight. Let us present to the north, at once, the alternative of letting slavery alone, in our midst, or of having it in all its power, terror, and "barbarism," turned loose upon its own homes, and firesides. Let Boston, and New York, and Philadelphia, be made to quake to their centres, in anticipation of the tread of a column of 300,000 negroes, marching upon their firesides next July. But, at the same time, let us hold aloft the olive branch, and say to them, let us alone, and we will not trouble you.[13]

Among Northern onlookers, who watched the Confederate debate on arming the slaves with no slight interest, only the Copperheads took such threats seriously. Convinced that the South could indeed organize hundreds of thousands of slaves for a military offensive against the Union, they regarded the prospect as yet one more reason for seeking a quick and peaceful resolution to the war. "Unable to do much more than hold our own against the white troops of the South, how can we expect to do so when they shall have been reinforced by 4 or 500,000 able-bodied negroes," asked the *New York News*, utterly heedless of Sherman's ongoing romp through Georgia. As that paper envisioned it, the North would soon rue the day "when 200,000 semi-civilized Africans, trained in life-long obedience to the officers by whom they shall be led," would sweep over the Northern states in an overwhelming "retaliatory invasion."[14] More generally, though, the Northern press saw the plan for arming the slaves for what it was—a desperate and almost laughable idea that exposed the bankruptcy of the Confederacy's founding principles. The *Troy Times* proclaimed:

There is no doubt the rebel authorities are about to arm the slaves. . . . What does the measure imply? First, the desperate straits of the rebellion. It shows that it has no more available white men left to draw upon for replenishing its armies. It must make the negroes fight its battles or ignobly fall. To this precarious condition is it reduced at last.

Second, in arming the slaves, it surrenders the vital principle upon which the confederacy is based. It must necessarily give up slavery, which Vice President Stephens declared to be the "corner-stone" of the rebel Government. Yielding so much as this, it of course abandons the cause of the war, acknowledges before the world that it is beaten, and that it only hopes, by adopting the principle of its enemy at this eleventh hour, to save itself from destruction.

Third, it ignores the doctrine of State rights in impressing slaves into its military service and arming them. [The Confederacy] has from the beginning assumed that the central Government had no right to interfere in any way with slavery; that it was peculiarly a State institution. . . . Yet, it now lays violent hands upon it, and drags the slaves into the military service without the leave of masters, or obtaining permission from the States. It strikes down the very foundations of its own superstructure of State rights.

Fourth, the placing of the slaves in its armies as soldiers is a recognition of their manhood; it carries with it, of course, the concession of their freedom; it refutes the charge of uncivilized warfare on the part of the United States in receiving black men as soldiers in our army.

Thus we see that in arming and emancipating their slaves, the traitor Government at Richmond abandons [every] principle it has ever professed in making war upon the Union. . . .

But will the negroes fight for the traitors? Time will determine. We believe they will only fight as

Farmers, come forward at once and tender your able-bodied and most intelligent negroes to the Government, and by so doing, you will keep them from falling into the hands of the enemy, who will use them for your own destruction.—Better give up half your negroes to defend your homes than let them all fall into the clutches of the North, to be used as spies, and guides, and to aid in your utter ruin. It is desired that the owners shall pledge themselves to emancipate such negroes as will volunteer in the Confederate service, promising them after we shall gain our independence, and they should desire to return to their old homes, that proper provisions will be made for them and their families, and fair wages given.

Augusta Constitutionalist, April 20, 1865. Southerners who advocated arming and emancipating the slaves did so not because they believed it was morally right but rather as a practical measure, to stop them from running away to aid the Union side.

> they are compelled to; we believe they will prove an element of demoralization in the rebel service which must hasten the overthrow of the confederacy; we believe they will desert by wholesale whenever they are put forward to fight for the rebels, even if they do not turn upon their old oppressors and shoot them down. . . . We do not regret that the rebels have resolved to arm their slaves. Surely the end of the rebellion cannot be far off.[15]

Southern papers that supported the use of black soldiers refused to concede that it spelled the end for the Confederacy—or for slavery. Some even hoped that battlefield training might *enhance* the South's slavery system. For as they saw it, blacks would serve in the army under conditions that fully mimicked slavery. Army life would be made to feel just like plantation life: hard work and strict regimentation, maintained under the watchful eye of white superiors who would enforce discipline and good behavior. Consequently, as a North Carolina farmer explained in a letter to the *Raleigh Confederate*, slavery was really the perfect training ground for blacks entering military service, and military service, in turn, would help make them better slaves after the war:

> Now, let us examine the objections alleged by some, against the use of this most important item of our defence against our inhuman enemy. . . . The first, and really as far as I can judge, the only plausible one is, that instead of fighting for *us*, they will desert to the enemy in the hour of extremity, unless we pledge them their liberty after the war. This objection . . . is not founded on truth, and certainly is not in our experience. Look at the thousands who have had every chance to escape and *with safety*, at those who have followed their masters to the war, or who have been employed as teamsters, cooks, &c., &c. How wonderfully few have deserted! It is true that if left to the seductions and lies of the Yankee, many have left their plantations to go over to the enemy, but most of them have been forced to do so by one means or another. But surrounded by white troops and under the eye of these whom they have been accustomed to obey, and where there is no chance of escape, the case would be very different. . . . To prevent their escape privately, it may be necessary to employ unusual vigilance and severe punishment. As to giving our negro soldiers their liberty, after the war, as a *reward*, it can only be the idea of a visionary and thoughtless enthusiast. If we are honest in saying what we do, and believing as all do; all who understand the negro character, that he is better off in slavery than in being compelled to look out and care for himself, then we are repaying a service by a *wrong*—no, it would be a *criminal folly* to do this. He can be rewarded, and in a mode far more congenial to his tastes and conducing far more to his happiness. He can be allowed by law a ration of tobacco, sugar and whiskey, for life; he can be furnished with

a suitable ornamental suit of extra clothing once a year; will have by law every Saturday in the year for his own time, with hospitals for the maimed, all to be distributed under the superintendence of his master, or in many other ways. But to give him liberty, that useless thing *to him*, would be to raise the class of free negroes in our country to a power that would be dangerous. . . .

Another objection alleged by some timid men is, that after having borne arms, the negro can never be afterwards made to return to his labors. This is nothing more or less than a downright mistake. What is there in the habit of strict obedience to unfit him from continuing to that discipline so necessary to all well regulated plantations? What is there in the habit of quick and thorough obedience to military orders, to induce a disobedience or unwillingness in obeying the orders of a master? What is there in the habits of cleanliness and carefulness of the soldiers to injure the worth of a negro on the plantation? I have been bred a military man from my earliest youth. I am the owner of one of the largest bodies of negroes in the country, and I would, as a matter of *policy*, have all my negroes brought up to habits of military discipline and order, and would consider them more manageable and more valuable. No! there can be no reasonable doubt as to the decision on the question, whether *we* shall use the negroes as soldiers against the Yankee negroes and soldiers, or whether by our folly and hesitation they shall use them as soldiers against us. . . . Let full 100,000 men be sent to the various camps of instruction as soon as practicable; let them be put under drill and discipline forthwith, and we shall be able in the early spring to place under that great master, Gen. R.E. Lee, 100,000 strong, able-bodied men, to serve in our noble cause. . . .

The coming spring is to be the crisis of this war. If Grant, by dint of overwhelming numbers, even of *negroes* and mobs, is able to drive Lee before him, he turns these negroes and mobs loose upon the no longer defended cities of Richmond and Petersburg, to plunder and destroy. . . . On the other hand, General Lee, with the addition of 100,000 able-bodied troops, fairly disciplined, will be able to defeat all Grant's purposes and roll back the tide of war, and finally bring the North to a knowledge of the fact that we are not to be subjugated by all the powers he can bring to bear, but are ready to make any and all sacrifices to protect ourselves in independence of her hateful tyranny and despotism.[16]

The debate on arming the slaves begs one vital question: how could these Southerners actually believe that their slaves—the men they held in subjection and ruled over with a whip—would want to

On the question of policy, it may be remarked, first, that the difficulty to the South, arising from the scattered paucity of her population, in obtaining men to fill her armies, renders the conscription of her colored people *now* necessary; and, *second*, that the danger of the North's capturing and forcibly arming her negroes against her, enforces this unexpected effort for self-preservation and independence. And, too, the negroes have a vital interest, present and future, in defending the soil and climate, their products, and the system of slave labor which produces them, as the only reliable and permanent sources of their own subsistence and well-being. Nor should, nor will, they be unmindful of those "domestic relations" which bind them to their homes, their owners, their wives and children, or of that lasting peace which is so essential to their happy lives and thriving condition. They may assuredly understand that Yankeedom will not leave them any of these blessings, and that the North intends to dispossess both them and their owners of their favored country.

South Carolinian, January 16, 1865.
For some Southerners, employing slaves as soldiers was more than a matter of necessity. They genuinely believed that slaves understood the benefits they derived from slavery, and sympathized with the needs and interests of their white masters.

fight for the Confederacy and for the enslavement of their own people? From an outsider's perspective it seems delusional. However, the employment of blacks as soldiers did not contradict the South's ideas about slavery. It brought those ideas to perfect fulfillment. In the decades before the war, proslavery theorists had argued that the relationship between planters and their bondsmen was based fundamentally on affection and sympathy. Good white masters cared for their slaves as if they were part of the family, and the slaves (when they were not being misled by abolitionist propaganda) received this care gratefully. Slavery, as Southerners idealized it, was about racial harmony. And when the war erupted in 1861, the Southern press had declared proudly that by securing its independence, the Confederacy would be able to take this harmony to an even higher level. The new nation would shape itself into a biracial utopia in which Southern whites could cultivate idyllic relationships with their slaves, free from the poisoning influence of abolitionism. What better way was there to demonstrate the dawning of this new era in Southern race relations than to have blacks and whites fighting side by side for the Confederacy's survival? Would not the experience of common military service make the bonds between the two races stronger than ever? As envisioned by one Southern man—a soldier in Lee's army—when the war was over and the Confederacy stood triumphant, "the memory of the faithful slaves who did their duty defending their masters even 'to the bitter end'" would give the institution of slavery a luster it never before possessed. "Slavery will still exist only in a nobler and higher form, the master and negro mutually feeling that each . . . is prepared to sacrifice even unto life for the other."[17]

This spirit of racial harmony represented not just slavery at its best but slavery at its holiest, for its achievement was part of what the South conceived as God's plan for the black race. Both before and during the war, the Southern churches had maintained that slavery was ordained by God. It was *His* will that the children of Ham should serve the needs of the white race. Now, blacks would take their natural position of servitude to an even more exalted level by coming to the aid of their white masters in wartime, when their help was so desperately needed. The *Southern Christian Advocate* elaborated:

> Without doubt, we are in a crisis. . . . The time has arrived in the history of this gigantic struggle, when the intellect of our country is profoundly agitated as the means and measures best to be adopted to repair our recent disasters and infuse freshness of purpose, vitality of will, inflexible constancy and heroic energy, into the grand cause which now . . . calls for a heavier draft upon those resources which Providence has placed in our hands.
>
> How much of a crisis then exists? Just so much as our want of valiant will and persistent endurance allows to exist,—so much and no more. The crisis ends the moment we rise to the full height of manhood and show our entire competency to use against our adversaries, that repelling power which God has committed to our trust. Slavery has done us vast service in the war by sustaining, in large part, the productive industry of the country. But the crisis in this utility of slavery has now come in the advantages it offers for throwing into the field such a body of slaves as soldiers, as may answer the purpose of terminating this struggle. No fact is clearer, than that relatively to the Yankees, we . . . have but to convert our slaves into soldiers to put us upon equal ground with them; and whenever the Yankee sees that we occupy this ground of equality, he will feel the force of an argument which he never imagined could have an existence. Our supposed weakness has been his battle cry. Silence that and his enthusiasm will begin to expire. The only way to silence him is to fight him with his pet hobby, the negro.
>
> One fact is past argument, viz., the negro will be the future soldier of the war. If not on our side, then against us. Whether he ought to be a soldier,

is not the question. A soldier he is, despite of us. Lincoln has no recruiting material but Southern negroes; and if we falter now, if we fail to seize the moment to cut off his supplies, if we hesitate to use the negro for our cause, we simply invite our enemy to pursue his work of destruction. Viewed as an abstract matter, we might oppose his conversion into a soldier; but when the real state of the case is, whether our foes shall use him or we ourselves, every sentiment of self-preservation and of self-regard, every motive of humanity, every obligation of Christian principle, points out the course to be adopted.

All of us agree that slavery is a providential institution, that it rests upon Christian ground, that we are solemnly responsible for its guardianship, and that its uses, if rightly employed, are mutually advantageous to slaveholder and slave. Starting from this point, we proceed to say, that the institution is capable of benefiting both slaveholder and slave *as a fighting institution*, in a degree more vital to all interests and inclusive of more favorable results than it has ever hitherto been as an agricultural and domestic power. Has slavery made our wealth? It can now do more; for . . . it is now reduced almost to a certainty, that *we must employ slavery if we expect to perpetuate slavery*. Employ it, we mean, as a military force. The refusal therefore to use slavery in this way will be tantamount to abolition, and moreover, in the worst form that abolition can assume. Whatever may be the future fortunes of slavery, it is very clear that it should survive the war. Humanity, Philanthropy, Christianity, all indicate this as essential to the well being of all parties . . . and hence, to secure this continuance, we should promptly organize a suitable number of our slaves to fight side by side with us in this struggle.

If these views are just and true, our slaves now stand in a new providential light. They are more important to us than ever before. They are more essential to us than ever before. They are more than ever providentially ordained *for our auxiliaries and helpers*. Disguise it as we may, these are the facts,—stern, solid, stubborn facts, from which, no patriot, no christian, will dare avert his eyes. Prejudices may hide the truth from our reason, but this is no time for prejudices. Prejudices are costly follies, aye, costly crimes in the midst of such a struggle as we are now enduring. If then we manfully . . . examine this great subject in the light which the Providence of the Present, not the Providence of the Past, sheds upon it, we can hardly fail of the conclusion that duty to ourselves, and to the negro, to the civilization of the continent, demands of us the immediate arming of our slaves. Should it please the All-wise Disposer of events to prosper the earnest and heroic effort of our brave people, crowning it with that success which our prayers . . . crave and entreat, then indeed shall slavery emerge from this Revolution with yet higher and holier claims upon our Christian care and sympathy.[17]

Despite such holy motivations for enlisting the slaves, the idea might have fizzled totally had Robert E. Lee not entered the discussion. In February 1865, as the Confederate Congress debated a bill on black enlistment, Lee wrote a letter to Representative Ethelbert Barksdale of Mississippi, the author of the bill, offering his straightforward support for it. Between the Union's numerical advantage over the Confederacy, its success in recruiting black soldiers, and the exhaustion of Southern manpower and resources, Lee did not see any alternative but to call upon the slaves for military service—and to give freedom to those who fought. With Lee's position clear, many Southern newspapers threw themselves in line behind him, ever ready to trust in his guidance on military matters.[19] The Confederate Congress, however, narrowly fell short on following his lead. After the House passed the "negro enlistment bill," authorizing Davis to requisition a quota of black soldiers from every state in the Confederacy, the Senate

PROSPECTS OF THE SOUTHERN SAMBO.

LEE—"*Hold on there, Driver, we want Sambo now to fight for Liberty and Independence. You can thrash him as much as you like when he comes back.*"

Frank Leslie's Illustrated Newspaper, March 25, 1865. As Northerners well understood, it was illogical to expect blacks to fight for the country that enslaved and brutalized them. In this cartoon, General Robert E. Lee has come to requisition slaves as soldiers, and tells the overseer: "Hold on there, Driver, we want Sambo now to fight for Liberty and Independence. You can thrash him as much as you like when he comes back."

defeated it by a single vote. Lee's home state of Virginia, however, showed no such hesitation. On March 13, the state legislature passed its own resolution to employ black troops, although it still held back from requiring that enlisted slaves be given their freedom. Even at its most dire moment, the Confederacy could not let go of slavery.

Nevertheless, this act by Virginia brought to fulfillment a remarkable shift in the wartime role of blacks. In 1861, the North and South had entered into a white man's war—one that was about slavery, but in which the slaves themselves were to play only a marginal part. Over the course of the conflict, however, the situation had changed completely. Now the South was competing against the North for the indispensable help of blacks in waging its battles. As one Southern editor recognized, "It is now evident that the negro slave is to be a sort of balance power in this contest, and that the side which succeeds in enlisting the feeling and securing the active operation and services of the four millions of blacks, must ultimately triumph."[20]

Virginia had positioned itself to lead the South in soliciting this cooperation from the slaves. In the final weeks of the war, the state quickly organized two companies of black soldiers, consisting mostly of slaves. But according witnesses, the process of enrolling them was tricky indeed. Surveying the efforts to organize these new recruits, the *Richmond Examiner* candidly reported that "the conscription of negroes in Richmond and Petersburg is carried on with difficulty." At their new barracks in the Confederate capi-

> "I am willing to enlist a portion of my able-bodied colored men, with the promise of their freedom after the war, provided they stand and fight it out like true and loyal soldiers. I think that all true and loyal Virginians should be willing to adopt this principle and carry it out to the letter. Unless something of the kind is offered our slaves, we had as well send them off to Gen. Grant; because the North offers them freedom, and I am convinced that we cannot induce them to *fight* to perpetuate their own slavery."

Richmond Whig, March 25, 1865. After Virginia authorized the enlistment of black troops, one slaveholder offered his personal support for the measure and frankly admitted that freedom, not slavery, was what Southern blacks desired.

tal, "the colored soldiers are kept under strict surveillance, but many get away in spite of all precaution." The attempt to enlist them had evidently caused "a great panic among the blacks," who did not appear eager to fight for the proslavery Confederacy's survival.[21] The *Examiner*'s observations paint a pathetic and sordid picture of Confederate society at war's end. With Southern whites having deserted the army in droves, and with slaves now being brought into it by compulsion, the Confederacy had fallen far from its lofty beginnings. Conceived as a grand social experiment—the creation of a perfectly ordered and wondrously prosperous biracial slave society—it lay exposed as a complete abortion.

The Detroit Free Press.

VOLUME XXVIII. DETROIT, MICHIGAN, MONDAY MORNING, APRIL 10, 1865. NUMBER 26[illegible]

[T]he Free Press.

WALKER, BARNS & CO.,
[PUB]LISHERS AND PROPRIETORS.

[illegible] Free Press, $10; the Tri-Weekly, $6; the [illegible] Daily to city subscribers, $12, or [illegible] cents per week.

Single Copies Five Cents.

[LO]CAL INTELLIGENCE.

Town Gossip.

Ap[ril], a [illegible], half tears, half smiles
[illegible] little playful wiles;
[illegible] her rainbow hood
[illegible] the word.

[illegible] the past week, April, the capricious [illegible] in succession fleecy skies, [illegible] boisterous winds, clouds of [illegible], nipping airs. We live in a [illegible] extremes, for no change could have [illegible] than from the really oppressive [illegible] Monday, to the pinching cold of Fri[day]. [illegible] that this month ends the long struggle [illegible] the seasons. A few more weeks, per[haps] only days, and that beautiful tender green, [illegible] no future luxuriance can ever lend [illegible] charm, will appear. The trees, [illegible] but full of vegetable blood, will be [illegible] to burst into full foliage, and the wind [illegible] sighs through their bare branches, [illegible] amidst unnumberable leaves. [illegible] will pour out floods of melody, and [illegible] throats of thousands of feathered [songs]ters will sweet songs greet the purple [illegible] and mingle with the yellow sunshine in [illegible] sweetness. Sad and lorn indeed [is] the heart that will have no visitings of [illegible] thoughts when all creation [illegible]. What has the earth to equal the [illegible] springtime sprightliness? Summer [illegible] present, and thinks not of the fu[ture] [illegible] conservative; Win[ter] [illegible] its faith, and clings tremu[lously] [illegible]. But Spring, with its [illegible] of life, is the true emblem of hope, [illegible] and immortality.

[Spr]ing gives pleasure, Summer treasure,
Autumn gladness, Winter sadness;
[Spr]ing revives, Summer thrives;
[Aut]umn pleases, Winter freezes.

[The we]ek just passed has been a stirring and [illegible]. As smaller things must give [place] to greater, so we shall pass over the elec[tion] [illegible] Associate Justice of the Supreme [Court], [illegible] Regents, and officers of the Young [Men's] Association, Professor Anderson's won[derful fea]ts, the attractions at the Athenæum, [illegible]

[illegible]

The Siegel Case.

[illegible]

---

ward rapidly, and the wheat is looking fine, though it is in need of warm "April showers."

ATHENÆUM.—The great moral drama of "Ten Nights in a Bar Room," brought out a good house Saturday night. It has on a previous occasion attracted more than passing attention, and the scenes contained therein being such as are every day enacted, could we but lift the veil which skims the surface of the deplorable condition of thousands who are now plunging deeply into the vortex of intemperance and ruin. The piece was in good hands and was well brought out. The tableaux were an agreeable feature. On Monday night, the beautiful fairy drama of the "Lakes of Killarney," and the "Foster Sister," is announced. The bill is an attractive one.

Owing to certain improvements now going on at the Athenæum building, on and after Wednesday night, the place will be closed for a brief season. In the interim the Young Men's Hall's will be the scene of operations of the company, Manager Hough having engaged that Hall to accommodate his patrons. On the opening night something new and startling will be produced.

DETROIT BASE BALL CLUB.—At the adjourned meeting held Saturday evening at the Fire Marshal's office, the report of the Directors on procuring a ground for the use of the club during the season, was presented. It was stated that Capt. Ives had offered his skating park for the sum of $300, and that a very fair piece of ground could be obtained on the Brush farm, immediately in the rear of Harper Hospital. The former proposition met with the most favor, although the price was considered too high. The advantages it possesses in the way of location, fitness of the ground and conveniences generally were all considered, and finally the Directors were requested to confer again with the proprietor with power, and ascertain his most liberal terms, and report at another meeting on Monday night. Several new members entering upon the lists, and more proposed. With a smart effort, a lively season at the invigorating game can be enjoyed. It is proposed, should an engagement with the owner of the park be effected, to have the first toss with the ball on Wednesday next.

"KNOW THYSELF."—A magnificent lottery scheme being on the boards a while since, one of our citizens determined to make a ten strike, and get the piano sure. He thereupon speedily divested himself of a ten dollar greenback and purchased ten tickets, arguing that if one ticket be a good thing in a lottery, what an invaluable possession would ten tickets be. Imagine his chagrin, when, instead of a splendid piano, there were handed out to him, ten copies of a cheap Sunday School pamphlet, entitled, "Know Thyself." The invaluable treasure was placed under his arm, and the fortunate individual started on his way, not rejoicing. He could not help but reflect upon the singular title of the work and its peculiar, personal application. The reflection caused a sudden muscular application which suddenly lodged the valuable library in the gutter, with the audible ejaculation of "Know thyself, yes, I think I do, and this is the last lottery ticket *I* purchase."

BOARD OF TRADE.—The prospects of the forthcoming convention of delegates of the different Boards of Trade of the several cities of the north and west, to be holden in this city in July, give earnest of a good attendance. The convention will be a very important one, as matters will come before the Board of vast moment to the commercial interests of the country. It will be remembered that the Detroit Board of Trade have issued circulars inviting such a conference. Yesterday, at a meeting of the Detroit Board, favorable responses were read from the Presidents of the Boards of Trade of Buffalo and Oswego, giving assurance that delegates would be sent, and fully indorsing the necessity and propriety of such a convention.

THE HOLT TRIAL.—The following is a copy of the motion upon which the prisoner's counsel asks for a new trial in the case:

"That on the trial of said cause, one Frederick H. Eberts was called as a juror, who upon his oath was examined relative to his competency to sit as a juror, and upon his oath aforesaid did say: 'I have formed a partial opinion of the guilt or innocence of the person from rumors heard on the street.' The counsel for the prisoner thereupon challenged said Eberts for cause, and thereupon the court ruled said Frederick H. Eberts was competent to sit as a juror in said cause. That the court erred in allowing said Frederick H. Eberts to sit as juror. To which ruling of the court, the defendant, by his counsel then and there excepted."

WHEAT LANDS.—From careful estimates made by merchants, millers and others, who have means of knowing, it is believed full half of last year's wheat crop is still in the hands of farmers in this State. The large crop, of say from 1,000 to 2,000 bushels, are generally unsold, and there is no disposition to sell at the present reduced prices. We have advices from Illinois which state that the same facts, only to a greater degree, apply to that State.

THE SPECIAL INCOME TAX—IMPORTANT NOTICE.—By advertisement in another column from the office of the Collector of Internal Revenue, it will be seen that any person neglecting to pay the special tax on the incomes of 1863, now due, are liable to be charged ten per cent. penalty on the amount after the 10th inst. Those who do not wish to be subjected to this additional burden, should at once attend to this notification.

METROPOLITAN POLICE.—The following appointments have been made since those last mentioned: J. S. Booth, Second Ward; J. T. Hewson, Andrew Huber, and John Ochs Tenth Ward. No further selection will be made until Tuesday next, when it is probable the balance required will be announced. Including those named above, thirty-four members have passed the Board of Commissioners.

THE GREENFIELD OIL WELL.—Parties that arrived last evening from the Greenfield oil well, report the discovery of naptha, and also that oil has been found in considerable quantities. The proprietors of the well feel considerably elated at the present prospect of the discovery of petroleum in paying quantities.

"PUTTY AND VARNISH."—Josh Billings, the humorous writer and lecturer, appears at Young Men's Hall Tuesday night. "Josh" is a Michigan man, and has always been noted for his original wit and eccentricities. Many laughable stories are told by his old companions of the innumerable practical jokes and "drives" perpetrated by him.

WORKING MEN'S MASS MEETING.—The

SUNDAY'S MORNING EDITION.

THE ENEMY PUSHED FROM THE ROAD TOWARDS DANVILLE.

They are Now Pursued Towards Lynchburg.

Grant Confident of Receiving the Surrender of Lee and What Remains of his Army.

REPORT THAT THE PRESIDENT WILL ISSUE ANOTHER AMNESTY PROCLAMATION.

&c., &c., &c.

[BY THE WESTERN UNION LINE.]

FROM WASHINGTON.

Dispatch to the Associated Press.

NEW YORK, April 8.

The *Post's* special says: There is no doubt that ex-Senator Hunter and Judge Campbell remained in Richmond to see what can be done about peace.

The President will probably soon issue another proclamation about amnesty.

The Richmond *Whig* says: Gov. Smith on Sunday said the rebel troops were victorious and Richmond should not be evacuated, and then left on horseback.

A large number of rebel prisoners arrived in Washington this morning, desirous of taking the oath of allegiance.

The correspondence of the Washington *Morning Chronicle*, from Wilmington, April 2d, says: It is a mistake to suppose Wilmington was left bare. Large quantities of cotton are being found in private houses, and both British and American gold abound, and silver is not scarce.

The most interesting item of the week has been the arrest of twenty pilots formerly employed in the Nassau blockade running trade. Most of them resided in Smithfield, at the mouth of Cape Fear river. They came from Nassau to Beaufort, having taken the oath of allegiance at Nassau before the United States Consul. On leaving they, however, were arrested as soon as they reached Beaufort, and are now in custody.

A letter from Richmond, dated April 6, says: The new state of affairs in this city gives general satisfaction to the residents, who, to show their gratitude, tender every attention and information to our soldiers, and on the soldiers' part they are kind and courteous, thus giving contradictions to the false assertions of the rebel press. The streets after taps are free from soldiers, except a patrol or changing of guards. No barroom has yet been allowed to be opened, and what whisky is found is confiscated and poured into the streets. Perfect order prevails. The scarcity of flour and wheat continues extreme, and consequently trade does not improve much.

Mr. Plouty, District Attorney of Florida, arrived here this afternoon. He saw at Savannah a prominent member of the Georgia Legislature, who had just left Augusta. The leading members of the Legislature admitted that the rebellion was near its end. The opinion prevailed that Lee and Johnston and Davis would retreat to Georgia, and then across the Mississippi River. The United States District Court at Key West, has condemned $25,000 worth of property since March 1st.

Special Dispatch to the Western Press.

WASHINGTON, April 8.

Notice has been posted at the War Department that no passes to Richmond will be granted under any circumstances.

The body of Gen. Winthrop, killed in front of Petersburg, was brought here to-day. Over 500 rebel officers, of all grades, are now in Old Capitol Prison. Gen. Barringer and several others are being sent to Fort Delaware.

Convalescents in and around Washington are being removed to Philadelphia and New York from the hospitals, to make room for the constantly arriving wounded from City Point.

Information has been received that 5,000 Union prisoners, of those held by the rebels in Georgia, have arrived at or near Dalton, to be delivered to us on Thursday.

President Lincoln has paid another visit to Richmond, accompanied by his wife and Senators Sumner and Harlan, and others of the party.

FROM NEW ORLEANS.

Dispatch to the Associated Press.

CAIRO, April 8.

New Orleans dates to the 2d are received.

The *Times* says: The monitors Osage and Milwaukee were sunk by torpedoes in Mobile Bay, while attempting to get in range of Spanish Fort. They are not very materially damaged, and can easily be raised and repaired.

The *True Delta* says it was the Essex and Milwaukee that were sunk, and probably only about six lives were lost.

The *Delta* says Forrest's army is breaking up; large numbers daily deserting and going home, mostly Texans. One hundred and fifty deserted in one day.

The steamship Liberty sailed on the 2d for New York, via Havana, with a full load of cotton.

Baton Rouge advices of the 3d represent the river rising. The crevasse, six miles above Baton Rouge, on the west side, is one mile wide and quite deep, and still widening. The country back is overflowed to the depth of sixteen feet.

The troops at Morganza have been placed on steamboats, fears being entertained for the fort. General Herron has a large working party on the levee at Morganza, and hopes to prevent a break there.

A meeting on the west side terminated in a determination to exterminate the jay-hawkers and murderers who are infesting that section. The flood on the 6th washed away the span of the Memphis and Charleston Railroad Bridge between Collierville and Layfayette. A locomotive and three cars on the westward train were precipitated into the water, several were killed and injured.

The steamers Liberty and Cairo, from Memphis, the former for Evansville with 300 bales of cotton and the latter for St. Louis with 88 bales, passed up.

Steamers from Yazoo, at Vicksburg, on the 4th, brought 340 bales of cotton. The Zephyr, from Red River for Memphis, had 770 bales.

FROM THE FRONT.

Special Dispatch to the Western Press.

NEW YORK, April 8.

The *Herald's* correspondent, who ascended James River from City Point to Richmond, says: Just below Chapin's farm there was a new iron-clad unfinished ram, the Texas. She had a plain flush deck, no armament or engines [illegible]

Fort Sumpter, was deemed a most appropriate occasion for thanksgiving, prayer and praise to Almighty God for our national successes, and the bright prospects of returning peace and fraternal harmony. In deference, however, to the wishes now made known to me of many patriotic persons representing some of our religious denominations, that the designated day be solely devoted to the solemn observance of their church ceremonies, I, Reuben E. Fenton, Governor of the State of New York, do hereby amend my proclamation, and set apart Thursday, the 20th inst., for the purpose therein recommended.

(Signed,) R. E. FENTON.

Address of the Citizens of New York to the President in Reference to a Public Celebration.

Dispatch to the Associated Press.

NEW YORK, April 8.

The Committee appointed at the Wall street meeting of Monday, to make arrangements for a public celebration, met at the Custom House, collector Draper in the chair. The following address and accompanying resolutions were adopted.

ADDRESS TO THE PRESIDENT.

The Citizens of New York, to Abraham Lincoln, President of the United States:

With devout thankfulness to Almighty God for the gracious protection he has vouchsafed to us as a nation during the perils and conflict of the civil war, we desire to acknowledge his merciful goodness, and to join in reverence for His holy name. In the confident belief that the measure will be in accordance with the principles which have guided your counsels in the execution of the great and important trust committed to your hands, we respectfully request that a day be designated in your own good time, which may be set apart when the whole people may be invited to assemble and meet together to offer praises and thanksgivings for the brilliant successes, which, under divine providence, have been secured to us by the energy, sagacity and fidelity of the government, and by the skill, intrepidity and self-sacrificing devotion of the army and navy engaged in maintaining the honor and preserving the life of the nation, for the countless blessings we enjoy under the benign influence of free institutions, and for the cheering prospects opening before us of an even more united and prosperous and happy country; and we remain your friends and fellow-citizens.

RESOLUTIONS.

Resolved, That the address be duly authenticated with the signatures of the committee of arrangements, and such other citizens as may desire to unite in this measure of grateful duty and transmit it to the President.

Resolved, That the people of New York are filled with admiration at the splendid combination and dashing bravery which has marked the movements of the conflicts on the battlefields of Virginia, Georgia, and the Carolinas, and that Lieut. Gen. Grant, with Maj. Gen. Sherman and the soldiers and officers under his command, have crowned themselves and the American people with imperishable renown.

Resolved, That while all the commanding Generals who have borne the national colors over fields of victory deserve and will receive the plaudits of a grateful people, their names, which shine out with peculiar lustre, our hearts are full and our eyes suffused whenever we utter the name of Sheridan, the soldier, the successful leader, and chosen warrior, Grant, and of Sherman and Thomas, Schofield and Terry, Meade and others who have filled the measure of the country's glory.

Resolved, That the general committee, in conformity with the terms of the resolution under which it is appointed, will select a fitting time and an appropriate manner, to be hereafter determined, to celebrate the victories achieved in securing the final triumph of the Union cause, to the end that the people of the State of New York may have the opportunity to evince their gratitude and affection for the great leader of the American army, Ulysses S. Grant, and the gallant officers and soldiers whose deeds have rendered his name immortal.

Resolved, That a select committee of five citizens be appointed by the chair, to be announced hereafter, to carry into effect the last preceding resolution.

Resolved, That copies of these proceedings be transmitted to the President and Lieutenant General Grant, and published; that the address to the President be engrossed and signed by the members of the committee present, including Hamlin Fisher, Moses Taylor, Moses H. Grinnell, Hiram Walbridge, A. T. Stewart, Simeon Draper, Col. Howe, Samuel Sloan, P. M. Wetmore, and others.

It was resolved to place the address in the rotunda of the Custom House on Monday, where all citizens will have an opportunity to sign it before it is forwarded to the President.

Finance and Trade.

Special Dispatch to the Western Press.

NEW YORK, April 8.

The speculative feeling in stocks is less buoyant this morning, and there is a slight irregularity in quotations, with the feeling prevailing towards a decline. This appears to be only the result of the usual check to speculative operations experienced on the closing day of the week. Governments quiet and steady. Coal and miscellaneous shares strong, with a rise in Cumberland. The gold room was steady throughout the morning, with the tendency slightly upward. The market suddenly fell this afternoon, from 150½ to 148¼, without any apparent cause, but afterward it went up a little. Money continues quite easy at 6 per cent on call. Moderate demand for petroleum stocks; sales, Oceanica 220; United States 870; Rynd Farm 325; Cherry Run 65; Tack 210; Buchanan Farm 45; Excelsior 400; Germania 74. Petroleum inactive; 34 for crude; 52@53 for refined in bond; and 72@73 free. The first auction sale of Savannah cotton by the government is announced for Tuesday next. There will be 5,000 bales offered, ranging in quality from pickings to good middlings. Sales will be for gold. European steamers are bringing intelligence of failures in consequence of cotton speculations. The fall of Richmond will cause still lower prices in the Liverpool market. The dry goods market has been quite active throughout the week, especially domestic cotton fabrics. A large business has been transacted. Jobbers have supplied themselves freely at auction sales, but they have been selling freely for distribution, and their stock has been steadily reducing prices. Cotton fabrics further declined at the sales Friday, and very low prices were touched in domestic woolens and flannels. Trade is dull and the market low. Manufacturers are curtailing their productions, and in some cases trade will be stopped entirely unless the market looks brighter. For foreign goods there has been comparatively a falling off in prices. Desirable dress goods are scarce, and command full prices. In millinery goods and trimmings the demand is firmer. The produce and merchandise market has been generally dull and heavy throughout, with occasional reactions. There is no speculative feeling in any direction. Buyers are only purchasing to supply their immediate wants, having little or no confidence in the present values being sustained in the future.

Proclamation by the Governor of Ohio.

[illegible]

---

pushed from the road towards Danville, and are now pursued towards Lynchburg, and that he is very confident of receiving the surrender of Lee and what remains of his army.

E. M. STANTON, Sec. of War.

FROM WASHINGTON.

WASHINGTON, April 8.

A notice is posted at the War Department that no passes to Richmond are granted under any circumstances.

Over 500 rebel officers of all grades are now in the Old Capitol prison.

Information is received that 5,000 Union prisoners of those held by the rebels in Georgia, have arrived at or near Dalton, to be delivered to us.

On Thursday President Lincoln paid another visit to Richmond, accompanied by his wife, Senators Sumner and Harlan and others of the party.

From San Francisco.

Dispatch to the Associated Press.

SAN FRANCISCO, April 7.

The steamer John L. Stephens, from Mazatlan, brings $93,000 in treasure and 1,000 bags of silver ore.

The Mazatlan *Times*, imperial organ, gives a report that Juarez was en route for Cape St. Lucas, whence he would sail for San Francisco, on his way to Washington.

The French naval expedition has sailed, it is supposed for Guaymas.

An Imperial force has moved to the Pacific.

The Sinaloa correspondent of the San Francisco *Bulletin*, writing from Mazatlan, March 30, says that Jurez is still at Chihuahua, with his ministers, raising troops, though cash, arms and ammunition are scarce.

The French war steamer Victoria, and transport du Rhine, are at Santa Barbara, on the coast of California. They hope to obtain supplies of coal at San Francisco.

The daily overland mail hence to Salt Lake resumed its trips yesterday. The first mail this way since the interruption arrived last night.

Recent meetings on behalf of the Christian Sanitary Commission resulted in remittances by telegraph of $20,000 the past few days in gold.

From the Pacific.

Dispatch to the Associated Press.

SAN FRANCISCO, April 5.

The Union Convention of Oregon have nominated A. A. Denny as Territorial delegate. The military celebration was held throughout the state to-day. A mass meeting in aid of the Soldiers' Relief Association was held to-night.

Sailed.

NEW YORK, April 8.

The steamers City of Manchester and America sailed to-day for Europe with $400,000 in specie.

FROM THE NINETEENTH MICHIGAN.

Special Correspondence of The Detroit Free Press.

NEAR GOLDSBORO, N. C., March 31.

In the battle of Smith's Ford our regiment suffered severely. Capt. Leonard Gibbon was instantly killed while gallantly leading his men. He was struck near the nose, the ball passing entirely through his head. He is buried in a pleasant place, with a head-board to mark his resting place. Lieut. Charles Pursell, commanding Co. I, was killed, being struck between the eyes. Color Corporal Car[illegible] was also killed while nobly protecting our battered flag. They were all buried side by side, each grave being marked with an inscription. W. R. Beebe was wounded slightly across the breast. He walked off the field laughing at his escaping so well.

The following is a complete list of the casualties:

A. G. Crawford, company A, slightly wounded in hip; B. Borling, company A, slightly wounded in head; C. Hogeboome, company B, wounded in left forearm; Corp. S. Ostrander, company B, right fore arm; First Lieut. Chas Pursel Schoolcraft company F, killed; Elias E. Gilpin, company G, killed; Lake Stallings, company H, wounded; Henry Sanford, company H, left lower limb, amputated; Capt. Leonard Gibbon, company I, killed; H. Beaman, L. C. Northrup, J. Clamfoot, Anson Stone, J. Pomfrey, company I, wounded; C. T. Bean, colored Corporal, company H, killed; Corp. W. R. Beebee, company H, slight flesh wound across the breast—doing well.

We are encamped upon the Newbern railroad, about three miles southeast of the town. We have communications with Newbern and Wilmington. Trains are running to Newbern and supplies are pouring in quite rapidly. The entire army must be clothed, many of our boys wearing rebel clothing, as they have drawn none since they left Atlanta. We expect another active campaign, but not until we are rested and refitted. When we start out again there will be something done. I think it will be the last campaign of the war. We shall have a very large army, though of course it would not be proper to state the exact number. When Sherman hammers at the back door you may expect the thing is over. That knocking will not long be delayed.

M. B. DUFFIE.

NEWS BREVITIES.

During the week ending Saturday last, thirty-eight National Banks were established, with an aggregate capital of $9,112,000. The number of these institutions in operation is 973, with a capital of about $125,000,000.

It is reported that the Chicago *Post* has been purchased by republicans, and will assume the character of a republican journal on the 1st of May.

Austria and Prussia, it has been stated, have agreed upon the flag for the mercantile marine of Schleswig-Holstein. It is composed of three horizontal bands, the upper one blue, that in the middle white, and the lower one red. The blue band is said to have a yellow square by the side of the staff.

A rival for the Armstrong gun is announced in Pittsburg, Pa. The inventor has challenged Sir William Armstrong to a trial in November next, each piece to be fired two hundred consecutive times.

The U. S. Assessor of Chicago has pounced upon a number of business houses in that city for making fraudulent returns of incomes, and they have been mulcted heavily, by being required to pay their full income tax and heavy fines besides. One house was obliged to "fork over" $8,000.

The Commissioner of Agriculture at Washington has some superior tobacco seed for distribution. It was obtained by our Consul at Havana.

Slopped Over.

From the Cincinnati Commercial (Rep.).

Some of the speakers at the jubilation in Washington over the fall of Richmond, slopped over. They couldn't contain themselves. They talked as though the war were concluded, our domestic affairs on a solid footing, our debts paid off, and the nation ready to settle accounts with the rest of the world. They defied France, threatened England, patronized Mexico, and glowered at mankind generally.

It is fortunate, perhaps, for our future welfare that these sort of people are understood abroad as thoroughly as at home, and about the same estimate placed upon their value. On one occasion they blaze up in [illegible]

MONDAY'S MORNING EDITION.

GLORY! GLORY!! GLORY!!!

THE REBELLION ENDED!

LEE'S WHOLE ARMY SURRENDERED.

THE SURRENDER EFFECTED SUNDAY AFTERNOON.

Correspondence Between Generals Grant and Lee.

ALL ARMS AND PUBLIC PROPERTY TO BE DELIVERED UP.

The Officers to Retain their Private Property and Side Arms.

EACH OFFICER AND SOLDIER TO BE ALLOWED TO GO HOME ON PAROLE.

Grant Pledges that they Shall Not be Disturbed as Long as they Do not Take Arms against the United States.

A Salute of Two Hundred Guns Ordered Fired at Every Post and Arsenal in the United States.

THE PRESIDENT'S INTERVIEW WITH REBEL OFFICIALS.

THE BOMBARDMENT OF MOBILE ACTIVELY PROGRESSING.

&c., &c., &c.

SURRENDER OF LEE'S ARMY.

[OFFICIAL.]

WASHINGTON, April 9—9 P. M.

To Major General Dix, New York:

This department has received the official report of the surrender this day of Gen. Lee and his army to Lieut. Gen. Grant, on the terms proposed by Gen. Grant.

(Signed) E. M. STANTON, Secretary of War.

HEADQUARTERS ARMIES OF THE UNITED STATES, April 9—4:30 P. M.

To Hon. Edwin M. Stanton, Secretary of War.

General Lee surrendered the army of Northern Virginia this afternoon upon the terms proposed by myself. The accompanying additional correspondence will show the conditions fully.

U. S. GRANT, Lieutenant General.

April 9, 1865.

GENERAL—I received your note of this morning on the picket line, whither I had come to meet you, and ascertain definitely what terms were embraced in your proposition of yesterday with reference to the surrender of this army. I now request an interview in accordance with the offer contained in your letter of yesterday for that purpose.

Very respectfully, your obedient servant,

R. E. LEE, General.

To Lieut. Gen. Grant, commanding United States Armies:

April 9, 1865.

Gen. R. E. Lee, commanding Confederate States Armies:

Your note of this date is but this moment, 11:50 A. M., received. In consequence of my passing from the Richmond and Lynchburg road to the Farmville and Lynchburg road, I am at this writing about four miles west of Walter's Church, and will push forward to the front for the purpose of meeting you. Notice sent to me on this road, where you wish the interview to take place, will suit me.

Very respectfully, your obedient servant,

U. S. GRANT, Lieut. Gen.

APPOMATOX COURT HOUSE, April 9, 1865.

Gen. R. E. Lee, Commanding C. S. A.:

In accordance with the substance of my letter to you of the 8th inst., I propose to receive the surrender of the army of Northern Virginia on the following terms, to wit: Rolls of all the officers and men to be made in duplicate, one copy to be given to an officer designated by me, the other to be retained by such [illegible]

---

army of Northern Virginia in t[illegible] gle. I feel that it is so, a[illegible] it as my duty to shift from myself t[illegible] sibility of any further effusion o[illegible] asking of you the surrender of that [illegible] the Confederate States Army know[n as the] army of Northern Virginia.

Very respectfully your obedient serv[ant],
U. S. GRANT, Li[eut. Gen.],
Commanding Armi[es]

Apr[illegible]

GENERAL—I have received you[r] [illegible] this date. Though not entirely of t[illegible] you express of the hopelessness of [illegible] sistance on the part of t[illegible] of Northern Virginia, I [illegible] your desire to avoid useless [illegible] of blood, and therefore, bef[ore con]sidering your proposition, ask the [illegible] will offer on condition of its surrende[r].

R. E. L[EE], G[eneral].

To Lieut. Gen. Grant, Commanding Ar[mies] United States:

Apr[illegible]

To Gen. R. E. Lee, Commanding, C. S. [A.]:

GENERAL—Your note of last evenin[g] [illegible] to mine of the same day, asking on [what con]dition I will accept the sur[render of] the army of Northern Vir[ginia is] received. In reply I wo[uld say] that, peace being my first desire, [there is] but one condition that I insist upon, [viz:] the men surrendered shall be disqu[alified for] taking up arms again against the g[overnment] of the United States, until properly e[xchanged]. I will meet you, or designate office[rs to meet] any officers you may name, for the [pur]pose, at any point agreeable to you, f[or the pur]pose of arranging definitely the te[rms upon] which the surrender of the Army of [Northern] Virginia will be received.

Very respectfully, your obedient serv[ant],
U. S. GRANT, Lieut Gen. Comm[anding]
Armies of the Unit[ed States].

Ap[illegible]

GENERAL—I received at a late [hour your] note of to-day, in answer to mine of [illegible]. I did not intend to propose the surren[der of the] Army of Northern Virginia, but [to ask the] terms of your proposition. To be fr[ank, I do] not think the emergency has arisen [to call for] the surrender, but as the restoration [of peace] should be the sole object of all, [I desire] to know whether your proposa[ls would] tend to that end. I cannot, therefor[e, meet you] with a view to surrender the army o[f Northern] Virginia, but as far as your propo[sal may] effect the Confederate States forces [under my] command, and tend to the restoration [of peace,] I should be pleased to meet you a[t illegible] to-morrow, on the old stage road to [illegible] between the two armies.

Very respectfully, &c., R[illegible]

To Lieut. Gen. Grant.

April [illegible]

To Gen. R. E. Lee, Commanding C. S. A.

GENERAL—Your note of yesterd[ay is re]ceived. As I have no authority to [treat on] the subject of peace, the meeting pro[posed for] 10 A. M. to-day could lead to no goo[d. I will] state, however, General, that I ar[illegible] anxious for peace with yourself, [and the] whole North entertain the same feel[ing. The] terms upon which peace can be [had are] well understood. By the South [laying] down their arms they will hasten [that most] desirable event, save thousands o[f human] lives, and hundreds of millions of pr[operty not] yet destroyed—sincerely hoping th[at all our] difficulties may be settled without [the loss of] another life, I subscribe myself,

Very respectfully, &c.,
U. S. GRANT, Li[eut. Gen.]

WAR DEPARTMENT, WA[SHINGTON], April 9—9:30 [illegible]

To Lieut. Gen. Grant:

Thanks be to Almighty God for [the great] victory with which He has this day [crowned] you and the gallant armies under [your com]mand. The thanks of this departme[nt and of] the government, and of the peopl[e of the] United States, their reverence and ho[nor, have] been deserved, and will be rendered t[o you and] the brave soldiers and gallant office[rs of your] army for all time.

E. M. STANTON, Secretary [of War].

WAR DEPAR[TMENT], WASHINGTON, April 9—10 [illegible]

Ordered that a salute of two hun[dred guns] be fired at the headquarters of every [army and] navy department, and at every post [and arse]nal in the United States, and at [the mili]tary academy at West Point [on the] day of the receipt of this [order, in] commemoration of the surrender of G[en. R. E.] Lee and the Army of Northern Vi[rginia to] Lieut. Gen. Grant, and the army [under his] command. Report of the receipt a[nd execu]tion of this order to be made to th[e Adjutant] General at Washington.

E. M. STANTON, S[ecretary of War].

FROM NEW YORK.

NEW YORK, [illegible]

The steamship Matanzas arrived [illegible] ing from City Point, with 900 rebel [illegible] Part of these were captured at Be[illegible] Goldsboro and Columbia. Among t[illegible] ers is Col. Rhett, of Fort Sumpter n[illegible]

The *Times'* Petersburg correspon[dent con]tradicts the statement that the ra[ilroad to] Richmond was nearly repaired. No [illegible] man has been put upon it. The [illegible] Railroad is to have its guage change[d to] take upon it our rolling stock.

Petersburg was in command of G[illegible] ren until the 5th, when Gen. Hartsu[ff was as]signed to the command as Military [illegible]

The *Herald's* Richmond correspond[ent says] Mr. Lincoln was on the 4th informed [by Gens.] Weitzel and Shepley, that promine[nt rebels] desired an interview with h[im. He] replied that he was willing [to grant] the interview, but in the presence o[f illegible]. After the reception of the officers of [the army] and navy, it was announced to the [illegible] that Judge Campbell, Assistant rebel [Secreta]ry of War, and Mr. Myers, membe[r of the] late rebel Congress, were awaiting an [interview] with the President in another roo[m. The] President, accompanied by Gen. We[itzel, im]mediately retired to the room, and h[eld a con]ference, which lasted but a short time [and was] adjourned to the flag-ship Malvern. [The re]sult of these conferences cannot [be] known, but auspicious results are [said to] be about to accrue from them.

The *Herald* has Mobile Bay corres[pondence] up to the 31st ult. It appears that [illegible] and Smith's corps marched from Dan[illegible] on the 25th, for Blakely, meeting slig[ht oppo]sition only on the first day. On the [illegible] 13th corps moved toward the Spanis[h Fort, a] strong earth-work commanding Min[illegible], encountering and driving in the rebe[l pickets,] and in the evening Granger encampe[d on the] left of that fort. The 13th corps co[ntinued] towards Blakely, encamping at Sible[y's Mills,] five miles from that town on the 26th. [On the] morning of the 27th our forces advanc[ed upon] Spanish Fort, driving in the rebels, [illegible] rifle pits, and establishing our batteri[es within] 400 yards of the fort. On the 29th, o[ur men] were intrenched within seventy yar[ds of the] fort. Several lives had been lost by t[orpedoes,] which are thickly strewn forward. [illegible] averages 150 per day. Three hundre[d illegible] enemy had been cut off by a portio[n illegible]

Part Six Endings and Beginnings

Chapter 14

In the Loss of Lee, They Lose Everything

The possible arming of the slaves notwithstanding, the hopes of the Confederacy ultimately came to rest on the skill and daring of its most revered commander, Robert E. Lee. The legend of Lee's greatness emerged early in the war. In 1862, while the Tennessee and Mississippi Valleys had come under the increasing domination of the Federals, Lee had successfully protected Virginia and the Confederate capital at Richmond, winning as well the trust and admiration of the Southern public. Even after his loss at Gettysburg, the respect of Southerners for his military genius remained unbounded. As one newspaper declared at the end of 1863, Lee was "certainly the anchor of hope of the Confederacy"—the one man who could deflate the swelling power of the Union and "roll the stone from the grave" for the South's "resurrection." It was a mystique that only grew with time, and in the winter of 1864–65, with Sherman marching through the heart of Georgia and the Carolinas, Southerners continued to believe that so long as Lee remained in the field, all hopes were not lost. "He is indeed the main prop of our cause," declared the *Macon Telegraph & Confederate*. "With him between them and the vandal hordes, men sleep in peace at night and dream of victory."[1] No matter how devastating Sherman's march was, nothing promised to be so disheartening to Southerners—or uplifting for Union men—as securing the surrender of Lee's Army of Northern Virginia.

Grant had been attempting to achieve this very result since the spring of 1864, after Lincoln put him in charge of operations in the eastern theater. In bringing Grant east, Lincoln had promoted him to the rank of lieutenant general—a title that had been held only once before, by George Washington—and the

GENERAL ROBERT EDMUND LEE.

Southern Illustrated News, October 17, 1863. Portrait of Robert E. Lee.

president expected that he would prove as successful as Washington in finally carrying the country to victory. Grant quickly took the offensive and crossed the Rapidan on May 4, in hopes of engaging Lee's army in a showdown somewhere south of the densely covered wilderness that bordered the river. Lee surprised him, however, with an attack near Chancellorsville, and the two armies contended with each other in two days of uncoordinated fighting. Although Lee's men were badly outnumbered, 115,000 to 64,000, the thick woods negated the Union's advantage in manpower and artillery, and the Battle of the Wilderness ended in a draw, with both armies suffering a high percentage of casualties. Nevertheless, Grant was undeterred and instead of retreating, continued to press southward in pursuit of Lee, who had entrenched his troops around Spotsylvania. There, Grant attempted a series of ill-fated assaults on the Confederate trenches—maneuvers involving close-range, hand-to-hand fighting that the surviving soldiers regarded as the most horrific they had yet experienced. Having failed at Spotsylvania, Grant then attempted to lure Lee out of the trenches by moving the engagement further south, to Cold Harbor, just outside of Richmond. As they had at Spotsylvania, the Confederates dug themselves into another line of trenches, against which Grant ordered an all-out direct offensive on June 3. The men in blue knew they were entering a slaughter pen—hundreds of them wrote their names on pieces of paper and pinned them to their chests so that their bodies could be properly identified later. Their premonitions were tragically correct. Grant's defeat at Cold Harbor was terribly costly; in one day of fighting, the Union suffered 7,000 casualties. All told, this month-long series of engagements took a heavy toll on both sides, as Grant and Lee each lost *half* of their armies.

Determined to drive Lee into open combat, Grant continued to lead his troops southward over the James River to threaten Petersburg, a primary railroad hub that was essential to maintaining Virginia's lines of communication and food supplies. Lee outmaneuvered him, however, and got to the town first to fortify it. This time, both armies built trenches that eventually stretched for over fifty miles around Petersburg, and settled into siege warfare—an unrelenting and enormously destructive mode of combat that would typify the world wars of the twentieth century. The fighting in Virginia thus became a war of attrition.

Over the next nine months, Grant slowly extended the length of the Union trenches, tightening a noose around Lee and Petersburg. One by one, the roads leading into the town fell under the control of Grant's men, and on April 2, 1865, they broke through the Confederate line and seized the last open railroad, thereby severing Lee's only remaining supply link with the rest of the Confederacy. In order to avoid being completely encircled, Lee had to evacuate, which meant abandoning not only Petersburg but nearby Richmond too. The Confederate general sent a telegram to Jefferson Davis to inform him that the capital was now defenseless, and everyone capable of leaving Richmond did so quickly, including Davis and his cabinet, who escaped the city with the all the gold from the Confederate treasury. In order to ensure that the Union gained nothing of value from taking Richmond, the city was torched as the government departed. On April 3, when the Yankees triumphantly marched into town, with Abraham Lincoln in tow, much of the Confederate capital was in ruins, cannibalized by its own people.[2]

With Lee in retreat, Davis on the run, and the rebel seat of power now in Union hands, the North could hardly contain its exultation. Expressions of joy, patriotism, and sheer relief exploded in colorful public displays reminiscent of the type that had followed the fall of Fort Sumter four years previously. The *Herald* in New York City reported:

> It would be impossible through the medium of pen, ink and paper to convey to our readers anything like a full description of the unbounded enthusiasm that prevailed in this city yesterday. . . . There is no language capable of expressing the wild scenes of excitement and the joyful demonstrations of patriotism, from the Battery to Spuyten Duyvel creek. People fairly danced in the excess of enthusiasm. To state that they howled would sound harshly and flat, but it would nevertheless be a simple truth. Some are so organized that under extraordinary emotions words will not suffice for their purpose; they must roar, or choke in the effort to express themselves through the customary channels.—This scientific theory is the best we can offer in explanation of the patriotic exhaustion of lungs that occurred yesterday. Huzzaing and cheering were heard as never they were heard before. Singing also formed part of the popular mode of letting off the exuberant feelings of the masses. Down on Wall street . . . ten thousand human beings chanted, as with one voice, the now favorite national hymn of "Glory Hallelujah," with an accompaniment of shouting and jumping and stamping beyond all description. Those who did not hear it will have to imagine the effect of such a union of throats in a locality where such different performances are generally witnessed.
>
> The rage for flags was immense. The news of Saturday and Sunday had the effect of inducing hundreds to make a raid on the flag stores early yesterday morning, and the consequence was that the supply on hand was very nearly exhausted before the intelligence of Richmond's fall arrived. Half an hour after the receipt of the capture of the rebel capital there was not a single large flag of national character in the whole city left unpurchased. Every housekeeper showed his loyalty and satisfaction by exhibiting the Stars and Stripes from some portion of his establishment. The City Hall proudly displayed her usual quota of national, State and municipal banners. The Custom House, Post Office, exchanges, hotels, churches and all public buildings were crowned with the victorious ensign of the Union. Some houses had a flag from every window, two or three on the roof and more over the stoops and doorways. The railway cars and horses were decorated with miniature flags. Carts, stages and wagons all over the city displayed the same symbol of loyalty. . . . Every spot where a piece of bunting could properly be fastened was so decorated.[3]

The public jubilation roared to a crescendo over the following week, as Lee's surrender went from being imminent to actual. After evacuating Petersburg, Lee

THE WAR ENDED

GOD HAS GRANTED

VICTORY.

GLORIOUS NEWS

SURRENDER OF

LEE'S ARMY

Harrisburg Telegraph, April 10, 1865.
For Northerners, Lee's surrender represented more than a military triumph. It was a God-given moral victory that reflected the righteousness of the Union cause.

PEACE!!!

LEE SURRENDERS.

THE REBELLION CRUSHED!

END OF THE WAR!

THE UNION RESTORED!

Liberty Triumphant!

Philadelphia North American & United States Gazette, April 10, 1865.
In 1861, the Northern press had proclaimed that the Union was fighting for liberty—meaning the supremacy of the federal government over states' rights. With the war over, the press now proclaimed the triumph of liberty as Northerners understood it.

had attempted to get to the town of Danville, where he could combine his troops with those of Joseph E. Johnston, but Grant outpaced him, forcing Lee to shift direction and head toward Lynchburg and the old village of Appomattox. There, with Union troops surrounding him, and possessed of an army that was severely weakened by despondency and exhaustion, and depleted by desertion and want of food, Lee sent a note to Grant on April 9, offering to surrender. As far as Northerners were concerned, this was the end of the war. The rebels had banked their hopes on Lee, and without him, their power of resistance was destroyed. "In the loss of Lee, they lose everything," the *New York Tribune* declared triumphantly. "The Rebellion is over; suppressed,—overwhelmed,—destroyed,—fought down,—by strong arms, and stout hearts, and wise heads—ended as rebellion should be by utter destruction." For the North, this was more than just a military victory; it was a *moral* one that vindicated the Union and the ideals of liberty and free government for which it stood:

> After four years of awful strife free Government is saved, the right of the majority to rule is vindicated, and the duty of the minority to submit to the popular will constitutionally expressed, is enforced. And Republican Government justly administered, is proven to be the strongest form of Government ever devised by man. The war has shown that the people, when acting together in behalf of human equality, constitute the dominant power of the State. They are able to crush any aristocracy or oligarchy that plots or conspires against their rights.
>
> The strength of the resolve to put down the rebellion at whatever cost of blood and treasure could be seen in the spontaneous jubilation of the people. It was like the steam of a herculean locomotive, being blown off when it reaches the end of its journey. It was that pent-up power that propelled the engine. The tumultuous raptures of yesterday [were] the sudden letting loose of the feeling which for four years has nerved the heart of the people to fight on and to hold out and when the first born fell, to send to the battle the second and the third born. It was this unconquerable spirit in the common people to save their Union, unconditionally, which won the contest. It was this high resolve that caused Chicago alone to contribute twenty-two thousand of her sons to the war for the Union, the State of Illinois two hundred and thirty thousand, and the loyal States more than two million of men to combat treason and oligarchy; and while this love of liberty and equal rights animates the breasts of the masses, the great Republic can not be destroyed by human foes.[4]

These victory celebrations carried special meaning for Northern blacks, who saw in the Union's triumph

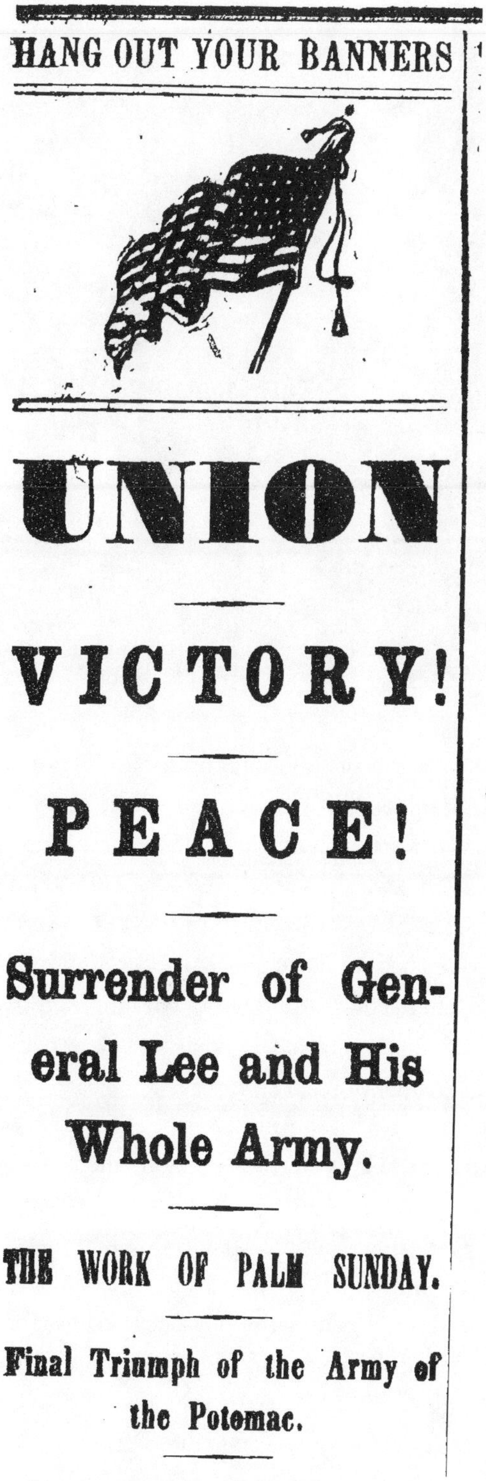
HANG OUT YOUR BANNERS

UNION

VICTORY!

PEACE!

Surrender of General Lee and His Whole Army.

THE WORK OF PALM SUNDAY.

Final Triumph of the Army of the Potomac.

New York Times, April 10, 1865.

Frank Leslie's Illustrated Newspaper, April 22, 1865. As New Yorkers poured into the streets to celebrate the end of the war, they came together in a spirit of unity that they had not shared since 1861.

the affirmation of their own honor and manhood. The patriotic rallies that had occasioned the outbreak of the Civil War were all-white affairs. Northerners were set to embark on a war to save the Union, not to end slavery, and as blacks were not even permitted to serve in the army, they had no place in them. Now, the situation had totally changed. At the victory parades in 1865, blacks not only watched from the sidelines but actively participated, without any apparent resistance from their white compatriots. Although it was not clear how long such feelings of amity would last, they seemed to augur well for the future of blacks in the North. A correspondent for the *Anglo-African* reported from Cincinnati:

> The celebration of the day began at an early hour, the firing off of cannons and ringing of bells, foretelling the jubilee of the day. Flags, tri-colors, and mottoes were shown from every dwelling. . . . Each one vied with another in the gay decorations of their homes and places of business. The street cars, omnibusses and other conveyances were dressed gaily in red, white and blue. Our colored citizens were not behind in their decorations, but showed both taste and appreciation of the beautiful in their arrangements.
>
> The most important feature of the day was the grand procession in the p.m., in which *our people* took part. The whole turn out was *grand*, but I will only particularize *our people*. I was justly proud of the display made by our colored citizens. They marched with the general procession, some in carriages or coaches, and for the most part on foot. . . . A most beautiful feature was the cars, with little girls dressed in white, and gayly decorated with the tri-colors; wreathes upon their heads, and flags innumerable protruding, one in each tiny hand. The cars bore the following mottoes: "All men were created of one blood." "All men are born equal." "God is for us, who can be against us?" "No negro rebels." "The time has come.". . .
>
> A beautiful standard was borne by one of the men, with an eagle and the Goddess of Liberty, holding a scroll upon which was inscribed, "Liberty, Equality."

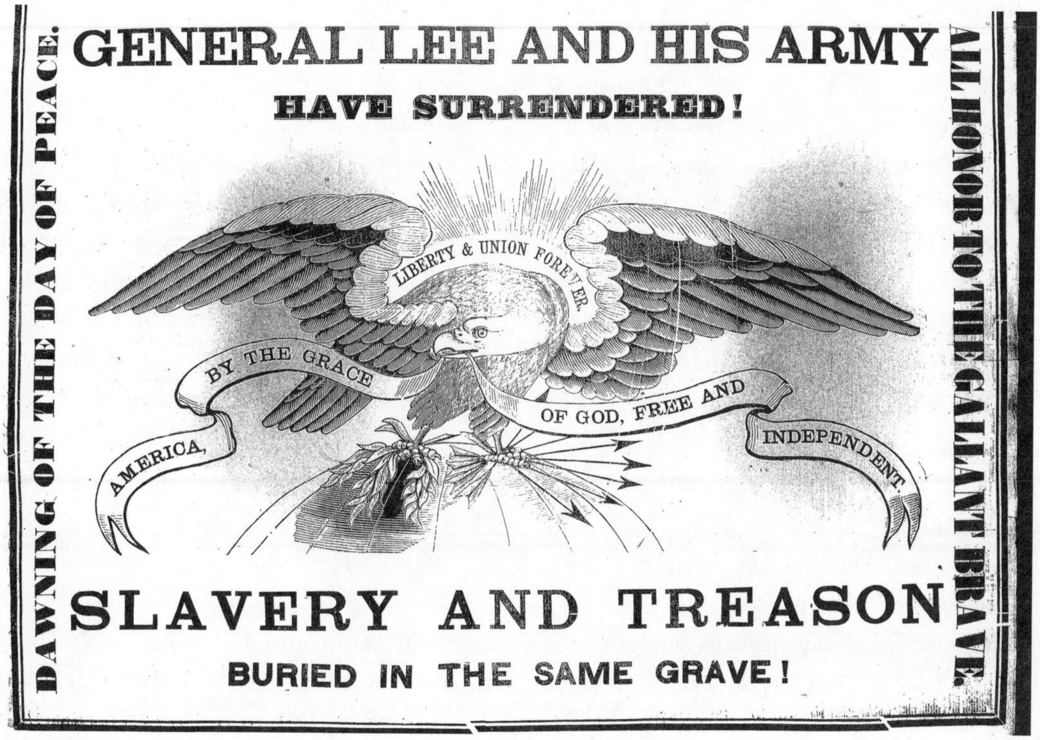
GENERAL LEE AND HIS ARMY
HAVE SURRENDERED!
LIBERTY & UNION FOREVER.
AMERICA, BY THE GRACE OF GOD, FREE AND INDEPENDENT.
SLAVERY AND TREASON
BURIED IN THE SAME GRAVE!
DAWNING OF THE DAY OF PEACE.
ALL HONOR TO THE GALLANT BRAVE.

Albany Evening Journal, April 10, 1865.
The defeat of Lee, the squelching of the rebellion, the death of slavery, and the vindication of the Union were all interconnected in the minds of Northern Republicans, and all were causes for celebration.

Our turn out, I learn, was treated on the whole line of march with the utmost courtesy. No sneers at the negro, and well that it was so, for have we not won for ourselves a place in the ranks of mankind? But we must be up and watching, for not yet is our mission o'er. It was a matter of surprise to ourselves, the manner in which our turn out was received by the whites. Hats and handkerchiefs waved from all sides. . . . This was, by far, the most impressive feature of yesterday's glorious celebration.[5]

Black Americans had good reason to remain a bit wary amid the welcoming and celebratory mood of the moment, for despite the overwhelming joy exuded by the Northern people, differences of opinion—particularly on the issue of emancipation—still remained. Members of the highly conservative peace wing of the Democratic party were certainly relieved to see the fighting come to an end. But they were far from happy about what the war had cost, and could not embrace the changes it had wrought with regard to slavery. As the *Harrisburg Patriot & Union* explained solemnly:

> Why should the Democrats rejoice over the fall of Richmond and the surrender of Gen. Lee and his army? Not for the carnage wrought in accomplishing that result; not that the South is humbled and subdued; not that the anti-slavery dogmas and the anti-democratic heresies of the dominant [Republican] party are now nearer their final realization; but that the reign of blood is nearly over and peace—in some form—is about to beam once more upon the land. It

has been the part of the Democracy of the North, for the past four years of trial and carnage, to pray and work for peace—to still the troubled elements—to modify the violent measures of extremists—to stay the tide of blood—to save the poor men of the land from the remorseless conscription, their wives from widowhood and their children from destitute orphanage. . . . Their efforts were seconded by but few in the ranks of the opposite political party, and the war has gone on, steeping the land in misery, . . . and, as the end of the rebellion is now approaching by the channel of blood, without any hope of peaceful negotiation, it becomes useless any longer to hope or ask for an amicable adjustment. The Democracy can only rejoice that peace is coming, and that the reign of Destruction is passing away—no more. They would gladly, also, rejoice at the re-establishment of the Union, but they know not what shape the new Union will be made to assume by the leaders of the Abolition party.[6]

Although they had failed to temper or control how the war effort had been conducted, the Copperhead press nevertheless hoped to exert a taming influence over the process of reunion. At the start of the conflict, the peace party had insisted that the North and South could never be forced back together again. Not only was a war of coercion antithetical to the nation's democratic ideals, but they believed that even if it succeeded, the experience would so alienate the South from the North that any lasting union between the two would be impossible. Now they again cautioned that reconciliation could not be forced. Reconstructing the country would require that the Republicans in power soothe the wounds of war by treating the Southern people with leniency and respect. The Copperheads *denied* that the Union had won any kind of moral victory over the rebels; Northerners had triumphed not because they were better or more deserving of success than Southerners, but only because they were more powerful. And while overwhelming force had lifted the Union to victory in war, mercy, warned the *New York News*, was the only true basis for peace:

> In dealing with a foreign enemy, supremacy in arms may bring about a settlement of the questions in dispute. The trial by battle ended, the combatants quietly resume their respective separate missions in the family of nations. Not so in a domestic quarrel. If, after a peace has been conquered by the stronger party, the contestants are to live under the same political roof, . . . something more is essential beside triumph upon the field of battle. Those who have confronted each other in deadly conflict are not made friends by the simple act of sheathing their swords. The hearts so lately inflamed with the passions of the civil strife must be attuned to the harmonies of tranquil companionship. The hands that have wielded the weapons of destruction must be clasped in concord. The hatchet must be buried. . . . Until that is done, it cannot be said that peace dwells in the land.
>
> The North has not passed unscathed the ordeal of war. Triumph has been achieved at such a cost that the pride of victory is subdued by painful memories, and exultation yields to the solemn emotions inspired by retrospection. The chimes will be rung, the cannons will boom, and the millions will wear holiday faces, but beneath the surface of popular rejoicing there will be an irrepressible sentiment of awe and sadness, a people's tribute to the countless fallen and bereaved. There are too many drops of blood and too many bitter tears upon the laurels of the North to permit us to display them vauntingly. . . .
>
> To overcome the physical resistance of the South was, after all, an affair of force.—In their valor, their endurance, their martial skill and their faith in the justice of their cause, they were equal to the North. They have been subdued by overwhelming numbers. But to overcome their resentments and secure their future amity will be found a most difficult and delicate task. . . . If they should be compelled to enter the

Union with the deprivation of a single privilege that was theirs at the commencement of this struggle, the spirit of sectional antagonism will remain and will be nursed and encouraged with the recollection of defeat. The history of this war will be taught to Southern children as the record of a struggle not yet ended, and the coming generation will be educated to hate the conquerors of their fathers, and to rekindle the flame of strife at the first opportunity. . . .

Such are the perils that threaten the Republic as it emerges, shattered and impoverished, from the furnace of civil war. But the danger may be averted by removing at once, between the North and the South, the relations of conqueror and conquered.—Let perfect political equality between the sections be established, let the sovereignty of the States be acknowledged, let the necessity for a standing army be canceled, and a policy of conciliation inaugurated, and the Republic may resume its natural career of freedom, prosperity and progress.[7]

This was an attitude that many voices in the Republican camp were actually quick to embrace. Despite the severity with which the war had been waged, newspapers back home still fancied the idea that the majority of Southerners were not rebels at heart, but rather had been misled and "duped" into it by their evil-minded, slave-owning leaders. In dealing with the general population of the South, the *Albany Evening Journal* therefore hoped that Lincoln would issue a generous amnesty to encourage their loyalty to the Union:

Now that the war has virtually ended, and we have no more need to make draughts upon the resources of military skill, we enter upon an epoch in which statesmanship of the highest order will be demanded. We have shown how terrible we could be in War; let us hope we shall be able to prove that we can be grand in the era of Peace. So long as Treason was organized, arrogant, defiant, we could not exhibit before it a single element of weakness; now, when it is prostrate and incapable of further harm, we can afford to be magnanimous and charitable. . . . We have Government to establish; social institutions to reconstruct; a wasted and ravaged country to restore to prosperity. In order to accomplish this, we must forego passion and forget hatreds. We must learn to love each other again—to work together for the good of one country, one cause, one destiny.

Such are the considerations that are soon to present themselves and demand action. . . . Above all things, let us cherish no revenges. To forgive, is noble. We would approach the Southern people, not with the Halter, but with the Constitution; we would build upon their conquered soil, not the scaffold, but the school-house; we would pronounce to them not the terrible sentence of the Mosaic law, "An eye for an eye and a tooth for a tooth," but the tender invitation of the Prince of Peace, "Arise, thy sins, which are many, are all forgiven thee.". . . We would point out to them acres of unnamed graves, ruined cities, desolated hamlets, blasted fields, destitution and misery everywhere, saying, "Behold your work." And then we would invite them, by every consideration we can appeal to honorable manhood, to prove themselves repentant of their grave error, and redeem the dark and bloody past by the lustre of their future. Thus we shall show ourselves worthy of the glory we are permitted to enjoy.

We hope and believe that the President will issue a Proclamation setting forth the terms upon which the Rebel masses will be welcomed back to their allegiance,—and that these terms will be made broad and liberal, as is becoming the temper of a great people. . . . Nor is it too much to believe that the Southern people, relieved from the domination of a hateful and imperious oligarchy, enlightened respecting the great errors into which their ambitious and wicked leaders have beguiled them, and convinced of the futility of further resistance, will gladly welcome such a step on the part of the

Government, and conform to the circumstances of their situation.

The morning breaks brightly, and darkness fleeth before the rising sun. Let us welcome the auspicious day, and go forth cheerily and prayerfully to meet its responsibilities and perform the work it brings us![8]

This spirit of magnanimity toward the common people of the South was commingled with deep feelings of respect for Lee and the Army of Northern Virginia. In this, the Northern press followed the example set by Grant at Appommatox. The terms of Lee's surrender had been very generous. Grant paroled all of the rebel soldiers, promising that they would never be "disturbed by U.S. authority" so long as they ceased all resistance to the federal government and obeyed the laws of the land—essentially, assurance that they would not be prosecuted in the future for treason. In addition to showing great mercy toward Lee's soldiers, Grant was careful to shelter their pride. When Union troops began sounding off their guns to celebrate the surrender, Grant silenced them, acknowledging that the Southern men were no longer enemies but fellow Americans once again. Voicing its approval, the *Philadelphia North American & United States Gazette* wrote:

General Lee surrendered his whole army, with all its artillery, baggage train, munitions of war, small arms, etc., and Grant, with a proper spirit of respect for brave soldiers, treats the officers and men with due courtesy, and gives them liberty on their parole of honor. . . .

We treat this as virtually ending the struggle, because it is not conceivable that any of the confederate generals will feel inclined to protract the war and waste more rivers of blood after their commander-in-chief, whose tremendous resistance in Virginia has been the main stay of the rebellion, has abandoned all hope, and thrown himself and his army upon the generosity of the victorious Grant. The people of the south were long since weary of the war, and yearning for its close. They have seen their best and bravest torn from their homes to waste their lives in a vain conflict. They have seen mourning domesticated at every hearth, and ruin and desolation stalk rampant over all their broad domain. . . . It will be seen by the correspondence between Grant and Lee that Lee himself says that his object in proposing to treat was peace, and . . . it is plain from the whole tenor of the correspondence that the surrender means peace emphatically. We say, then, to the people of the United States, who have looked forward with anxious hearts to the wished-for dawn of peace, rejoice now, for it has come at last. The awful horrors of this frightful but still glorious contest may now be considered as passing into the domain of history. Freedom and slavery have fought out their great battle, and slavery is in the dust forever.

If ever a beaten and surrendered army, fighting in a bad cause, earned for itself the respect of those against whose banners it had been arrayed, it surely is the confederate army just given up by General Lee into the hands of the victorious Grant. The men of that army on many an ensanguined field—on many a perilous march—on many a day of suffering and hardship, have proved themselves soldiers worthy of the proud American race. . . . And now, at the close of the mighty struggle, when this mighty army, which has been for four years the very bulwark of the rebellion, has ended the reign of sorrow and blood by bringing us peace as it once brought us war, we feel that we should be churlish and narrow-minded indeed, could we refuse this parting tribute to the soldiers of the great Confederate army of Northern Virginia. They fought well, so long as there was a hope of success for their cause, and in their discipline, their courage, their steadfastness, their perseverance and endurance, they exalted the American name in the eyes of all the world not less than did our own gallant veterans. The men who have fought out such a conflict can afford to close it without heart-burnings or hatred. They have met in deadly strife, and know each other henceforth to be men worthy of the American race.

We speak now of the soldiers of the rebel armies. Of the political chiefs who have driven them on, ever fierce, we do not now care to speak. We fought for liberty and peace, and having secured them both, we shall deal with becoming magnanimity with the soldiers of the conquered armies.[9]

While the North was quick to support the merciful treatment of the Southern masses, the dominant attitude toward the leaders of the rebellion—men such as Jefferson Davis—was much harsher. There was no general demand for their execution; that would only serve to inflame the ire of the Southern people and make them look at reunion with dread. But many felt that those who headed the Confederate government had to be stripped of their political power, and perhaps divested of their property, in order to ensure that they would never again have the means to whip up another insurrection against the Union. As the *Cincinnati Gazette* emphatically opined, it was important that the North not allow itself to become so softhearted as to forget to punish this "rebel class" thoroughly:

How shall we execute justice for the crime which has turned the land into a sea of woe, so that it shall be a warning to rebellion for all time? How shall we temper justice with mercy so that the sum of all crimes shall not mock our ideas of justice with impunity? How shall we build up civil Government out of anarchy, . . . and establish peace on such foundations that the blood and treasure which it has cost shall not be thrown away?

We see manifestations on the part of many well-meaning but weak-minded persons . . . to assume that the whole matter may be settled by a gush of the emotions and by fine sentiments; that the end of all this slaughter and devastation of society is to be simply a re-enactment of the Prodigal Son, in which the Government, overflowing with parental affection, shall run to meet the Southern rebel, and shall fall on his neck and kiss him, bring him back to the parental mansion, give him the place of honor, kill the fatted calf, and drown all the terrible events of the past four years in the oblivion of our convivialities. . . .

Has the power of the rebel class been merciful to the South or to the whole country that we should seek to restore it in mercy? Is it a desire for more bloodshed that would deprive this bloody class of their destructive power? Is justice to those whose crime has drenched the land with blood, to be stigmatized as vengeance? We had to subjugate the rebels. They were impressible only by that argument. It is necessary that they should be made to feel that they are subjugated. The realization of subjugation must come before submission to the Government will begin. It is necessary that we deprive the rebels of political power in the local governments and in the nation, until they have gone through a probation and have shown . . . repentance. If this be holding States as Territories, let them make the most of it, for anything less is to restore the conquered rebels to political power.

There is a cruelty more heartless than stern justice or vengeance, more indifferent to blood than the most brutal soldiery; it is the heartlessness of political triflers who, untouched in their own persons by the nation's calamity, are generous in the blood of the brave patriots who have fallen in their country's cause; who are magnanimous to forgive crimes that others have suffered. . . . Some of these are crying out that we must moderate our [delight] over victories that are crushing the rebellion; that we must spare the rebels the conviction that they are conquered, or we shall make them implacable; and that if we cannot recover their love, we shall yet fail to restore the Union.

. . . We have destroyed their great Southern Empire, whose corner stone was to be slavery, and

> whose superstructure [was] military prestige and power. It is necessary to make them realize their subjugation. . . . Anything less than this will but restore defeated rebels to political power to renew the conflict.[10]

All of the North's projections about the coming peace left out one important consideration: would the South fall into line behind Lee and finally give up the fight? There is no doubt that most Southerners regarded Lee's surrender as the end of the war. But Jefferson Davis remained at large, and several armies, including those of Joseph Johnston and Kirby Smith, were still in the field. With a spirit of indignation, the *North Carolina Standard*, which for the past two years had agitated against the war, demanded that the military leaders of the Confederacy now submit to the Union—and suffer whatever consequences befell them—so that the Southern people might enjoy the blessings of peace and reconciliation:

> When Gen. Lee surrendered to Gen. Grant every thoughtful and reasonable war man in the Confederate States, at once felt that further resistance to the armies of the Union would be in vain. . . . It had been apparent to us for years that there was no ground for hoping for Confederate success, and we foresaw that unless the Union could be restored on the basis of the Constitution, subjugation would certainly be the result.—But our warning voice was unheeded, and hence the sufferings and the sorrows in which we are now plunged. Those who took the view we did, and labored to avert subjugation by accepting restoration [of the Union], have proved themselves the best friends of the South and of human liberty; and those who took a different view, and urged the war to the last extremity, have proved themselves the worst enemies our people have ever had.
>
> It is folly—it is a crime on the part of any of the commanders of the Confederate forces to hold out longer. They owe it to their own character, to the brave men whom they command, and to an afflicted people who must suffer in proportion to the prolongation of the contest, to surrender at once. No wise or good commander will hurl one man against eight to ten men, flushed with success and confident of victory. In the name of God and humanity let the conflict cease, and let the bow of reconciliation, now spanning the heavens, be regarded as a sign of endless peace and brotherhood. Who is Davis, or [Secretary of State] Benjamin, . . . or any other mere civilian, that the lives of thousands of gallant men should be sacrificed in the vain hope of protecting them? Let the soldiers be surrendered and sent to their homes, and let these desperate, ungodly, wicked men incur the legitimate consequences of their conduct.[11]

In this view of the situation, Southerners were not to begrudge Lee's surrender, but rather embrace it. They had to acknowledge the wisdom—even the dignity—of following the lead of their most beloved military figure. The *Augusta Chronicle & Sentinel* envisioned that by ceasing to support the rebellion and proactively withdrawing from the Confederacy, the people of Georgia might still be able to control their future and shape the way in which they reentered the Union:

> The example set . . . by Gen. Lee ought to be promptly followed. He saw that the hour had come for yielding up the struggle, and he had the magnanimity to acknowledge it. There was a blended dignity and wisdom in his course. It inspired respect, even in his enemies. It was doubtless one of the most painful duties of his life to ride up to Gen. Grant and tender that sword which so many victories had illuminated. But it was one of the noblest acts of his splendid career. He saw that to protract the struggle, was to sacrifice human life wantonly. He was too great and too good for that.

It is high time that this struggle should now end. Such is the peculiarity of our condition, that each State must now act for itself. We have all the while insisted that this was the true theory of our government. Georgia must meet in Convention and adjust herself to the new order of things. To be inactive is to drift. It is to abandon the great ship to the mercy of the waves; no eye fixed on the compass; no hand grasping the helm. The Convention should assemble with as little delay as possible. . . . In short, at this moment of [the] revolution, . . . it is important that Georgia should be in a position to exert her sovereign will.[12]

Other voices in the Deep South, however, continued to deny the inevitability of defeat. Whereas the *Chronicle & Sentinel* endorsed "yielding up the struggle," its compatriots at the *Augusta Constitutionalist* took the opposite approach. The dire implications of Lee's decision to surrender were not to be acknowledged—let alone honored—but instead downplayed. They "by no means necessitate our abandonment of the struggle or the folding of the hands of the people in mute despair," the *Constitutionalist* commanded. Southerners simply had to take "more determined and united action" to defend themselves. How exactly they were to do this, though, with their armies so dreadfully reduced and disorganized, vast areas of the country in ruins, and the Richmond government on the lam, was a mystery.[13]

It is difficult to assess how generally this defiant attitude permeated the Confederacy. By April 1865, many newspapers had been driven out of circulation or had been suspended temporarily by the Union armies until loyal editors could be installed to lead them. In Texas, however, the press remained vital and totally devoted to sustaining the rebellion at all costs. Texas had been spared the devastation suffered by other states in the Confederacy, as the Union armies had focused their efforts in the West on the area immediately around the Mississippi River. Consequently, Texas seemed as high-spirited in 1865 as it had been four years earlier, and newspapers there responded to the loss of Lee's army with a virulent determination to fill the breach. As the governor of the state envisioned in a public letter to his people, Texans would save the rest of the Confederacy from the doom that seemed to be hovering over it:

My *Countrymen*: Disaster has befallen our arms in Virginia! Our chosen Chieftain, Robert E. Lee, victorious on so many glorious fields, is a prisoner of war, and a portion of his army has surrendered!

THE CAPITULATION OF GEN'L LEE.

Rumors of a very painful and depressing character have been prevalent in our city the past day or two, involving the loss by capture of a portion of the gallant Army of Northern Virginia, and the capitulation of the heroic General Lee to the enemy. Reluctant to give credence to these stories of disaster, and hoping against hope that they might prove false, we have refrained from giving them publicity. It is, however, no longer the part of wisdom or prudence to withhold the facts of the case, so far as they have reached us—facts that are gloomy enough in all conscience, but which by no means necessitate our abandonment of the struggle or the folding of the hands of the people in mute despair. Rather should they nerve men resolved to be free to more determined and united action.

Augusta Constitutionalist, April 21, 1865.
Southern papers greeted the news of Lee's surrender in a subdued fashion. Nevertheless, some tried to maintain a brave face and insisted that it did not really signify the end of the Confederacy.

These unforeseen calamities impose additional responsibilities on the State of Texas. My object now is briefly to point you to the path of duty—to exhort you by all the considerations which make life desirable, or existence tolerable, to pursue that path, without faltering or flinching.

Your faith, your honor, and your manhood, are pledged to your brethren east of the Mississippi; for four years they have fought your battles, and stood [as] a wall of fire, between you and the invader. Their cause is your cause—their fate is inseparably yours. They look now with eager eyes and anxious hearts, to the people and the armies of this Department, for rescue and deliverance. They will not—they must not look in vain!

With God's blessing, it may yet be the proud privilege of Texas, the youngest of the Confederate sisters, to redeem the cause of the Confederacy from its present perils.

In extent and resources, Texas constitutes an Empire in herself. Favored of nature, she is inaccessible to her enemies; her soil is unsullied by the tread of an invading enemy—her great resources, if prudently husbanded, and wisely applied, are equal to any emergency.

Accepting in their full significance the facts of our situation, there is no reason for yielding, even to a momentary panic, still less for giving way to unmanly despair. . . . Let every man resolve to do his whole duty; and, renewing his vows for fidelity to the cause of his country, he will draw fresh inspiration from the urgency of the occasion. I tell you, frankly, that every man has a personal and individual interest in this struggle. Be not cajoled or deceived, my countrymen, by false hope and fair promises. Look at the bloody and desolate track of the invader through Georgia and South Carolina, and see the fate that awaits you—cities sacked, and in ruins—the country swept by the besom of destruction—thriving villages, and once happy homes, reduced to ashes—their helpless inmates stripped of their property—turned adrift to beg or starve; this, too, not unfrequently attended with such brutality as the tongue cannot pronounce, nor the pen record. . . .

There are critical conjunctures in the history of all great Nations, when the people must rise into heroism, or sink into servile insignificance and national degradation. Such a crisis is now upon us. . . . I conjure you, my countrymen, by all the proud memories of the past—by the unforgotten glories of San Jacinto and the Alamo—by the fresh laurels your valor has plucked from bloody fields, stretching from the Potomac to the Rio Grande—by your love for your wives and little ones—your mothers and your sisters—by all your future hopes and your faith in Heaven—to stand fast and firm by your colors and your country.

They lie, who say our cause is hopeless. Unless all history is false, . . . we cannot be conquered if we remain united and true to ourselves.[14]

Beyond calling upon the honor and power of Texan men, political leaders also continued to place high demands on women. In order to continue financing military operations against the Union, Confederate treasury secretary George A. Trenholm had issued a public appeal imploring the people of the state to give not only money but all silver plate and jewelry—the prized possessions of any Southern lady—to refill the nation's coffers. At the moment, Jefferson Davis was struggling to get to Texas to reestablish a seat of power for the Confederate government, and while he had escaped Richmond with the remaining money in the treasury, he was bound to need more. It was a requisition that Aurelia Hadley Mohl, a prominent writer and journalist from Houston, avidly seconded:

Come Texan women, let us give up our jewels; I am almost ashamed to urge you thus to a sacrifice so slight, after the costly offerings that have already been laid upon the sacred altar of our country's freedom, almost ashamed to beg you to give up your gold and gems, after you have given up your dear ones for your land; but the result will prove which we esteem the greater treasure, our [national] or our golden jewels.

Some whom I address, may think they have too little jewelry to do any good. Why, if every woman in the Confederacy gives one article, a ring, a broach, a bracelet, a silver spoon, how many hundred thousand offerings would there be? The President would have the two millions with which he says he can "feed the army and save the country," *we, the women of the South, will have saved our country*. What a grand thought! and the best of it is, the thought is a practical one and can be carried out.

But there may be a few who are embarrassed with riches, and have so many elegant jewels, they cannot bear to part with any. I hardly know what to say to these. "What! give up my superb silver that I have inherited from my ancestors." Dear lady, the alternative is to give it to your own people or have it stolen from you by the Yankees. Let us give up all if need be. Have you but your bridal ring left, matron? Let it wed you anew to your country's honor. Gentle maiden, have you nought but the glittering circlet of a betrothal? Offer it as the next dearest treasure to him who gave. If he is a soldier he will be benefitted by it. If he is not, he deserves to lose you and the ring both. But that any southern maiden should betroth herself to a young man who will not fight for his country now, is almost incredible.

Travelling down the Rhine, one lovely July day, I saw an old woman very plainly dressed, who wore upon her bosom an iron broach of curious workmanship. I had read of the women of Hungary and the Netherlands who gave up their jewels to their country and received iron ones in return; so I went to her and asking pardon for the seeming impertinence, I begged her to tell me where she got that quaint broach. "Madam," she answered, "it has descended to me from a Dutch ancestress who received it as an equivalent for many thousand florens worth of plate and jewelry, which she gave to her country in its hour of peril. Since then . . . there has not been one base enough to sell this 'jewel for gold.'" Perhaps we too may receive some such token from our government. At all events we will get a receipt or certificate of some kind which we can frame and transmit to future generations, a more precious heirloom than glittering gems and costly laces. But do not let it be said that women of any nation excel us in devotion to their country. I beg you all when you read this, to make up a bundle of your jewels, seal it and write upon it "for my country." Very soon we will receive directions how and where to send our offerings. Let us be ready when the orders come. . . .

We, women, wield a tremendous influence. Let us be very careful to use it properly. I fear we have never appreciated our power in this war. Let us learn to do so. I am afraid we have been too lenient to shirkers, and not kind enough to soldiers. Let us determine to use all our influence to bring every man into the army who is able to go. Let us be encouraging, earnest and hopeful, never entertaining, for a moment, any idea of compromise with our enemies. Let us never think of any terms of peace but entire and complete independence.[15]

One woman who intended to answer the call for jewelry donations added these do-or-die thoughts in an anonymous letter to the *Galveston Tri-Weekly News*:

Would to God that I had the power to arouse every man, woman and child throughout the land to a sense of the obligations they are under, to come to the rescue of our suffering cause at this fearful crisis. . . . Lee, the Christian warrior, the man to whom all eyes have been turned, as the one who was to lead our brave troops to final triumph, has capitulated; and while it wrings our hearts with anguish, to contemplate the fact, let it nerve us with a higher, deeper, holier resolve never to yield this fight, until

Galveston Tri-Weekly News, April 23, 1865. With the Confederacy so clearly in desperate straits, the press relied on memories of the destruction wrought by the Union armies to rally Southerners for renewing the fight.

Wherever they have passed over the surface of our fair land, the blackness of desolation has marked their path, and such barbarous desolation has been their devilish boast. Public records have been destroyed — institutions of learning, public libraries, pillaged or burned, and the temples of God sacrilegiously defiled.

Fellow-countrymen, will you, can you ever submit to be ruled by such a people? Can you ever join hands with them in fraternal union? Can you, with all these things freshly before you—daily occurring on your native soil—ever return to political union with these despoilers of your houses—these violators of your wives and daughters? Never! A dark crimson stream divides you, which all the skill of negotiation can never bridge over. The Southern people have determined to be free and independent, and if their fortitude and courage do not fail them, it is impossible to doubt the issue.

we win for ourselves a triumphant vindication of our cause on the broad basis of our national independence. Let none say that we are vanquished. The loss of our commander-in-chief in the field, is a great calamity, greater still might overtake us, but we are not vanquished, so long as we remain defiant, and are willing to perish rather than be subjugated. Let every man throw down his certificate of exemption, and trample it under his feet as something unworthy of men. . . . Let them gird on the armor of war . . . and go at once to the field. Wives, mothers, daughters, send your loved ones, that are yet at home, to swell the ranks of our host and we will yet overwhelm the insolent foe, and teach them that we are invincible. Bid them go and leave with you their business affairs, and if they should come no more, it will be an inheritance sufficiently glorious for you and your children to know, that they died defending the holiest cause for which the sword was ever unsheathed. . . . A word of encouragement, fitly spoken, may arouse some desponding one to action, and one more soldier will be added to our ranks. Remember, our armies are composed of individuals, and each individual has his part to act in this momentous drama, that has the world for its audience and a land made red with the blood of slaughtered patriots for its theater of action.

Put your hand upon your lips, and be silent when you would say it may be too late to struggle now. I tell you it is not too late. . . . Let all bring their treasures, be they great or small, and devote them to the call of our President. The offering will elevate and enable our own souls; it will strengthen the armies, and cheer the hearts of our troops, and teach our hated foe that there is no sacrifice, however costly, that we are not willing to make to secure that blessing without which all others are valueless—priceless liberty. My offering is indeed the widow's mite. It is a simple gold ring, it is all I have to give, but dearer is it to me than the gems and gold of earth or the pearls of the ocean. It is the bequest of an adored sister. She took it from her precious finger, awhile before dying and sent it to me with her blessing, and a request that I should wear it as long as I live. It is hard to part with it, yet I feel that she would approve of the disposition I now make of it. After we have made our offerings, let each one renew their vows and swear eternal fidelity to our country. When we have done this, and done all that mortals can do, if it will not purchase the desired boon, let us gather ourselves together on the last spot of earth that freedom holds, and there perish, and leave our bleaching bones to tell to coming ages, that we lived and died, free men, and free women.[16]

Those who continued to support the fight for Confederate independence insisted that individual effort still mattered. Lee's army had been disbanded, the Union controlled huge swaths of Confederate territory, and Southern soldiers had deserted their posts in droves, but still, the combined actions of each man and each woman in the South could turn the tide. Their manpower, their jewelry, their money, and their devotion to the cause could save the Confederacy. The people simply had to tap all of their reserves, including the wellsprings of their faith. As another Texan explained in a letter to the *Houston Tri-Weekly Telegraph*:

> Mr. Editor.—Feeling that in the present state of the public mind, depressed by apparently the most disastrous news received during the struggle, I believe it to be the duty of every one who can advance a thought to allay public fear and prevent national demoralization, to give it expression. . . . Some have seen in the recent disasters a train of providences which indicate that we are forsaken of God. They tell us that the loss of General Lee—a God-fearing man—with an army, bears this impress. A few remarks in an examination of this view, I trust, will tend to dissipate this fallacy.
>
> . . . By all the means at our disposal of reading God's will, we *do* feel that God does sympathize with the fundamental principles which underlie our cause—the right of self-government, the liberty of action, the freedom of conscience. If this be so—if these are principles the success of which will most glorify God and conduce to human happiness—they must ultimately succeed. The question, then, is not upon the final result, but upon the instrumentalities employed. When Israel had reached the very borders of the promised land, their fears and unbelief consigned them to a dreary wandering of forty years in the wilderness. God's promise had not failed, the designs of the Almighty had not been frustrated, but that generation was denied the benefits of the promise—the instrumentalities had failed. The Confederate States are the present instruments; if they fail, they will fail from the same cause. We stand now upon the very borders of the promised land. . . . What shall we do? The Confederate cause seems under a cloud; we lament our state, and think it worse now than ever before. Not so! it is an hour of trial; it is a crisis in the struggle; if we read the lesson aright, it may be the moment of our triumph. It thunders in the Confederate ear—"Have faith in God!" It is the extremity with us—the weak moment—if we are exorcised by it as we should be, it may be, yea will be, the moment of strength. It calls upon us to double our diligence toward the goal, and add . . . to that faith in the overruling Providence of God which promises victory. Let us but do this, and help will come.[17]

The Union may have succeeded in defeating Lee, but pacifying the entire scope of Southern public opinion would be another matter entirely.

The New-York Times.

VOL. XIV......NO. 4231. NEW-YORK, MONDAY, APRIL 17, 1865. PRICE FOUR CENTS

OUR GREAT LOSS

The Assassination of President Lincoln.

DETAILS OF THE FEARFUL CRIME.

Closing Moments and Death of the President.

Probable Recovery of Secretary Seward.

Rumors of the Arrest of the Assassins.

The Funeral of President Lincoln to Take Place Next Wednesday.

Expressions of Deep Sorrow Throughout the Land.

OFFICIAL DISPATCHES.

WAR DEPARTMENT, WASHINGTON, April 15—4:10 A. M.

To Major-Gen. Dix:

The President continues insensible and is sinking.

Secretary SEWARD remains without change.

FREDERICK SEWARD'S skull is fractured in two places, besides a severe cut upon the head.

The attendant is still alive, but hopeless. Maj. SEWARD'S wound is not dangerous.

It is now ascertained with reasonable certainty that two assassins were engaged in the horrible crime, WILKES BOOTH being the one that shot the President, and the other, a companion of his, whose name is not known, but whose description is so clear that he can hardly escape. It appears from a letter found in BOOTH'S trunk that the murder was planned before the 4th of March, but fell through then because the accomplice backed out until "Richmond could be heard from." BOOTH and his accomplice were at the livery stable at 6 o'clock last evening, and left there with their horses about 10 o'clock, or shortly before that hour.

It would seem that they had for several days been seeking their chance, but for some unknown reason it was not carried into effect until last night.

One of them has evidently made his way to Baltimore—the other has not yet been traced.

EDWIN M. STANTON,
Secretary of War.

WAR DEPARTMENT, WASHINGTON, April 15.

Major-Gen. Dix

ABRAHAM LINCOLN died this morning at twenty-two minutes after seven o'clock.

EDWIN M. STANTON,
Secretary of War.

WAR DEPARTMENT,
WASHINGTON, April 15—3 P. M.

Maj. Gen. Dix, New-York

Official notice of the death of the late President ABRAHAM LINCOLN, was given by the heads of departments this morning to ANDREW JOHNSON, Vice-President, upon whom the constitution devolved the office of President. Mr. JOHNSON, upon receiving this notice, appeared before the Hon. SALMON P. CHASE, Chief-Justice of the United States, and took the oath of office, as President of the United States, assumed its duties and functions. At 12 o'clock the President met the heads of departments in cabinet meeting, at the Treasury Building, and among other business the following was transacted:

First—The arrangements for the funeral of the late President were referred to the several Secretaries, as far as relates to their respective departments.

Second—WILLIAM HUNTER, Esq., was appointed Acting Secretary of State during the disability of Mr. SEWARD, and his son, FREDERICK SEWARD, the Assistant Secretary.

Third—The President formally announced that he desired to retain the present Secretaries of departments of his Cabinet, and they would go on and discharge their respective duties in the same manner as before the deplorable event that had changed the head of the government.

All business in the departments was suspended during the day.

The surgeons report that the condition of Mr. SEWARD remains unchanged. He is doing well.

No improvement in Mr. FREDERICK SEWARD.

The murderers have not yet been apprehended.

ters was to paralyze the country by at once striking down the head, the heart and the arm of the country.

As soon as the dreadful events were announced in the streets, Superintendent RICHARDS, and his assistants, were at work to discover the assassin.

In a few moments the telegraph had aroused the whole police force of the city.

Mayor WALLACH and several members of the City Government were soon on the spot, and every precaution was taken to preserve order and quiet in the city.

Every street in Washington was patroled at the request of Mr. RICHARDS.

Gen. AUGUR sent horses to mount the police.

Every road leading out of Washington was strongly picketed, and every possible avenue of escape was thoroughly guarded.

Steamboats about to depart down the Potomac were stopped.

The *Daily Chronicle* says:

"As it is suspected that this conspiracy originated in Maryland, the telegraph flashed the mournful news to Baltimore, and all the cavalry was immediately put upon active duty. Every road was picketed and every precaution taken to prevent the escape of the assassin. A preliminary examination was made by Messrs. RICHARDS and his assistants. Several persons were called to testify and the evidence as elicited before an informal tribunal, and not under oath, was conclusive to this point. The murderer of President LINCOLN was JOHN WILKES BOOTH. His hat was found in the private box, and identified by several persons who had seen him within the last two days, and the spur which he dropped by accident, after he jumped to the stage, was identified as one of those which he had obtained from the stable where he hired his horse.

This man BOOTH has played more than once at Ford's Theatre, and is, of course, acquainted with its exits and entrances, and the facility with which he escaped behind the scenes is well understood.

The person who assassinated Secretary SEWARD left behind him a slouched hat and an old rusty navy revolver. The chambers were broken loose from the barrel, as if done by striking. The loads were drawn from the chambers, one being but a rough piece of lead, and the other balls smaller than the chambers, wrapped in paper, as if to keep them from falling out.

LAST MOMENTS OF THE PRESIDENT.

Interesting Letter from Maunsell B. Field, Esq.

On Friday evening, April 14, 1865, I was reading the evening paper in the reading-room of Willard's Hotel, at about 10½ o'clock, when I was startled by the report that an attempt had been made a few minutes before to assassinate the President at Ford's Theatre. At first I could scarcely credit it, but in a few minutes the statement was confirmed by a number of people who came in separately, all telling the same story. About fifteen minutes previously I had parted with Mr. MELLEN, of the Treasury Department, and he had retired to his room. Immediately on receiving this intelligence I notified him of it, and we together proceeded to the scene of the alleged assassination. We found not only considerable crowds on the streets leading to the theatre, but a very large one in front of the theatre, and of the house directly opposite, where the President had been carried after the attempt upon his life. With some difficulty I obtained ingress to the house. I was at once informed by Miss HARRIS, daughter of Senator HARRIS, that the President was dying, which statement was confirmed by three or four other persons whom I met in the hall; but I was desired not to communicate his condition to Mrs. LINCOLN, who was in the front parlor. I went into this parlor, where I found Mrs. LINCOLN, no other lady being present, except Miss HARRIS, as already mentioned. She at once recognized me, and begged me to run for Dr. STONE, or some other medical man. She was not weeping, but appeared hysterical, and exclaimed in rapid succession, over and over again: "Oh! why didn't he kill me? why didn't he kill me?" I was starting from the house to go for Dr. STONE, when I met at the door, Major ECKERT, of the War Department, who informed me he was going directly to STONE'S house, STONE having already been sent for, but not having yet arrived. I then determined to go for Dr. HALL, whose precise residence I did not know. Upon inquiring of the crowd, I was told it was over FRANK TAYLOR'S bookstore, on the avenue. This proved to be a mistake, and I was compelled to return to his actual residence on the avenue, above Ninth-street. I found the doctor at home and dressed, and he at once consented to accompany me. Arrived in the neighborhood of the house, I had great difficulty in passing the guard, and only succeeded at last in having the doctor introduced, admission being refused to myself. I returned to Willard's, it now being about 2 o'clock in the morning, and remained there until between 3 and 4 o'clock, when I again went to the house where the President was lying, in company with Mr. ANDREWS, late Surveyor of the port of New-York. I obtained ingress this time without any difficulty, and was enabled to take Mr. ANDREWS in with me. I proceeded at once to the room in which the President was lying, which was a bedroom in an extension, on the first or parlor floor of the house. The room is small, and is ornamented with prints—a very familiar one of LANDSEER'S, a white horse, being prominent directly over the bed. The bed was a double one, and I found the President lying diagonally across it, with his head at the outside. The pillows were saturated with blood, and there was considerable blood upon the floor immediately under him. There was a patchwork coverlet thrown over the President, which was only so far removed, from time to time, as to enable the physicians in attendance to feel the arteries of the neck or the heart, and he appeared to have been divested of all clothing. His eyes were closed and injected with blood, both the lids and the portion surrounding the eyes being as black as if they had been bruised by violence. He was breathing regularly, but with effort, and did not seem to be struggling or suffering.

The persons present in the room were the Secretary of War, the Secretary of the Navy, the Post-

the room were all profoundly affected. The President's eyes after death were not, particularly the right one, entirely closed. I closed them myself with my fingers, and one the surgeons brought pennies and placed them on the eyes, and subsequently substituted for them silver half-dollars. In a very short time the jaw commenced slightly falling, although the body was still warm. I called attention to this, and had it immediately tied up with a pocket handkerchief. The expression immediately after death was purely negative, but in fifteen minutes there came over the mouth, the nostrils, and the chin, a smile that seemed almost an effort of life. I had never seen upon the President's face an expression more genial and pleasing. The body grew cold very gradually, and I left the room before it had entirely stiffened. Curtains had been previously drawn down by the Secretary of War.

Immediately after the decease, a meeting was held of the members of the Cabinet present, in the back parlor, adjacent to the room in which the President died, to which meeting I, of course, was not admitted. About fifteen minutes before the decease, Mrs. LINCOLN came into the room, and threw herself upon her dying husband's body. She was allowed to remain there only a few minutes, when she was removed in a sobbing condition, in which, indeed, she had been during all the time she was present.

After completing his prayer in the chamber of death, Dr. GURLEY went into the front parlor, where Mrs. LINCOLN was, with Mrs. and Miss KINNEY and her son ROBERT, Gen. TODD, of Dacotah, (a cousin of hers,) and Gen. FARNSWORTH, of Illinois. Here another prayer was offered up, during which I remained in the hall. The prayer was continually interrupted by Mrs. LINCOLN'S sobs. Soon after its conclusion, I went into the parlor, and found her in a chair, supported by her son ROBERT. Presently her carriage came up, and she was removed to it. She was in a state of tolerable composure at that time, until she reached the door, when, glancing at the theatre opposite, she repeated three or four times: "That dreadful house!—that dreadful house!"

Before I myself left, a guard had been stationed at the door of the room in which the remains of the late President were lying. Mrs. LINCOLN had been communicated with, to ascertain whether she desired the body to be embalmed or not, and the Secretary of War had issued various orders, necessary in consequence of what had occurred.

I left the house about 8.30 o'clock in the morning, and shortly after met Mr. Chief-Justice CHASE, on his way there. He was extremely agitated, as, indeed, I myself had been all through the night. I afterward learned that, at the Cabinet meeting referred to, the Secretary of the Treasury and the Attorney-General were appointed a committee to wait on the Vice-President, which they did, and he was sworn into office early in the morning by the Chief-Justice.

MAUNSELL B. FIELD.

THE GREAT CALAMITY.

WASHINGTON, April 16.

THE CORPSE.

The corpse of the late President has been laid out in the room known as the "guests' room," northwest wing of the White House. It is dressed in the suit of black clothes worn by him at his late inauguration. A placid smile rests upon his features, and the deceased seems to be in a calm sleep. White flowers have been placed upon the pillow and over the breast.

The corpse of the President will be laid out in state in the east room on Tuesday, in order to give the public an opportunity to see once more the features of him they loved so well. The preparations are being made, to that end, under the supervision of the upholsterer. The catafalque upon which the body will rest is to be placed in the south part of the east room, and is somewhat similar in style to that used on the occasion of the death of President HARRISON. Steps will be placed at the side to enable the public to mount to a position to get a perfect view of the face. The catafalque will be lined with fluted white satin, and on the outside it will be covered with black cloth and black velvet.

THE FUNERAL.

The funeral of President LINCOLN will take place on Wednesday next. Rev. Dr. GURLEY, of the New-York-avenue Presbyterian Church, where the President and his family have been accustomed to worship, will doubtless be the officiating clergyman.

The remains will be temporarily deposited in the vault of the Congressional Cemetery, and hereafter taken to Mr. LINCOLN'S home at Springfield, Illinois.

THE FUNERAL CAR.

The funeral car, which is being prepared for the occasion, is to be a magnificent affair. It is to be built on a hearse body. Its extreme length will be fourteen feet. The body of the car will be covered, with black cloth, from which will hang large festoons of cloth on the sides and ends, gathered and fastened by large rosettes of white and black satin over bows of white and black velvet. The bed of the car, on which the coffin will rest, will be eight feet from the ground, in order to give a full view of the coffin; and over this will rise a canopy, the support of which will be draped with black cloth and velvet. The top of the car will be decorated with plumes. The car will be drawn by six or eight horses, each led by a groom.

BOOTH NOT ARRESTED.

Up to this time it has not been ascertained that the assassin of the President has been captured.

THE PRESIDENT'S PLACE OF WORSHIP.

This morning, at the New-York-avenue Presbyterian Church, which Mr. LINCOLN formerly attended, a large crowd of persons assembled in anticipation that the pastor, Rev. P. D. GURLEY, D. D., would make some allusion to the nation's great calamity. The pulpit and the choir, and the President's pew were draped in mourning.

THE ASSASSINATION A CONSPIRACY.

The *Extra Star* has the following:

"Developments have been made within the past twenty-four hours, showing conclusively the existence of a deep laid plot of a gang of conspirators, including members of the order of the Knights of the

him only on the importunity of his friends as a matter of precaution.

The President before retiring to bed, would, when important military events were progressing, visit the War Department, generally alone, passing over the dark intervening ground, even at late hours, on repeated occasions; and after the warning letters had been received, several close and intimate friends armed for any emergency were careful that he should not continue his visits without their company. For himself, the President seemed to have no fears.

The above facts have heretofore been known to the writer of this telegram, but for prudential reasons, he has not stated them until now.

THE LAST HOURS OF THE PRESIDENT.

As everything pertaining to the last hours of the late President must be interesting to the public, the following incidents of the last day of his life have been obtained from several sources.

His son, Capt. LINCOLN, breakfasted with him on Friday morning, having just returned from the capitulation of LEE, and the President passed a happy hour listening to all the details. While at breakfast he heard that Speaker COLFAX was in the house, and sent word that he wished to see him immediately in the reception room. He conversed with him nearly an hour about his future policy as to the rebellion, which he was about to submit to the Cabinet. Afterwards he had an interview with Mr. HALE, Minister to Spain, and several Senators and Representatives.

At 11 o'clock the Cabinet and Gen. GRANT met with him, and in one of the most satisfactory and important Cabinet meetings held since his first inauguration, the future policy of the Administration was harmoniously and unanimously agreed on. When it adjourned Secretary STANTON said he felt that the government was stronger than at any previous period since the rebellion commenced.

In the afternoon the President had a long and pleasant interview with Gen. OGLESBY, Senator YATES, and other leading citizens of his State.

In the evening Mr. COLFAX called again, at his request, and Mr. ASHMUN, of Massachusetts, who presided over the Chicago Convention of 1860, was present. To them he spoke of his visit to Richmond; and when they stated that there was much uneasiness at the North while he was at the rebel capital, for fear that some traitor might shoot him, he replied jocularly that he would have been alarmed himself if any other person had been President and gone there, but that he did not feel any danger whatever. Conversing on a matter of business with Mr. ASHMUN, he made a remark that he saw Mr. ASHMUN was surprised at; and immediately with his well-known kindness of heart said, "You did not understand me, ASHMUN, I did not mean what you inferred, and I will take it all back and apologize for it." He afterward gave Mr. ASHMUN a card to admit himself and friend early the next morning, to converse further about it.

Turning to Mr. COLFAX he said: "You are going with Mrs. LINCOLN and me to the theatre, I hope." But Mr. COLFAX had other engagements, expecting to leave the city the next morning.

He then said to Mr. COLFAX, "Mr. SUMNER has the gavel of the Confederate Congress, which he got at Richmond, to hand to the Secretary of War. But I insisted then that he must give it to you; and you tell him for me to hand it over." Mr. ASHMUN alluded to the gavel which he still had, and which he had used at the Chicago Convention, and the President and Mrs. LINCOLN, who was also in the parlor, rose to go to the theatre. It was half an hour after the time they had intended to start, and they spoke about waiting half an hour longer, for the President went with reluctance, as Gen. GRANT had gone North, and he did not wish the people to be disappointed, as they had both been advertised to be there. At the door he stopped, and said: "COLFAX, do not forget to tell the people in the mining region as you pass through them, what I told you this morning about the development, when peace comes, and I will telegraph you at San Francisco." He shook hands with both gentlemen with a pleasant good-bye, and left the Executive Mansion, never to return to it alive.

The President and Cabinet, at the meeting, to-day, intrusted to Assistant Secretary of the Treasury, HARRINGTON, the general arrangement of the programme for the funeral of the late President. Maj. FRENCH, the Commissioner of Public Buildings, will attend to the carrying out of so much of it as directly appertains to the corpse, and Maj.-Gen. AUGUR, in charge of the defences of Washington, will be in charge of the military part of the procession. Assistant Secretary HARRINGTON has been in consultation, to-night, relative to the arrangements, with Gov. OGLESBY, Senator YATES and Ex-Representative ARNOLD, of Illinois, and Gens. GRANT, HALLECK and AUGUR and Admirals FARRAGUT and SHUBRICK.

The funeral ceremonies of the late President will take place on Wednesday. The time for the remains to leave the city, as well as the route by which they will be taken to Springfield, is as yet undetermined. The procession will form at 11 o'clock, and the religious services will commence at noon, at which hour throughout the whole land, the various religious societies have been requested to assemble in their respective places of worship for prayer. The procession will move at 2 P. M. Details will be made known as soon as perfected.

The acting Secretary of State has issued the following address.

To the People of the United States:

The undersigned is directed to announce that the funeral ceremonies of the lamented Chief Magistrate will take place at the Executive Mansion, in this city, at 12 o'clock noon on Wednesday, the 19th instant.

The various religious denominations throughout the country are invited to meet in their respective places of worship at that hour for the purpose of solemnizing the occasion with appropriate ceremonies.

(Signed) W. HUNTER,
Acting Secretary of State.

DEPARTMENT OF STATE, WASHINGTON, April 17, 1865.

WASHINGTON, Saturday, April 15.

inches from the orifice. The ball lay still further in advance. The wound was half an inch in diameter.

A silver plate upon the coffin over the breast bears the following inscription:

ABRAHAM LINCOLN.
SIXTEENTH PRESIDENT OF THE UNITED STATES.
Born July 12, 1809.
Died April 15, 1865.

The remains have been embalmed.

A few locks of hair were removed from the President's head for the family previous to the remains being placed in the coffin.

THE NEW PRESIDENT.

INAUGURATION OF ANDREW JOHNSON.

BRIEF AND IMPRESSIVE CEREMONIES.

The Oath of Office Administered on Saturday by by Chief-Justice Chase.

PRESIDENT JOHNSON'S INAUGURAL ADDRESS.

WASHINGTON, Sunday, April 16.

Yesterday morning Attorney-General SPEED waited upon Hon. ANDREW JOHNSON, Vice-President of the United States, and officially informed him of the sudden and unexpected decease of President LINCOLN, and stated that an early hour might be appointed for the inauguration of his successor. The following is a copy of the communication referred to:

WASHINGTON CITY, April 15, 1865.

SIR: ABRAHAM LINCOLN, President of the United States, was shot by an assassin last evening at Ford's Theatre, in this city, and died at the hour of twenty-two minutes after seven o'clock. About the same time at which the President was shot, an assassin entered the sick chamber of Hon. W. H. SEWARD, Secretary of State, and stabbed him in several places in the throat, neck and face, severely, if not mortally, wounding him. Other members of the Secretary's family were dangerously wounded by the assassin while making his escape.

By the death of President LINCOLN, the office of President has devolved, under the Constitution, upon you. The emergency of the government demands that you should immediately qualify, according to the requirements of the Constitution, and enter upon the duties of President of the United States. If you will please make known your pleasure, such arrangements as you deem proper will be made.

Your obedient servants,

HUGH McCULLOCH,
Secretary of the Treasury.
EDWIN M. STANTON,
Secretary of War.
GIDEON WELLES,
Secretary of the Navy.
WILLIAM DENNISON,
Postmaster-General.
J. P. USHER,
Secretary of the Interior.
JAMES SPEED,
Attorney-General.

To ANDREW JOHNSON, Vice-President of the United States.

Mr. JOHNSON requested that the ceremony take place at his rooms at the Kirkwood House, in this city, at 10 o'clock in the morning.

Hon. SALMON P. CHASE, Chief-Justice of the Supreme Court of the United States, was notified of the fact, and desired to be in attendance to administer the oath of office.

At the above-named hour the following gentlemen assembled in the Vice-President's room to participate in the ceremony:

Hon. SOLOMON P. CHASE.
Hon. HUGH McCULLOCH,
Secretary of the Treasury,
Mr. Attorney-General SPEED,
F. P. BLAIR, Senior,
Hon. MONTGOMERY BLAIR,
Senator FOOT, of Vermont,
Senator YATES, of Illinois,
Senator RAMSAY, of Minnesota,
Senator STEWART, of Nevada,
Senator HALE, of New-Hampshire,
Gen. FARNSWORTH, of Illinois.

After the presentation of the above letter, the Chief Justice administered the following oath to Mr. JOHNSON:

"I do solemnly swear that I will faithfully execute the office of President of the United States, and will, to the best of my ability, preserve, protect and defend the Constitution of the United States."

After receiving the oath, and being declared President of the United States, Mr. JOHNSON remarked:

ADDRESS OF PRESIDENT JOHNSON.

"Gentlemen, I must be permitted to say that I have been almost overwhelmed by the announcement of the sad event which has so recently occurred. I feel incompetent to perform duties so important and responsible as those which have been so unexpectedly thrown upon me. As to an indication of any policy which may be presented by me in the administration of the government, I have to say that that must be left for development as the Administration progresses. The message or declaration must be made by the acts as they transpire. The only assurance that I can now give of the future is by reference to the past. The course which I have taken in the past in connection with

ent perils. I feel in making this request that it w... be heartily responded to by you and all other pa...ots and lovers of the rights and interests of a f... people."

At the conclusion of the above remarks, the Pr...dent received the kind wishes of the friends by wh... he was surrounded.

A few moments were devoted to conversation. ... were deeply impressed with the solemnity of the o...casion, and the recent sad occurrence that cau... the necessity for the speedy inauguration of ... President was gravely discussed.

Mr. JOHNSON is in fine health and has an ear... sense of the important trust that has been conf... in him.

WM. HUNTER, Esq., the Chief Clerk of the S... Department, has been appointed Acting Secretar... State.

A special meeting of the Cabinet was held at ... Treasury Department, at 10 o'clock this morning.

NEWS FROM WASHINGTON.

Special Dispatches to the New-York Time...
WASHINGTON, Sunday, April ...

APPROPRIATE RELIGIOUS SERVICES.

Easter Sunday has been, for the most part, a c... and fair, and sunny, and breezy day; yet the t... of all voices have been low, and the great bere...ment has been the subject of all conversation. ... GURLEY'S Church, where Mr. LINCOLN attended, ... overflowingly full at an early hour. The pulpit, ... front of the choir, gallery and the vacant pew ... heavily draped in mourning.

The day had been set apart for sacramental ...poses, but the Rev. Doctor prefaced the serv... with some feeling remarks upon the death of ... LINCOLN. He urged the audience to look beyon... hand of the assassin to the hand of the wise ... who overrules all things, and makes even the w... of man to praise him. He admitted the sorrow... this affliction, but doubted not that time would ... God's purpose in bringing it upon us.

Most of the churches of the city are drap... mourning, and in each of them was to-day appr...ate and touching remembrance of the nat... sorrow.

A meeting of all clergymen in the city is call... nine o'clock, to-morrow morning, to take such a... as becomes a Christian community at this ... Meetings are also called for to-morrow, of a ... number of State, social, literary, benevolent an... ligious organizations, to take action appropria... the occasion.

THE INVESTIGATION OF THE MURDER.

The city and military authorities have been co... pursuing investigations since yesterday mor... and persons conversant to some extent with th... sults thereof, are very confident that the murd... Mr. LINCOLN and the attempted murder of Mr. ...ARD, are only part of the fruits of a carefully pl... conspiracy that intended the murder also of ... members of the Cabinet, and the destruction of ... of the public buildings, and perhaps certain sec... of the city. Nothing has yet been brought to ... calculated to fix the identity of the assassin o... SEWARD, though various parties have been arr... and examined, and two or three are held for fu... examination.

RUMORS OF BOOTH'S ARREST.

Rumor has arrested BOOTH a dozen times alr... and many persons will retire to-night in the con... belief that he is confined on a gunboat at the N... yard, but so far as can be learned from the au... ties he not only has not been arrested, but very ... is known as to the route he took in escaping. ... aggregate reward now offered here for the arr... these men is thirty thousand dollars.

MRS. LINCOLN.

Mrs. LINCOLN is yet much depressed, thoug... so than yesterday. She remains at the White H... Hon. MONTGOMERY BLAIR has tendered to her th... of his house till such time as she leaves the ... and President JOHNSON has communicated t... that he expects her to occupy the White House ... she remains in Washington.

THE BODY OF MR. LINCOLN.

The body of Mr. LINCOLN, dressed in the ... black suit he wore on inauguration day, is ly... the northwest corner room of the second floor ... White House. The head lies amidst white flo... and the features wear the calm peaceful expr... of deep sleep. The corpse will be laid in s... the east room on Tuesday, and the funeral w... held on Wednesday.

Hundreds of instances of Mr. LINCOLN'S pe... kindness and graceful courtesy have come t... within the last two days. The *Intelligencer* sa... last official act was to sign a permit allowing ... THOMPSON, late Secretary of the Interior, to lea... country for Europe.

LIEUT.-GEN. GRANT.

Gen. GRANT is still here and at Willard's. H... been in consultation to-day some time wi... President and Cabinet. It is said that as soon ... arrived yesterday he ordered the arrest at Rich... of various prominent late rebels.

ARRIVALS IN THE CITY.

There are numerous arrivals of distinguishe... sons from the North, consequent upon the na... bereavement. Among others are Hon. L. F. S... TER, Senator and Vice-President pro tem., and ... BUCKINGHAM and Staff, of Connecticut.

INTENSE FEELING OF SORROW.

There is intense feeling in all parts of the cit... any man showing the least disrespect to the m... of the universally lamented dead, is su... find rough treatment. One of the ... haired wandering preachers, named T... son, and hailing from Buffalo, while sp... at a soldier's camp, this afternoon, indulged ... remark that if the new President pursued Mr ...COLN'S policy he would meet Mr. LINCOLN'S ... two weeks. He was immediately set upon ... soldiers, and only escaped severe bodily har... cause he was at once arrested. I... other case, a crowd of curious p...

Chapter 15

The Greatest Crime of Modern Times

The triumphal celebrations in the North following Lee's surrender were short-lived, their gaiety shattered by what seemed like an unthinkable act of violence—the assassination of Abraham Lincoln by John Wilkes Booth. Booth, who hailed from a famous theatrical family, had been born and raised in Maryland, and like many others in the border slave states, the Booth family had been divided over the war. While Booth's brothers backed the Union, John Wilkes, as a fervent believer in slavery and white supremacy, aligned himself with the Confederacy. Although Booth never aided the South militarily, he seethed with hatred for Lincoln, particularly in light of the president's support for emancipation. Anxious to know what Lincoln planned to do about the freedmen, Booth was in Washington on April 11, 1865, to hear what would be the president's last public speech. Lincoln was taking the opportunity to offer some preliminary thoughts about reunion, and in it, he expressed his hope that at least some black Americans—those who had fought for the Union as well as others who were sufficiently educated—would be given the right to vote. Booth shuddered at the thought. Already bereft by the news of Lee's capitulation to Grant, and pained by his own failure to contribute anything substantive to the Confederate cause, Booth found Lincoln's endorsement of limited black suffrage more than he could bear. Since at least the summer of 1864, Booth had been concocting an elaborate plot to assist the South by kidnapping Lincoln. Now, to avenge the fallen Confederacy and prevent the president from promoting "nigger citizenship," he resolved to kill him.

Booth found the venue for enacting his assassination scheme in the newspapers, which announced on April 14 that Lincoln and his wife would be attending Ford's

Frank Leslie's Illustrated Newspaper, May 6, 1865. After shooting Abraham Lincoln in the back of the head, assassin John Wilkes Booth falls to the stage of Ford's Theater as the stunned audience looks on.

Theater that evening for a performance of *My American Cousin*. Despite the hatreds that the war had unleashed, Lincoln took a fatalistic view toward his personal security and made no special precautions to protect himself from possible violence. The presidential box at the theater was therefore unguarded. During the third act, Booth stealthily approached Lincoln and shot him at close range, in the back of the head. With dramatic flair, he then leaped from the balcony box to the stage, intending to proclaim his triumph to the audience. However, in an odd and heavily symbolic turn of events, the spur of Booth's boot snagged the American flag hanging by the side of the theater, causing him to lose his balance and break his leg upon hitting the stage. When Booth picked himself up, he brandished a dagger and shouted the state motto of Virginia, "*Sic semper tyrannis*" (thus always to tyrants), before fleeing the theater.

The shooting of Lincoln was actually part of a grander scheme. While Booth was at Ford's theater, an accomplice named Lewis Thornton Powell approached the home of the secretary of state, William H. Seward, armed like Booth with both a pistol and a knife. Seward was confined to his bed, recovering from a carriage accident, and Powell gained access to the house by posing as a doctor bearing medication. When Seward's son Frederick asked him to just leave the medicine and depart quietly, Powell bludgeoned him with his gun, raced into the secretary of state's bedroom, and attacked him as he rested, slashing him on the face and neck. The tumult awakened others in the house, who came to Seward's aid and tried to subdue Powell, but the intruder succeeded in getting away for the moment. In the end, Seward would survive his wounds; the president, however, was pronounced dead the next morning.[1]

Today, in an age when presidents are commonly the objects of assassination plots, the targeting and killing of Lincoln may not seem shocking. But for Americans who were living through it, it was inconceivable. This was the first presidential assassination in U.S. history. Before this time, many Americans believed that political killings would *never* happen in this country, since citizens had the opportunity every four years to remove presidents from office through peaceable elections. The following article from the *Springfield Republican*, in addition to conveying the details of the assassination, aptly captures the utter surprise of the people who witnessed it:

> During the third act, and while there was a temporary pause for one of the actors to enter, a sharp report of a pistol was heard which merely attracted attention, but suggested nothing serious, until a man rushed to the front of the president's box, waving a long dagger in his right hand and exclaiming *Sic Semper Tyrannis*, and immediately leaped from the box, which was in the second tier, to the stage beneath and ran across to the opposite side, making his escape amid the bewilderment of the audience. . . . The screams of Mrs Lincoln first disclosed the fact to the audience that the president had been shot, when all present rose to their feet, rushing towards the stage, many exclaiming, "Hang him! hang him!"
>
> The excitement was of the wildest possible description, and of course there was an abrupt termination of the theatrical performance. There was a rush towards the president's box, when cries were heard, "Stand back and give him air," "Has any one any stimulants?"
>
> On a hasty examination it was found that the president had been shot through the head, above and back of the temporal bone, and that some of the brain was oozing out. The president was moved to a private house, and the surgeon-general of the army and other surgeons [were] sent for to attend to his condition.
>
> On an examination of the private box, blood was discovered on the back of the cushioned rocking chair on which the president had been sitting; also on the partition and the floor. A common single-barreled pocket pistol was found on the carpet. A military guard was placed in front of the private residence to which the president had been conveyed. An immense crowd was in front of it, all deeply anxious to learn the condition of the president. It had been previously announced that the wound was mortal, but all hoped otherwise.[2]

The public response to the assassination looked like a solemn, subdued version of the patriotic displays that had appeared across the North *exactly* four years previously, after the firing on Fort Sumter. Back then, Northern communities had swathed themselves in red, white, and blue in demonstrating their enthusiastic support for war; now, these same cities and towns were blanketed in black. In Albany, the *Atlas & Argus* described the public mood in this way:

> The intelligence of the President's death reached this city about nine o'clock yesterday morning. The people generally were prepared for the announcement from the tenor of the news in the morning papers. The impression created, was one of universal sadness, and every countenance wore a look of sorrow. The streets began to fill up rapidly, and in a short space of time, large crowds were collected about the various newspaper offices and bulletin boards. Flags throughout the city were soon draped in mourning and suspended at half mast. Nor was this all. Signs of mourning were exhibited in every conceivable way. The Dry Goods stores were besieged for white and black cloth, and in a few hours there was scarcely a street in the city that did not give evidence of sorrow in view of the great national calamity. The Capitol, City Hall, State Hall, State Library, Agricultural Rooms, and other public buildings were hung in black. All the Banks,

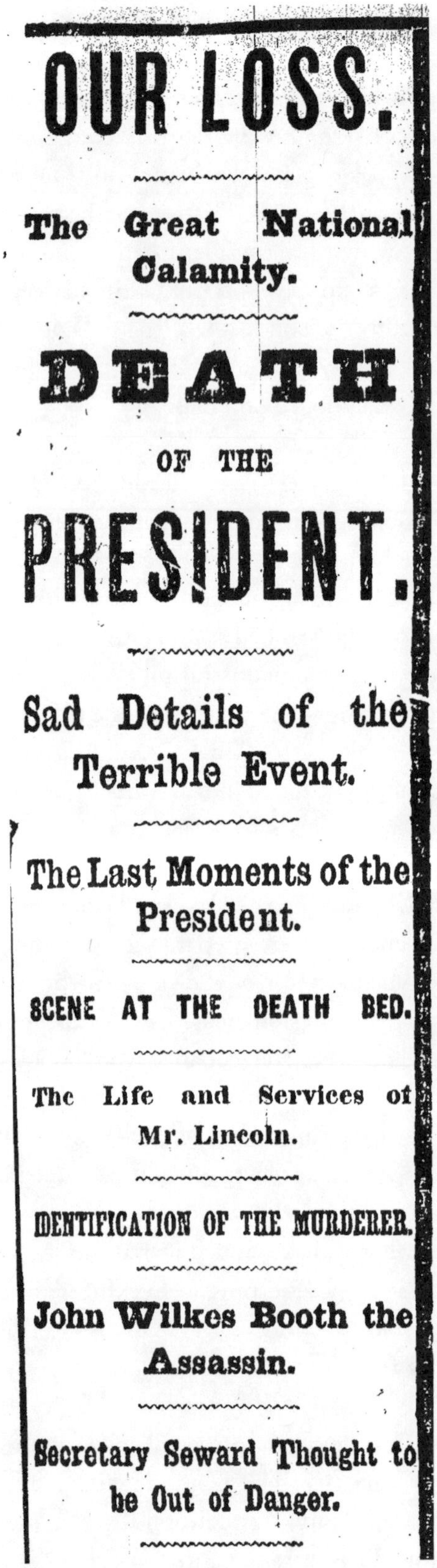
OUR LOSS.

The Great National Calamity.

DEATH OF THE PRESIDENT.

Sad Details of the Terrible Event.

The Last Moments of the President.

SCENE AT THE DEATH BED.

The Life and Services of Mr. Lincoln.

IDENTIFICATION OF THE MURDERER.

John Wilkes Booth the Assassin.

Secretary Seward Thought to be Out of Danger.

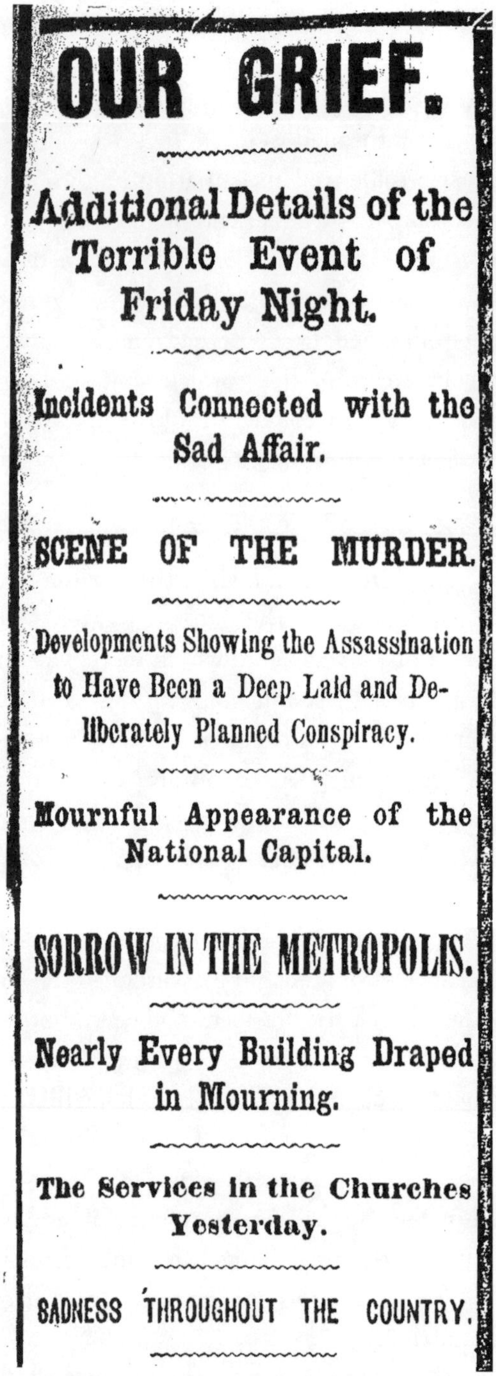
OUR GRIEF.

Additional Details of the Terrible Event of Friday Night.

Incidents Connected with the Sad Affair.

SCENE OF THE MURDER.

Developments Showing the Assassination to Have Been a Deep Laid and Deliberately Planned Conspiracy.

Mournful Appearance of the National Capital.

SORROW IN THE METROPOLIS.

Nearly Every Building Draped in Mourning.

The Services in the Churches Yesterday.

SADNESS THROUGHOUT THE COUNTRY.

LEFT *New York Herald,* April 16, 1865.
Northern newspapers showed their grief by lining their columns with thick black borders, much as private citizens draped black cloth outside the windows and across the balconies of their homes.

ABOVE *New York Herald,* April 17, 1865.

Printing establishments, Hotels, and the stores on Broadway, State street and Pearl street, were draped in mourning in a like manner, as were also hundreds of private residences in every part of the city. In every direction demonstrations of sorrow were to be witnessed. . . .

Throughout the city there was but little desire to transact business.

The Washington tragedy absorbed all thought and all conversation. In the stores, on the street corners, in the railroad cars, men, women and children of all classes, could talk of nothing else. All agreed that the crime that has been committed was the greatest of modern times.[3]

Many Northerners instinctively presumed that Booth had acted in cahoots with the rebels, and figured that Jefferson Davis himself might have been involved in planning the assassination. In actuality, Booth had received no help or encouragement from the Confederacy, but his onstage declaration of "*Sic semper tyrannis*" certainly left no doubt as to where his sympathies lay. It was therefore easy to conclude that at the very least, Booth had acted in the name of the rebellion—that, as one Northerner put it, the "spirit of the Rebellion" had motivated his "stealthy deed in Ford's theater." And for Northern Republicans, at least, there was no mistaking what that "spirit" was. It was slavery. All the horrible events of the war went back to this one thing. Slavery had not only motivated the rebels to make their bid for independence but inspired them to fight atrociously against Northerners for it. "The barbarities practiced on the black man prepared the way for the barbarities since practiced on the white," explained the *New York Times*. "The devilish spirit" of slavery had seemed to manifest itself early in the war, after the Battle of Manassas, "in the murder of wounded men, the desecration of the dead, and the manufacture of rings and drinking-cups out of the bones and skulls of Union soldiers." Now, Lincoln's assassination stood as a final, hateful act committed in slavery's defense. It was the type of "last desperate resort" that "the brutalizing institution of slavery alone could produce."[4] In a letter to William Lloyd Garrison, abolitionist Henry C. Wright therefore hoped that all Americans might finally realize just how dangerous and malicious the institution of slavery truly was:

Dear Garrison—The assassination of President Lincoln is accomplished. Slaveholders and their allies have done the deed. Slavery, that instigated the rebellion, that began and for four years has carried on this civil war, has done it. The spirit that has assassinated and mutilated five hundred thousand of our sons and brothers and fathers and husbands on the battlefield, . . . and carried desolation and anguish to the homes and hearts of the whole land, has done it. . . . The man who can buy and sell men and women, and hold and use them as chattels, is an assassin at heart. So are those who plead or apologize for slavery. There is no conceivable crime which they will not commit, if an opportunity offers. . . .

President Lincoln is a martyr to free labor. Hundreds of thousands have been sacrificed to slavery as soldiers, in prisons and in battles. Now the slaveholder's dagger has pierced the heart of the representative man of the nation. Will this open the eyes of the North to see slavery as it is? . . . SLAVERY IS THE ASSASSIN! The ball that pierced the brain of our kind-hearted and noble President was aimed by slaveholding rebels and their sympathizing allies. The man who apologizes for slavery, apologizes for the assassin, and makes himself an accessory to the murderous deed. This assassin, (slavery) is the monster that has been held up . . . as approvingly ordained of God, and the Heaven-sent missionary to carry salvation . . . to Africa! President Lincoln, as the people's right hand, gave this assassin of the negro, of freedom, justice and free institutions, the death-blow. Now the surviving tools and minions of that assassin, instigated by the same spirit of murderous "hatred to free labor, free schools, free press, free

Frank Leslie's Illustrated Newspaper, May 13, 1865.
Abraham Lincoln's twenty-day funeral procession retraced the 1,600-mile route he had taken in 1861 between his home in Springfield, Illinois, and his office in Washington. An estimated one million Americans came out to view the casket, and, as pictured here, immense crowds lined Broadway as the procession made its way through New York City.

society, free thought and speech and a free Republic," have slain the *political* embodiment of freedom to labor and the laborers of the nation, the continent and the world. In so doing they have given to President Lincoln a name and a place in the history of nations, and in the great human heart, never before given to man.[5]

This conception of Lincoln as a martyr seemed particularly fitting, for as fate would have it, the assassination occurred on Good Friday. The similarity between the killing of Christ and the murder of Lincoln was too striking for Northern Christians to ignore. Like Christ, Lincoln was a man of mercy, one who seemed ready to extend a liberal amnesty to the people of the rebellious South. And, like Christ, Lincoln's goodness had been foully betrayed by his enemies. As the *Chicago Tribune* proclaimed, Lincoln was thus a martyr to freedom, no less so than Christ was a martyr to his faith:

The nation mourns. Its agony is great. Its grief is dumb. Never before have the American people been so stricken. The ball that pierced the President has pierced the hearts of all of us. The assassin aimed well if he thought to fill with unutterable sorrow all lovers of the Union, of Liberty, and of mankind. President Lincoln—whose life was covered with glory by his faithfulness to his country—has ascended to his God. Pale in death, murdered by the hellish spirit of Slavery, which has already drunk the heart's blood of so many whom we loved, his body lies at the nation's capital—a new sacrifice upon our country's altar. All the land weeps. For we loved none as we loved him. He was so great where men are rarely great—in his simplicity, his integrity, his purity of patriotic purpose, his kindliness of heart—especially toward the class of offenders before whose malignity he falls a martyr. There are none in the councils of the nation . . . who would have suffered from them so much, yet forgiven them so freely as he. Already the complaint was upon the lips of the nation that he was in danger of sacrificing justice and security to leniency, when he is struck down by those whom he was lifting up. He is murdered by those whom he would have spared and reconciled. . . .

The spectacle is sickening. The human heart, revolting from it with disgust, loses faith in humanity, and sinking back like a child into the arms of its parent, we cry unto the God of the bereaved: Thou God reignest! Fulfill this day to a nation in tears, thy holy promise—"Blessed are they that mourn, for they shall be comforted." "Blessed are they that are persecuted for righteousness sake, for theirs is the kingdom of Heaven."

On the sacred anniversary of the day made holy by the crucifixion of Him who uttered these words, we mourn another martyrdom. . . . Our President has fallen, in the prime of his energy and usefulness, another martyr to the demon—Slavery. His fame undimmed will shine brighter and brighter, as rebellion disappears and the Union survives—clearer and holier, as slavery passes into history and Liberty fills the world.

Those who thought to end his career have crowned his pure fame with immortality. Those who thought to crucify the Spirit of Freedom will behold it roll away the stone from the sepulchre, and visit, with a Pentecostal effusion, its disciples, inspiring them with a faith that shall overturn the world. Hitherto the name of Washington has stood first in war, first in peace, first in the hearts of his countrymen. His star shall not decrease, but that of another shall increase, until, richer and more heavenly than the fame of him who emancipates his country will be the glory of him who gave emancipation to an outcast race and people. The first was manly and patriotic; the last was Christ-like and divine. Those who are now young will but live to see the dawning of the fame and power of the martyred Lincoln.[6]

In life, Lincoln had continually been the object of criticism, scorn, and malice. In death, however, he secured a place of honor within the pantheon of American heroes. Particularly within the hearts of his fellow Republicans, Lincoln embodied not only the hallowed virtue of self-sacrificing patriotism but the righteous cause of liberty itself. Americans before the war had identified these traits with the memory of George Washington. Now Washington was no longer alone in commanding the veneration of the American people. The *Albany Evening Journal* explained:

The comparison is suggested between George Washington and Abraham Lincoln. Both were men of irreproachable personal character. Both were almost idolized by the people. Both led the Nation through a great crisis of suffering to victory. Both stamped themselves ineffacebly upon the thought and action of the times in which they lived. The work of one was a supplement of that performed by the other. Washington's mission was to instill into the hearts of his fellow-countrymen a love for

Union—to create and fix the spirit of Americanism—to lay the bases of that compact democracy which has been able to withstand, unimpaired, the mightiest whirlwind of Revolution. Lincoln's task was to purify the Government, and remove from its escutcheon the dark stain of Slavery—to bring its life into harmony with the great principles of human Freedom—to establish justice and promote equity. We cannot think of Washington without remembering that his sword saved the infant Republic, and his wise statesmanship laid the foundations of "a more perfect Union." Future generations will immortalize Lincoln as the Great Emancipator, who struck the hateful chains of bondage from the limbs of the Nation; who gave emphasis in policy to the declaration of our forefathers, that "all men are created free and equal."

Henceforth, the tomb of Abraham Lincoln will be, like Mount Vernon, a Mecca to the American people. As peace returns—as the furrows of sanguinary war are covered with the ripened growths of already up-springing industries—as the teeming millions who throng to our shores from every foreign clime, add strength to our sinews and energy to our character—as the fruits of his wonderful work are developed in the blessings the land will be permitted to enjoy—then, in the white light of history, when all differences are forgotten and the asperities which even still exist have passed into the gloom of oblivion—they who love best the cause of humanity, will make haste to inscribe upon the tablet of fame, beside the name of Father of his Country, that of the Savior of its Liberties.[7]

Obviously, this appellation of Lincoln as the "Great Emancipator" would not arouse the same feelings in all Americans. Northern whites were far from universal in embracing the end of slavery. But for blacks throughout the country, Lincoln's stance on emancipation made him truly beloved. The *Black Republican*, a newly created newspaper in New Orleans, conveyed not only reverence for the deceased president but a clear sense of indebtedness to him. In commenting upon the killing of Lincoln and the attack on Seward, the paper declared:

> These dreadful deeds are a fitting finale of this brutal and bloody rebellion. They are the natural results of it. . . . They are the fell spirit of slavery. . . . [S]lavery, that for two hundred years has educated whole generations in cruelty and the spirit of murder; that, in the end, drove half a nation to a rebellion to destroy liberty, now whets the knife of the assassin to murder, in cold blood, the most illustrious exemplar of freedom.
>
> Rebels may condemn these horrible acts; they may seek to run down the responsibility to some individual insanity, but they can never clear the skirts of the rebellion of the responsibility for the madness of the murderers. The assassins are the natural outcrop of that vast stratum of cruelty and of crime which slavery has been so long depositing below the surface of society. The greatest earthly friend of the colored race has fallen by the same spirit that has so long oppressed and destroyed us. In giving us our liberty he has lost his own life. . . . He has sealed with his blood his Divine commission to be the liberator of a people. Hereafter, through all time, wherever the Black Race may be known in the world; whenever and wherever it shall lay the foundations of its power; build its cities and rear its temples, it will sacredly preserve if not deify the name of *"Abraham, the Martyr."*[8]

Not all Northerners were so bereft by the loss of Lincoln. The animosities that many Democrats felt toward him during the war did not simply vanish. While the editors who ran the presses universally condemned the assassination, individual men and women who had hated Lincoln before continued to voice their detestation of him. Republicans naturally were incensed by such "treasonable" talk and condemned it

A MONUMENT

IN HONOR OF

ABRAHAM LINCOLN,

THE FRIEND OF HUMANITY.

To the Colored Citizens of the State of New York:

As there is to be a monument erected in honor of our good President—one we loved so much when living, and whose memory we still cherish, because he was the friend of the bondman, and died a martyr to liberty—the Committee of the Union Emancipation Jubilee will have subscription books open to enable our citizens to pay a lasting tribute of respect to the honored dead, by contributing towards the erection of the monument.

Let every man, woman and child come on Tuesday, August 1st, 1865, to Hanft's Myrtle Avenue Park, Brooklyn, and comply with the above request.

Yours, truly, J. A. Trower,

Chairman of Committee.

Anglo-African, May 13, 1865.
On account of the Emancipation Proclamation, black Americans felt a unique bond with Lincoln and were left bereft by his death. Efforts to raise money for memorializing Lincoln emerged quickly, and the first statue of the president erected after the war was indeed financed by contributions from freed slaves.

angrily in the columns of their newspapers. "No one finds satisfaction in the death of Abraham Lincoln, who is not at heart a malignant rebel. Therefore the authors of all such treasonable speech should be visited with summary punishment," resolved the editor of the *Hampshire Gazette & Northampton Courier*. Citizens that "talk treason in public places" had to be dealt with sternly and "forced into a respectful silence." According to the papers, those who voiced their cheery approval for the assassination were liable to be accosted, beaten, or even arrested. In describing the wrath they courted, the *Troy Times* wrote:

> A loyal people will not endure expressions of approval of the assassination of President Lincoln. They will not endure disloyalty. The public mind is fearfully aroused, and the indignation felt towards the enemies of the Union is terrible. But we are glad to see that in most communities there is a disposition to uphold the law and to repress all forms of personal violence. Let the law in all its full majesty be enforced against the miscreants who show themselves unmistakably in sympathy with disloyal assassins. In New York, several arrests have been made.—Three men were sentenced to the penitentiary six months each, on Saturday, for disloyal and brutal utterances. On Monday, four others, including James Britton, treasurer of a theatre, were sentenced for like terms to the penitentiary, for treasonable talk. We presume they were convicted upon the ground of disorderly conduct. In some places there were exhibitions of mob violence, which cooler judgment will no doubt regret and condemn. At Poughkeepsie, a well known rebel sympathizer was seized by a mob and made to carry an American flag. A woman and a young man were placed in jail by the authorities for uttering treasonable language. . . . At Springfield, Mass., a man expressed joy over Mr. Lincoln's death, and although escorted home under the protection of the Sheriff, a crowd of two hundred followed him and when they arrived at his home they required him to get down upon his knee on the piazza and with uncovered head and right hand uplifted, swear, "I am sorry Abraham Lincoln was shot. So help me God.". . . At San Francisco there was [a] most intense feeling of grief and horror, and several rebel brawlers were only saved from lynch law by the prompt action of the police. . . . We say to all, uphold the law, give no sanction to anything that partakes of a mob spirit. The law is our protection, it is the safety of the Republic, and it must be maintained. The disorderly creatures who dare mock the bereaved hearts of loyal people by exhibiting sympathy with traitor assassins, may be properly arrested and dealt with by the legal tribunals as in

> New York. That is the way to rebuke and punish them.[9]

However infuriating they were, Northerners who publicly applauded Lincoln's death were the exception, not the rule. Even the leading voices among the Copperheads lamented it, for if Lincoln had lived, he very likely would have initiated a lenient and forgiving policy toward the South. When Lee had surrendered, the president supported the generous terms that Grant extended to him. And previously, in December 1863, Lincoln also had issued a plan for reconstruction that included a general amnesty for all common citizens in the South who took an oath of allegiance to the Union. Even after Lee's surrender, with the rebellion finally crushed, Lincoln never so much as hinted about imposing a vindictive peace. His apparently forgiving attitude toward the South transformed him in the eyes of his Copperhead opponents from an enemy into a friend. They had just started looking to Lincoln as a man of mercy capable of reestablishing ties of goodwill with the Southern people. Now Copperhead papers such as the *New York News* feared that that the assassination would unleash a call for vengeance in the North that would crush the spirit of reconciliation Lincoln had begun to foster:

> Mr. Lincoln, of those in power, was the best friend of the South. In his kindheartedness, he withstood and baffled the vindictiveness and fanaticism of the radicals of his party. It is known that he had prepared and was about to publish a proclamation of general amnesty, so conciliatory in its tone and so honorable in its conditions, that it would have been acceptable to a large portion of the South as well as to the conservative people of the North. What of that proclamation? Will it be ignored now that its author lies cold in death? We trust not. It is among the legacies he leaves the Republic. Those who have power cannot pay a better tribute to his memory than to fulfill his wishes. . . . The living do honor to the dead in completing the unfinished labor of love. No fitter requiem to Abraham Lincoln [exists] than the song of peace swelling from the grateful hearts of his countrymen.
>
> He asks no hecatombs—let his grave be unpolluted by the blood of Americans slaughtered in revenge. . . . Shall the legitimate sorrow of the people for the loss of one whom they trusted and honored degenerate into a savage vindictiveness toward a race guiltless, and, at this day, unconscious of the crime that has been perpetrated? . . . No; let our statesmen and our people resume the conciliatory temper that prevailed before the dreadful tidings came. . . . Let it be said that the germ of peace was planted by the hand of Abraham Lincoln. Let it live and flourish and become a monument to his fame.[10]

For some Republicans, this turnaround on Lincoln could not overshadow the fact that for years, these conservative Democratic journals had vilified the president. In their mind, the Democrats carried a great deal of responsibility for the assassination; through their repeated attacks on him, they had planted their hatred of the president into Booth's mind and thus inspired him to violence. Consequently, Republicans sought to use Lincoln's death as an opportunity to promote restraints on free speech that many citizens before the Civil War would have regarded as un-American. Without denying the genuineness with which the "Anti-Administration journals" mourned Lincoln's death, the *New York Times* admonished:

> How many of them can honestly say that they have had no agency in supplying the motive which impelled this damnable deed? What that motive was is certain. It was the belief that Abraham Lincoln was a tyrant. Booth's utterance, *Sic semper tyrannis*, on the instant after committing the deed, . . . place[s] this beyond all doubt. The man's brain was fired with the idea that President Lincoln was the oppressor of

> the country. . . . Whence came that idea? . . . We cannot tell; but this we know, that it was an idea which very many of the Democratic presses of the North have sought to make current. They have countless times, during the last four years, applied to President Lincoln the very words *tyrant* and *oppressor*.
>
> Nothing was further from their design than an instigation to personal violence. Yet they have no business to wonder that personal violence has followed. . . . Indeed, we ourselves are free to confess that if all that has been said against Mr. Lincoln by the so-called Democratic journals of the North were literally, strictly, true, we should have considered no fate too severe for him. Better, in our judgment, that he should have died a thousand such deaths than that he should destroy our republican liberties, as he was charged with doing. We say, then, that to declare Mr. Lincoln a tyrant and a liberty-destroyer, to declare this unqualifiedly, systematically, persistently, as was done by a large portion of the Democratic press, was to expose him to just such a death as he experienced. . . .
>
> We do not write this with any desire to excite odium for the past. Let it all rest. What has been written, has been written. But we do most earnestly hope that this assassination will restrain license of speech against President Johnson and all future Presidents.[11]

Others within the Republican camp were more willing to forgive the past, choosing instead to focus on the present state of mourning that united Northerners. The soft stance taken by the Copperhead press was truly striking. As a paper in Philadelphia described, it was as if the North had come full circle, returning again to the spirit of patriotic unanimity that had swept over it four years earlier:

> Here is a fresh marvel. As the nation suddenly uprose in its majesty at the fall of Sumter, casting away all local dissensions or party feelings, so it has once more become fused into one harmonious, patriotic mass. Never was there such an overwhelming public sentiment . . . in favor of our slain President and the sublime truths he taught, as is now prevalent all over the land. It is folly to say that it is not genuine. There never was a more earnest expression of grief than this, and it must be accepted as the voice of the whole American people. Something of this kind, perhaps, was needed to bring us back to that unity of which the nation was so proud in 1861. . . . When the men who for four years reviled and assailed him manifest such undoubted grief at his loss, it is very clear that the past, for the time at least, is wiped out; that the nation stands as a unit at the bier of its murdered hero.[12]

Interestingly, Lincoln's death did not change the attitude of the Northern press toward the people of the South. As before, the papers continued to draw a clear distinction between "the loyal masses," who deserved clemency, and their evil-minded leaders, who needed to be humbled and punished. The following thoughts, taken from a sermon by a Presbyterian preacher in New York and later published in the *Evangelist*, are representative of how many papers in the North dealt with the question of retribution:

> I would grant a general amnesty to the masses; but I would punish the leaders of the rebellion with death or with expatriation and confiscation. I would do this not from any spirit of revenge or personal hate, but because I believe the life and health of the State demand it. There is no safety in permitting them to remain in the country. I would hang them outright, or I would banish them with the sentence of death if they ever returned. Go look upon the prostrate form of our martyred President, and view the mangled person of our revered Secretary, and learn from thence the diabolism of treason, and then decide what the weal of the country demands should be done with traitors. Such men as Jefferson Davis . . .

and numerous others of the same class, would make rather hard material for reconstruction. And the same thing is true of Robert E. Lee. . . . That Robert E. Lee is a gentleman in his manners, and an able general, all will admit, but that he is an intelligent, far-reaching, thorough-paced traitor, cannot be denied. He lifted his traitorous sword against his country and his government, after having been educated at the nation's expense and received into her armies as a child of the Republic. I have been surprised at certain apologetic opinions, which I have heard expressed by individuals, good and true to their country, in regard to this chief of rebel generals. Were I going to select two men, one from civilians and the other from the army, to be executed for treason, I would take Jefferson Davis and Robert E. Lee.

> . . . Let us act like men and not like children in giving form and character and stability to this great nation after it has passed through such a baptism of fire and blood. Let us not forget the claims of justice in our haste to dispense mercy.[13]

Even the soldiers—who were Lincoln's greatest supporters—continued to focus their feelings of retribution against the leading figures of the Confederacy, not against the people generally. An army correspondent in Knoxville, Tennessee, expressed the mood among the troops in these terms:

> I have never seen anything like the profound, universal sorrow which fell, like a pall, over the army on the receipt of the news of the assassination of President Lincoln. The jubilee of rejoicing at the downfall of the Rebellion had hardly died away when, like a thunder-stroke, the appalling news flashed over the wires that our President and Secretary of State had fallen, by the hands of assassins. O, the magnitude and infamy of the crime, and the irreparable loss of a nation in mourning!
>
> The deepest feelings of sorrow were manifested everywhere, in the army and out of it. . . . The soldiers—I suppose it is human nature with them—swear vengeance, and will not believe that the Rebel leaders are not the instigators of the foul deed. It is so completely in keeping with the whole spirit of the Rebellion . . . that it certainly calls for an extraordinary stretch of charity on the part of the nation's defenders, to view with anything like forbearance or equanimity, at least the more prominent and culpable of the insurgent leaders. And here it may not be out of place to state that, apart from the present excited state of feeling elicited by a great national calamity, the officers and soldiers generally in this Department are decidedly in favor of meting out some sort of punishment to the infamous wretches who have been the cause of the untold suffering, desolation, and bloodshed of the last four years. It is only natural to suppose that the question, "What shall be done with the Rebel leaders?" should be generally discussed and commented on in the army, and . . . the common, unanimous sentiment is emphatically against a free pardon for all.[14]

Beyond inspiring feelings of vengeance, Lincoln's death also caused Northerners to think more introspectively. They wanted a moral explanation for it, and in searching for an answer, some came to believe that God had expressly willed it, in order to ensure that the rebel leaders would suffer the stern retribution they deserved. Perhaps, in light of Lincoln's apparent penchant for forgiveness, God had allowed Booth to consummate his bloody plan. The vice president, Andrew Johnson, was a Tennessee Unionist—a man who had been physically threatened by the rebels for his refusal to support the Confederacy. He seemed to be someone who could be trusted with the job of punishing traitors. Maybe God had struck Lincoln down so that Johnson could ascend to the helm. The Reverend M. L. P. Thompson had elaborated upon this idea in a sermon he preached two weeks after the assassination, which the *Cincinnati Gazette* promptly published:

God is not the author of crimes. The responsibility for them rests solely and forever on the guilty perpetrators of them. But God permits bad men to conceive wickedness in their hearts, and He permits them to execute the wickedness which they have conceived, and He uses their wicked doings for the furtherance of His own designs. . . . The assassination of Mr. Lincoln was unforeseen and undreamed of by himself or us. The conspiracy that culminated in that fatal pistol shot was hatched and ripened in the dark. . . . But did not God know? . . . Was not His eye upon the assassin all the hours of that dreadful day? . . . Up to the very moment when he did the deed, was not God looking at him and perfectly cognizant of his horrible design? And can any of you doubt whether it was in God's power to stay him? Could not He, without whom not a sparrow falleth to the ground, and who numbereth our very hairs, have interposed some shield to guard that precious life, if it had not been His own purpose . . . that Mr. Lincoln on that day, at that hour, in that place, and by that assassin hand, should die? We must attribute the death of the President, and all the circumstances of it, to a Divine purpose, and plan, and agency. . . .

Why has God thus smitten us? . . .

Mr. Lincoln was simply an instrument in the hand of God. Four years ago, at the outbreak of this great rebellion and unparalleled civil war, he was called under the direction of the divine providence to preside over the nation as its chief magistrate and political head. . . . We are to suppose that he was selected of God on account of some peculiar suitableness which he possessed for the particular work which was then to be accomplished. . . . We now see that in many very important particulars, . . . Mr. Lincoln was the very man for his period. . . . I attach the utmost value to those traits of his remarkable character which has won for him the prenomen of *Honest*. . . . There have been more times than one, I am absolutely certain, when the only bond that has held us together in the strife, was the confidence which all felt, alike, in the perfect integrity of our leader and the patriotic purity of his intentions, when, if we had distrusted these, we should have fallen into hopeless divisions, and of necessity abandoned the war, and the nation would have perished.

But was Mr. Lincoln the man for the new crisis which now arises? Was he the man for the future? . . . No man could be animated by a more steadfast purpose against rebels in arms than he, but was he capable of the sternness which was demanded for vindicating the principles of eternal justice . . . against rebels vanquished and prostrate at his feet? Against treason organized for war, his face was adamant, and his hand was gauntleted with iron; but could he have been relied upon to set the fatal seal of God's abhorrence and utter condemnation on the traitors conquered, seized and in his power? . . . Had not Mr. Lincoln committed himself to a course of conduct . . . which would have left public justice unappeased and law dishonored? We may not love him less for this, or mourn less tenderly for his fate, but may we not suppose that for such a reason as this he was not approved of heaven as a leader for the period that is now opening before the nation?[15]

Others interpreted the workings of God in more benevolent ways. Rather than being a matter of divine judgment *against* Lincoln, maybe death was a blessing bestowed upon him—a welcome release from the struggles of this world. As one paper affirmed, "Abraham Lincoln was God's chosen instrument to lead the Nation through the tribulation of the past." But now that this glorious work was finished, "he has been called away to an infinitely better reward and a higher sphere of glory" in heaven. Or, possibly, God was using Lincoln's demise to serve a grander purpose. Perhaps the assassination was meant to shock Northerners and Southerners into realizing just how horrible their conflict was, and thus to help them come together with common feelings of sorrow and regret. The *Springfield Republican* conjectured:

We have a feeling, rising almost to assured conviction, that the cruel death of President Lincoln . . . will prove the occasion and the means of reconciliation. We need a common starting point of sympathy and feeling with the southern people—shall we not find it in united execration of the foulest deed ever wrought upon our soil, wrought in behalf of treason and its fell spirit. . . . We cannot doubt that the prevailing feeling at the South will be one of horror and indignation; that those so steeped in the poison of rebellion as to rejoice in it will be but a small minority, and that the exhibition of such fiendish malignity will cause them to be marked and shunned as infamous. The majority of the southern people have been ready to fight for independence, misled by false notions of their political rights and duties, but now that the effort has manifestly failed, they will have no sympathy with those who would inaugurate a reign of murder and brigandage from motives of revenge. . . . It will appal the southern people; it will awaken their indignation and grief; it will resuscitate all the better impulses so long suppressed, and thus prepare them to accept the magnanimous offer of the government and give their efforts for a true and permanent peace. So light shall rise in the darkness, and hope blossom out of despair. So shall our lamented president be twice the savior of his country—once by his life, and more truly by his death.[16]

The expectations of the *Springfield Republican* were realized only to a very limited extent. Some in the South—particularly those that had been strong proponents for peace—were indeed appalled by the assassination. However, their horror was not just a response to the act itself but also a reflection of their fear that a vengeful North would make Southerners suffer bitterly for it. The *North Carolina Standard* was thus quick to disavow that anyone in the South had any interest or desire to see Lincoln killed:

We announce with profound grief the assassination of the President of the United States! Humanity is shocked, and the heart bleeds at the announcement. . . .

Abraham Lincoln was the best friend the South had in all the North. We pray God that his untimely and cruel death may not add to the miseries of our afflicted State. North Carolina had no agency in the awful deed. We wash our hands of this blood guiltiness; and we call heaven to witness that we deplore it as the saddest event in the history of this continent. . . . Let the friends of the Union bear this stroke as best they may, and not let the innocent be held responsible for the acts of the guilty. His assassins will be pursued by the stern purpose of the avenger of blood, and no country, however remote, will be able to shield them from the condign punishment that awaits them. The secession of the Cotton States, which commenced in crime, has ended in assassination.—We thank God that we are not responsible for either the commencement or the termination of this horrid business.[17]

However, if the Northern people expected Southerners to weep en masse over Lincoln's demise, they were fooling themselves. Some papers gave the assassination scant attention, doing little more than confirming that it had occurred and affirming that no one in the Confederacy was to blame.[18] With the federal government now standing over them as a conqueror, perhaps they felt it was better to keep their opinions about Lincoln to themselves. Others, however, were less reticent in letting their feelings show. After giving its readers a few details on the assassination, the *Augusta Constitutionalist* made light of it, deriding it as just another "little dramatic spectacle," one "not announced in the bill" of the playhouse that fateful evening.[19] But it was the papers in Texas—fiery, unrepentant, ever-defiant Texas—that gloried the most flagrantly in Lincoln's death. "It is certainly a matter of congratulation that Lincoln is dead, because the world

Assassination of President Lincoln.—Since the suspension of the *Telegraph and Confederate*, information of the assassination of President Lincoln has reached all classes of the people. A general regret, after reflection, is now felt at this atrocious occurrence.

Macon Telegraph, May 11, 1865. Some Southern newspapers had little to say about Lincoln's assassination. This death notice, expressing regret for the crime only "after reflection," falls far short of the outrage that Northerners conveyed.

is happily rid of a monster that disgraced the form of humanity," hissed the *Texas Republican*. Lambasting the "twaddle" printed by other Southern papers that lamented the assassination, the *Republican* vehemently defended its own feelings of relief and joy:

> We were under the impression there was no proposition more fully admitted than the right, if not the duty, of individuals to destroy the life of tyrants. By no other means than by individual daring and bravery can such men be reached. They are not to be found in the van of battle, or at posts of danger, but in places of security, difficult and dangerous of approach, where they remain to carry out their iniquitous designs. The man, therefore, who has the high moral and physical courage to brave all the consequences attending such an act, and to strike down a tyrant when panoplied in his strength and power, is not, as we conceive, an assassin or murderer, but a hero. If we are to judge of a transaction by the motives which seem to govern it—the purity of purpose, the lofty impulse, the total abnegation of self and of personal security, how noble, how chivalric the conduct of Booth? He killed Lincoln, in the midst of his minions, any and all of whom were ready to crush him, and then, instead of skulking away, paused to proclaim the heroic sentiment of patriotism that impelled the deed. "Sic Semper Tyrannis, the South is avenged!" will live to be admired in eloquence and song. . . .
>
> There is no reason to believe that Booth, in killing Lincoln, was actuated by malice or vulgar ambition. He slew him as a tyrant, and the enemy of his country. Therefore we honor the deed. . . . For upwards of four years this man, remarkable for his iron will and malice, had carried on a war against these States, without a parallel in modern history for its atrocity and barbarism, with the declared purpose of subjugation or extermination. But at the very time when in his heart he was exulting over the supposed prostrate condition of the South, he fell by the hand of one of his own people. How prophetically the lines, which he applied to the South, refer to himself: "It must needs be that offences come, but woe to that man by whom the offence cometh."[20]

The *Houston Tri-Weekly Telegraph* was only slightly more generous. While that paper could at least concede that Lincoln possessed some redeeming personal qualities, it nevertheless reveled in the knowledge that he had paid the ultimate price for his political misdeeds:

> From now until God's judgment day, the minds of men will not cease to thrill at the killing of Abraham Lincoln, by the hand of Booth, the actor, in the theatre at Washington, on the night of April 14th, 1865. . . . Mr. Lincoln was, it is true, . . . natively a kindly, genial man. We do not suppose a love of oppression, or tendency to wrong, any part of his original disposition. We believe he thought at

the beginning, that the great movement of the Southern people for self-government was a mere passionate outbreak, caused by designing leaders, and that the hearts of the great mass of the people would soon return to the Union. . . . No doubt he expected the Union soon to be re-established, and an era of good feeling to prevail. . . .

Fully embarked, however, in the war, the change came upon Mr. Lincoln, which has ever come upon the souls of men over which any great end of ambition or fanaticism obtains control. . . . Abraham Lincoln came to think that the one great and supreme object—it may be he thought it the object of real and ultimate good to mankind—was the complete and unresisted re-establishment of the power of the government of the United States . . . over the people of the Southern States. No constitution, no law, no right, no humanity stood in the way of this end. Treasure was nothing, human life was nothing, old and cardinal principles of liberty and sentiments of right were nothing, in order to effect it. We saw successively in his public documents how superruling became his purpose, and how callous to all the usual motives of humanity he grew. 75,000 men, 300,000 men, 500,000 men—men—victims without number. Our slaves to be freed and armed against our lives, our cities burned, our fields ravaged, all that would sustain life wasted and destroyed. . . . He may have felt pity, but no remorse; and to fasten despotism upon a people free as himself, entitled to life and liberty and the pursuit of happiness like himself, he would have stood unmoved and inflexible, and with no eye turned to heaven, would have seen them swept from the earth. . . .

Doubtless if the South had bowed a submissive knee and kissed the rod of its masters, Mr. Lincoln's good humor would have largely returned. Conquered and loyal, behaving ourselves quietly, bending meekly to the burdens put upon our backs, and drawing smoothly under the yoke fastened upon our necks, Mr. Lincoln would have imagined himself friendly and patronizing towards us. . . . With all allowance for his amiable personal qualities, we yet know it to be true that Abraham Lincoln had as fell a purpose as ever existed in the bosom of despotism, that the Southern people were to be bereft of their liberties, subjugated to a government hateful to their inmost souls, and ruled forever, not by their own free will, but by the bayonets and the votes of the more populous North. He was the instrument of the North to effect upon us and our children this destructive, ruinous object.

We feel that we can not read all the dark riddle, and solve the hidden arcanum of this bloody tragedy. Its effect may be to stimulate the passions at work on both sides to ten-fold strength. The purpose to avenge his blood in still deeper atrocities upon innocent Southern people may infuriate the North. . . . What sacrifices, by flame and sword, by insult, confiscation, exile and death, and by all the wrongs which make oppression bitter, shall be required of us as the expiation, we know not. All of them we defy. Not a soldier, nor a woman, an old man nor a lisping child with true heart to this Southern land but feels a thrill, electric, divine, at this sudden fall, in his own blood, of the chief of our oppressors. . . . If the reign of despotism is again to be re-inaugurated at this day and over this people, then let despotism and whoever may be its minions beware the deserved fate of tyrants.[21]

One Texan, writing from his home in Galveston to the editor of the *Tri-Weekly News*, went so far as to suggest that Lincoln's assassination might bring the North to finally negotiate a compromise with the Confederacy. It was a delusional thought. As his words reveal, the author was not only ill-informed about Henry Seward's survival of the attempt against his life but also totally unaware of the tone of Northern public opinion and the true fate of the Confederacy:

Lincoln and Seward more than all others had placed themselves (as they doubtless thought) out of harm's way. They had incited all the worst passions of the people; for many years they had stirred the popular mind of the North against the South; they enjendered and fostered a spirit of deadly hate of one section towards the other, more intense than that of Carthage against Rome, and finally seized the reins of government and plunged the nation into civil war more horrid and cruel than any that has hitherto marred the pages of ancient or modern history. They have eclipsed the tyranny of a Caligula, Herod or [N]ero. . . . They have made very many women widows, and children fatherless. They have reduced our once fruitful and happy land, the abode of high civilization and a refined intelligence, to a heap of ruins and pyramids of chimneys, leaving only the sky and the land in their wake; they have driven thousands of helpless women and children from their homes and domicils in a country that they had desolated with fire and sword, to starve and perish by the inclemencies of the season. . . . They have subsidized the mercenary hordes of Europe and America, and armed our own slaves for our destruction, and led them into our fair land for the purpose of committing the worst atrocities such as this page would blush to contain and for four long years they have enacted this inhuman tragedy, with fiendish satisfaction that would have made a Herod or a Nero blush for shame. The wonder is that some avenging hand did not overtake these enemies of the human race long ere this. But at last that terrible retribution, which is sometimes slow but always certain, has fallen upon the doubly guilty in the form of the assassin's hand, and these enemies of human liberty are hurled from a life they had made infamous. . . . I see, in the distant horizon of the North, the dark and sombre cloud, which has lowered over us for four long gloomy years, beginning to break, and the Star of Peace, darting a few feeble rays, tells us of the approaching halo, that may soon spread joy and gladness over our once happy but now [afflicted] country.

The tyrants that afflicted us are gone; history will award them a place amongst the enemies of the human race, and to those who wielded the implements of death against these human monstrosities, will be awarded a place among the chivalric and heroic benefactors of mankind—to rank not as assassins, or murderers, but as benefactors of mankind.[22]

The diaries and personal papers of Southerners reveal that while the sentiment was not universal, many indeed reacted to the news of Lincoln's death with relief, gladness, and even feelings of joyous retribution.[23] Although April had started off dreadfully for the defenders of the Confederacy, they finally had something to cheer about.

New-York Tribune.

VOL. XXV.....No. 7,493. NEW-YORK, WEDNESDAY, APRIL 12, 1865. PRICE FOUR CENTS.

FROM RICHMOND!

Important and Interesting News from the Late Rebel Capital.

WASHINGTON, Tuesday, April 11, 1865.

The Richmond Whig of Monday, the 10th instant, is received. It says:

Whatever may be the fate of the Constitutional Amendment, it is as certain as sunrise that Slavery in Virginia is dead.

A National Bank of the United States is to be immediately established in Richmond, where shares in United States stocks will be sold at the rates established in Northern cities.

The aggregate value of the property destroyed in Richmond foots up $2,146,240. Imposing as these figures appear, they are far short of the truth for the reason already stated, that real estate was before the war invariably assessed much below the value which it would have commanded in the market. Our list covers no more than the value of the bricks and mortar.

All the hospitals of Richmond have been taken possession of by the military authorities and are used for the care and comfort equally of the Union and Confederate sick and wounded.

A number of Confederate surgeons left in the city have been paroled to attend to the Confederate sick and wounded.

The Chimborazo, Winder, Jackson and Howard's Grove hospitals, four of the principal Confederate hospitals, are used for the accommodation of the Union wounded. Their accommodations are for about twenty-four thousand beds, which accommodations were left entirely by the Confederate authorities.

Confederate prisoners to the number of 800 or 1,000 have been received in the city within the past 48 hours and consigned to the Libby Prison.

More than half of Gen. Pickett's Division has been brought in or captured, and the country between Richmond and Amelia County is said to be full of Confederate soldiers, nearly all of them Virginians, making their way to their homes.

The Castle is used as a receptacle for citizen prisoners, of whom quite a number are gathered there.

Manchester was not at all disturbed by the villagers on Monday morning last, neither did the fire reach that trans-James District.

A pontoon bridge spans the river now and connects Richmond with Manchester, and we hope that business will soon revive and pervade both sections alike.

The churches of all the religious denominations whose pastors remained in the city, were opened yesterday, and services were conducted in them as usual in presence of large congregations, a good proportion being composed of the officers and soldiers of the Union Army of occupation.

In the Episcopal churches the regular form of service was observed, with the single exception of the prayer for the President of the Confederate States, as inserted in the Liturgy, which was made instead, "for all in authority." As the United States is the power in authority, the prayer for the President of the United States was of course implied, if not said.

The sermons preached exhibited generally a very high order of talent, eminently practicable and religious in their tone, and we are glad to know that all the Union officers and privates who were listeners entertained a high opinion of the pulpit eloquence of the clergymen of Richmond.

Saturday afternoon was rendered a memorable day in Richmond by the first review and parade of the United States forces occupying the city.

These troops comprised the Third Division of the Twenty-fourth Army Corps of the Army of the James, commanded by Major-Gen. Godfrey Weitzel, in absence of Gen. Ord.

The troops were under the immediate command of Brig.-Gen. Charles Davies.

The review was appointed for 2 o'clock on East Main-st., the left of the procession to rest on the outskirts of the city, and the right westward, toward the heart of the city.

By the hour of noon hundreds of citizens, male and female, had taken favorable positions from which a view of the military spectacle could be obtained. The windows and doors for more than a mile along Main-st. were crowded with spectators, who watched with interest the maneuvers of the various regiments, batteries and squadrons, as they appeared, wheeled into line and took up their positions, until the line, far as the eye could reach, shone in the sun a glittering hedge of bayonets.

Gay banners and bands interspersed the line at intervals, and couriers went and came, carrying orders and keeping both wings in communication.

An hour beyond the time appointed passed, and yet Brig.-Gen. Devins and staff, who were first to review the troops had not made his appearance. Finally, however, a flourish of trumpets announced his approach, and the General, with a splendidly-mounted and appearing staff, approached the line from the left, the mounted band on the extreme right striking up "Hail to the Chief who in triumph advances."

During the performance of this air Gen. Devins and staff rode down the right, but made a detour through Fifteenth and Carey-sts., and rode rapidly to the extreme left of the line on the outskirts.

From this point the review was accomplished, the General and staff galloping from left to right, the line coming to a "present arms" as he passed, and the bands striking up.

Gen. Devins alone carried his hat in his hand, and this distinction caused him to be easily recognized by the citizens.

At points on the line he was heartily cheered by the troops.

Long accustomed as Confederate eyes have been to the once all-pervading "gray," we do not believe that the sudden substitution of "blue" as the pervading color is distasteful to many of our citizens, thousands of whom looked on the military spectacle of Saturday not as the display of prowess on the part of a triumphant foe, but as an exhibition of the military genius and resources of the United States, which all can again contemplate with pride.

None of the colored troops appeared on the parade or review, but it is said that a separate display of them will probably take place before long.

One feature of the display was evident to every observer, and that was the superior drill, morale and discipline manifested by the men in their marching and soldierly bearing, the perfect condition of their arms and equipments, burnished to a dazzling brightness, the batteries drawn by well-trained horses, fat and sleek, and substantially caparisoned, all in striking contrast to what the citizens have been accustomed for the four years during which Richmond was held by the Confederate Army.

The reporter passed over the greater part of the parade, and did not witness or hear of a single unpleasant incident to mar the general harmonious character of the day.

The citizens viewed the military pageant with silent interest from their side-walks, doors and windows, and if they did not openly rejoice at the appearance of the "Old Flag of the Union," there were no expressions that could be construed into derision or contempt for it.

The soldiers on the other hand abstained from those boisterous shouts of exultation that might have been expected, and marched orderly and quiet as though desirous of abstaining from any unnecessary demonstrations that might tend to give offense to citizens.

Altogether citizens and soldiers have cause to congratulate themselves on the result of the first review and parade of the United States troops in the capital of Virginia.

Mosby's Guerrillas Badly Beaten.

PHILADELPHIA, Tuesday, April 11, 1865.

The following is a special dispatch to *The Bulletin*:

WASHINGTON, April 11, 1865.

An engagement with Mosby's guerrillas took place yesterday 14 miles from this city. The guerrillas were badly beaten.

NEWSPAPER ACCOUNT.

From The Washington Chronicle, April 11.

For some time past there have been at Burke's Station, on the Orange and Alexandria Railroad, a large number of mules, used for hauling wood to the railroad from various parts of the adjacent country, for Government use. At said Station, which is about 14 miles from Alexandria, there are posted two companies of the 202d Pennsylvania, and a detachment of the 8th Illinois Cavalry, numbering some 45 men.

On Saturday last, two guerrillas appeared in the vicinity of the station, to reconnoiter, having been sent there from Loudon County, by Mosby, to ascertain what was the force on guard, and what was the feasibility of capturing the mules and any other valuables that might be in the vicinity. These scouts were very wary, and rapidly departed, after having accomplished their mission. Upon their return to Mosby's quarters, he ordered an expedition for the capture of the mules. This expedition, in number about two hundred, left Loudon on Sunday evening, and appeared in the vicinity of Burke's station yesterday (Monday) morning, about 6½ o'clock.

Virginia cavalry, and had arrived at Mosby's quarters on Saturday, having been ordered to join him from the army of Lee but a few days ago.

REBEL PRISONERS.

The Herald publishes the following alphabetical list, embracing the names of the general officers of Lee's army who surrendered to Gen. Grant on the 8th and 9th inst. The names marked with an asterisk are those of graduates of the West Point Academy or former officers of the United States Army:

COMMANDER-IN-CHIEF.

*General Robert E. Lee of Virginia, Commander-in-Chief of the Rebel armies; Graduated 1829; March 16, 1861, promoted Colonel First United States Cavalry; April 25, 1861, resigned; April, 1861, appointed Commander Virginia military and naval forces; September 26, 1861, assumed command in Western Virginia; June, 1862, assumed command of the Army of Western Virginia; February 6, 1865, assumed command of the armies of the Confederate States; April 9, 1865, surrendered to General Grant.

STAFF.

*Brigadier-General R. H. Chilton, Chief of Staff.
Major C. T. Venable, Aid-de-Camp.
Colonel W. H. Taylor, Aid-de-Camp.
Major C. Marshal, Private Secretary.
Brigadier-General A. L. Long, Chief of Artillery.
Lieutenant-Colonel F. G. Baldwin, Chief of Ordnance.
Lieutenant-Colonel Murphy, Inspector General.
Major Henry O. Tayton, Assistant Inspector General.
Lieutenant-Colonel J. L. Corbey, Chief Quartermaster.
Lieutenant-Colonel A. A. Cole, Chief Commissary.
Surgeon S. Guild, Medical Director.

SUBORDINATE COMMANDERS.

Anderson, Brigadier-General Thomas, of Georgia, commanded Brigade Longstreet's Corps. Wounded at Weldon Railroad, August 20, 1864.

*Anderson, Lieutenant-General R. H., of South Carolina, West Point, 1842. Captain Second Dragoons, 1861. Resigned March 3, 1861. Colonel First South Carolina. Brigadier General, 1861. Major-General, 1862. Wounded at Antietam. Lieutenant-General, May, 1864. Commanded Fourth Corps Lee's Army.

Bankhead, Brigadier-General, of Mississippi.

Barksdale, Brigadier-General, commanding brigade Second Corps.

Barringer, Brigadier-General Rufus, of Georgia, commanding brigade W. F. Lee's Cavalry.

Barton, Brigadier-General Seth, of Virginia. West Point, 1849. Captain First Infantry. Resigned June 11, 1861. Commanding Walker's Brigade, Heth's Division.

Battle, Major-General Cullen A., of Alabama, Colonel Third Alabama, August 20, 1862. Promoted Brigadier-General, June 3, 1864. Wounded at Coal Harbor September 19, 1864, Commanding Rhodes' Division at Winchester, October 19. Wounded at Cedar Creek, commanding a division Gordon's Second Corps.

Benning, Brigadier-General Henry L., of Georgia, May 5, 1864. Wounded at Wilderness, March 8, 1865. Commanding brigade Longstreet's First Corps.

Ross, Colonel F. S., of Texas, commanding brigade.

Bryant, Brigadier-General, commanding brigade Kershaw's Division.

Bryan, Brigadier-General Goode, of Georgia, Colonel Sixteenth Georgia, August 29, 1863. Promoted Brigadier-General.

Capers, Brigadier-General Ellison, of South Carolina. Promoted Brigadier-General March 3, 1865.

Carter, Brigadier-General T. H., Chief Artillery, Second Army Corps.

Chilton, Brigadier-General Robert H., of Virginia, Chief of Staff to General Lee. West Point, 1837. Paymaster United States Army. Resigned April 29, 1861.

Cooke, Brigadier-General Philip, of Georgia, commanding brigade Heth's Division.

Conner, Brigadier-General James, of South Carolina, commanding brigade Kershaw's Division.

Corse, Brigadier-General, of Virginia, commanding brigade Pickett's Division.

Cosby, Brigadier-General, commanding cavalry.

Cox, Brigadier-General W. R., commanding Ramseur's old brigade.

Davis, Brigadier-General Joseph R., of Mississippi.

Dearing, Brigadier-General, commanding cavalry brigade.

De Bose, Brigadier-General, of Georgia, commanding brigade, Kershaw's division.

Echols, Brigadier-General, commanding brigade, Kershaw's division.

*Elzey, Major-General Arnold J., of Maryland. West Point, 1837. Captain Second Dragoons; resigned 1861. Colonel First Maryland, July 1, 1861; Brigadier-General at Bull Run, 1861; disabled; retired from active duty.

*Evans, Major-General Nathan G., of South Carolina. West Point, 1848. December, 1860, resigned captaincy United States Army. February 6, 1865, commanding division, Gordon's corps, at Hatcher's Run.

*Ewell, Lieutenant-General Richard S., of Virginia. Graduated 1840. May 7, 1861, resigned captaincy United States Army. July 21, Brigadier-General at Bull Run. May, 1863, promoted Lieutenant-General. May 6, relieved command Second Corps; assumed command Department Henrico.

*Field, Major General Charles W., of Kentucky. West Point, 1849. February 12, 1864, commanding Division, Longstreet's Corps.

Finnegan, Brigadier General, Caesar, of Florida, formerly private United States Army, commanding brigade, Mahone's Division.

Forsyth, Colonel Charles, of Alabama, commanding brigade.

*Gardner, Brigadier-General W. M., of Georgia. West Point, 1846; captain, Second Infantry; resigned 1861. November 14, promoted Brigadier-General Rebel Army. July 7, 1864, commanding post, Richmond, Va.

Gary, Brigadier-General, of South Carolina, commanding brigade cavalry.

*Gerald, Major, C. B., of Mississippi, commanding Humphrey's old Brigade.

Gordon, Major-General, of Georgia, commanding Second Corps, Lee's army.

*Gorgas, Brigadier-General, of Virginia. West Point, 1841. Chief of Ordnance, Confederate States Army.

Grymes, Major-General, of Georgia. February 1, 1865, promoted Major-General, commanding Division, Gordon's Corps.

*Heth, Major General Henry, of Virginia. West Point, 1847. Resigned captaincy of 10th Infantry April 25, 1861. May 24, 1863, promoted Major-General Confederate States Army, commanding Division in A. P. Hill's Corps.

Hoffman, Colonel John S., of Virginia, commanding Infantry Brigade, Pegram's old Division.

Hunter, Brigadier-General Eppa, of Virginia. Colonel 8th Virginia, August 9, 1863, promoted Brigadier-General; commanding Brigade, Pickett's Division.

*Johnson, Major-General Bushrod R., of Tennessee. Graduated 1840. Resigned first lieutenancy October 22, 1847. January 24, promoted brigadier-general. Captured by Grant at Fort Donelson, at Shiloh. Promoted major-general 1864. Commanding division in Anderson's (Fourth) Corps.

*Jordan, Brigadier-General Thomas, of Virginia. Graduated 1840. Captain and Acting Quartermaster United States Army. Resigned May 21, 1861. Chief of Staff to Beauregard. Promoted brigadier-general in 1864.

Kasey, Lieutenant-Colonel J. G., commanding Pegram's old brigade.

Kemper, Major-General J. L., of Virginia. Colonel of Seventh Virginia. Promoted brigadier-general in 1863. Captured at Gettysburg. Promoted major-general in 1864. Commanding Reserves of Virginia.

Kershaw, Major-General J. B., of South Carolina. Colonel Second South Carolina, February 13, promoted Brigadier-General. Promoted Major-General in 1864. Commanding Division in Longstreet's Corps.

Lane, Brigadier-General, commanding Brigade, Kershaw's Division.

*Lawton, Brigadier-General Alex. R., of Georgia. Graduated 1839. Second Lieutenant First Artillery. Resigned December 31, 1840. Colonel Georgia Infantry May 14, 1861. Brigadier-General, commanding Military Division of Georgia. September 17, wounded in leg at Antietam. Ex-Quartermaster-General Confederate States Army.

Lee, Colonel John W., of North Carolina, commanding Johnston's old Brigade.

*Lee, General R. E., of Virginia. (See above).

*Lee, Brigadier-General G. W. Custis, of Virginia. Graduate 1854; First-Lieutenant Engineers; resigned May 2, 1861; Colonel on Davis's staff; promoted Brigadier-General 1864; commanded Division Ewell's command.

*Lee, Major-General Fitz Hugh, of Virginia. Graduate 1856; First-Lieutenant Cavalry, May 21, 1861, resigned; Colonel First Virginia Cavalry, July 24, 1862; promoted Brigadier-General August 3, 1863; promoted Major-General, commanding Corps of cavalry.

Lilly, Brigadier-General Robert D. Commanding Pegram's old Brigade.

Lomax, Major-General Lunsford L., of Virginia. Colonel Virginia Cavalry; July 22, 1863, promoted Brigadier-General; February 20, 1863, confirmed Major-General; commanding Division cavalry.

Long, Brigadier-General A. L., of Virginia. Chief Artillery, Lee's Army.

*Longstreet, Lieutenant-General James B., of Alabama. Graduate 1842; Second Lieutenant Eighth Infantry, March 4, 1845; brevet Captain, August 20, 1847, for gallantry at Cherubusco; brevet Major, September 8, 1847, for gallantry at Molino del Rey; wounded at Chapultepec, September 13, 1847; Paymaster United States army; resigned June 1, 1861; promoted Brigadier-General Confederate States Army, October 1, 1861; promoted Major-General, June 17, 1862; promoted Lieutenant-General, May 8, 1864; wounded at the Wilderness; commanding First Corps Lee's army.

Mahone, Major-General William, of Virginia. November 16, promoted Brigadier-General; March, 1864, in charge of all military railroads in the South; August 13, 1864, promoted Major-General; commanding Division A. P. Hill's Corps.

*Pemberton, Lieutenant-Colonel John C., of Virginia; graduate 1837; Captain U. S. A. September 15, 1850; resigned April 1861; Colonel and Assistant Adjutant-General to Joe Johnston; promoted Brigadier-General 1862; commanding at Charleston; promoted Lieutenant-General, July 4, 1863, surrendered Vicksburg and army to Grant; May 14, 1864, resigned commission; appointed Lieutenant-Colonel artillery; on duty as inspector artillery.

*Pendleton, Brigadier General William N., of Virginia; graduate 1830; resigned lieutenancy U. S. A. October 3, 1833; clergyman of Protestant Episcopal Church from 1837 to 1839; rector of Episcopal Diocesan School of Virginia, Alexandria, Va., from 1839 to 1844; captain of battery in Joe Johnston's army July, 1861; colonel of reserve artillery at Manassas, 1862; chief of artillery of Army of the Valley.

*Pickett, Major-General George E., of Virginia; graduate 1846; captain Ninth infantry regiment; resigned July 25, 1861; appointed brigadier general in regular army September, 1863; major-general commanding division of Longstreet's corps.

Preston, Brigadier-General John A., of Virginia, commanding Bureau of Conscription.

Ransom, Brigadier-General M. W., of North Carolina, commanding brigade of infantry.

Rosser, Major-General Thomas L., of Texas, Major-General February 20, 1865, commanding Division of Fitzhugh Lee's Corps of cavalry.

*Ruggles, Major-General Daniel, of Virginia, native of Massachusetts; graduate 1833; Captain and Brevet Lieutenant-Colonel 1861; resigned May 5, 1861; Brigadier-General C. S. A.; promoted Major-General 1862; lately on duty at Fredericksburg.

Smith, Colonel Thomas, of Virginia, commanding Brigade of Wharton's Division.

Sorrell, Brigadier-General G. M., of Georgia, Assistant Adjutant-General to Longstreet; November 2, 1864, promoted Brigadier-General; February 6, 1865, wounded at Hatcher's Run; February 21, recovered from wound; commanding Brigade of A. P. Hill's Corps.

*Stuart, Brigadier-General George H., of Maryland; graduated 1848; resigned captaincy First Cavalry, April 22, 1861; Colonel of Maryland Volunteers, C. S. A.; promoted brigadier-general, 1863; captured at Wilderness, May 5, 1864; commanding brigade of Pickett's Division.

St. John, Brigadier-General Isaac M., of Virginia, Commissary General, Confederate States Army.

Weisiger, Brigadier-General D. A., of Virginia. November 14, 1864, promoted from colonel of Twelfth Virginia to brigadier-general; commanding brigade of Mahone's Division.

Wharton, Brigadier-General G. C., of Virginia, colonel commanding First Brigade, Floyd's Division, at Donelson, July 8, 1863, promoted brigadier-general; September 19, 1864, wounded at Winchester. Commanding division Second Corps.

Wickham, Brigadier-General Wm. C., of Virginia, colonel Virginia Cavalry. Promoted brigadier-general September 1, 1861; resigned November, 1863, to take seat in Legislature of Virginia.

Wilcox, Major-General Cadmus M., of Alabama. Graduated 1846; resigned captaincy Seventh Infantry June 8, 1861. October 21, 1861, appointed brigadier-general Confederate States Army; August 3, 1863, promoted major-general, commanding Division A. P. Hill's (Third) Corps.

Wise, Brigadier-General Henry A., of Virginia. Member of United States Congress. June 18, 1861, appointed brigadier-general Confederate States Army, commanding brigade of infantry Ewell's command.

RECAPITULATION.

General captured	1
Lieutenant-Generals captured	3
Major-Generals captured	17
Brigade Commanders	61
Total General officers	82

The number of men actually surrendered by General Lee is from twenty thousand to twenty-two thousand of all arms.

Within the past two weeks over twenty thousand Rebel prisoners have been sent away from City Point, and a large number still remain there.

FROM NEW-ORLEANS AND THE SOUTH-WEST.

By the arrival of the Liberty we have New-Orleans papers of April 2. The purser, Mr. Donaldson, has our thanks for customary favors.

The Times says the monitors Osage and Milwaukee sank in shoal water in Mobile Bay, while attempting to get in range of Spanish Fort; that they were not materially damaged, and can easily be raised and repaired.

Baton Rouge advices represented the river rising, with a crevasse just above the town, from which great damage had ensued. The cotton trade was animated, and the arrival and departure of way steamers was duly chronicled.

Respecting the organization of the judiciary of Louisiana *The True Delta* says:

The organization of the Judiciary of the State has been completed, so far as the appointment of a full bench of the Supreme Judges, the District Courts of New-Orleans, and the Second and Third Judicial Districts, can make it so. The refusal of Mr. Roselius to accept the office of Chief-Justice necessitated a reconstruction of the Court, as it was first announced. It now stands as follows: Chief-Justice, William B. Hyman; Associate Judges, Labauve, Ilsley, Jones and Howell. We learn that there will be a meeting of the Court for the purpose of fully organizing on Monday next.

The District Courts have been reconstructed, by making some changes and filling the two vacancies formerly existing in the Fourth and Fifth. The following are the Judges of the District Courts of New-Orleans: First District, Edmund Abell; Second, John W. Thomas; Third, Ernest T. Fellows; Fourth, Paul E. Theard; Fifth, Guy Duplantier; and Sixth, Charles Leaumont. The Second and Third Judicial Districts have also been recognized by the appointment of Judge A. Cazabat to the bench of the former, and R. T. Posey to the latter. The Second Judicial District comprises the parishes of Jefferson, St. Bernard and Plaquemines; the Third those of Baton Rouge, East and West, St. Charles, St. James, etc.

With the exception of Judge Howell, the Supreme Court is composed of Judges heretofore appointed, as noticed by us at the time. Judge Howell is well known to our citizens as the Judge of the Sixth District Court from 1859 until his transfer to the Second District, on the resignation of Judge Whitaker. He occupied this position but a short time, when he resigned and resumed the practice of law. His appointment to the Supreme Bench is, in our opinion, a decided acquisition to that high tribunal.

A correspondent of *The Times* at Cairo, Ill., writing March 26, narrates the following, respecting the operations among guerrillas in Kentucky:

Capt. Gregory, commanding a company of newly recruited Kentuckians, started from Paducah on the 21st inst., bound on a guerrilla hunt, taking with him 20 men. When 25 miles from the city, Col. Cunningham, volunteer aid to Capt. Gregory, received information that the notorious bushwhacker, Capt. McDougal, with 75 men, was quartered at a house some two miles distant. Hastily assembling his small force, which was in squads scouring the country in different directions, Capt. Gregory started toward the spot indicated, which he neared at 10 o'clock at night. When about a quarter of a mile from the house the men were dismounted, and their horses concealed in the woods; the troops were instructed to crawl up and surround the house, trusting to the darkness and caution to effect a surprise.

Fearing that in the hand to hand encounter, that was likely to ensue friends might be mistaken for foes, a password was given out, with instructions that any one failing to give it when challenged was to be shot down.

These arrangements being completed, the heroic little band moved cautiously forward, when within easy pistol range of the house they were discovered and the alarm given. Immediately there were signs of commotion in the house and attempts made to escape—but Gregory had completely surrounded them, and every one who had the temerity to show his head was shot. Captain Gregory, with an Ellsworth's rashness, rushed to the door alone, almost at the guerrillas and pulled trigger, but for some cause unknown the gun did not go off, whereupon the guerrillas fired and the brave Captain fell dead, pierced by a bullet through the brain.

The death of their leader so exasperated the men that they rushed upon the enemy with a shriek of revenge, and commenced an indiscriminate slaughter. But the enemy, as soon as they discovered the actual strength, of the Unionists, rallied and drove them out of the house, but dare not pursue beyond the friendly shelter of its walls. Our men resumed their old position around the house, where they remained until near morning, when, learning that the enemy were receiving reinforcements from another band about a mile distant [illegible]

RECONSTRUCTION.

IMPORTANT SPEECH BY THE PRESIDENT.

WASHINGTON, Tuesday, April 11, 1865.

The Executive Departments, including the President's mansion, were again illuminated to-night, and adorned with transparencies and national flags, as were also many places of business and private dwellings. Bonfires blazed in many parts of the city, and rockets were fired. Thousands of persons of both sexes repaired to the Executive Mansion, and after several airs had been played by the band, the President, in response to the numerous calls, appeared at an upper window. The cheering with which he was greeted having ceased, he spoke as follows:

We meet this evening, not in sorrow, but in gladness of heart. The evacuation of Petersburg and Richmond, and the surrender of the principal insurgent army, give hope of a righteous and speedy peace, whose joyous expression cannot be restrained. In the midst of this, however, He from whom all blessings flow must not be forgotten. A call for a National Thanksgiving is being prepared, and will be duly promulgated. Nor must those whose harder part gives us the cause of rejoicing be overlooked. Their honors must not be parceled out with others. I, myself, was near the front and had the high pleasure of transmitting much of the good news to you. But no part of the honor for plan or execution is mine. To Gen. Grant, his skillful officers and brave men all belong. The gallant navy stood ready, but was not in reach to take active part. By these recent successes the re-inauguration of the national authority—reconstruction, which has had a large share of thought from the first—is pressed much more closely upon our attention. It is fraught with great difficulty. Unlike a case of war between independent nations, there is no authorized organ for us to treat with. No one man has authority to give up the rebellion for any other man. We simply must begin with and mold from disorganized and discordant elements. Nor is it a small additional embarrassment that we, the loyal people, differ among ourselves as to the mode, manner, and measure of reconstruction. As a general rule, I abstain from reading the reports of attacks upon myself, wishing not to be provoked by that to which I cannot properly offer an answer. In spite of this precaution, however, it comes to my knowledge that I am much censured for some supposed agency in setting up and seeking to sustain the new State government of Louisiana. In this I have done just so much and no more than the public knows. In the annual message of December, 1863, and the accompanying proclamation, I presented a plan of reconstruction, as the phrase goes, which I promised, if adopted by any State, would be acceptable to and sustained by the Executive Government of the nation. I distinctly stated that this was not the only plan which might possibly be acceptable; and I also distinctly protested that the Executive claimed no right to say when or whether members should be admitted to seats in Congress from such States. This plan was in advance submitted to the then Cabinet and approved by every member of it. One of them suggested that I should then, and in that connection apply the emancipation proclamation to the theretofore excepted parts of Virginia and Louisiana, that I should drop the suggestion about apprenticeship for freed people, and that I should omit the protest against my own power in regard to the admission of members of Congress. But even he approved every part and parcel of the plan which has since been employed or touched by the action of Louisiana. The new Constitution of Louisiana, declaring emancipation for the whole State, practically applies the proclamation to the part previously excepted. It does not adopt apprenticeship for freed people, and is silent, as it could not well be otherwise, about the admission of members to Congress. So that as it applied to Louisiana, every member of the Cabinet fully approved the plan. The message went to Congress, and I received many commendations of the plan, written and verbal, and not a single objection to it from any professed emancipationist came to my knowledge until after the news reached Washington that the people of Louisiana had begun to move in accordance with it. From about July, 1862, I had corresponded with different persons supposed to be interested in seeking a reconstruction of a State Government for Louisiana. When the message of 1863 with the plan before-mentioned reached New-Orleans, Gen. Banks wrote me that he was confident that the people, with his military coöperation, would reconstruct substantially on that plan. I wrote to him and some of them to try it. They tried it, and the result is known. Such has been my only agency in getting up the Louisiana Government. As to sustaining it, my promise is out, as before stated; but as bad promises are better broken than kept, I shall treat this as a bad promise, and break it whenever I shall be convinced that keeping it is adverse to the public interest, but I have not yet been so convinced. I have been shown a letter on this subject (supposed to be an able one), in which the writer expresses regret that my mind has not seemed to be definitely fixed on the question, whether the seceded States, so called, are in the Union or out of it. It would, perhaps, add astonishment to his regret were he to learn that since I have found professed Union men endeavoring to answer that question, I have purposely forborne any public expression upon it. As appears to me, that question has not been, nor yet is, a practically material one, and that any discussion of it, while it thus remains practically immaterial, could have no effect other than the mischievous one of dividing our friends. As yet, whatever it may become, that question is bad as the basis of a controversy, and good for nothing at all—a merely pernicious abstraction. We all agree that the seceded States, so called, are out of their proper practical relation with the Union, and that the sole object of the Government, civil and military, in regard to those States, is to again get them into that proper practical relation. I believe that it is not only possible but, in fact, easier, to do this without deciding or even considering whether those States have ever been out of the Union than with it. Finding themselves safely at home, it would be utterly immaterial whether they had been abroad. Let us all join in doing the acts necessary to restore the proper practical relations between these States and the Union, and each forever after innocently indulge his own opinion, whether in doing the acts he brought the States from without, into the Union, or only gave them proper assistance, they never having been out of it. The amount of constituency, so to speak, on which the new Louisiana Government rests, would be more satisfactory to all if it contained 50,000, 30,000, or even 20,000, instead of only about 12,000, as it does. It is also unsatisfactory to some that the elective franchise is not given to the colored man. I would myself prefer that it were now conferred on the very intelligent, and on those who serve our cause as soldiers. Still the question is not whether the Louisiana Government, as it stands, is quite all that is desirable. The question is, will it be wiser to take it as it is and help to improve it, or to reject and disperse it? Can Louisiana be brought into proper practical relation with the Union sooner by sustaining or by discarding her new State Government? Some twelve thousand voters in the heretofore Slave State of Louisiana have sworn allegiance to the Union, assumed to be the rightful political power of the State, held elections, organized a State Government, adopted a Free State Constitution, giving the benefit of the public schools equally to black and white, and empowering the Legislature to confer the elective franchise upon the colored man.

This Legislature has already voted to ratify the Constitutional Amendment recently passed by Congress abolishing Slavery throughout the Nation. These twelve thousand persons are thus fully committed to the Union, and to perpetuate freedom in the State, committed to the very things, and nearly all things the Nation wants, and they ask the Nation's recognition and its assistance to make good this committal.

Now, if we reject and spurn them, we do our utmost to disorganize and disperse them. We, in fact, say to the white man, You are worthless, or worse; we will neither help you nor be helped by you. To the blacks we say, This cup of liberty, which these, your old masters, hold to your lips, we will dash from you, and leave you to the chances of gathering the spilled and scattered contents in some vague and undefined when, where and how.

If this course, discouraging and paralyzing both white and black, has any tendency to bring Louisiana into popular practical relations with the Union, I have so far been unable to perceive it. If, on the contrary, we sustain and recognize the new government of Louisiana, the converse of all this is made true. We encourage the hearts and nerve the arms of 12,000 to adhere to their work and argue for it, and feed it, and it, and grow it, and ripen it to a complete success.

The colored man, too, in seeing all united for him, is inspired with vigilance, and energy and daring to the same end. Grant that he desires the elective franchise, will he not attain it sooner by saving the already advanced steps toward it than by running backward over them? Concede that the new Government of Louisiana is only to what it should be as the egg is to the fowl, we shall sooner have the fowl by hatching the egg than by smashing it. [Laughter.]

Again, if we reject Louisiana we also reject our vote in favor of the proposed amendment to the National Constitution. To meet this proposition, it has been argued that no more than three-fourth of those States which have not attempted secession are necessary to validly ratify the amendment. I do not commit myself against this further than to say that such a ratification would be questionable and sure to be persistently questioned, while a ratification by three-fourths of all the States would be unquestioned and unquestionable.

I repeat the question, can Louisiana be brought into practical relation with the Union sooner by sustaining or by discarding her new State Government? What been sold of Louisiana will apply to other States. And yet so great peculiarities pertain to each State and such important and sudden changes occur in the same State, and withal so new and unprecedented is the whole case, that no exclusive and inflexible plan can safely be prescribed as to details and collaterals. Such exclusive and inflexible plan would surely become a new entanglement.

Important principles may and must be inflexible. In the present situation, as the phrase goes, it may be my duty to make some new announcement to the people of the South. I am considering and shall not fail to act when satisfied that action will be proper.

The President, during the delivery of the above speech, was frequently interrupted by applause, and on its conclusion, in the midst of the cheering the band struck up a patriotic air when he bowed and retired.

There were repeated calls for Senator Sumner, but he was not present.

Senator Harlan of Iowa was then called for, and after the applause had subsided he directed attention to two principles settled or to be settled by the closing contest: First, the American people had decided that the majority of the voters of the Republic should control its destinies and the incipient processes of making its laws. Second, that no part of the Republic should ever be permitted by force to divide it.

The punishment of traitors lay in the hands of Congress, and the Constitution pointed out clearly what constituted treason. Those who hatched the treason should suffer the penalty, and under Congress he was willing to trust the future in the hands of the citizens elected a second time to see the laws faithfully executed.

Senator Harlan's remarks were applauded.

The assemblage dispersed after vociferous huzzas and the performance by the band. A larger and more enthusiastic meeting has seldom if ever before been held in front of the Executive Mansion.

ADMIRAL FARRAGUT IN BALTIMORE.

His Reception by the City Authorities.

BALTIMORE, Tuesday, April 11, 1865.

Vice-Admiral David G. Farragut, U. S. Navy, arrived here at 8 o'clock this morning from Fortress Monroe, in the steamer Louisiana, Captain Porter, and was received at the wharf by a large detachment of military, ordered out by Gen. W. W. Morris, the Mayor and Committee, and many citizens.

He was accompanied by his wife and Mrs. Captain Pinnock, Miss Curtiss, Miss Buttrick, and Mrs. Col. Lamb.

As soon as the steamer was announced to be at the wharf, Mayor Chapman proceeded to welcome the Admiral to the city, accompanied by the Committees of the two branches.

The procession was then formed and the Admiral was escorted to the Eutaw House, receiving on his way thither enthusiastic greetings from the citizens.

The city Councils gave him a public dinner this afternoon. He leaves to-morrow for New-York.

From Fortress Monroe.

FORTRESS MONROE, Monday, April 10, 1865.

The steamship Arago arrived here at 6:30 o'clock yesterday evening, with Henry Ward Beecher and party, from New-York bound to Fort Sumter. Owing to the south-easterly wind, the Arago was somewhat later in reaching here than was expected.

Judge Holt, Provost-Marshal General Fry and others were here yesterday, awaiting the arrival of the Arago. The entire party subsequently put to sea. At the time the weather indicated the approach of a storm. To-day the storm set in. It has rained heavily all day, and a dense fog now prevails.

Jeff. Davis at Danville.

From The Washington Republican, April 11.

Parties have arrived from Danville within our lines, who report that the fugitive insurgent, Jeff. Davis, arrived at Danville on Monday afternoon last, covered with dust and perspiration. His only baggage consisted of three dilapidated trunks, which looked hardly fit for a journey to Mexico.

Jeff. was accompanied by two or three members of his Cabinet, and the whole party seemed to be in an extremely demoralized condition.

Breckinridge, the Rebel Secretary of War, had not turned up, and was not heard from, although diligent [illegible]

A PROCLAMATIO[N]

Treatment of National Vessels [by] Foreign Powers.

WASHINGTON, Tuesday, April 11, 186[5].

Another important proclamation is issued [to-]day, claiming that our vessels of war in foreign p[orts] shall no longer be subjected to restrictions as at pre[sent], but shall have the same right and hospitalities w[hich] are extended to foreign men-of-war in the ports of [the] United States, and declaring that hereafter the cru[isers] of every nation shall receive the treatment which those ports they accord to ours, as follows:

Whereas, For some time past vessels-of-war of [the] United States have been refused in certain ports p[rivi]leges and immunities to which they were entitle[d by] treaty, public law, or the comity of nations, at the s[ame] time that vessels-of-war of the country wherein said privileges and immunities have been with[held] have enjoyed them fully and uninterruptedly in ports of the United States, which condition of th[ings] has not always been forcibly resisted by the U[nited] States, although, on the other hand, they have no[t at] times failed to protest against and declare their di[ssat]isfaction with the same. In the view of the U[nited] States no condition any longer exists which can [be] claimed to justify the denial to them by any one of [such] nations of the customary naval rights such as has [here]tofore been so unnecessarily persisted in; now, th[ere]fore, I, Abraham Lincoln, President of the U[nited] States, do hereby make known that if, a[fter] a reasonable time shall have elapsed [for] the intelligence of this proclamation to [have] reached any foreign country in whose [ports] the said privileges and immunities shall have b[een] refused as aforesaid, they shall continue to be so refu[sed], then and thenceforth the same privileges and imm[uni]ties shall be refused to the vessels-of-war of the cou[ntry] in the ports of the United States, and this refusal [shall] continue until the war vessels of the United States have been placed upon an entire equality in the for[eign] ports aforesaid with similar vessels of other coun[tries]. The United States, whatever claim or pretense [may] have existed heretofore, are now at least entitle[d to] claim and concede an entire and friendly equal[ity of] rights and hospitalities with all maritime nations.

In witness thereof, I have hereunto set my hand, and c[aused] the seal of the United States to be affixed. Do[ne at] the City of Washington, this eleventh day of Ap[ril, in] the year of Our Lord 1865, and of the Independe[nce of] the United States of America, the eighty-ninth.

ABRAHAM LINCOL[N].

By the President: WILLIAM H. SEWARD, Secretary of S[tate].

REJOICINGS.

In New-York City.

PRAISE TO GOD AT OLD TRINITY.

Trinity Church was never more sorely t[ried] than yesterday. Long before noon, the devout [wor]shipers who are at all times glad to utter praise [to] Omnipotence for mercies given began to fill the se[ats], but when the hour appointed for the *Te Deum* and o[ther] exercises arrived, not only were the seats filled and aisles crowded, but the entire surroundings of [the] building presented much such a spectacle as do[es the] doorsteps of a Romish Cathedral on Sabbath morn[ing]. It was not the vulgar crowd merely, either. W[ell,] many of the noblest and fairest of our metropolis [had] been wise in time and had found admission, there [were] more than twice fifty times "five foolish virgins" [who] besought piteously but in vain for entrance. So be[sieged was] the church, in front of the church, and on either si[de of] the church, both sexes, both colors and all ages c[row]ded together for one glance at a door or window.

We had intended to state, in this report, what di[stin]guished persons were present and took part in the [ex]ercises. We were saved that trouble; everybody [was] present, and as for the exercises—those who were [there] body will gladly excuse a recalling of the exercises [at] least so far as the congregational part was concerned.

At one o'clock p. m., the Rev. Dr. Haight commen[ced] the services by the reading of the fifth chapter of [Mat]thew (the Sermon on the Mount), followed by [the] Dr. Vinton in prayer. A psalm of thanks for vic[tory] was then sung by the choir, after which the remain[ing] prayers of the service for this occasion were recited.

The choir then sang the *Te Deum Laudamus* of B[...] in A.

Dr. Vinton announced the circumstances that [had] been the occasion of this service, and spoke brief[ly of] the influence which religion should have upon the m[inds] of all. Referring to the precepts of our Savior w[hich] had been read, in the sermon on the Mount, the spea[ker] expressed a devout hope that charity might preva[il in] the dispositions of all toward those who, misguided [and] erring though they be, are yet our brethren.

At the close of his remarks, Dr. Vinton made th[e re]quest that, in the singing of the *Gloria in Excelsis*, [every] individual voice in the assembly should be raise[d in] thanksgiving to Almighty God for the abundant [bless]ings which His grace has showered upon our na[tion] and ourselves.

Thereupon the great organ poured forth its thun[der] of music, under the skillful touch of Dr. Cutler; [and] under the guidance of the choir, the entire congre[gation] arose and chanted, with the heartiest unani[mity,] that noble anthem of the Episcopal Church, the *G[loria] in Excelsis* of Tallis in G. It is seldom in one's life that a scene of such tremendous significance is b[efore] him. We may hear, any Sabbath that we choose [to go] to Plymouth Church, 3,000 people in grand chorus [sing]ing the praise of our Lord; and we shall often [hear,] perhaps, the notes of the organ pealing forth [more] thrilling music than that which helps vocalize [the] words of the *Gloria*. But not once in a lifetime do [we see] men have the proud honor of standing, individuals [of a] vast nation, devoutly in the temple of the Lord, sin[ging] praise to Him for the triumph of a war of principle [over] the power of Satan.

The grass does not grow before the doors of Tri[nity;] business men hasten hither and thither as ever, [but] to accomplish business duties; but within these doo[rs a] congregation of the best and the fairest, of the [rich] and the poor, of the thoughtful and the careless, met to say, "For Thine abundant mercy in saving [the] Republic—for the destruction of tyranny, sla[very,] treachery—for Thy restoring this Thy land to us [rid]ded of at least one great evil—we give glory to Thee [in] the highest!"

After the Rev. Dr. Dix had pronounced the ben[edic]tion, Mr. W. Diller, assistant organist of Trinity, [per]formed Handel's "Hallelujah Chorus" upon the or[gan] as a fitting close of the service. The voluntary [after]ward consisted of national airs, pealing forth while [the] great assembly slowly melted away.

THE SALUTE AT UNION-SQUARE.

At 12½ o'clock yesterday, a detachment of [the] 75th Heavy Artillery made their appearance at U[nion-]square with four 24-pound howitzers, under the c[ommand] of Capts. Keim, of Battery B, and Stoughtenb[urg, of] Battery G. Three of the howitzers were place[d in] front of the Everett House, facing the square, and [a] salute of 100 guns was immediately proceeded [with,] shaking the ground, and threatening dire devast[ation] to windows in the neighborhood, and filling the [air] with a cloud that portended nothing but victory [and] thanksgiving.

In Hudson.

HUDSON, N. Y., Tuesday, April 11, 18[65].

Glory hallelujah! Glory to God in the h[igh]est! Every bell is ringing—every gun is speakin[g in] thunder tones—every heart is dancing with joy, [over] the surrender of Gen. Lee.

Nearly $800 was subscribed in five minutes at [the] Post-Office for the relief of our sick and wou[nded] soldiers, and contributions are flowing in freely fro[m all] sides for this object.

A grand celebration and illumination is the [pro]gramme for to-night.

The excitement is indeed intense, and old Huds[on is] one mass of patriotism and joy.

In Detroit.

DETROIT, Monday, April 10, 18[65].

Business to-day is entirely suspended throu[gh]out the State. The hearts of the people are thri[lled] with joy and gratitude over the surrender of Gen. [Lee]. The demonstrations in this city are the most ent[husi]astic and joyous ever known.

Chapter 16

From War to Peace

Abraham Lincoln's assassination was the capstone killing that finished off the deadliest conflict in American history. Around 620,000 soldiers perished by it—360,000 on the Union side, 260,000 on the Confederate. Additional tens of thousands of Southern civilians succumbed to either malnutrition or exposure. Although in absolute numbers, more Northern men died in the war, proportionally, the South suffered the greater loss. One-quarter of Southern white men of military age—3 percent of the entire Southern white population—were wiped out. For the Southern states, where the overwhelming majority of the combat occurred, the destruction went far beyond the loss of life. Apart from the wreckage of slavery, which had been the primary source of Southern wealth, half of the South's agricultural machinery and 40 percent of its livestock had been decimated, leaving its economy in ruins. In 1860, the South had been the richest region in the United States in terms of per capita income among whites. In 1865, it was the poorest region, a dubious distinction it still holds today. In the wake of all this destruction and upheaval, wrathful emotions had been unleashed on both sides—feelings that were bound to endure even though the military conflict was over. After what had passed between them over the course of a long and bloody war, how were the people of the North and South supposed to come together again as friends and compatriots?

As they had during the war, Southern newspapers entered the breach to guide their readers through what was a terribly chaotic and uncertain time. Most did so with a healthy dose of pragmatism and a clear understanding of the futility of further resistance. Shrill and vengeful expressions of hatred toward the Union disappeared quickly from the Southern press—even from those papers that still had the same editor as in wartime. Instead, they aspired to lead Southerners through the painful process of accepting defeat, and to help them see the positive benefits to be derived from the reimposition of federal authority. Despite its strong feelings of lamentation, the *Countryman* wrote:

> A stern and solemn, as well as unpleasant duty devolves upon us, as the editor[s] of a newspaper. Our people look, in some measure, to their public journalists for instruction, when in doubt as to the proper course to pursue. We will not withhold from the people the light that is in us, however little that light may be.
>
> We have pondered our present condition well. . . . We confess, in all candor, before our conquerors, as well as before our own people, that we are deeply mortified—chagrined beyond endurance at the failure of our cause—the striking of our colors. . . . We survive our flag—we have outlived our country—and new duties devolve upon us, under our new relations. . . . And what is that duty?—We are a conquered people, and, according to all the received laws of nations, the conquerors have a right to dictate terms to the conquered, and to govern them by the public law. And even whether they have the right or not, they have the power, and they are going to use it—depend upon that. *Might*, after all, is *right*.
>
> We frankly tell our conquerors that if we could see any chance under heaven to further resist them successfully, we would certainly avail ourselves of all the means in our power to do so. But we also tell our people that it is not only folly to make further resistance, but it is [a] crime. . . . It is the duty of all of us, now, to obey the "powers that be." The federal military officers in our midst are the "powers that be," until the federal civil authorities prepare some sort of government for us.
>
> Any sort of government, it matters not how despotic it be, is better than no government at all. As things now stand, we have, in our midst, no immediate government. Everything is anarchy, and confusion. Mob law reigns with worse than tyranny; and the only law left us is the law of the robber, and the highwayman. There is no security for life, nor property. Our own people, turned loose without restraint, are biting and devouring each other. We have more cause of immediate dread from the factions and feuds in the bosom of our own society, than from any other cause.
>
> In this view of the case, we consider it the duty of our conquerors to give us some sort of government. As we are satisfied in our mind that this must come at last, we wish it to come immediately. . . . Thus our people may have *some* protection against the bands of freebooters all over the country, as often under confederate, as federal colors.
>
> When the federals establish their government, we assure our people it is best for them to obey it. No possible good can come from resisting it. They should acquiesce in its mandates promptly, if they cannot do so cheerfully. And then every time any of their rights, under the terms of capitulation . . . are violated, they should approach the federal authorities with boldness and confidence, but with respect, for a redress of their grievances. This is the course we have marked out for ourself, and we recommend all others to pursue the same.
>
> We do not recommend anyone to evince any slavish fear of the yankees; we do not advise our people to go forward like the meek ox, with neck extended, and invite the yoke. People who would do this . . . we do not consider good enough for us to spit upon, nor for us to walk upon, if they would lie down for us to trample them under foot. Should they offer their vile carcasses as a pavement to save our sandals from the mire, we would avoid the contamination thus proffered our soles, and tread aside into the mud. Any gentlemanly yankee would kick such people promptly for proving themselves such debased lickspittles.
>
> What we recommend to our people is, to promptly obey the "powers that be," at the same

time that they preserve the dignity, and manly personal independence of gentlemen who have failed in a good cause. . . . Let it be understood, by all parties, that we are the friend of law and order.[1]

Sensing that the pulse of public opinion was sullen, spiteful, and averse to cooperating with the North, the *Macon Telegraph* similarly tried to remind its readers that self-interest, as well as self-pride, demanded that they adopt a more amicable attitude toward their former enemies:

> Some may think it more compatible with personal dignity and the spirit of freemen, to maintain a position of imbecile and ineffective defiance—a sullen and vindictive demeanor toward the victor—a resolute determination to hold no intercourse with him, either social, commercial or political—to refuse all co-operation even in the essential matters of preserving public order. . . . These ideas and purposes seem to float in many brains, but in our judgment they are the offspring of an excusably wounded pride, disappointment and temporary passion, and not of common sense or sound discretion. If your house be in flames, no matter who set it on fire, the best thing you can do is to join in with anybody, who will help you save the building, or even a portion of it. So we believe it is now the part of interest and of true dignity and manhood for every Southern man to assist in restoring peace and public order under the new condition of things. The fact that our purposes have been defeated, does not release us from a common obligation to God, society and ourselves, to do the best we can under the situation. . . . Is it hard? Grant it—but is there any better, more rational, more dignified course left open to us?[2]

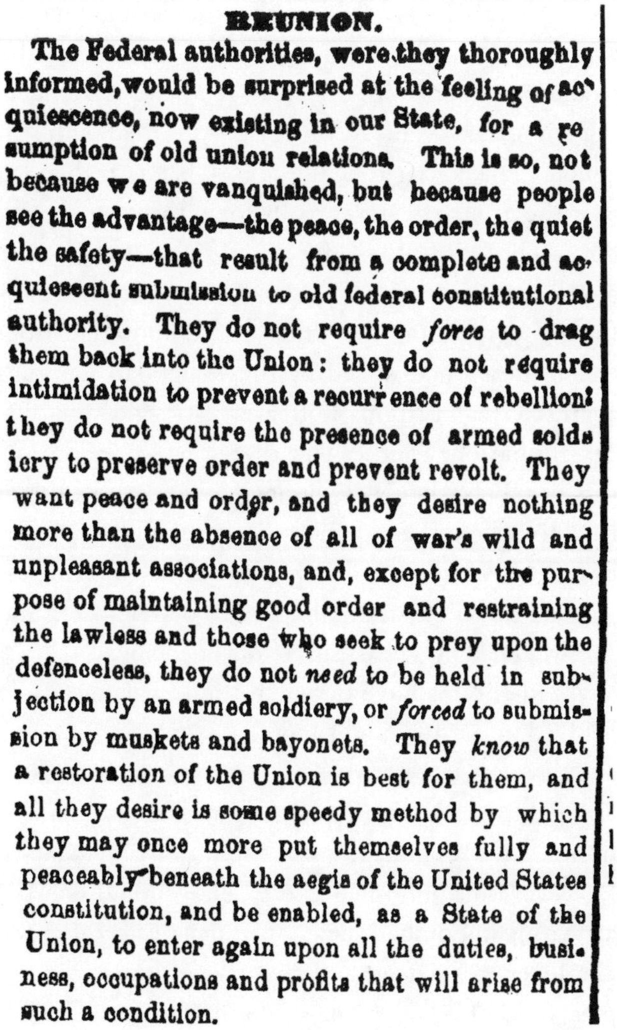

REUNION.

The Federal authorities, were they thoroughly informed, would be surprised at the feeling of acquiescence, now existing in our State, *for a re*sumption of old union relations. This is so, not because we are vanquished, but because people see the advantage—the peace, the order, the quiet the safety—that result from a complete and acquiescent submission to old federal constitutional authority. They do not require *force* to drag them back into the Union: they do not require intimidation to prevent a recurrence of rebellion: they do not require the presence of armed soldsiery to preserve order and prevent revolt. They want peace and order, and they desire nothing more than the absence of all of war's wild and unpleasant associations, and, except for the purpose of maintaining good order and restraining the lawless and those who seek to prey upon the defenceless, they do not *need* to be held in subjection by an armed soldiery, or *forced* to submission by muskets and bayonets. They *know* that a restoration of the Union is best for them, and all they desire is some speedy method by which they may once more put themselves fully and peaceably beneath the aegis of the United States constitution, and be enabled, as a State of the Union, to enter again upon all the duties, business, occupations and profits that will arise from such a condition.

Macon Telegraph, May 20, 1865.
In trying to serve as voices of reason, many Southern newspapers quickly embraced reunion and welcomed the return of peace.

The attitude of the Southern press toward reunion was somewhat ambivalent. On one hand, they pragmatically accepted defeat as a fact that could not be denied or avoided. At the same time, though, they remained resistant to admitting that the South had done anything wrong. According to the newspapers, the Southern people were supposed to submit to federal authority, but never were they to *behave* submissively or shamefully. They still had their dignity to protect. This preoccupation with Southern honor would, over time, give birth to an interpretation of the Civil War that has come to be called the Lost Cause. The Lost Cause offered Southerners a framework for understanding the war that acknowledged the glory and goodness of the Confederate war effort, despite its failure. It is a rendering of wartime events to which many in the South still adhere. The cornerstone of the Lost Cause is the idea that the Southern states really fought not for slavery but rather for freedom—for states' rights, irrespective of the slavery issue. In this way, the South's bid for independence from the Union was no different from the contest once waged by the American colonies against Great Britain. Both were struggles for self-determination. Southerners, therefore, were not traitors or rebels; they were honorable citizens who had tried to uphold the American heritage of liberty. Even though they lost the fight, their cause was nevertheless just and right. They had simply been outnumbered and overwhelmed by a physically stronger enemy.

As historians have detailed, the Lost Cause fully evolved in the 1870s and 1880s, as Confederate veterans developed a network of fraternal organizations and published a corpus of stories and testimonials to honor and commemorate their wartime deeds. However, this notion of a Lost Cause actually started appearing in Southern newspapers *immediately* after the Confederacy's defeat, and grew out of ideas that the press had helped to popularize during the war.[3] The following statement from the *Galveston Tri-Weekly News* embodies it perfectly:

> We have conversed with many of our soldiers. . . . They all admit that the superior power of the enemy has made it necessary that we relinquish our claims to a separate nationality, but they will not admit that they can be, or will submit to be, treated as felons deserving punishment, because they attempted to maintain their claim to independence. Our people believe that they had as much right to assert such a claim as our forefathers had. . . . Our people will never admit that they have made themselves criminals, by attempting to do the same thing that our fathers did before us.
>
> The fact that they have been overpowered proves nothing in regard to the right and justice of their cause. The right to a government of our own choice is a great American right, asserted for us by the fathers of the revolution of 1776, and was made the only ground of justification for their rebellion against the mother country. If three millions of people had the right to rebel and set up a government of their own, have not eight millions of people as perfect a right to do the same thing? Our fathers were aided by France and succeeded in getting their claim acknowledged; we could get neither aid nor encouragement from any nation on earth, and after having resisted the most cruel and desolating war ever prosecuted since the dark ages, for four years, we are compelled to admit that we have been overpowered. In this there is nothing dishonorable, but on the contrary, we believe that the deeds of the Confederate armies, in their unparalleled struggle for civil liberty, will be the admiration of posterity for all time to come. There are those who may stigmatize us as traitors and rebels at the present day, but so were Washington and his compatriots of '76, stigmatized in their day.
>
> We have been acting precisely upon the very same principles which governed them, and it is not in the power of human ingenuity to disguise that great truth; that truth, though temporarily ignored, must yet prevail and vindicate the righteousness of our cause. We must simply yield to superior power, but we contend that while we must all now return to our allegiance to the former government, . . . no true Southern man can ever have occasion to blush for the struggle we have made to establish a separate government; nor can any true patriot of the South ever join in any attempt to dishonor the memory of the great generals and brave soldiers who have fallen in this struggle. . . . As the passions and prejudices of the present day subside, it will be seen and admitted by all that the people of the South have been actuated by their honest convictions of duty as patriots

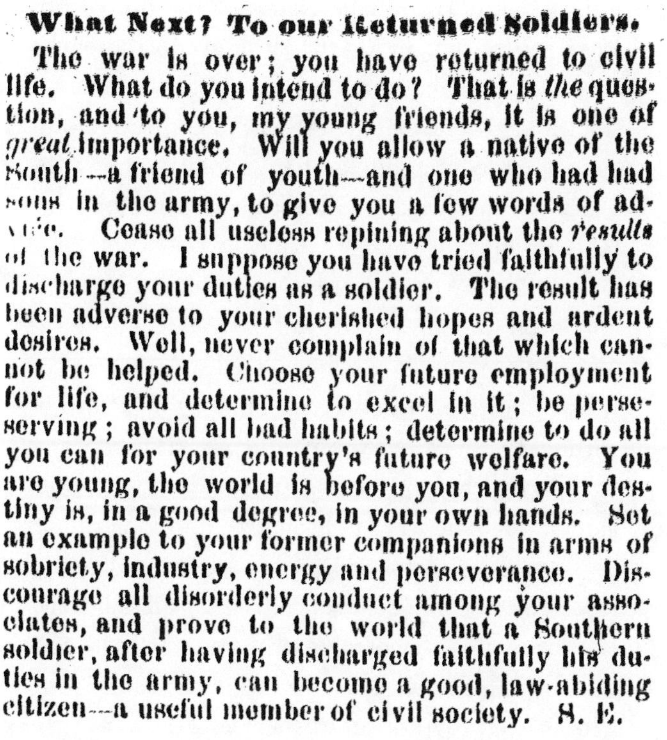

What Next? To our Returned Soldiers.

The war is over; you have returned to civil life. What do you intend to do? That is *the* question, and to you, my young friends, it is one of *great* importance. Will you allow a native of the South—a friend of youth—and one who had had sons in the army, to give you a few words of advice. Cease all useless repining about the *results* of the war. I suppose you have tried faithfully to discharge your duties as a soldier. The result has been adverse to your cherished hopes and ardent desires. Well, never complain of that which cannot be helped. Choose your future employment for life, and determine to excel in it; be persevering; avoid all bad habits; determine to do all you can for your country's future welfare. You are young, the world is before you, and your destiny is, in a good degree, in your own hands. Set an example to your former companions in arms of sobriety, industry, energy and perseverance. Discourage all disorderly conduct among your associates, and prove to the world that a Southern soldier, after having discharged faithfully his duties in the army, can become a good, law-abiding citizen—a useful member of civil society. S. E.

Galveston Tri-Weekly News, June 2, 1865.
Now that the war was over, soldiers were advised to put aside any lingering feelings of hostility toward the Union and to return to their places as peaceable citizens of the United States.

> and as freemen, and that they have conscientiously believed that their cause was the cause of justice, of truth and of human liberty. We may and should yield obedience to the authorities established over us by superior power, but we cannot (if we would) yield our honest convictions that we have been struggling in a righteous cause.[4]

The Southern press was prickly and defensive in considering the reasons for the Confederacy's failure. Throughout the war, they had constantly harped against the selfishness of extortioners and the despondency of "croakers" who sapped the strength and will of the Southern people. Now such complaints disappeared from the newspapers. As far as they were concerned, the Confederacy had not fallen apart internally; the Union had smashed it with overwhelming military force. Defeat did not signify "a want of patriotism or bravery on the part of our soldiery," a Louisiana paper affirmed; Southerners surrendered "through compulsion only, to a force superior in numbers." And that superior physical power had been applied brutally and ruthlessly against the Southern people. The Union had not won an honorable victory; rather, as the *Countryman* described, "the yankees have overpowered us, as the *beasts* in the African jungle overpower the *man* that crosses their track." Southerners believed that, in a fair fight, the Confederacy would have won.[5]

As the newspapers of the time indicate, Southerners also deeply resented being branded as rebels and traitors. Convinced that the Southern people had been right to secede from the Union, the press not only commanded them to hold their heads high in accepting defeat but also demanded that Northerners show them proper respect in welcoming them back into the Union. The *Texas Republican* declared imperiously:

> While it would be essentially wrong and unwise to do anything to revive or keep alive the spirit of animosity created by this war, it would be equally disgraceful to exhibit a truculent, mean-spirit. We trust that none of our citizens will ever by any such conduct, forfeit their own self-respect or the respect of their friends.
>
> Men must not suppose, that because the Southern Confederacy is dead, its memory will become odious either to this generation or to generations that are to follow. The moving spirit which impelled the revolution sprung from an exalted attachment to free institutions, and, whatever opinions may be entertained as to the causes which produced the struggle, the revolution itself will be honorable as long as virtue and heroism are admired among men. . . . It may be the policy of our conquerors to stigmatise the conduct of our people as treason and endeavor

to render it and them odious by punishments due only to infamy. But such treatment will fail of its object. . . . The Southern people have nothing to be ashamed of or to regret except failure, which is to be attributed to their having encountered the most powerful and determined people on the globe. Even our late enemies must respect and honor the heroism which has protracted a struggle for four years against such fearful odds.

The war is now over, and what sensible, good men of both sections, most desire, is peace and good will. There can be no peace and good will unless accompanied with kind actions. Let us meet the North in that spirit, with the hope that as they profess to love the Union, they will endeavor to so control its destinies that it may afford the blessings of good government to all.[6]

The underlying message was that the reimposition of federal authority was not such a terrible thing. If both sides embarked upon reunion in the right spirit—a spirit that acknowledged the equality and honor of the South—then the transition from war to peace could be smooth and seamless. It was a very different tune from the one whistled by the press during the war. For four years, Southern newspapers had constantly and vividly described the consequences of defeat in the most horrific terms. Now they aspired to put all of these fears—fears that they themselves had exacerbated—to rest. As the *Montgomery Mail* explained, "tabooists" in the Confederacy had really misled the public into believing that "subjugation" would be followed by the perpetration of unending atrocities by the Yankees:

> Those who advocated eternal war against the "Yankees," were eloquent in drawing frightful pictures of the consequences of "subjugation.". . . The word was a harsh one and expressed bondage, like that of the ox working for its master and bearing the yoke of labor upon its neck. We were to be, according to the tabooists, bondsmen to Northern masters, and despoiled of every right. . . . The war, they said, must go on until "independence or extermination" was wrought out, and in the latter event, those who survived the extermination would be at the mercy of the subjugator. We are left, then, to conjecture only as to what will be the Southern condition [after the war], but we think it will not be so terrible as the tabooists portray it. . . .
>
> Subjugation would only subject us to the same condition we left in 1861; will only subject us to the Constitution under which we lived so long. . . . But it was said that our constitutional rights would be withheld from us. We think otherwise. It is very true that during the war the constitution has been disregarded; that the war has been waged in violation of civilized usages; that its spirit has been savage and truculent, not to say diabolical. This is all sadly true. But the same is true of all internecine wars. The civil wars in England were conducted in the same spirit. The French revolution was worse. The war of the revolution of 1776 was equally as bad. But after these wars justice and humanity were restored. . . . Nor is there any more reason to suppose that the United States will be a despotism after peace is restored. The constitution will then be the shield and protection of all. The New Englander and the Western man will have the same interest in preserving it as the Southern man. . . .
>
> Our conclusion is, that "subjugation" is nothing worse than restoring the constitution which once protected us, and will protect us again; that subjugation is "a painted devil" to frighten the imaginations of the weak. It is certainly cheering to believe that the condition to which our disasters seem to have hurried us will not be so bad as the art of tabooism would make it.[7]

This effort to allay popular anxieties was natural enough. With the Confederate government gone and its armies disbanded, what else could the press legitimately do? Whipping up a public hysteria against reunion would only further embarrass the South and elicit the anger of the North. By promoting public tranquility, the newspapers hoped to convince the federal government that it did not need to station standing armies throughout the Southern states in order to pacify them. They believed that if Southerners showed goodwill towards their conquerors, they might be spared that humiliation. On a more positive note, the papers also emphasized that the restoration of peace gave the ruined Southern states a second chance—an opportunity to start again and recapture their former prosperity, with the help of their former enemies. The *North Carolina Standard*, already a long time disillusioned by the war, was quick to encourage its readers to think of reunion in such hopeful terms:

> Our people are just emerging from a desolating war, and a large majority of them are destitute not only of the comforts but of the necessaries of life. They have been compelled to drink the cup of "peaceable secession" to the dregs. They have lost life, property, comforts, everything but honor; and at one time many of them feared that even hope was gone. The contest is now virtually at an end, and it is the duty of every good citizen to strengthen the arm of just authority, and to aid in bringing order from chaos, so that industry may be protected and rewarded and our former prosperity and happiness restored. Up to the hour when the States south of us madly shot from their appropriate orbits in the federal system, the hand of the federal government had never been laid upon them but to protect and benefit them. The old flag never waved, whether on land or sea, but for their protection. And now, after a long and most desolating war between brethren, let us hope that the same flag, restored to its original place in the heavens, will wave as *our* flag once more and forever, protecting every one who may rest or labor under its gorgeous folds. We feel sure that it will. We feel sure that our recent enemies are now generous friends. We see, and hear, and feel this in all they say and do in our midst. But the ocean, after a storm, does not immediately subside. . . . It is so with society. Our people will need, for months to come, the strong arm of military power to protect them in their pursuits and to restore order to society. It is not for us to say by what mode this shall be accomplished, but only to declare our conviction that it is indispensable. Under proper auspices, and with the inducement to renewed labor which all our people will have, we may hope again to see our fields growing green for future harvests, our workshops crowded with industrious mechanics and artizans, our commerce whitening our waters, our schools resuming their operations, and plenty and happiness beaming among us. Let us look forward with hope to the good day which seems to be ahead of us, and endeavor to forget the sufferings through which we have passed. "The gods help those who help themselves." Let us all cheerfully "accept the situation," and go to work to improve our condition. We are all comparatively poor, but we have friends who will aid us,—we shall have the protection of a strong and good government, one that will extend to us credit for what we may need, and take pleasure in encouraging us in our efforts to restore our former prosperity.[8]

When the Confederacy had been struggling for independence, the notion of relying on the North for anything had been anathema. Allowing Northerners to establish a foothold on Southern soil was even more repellent. As the newspapers had described it, Southerners were supposed to fight to the death rather than see Yankees take over their lands and farms. With the dawning of peace, however, this attitude changed quickly, as the press looked forward to seeing Northerners, including those who had fought in the Union armies, settle in the Southern states and initiate an influx of labor and capital to rebuild them. According to the *Montgomery Mail*:

> The secession movement has been entirely crushed, and its advocates sentenced to silence and to shame.

This is a proper retribution, and the law of retribution is inexorable in its decrees. Four years since, the South was in the enjoyment of a prosperity and social quiet and happiness unequalled in the history of any people whose society rested on a slave basis. . . . With a climate not only favorable to the maintenance of life without much exertion, but courting an indulgence in tropical ease and eastern luxury, a soil in admirable adaptation to those ends, and a peculiar labor system that sympathised and affiliated with the people, the climate and the soil, it sustained the Southern sybarite in his lounging, lordly *abandon*.

But what to-day is the picture? It bears no drawing in detail. We can only give a few prominent points in the scene and forbear. The baronial hall in ashes, the bones of its lord lie whitening on the hills, and its sons and daughters, outcasts and wanderers in the valleys. These we say, are the prominent points in the picture, the relief is drawn in colors of humiliation and degradation, unequalled in the history of any christian people of modern days. . . .

Having a personal appreciation of the associations and relationships which will necessarily grow up in the future, between those who seriously differed in the past, . . . we very respectfully counsel the practice of the highest amenity both public and private, in the intercourse of the two people, and the practice of lenity in the exercise of [Union] authority. The people of the South are prostrate at the foot of their own proper and legitimate government, and however erring and criminal they may be supposed to be, they yet have the christian's right to demand *mercy* of a christian government, and nothing will so quickly restore weakened affection and loyalty, as granting it. . . .

The nature of the war has created a vacuum both in the population and the wealth of the South—on the other hand *both have increased* in the States of the North—wealth is overgrown, population is teeming, and these, like the waves of the sea ever seek their level. Millions of capital and thousands of men have already set in, in one united current, for the South—capital for investment, and men for homes; and we welcome them. In view of these facts, we suggest to the present authorities and the government of the United States, to deal as gently with the South, in its fallen estate, as is possible; for men in the North, yes, thousands of the very armies now in the South, will make their homes here, and the pleasantness or unpleasantness of their future lives very materially depends upon . . . the course of the government towards us. Treat us as a defeated people, but not as a subjugated one, and friendship and harmony will soon be restored, and the war forgotten.[9]

In attempting to guide and shape public opinion in the conquered Confederacy, newspapers adopted a realistic attitude. Instead of wallowing in the South's failures, they aimed to ready their readers for reunion, and to help them see the cheering possibilities that existed for them in the future. In part, doing this meant breaking with the past and abandoning the ranting anti-Northern rhetoric that had dominated wartime news coverage. However, other ideas that editors had used to fire up Southerners for war were more malleable and could be reconfigured to promote peace instead. This was particularly true of the South's religious beliefs. Throughout the fighting, the press had tried to stiffen the resolve of anxious and desponding Southerners with the knowledge that that if they behaved rightly, God would be on their side and bless their beleaguered country with success. The fall of the Confederacy did not negate these articles of faith; it just gave them a new spin. As the *Macon Telegraph* conceded, God obviously had withdrawn His support from the Confederacy. But by accepting this act of divine judgment against them and reforming their ways, the Southern people could return to His good graces and propel the South to new heights of glory in the postwar period:

Let us see what is our *actual condition* at present. We are at the *close of the war*. The red waves of destruction no longer surge over our land. The cannon's roar no longer reverberates among our hills and mountains, and the flames of burning cities do not now light up the midnight heavens. Death is not stalking abroad in our land, and destruction and dismay have ceased to hold high carnival in our midst. For all this we thank God. . . .

We labor, just now, under a great depression of business. . . . Trade is almost at a stand still and a mighty incubus seems to rest upon the public mind. The future is dark and uncertain; and these beget apprehension. Actual want is staring many of us in the face, and few avenues of relief appear to be left open to us. In addition, we know not what measures may be adopted by the general government: they may be severe; they may be intended as punishment for rebellion—we know not. But dread uncertainty casts a pall over the hearts of all. Nevertheless, we accept the new state of things: we bow to the Federal authority: we yield allegiance to the stars and stripes: we confess ourselves to be in the hands and subject to the power of the federal government: and to whatever it allots we submit gracefully. We willingly return to the old government and acknowledge that to do so is best for us. In the meanwhile we submit that mercy becometh a great and victorious people. We [believe] that the government at Washington really desires the well-being of the recovered States; and we here avow that, if *clemency* is exercised and *liberal measures* devised, a revival of prosperity will soon gladden the land, brotherhood will speedily cement the reunion, and the desire for peace and union which is now universal will give way to a higher feeling of respect and good will.

Under such circumstances as these, . . . what is our duty as a Christian people?

1. To accept our condition as an appointment of God. He has permitted, nay, guided the course of events. He ruled over us and for our good, and to what he assigns our lot we should yield a graceful acquiescence.

We are not a fanatical people. We have thought that God willed a severance of the Union; but since events have proven that He does not, it becomes us to bow in submission, and with cheerfulness. The actual state of fact cannot be gainsayed or denied—we are living within the Federal Union, and to the Constitution and Laws of that Union we should render unhesitating obedience; we owe allegiance to the Federal Government, and as law-abiding citizens and Christians, we should promptly respond to the calls of duty.

2. *Humility, repentance and reformation become us.* We have esteemed ourselves too highly—have prided ourselves upon our piety, wealth, respectability and chivalry, and God has abased us. We have hastened to be rich, and consequently have been pierced through with many sorrows. Let us confess our faults, and repent in the sight of God, and reform our conduct; then we may hope for his blessing and regain his favor. Sorely he has scourged us; but of little benefit will that scourging prove, if it lead not to reformation. Let us be a nation of Christian citizens—loyal to earthly and heavenly government, and then shall we be the happiest and the best of nations.

3. And this brings us to our last point. . . . Let true religion in all her forms receive the highest encouragement; let individual piety be made to assume a lofty rank; let public virtue, as a result of Christianity, vivify all the ramifications of society, and purify all the members of the body politic. Religion and morality are, indeed, the only safeguards of liberty, happiness and prosperity. . . . Let religion, then, be cultivated; let God be honored, and his reign acknowledged; let the forms and proprieties of morality prevail, and soon the dire effects of our late sad years will pass away, and industry and comfort, and success and honor, and contentment and happiness and prosperity will beam upon our land, and light up all its long future path to greatness and to glory.[10]

The South, in other words, would rise again.

In many ways, Northern papers depicted America's postwar future in terms that perfectly complemented the expectations of their Southern counterparts. As members of the Southern press had hoped, Northern observers looked at the defeated Confederacy as a land overflowing with opportunities that they were eager to exploit and enjoy. With the war over, the *Troy Times* envisioned that "the South can be made to blossom like the garden of Eden." Despite the enormous destruction wrought across the South—between the ruined fields, wasted livestock, demolished buildings, wrecked bridges and rail lines, and lost property of all kinds—hope sprang eternal in the North. Millions of plantation acres would now come under Northern cultivation, with millions of dollars in profit to be gained:

> Our people have always manifested a bold and adventurous spirit in the pursuit of wealth and power. When California opened to the world the magnificent treasures of her mountains and valleys, the dangers of a sea-passage "around the horn," and the rugged, forbidding life [of] the settler . . . were counted as naught compared to the glittering prospect, uncertain though it was, of gaining riches and position in the Eldorado State. In less than five years after the rush began, California was a full-grown, powerful State, admitted to an equality with the other States in the Federal Union. . . .
>
> The South opens a wider field with a more certain prospect of success to the immigrant. In agricultural resources, in mineral wealth, in the extent and variety of its productions, and its monopoly of some of the staples of commercial and manufacturing enterprise,—in the beauty of its climate—we may justly regard the Southern States as the fairest and most inviting portion of our vast domain. Virginia is rich in timber, mineral wealth, agricultural productions, and commercial developments. North Carolina has her turpentine and rosin, and her coal mines still untouched. South Carolina is less inviting, but grows along her sea coast the finest cotton in the world. Georgia, Louisiana, Alabama, and Mississippi produce cotton, rice, sugar and molasses, to an indefinite amount, and the former, in addition, sends to market the best pine and ship timber in the country. Florida produces little that is valuable except timber, though the missionary would find a field of labor among her ignorant, degraded population, and the student of natural history might be edified with a view of her sand-flies, moccasins and alligators that exist *ad libitum*. . . . Here we have a field for development as extended as, and more promising than, any other section of our country.
>
> The South, we know, has never been developed to anything like one-fifth its capacity. The system of labor and the policy of large estates forbade this. With free labor in the future, . . . and with land more generally distributed among the people, together with the introduction of useful agricultural and mechanical improvements in the work of production, the South will soon become . . . the most beautiful and productive country in the world. . . . On the Red River, on the Brazos, and on numberless bayous in Mississippi and Texas, there are millions of unredeemed acres that can be converted into splendid sugar estates. Cotton has ceased to be King, but it will always have a position in the markets of the world second to no other raw article of production. In 1860, the export of this staple amounted, at less than *eleven* cents per pound, to *one hundred and ninety-two million dollars!* . . . What an illimitable and exhaustless field is here opened up to the developing enterprise of the American people! The mind cannot grasp that magnificence of the prospect that is before us as a nation, if we make a proper use of the capabilities and resources of the country.[11]

These rich opportunities were not for the North only. They would redound to the benefit of both regions, making them equal partners in transforming the United States into the greatest and most resplendent nation on earth. Although Northerners and Southerners might be estranged for the moment, the *Albany Evening Journal* was confident that their future together would be harmonious and bright:

> The failure of their cause, is naturally keenly felt by the great mass of the Southern people. . . . But this feeling will be only temporary. The Southern people will gradually emerge from the pit of despondency into which they are now plunged. The "sober second thought" will reveal to them their situation in a new light. They will see that what seemed to them in the hour of defeat a great loss, may, if rightly improved, be a great gain. . . .
>
> . . . Their fate is indissolubly linked to ours. They may become partakers with us in all the blessings that the future has in store for a great nation. Our triumphs will become their triumphs; our glory will be theirs as well. They will enjoy with us all the blessings which follow in the footsteps of Peace. The new career of development which opens to and invites us, they may tread, not as inferiors, not as subjects, but as equals and partners.
>
> The South itself will be regenerated and redeemed. Emancipated from the curse that has so long fettered and withered it, it will enter upon a nobler and higher stage of progress. . . . A more healthful civilization will rise from the ruins of semi-feudalism by which it has been so long cursed. The very earth itself will feel the quickening breath of the new social dispensation. The soil, once blighted by Slavery, will recover its richness, and the half desert wastes will blossom like the rose.
>
> What a grand future—what a bright destiny, for the North and South! The war ended; the *cause* of the war forever removed;—the triumphs of peace will begin. A whole continent at our disposal; the best blood and sinew of all lands coming to our shores; illimitable vistas of wealth opening before us on every side; boundless resources at our command; the opportunity to become the greatest Power the sun ever shone on are ours![12]

Northern talk about reunion was remarkable in its naiveté, particularly with regard to the consequences of emancipation. The destruction of slavery, rather than causing tremendous bitterness and economic stagnation, was supposed to magically transform the South. Plantation agriculture would come to an end, large tracts of land would be magnanimously divided between white and black farmers, and black workers of all kinds—including black migrants from the North—would blaze new trails toward success. As the *Springfield Republican* proclaimed, there was no reason to feel apprehensive about the future; Northerners and Southerners, and blacks and whites, would all live and prosper together in a new era of sectional and racial harmony:

> Slavery thus eliminated the problem of reconstruction and unity becomes easy. We are of the same stock. We have a common interest in the strength and glory of the nation and . . . our material interests will be more closely connected than ever before. As soon as the southern people return to peaceful pursuits the demand for northern manufactures will be unprecedented. The business of the South will be more than ever before in the hands of northern men. The fertile but desolate sections of the country will attract thousands of our discharged soldiers for settlement, and southern society will be rapidly changed. The great plantations of the South will inevitably be broken up into small farms, as a consequence of the impoverishment of the planters and the power of the negroes to make their own terms for labor. The negroes themselves will gradually become land owners, and the planting aristocracy will disappear. This change is a great one, but all the circumstances conspire to make it rapid beyond all precedent in history. The elements are all separated and everything is in fermentation in the South, and

A MAN KNOWS A MAN

"Give me your hand, Comrade! We have each lost a LEG for the good cause; but, thank GOD, we never lost HEART."

Harper's Weekly, April 22, 1865. In the immediate aftermath of the war, there was a feeling that blacks and whites, by virtue of their common combat experiences, would move into the future with new feelings of amity and brotherhood—much as the veterans pictured here clasp hands to congratulate each other on a job well done.

the infusion of northern population and the training already given to so many of the negroes in the use of arms and in habits of self-reliance will be a sufficient guaranty against the crystallization of affairs into anything like their old forms. . . . Not only will there be a large white emigration from the North and West and from Europe into the southern states after the war is over, but the colored people of the North will be largely attracted thither. They prefer the southern climate; many of them have relatives in the South, and to all educated colored men there will be abundant opportunities there for benevolent labor as well as for the acquisition of wealth. Our northern free schools can furnish thousands of colored teachers and missionaries to the freedmen of the South, and they should arouse themselves to the greatness of their opportunity and enter at once into the field so full of rewards for energetic and faithful effort. By these and many other instrumentalities is the reconciliation and renovation of the South to be accomplished. We have no fears for the future. There will be some prejudices to overcome and some enmities to be obliterated only by time, but when the war ends the North and the South will speedily become one nation—one in character, purpose, and common effort and hope, as never before.[13]

The North, which had always been deeply prejudiced against blacks, was not inclined to give the ex-slaves of the South any special treatment or assistance as they set out to forge new lives for themselves. In Northern eyes, the slaves had been given their freedom; what they did with it was purely up to them. Even William Lloyd Garrison, the abolitionist leader who had struggled for decades to promote the ideals of universal freedom and racial equality, withdrew from the

American Anti-Slavery Society in 1865 and shut down his newspaper, the *Liberator*. As far as he was concerned, the work of abolition was finished. At the end of the war, the federal government did set up the Freedmen's Bureau to help oversee the transition of blacks out of slavery. The work of the bureau was incredibly humane, but to the *New York Tribune*—a strongly antislavery paper—its services were still excessive. "We know that many blacks are poorly fitted for freedom," the paper conceded. "But all coddling, and pampering and guardianship, tend to perpetuate some of the worst abuses of slavery." In addressing the question of how the freedmen ought to be treated, the *Tribune* offered this simple, laissez-faire answer:

> Treat them exactly like any other people.—Judge each according to his conduct rather than his color. If you want their work, hire and recompense them; if you desire products of their labor, buy and pay for them; if they want your lands or goods, require pay from them. Help them to work if they are needy; give alms to the sick or disabled; but teach them that every thing good has its price, and that they can only obtain what they want by paying for it. The lesson is simple, and no one, though a negro, need be long in learning it. . . .
>
> Freedom and Opportunity—these are all that the best Government can secure to white or black. Give every one a chance, and let his behavior control his fate. If negroes will not work they must starve or steal; and, if they steal, they must be shut up like other thieves. If there be any among them who fancy that they, being free, can live in comfort without work, they have now entered a school in which they will certainly and speedily be taught better.
>
> There is just one thing necessary at present—a frank, cheerful, ungrudging recognition of the fact that slavery has ceased in this country—that all our people are free. We believe this recognition is being generally and heartily made by the Southern whites lately in rebellion, and we will do all in our power to encourage them in this course. Only clear away the wreck of slavery, dispel the lingering fear of a return to it, and we may soon break up our Freedmen's Bureaus and all manner of coddling devices, and let negroes take care of themselves.[14]

With good reason, the *Anglo-African*, as a defender of civil rights for blacks, looked toward the future nervously. Given the evident attitudes of Northern newspapers—their spirit of mercy toward the common people of the South and their lack of sympathy with the plight of the freedmen—the prospects for the black race in America seemed precarious at best. That newspaper thus admitted:

The North has taken upon itself the care, custody and mastership of the negro, and must stand to its bargain. It will make them citizens of the Union, with equal rights with the whites. As such, they cannot be excluded from the Northern States. They love town life, and will abound most where there are most towns. They, especially as the rigid rule and espionage of the South will not be kept up at the North, will fill up your cities to repletion with cheap labor, and starve your white workingmen if they continue to submit to the rule and the lead of the Abolitionists. The North, by freeing our negroes, has lost the most valuable slave colonies in the world; for, whatever the political relations of the sections, we were commercially your slave colonies, and had built up your wealth, just as the wealth of most of the nations of Western Europe has been built up. Indeed, ancient and medieval wealth, refinement and civilization were derived from Asiatic trade; and Asiatic laborers have always been essentially slaves. You have but one safe, one fair and honorable, one constitutional course to pursue, and that is, to send the negroes home to their masters.

Letter from Richmond in the *New York News*, May 25, 1865.
Although Southerners seemed to accept defeat, they clung to their memories of slavery and hoped to enlist the aid of the North in keeping the black race in a position of subservience.

WHAT SHALL BE DONE WITH THE NEGROES?

"WHAT SHALL BE DONE WITH THE NEGRO?"

This old stale and malicious slaveholder's question is now being asked by some white men who grudge us the liberty which God and our government have given us. If we saw fit to indulge in a retaliation spirit, we might ask, in return, *what shall be done with many white men?* **But we prefer to meet the question in a more manly way. And we ask all such,** *what do you want to do with the negro? What has he done to you, that you should be so opposed to his being free, like your own people? Did not the same God make him who made you? and did He not make him free, as he made you?*

TOP *New York Tribune,* May 25, 1865.
In the postwar North and South alike, this was one of the most urgent questions playing on the public mind.

LEFT *Anglo-African,* June 10, 1865.
The quibbling among Northern and Southern whites concerning "what to do with the Negro" angered and frustrated the black community, which had expected that their wartime service for the Union would earn them an equal place in American society.

If we feel less disposed to join in the shouts of victory which fill the skies, it is because with the cessation of the war our anxieties begin. Is the public mind sufficiently penetrated by the lesson of the day, thoroughly and adequately, to profit by it? Will the "reconstruction" be based not only on mercy and kindness to the whites, but also in love and justice to the blacks? . . .

Our fear is that the government will not be equal to its duty in the premises. It will not act up to that mandate of the Constitution which obliges it to "guarantee to THE PEOPLE of each state a republican form of government." While simply insisting on the abolishment of slavery as the condition in which the rebel States shall be readmitted into the Union, an immense margin for oppression akin to slavery is left to the evil disposed in those States. To be sure, there will be no actual slavery, . . . but the old habitudes, the odor of slavocracy will be left behind with unlimited power to enact laws to suit itself. . . . No one can mistake the spirit in which the ruling class of the South regard the termination of this civil war. No one can doubt that they lay down their arms today in the hope of taking them up again at a future day in which . . . they may resume the struggle with larger hopes of success. The very women brood rebellion, and their offspring will come into the world ripe for it. The now rising generation hate the Yankees as part of their creed, and the South is studded all over with battle-fields, which . . . bid the wayfarer to halt and breathe a prayer for independence. . . .

Let the North beware; let it be careful not to fritter away the present chance to secure a lasting peace. Let it secure, by granting [the freedmen] "equality before the law," the only portion of the Southern people who now are and . . . will continue to be loyal themselves and will insure the loyalty of the rest.[15]

Indeed, the "odor of slavocracy" continued to waft across the defeated South, poisoning the whole atmosphere of peace. Northerners present in the South in 1865 saw what folks at home in the North could not—that anti-Yankee and antiblack sentiment there was ubiquitous. Even those Southerners who had been made destitute by the war seemed to seethe with resentment and hatred. A correspondent from the *New York Times*, after traveling through Alabama by rail from Montgomery to Mobile, posted a report recounting not only the bitter attitudes of the white people he met but also the violence they perpetrated against the ex-slaves. The cruelties he describes evoke the severe punishments that were part of slavery and foreshadow the brutality of white supremacist Klan violence against blacks during Reconstruction:

> The appearance of the country fully justifies the belief that the greatest distress prevails among the people. And yet it is strange how terribly bitter the returned rebels are. Even on their way to the government Commissary to procure rations they abuse the government and people of the United States. Terms as unmerciful as any we have heard for months were used by this mad people.
>
> The colored people will be murdered and driven to untimely graves if the government does not keep provost guards at the country seats and the cities. So great is the madness of the old slaveholders over defeat and subjugation, that, on their return home, they amuse themselves by cutting off the ears, noses and lips of their former slaves. This is not a dream. It is a terrible fact. . . . At Montgomery five men came in one day with ears cut off and in an almost nude state. Others came in with throats cut, while others appeared terribly marked over their bodies with blows from sticks and stones. The perpetrators are "chivalrous" men, high-minded, well-bred gentlemen, no doubt. Thank heaven, the dominion of such gentry is at an end. . . . But these cases are only samples. All officers and soldiers of the army here are filled with the deepest horror over these awful deeds, and are resolved that they must end.
>
> When the train stops on the railroad, or when a boat stops at a landing, the delay is usually spent in tormenting poor colored persons who may be attempting to come on board. The only exceptions are known when a sufficient number of Union officers and soldiers are on board to give protection to the poor refugees.
>
> I am of the opinion, candidly, that one-twentieth of these awful deeds will never be known.[16]

While slavery in the South had come to an end, the antiblack prejudices that underlay it remained as vital as ever. Southerners did not accept emancipation graciously. Instead, they looked expectantly to the North to help them reestablish white control over blacks—to help them keep as much of the old system of slavery as they could. Southerners were certain that without strict control, the freedmen would refuse to work and would become vagrants, roaming the countryside and stirring up trouble. As one Virginian put it, "From mere habits, the liberated slaves will work a little at first, but they will grow more and more indolent daily" and regress back to a "savage, idle state" of being. "They are savage by nature." The only "fair and honorable" course for the federal government to pursue, therefore, was "to send the negroes home to their masters," who would ensure that they remained productive and submissive. In this way, the collapse of the Confederacy did nothing to crush the Southern dream of building a perfectly ordered and prosperous biracial society, one composed of white masters and black workers. No less than before, "[t]he great question now before our people is how to appropriate all the African labor of the country" so as to ensure "the best possible good" for the South, explained the *Macon Telegraph*. Emancipation need not prevent Southerners from achieving this ambition, "for the white people . . . are the dominant party" and "with wholesome laws, will solve the question of harmony between the two races." As before, it would be a "harmony" based on rigid racial hierarchy. And while the federal armies remained in the South, it was hoped that they would help foster it by reminding the freedmen that they would never really be free of white authority.[17] The *Galveston Tri-Weekly News* was emphatic on this point:

> Of all the questions vitally affecting the welfare of the State, . . . there is none in which the future happiness and prosperity of our country are so deeply involved as in the relative position which the white and black races are hereafter to occupy. For more than twenty years we have been discussing the great question of abolition. . . . This attempt to overthrow an institution that has become a part of our social system, and which our entire population has believed essential to the welfare of both races, led to the war that has just terminated in our defeat, and the only thing now left for us to do, and all we can do in our present entire dependence on the clemency of our conquerors, is to repeat to them what we have been urging for so many years, namely: that the attempt to set the negro free from all restraint and make him, politically, the equal of the white man, will be most disastrous to the whole country and absolutely ruinous to the South. . . .
>
> If the policy of emancipation is to be carried out, the cause of humanity and the true interests of all parties require that the poor negro should no longer be deceived on the subject. He should be told plainly . . . that if he chooses to leave home and go among strangers, he will still have to work, and perhaps harder than ever before, and that whether he is able to work or not, he must still take care of himself, as he will have no one else to look to. He should be told . . . that if he leaves his old home and the service of his master, he must go to work on some other plantation, and for another white man, as he must have a steady home and steady work somewhere. He should be told plainly that his being free is not the privilege of being idle, or doing as he pleases, but simply the privilege of working for another man and taking care of himself and family as best he can. If the negroes are told these truths, and further informed that their freedom can never make them the equals of the white race, ... they will soon cease to run away from their homes, as many are now doing. . . . If this be not done soon, our whole country will be overrun with vagrant negroes, congregating in towns and villages, ... and soon they will be suffering from want and every kind of destitution, and next they will resort to thefts and robberies to save themselves from starvation, rather than go to work. We would most earnestly admonish the Federal authorities that they should not lose a moment in adopting proper regulations in regard to our negroes, if they would save the country from the disastrous consequences of releasing so many slaves from every necessary and wholesome restraint.
>
> We do not believe there is an intelligent planter in the South who would not most cheerfully surrender all right of property in his negroes, if he could do so, and at the same time secure the same services by the payment of such low wages as is paid for agricultural labor in other countries. . . . But they believe—indeed, they know—that they can never get such labor, if their negroes are permitted to . . . be idle, and to wander from place to place, at pleasure. They know that in such case, their plantations will never be cultivated, and will have to be abandoned. . . . But to the people of the South the consequences of abolition, in a moral and social point of view, are far more to be dreaded than the loss of property, even though that may reduce them to the most abject poverty. They have become accustomed to heavy losses of property. . . . But to be compelled to live with their own slaves, when forced by the strong arm of power, into a social and political equality with themselves, is what no people on earth have ever yet submitted to. . . . No instance can be found in the history of the world where two races so distinct in

> color, physological characteristics and mental capacities, ever lived together as equals, and the attempt to make the experiment in this case, must inevitably lead to the utter extermination of one race or the other, and it requires no prophet to tell which race it will be.[18]

When the Civil War began, the North had recognized that to save the Union, it would not be enough to crush the rebellion militarily. The *spirit* of the rebellion had to be exorcised as well. On this point, as with so many issues that had erupted in wartime, the newspapers in 1865 tell an intriguing, and ultimately sad, story. If Northerners had read the situation carefully, they would have seen that with respect to matters of race, the rebel spirit remained alive and well. It was a temperament that the North, tired of war and tinged by its own ideas about white supremacy, would not resist for long. Slavery had torn the United States apart and plunged the North and South into a bloody and highly controversial civil war. The legacy of slavery would prove no less brutal, tragic, and divisive for the nation.

Notes

Introduction

1. George Templeton Strong, *The Diary of George Templeton Strong*, edited by Allan Nevins and Milton Halsey Thomas; abridged by Thomas J. Pressly (Seattle: University of Washington Press, 1988), pp. 181–183.
2. *Montgomery Daily Advertiser*, April 13, 1861; *New Orleans Picayune*, April 13, 1861; *Cincinnati Gazette*, April 16, 1861; *Hampshire Gazette & Northampton Courier*, April 23, 1861.
3. *Augusta Chronicle & Sentinel*, May 11, 1862.
4. Statistics taken from U.S. Census data for 1860, as published in Alfred McClung Lee, *The Daily Newspaper in America: The Evolution of a Social Instrument* (New York: The Macmillan Company), pp. 718, 725.
5. Richard J. Carwardine, *Evangelicals and Politics in Antebellum America* (New Haven: Yale University Press, 1993), pp. 38–39.
6. Some might argue that we cannot presume that newspapers reflect the opinions of their readers. Indeed, it is impossible to know how perfectly Civil War newspapers represented the thoughts and feelings of the masses. There is no polling data from the Civil War period to shed light on popular opinion. But given that people were likely to read and patronize newspapers that harmonized with their personal views, they are the best proxy we have for gauging public opinion.
7. Dwight Lowell Dumond, *Southern Editorials on Secession* (New York: The Century Company, 1931), pp. 363–479; Donald E. Reynolds, *Editors Make War: Southern Newspapers in the Secession Crisis* (Nashville: Vanderbilt University Press, 1966), pp. 161–209.
8. Howard Cecil Perkins, *Northern Editorials on Secession*, vol. 1 (New York: D. Appleton-Century Company, 1942), pp. 238–331.
9. *New York World*, April 17, 1862.
10. *Mobile Register* reprinted in the *Memphis Appeal*, June 1, 1862.
11. *New York News*, May 10, 1861.

Chapter 1

1. "Declaration of Causes Which Induced the Secession of South Carolina," in Frank Moore, ed., *The Rebellion Record* (New York: Putnam, 1862), I:4.
2. Don E. Fehrenbacher, ed., *Abraham Lincoln: A Documentary Portrait through His Speeches and Writings* (Stanford: Stanford University Press, 1964), p. 154.
3. For a more detailed treatment of secession in the South, see David M. Potter, *The Impending Crisis, 1848–1861* (New York: Harper & Row, 1976), ch. 17–18. On events leading up to the war, see Richard N. Current, *Lincoln and the First Shot* (Philadelphia: J. B. Lippincott Company, 1983), *passim*.
4. *Philadelphia Inquirer*, April 15, 1861; *Detroit Free Press*, April 18, 1861; *Independent*, May 2, 1861; *New York World*, April 19, 1861.

5. *Harrisburg Patriot & Union*, April 24, 1861. See also the *New York Times*, April 16, 1861.
6. *Troy Times*, April 25, 1861. See also the *Harrisburg Telegraph*, April 17, 1861; *Barre Gazette*, May 17, 1861.
7. *New York World*, April 23, 1861. For other views of the Union's relative strength, see the *Detroit Free Press*, May 17, 1861; *Troy Times*, April 23, 1861.
8. *Albany Evening Journal*, June 1, 1861, reprinted in the *Detroit Free Press*, June 8, 1861; *Harrisburg Telegraph*, June 8, 1861; *Evangelist*, June 27, 1861. See also the *Philadelphia North American & United States Gazette*, May 6, 1861; *New York Herald*, April 29, 1861.
9. *New York Times*, April 13, 1861; *Detroit Free Press*, April 24, 1861; *Troy Times*, April 22, 1861.
10. *Chicago Tribune*, April 22, 1861.
11. *Albany Evening Journal*, April 30, 1861. For a more secular view, see the *Detroit Free Press*, April 14, 1861.
12. *Barre Gazette*, April 26, 1861; *Troy Times*, May 1, 1861. See also the sermon by the Reverend Thompson, published in the *Cincinnati Gazette*, April 30, 1861.
13. *Princeton Standard*, May 31, 1861; *Cleveland Plain Dealer*, April 17, 1861. See also the *Chicago Tribune*, April 14, 1861.
14. *New York News*, April 29, 1861. See also the *New York Evening Day-Book*, April 20, 1861.
15. *Hampshire Gazette & Northampton Courier*, May 7, 1861.
16. *Richmond Dispatch*, June 26, 1861.
17. *Montgomery Daily Advertiser*, April 13 and April 15, 1861; *Eastern Clarion*, April 19, 1861. See also the *Rome Weekly Courier*, April 19, 1861; *Vicksburg Evening Citizen*, April 16, 1861.
18. *Memphis Avalanche*, April 26, 1861. See also the *North Carolina Semi-Weekly Standard*, July 24, 1861; *Montgomery Daily Advertiser*, April 15, 1861; *Vicksburg Evening Citizen*, May 10, 1861.
19. *Memphis Bulletin* in the *Houston Weekly Telegraph*, June 26, 1861. See also the *Macon Telegraph*, April 23, 1861; *Rome Weekly Courier*, July 5, 1861.
20. *Hillsborough Recorder*, June 26, 1861. See also the *South-Western Baptist*, April 25, 1861; *Rome Weekly Courier*, May 10, 1861.
21. *Richmond Dispatch*, May 18, 1861; *Rome Weekly Courier*, July 16, 1861.
22. *Richmond Enquirer*, May 17, 1861. See also the *New Orleans Bee*, May 20, 1861; *Macon Telegraph*, May 18, 1861.
23. *Columbus Sun*, June 20, 1861.
24. *Augusta Chronicle & Sentinel*, April 25, 1861.
25. *Richmond Examiner*, July 4, 1861. See also the *Rome Weekly Courier*, May 3, 1861.

Chapter 2

1. The discussion of liberty in this chapter draws upon several sources: James M. McPherson, *For Cause & Comrades: Why Men Fought in the Civil War* (New York: Oxford University Press, 1997), pp. 104–114; Randall C. Jimerson, *The Private Civil War: Popular Thought during the Sectional Conflict* (Baton Rogue: Louisiana State University Press, 1988), pp. 32–36; Reid Mitchell, *Civil War Soldiers: Their Expectations and Their Experiences* (New York: Viking, 1988), pp. 11–14; Earl J. Hess, *Liberty, Virtue and Progress: Northerners and Their War for the Union* (New York: New York University Press, 1988), pp. 23–28.
2. Manisha Sinha, *The Counter-Revolution of Slavery: Politics and Ideology in Antebellum South Carolina* (Chapel Hill: University of North Carolina Press, 2000), pp. 221–250; Drew Gilpin Faust, *The Creation of Confederate Nationalism: Ideology and Identity in the Civil War South* (Baton Rouge: Louisiana State University Press, 1988), pp. 58–60.
3. *Montgomery Daily Advertiser*, April 13, 1861. See also the letter from W. H. Watkins to W. H. Seward, printed in the *Natchez Daily Courier*, May 14, 1861. For a religious view, see the sermon by the Reverend T. B. Wilson in the *Texas Republican*, May 24, 1861.
4. *Eastern Clarion*, April 12, 1861.
5. *New Orleans Crescent*, April 16, 1861. See also the *Houston Weekly Telegraph*, April 30, 1861; *Southern Federal Union*, April 23, 1861.
6. *Memphis Appeal*, April 13, 1861; *Nashville Union & American*, April 16, 1861. See also the *North Carolina Semi-Weekly Standard*, April 20, 1861.
7. *Richmond Dispatch*, May 6, 1861. See also the *Montgomery Weekly Advertiser*, May 11, 1861; *Charleston Mercury*, April 22, 1861; *Southern Confederacy*, May 11, 1861.
8. *Richmond Whig*, May 2, 1861. See also the *Nashville Republican Banner*, May 25, 1861; *Southern Federal Union*, May 21, 1861.
9. *Memphis Avalanche*, April 17, 1861.
10. *Memphis Appeal*, May 18, 1861. See also the *Rome Weekly Courier*, July 26, 1861.
11. *Richmond Whig*, April 30, 1861. See also the *Richmond Dispatch*, May 2, 1861; *Texas Republican*, May 18, 1861; *Montgomery Daily Advertiser*, April 26, 1861; *Natchez Daily Courier*, May 2, 1861; *Milton Chronicle*, July 12, 1861.
12. *New York Herald*, April 28, 1861, reprinted in the *Columbus Sun*, May 9, 1861; *Memphis Avalanche*, May 30, 1861; *Richmond Whig*, May 11, 1861; *New Orleans Bee*, May 7, 1861; *Memphis Appeal*, May 9, 1861; *South-Western Baptist*, May 16, 1861.
13. *Eastern Clarion*, May 10 and May 17, 1861; *Nashville Union & American—Extra*, May 20, 1861. See also the *Houston Weekly*

Telegraph, May 14, 1861; *Southern Federal Union*, May 7 and 14, 1861.

14. New Orleans *Delta*, reprinted in the *Selma Morning Reporter*, June 4, 1861, and the *Texas Republican*, June 15, 1861.

15. *Augusta Constitutionalist*, April 24, 1861.

16. *Charleston Mercury*, June 27, 1861. See also the *Shreveport Weekly News*, July 8, 1861; *Memphis Appeal*, July 4, 1861.

17. *Hampshire Gazette & Northampton Courier*, May 7 and May 14, 1861; *Barre Gazette*, April 19, 1861. See also the *Cleveland Plain Dealer*, April 19, 1861; *Detroit Free Press*, June 26, 1861.

18. *Rutland Herald*, April 30, 1861. See also the *Chicago Tribune*, April 26, 1861.

19. *Louisville Journal*, reprinted in the *Wheeling Intelligencer*, June 24, 1861. For an Irish perspective, see the *Irish-American*, April 20, 1861.

20. *Evangelist*, August 1, 1861. See also the *Chicago Tribune*, June 18, 1861.

21. *Wellsburg Herald*, May 24, 1861. See also the *Wheeling Intelligencer*, April 29 and May 14, 1861.

22. *Philadelphia North American & United States Gazette*, May 11, 1861. See also the *Chicago Tribune*, April 25, 1861; *New York Times*, May 10, 1861; *New York Evening Post*, April 30, 1861; *Independent*, July 25, 1861; *Cleveland Plain Dealer*, May 25, 1861.

23. *Independent*, May 2, 1861.

24. *New York Evening Day-Book*, May 9, 1861. See also the *Louisville Courier*, April 30, 1861.

25. *New York News*, May 27, 1861. See also the *Crisis*, June 13, 1861.

26. *Anglo-African*, September 14, 1861.

Chapter 3

1. *Augusta Constitutionalist*, March 30, 1861.

2. Drew Gilpin Faust, ed., *The Ideology of Slavery: Proslavery Thought in the Antebellum South, 1830–1860* (Baton Rouge: Louisiana State University Press, 1981), pp. 4–6; Eric Foner, *Free Soil, Free Labor, Free Men: The Ideology of the Republican Party before the Civil War* (New York: Oxford University Press, 1970), pp. 11–39.

3. *Nashville Union & American*, April 13, 1861; *Richmond Examiner*, June 1, 1861.

4. *Richmond Examiner*, July 17, 1861. See also the letter by Joseph E. Brown, governor of Georgia, to David Walker, published in the *Southern Federal Union*, April 30, 1861.

5. Mitchell Snay, "American Thought and Southern Distinctiveness: The Southern Clergy and the Sanctification of Slavery," *Civil War History* 25 (December 1989), pp. 326–327; Faust, *Ideology of Slavery*, p. 11.

6. *South-Western Baptist*, May 30, 1861. For other biblical arguments, see the *Macon Telegraph*, May 9, 1861.

7. *Memphis Avalanche*, May 22, 1861; New Orleans *Delta* in the *Troy Times*, May 2, 1861. See also the *Vicksburg Evening Citizen*, May 2, 1861; *Rome Weekly Courier*, May 31, 1861.

8. *Memphis Avalanche*, May 30, 1861; *Rome Weekly Courier*, June 7, 1861.

9. *Rome Weekly Courier*, June 28, 1861.

10. *New Orleans Bee*, January 17, 1862, reprinted in the *Richmond Whig*, January 30, 1862. See also the *Macon Telegraph*, May 18, 1861. My ideas regarding the Confederacy's scheme to build a biracial utopia have been influenced by the following articles: Donald G. Matthews, "Charles Colcock Jones and the Southern Evangelical Crusade to Form a Biracial Community," *Journal of Southern History* 41 (August 1975), pp. 299–320; Jack Maddex, Jr., "Proslavery Millennialism: Social Eschatology in Antebellum Southern Calvinism," *American Quarterly* 31 (Spring 1979), pp. 46–62.

11. *Anglo-African*, May 4, 1861.

12. *Hampshire Gazette & Northampton Courier*, June 4, 1861.

13. *Liberator*, May 3, 1861.

14. *New York Courier & Enquirer*, April 30, 1861.

15. *Harrisburg Patriot & Union*, June 7, 1861; *Detroit Free Press*, May 4, 1861.

16. *Albany Atlas & Argus*, April 30, 1861, reprinted in the *Harrisburg Patriot & Union*, May 3, 1861. See also the *Providence Post*, May 4 and May 10, 1861; *Rutland Herald*, May 22, 1861.

17. *Louisville Journal*, July 31, 1861.

18. *Chicago Tribune*, August 19, 1861. See also the *New York Evening Post*, April 30, 1861; *New York Times*, April 21 and July 29, 1861.

19. *New York World*, June 4, 1861.

20. *Evangelist*, May 23, 1861. See also the *Independent*, May 9, 1861.

21. *New York Times*, August 9, 1861.

22. *National Principia*, May 4, 1861.

Chapter 4

1. The battle narrative in this chapter relies on information from the following sources: Ethan S. Rafuse, *A Single Grand Victory: The First Grand Campaign and Battle of Manassas* (Wilmington: Scholarly Resources, 2002), pp. 44–47, 54–58, 191–204; James M. McPherson, *Battle Cry of Freedom: The Civil War Era* (New York: Oxford University Press, 1988), pp. 335–350.

2. *Greensborough Patriot*, June 4, 1861.
3. *Rome Weekly Courier*, August 30, 1861.
4. *Shreveport Weekly News*, August 19, 1861; correspondence from the *New Orleans Picayune* printed in the *Eastern Clarion*, August 9, 1861.
5. Correspondence from the *Southern Confederacy* printed in the *Natchez Weekly Courier*, September 11, 1861. See also the *Weekly Mississippian*, August 14, 1861.
6. *Charleston Courier*, July 27, 1861; *Memphis Avalanche*, August 17, 1861. For other sermons, see the *Richmond Examiner*, July 29, 1861.
7. *Savannah Republican*, August 3, 1861. See also the *Richmond Whig*, July 25, 1861.
8. *Charleston Mercury*, August 1, 1861. See also the *Richmond Whig*, July 23, 1861, reprinted in the *Eastern Clarion*, August 2, 1861.
9. *South-Western Baptist*, August 8, 1861. See also the *Memphis Avalanche*, July 25, 1861; *North Carolina Semi-Weekly Standard*, July 27, 1861.
10. *Richmond Enquirer*, August 2, 1861. See also the *Memphis Avalanche*, August 2, 1861; *Macon Telegraph*, July 24, 1861.
11. *New York News*, July 23 and July 24, 1861. For other pro-peace views, see the *Cincinnati Enquirer*, July 23, 1861; *Louisville Courier*, July 13, 1861; *New York Evening Day-Book*, August 1, 1861.
12. *Albany Atlas & Argus*, August 5, 1861, reprinted in the *Pittsfield Sun*, August 15, 1861.
13. *Philadelphia Evening Bulletin*, July 24, 1861; *Albany Evening Journal*, July 23, 1861; *Providence Post*, July 24, 1861.
14. *Springfield Republican*, July 25, 1861. See also the *Boston Evening Transcript*, July 24, 1861; *Barre Gazette*, July 26, 1861; *Princeton Standard*, July 26, 1861; *Albany Evening Journal*, July 26, 1861.
15. *New York Times*, July 24, 1861; *The Evangelist*, July 25, 1861. See also the *National Principia*, July 27, 1861.
16. *Cleveland Plain Dealer*, July 29, 1861.
17. *New York Tribune*, July 28, 1861.
18. *Troy Times*, May 3, 1862; *New York World*, May 2, 1862; *Cincinnati Enquirer*, May 2, 1862; *Louisville Journal*, May 7, 1862; *Hampshire Gazette & Northampton Courier*, May 6, 1862; *New York Times*, May 1, 1862; *Boston Evening Transcript*, May 2, 1862.
19. *Springfield Republican*, May 3, 1862.

Chapter 5

1. This chapter's narrative on the capture and occupation of New Orleans draws on information from Stephen V. Ash, *When the Yankees Came: Conflict and Chaos in the Occupied South, 1861–1865* (Chapel Hill: University of North Carolina Press, 1995), pp. 17–18, 40–43, 197–198; Chester G. Hearn, *When the Devil Came Down to Dixie: Ben Butler in New Orleans* (Baton Rouge: Louisiana State University Press, 1997), pp. 60–70, 103–105; Gerald M. Capers, *Occupied City: New Orleans Under the Federals, 1862–1865* (Lexington: University of Kentucky Press, 1965), pp. 35–51, 67–69.
2. *New Orleans Bee*, May 1, 1862; *New Orleans Crescent*, May 1, 1862. See also the New Orleans *Delta*, May 1, 1862, reprinted in the *Galveston Tri-Weekly News*, May 10, 1862.
3. *Wilmington Journal*, May 3, 1862.
4. *Richmond Enquirer*, May 7, 1862. See also the thoughts of the Reverend J. H. Thornwell in the *Greensborough Patriot*, May 8, 1862, and the *South-Western Baptist*, May 22, 1862.
5. *Raleigh State Journal*, May 3, 1862, reprinted in the *Richmond Dispatch*, May 6, 1862. See also the *Lynchburg Republican* in the *Memphis Appeal*, May 4, 1862; *Richmond Enquirer*, April 28, 1862.
6. *Augusta Constitutionalist*, April 27, 1862, reprinted in the *Wilmington Journal*, May 7, 1862. See also the *Houston Weekly Telegraph*, June 14, 1862; *Galveston Tri-Weekly News*, June 12, 1862.
7. *Memphis Appeal*, May 10, 1862. See also the *Montgomery Daily Advertiser*, April 30, 1862; *Salisbury Watchman* in the *North Carolina Semi-Weekly Standard*, May 3, 1862.
8. The age range affected by the conscription act widened over the course of the war. In September 1862, the Confederate Congress raised the age limit from thirty-five to forty-five; in February 1864, the limits were expanded again, so that all white men between the ages of seventeen and fifty were liable for conscription.
9. *Memphis Avalanche*, April 29, 1862; Albert Burton Moore, *Conscription and Conflict in the Confederacy* (New York: Macmillan, 1924), p. 21.
10. *Savannah Republican* in the *Memphis Appeal*, May 21, 1862. See also the *Texas Republican*, April 26, 1862.
11. *Richmond Whig*, April 29, 1862, reprinted in the *Wilmington Journal*, May 13, 1862.
12. *Augusta Chronicle & Sentinel*, May 11, 1862. See also the *Richmond Whig*, May 15, 1862; *Memphis Appeal*, June 1, 1862.
13. *New York Times*, May 29, 1862.
14. *Harrisburg Union & Patriot*, May 1, 1862.
15. *New York World*, April 30, 1862.
16. *Springfield Republican*, May 24, 1862.
17. *Louisville Journal*, June 7, 1862; *New York Times* in the *Detroit Free Press*, May 31, 1862. For Butler's perspective, see the *Pittsfield Sun*, July 24, 1862.
18. *Albany Evening Journal*, June 4, 1862, reprinted in the *Cincinnati Gazette*, June 10, 1862. See also the *New York World*, May 30, 1862; *Springfield Republican*, May 26, 1862.
19. *Richmond Dispatch*, May 27, 1862. See also the *Memphis Avalanche*, May 22, 1862.

20. *South-Western Baptist*, May 29, 1862; *Countryman*, June 3, 1862.

21. *Daily Mississippian*, May 29, 1862, reprinted in the *Galveston Tri-Weekly News*, June 14, 1862.

22. *North Carolina Semi-Weekly Standard*, June 25, 1862, reprinted also in the *Daily Mississippian*, June 6, 1862; *Natchez Daily Courier*, June 14, 1862.

23. *Richmond Whig*, May 22, 1862, reprinted in the *Memphis Appeal*, May 31, 1862. See also the *Greensborough Patriot*, June 12, 1862; *Southern Federal Union*, May 27, 1862; *Richmond Examiner*, May 21, 1862.

24. *Church Intelligencer*, August 29, 1862. See also the *South-Western Baptist*, July 10, 1862; *Houston Weekly Telegraph*, May 28, 1862.

Chapter 6

1. Allen C. Guelzo, *Lincoln's Emancipation Proclamation: The End of Slavery in America* (New York: Simon & Schuster, 2004), pp. 120–169; William E. Gienapp, *Abraham Lincoln and Civil War America* (New York: Oxford University Press, 2002), pp. 110–115; Richard J. Carwardine, *Lincoln: Profiles in Power* (London: Pearson, 2003), pp. 198–212.

2. *Liberator*, September 26, 1862. See also the *Independent*, September 25, 1862.

3. *New York World*, September 24, 1862, reprinted in the *Crisis*, October 1, 1862; *Louisville Journal*, September 24, 1862.

4. *Cincinnati Enquirer*, October 10, 1862. See also the *Harrisburg Patriot & Union*, October 3, 1862; *Cincinnati Enquirer*, October 12, 1862.

5. *Weekly Caucasian*, October 11, 1862. As a standard rule, the *Caucasian* used quotation marks around the word *slavery*. Its editor, John H. Van Evrie, believed that *slavery* was a pejorative term, one that defined a relationship as oppressive and unjust. Since, in his view, blacks were naturally inferior and benefited from serving white masters, their state of bondage was not cruel or wrong—it was not really "slavery."

6. *Harrisburg Patriot & Union*, September 25, 1862.

7. *Rutland Herald*, September 29, 1862. See also the *Harrisburg Telegraph*, September 23, 1862.

8. *New York Evening Post*, November 13, 1862.

9. *Harrisburg Telegraph*, September 24, 1862; *Troy Times*, September 27, 1862. See also the *Cincinnati Gazette*, September 25, 1862; *Chicago Tribune*, September 23, 1862.

10. *Springfield Republican*, reprinted in the *Anglo-African*, January 3, 1863.

11. *Providence Post*, January 15, 1863, *Cleveland Plain Dealer*, January 31, 1863, reprinted in the *Crisis*, March 11, 1863. See also the *Cincinnati Enquirer*, March 6, 1863.

12. *Hampshire Gazette & Northampton Courier*, February 10, 1863.

13. *New York Times*, June 14, 1863, reprinted in *Harper's Weekly*, July 4, 1863. See also the *Independent*, June 4, 1863.

14. *Troy Times*, January 13, 1863, reprinted in the *New York Tribune*, January 17, 1863. See also the *Harrisburg Telegraph*, July 29, 1863. A reprint of the article from the *Atlantic Monthly* can be found in the *Cincinnati Gazette*, July 1, 1863. The Col. Richardson mentioned in Mary Clarke's letter is John Peter Richardson, who was governor of South Carolina in the early 1840s.

15. *Liberator*, December 26, 1862; *Harrisburg Telegraph*, September 23, 1862; *New York Times*, March 29, 1863.

Chapter 7

1. *Charleston Courier*, October 3, 1862; *South-Western Baptist*, October 16, 1862; *Greensborough Patriot*, October 16, 1862. See also the *Montgomery Weekly Advertiser*, October 8, 1862; *Richmond Enquirer*, September 30, 1862.

2. *Southern Confederacy*, October 30, 1862, reprinted in the *Columbus Sun*, October 31, 1862; *Confederate Union*, November 4, 1862; *Rome Weekly Courier*, November 7, 1862.

3. *Richmond Examiner*, January 7, 1863.

4. *Memphis Appeal*, October 3, 1862. See also the *Richmond Whig*, October 16, 1862; *Richmond Enquirer*, October 17, 1862.

5. *Augusta Constitutionalist*, January 16, 1863. See also the *Richmond Dispatch*, January 6, 1863.

6. *Daily Mississippian*, January 3, 1863.

7. *Natchez Daily Courier*, January 9, 1863, reprinted in the *Natchez Weekly Courier*, January 14, 1863.

8. *Religious Herald*, October 9, 1862.

9. *Richmond Whig*, November 13, 1863. The full text of the sermon was published in pamphlet form: J. D. Renfroe, *"The Battle Is God's." A Sermon Preached from Wilcox's Brigade, on Fast Day, the 21st August, 1863* (Richmond: MacFarlane & Ferguson, 1863).

10. *Charleston Mercury*, January 29, 1864.

11. *Columbus Sun*, August 8, 1863; *Richmond Examiner*, May 28, 1863.

12. *Charleston Courier*, January 31, 1863.

13. *Columbus Sun*, August 6, 1863. See also the *Rome Weekly Courier*, October 30, 1863.

14. Walter Johnson, *Soul by Soul: Life Inside the Antebellum Slave Market* (Cambridge: Harvard University Press, 1999), p. 19.

15. Drew Gilpin Faust, *The Creation of Confederate Nationalism:*

Ideology and Identity in the Civil War South (Baton Rouge: Louisiana State University Press, 1988), pp. 76–81; Bell Irvin Wiley, "The Effort to Humanize the Institution of Slavery During the Confederacy," *Emory University Quarterly* 5 (December 1949), pp. 207–220.

16. *Christian Index*, September 18, 1863. See also the *Galveston Tri-Weekly News*, November 7, 1864.

17. *Southern Christian Advocate*, January 21, 1864. See also the *Southern Confederate Union*, October 28, 1862; *Columbus Sun*, March 15, 1863.

18. *Christian Index* in the *Countryman*, March 29, 1864. See also the *South-Western Baptist*, February 19, 1863.

19. *Daily Mississippian*, October 10, 1863.

Chapter 8

1. Joseph T. Glatthaar, *Forged in Battle: The Civil War Alliance of Black Soldiers and White Officers* (New York: The Free Press, 1990), p. 227.

2. *Troy Times*, January 30, 1863; *Hampshire Gazette & Northampton Courier*, February 10 and January 6, 1863. See also the *Albany Evening Journal*, April 19, 1862.

3. Black soldiers successfully protested the inequity in their pay, and many refused to accept the lesser pay at all, until Congress in 1864 equalized the pay of black and white soldiers. Back pay, however, was given only to those black soldiers who had been free men at the start of the war.

4. *Anglo-African*, March 14, 1863. See also the *Anglo-African*, January 17 and March 7, 1863; *Independent*, March 12, 1863.

5. *Albany Evening Journal*, February 12, 1863.

6. *Hampshire Gazette & Northampton Courier*, February 24, 1863.

7. *Anglo-African*, April 18, 1863.

8. *Detroit Free Press*, February 23, 1863.

9. *Cincinnati Enquirer*, July 8, 1863.

10. *Crisis*, March 18, 1863. Portions of this narrative also appeared in the *Harrisburg Patriot & Union*, October 14, 1862; the *Cincinnati Enquirer*, October 5, 1862; and the *Weekly Caucasian*, July 19 and July 26, 1862, and February 14, 1863.

11. *Richmond Examiner*, February 18, 1863, reprinted in the *Daily Southern Crisis*, March 4, 1863.

12. *Confederate Union*, December 30, 1862; *Augusta Constitutionalist*, January 7, 1863, reprinted in the *Daily Southern Crisis*, February 3, 1863.

13. *Augusta Chronicle & Sentinel*, April 9, 1863, reprinted in the *Daily Mississippian*, April 14, 1863.

14. *Savannah Republican*, March 14, 1863.

15. Glatthaar, *Forged in Battle*, pp. 155–157; James M. McPherson, *Battle Cry of Freedom: The Civil War Era* (New York: Oxford University Press, 1988), p. 634.

16. *New York Herald*, June 6, 1863; *New York Times*, June 11, 1863; *Chicago Tribune*, June 16, 1863.

17. *New York Times*, June 11, 1863.

18. James Hollandsworth, Jr., *The Louisiana Native Guards: The Black Military Experience During the Civil War* (Baton Rouge: Louisiana State University Press, 1995), p. 65.

19. *Columbus Sun*, October 28, 1863.

20. *Daily Mississippian*, August 27, 1863, reprinted in the *Natchez Semi-Weekly Courier*, December 18, 1863. See also the *Selma Morning Reporter*, August 19, 1863. For a more mainstream view against the use of black soldiers, see the *Montgomery Weekly Advertiser*, August 12, 1863.

Chapter 9

1. James M. McPherson, *For Cause and Comrades: Why Men Fought in the Civil War* (New York: Oxford University Press, 1997), ix.

2. Albert Castel, *General Sterling Price and the Civil War in the West* (Baton Rouge: Louisiana State University Press, 1968), pp. 3–5, 60–61. *The War of the Rebellion: A Compilation of the Official Records of the Union and Confederate Armies*, ser. 1, vol. 8 (Washington: Government Printing Office, 1883), pp. 695–697.

3. *Weekly Cotton States* in the *Natchez Weekly Courier*, March 5, 1862. See also the *Memphis Avalanche*, March 11, 1862.

4. *Memphis Avalanche*, May 14, 1862. See also the *Texas Republican*, May 10, 1862.

5. *North Carolina Weekly Standard*, October 29, 1862, reprinted in the *Greensborough Patriot*, October 30, 1862. See also the *Galveston Tri-Weekly News*, May 12, 1863.

6. *North Carolina Weekly Standard*, November 5, 1862.

7. John Solomon Otto, *Southern Agriculture during the Civil War Era, 1860–1880* (Westport: Greenwood Press, 1994), pp. 30–32; James L. Roark, *Masters Without Slaves: Southern Planters in the Civil War and Reconstruction* (New York: W. W. Norton & Co., 1977), pp. 39–42; Stanley Lebergott, "Why the South Lost: Commercial Purpose in the Confederacy, 1861–1865," *Journal of American History* 70 (June 1983), pp. 61–63.

8. *Columbus Sun*, March 25, 1863. See also the *Daily Southern Crisis*, March 30, 1863; *Montgomery Weekly Advertiser*, March 25, 1863; *Countryman*, March 4, 1862; *Southern Federal Union*, May 6, 1862; *Macon Telegraph*, November 6, 1862.

9. *Lynchburg Republican* in the *Richmond Whig*, May 3, 1861, reprinted in the *Huntsville Southern Advocate*, May 15, 1861, and

Rome Weekly Courier, November 22, 1861. See also the *Vicksburg Evening Citizen*, May 11, 1861.

10. *Richmond Whig*, October 22, 1861; *Southern Confederacy*, October 12, 1861; *Memphis Avalanche*, March 31, 1862; *Greensborough Patriot*, April 3, 1862; *Rome Weekly Courier*, January 30, 1863; *Columbus Sun*, March 26, 1863; *Richmond Dispatch*, January 29, 1863.

11. *Eastern Clarion*, May 2, 1862; *Rome Weekly Courier*, October 31, 1862.

12. *Macon Telegraph*, November 7, 1862, reprinted in the *Rome Weekly Courier*, November 21, 1862, and the *Richmond Whig*, November 11, 1862. See also the *Milton Chronicle* in the *Rome Weekly Courier*, April 11, 1862; *Richmond Disptach*, April 15, 1863; *Selma Morning Reporter*, October 20, 1862.

13. *Religious Herald*, December 4, 1862; *South-Western Baptist*, October 10, 1861; *Galveston Tri-Weekly News*, March 14, 1863; *Weekly Mississippian*, November 20, 1862; *Weekly Mississippian*, March 5, 1862; *Confederate Union*, March 24, 1863; *South Carolinian*, November 10, 1863.

14. *Augusta Chronicle & Sentinel*, July 15, 1862, reprinted in the *Rome Weekly Courier*, July 25, 1862.

15. *Houston Weekly Telegraph*, January 21, 1863.

16. David Williams, *Rich Man's War: Class, Caste, and Confederate Defeat in the Lower Chattahoochee Valley* (Athens: University of Georgia Press, 1998), p. 119.

17. *Columbus Sun*, September 29, 1862. See also the *Montgomery Weekly Advertiser*, October 22 and November 11, 1862; *Rome Weekly Courier*, November 14, 1862; *Greensborough Patriot*, October 23, 1862.

18. *Milton Chronicle* in the *Greensborough Patriot*, November 20, 1862; *Daily Southern Crisis*, January 16, 1863; *Rome Weekly Courier*, April 11, 1862. See also the *Galveston Tri-Weekly News*, January 20, 1863; *South-Western Baptist*, November 6, 1862.

19. Paul D. Escott, *After Secession: Jefferson Davis and the Failure of Confederate Nationalism* (Baton Rouge: Louisiana State University Press, 1978), p. 126.

20. *Selma Morning Reporter* in the *Southern Confederacy*, February 11, 1863, and *Augusta Chronicle & Sentinel*, February 14, 1863. See also the *Rome Weekly Courier*, October 30, 1863; *Greensborough Patriot*, March 12, 1863.

21. *Greensborough Patriot*, April 16, 1863. For an account of the Milledgeville riot, see the *Augusta Chronicle & Sentinel*, April 12, 1863.

22. *Columbus Sun*, April 8 and April 11, 1863; *Richmond Examiner*, April 4, 1863; *Richmond Whig*, April 6, 1863; *Countryman*, April 21, 1863; *Milton Chronicle*, April 10, 1863; *Confederate Union*, April 14, 1863.

23. *North Carolina Semi-Weekly Standard*, March 25, 1863.

24. *Vicksburg Whig*, April 11, 1863. See also the *Augusta Chronicle & Sentinel*, April 4, 1863; *Richmond Whig*, April 6, 1863, reprinted in the *Columbus Sun*, April 10, 1863.

25. *New York Times*, April 21 and April 20, 1863. See also the *Albany Evening Journal*, April 28, 1863.

26. *New York Tribune*, April 11, 1863.

27. *Montgomery Weekly Advertiser*, May 13, 1863.

28. *Confederate Union*, November 24, 1863, reprinted in the *Rome Weekly Courier*, December 4, 1863; *Richmond Whig*, November 6, 1863; *Carolina Spartan*, September 24, 1863. See also the *Milton Chronicle*, November 9, 1863; *Hillsborough Recorder*, September 23, 1863.

Chapter 10

1. The narrative in this chapter draws on information from Duane Schulz, *The Most Glorious Fourth: Vicksburg and Gettysburg, July 4, 1863* (New York: W. W. Norton, 2002), ch. 5, 9; James M. McPherson, *Battle Cry of Freedom: The Civil War Era* (New York: Oxford University Press, 1988), pp. 627–631, 654–665; Everard H. Smith, "Chambersburg: Anatomy of a Confederate Reprisal," *American Historical Review* 96 (April 1991), pp. 441–443; Herman Hattaway, *Shades of Blue and Gray: An Introductory Military History of the Civil War* (San Diego: Harcourt Brace & Company, 1998), pp. 132–150.

2. *Daily Mississippian* in the *Wilmington Journal*, January 27, 1863, *Daily Southern Crisis*, January 28, 1863, reprinted in the *Vicksburg Daily Whig*, January 30, 1863; *Richmond Enquirer*, May 30, 1863.

3. *Cincinnati Gazette*, June 26, 1863.

4. Correspondence of the *Philadelphia Evening Bulletin* in the *New York Times*, June 19, 1863; *Boston Evening Transcript*, June 26, 1863; *New York Times*, June 16, 1863.

5. *Charleston Courier*, June 27, 1863.

6. *Savannah Republican*, July 14, 1863. For another Confederate soldier's account, see the *Mobile Register & Advertiser*, August 9, 1863. For a Northern view of what occurred in Chambersburg, see the *Harrisburg Telegraph*, July 2, 1863.

7. *Richmond Dispatch*, June 26, 1863, reprinted in the *Wilmington Journal*, June 30, 1863. See also the *Savannah Republican*, June 26, 1863; *Charleston Courier*, June 25, 1863; *Richmond Examiner*, July 11, 1863; *Richmond Whig*, July 2, 1863.

8. Correspondence of the *Missouri Democrat* in the *Cincinnati Enquirer*, July 16, 1863.

9. *New York Times* in the *Boston Evening Transcript*, July 7, 1863; *Hampshire Gazette & Northampton Courier*, July 28, 1863.

10. *New York Evening Post*, July 8, 1863.
11. *New York News*, July 8, 1863. See also the *Harrisburg Patriot & Union*, July 6, 1863.
12. *Philadelphia Evening Bulletin*, July 7, 1863. See also the *New York Times*, July 8, 1863; *Rutland Herald*, July 8, 1863.
13. *Evangelist*, July 9, 1863. See also the *Independent*, July 9, 1863.
14. *Richmond Dispatch*, July 9, 1863; *Augusta Chronicle & Sentinel*, August 6, 1863. See also the *Galveston Tri-Weekly News*, July 22 and August 5, 1863; *Richmond Examiner*, July 9, 1863; *Richmond Dispatch*, July 9, 1863.
15. *North Carolina Semi-Weekly Standard*, July 17, 1863.
16. *North Carolina Semi-Weekly Standard*, August 7, August 11, August 21, 1863; correspondent from the *Savannah Republican* in the *Selma Morning Reporter*, August 14, 1863. For other reports of "croaking" and peace sentiment, see the *Mobile Register* in the *Columbus Sun*, July 26, 1863; *Confederate Union*, July 28, 1863; *Rome Weekly Courier*, August 7, 1863; *Memphis Appeal*, August 21, 1863.
17. *Augusta Constitutionalist*, July 18, 1863.
18. *Countryman*, July 28, 1863.
19. *Selma Morning Reporter*, July 18, 1863.
20. *Montgomery Mail*, July 16, 1863. See also the *Houston Weekly Telegraph*, July 14, 1863; *Savannah Republican*, July 12, 1863; *Lynchburg Virginian* in the *Rome Weekly Courier*, August 21, 1863; *Richmond Whig*, July 10, 1863; *Confederate Union*, July 14, 1863; *Greensborough Patriot*, July 23, 1863; *Augusta Constitutionalist*, July 11, 1863; *Charleston Courier*, July 14, 1863; *Columbus Sun*, August 1, 1863; *South-Western Baptist*, July 20, 1863; *Montgomery Weekly Advertiser*, July 15, 1863.
21. *Memphis Appeal*, August 28, 1863.
22. Paul D. Escott, *After Secession: Jefferson Davis and the Failure of Confederate Nationalism* (Baton Rouge: Louisiana State University Press, 1978), p. 127.
23. *Richmond Enquirer*, August 7, 1863.
24. *Richmond Enquirer*, August 5, 1863. See also the *Richmond Whig*, August 10, 1863.
25. *Rome Weekly Courier*, September 18, 1863; *Christian Index*, September 18, 1863.
26. *Charleston Courier*, July 17, 1863.

Chapter 11

1. The interpretation of the riots offered in this chapter relies on insights from the following sources: Iver Bernstein, *The New York City Draft Riots: Their Significance for American Society and Politics in the Age of the Civil War* (New York: Oxford University Press, 1990), ch. 1; Edward K. Spann, *Gotham at War: New York City, 1860–1865* (Wilmington: Scholarly Resources, 2002), ch. 8.
2. Joan E. Cashin, "Deserters, Civilians and Draft Resistance in the North," in Joan E. Cashin, ed., *The War Was You and Me: Civilians in the American Civil War* (Princeton: Princeton University Press, 2002), pp. 265–269; Ella Lonn, *Desertion During the Civil War* (Lincoln: University of Nebraska Press, 1998), p. 145.
3. *Detroit Free Press*, March 6, 1863. See also the *Albany Atlas & Argus*, February 27, 1863.
4. *New York Times*, July 13, 1863.
5. *New York News*, July 13, 1863.
6. *New York Tribune*, July 28, 1863.
7. *New York Herald*, July 15, 1863.
8. *Anglo-African*, August 1, 1863.
9. Ibid.
10. *New York Herald*, July 15, 1863.
11. *New York Times*, July 15, 1863.
12. *Hampshire Gazette & Northampton Courier*, July 21, 1863. For antiriot perspectives from Democratic papers, see the *Providence Post*, July 15, 1863; *Cleveland Plain Dealer*, July 15, 1863.
13. *New York Times*, July 15, 1863.
14. *Philadelphia North American & United States Gazette*, July 15, 1863. See also the *Harrisburg Telegraph*, July 14, 1863; *Cincinnati Gazette*, July 14, 1863; *Boston Evening Transcript*, July 14, 1863.
15. *Weekly Caucasian*, July 18, 1863. See also the *Cincinnati Enquirer*, July 16, 1863.
16. *New York News*, July 22, 1863. See also the *Weekly Caucasian*, August 1, 1863.
17. *New York World*, July 18, 1863.
18. *Charleston Courier*, July 21, 1863. See also the *Augusta Constitutionalist*, July 22, 1863.
19. *Richmond Enquirer*, July 18, 1863. See also the *Rome Weekly Courier*, July 31, 1863; *Richmond Dispatch*, July 18, 1863.
20. *Greensborough Patriot*, July 23, 1863.

Chapter 12

1. Edward Stanwood, *A History of Presidential Elections* (Boston: Houghton, Mifflin and Company, 1892), pp. 236–243.
2. *Columbus Sun*, September 13, 1864; *Augusta Chronicle & Sentinel*, September 8, 1864.
3. *The War of the Rebellion: A Compilation of the Official Records of the Union and Confederate Armies*, ser. 1, vol. 39, part 3 (Washington: Government Printing Office, 1892), pp. 378, 202.
4. Joseph T. Glatthaar, *The March to the Sea and Beyond: Sherman's Troops in the Savannah and Carolinas Campaigns* (New York: New York University Press, 1985), pp. 134–140; Mark Grimsley, *The*

Hard Hand of War: Union Military Policy Toward Southern Civilians, 1861–1865 (New York: Cambridge University Press, 1995), pp. 190–200; Charles Royster, *The Destructive War: William Tecumseh Sherman, Stonewall Jackson, and the Americans* (New York: Alfred A. Knopf, 1991), pp. 327–332, 340–348.

5. *Countryman*, January 10, 1865.

6. *Augusta Chronicle & Sentinel*, December 8, 1864.

7. Glatthaar, *The March to the Sea and Beyond*, pp. 73-74; Grimsley, *The Hard Hand of War*, p. 199.

8. *Columbus Enquirer* in the *Galveston Tri-Weekly News*, December 21, 1864; Correspondent for the *Augusta Constitutionalist* in the *Richmond Dispatch*, December 7, 1864. See also the *Richmond Whig*, February 11, 1865.

9. *Augusta Register*, December 2, 1864, reprinted in the *Raleigh Confederate*, December 7, 1864, and *Macon Telegraph & Confederate*, December 12, 1864.

10. *Macon Telegraph & Confederate*, December 21, 1864.

11. *Augusta Chronicle & Sentinel*, December 29, 1864; *Raleigh Confederate*, December 17, 1864. See also the *Savannah Republican*, October 1, 1864; *Macon Telegraph & Confederate*, December 13, 1864; *Hillsborough Recorder*, February 1, 1865.

12. *Raleigh Progress*, January 21, 1865.

13. *Columbus Sun*, January 25, 1865. See also the *Charleston Courier*, January 31, 1865; *Raleigh Confederate*, February 3, 1865.

14. On the breakdown of morale among Confederate women, see Drew Gilpin Faust, *Mothers of Invention: Women of the Slaveholding South in the American Civil War* (Chapel Hill: University of North Carolina Press, 1996), pp. 238–243.

15. *Charleston Courier*, January 20, 1865. See also the *Raleigh Confederate*, January 12, 1865.

16. *Cleveland Plain Dealer*, December 30, 1864.

17. *Harrisburg Telegraph*, February 9, 1865.

18. *New York Herald*, March 21, 1865.

19. *Raleigh Confederate*, March 24, 1865, reprinted in the *Richmond Whig*, March 30, 1865. See also the *Richmond Dispatch*, March 22, 1865.

20. Jacqueline Glass Campbell, *When Sherman Marched North from the Sea: Resistance on the Confederate Home Front* (Chapel Hill: University of North Carolina Press, 2003), pp. 50–57, 71–73.

21. *Galveston Tri-Weekly News*, March 20, 1865.

22. *Raleigh Confederate*, March 20, 1865. The *Confederate* states that the letter was addressed to William H. Care, a soldier in the 30th Regiment of North Carolina Infantry. However, that name does not appear within the printed or electronic rosters of North Carolina soldiers. These rosters do not offer perfect information; they are not complete lists of the soldiers who served, and often include misspelled surnames. *North Carolina Troops, 1861–1865*, a roster complied by Louis H. Manarin, does have an entry for a William H. Case, but does not indicate the regiment to which that soldier belonged. More information on the identity of William H. Care therefore remains elusive. As for the suggestion that Confederate soldiers were crossing into enemy territory, recent research on Georgia soldiers indicates that many of them indeed went behind Union lines to desert. See Mark A. Weitz, *A Higher Duty: Desertion among Georgia Troops during the Civil War* (Lincoln: University of Nebraska Press, 2000), pp. 65–79.

23. *Army Argus & Crisis*, February 18, 1865, reprinted in the *Montgomery Daily Advertiser*, March 5, 1865, and *Galveston Tri-Weekly News*, April 23, 1865.

24. *Philadelphia North American & United States Gazette*, March 17, 1865.

25. *New York News*, March 23, 1865.

Chapter 13

1. *Mobile Tribune* in the *Columbus Sun*, October 14, 1864. For a more extended discussion of the Confederate debate on emancipation, see Robert F. Durden, ed., *The Gray and the Black: The Confederate Debate on Emancipation* (Baton Rouge: Louisiana State University Press, 1972).

2. *Richmond Enquirer*, October 6, 1864.

3. *New York Times*, October 21, 1864.

4. *Raleigh Progress*, in the *North Carolina Weekly Standard*, October 26, 1864.

5. *Lynchburg Republican*, reprinted in the *North Carolina Weekly Standard*, November 2, 1864. See also *Richmond Dispatch*, November 9, 1864; *Macon Telegraph & Confederate*, January 6, 1865.

6. *Macon Telegraph & Confederate*, October 27, 1864.

7. *Richmond Enquirer*, November 15, 1864. For other army views, see the *Richmond Enquirer*, November 4, 1864.

8. *Army Argus & Crisis*, in the *Columbus Sun*, October 28, 1864. See also the *Raleigh Confederate*, October 30, 1864; *Mobile Register*, in the *Macon Telegraph & Confederate*, January 5, 1865.

9. Durden, *The Gray and the Black*, pp. 102–106.

10. *Columbus Sun*, November 18, 1864; *Richmond Whig*, November 10, 1864. See also the *Galveston Tri-Weekly News*, December 14, 1864.

11. *Charleston Mercury*, November 12, 1864. For a similar view, see the *Shreveport Weekly News* in the *Galveston Tri-Weekly News*, January 6, 1865.

12. *Columbus Sun*, January 28, 1865. See also the *Raleigh Confederate*, November 16, 1864.

13. *Countryman*, January 17, 1865, reprinted in the *Clarion*, January

28, 1865. See also the *Richmond Dispatch*, January 24, 1865.

14. *New York News*, November 7, 1864. See also the *Crisis*, October 19, 1864; *Missouri Republican*, December 10, 1864.

15. *Troy Times*, December 23, 1864. See also the *Cincinnati Gazette*, February 27, 1865; *Rutland Herald*, December 29, 1864.

16. *Raleigh Confederate*, January 13, 1865.

17. *Richmond Enquirer*, November 15, 1864. For a similar view on the common interests of masters and slaves, see the *South Carolinian*, January 16, 1865.

18. *Southern Christian Advocate*, February 2, 1865.

19. *Columbus Sun*, February 10, 1865; *Richmond Dispatch*, February 27, 1865. For a copy of Lee's letter to Barksdale, see the *Richmond Whig*, February 25, 1865.

20. *Columbus Sun*, March 22, 1865. See also the *Augusta Constitutionalist*, January 24, 1865.

21. *Richmond Examiner* quoted in the *Hampshire Gazette & Northampton Courier*, March 28, 1865.

Chapter 14

1. *Carolina Spartan*, December 10, 1863; *Macon Telegraph & Confederate*, December 19, 1864, reprinted in the *Wilmington Journal*, January 12, 1865, and *Richmond Dispatch*, January 20, 1865. Gary W. Gallagher, *The Confederate War* (Cambridge: Harvard University Press, 1997), pp. 85–88.

2. James M. McPherson, *Battle Cry of Freedom: The Civil War Era* (New York: Oxford University Press, 1988), pp. 724–743, 844–850; Herman Hattaway, *Shades of Blue and Gray: An Introductory Military History of the Civil War* (San Diego: Harcourt Brace & Company, 1998), pp. 208–217, 236–238.

3. *New York Herald*, April 4, 1865. See also the *Rutland Herald*, April 4, 1865.

4. *New York Tribune*, April 10, 1865; *Chicago Tribune*, April 11, 1865. See also the *Harrisburg Telegraph*, April 10, 1861; *Troy Times*, April 10, 1865; *Providence Post*, April 10, 1865.

5. *Anglo-African*, April 21, 1865.

6. *Harrisburg Patriot & Union*, April 13, 1865. See also the *Cincinnati Enquirer*, April 11, 1865.

7. *New York News*, April 11, 1865. See also the *Crisis*, April 19, 1865.

8. *Albany Evening Journal*, April 10, 1865, reprinted in the *Albany Atlas & Argus*, April 11, 1865.

9. *Philadelphia North American & United States Gazette*, April 10, 1865.

10. *Cincinnati Gazette*, April 12, 1865. See also the *New York Evening Post*, April 11 and April 14, 1865; *Troy Times*, April 11, 1865; *Independent*, April 13, 1865.

11. *North Carolina Daily Standard*, April 27, 1865.

12. *Augusta Chronicle & Sentinel*, April 19, 1865. See also the *Confederate Union*, April 25, 1865.

13. *Augusta Constitutionalist*, April 21, 1865. See also the *Shreveport Weekly News*, May 9, 1865.

14. *Houston Tri-Weekly Telegraph*, May 10, 1865.

15. *Galveston Tri-Weekly News*, April 26, 1865.

16. *Galveston Tri-Weekly News*, April 26, 1865.

17. *Houston Tri-Weekly Telegraph*, May 1, 1865.

Chapter 15

1. William Hanchett, *The Lincoln Conspiracies* (Urbana: University of Illinois Press, 1983), pp. 37–54; Elizabeth D. Leonard, *Lincoln's Avengers: Justice, Revenge, and Reunion after the Civil War* (New York: W. W. Norton, 2004), pp. 5–7. Lewis Powell also went by the alias Lewis Paine.

2. *Springfield Republican*, April 15, 1865.

3. *Albany Atlas & Argus*, April 17, 1865.

4. *Cincinnati Gazette*, April 17, 1865; *New York Times*, April 20, 1861; *Rutland Herald*, April 17, 1865.

5. *Liberator*, April 28, 1865. See also the *Independent*, April 27, 1865.

6. *Chicago Tribune*, April 17, 1865. See also the *Harrisburg Telegraph*, April 17, 1865; *Troy Times*, April 15, 1865; *Independent*, April 20, 1865.

7. *Albany Evening Journal*, April 19, 1865.

8. *Black Republican*, April 22, 1865. See also the *Anglo-African*, April 21 and May 20, 1865.

9. *Hampshire Gazette & Northampton Courier*, April 18, 1865; *Troy Times*, April 18, 1865. See also the *Chicago Tribune*, April 21, 1865.

10. *New York News*, April 17, 1865. See also the *Crisis*, April 19, 1865; *Harrisburg Patriot & Union*, April 17, 1865.

11. *New York Times*, April 21, 1865. See also the *Harrisburg Telegraph*, April 20, 1861.

12. *Philadelphia North American & United States Gazette*, April 22, 1865.

13. *Evangelist*, May 4, 1865. See also the *Liberator*, April 21, 1865; *New York Times*, April 16, 1865; *Albany Atlas & Argus*, April 17, 1865.

14. *New York Tribune*, April 26, 1865.

15. *Cincinnati Gazette*, April 25, 1865, reprinted in part in the *Crisis*, May 17, 1865.

16. *Troy Times*, April 17, 1865; *Springfield Republican*, April 20, 1865.

17. *North Carolina Daily Standard*, April 18, 1865. See also the *Raleigh Progress* in the *North Carolina Daily Standard*, April 21, 1865; *Montgomery Mail*, April 24, 1865.
18. *Confederate Union*, May 2, 1865; *Shreveport Weekly News*, May 2, 1865; *Macon Telegraph*, May 11, 1865.
19. *Augusta Constitutionalist*, April 23, 1865.
20. *Texas Republican*, April 18 and May 5, 1865. See also the *Chattanooga Rebel*, April 20, 1865, printed in the *Troy Times*, May 11, 1865.
21. *Houston Tri-Weekly Telegraph*, April 25, 1865.
22. *Galveston Tri-Weekly News*, May 3, 1865.
23. Thomas Reed Turner, *Beware the People Weeping: Public Opinion and the Assassination of Abraham Lincoln* (Baton Rouge: Louisiana State University Press, 1982), pp. 96–99; Carolyn L. Harrell, *When the Bells Tolled for Lincoln: Southern Reaction to the Assassination* (Macon: Mercer University Press, 1997), pp. 34–36, 59–60, 68–73.

Chapter 16

1. *Countryman*, May 16, 1865. See also the *Augusta Constitutionalist*, May 6, 1865.
2. *Macon Telegraph*, May 11, 1865. See also the *Augusta Chronicle & Sentinel*, May 5, 1865; *Augusta Constitutionalist*, April 26, 1865.
3. Gary W. Gallagher, *Lee and His Army in Confederate History* (Chapel Hill: University of North Carolina Press, 2001), pp. 268–270; David W. Blight, *Race and Reunion: The Civil War in American Memory* (Cambridge: Harvard University Press, 2001), pp. 258–264; Gaines M. Foster, *Ghosts of the Confederacy: Defeat, the Lost Cause, and the Emergence of the New South* (New York: Oxford University Press, 1987), pp. 104–114.
4. *Galveston Tri-Weekly News*, May 26, 1865; *Texas Republican*, May 26, 1865.
5. *Shreveport Weekly News*, May 16, 1865; *Countryman*, May 2, 1865.
6. *Texas Republican*, May 29, 1865.
7. *Montgomery Mail*, April 26, 1865.
8. *North Carolina Daily Standard*, April 20, 1865. See also the *Augusta Chronicle & Sentinel*, May 12, 1865; *Montgomery Daily Advertiser*, July 30, 1865.
9. *Montgomery Mail*, May 15, 1865.
10. *Macon Telegraph*, May 14, 1865.
11. *Troy Times*, May 8 and May 10, 1865.
12. *Albany Evening Journal*, May 10, 1865.
13. *Springfield Republican*, April 11, 1865. For another similarly naive view, see the *Cincinnati Gazette*, April 19, 1861.
14. *New York Tribune* in the *Philadelphia Age*, April 11, 1865; *New York Tribune*, May 25, 1865.
15. *Anglo-African*, April 15, 1865. See also the *Black Republican*, April 15, 1865.
16. *New York Times*, June 12, 1865. The startling bodily mutilations and humiliations inflicted upon Southern freedmen during Reconstruction are examined in Lisa Cardyn, "Sexualized Racism/Gendered Violence: Outraging the Body Politic in the Reconstruction South," *Michigan Law Review* 100 (2002), pp. 704–762.
17. Richmond letter published in the *New York News*, May 25, 1865, and the *Cincinnati Enquirer*, May 29, 1865; *Macon Telegraph*, June 8, 1865.
18. *Galveston Tri-Weekly News*, June 21, 1865.

Index

Note: Page numbers in italics refer to newspaper images and captions.